Medical Physics Department
Royal United Hospital
Combe Park
BATH BA1 3NG
Tel: (0225) 824082
Fax: (0225) 447535

D1550323

DIGITAL
IMAGE
PROCESSING

DIGITAL IMAGE PROCESSING

Rafael C. Gonzalez
University of Tennessee
Perceptics Corporation

Richard E. Woods
Perceptics Corporation

ADDISON-WESLEY PUBLISHING COMPANY

Reading, Massachusetts · Menlo Park, California · New York
Don Mills, Ontario · Wokingham, England · Amsterdam · Bonn
Sydney · Singapore · Tokyo · Madrid · San Juan · Milan · Paris

World Student Series

Reprinted with corrections September, 1993

Copyright © 1992 by Addison-Wesley Publishing Company, Inc.
All rights reserved. No part of this publication may be reproduced, stored in a retrieval system, or transmitted, in any form or by any means, electronic, mechanical, photocopying, recording, or other-wise, without the prior written permission of the publisher. Printed in the United States of America.

ISBN 0-201-60078-1
  3 4 5 6 7 8 9 10-MA-99 98 97 96 95

To Connie, Ralph,
and Robert

and

To Janice, David,
and Jonathan

PREFACE

The field of digital image processing is continually evolving. During the past five years, there has been a significant increase in the level of interest in image morphology, neural networks, full-color image processing, image data compression, image recognition, and knowledge-based image analysis systems. These topics form the core of a major modernization effort that resulted in the current text, a third-generation book which builds upon the popularity of the 1977 and 1987 editions of *Digital Image Processing* by Gonzalez and Wintz, and a decade of successful commercialization of digital image processing by the present authors at Perceptics Corporation. The academic flavor of the book again has been influenced by our teaching and research activities at the University of Tennessee.

The text now contains comprehensive new discussions on binary and gray-scale image morphology, neural networks, and full-color image processing. Our coverage of image data compression was completely redone in a more modern treatment of this subject matter, including image compression standards. A new chapter dealing with image recognition and knowledge-based image interpretation was added to the book. Other parts of the text also have undergone major changes ranging from expanded coverage of some traditional topics to revised examples using new images of higher resolution. In total, the book has 151 new sections, over 250 new drawings and images, 95 new problems, and 152 new references. An expanded instructor's manual, available from the publisher, contains detailed solutions to all problems and provides curriculum guidelines and project suggestions.

As before, the present edition of *Digital Image Processing* was prepared with students and instructors in mind. Thus, the principal objectives of the book continue to be to provide an introduction to basic concepts and methodologies for digital image processing, and to develop a foundation that can be used as the basis for further study and research in this field. To achieve these objectives, we retained a focus on material that we feel is fundamental and has a scope of application that is not limited to the solution of specialized problems. In addition, the mathematical complexity of the book remains at a level well within the grasp of college seniors and first-year graduate students in technical disciplines, such as engineering and computer science, that require introductory preparation in mathematical analysis, matrix theory, probability, and computer programming.

A brief overview of the new material is as follows. The discussion in Chapter 1 dealing with the elements of image processing systems has been updated to keep pace with new developments in image-processing hardware and software. A new section dealing with the extraction of connected components was added to Chapter 2. The topic of connected components is an area of considerable interest in binary image processing for automation, document imaging, and character recognition. Chapter 3 was expanded to cover more image transforms than in the past, including the slant and Haar transforms. Coverage of the discrete cosine transform also was expanded. This particular transform has become quite popular in the past few years in connection with worldwide standards for image data compression. Chapter 4 was restructured significantly. Several enhancement techniques were added, including simple methods for enhancement by point processing, such as gray-scale mappings for image negatives, contrast stretching, compression of dynamic range, gray-level slicing, and bit-plane slicing. A discussion of image subtraction and new results for image averaging were also included. The new organization of Chapter 4 treats enhancement by spatial and transform techniques separately. A comprehensive discussion on the fundamentals of spatial filters was added, including important variations of smoothing and sharpening filters. Coverage of enhancement in the frequency domain is now complemented by new images of higher quality and resolution. Several new sections dealing with color models and full-color image processing also were added to Chapter 4. With the exception of updates in reference material and the addition of more exercises, Chapter 5 was left in essentially its original form, which has as a basis a unified approach to restoration based on algebraic techniques. Chapter 6 was completely rewritten. The coverage includes an overview of basic information theory, a discussion of binary and continuous tone (monochrome and color) compression techniques, error-free and lossy compression methods, and image compression standards. Although the subject of image data compression has been included in digital image processing books for years, it is only recently that this topic has become an area of active commercial interest. The factors driving this interest are facsimile transmission requirements and document imaging. Actual acceptance of the technology was driven by standards. Chapter 7 was revised slightly. The Hough transform, originally covered in Chapter 3, was moved to Chapter 7 where it is more applicable, and new references and problems were added. Chapter 8 was expanded to include a better explanation of Fourier descriptors. A new, comprehensive section on binary and gray-scale morphology also was added to this chapter. Although image morphology has been an active topic of research in Europe for over a decade, it is only in the past few years that a similar level of interest has been sparked in the United States. Our coverage of this topic is extensively illustrated with image examples designed to improve comprehension. Chapter 9 is new. It deals with recognition and interpretation, topics that are fundamental processes in image analysis applications. In particular, we cover a broad range of recognition techniques, starting with the classic minimum-distance, correlation, and Bayes recognition schemes, and progressing through perceptrons and neural networks. The latter is a topic of considerable recent attention in image processing. We also cover structural recognition techniques and conclude the chapter with a discussion of knowledge-based image interpretation, including predicate calculus, semantic networks, and expert systems.

It has been our experience that one of the principal features that attracts students to a course on image processing is the opportunity to implement and test with real data the concepts and algorithms developed in the classroom. The ideal environment for this is provided by an image processing system that includes an image digitizer, a general-purpose computer, and image display equipment. The appendices to this book provide an alternative route for instruction when such a system is not available. Appendix A covers various techniques for generating gray-scale images on commonly available output devices such as printers and binary monitors. These techniques lend themselves to straightforward implementation in almost any computer language. Appendix B contains a set of coded images suitable for experimenting with the methods discussed in the text. The material in these two appendices can be utilized in conjunction with a modestly equipped general purpose computer to yield a basic approach for gaining hands-on experience with image processing techniques through algorithm implementation and visual display of results.

We are indebted to a number of individuals in academic circles as well as in government and industry who have contributed in different, but important, ways to the preparation of this book. In particular, we wish to extend our appreciation to J.M. Googe, W.L. Green, the late F.N. Peebles, R. Weaver, W.T. Snyder, M.G. Thomason, R.C. Kryter, M.T. Borelli, W. Thornton, B. Rock, H. Alter, M.A. Abidi, D. Brzakovic, and E.R. Dougherty. We also wish to acknowledge the image processing results contributed by B. Fittes, T. Saba, D. Cate, C. Hayden, M. Goldston, R. Eason, A. Perez, J. Herrera, Z. Bell, F. Contreras, R. Salinas, A. Morris, and M.A. O'Neal. Special thanks go to Eileen Bernadette Moran and David Dwyer of Addison-Wesley for their commitment to excellence in all aspects of the publication of this book. Finally, we wish to acknowledge the individuals and organizations cited in the captions of numerous figures throughout the book for their permission to use that material.

This edition of *Digital Image Processing* is but a reflection of the significant progress that has been made in this field in just the past five years. As is usual in a project such as this, progress continues after work on the manuscript stops. One of the reasons earlier versions of this book have been so well accepted throughout the world is their emphasis on fundamental concepts, an approach that, among other things, attempts to provide a measure of constancy in a rapidly-evolving body of knowledge. We have tried to observe that same principle in preparing this edition of the book.

R.C.G.
R.E.W.

CONTENTS

CHAPTER 1

INTRODUCTION

> One picture is worth more than ten
> thousand words.
> *Anonymous*

1.1 BACKGROUND

Interest in digital image processing methods stems from two principal application areas: improvement of pictorial information for human interpretation,
and processing of scene data for autonomous machine perception. One of the
first applications of image processing techniques in the first category was in
improving digitized newspaper pictures sent by submarine cable between London and New York. Introduction of the Bartlane cable picture transmission
system in the early 1920s reduced the time required to transport a picture across
the Atlantic from more than a week to less than three hours. Specialized printing
equipment coded pictures for cable transmission and then reconstructed them
at the receiving end. Figure 1.1 was transmitted in this way and reproduced
on a telegraph printer fitted with type faces simulating a halftone pattern.

Some of the initial problems in improving the visual quality of these early
digital pictures were related to the selection of printing procedures and the
distribution of brightness levels. The printing method used to obtain Fig. 1.1
was abandoned toward the end of 1921 in favor of a technique based on photographic reproduction made from tapes perforated at the telegraph receiving
terminal. Figure 1.2 shows an image obtained using this method. The improvements over Fig. 1.1 are evident, both in tonal quality and in resolution.

The early Bartlane systems were capable of coding images in 5 distinct
brightness levels. This capability was increased to 15 levels in 1929. Figure 1.3
indicates the type of image that could be obtained using the 15-tone equipment.

1

Figure 1.1 *A digital picture produced in 1921 from a coded tape by a telegraph printer with special type faces. (From McFarlane [1972].)*

During this period, introduction of a system for developing a film plate via light beams that were modulated by the coded picture tape improved the reproduction process considerably.

Improvements on processing methods for transmitted digital pictures continued to be made du ing the next 35 years. However, it took the combined advents of large-scale digital computers and the space program to bring into focus the potential of image processing concepts. Work on using computer techniques for improving images from a space probe began at the Jet Propulsion Laboratory (Pasadena, California) in 1964 when pictures of the moon transmitted by Ranger 7 were processed by a computer to correct various types of image distortion inherent in the on-board television camera. These techniques served as the basis for improved methods used to enhance and restore images from the Surveyor missions to the moon, the Mariner series of flyby missions to Mars, the Apollo manned flights to the moon, and others.

From 1964 until the present, the field of image processing has grown vigorously. In addition to applications in the space program, digital image processing techniques now are used to solve a variety of problems. Although often

Figure 1.2 *A digital picture made in 1922 from a tape punched after the signals had crossed the Atlantic twice. Some errors are visible. (From McFarlane [1972].)*

Figure 1.3 *Unretouched cable picture of Generals Pershing and Foch, transmitted in 1929 by 15-tone equipment from London to New York. (From McFarlane [1972].)*

unrelated, these problems commonly require methods capable of enhancing pictorial information for human interpretation and analysis. In medicine, for instance, computer procedures enhance the contrast or code the intensity levels into color for easier interpretation of x-rays and other biomedical images. Geographers use the same or similar techniques to study pollution patterns from aerial and satellite imagery. Image enhancement and restoration procedures are used to process degraded images of unrecoverable objects or experimental results too expensive to duplicate. In archeology, image processing methods have successfully restored blurred pictures that were the only available records of rare artifacts lost or damaged after being photographed. In physics and related fields, computer techniques routinely enhance images of experiments in areas such as high-energy plasmas and electron microscopy. Similarly successful applications of image processing concepts can be found in astronomy, biology, nuclear medicine, law enforcement, defense, and industrial applications.

Figure 1.4 shows some typical examples of the results obtainable with digital image processing techniques. The original images are on the left, and the corresponding computer processed images are on the right. Figure 1.4(a) is an image of a cell heavily corrupted by electronic noise. Figure 1.4(b) shows the result after averaging several noisy images, a common technique used for noise reduction. Figure 1.4(c) is a picture of the Martian surface corrupted by interference during transmission to Earth by a space probe. The interference—in this case, a set of vertical, structured lines—can be almost completely removed by computer processing, as Fig. 1.4(d) shows. Figures 1.4(e) and (f) illustrate the improvement possible on an x-ray image by contrast and edge

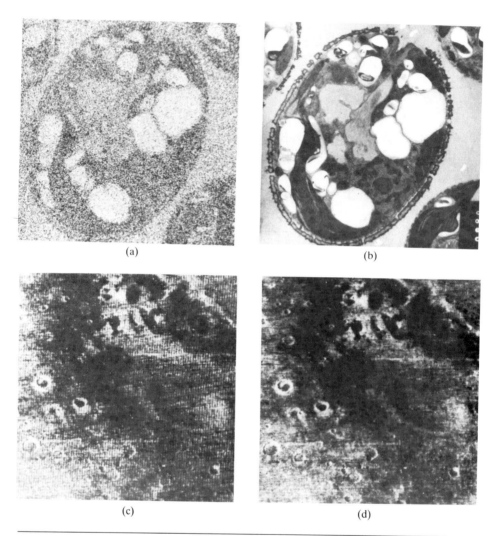

Figure 1.4 *Examples of digital image processing. Left column: original digital images. Right column: images after processing.*

enhancement. The image in Fig. 1.4(g) was blurred by uniform motion during exposure, and the image in Fig. 1.4(h) resulted after application of a deblurring algorithm. These illustrations are typical of those discussed in detail in Chapters 4 and 5.

These examples illustrate processing results intended for human interpretation. The second major area of application of digital image processing techniques mentioned at the beginning of this section is in solving problems dealing with machine perception. In this case, interest focuses on procedures for ex-

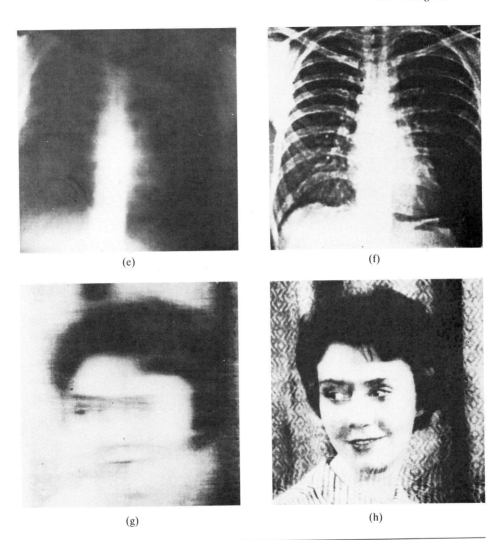

(e)

(f)

(g)

(h)

Figure 1.4 *(Continued)*.

tracting from an image information in a form suitable for computer processing. Often, this information bears little resemblance to visual features that human beings use in interpreting the content of an image. Examples of the type of information used in machine perception are statistical moments, Fourier transform coefficients, and multidimensional distance measures.

Typical problems in machine perception that routinely utilize image processing techniques are automatic character recognition, industrial machine vision for product assembly and inspection, military recognizance, automatic processing of fingerprints, screening of x-rays and blood samples, and machine processing of aerial and satellite imagery for weather prediction and crop assessment.

1.2   DIGITAL IMAGE REPRESENTATION

The term *monochrome image* or simply *image*, refers to a two-dimensional light intensity function $f(x, y)$, where x and y denote spatial coordinates and the value of f at any point (x, y) is proportional to the brightness (or *gray level*) of the image at that point. Figure 1.5 illustrates the axis convention used throughout this book. Sometimes viewing an image function in perspective with the third axis being brightness is useful. Viewed in this way Fig. 1.5 would appear as a series of active peaks in regions with numerous changes in brightness levels and smoother regions or plateaus where the brightness levels varied little or were constant. Using the convention of assigning proportionately higher values to brighter areas would make the height of the components in the plot proportional to the corresponding brightness in the image.

A *digital image* is an image $f(x, y)$ that has been discretized both in spatial

Figure 1.5   *Axis convention used for digital image representation.*

coordinates and brightness. A digital image can be considered a matrix whose row and column indices identify a point in the image and the corresponding matrix element value identifies the gray level at that point. The elements of such a digital array are called *image elements, picture elements, pixels,* or *pels,* with the last two being commonly used abbreviations of "picture elements."

Although the size of a digital image varies with the application, the following chapters demonstrate the many advantages of selecting square arrays with sizes and number of gray levels that are integer powers of 2. For example, a typical size comparable in quality to a monochrome TV image is a 512 × 512 array with 128 gray levels.

With the exception of the discussion in Chapter 4 on color techniques for image enhancement and a brief discussion in Chapter 7 dealing with the use of color in image segmentation, all the images considered in this book are digital monochrome images of the form previously described. Thus we do not cover three-dimensional scene analysis nor optical techniques for image processing.

1.3 FUNDAMENTAL STEPS IN IMAGE PROCESSING

Digital image processing encompasses a broad range of hardware, software, and theoretical underpinnings. In this section we discuss the fundamental steps required to perform an image processing task. Hardware and software issues are discussed in Section 1.4.

It will be helpful to use a "theme" example that runs throughout the discussion and serves to illustrate the material developed in this section. An application that is rather easy to conceptualize without any prior knowledge of imaging concepts is the use of image processing techniques for automatically reading the address on pieces of mail. Figure 1.6 shows that the overall objective is to produce a result from a problem domain by means of image processing. The *problem domain* in this example consists of pieces of mail, and the objective is to read the address on each piece. Thus the desired output in this case is a stream of alphanumeric characters.

The first step in the process is *image acquisition*—that is, to acquire a digital image. To do so requires an imaging sensor and the capability to digitize the signal produced by the sensor. As discussed in some detail in Section 1.4, the sensor could be a monochrome or color TV camera that produces an entire image of the problem domain every 1/30 sec. The imaging sensor could also be a line-scan camera that produces a single image line at a time. In this case, the object's motion past the line scanner produces a two-dimensional image. If the output of the camera or other imaging sensor is not already in digital form, an analog-to-digital converter digitizes it. The nature of the sensor and the image it produces are determined by the application. In terms of our example, mail reading applications rely greatly on line-scan cameras.

After a digital image has been obtained, the next step deals with *prepro-*

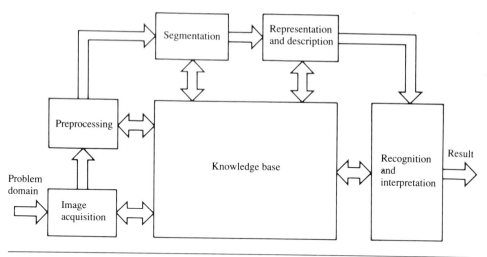

Figure 1.6 *Fundamental steps in digital image processing.*

cessing that image. The key function of preprocessing is to improve the image in ways that increase the chances for success of the other processes. In this example, preprocessing typically deals with techniques for enhancing contrast, removing noise, and isolating regions whose texture indicate a likelihood of alphanumeric information.

The next stage deals with segmentation. Broadly defined, *segmentation* partitions an input image into its constituent parts or objects. In general, autonomous segmentation is one of the most difficult tasks in digital image processing. On the one hand, a rugged segmentation procedure brings the process a long way toward successful solution of an imaging problem. On the other hand, weak or erratic segmentation algorithms almost always guarantee eventual failure. In terms of character recognition, the key role of segmentation is to extract individual characters and words from the background.

The output of the segmentation stage usually is raw pixel data, constituting either the boundary of a region or all the points in the region itself. In either case, converting the data to a form suitable for computer processing is necessary. The first decision that must be made is whether the data should be represented as a boundary or as a complete region. Boundary representation is appropriate when the focus is on external shape characteristics, such as corners and inflections. Regional representation is appropriate when the focus is on internal properties, such as texture or skeletal shape. In some applications, however, these representations coexist. This situation occurs in character recognition applications, which often require algorithms based on boundary shape as well as skeletons and other internal properties.

Choosing a representation is only part of the solution for transforming raw data into a form suitable for subsequent computer processing. A method must also be specified for describing the data so that features of interest are highlighted. *Description*, also called *feature selection*, deals with extracting features that result in some quantitative information of interest or features that are basic for differentiating one class of objects from another. In terms of character recognition, descriptors such as lakes (holes) and bays are powerful features that help differentiate one part of the alphabet from another.

The last stage in Fig. 1.6 involves recognition and interpretation. *Recognition* is the process that assigns a label to an object based on the information provided by its descriptors. *Interpretation* involves assigning meaning to an ensemble of recognized objects. In terms of our example, identifying a character as, say, a *c* requires associating the descriptors for that character with the label *c*. Interpretation attempts to assign meaning to a set of labeled entities. For example, a string of five numbers—or of five numbers followed by a hyphen and four more numbers—can be interpreted to be a ZIP code.

So far we have said nothing about the need for prior knowledge or about the interaction between the *knowledge base* and the processing modules in Fig. 1.6. Knowledge about a problem domain is coded into an image processing system in the form of a knowledge database. This knowledge may be as simple as detailing regions of an image where the information of interest is known to be located, thus limiting the search that has to be conducted in seeking that information. The knowledge base also can be quite complex, such as an interrelated list of all major possible defects in a materials inspection problem or an image database containing high-resolution satellite images of a region in connection with change-detection applications. In addition to guiding the operation of each processing module, the knowledge base also controls the interaction between modules. This distinction is made in Fig. 1.6 by the use of double-headed arrows between the processing modules and the knowledge base, as opposed to single-headed arrows linking the processing modules. This depiction indicates that communication between processing modules generally is based on prior knowledge of what a result should be. For example, in order for a machine to conclude that a string of characters is a ZIP code, the system must be endowed with the knowledge to recognize the significance of the location of the string with respect to other components of an address field. This knowledge guides not only the operation of each module, but it also aids in feedback operations between modules through the knowledge base. For instance, a string of numbers in the correct location but consisting of only four characters (one of which could not be recognized) might lead the interpretation module to "suspect" that two characters are joined. A feedback request through the knowledge base to the segmentation stage for another "look" is an example of knowledge utilization in performing image processing tasks.

Although we do not discuss image display explicitly at this point, it is important to keep in mind that viewing the results of image processing can take place at the output of any step in Fig. 1.6. We also note that not all image processing applications require the complexity of interactions implied by Fig. 1.6. Numerous practical applications are carried out by the functions provided in the outer path in Fig. 1.6. In fact, not even all those modules are needed in some cases. For example, image enhancement for human visual interpretation seldom goes beyond the preprocessing stage. In general, processing functions that include recognition and interpretation are associated with image analysis applications in which the objective is automatic—or even partially automatic— extraction of information from an image. Character recognition is but one example. We will encounter other applications throughout the rest of the book.

1.4   ELEMENTS OF DIGITAL IMAGE PROCESSING SYSTEMS _____

The elements of a general purpose system capable of performing the image processing operations discussed in Section 1.3 are shown in Fig. 1.7. This type of system generally performs image: (1) acquisition, (2) storage, (3) processing, (4) communication, and (5) display.

1.4.1   Image Acquisition

Two elements are required to acquire digital images. The first is a physical device that is sensitive to a band in the electromagnetic energy spectrum (such as the x-ray, ultraviolet, visible, or infrared bands) and that produces an electrical signal output proportional to the level of energy sensed. The second, called a *digitizer*, is a device for converting the electrical output of the physical sensing device into digital form.

As an example, consider the basics of x-ray imaging systems. The output of an x-ray source is directed at an object and a medium sensitive to x-rays is placed on the other side of the object. The medium thus acquires an image of materials (such as bones and tissue) having various degrees of x-ray absorption. The medium itself can be film, a television camera combined with a converter of x-rays to photons, or discrete detectors whose outputs are combined to reconstruct a digital image.

Another major sensor category deals with visible and infrared light. Among the devices most frequently used for this purpose are microdensitometers, image dissectors, vidicon cameras, and photosensitive solid-state arrays. The first device requires that the image to be digitized be in the form of a transparency (such as a film negative) or photograph. Vidicon cameras and solid-state arrays can accept images recorded in this manner, and they also can digitize natural images that have sufficient light intensity to excite the detector.

In microdensitometers the transparency or photograph is mounted on a flat bed or wrapped around a drum. Scanning is accomplished by focusing a beam of light (which could be a laser) on the image and translating the bed or rotating the drum in relation to the beam. In the case of transparencies the beam passes

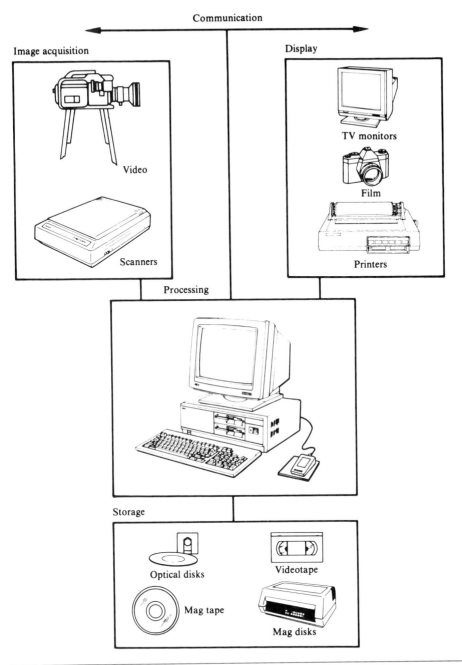

Figure 1.7 *Basic functional elements of an image processing system: acquisition, storage, processing, communication, and display. The components in each box are examples of devices used in such a system.*

through the film; in photographs it is reflected from the surface of the image. In both cases the beam is focused on a photodetector and the gray level at any point in the image is recorded by the detector based on the intensity of the beam. A digital image is obtained by allowing only discrete values of intensity and position in the output. Although microdensitometers are slow devices, they are capable of high degrees of position accuracy due to the essentially continuous nature of the mechanical translation used in the digitization process.

The operation of vidicon cameras is based on the principle of photoconductivity. An image focused on the tube surface produces a pattern of varying conductivity that matches the distribution of brightness in the optical image. An independent, finely focused electron beam scans the rear surface of the photoconductive target, and, by charge neutralization, this beam creates a potential difference that produces on a collector a signal proportional to the input brightness pattern. A digital image is obtained by quantizing this signal, as well as the corresponding position of the scanning beam.

Solid-state arrays are composed of discrete silicon imaging elements, called *photosites*, that have a voltage output proportional to the intensity of the incident light. Solid-state arrays are organized in one of two principal geometrical arrangements: *line scan sensors* and *area sensors*. A line-scan sensor consists of a row of photosites and produces a two-dimensional image by relative motion between the scene and the detector. For example, line-scan sensors are used extensively in flatbed image scanners. An area sensor is composed of a matrix of photosites and is therefore capable of capturing an image in the same manner as, say, a vidicon tube. A significant advantage of solid-state array sensors is that they can be shuttered at very high speeds (say, 1/10,000 sec.). This makes them ideal for applications in which *freezing* motion is required.

The technology used in solid-state imaging sensors is based principally on charge-coupled devices (CCDs). As Fig. 1.8(a) shows, a typical line-scan CCD sensor contains a row of photosites, two transfer gates used to clock the contents of the imaging elements into so-called transport registers, and an output gate used to clock the contents of the transport registers into an amplifier. The amplifier outputs a voltage signal proportional to the contents of the row of photosites.

Charge-coupled area arrays are similar to line-scan sensors, except that the photosites are arranged in a matrix format and a gate/transport-register combination separates columns of photosites, as Fig. 1.8(b) shows. The contents of odd-numbered photosites are sequentially gated into the vertical transport registers and then into the horizontal transport register. The content of this register is fed into an amplifier whose output is a line of video. Repeating this procedure for the even-numbered lines completes the second field of an interlaced TV image frame. Scanning is repeated 30 times per second.

Line-scan sensors with resolutions ranging from 256 to 4096 elements are not uncommon. The resolution of area sensors ranges from 32 × 32 elements

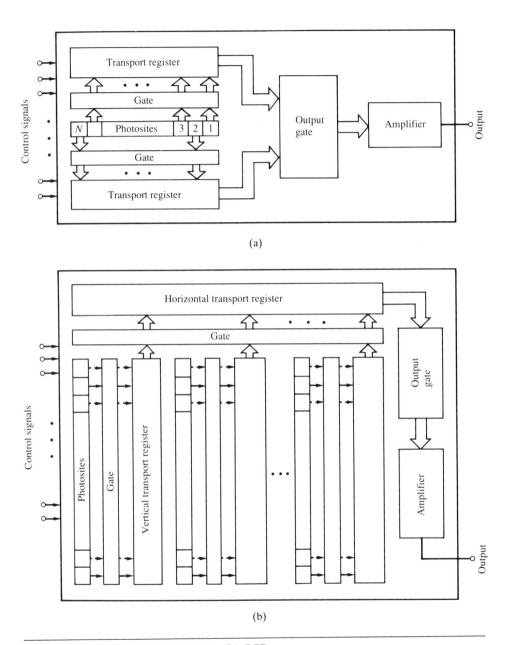

(a)

(b)

Figure 1.8   *(a) CCD line-scan sensor; (b) CCD area sensor.*

at the low end to 256 × 256 elements for a medium resolution sensor. Higher resolution devices with 640 × 480 elements are readily available, and sensors with resolutions on the order of 1280 × 1024 elements also are available commercially at relatively high, but often justifiable, prices. Specialty high-end sensors that use mechanical motion of a CCD chip to achieve resolutions on the order of 2048 × 2048 elements are available at premium prices. CCD arrays are typically packaged as TV cameras. Image digitization is achieved by feeding the video out of these cameras into a digitizer, as mentioned earlier.

1.4.2 Storage

An 8-bit image of size 1024 × 1024 pixels requires one million bytes of storage. Thus, providing adequate storage is usually a challenge in the design of image processing systems. Digital storage for image processing applications falls into three principal categories: (1) short term storage for use during processing, (2) on-line storage for relatively fast recall, and (3) archival storage, characterized by infrequent access. Storage is measured in bytes (eight bits), Kbytes (one thousand bytes), Mbytes (one million bytes), Gbytes (meaning giga, or one billion, bytes), and Tbytes (meaning tera, or one trillion, bytes).

One method of providing short term storage is computer memory. Another is by specialized boards, called *frame buffers*, that store one or more images and can be accessed rapidly, usually at video rates (30 complete images per second). The latter method allows virtually instantaneous image *zoom*, as well as *scroll* (vertical shifts) and *pan* (horizontal shifts). The amount of storage on a frame buffer card is limited by the physical size of the card and by the storage density of the memory chips used. Having 32 Mbytes of storage on a single frame buffer card is not unusual.

On-line storage generally takes the form of magnetic disks. Winchester disks with hundreds of Mbytes are common. A more recent technology, called magneto-optical (MO) storage, uses a laser and specialized materials technologies to achieve close to a Gbyte of storage on a 5¼-in. optical platter. The key factor characterizing on-line storage is frequent access to data. Thus magnetic tapes and other serial media are seldom used for on-line storage in image processing applications. Jukeboxes that hold 30 to 100 optical disks provide an effective solution for large-scale, on-line storage applications that require read–write capability. Optical jukeboxes operate on the same principle as the well-known musical jukebox, in the sense that a mechanical system is used to insert (retrieve) optical disks into (from) optical disk drives.

Finally, archival storage is characterized by massive storage requirements, but infrequent need for access. Magnetic tapes and optical disks are the usual media for archival applications. High-density magnetic tapes (6400 bytes/in.) can store a 1-Mbyte image in about 13 ft of tape. The key problem with magnetic tape is a relatively short shelf life—about seven years—and the need for a controlled storage environment. Current write-once-read-many (WORM) optical disk technology can store on the order of 1 Gbyte on 5¼-in. disks. Unlike MO, WORM disks with larger form factors are available, with the capability to store nearly 6 Gbytes on 12-in. disks, and slightly more than 10 Gbytes on 14-in. disks. Although they are not erasable, WORM disks have a shelf life that exceeds 30 years without special environmental requirements. When stored in a jukebox, WORM disks can also serve as on-line storage devices in applications in which read-only operations are predominant. One Tbyte of WORM storage is now possible in a jukebox that occupies a volume of less than 150 ft³. This capacity translates into 1 million 8-bit images of size 1024 × 1024.

The preceding paragraph dealt with archival storage in digital form. In applications for which retrieval in digital form is not a requirement, storing images in analog form, principally using photographic film or video tape, is not uncommon.

1.4.3 Processing

Processing† of digital images involves procedures that are usually expressed in algorithmic form. Thus, with the exception of image acquisition and display, most image processing functions can be implemented in software. The only reason for specialized image processing hardware is the need for speed in some applications or to overcome some fundamental computer limitations. For example, an important application of digital imaging is low-light microscopy. To reduce image noise requires performing image averaging over numerous images at frame rates (30 images per second in most cases). The bus architecture in all but a few high-performance computers cannot handle the data rate required to perform this operation. Thus today's image processing systems are a blend of off-the-shelf computers and specialized image processing hardware, with the overall operation being orchestrated by software running on the host computer.

As recently as the mid-1980s, numerous models of image processing systems being sold throughout the world were rather substantial peripheral devices that attached to equally substantial host computers. Late in the 1980s and early in the 1990s the market shifted to image processing hardware in the form of single boards designed to be compatible with industry standard buses and to fit into engineering workstation cabinets and personal computers. In addition to lowering costs, this market shift also served as a catalyst for a significant number of new companies whose specialty is the development of software written specifically for image processing.

Although large-scale image processing systems are still being sold for massive imaging applications, such as processing of satellite images, the trend continues toward miniaturizing and merging general purpose small computers

---

† A small computer to signify processing in Fig. 1.7 is used for illustration. Large main frame computers and specialized supercomputer systems are sometimes needed to solve large scale image processing problems.

equipped with image processing hardware. In particular, the principal imaging hardware being added to these computers consists of a digitizer/frame buffer combination for image digitization and temporary storage, a so-called arithmetic/logic unit (ALU) processor for performing arithmetic and logic operations at frame rates, and one or more frame buffers for fast access to image data during processing. A significant amount of basic image processing software can now be obtained commercially. When combined with other software for applications such as spread sheets and graphics, it provides an excellent starting point for the solution of specific image processing problems. Sophisticated display devices and software for word processing and report generation facilitate presentation of results. Often, solutions obtained with such systems are then ported to specialized, fast image processing boards that are compatible with the bus used during development.

Image processing is characterized by specific solutions. Hence techniques that work well in one area can be totally inadequate in another. All that the availability of powerful hardware and basic software does is to provide a starting point much farther along than it was less than a decade ago (and for a fraction of the cost). The actual solution of a specific problem generally still requires significant research and development. The topics covered in the following chapters provide the tools for exactly this type of activity.

1.4.4 Communication

Communication in digital image processing primarily involves local communication between image processing systems and remote communication from one point to another, typically in connection with the transmission of image data. Hardware and software for local communication are readily available for most computers. Most books on computer networks clearly explain standard communication protocols.

Communication across vast distances presents a more serious challenge if the intent is to communicate image data rather than abstracted results. As should be evident by now, digital images contain a significant amount of data. A voice-grade telephone line can transmit at a maximum rate of 9,600 bits/sec. Thus to transmit a 512×512, 8-bit image at this rate would require nearly five minutes. Wireless links using intermediate stations, such as satellites, are much faster, but they also cost considerably more. The point is that transmission of entire images over long distances is far from trivial. In Chapter 6 we show that data compression and decompression techniques play a central role in addressing this problem.

1.4.5 Display

Monochrome and color TV monitors are the principal display devices used in modern image processing systems. Monitors are driven by the output(s) of a hardware image display module in the backplane of the host computer or as

part of the hardware associated with an image processor, as discussed in Section
1.4.3. The signals at the output of the display module can also be fed into an
image recording device that produces a hard copy (slides, photographs, or
transparencies) of the image being viewed on the monitor screen. Other display
media include random-access cathode ray tubes (CRTs), and printing devices.

In random-access CRT systems the horizontal and vertical position of the
CRT's electron beam is controlled by a computer which provides the two-
dimensional drive necessary to produce an output image. At each deflection
point, the intensity of the beam is modulated by using a voltage that is proportional to the value of the corresponding point in the numerical array, varying
from zero intensity outputs for points whose numerical value corresponds to
black, to maximum intensity for white points. The resulting variable intensity
light pattern is recorded by a photographic camera focused on the face of the
cathode-ray tube.

Printing image display devices are useful primarily for low-resolution image
processing work. One simple approach for generating gray-tone images directly
on paper is to use the overstrike capability of a standard line printer. The gray
level of any point in the printout can be controlled by the number and density
of the characters overprinted at that point. Proper selection of the character
set achieves reasonably good gray-level distributions with a simple computer
program and relatively few characters. Appendix A contains examples of this
approach. Other common means of recording an image directly on paper include laser printers, heat-sensitive paper devices, and ink-spray systems.

1.5 ORGANIZATION OF THE BOOK

The material in this book is organized along the functional lines discussed
generally in Section 1.3. The book contains nine chapters, divided into three
broad topic areas: (1) background, (2) preprocessing, and (3) analysis.

The first three chapters cover background topics that are essential to understanding the material that follows in the remaining chapters. Chapter 2 deals
with foundations of visual perception and addresses topics in image resolution,
basic geometric relationships between pixels, the theoretic underpinnings of
imaging geometry, and some introductory concepts related to the properties
of photographic film. Chapter 3 deals with various image transforms, particularly the Fourier transform and some of its properties. Transforms are fundamental tools that are used extensively in image processing applications.

Chapters 4, 5, and 6 develop techniques for image preprocessing. Chapter
4 extensively treats image enhancement techniques, ranging from noise reduction and contrast enhancement to sharpening and color processing. Chapter 5
deals in detail with techniques for image restoration, which play a fundamental
role in recovering image information obscured by degradations, such as blurring. Chapter 6 deals with the important topic of data compression. As men-

tioned in Section 1.4, digital images contain large amounts of data, which serve as strong motivation for seeking methods capable of achieving data reduction. The methods discussed in Chapter 6 cover the spectrum of approaches available for this purpose.

Chapters 7, 8, and 9 cover techniques suitable for image analysis. Chapter 7 deals with segmentation, the first step in automated image analysis. As indicated in Section 1.3, segmentation is the process that subdivides an image into its basic constituent parts. Chapter 8 addresses the representation and description of segmented components. This material covers a broad range of topics, from simple descriptors (such as moments and signatures) to more complex descriptors based on image morphology. Finally, Chapter 9 deals with recognition and interpretation, the last two steps needed to complete an image analysis task. Chapter 9 covers numerous techniques for recognition, ranging from traditional statistical decision rules to more modern methods based on neural networks. The interpretation approaches presented in the final sections of the chapter are based on expert systems and other image modeling formulations.

Two appendices are included at the end of the book. Appendix A contains a discussion of halftoning techniques that can be used as the basis for developing gray-scale printing programs. If an image processing and display system is not available, such programs can be used to display on an ordinary line printer the results of image processing projects. Appendix B contains a set of low-resolution coded digital images that, together with a printing program, can be used as a basic tool for testing with image data the various image processing methods developed in the book.

REFERENCES

The references cited below are general in nature and cover the spectrum of available image processing techniques and their applications. References at the end of later chapters are keyed to specific topics discussed in the text. All references are cited by author, book, or journal name followed by the year of publication. The bibliography at the end of the book is organized in the same way and contains all pertinent information for each reference.

Some of the major journals that publish articles on image processing and related topics include: *Computer Vision, Graphics, and Image Processing, IEEE Transactions on Systems, Man and Cybernetics, IEEE Transactions on Pattern Analysis and Machine Intelligence, Pattern Recognition, IEEE Transactions on Medical Imaging, Journal of the Optical Society of America, IEEE Transactions on Information Theory, IEEE Transactions on Communications, IEEE Transactions on Acoustics, Speech and Signal Processing, Proceedings of the IEEE, Pattern Recognition Letters,* and issues of the *IEEE Transactions on Computers* prior to 1980.

Recommended books that complement our treatment of image processing include in chronological order by year:

Andrews, H. C., *Computer Techniques in Image Processing*, Academic Press, New York, 1970.

Lipkin, S., and Rosenfeld, R., *Picture Processing and Psychopictorics*, Academic Press, New York, 1970.

Duda, R. O., and Hart, P. E., *Pattern Classification and Scene Analysis*, Wiley-Interscience, New York, 1973.

Young, T. C. and Calvert, T. N., *Classification, Estimation, and Pattern Recognition*, American Elsevier Publishing Co., New York, 1974.

Tou, J. T., and Gonzalez, R. C., *Pattern Recognition Principles*, Addison-Wesley, Reading, Mass., 1974.

Andrews, H. C., and Hunt, B. R., *Digital Image Restoration*, Prentice-Hall, Englewood Cliffs, N.J., 1977.

Pavlidis, T., *Structural Pattern Recognition*, Springer-Verlag, New York, 1977.

Pratt, W. K., *Digital Image Processing*, Wiley-Interscience, New York, 1978 (Second ed., 1991).

Gonzalez, R. C., and Thomason, M. G., *Syntactic Pattern Recognition: An Introduction*, Addison-Wesley, Reading, Mass., 1978.

Hall, E. L., *Computer Image Processing and Recognition*, Academic Press, New York, 1979.

Castleman, K. R., *Digital Image Processing*, Prentice-Hall, Englewood Cliffs, N.J., 1979.

Duff, M. J. B., and Levialdi, S., *Languages and Architectures for Image Processing*, Academic Press, New York, 1981.

Fu, K. S., *Syntactic Pattern Recognition and Applications*, Prentice Hall, Englewood Cliffs, N.J., 1982.

Nevatia, R., *Machine Perception*, Prentice-Hall, Englewood Cliffs, N.J., 1982.

Pavlidis, T., *Algorithms for Graphics and Image Processing*, Computer Science Press, Rockville, Md., 1982.

Ballard, D. H., and Brown, C. M., *Computer Vision*, Prentice-Hall, Englewood Cliffs, N.J., 1982.

Rosenfeld, R., and Kak, A. C., *Digital Picture Processing*, 2nd ed., vols. 1 & 2, Academic Press, New York, 1982.

Levine, M. D., *Vision in Man and Machine*, McGraw-Hill, New York, 1985.

Dougherty, E. R. and Giardina, C. R., *Matrix Structured Image Processing,* Prentice Hall, Englewood Cliffs, N.J., 1987.

Jain, A. K., *Fundamentals of Digital Image Processing*, Prentice-Hall, Englewood Cliffs, N.J., 1989.

Schalkoff, R. J., *Digital Image Processing and Computer Vision*, John Wiley & Sons, New York, 1989.

CHAPTER 2

DIGITAL IMAGE FUNDAMENTALS

Those who wish to succeed must ask the right
preliminary questions.

Aristotle

The purpose of this chapter is to introduce several concepts related to digital images and some of the notation used throughout the book. The first section briefly summarizes the mechanics of the human visual system, including image formation in the eye and its capabilities for brightness adaptation and discrimination. Section 2.2 presents an image model based on the illumination–reflection phenomenon, which gives rise to most images perceived in normal visual activities. Section 2.3 introduces the concepts of uniform image sampling and gray-level quantization. Section 2.4 deals with relationships between pixels, such as connectivity and distance measures, which are used extensively in subsequent chapters. Section 2.5 contains a detailed discussion of imaging geometry and related topics. Finally, Section 2.6 contains an introduction to photographic film and some of its most important characteristics in terms of recording image processing results.

2.1 ELEMENTS OF VISUAL PERCEPTION

The ultimate goal of many of the techniques discussed in the following chapters is to help an observer interpret the content of an image. Hence developing a basic understanding of the visual perception process before proceeding is important. A brief account of the human visual mechanism follows, with particular emphasis on concepts that underpin much of the material presented in later chapters.

2.1.1 Structure of the Human Eye

Figure 2.1 shows a horizontal cross section of the human eye. The eye is nearly a sphere, with an average diameter of approximately 20 mm. Three membranes—the *cornea* and *sclera* outer cover, the *choroid*, and the *retina*—enclose the eye. The cornea is a tough, transparent tissue that covers the anterior surface of the eye. Continuous with the cornea, the sclera is an opaque membrane that encloses the remainder of the optic globe.

The choroid lies directly below the sclera. This membrane contains a network of blood vessels that serve as the major source of nutrition to the eye.

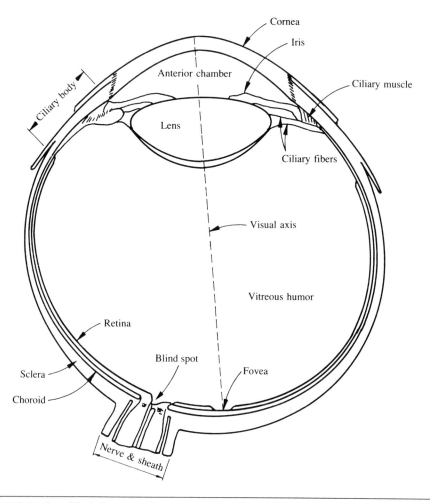

Figure 2.1 *Simplified diagram of a cross section of the human eye.*

The choroid coat is heavily pigmented and hence helps to reduce the amount of extraneous light entering the eye and the backscatter within the optical globe. At its anterior extreme, the choroid is divided into the *ciliary body* and the *iris diaphragm*. The latter contracts or expands to control the amount of light that enters the eye. The central opening of the iris (the *pupil*) varies in diameter from approximately 2 mm to 8 mm. The front of the iris contains the visible pigment of the eye, whereas the back contains a black pigment.

The *lens* is made up of concentric layers of fibrous cells and is suspended by fibers that attach to the ciliary body. It contains 60 to 70 percent water, about 6 percent fat, and more protein than any other tissue in the eye. The lens is colored by a slightly yellow pigmentation that increases with age. It absorbs approximately 8 percent of the visible light spectrum, with relatively higher absorption at shorter wavelengths. Both infrared and ultraviolet light are absorbed appreciably by proteins within the lens structure and, in excessive amounts, can cause damage to the eye.

The innermost membrane of the eye is the retina, which lines the inside of the wall's entire posterior portion. When the eye is properly focused, light from an object outside the eye is imaged on the retina. Pattern vision is afforded by the distribution of discrete light receptors over the surface of the retina. There are two classes of receptors: *cones* and *rods*. The cones in each eye number between 6 and 7 million. They are located primarily in the central portion of the retina, called the *fovea*, and are highly sensitive to color. Human beings can resolve fine details with these cones largely because each one is connected to its own nerve end. Muscles controlling the eye rotate the eyeball until the image of an object of interest falls on the fovea. Cone vision is called *photopic* or bright-light vision.

The number of rods is much larger: some 75 to 150 million are distributed over the retinal surface. The larger area of distribution and the fact that several rods are connected to a single nerve end reduce the amount of detail discernible by these receptors. Rods serve to give a general, overall picture of the field of view. They are not involved in color vision and are sensitive to low levels of illumination. For example, objects that appear brightly colored in daylight, when seen by moonlight appear as colorless forms because only the rods are stimulated. This phenomenon is known as *scotopic* or dim-light vision.

Figure 2.2 shows the density of rods and cones for a cross section of the right eye passing through the region of emergence of the optic nerve from the eye. The absence of receptors in this area results in the so-called *blind spot* (see Fig. 2.1). Except for this region, the distribution of receptors is radially symmetric about the fovea. Receptor density is measured in degrees from the fovea (that is, in degrees off axis, as measured by the angle formed by the visual axis and a line passing through the center of the lens and intersecting the retina). Note in Fig. 2.2 that cones are most dense in the center of the

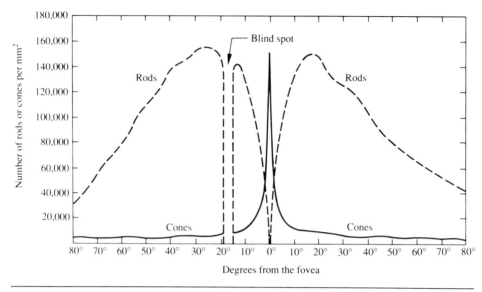

Figure 2.2 *Distribution of rods and cones in the retina. (Adapted from Graham [1965].)*

retina (in the area of the fovea). Note also that rods increase in density from the center out to approximately 20° off axis and then decrease in density out to the extreme periphery of the retina.

The fovea itself is a circular indentation in the retina of about 1.5 mm in diameter. However, in terms of future discussions, talking about square or rectangular arrays of sensing elements is more useful. Thus by taking some liberty in interpretation, we can view the fovea as a square sensor array of size 1.5 mm × 1.5 mm. The density of cones in that area of the retina is approximately 150,000 elements per mm^2. Based on these approximations, the number of cones in the region of highest acuity in the eye is about 337,000 elements. Just in terms of raw resolving power, a CCD imaging chip of medium resolution can have this number of elements in a receptor array no larger than 7 mm × 7 mm. While the ability of human beings to integrate intelligence and experience with vision makes this type of comparison dangerous, keep in mind that the basic ability of the eye to resolve detail is certainly within the realm of current electronic imaging sensors.

2.1.2 Image Formation in the Eye

The principal difference between the lens of the eye and an ordinary optical lens is that the former is flexible. As illustrated in Fig. 2.1, the radius of curvature of the anterior surface of the lens is greater than the radius of its posterior surface. The shape of the lens is controlled by the tension in the fibers of the ciliary body. To focus on distant objects, the controlling muscles cause the lens to be relatively flattened. Similarly, these muscles allow the lens to become thicker in order to focus on objects near the eye.

The distance between the focal center of the lens and the retina varies from approximately 17 mm to about 14 mm, as the refractive power of the lens increases from its minimum to its maximum. When the eye focuses on an object farther away than about 3 m, the lens exhibits its lowest refractive power, and when the eye focuses on a nearby object the lens is most strongly refractive. This information makes calculating the size of the retinal image of any object easy. In Fig. 2.3, for example, the observer is looking at a tree 15 m high at a distance of 100 m. If x is the size of the retinal image in millimeters, the geometry of Fig. 2.3 yields $15/100 = x/17$ or $x = 2.55$ mm. As indicated in Section 2.1.1 the retinal image is reflected primarily in the area of the fovea. Perception then takes place by the relative excitation of light receptors, which transform radiant energy into electrical impulses that are ultimately decoded by the brain.

2.1.3 Brightness Adaptation and Discrimination

Because digital images are displayed as a discrete set of brightness points, the eye's ability to discriminate between different brightness levels is an important consideration in presenting image processing results.

The range of light intensity levels to which the human visual system can adapt is enormous—on the order of 10^{10}—from the scotopic threshold to the glare limit. Considerable experimental evidence indicates that subjective brightness (brightness as perceived by the human visual system) is a logarithmic function of the light intensity incident on the eye. Figure 2.4, a plot of light intensity versus subjective brightness, illustrates this characteristic. The long solid curve represents the range of intensities to which the visual system can adapt. In photopic vision alone, the range is about 10^6. The transition from scotopic to photopic vision is gradual over the approximate range from 0.001

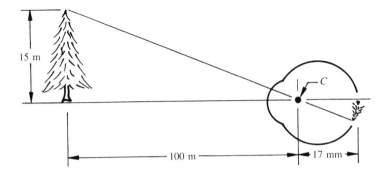

Figure 2.3 *Optical representation of the eye looking at a tree. Point C is the optical center of the lens.*

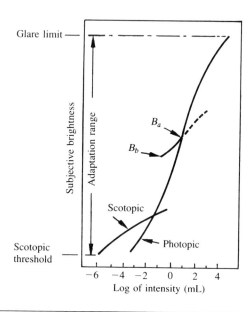

Figure 2.4   *Range of subjective brightness sensations showing a particular adaptation level.*

to 0.1 millilambert (-3 to -1 mL in the log scale), as the double branches of the adaptation curve in this range show.

The essential point in interpreting the impressive dynamic range depicted in Fig. 2.4 is that the visual system cannot operate over such a range *simultaneously*. Rather, it accomplishes this large variation by changes in its overall sensitivity, a phenomenon known as *brightness adaptation*. The total range of intensity levels it can discriminate simultaneously is rather small compared with the total adaptation range. For any given set of conditions, the current sensitivity level of the visual system is called the *brightness adaptation level*, which may correspond, for example, to brightness B_a in Fig. 2.4. The short intersecting curve represents the range of subjective brightness that the eye can perceive when adapted to this level. This range is rather restricted, having a level B_b at and below which all stimuli are perceived as indistinguishable blacks. The upper (dashed) portion of the curve is not actually restricted but, if extended too far, loses its meaning because much higher intensities would simply raise the adaptation level higher than B_a.

The ability of the eye to discriminate between *changes* in brightness at any specific adaptation level is also of considerable interest. A classic experiment used to determine the capability of the human visual system for brightness discrimination consists of having a subject look at a flat, uniformly illuminated area large enough to occupy the entire field of view. This area typically is a diffuser, such as opaque glass, that is illuminated from the back by a light source whose intensity, I, can be varied. To this field is added an increment of illumination, ΔI, in the form of a short-duration flash that appears as a circle in the center of the uniformly illuminated field, as Fig. 2.5 shows.

If ΔI is not bright enough, the subject says "No," indicating no perceivable change. As ΔI gets stronger, the subject may give a positive response of "Yes," indicating a perceived change. Finally, when ΔI is strong enough, the subject will give a response of "Yes" all the time. The quantity $\Delta I_c/I$, where ΔI_c is the increment of illumination discriminable 50 percent of the time with background illumination I, is called the *Weber ratio*. A small value of $\Delta I_c/I$ means that a small percentage change in intensity is discriminable. This represents "good" brightness discrimination. Conversely, a large value of $\Delta I_c/I$ means that a large percentage change in intensity is required. This represents "poor" brightness discrimination.

A plot of log $\Delta I_c/I$ as a function of log I has the general shape shown in Fig. 2.6. This curve shows that brightness discrimination is poor (the Weber ratio is large) at low levels of illumination, and it improves significantly (the Weber ratio decreases) as background illumination increases. The two branches in the curve reflect the fact that at low levels of illumination vision is carried out by activity of the rods, whereas at high levels (showing better discrimination) vision is the function of cones.

If the background illumination is held constant and the intensity of the other source, instead of flashing, is now allowed to vary incrementally from never being perceived to always being perceived, the typical observer can discern a total of one to two dozen different intensity changes. Roughly, this result is related to the number of different intensities a person can see at any one point in a monochrome image. This result does not mean that an image can be represented by such a small number of intensity values because, as the eye roams about the image, the average background changes, thus allowing a *different* set of incremental changes to be detected at each new adaptation level. The net consequence is that the eye is capable of a much broader range of *overall* intensity discrimination. In fact, we show in Section 2.3 that if the number of intensity levels used to represent a monochrome image is as small

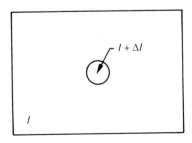

Figure 2.5 *Basic experimental setup used to characterize brightness discrimination.*

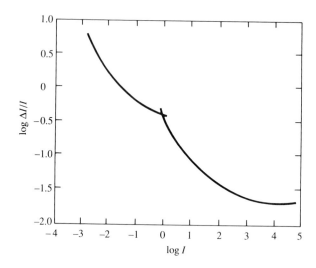

Figure 2.6   *Typical Weber ratio as a function of intensity. (Adapted from Graham [1965].)*

as one to two dozen levels, the eye is quite capable of detecting objectionable contouring effects.

Two phenomena clearly demonstrate that perceived brightness is not a simple function of intensity. The first, related to the images shown in Fig. 2.7, is based on the fact that the visual system tends to undershoot or overshoot around the boundary of regions of different intensities. Figure 2.7(a) shows a striking example of this phenomenon. Although the intensity of the stripes is constant, we actually perceive a brightness pattern that is strongly scalloped, especially near the boundaries. Figure 2.7(b) is called a *Mach band pattern*, named for Ernst Mach, who first described the phenomenon in 1865. The profile shows the real intensity distribution, but the brightness pattern perceived is a darker stripe in region *D* and a brighter one in region *B*.

The second phenomenon, called *simultaneous contrast*, is related to the fact that a region's perceived brightness does not depend simply on its intensity, as Fig. 2.8 demonstrates. All the center squares have exactly the same intensity. However, they appear to the eye to become darker as the background gets lighter. A more familiar example is a piece of paper that seems white when lying on a desk, but can appear totally black when used to shield the eyes while looking directly at a bright sky.

2.2   A SIMPLE IMAGE MODEL

The term *image* refers to a two-dimensional light-intensity function, denoted by $f(x, y)$, where the value or amplitude of f at spatial coordinates (x, y) gives

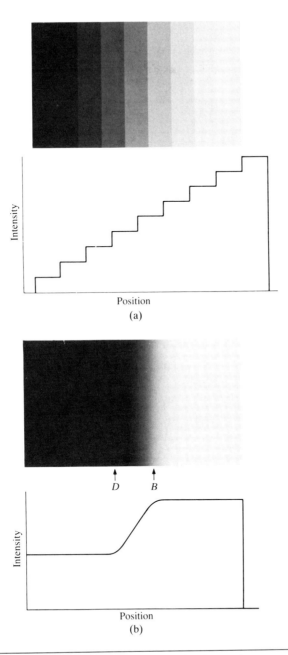

Figure 2.7 *Two examples showing that perceived brightness is not a simple function of intensity. (Adapted from Cornsweet [1970].)*

Figure 2.8 *Example of simultaneous contrast. All the small squares have exactly the same intensity, but they appear progressively darker as the background becomes lighter.*

the intensity (brightness) of the image at that point. As light is a form of energy, $f(x, y)$ must be nonzero and finite, that is,

$$0 < f(x, y) < \infty. \tag{2.2-1}$$

The images people perceive in everyday visual activities normally consist of light reflected from objects. The basic nature of $f(x, y)$ may be characterized by two components: (1) the amount of source light incident on the scene being viewed and (2) the amount of light reflected by the objects in the scene. Appropriately, they are called the *illumination* and *reflectance components*, and are denoted by $i(x, y)$ and $r(x, y)$, respectively. The functions $i(x, y)$ and $r(x, y)$ combine as a product to form $f(x, y)$:

$$f(x, y) = i(x, y)r(x, y) \tag{2.2-2}$$

where

$$0 < i(x, y) < \infty \tag{2.2-3}$$

and

$$0 < r(x, y) < 1. \tag{2.2-4}$$

Equation (2.2-4) indicates that reflectance is bounded by 0 (total absorption) and 1 (total reflectance). The nature of $i(x, y)$ is determined by the light source, and $r(x, y)$ is determined by the characteristics of the objects in a scene.

The values given in Eqs. (2.2-3) and (2.2-4) are theoretic bounds. The following *average* numerical figures illustrate some typical ranges of $i(x, y)$. On a clear day, the sun may produce in excess of 9000 foot-candles of illumination on the surface of the earth. This figure decreases to less than 1000 foot-candles on a cloudy day. On a clear evening, a full moon yields about 0.01 foot-candle of illumination. The typical illumination level in a commercial office is about 100 foot-candles. Similarly, the following are some typical values of $r(x, y)$: 0.01 for black velvet, 0.65 for stainless steel, 0.80 for flat-white wall paint, 0.90 for silver-plated metal, and 0.93 for snow.

Throughout this book, we call the intensity of a monochrome image f at coordinates (x, y) the *gray level* (l) of the image at that point. From Eqs. (2.2-2) through (2.2-4), it is evident that l lies in the range

$$L_{min} \leq l \leq L_{max}. \tag{2.2-5}$$

In theory, the only requirement on L_{min} is that it be positive, and on L_{max} that it be finite. In practice, $L_{min} = i_{min} r_{min}$ and $L_{max} = i_{max} r_{max}$. Using the preceding values of illumination and reflectance as a guideline, the values $L_{min} \approx 0.005$ and $L_{max} \approx 100$ for indoor image processing applications may be expected.

The interval $[L_{min}, L_{max}]$ is called the *gray scale*. Common practice is to shift this interval numerically to the interval $[0, L]$, where $l = 0$ is considered black and $l = L$ is considered white in the scale. All intermediate values are shades of gray varying continuously from black to white.

2.3 SAMPLING AND QUANTIZATION

2.3.1 Uniform Sampling and Quantization

To be suitable for computer processing, an image function $f(x, y)$ must be digitized both spatially and in amplitude. Digitization of the spatial coordinates (x, y) is called *image sampling*, and amplitude digitization is called *gray-level quantization*.

Suppose that a continuous image $f(x, y)$ is approximated by equally spaced samples arranged in the form of an $N \times M$ array as shown in Eq. (2.3-1), where each element of the array is a discrete quantity:

$$f(x, y) \approx \begin{bmatrix} f(0, 0) & f(0, 1) & \cdots & f(0, M-1) \\ f(1, 0) & f(1, 1) & \cdots & f(1, M-1) \\ \vdots & & & \\ f(N-1, 0) & f(N-1, 1) & \cdots & f(N-1, M-1) \end{bmatrix} \tag{2.3-1}$$

The right-hand side of Eq. (2.3-1) represents what is commonly called a *digital image*. Each element of the array is referred to as an *image element, picture element, pixel,* or *pel* as indicated in Section 1.2. The terms *image* and *pixels* will be used throughout the following discussions to denote a digital image and its elements.

Expressing sampling and quantization in more formal mathematical terms can be useful at times. Let Z and R denote the set of real integers and the set of real numbers, respectively. The sampling process may be viewed as partitioning the xy plane into a grid, with the coordinates of the center of each grid being a pair of elements from the Cartesian product $Z \times Z$ (also written as Z^2), which is the set of all ordered pairs of elements (a, b), with a and b being integers from Z. Hence $f(x, y)$ is a digital image if (x, y) are integers from $Z \times Z$ and f is a function that assigns a gray-level value (that is, a real number from the set of real numbers, R) to each distinct pair of coordinates (x, y). This functional assignment obviously is the quantization process described earlier. If the gray levels also are integers (as usually is the case in this and subsequent chapters), Z replaces R, and a digital image then becomes a two-dimensional (2-D) function whose coordinates and amplitude values are integers.

This digitization process requires decisions about values for N, M, and the number of discrete gray levels allowed for each pixel. Common practice in digital image processing is to let these quantities be integer powers of two; that is,

$$N = 2^n, \qquad M = 2^k \tag{2.3-2}$$

and

$$G = 2^m \tag{2.3-3}$$

where G denotes the number of gray levels. The assumption in this section is that the discrete levels are equally spaced between 0 and L in the gray scale. Using Eqs. (2.3-2) and (2.3-3) yields the number, b, of bits required to store a digitized image:

$$b = N \times M \times m. \tag{2.3-4}$$

If $M = N$,

$$b = N^2 m. \tag{2.3-5}$$

For example, a 128×128 image with 64 gray levels requires 98,304 bits of storage. Table 2.1 summarizes values of b from Eq. (2.3-5) for some typical ranges of N and m. Table 2.2 gives the corresponding number of 8-bit bytes.

Because Eq. (2.3-1) is an approximation to a continuous image, a reason-

Table 2.1 Number of Storage Bits for Various Values of N and m

N \ m	1	2	3	4	5	6	7	8
32	1,024	2,048	3,072	4,096	5,120	6,144	7,168	8,192
64	4,096	8,192	12,288	16,384	20,480	24,576	28,672	32,768
128	16,384	32,768	49,152	65,536	81,920	98,304	114,688	131,072
256	65,536	131,072	196,608	262,144	327,680	393,216	458,752	524,288
512	262,144	524,288	786,432	1,048,576	1,310,720	1,572,864	1,835,008	2,097,152
1,024	1,048,576	2,097,152	3,145,728	4,194,304	5,242,880	6,291,456	7,340,032	8,388,608

able question to ask at this point is: How many samples and gray levels are required for a good approximation? The *resolution* (the degree of discernible detail) of an image depends strongly on these two parameters. The more these parameters are increased, the closer the digitized array approximates the original image. However, Eq. (2.3-4) clearly points out the unfortunate fact that storage and, consequently, processing requirements increase rapidly as a function of N, M, and m.

In light of the preceding comments—and assuming square images for convenience—let us consider the effect that variations in N and m have on image quality. A "good" image is difficult to define, because image quality not only is highly subjective, but it is also strongly dependent on the requirements of a given application. We consider this problem in Section 3.3.9, in connection with image sampling, and in much more detail in Chapter 6, in the context of image data compression. For the moment, however, we are only interested in developing a general impression of how a digital image degrades as its spatial resolution and gray-level quantization are decreased.

Figure 2.9(a) shows a 1024 × 1024, 256-level digital image of a rose. Figures 2.9(b)–(f) show the results of reducing the spatial resolution from $N = 1024$ to $N = 512$, 256, 128, 64, and 32, respectively. In all cases, the maximum

Table 2.2 Number of 8-bit Bytes of Storage for Various Values of N and m

N \ m	1	2	3	4	5	6	7	8
32	128	256	512	512	1,024	1,024	1,024	1,024
64	512	1,024	2,048	2,048	4,096	4,096	4,096	4,096
128	2,048	4,096	8,192	8,192	16,384	16,384	16,384	16,384
256	8,192	16,384	32,768	32,768	65,536	65,536	65,536	65,536
512	32,768	65,536	131,072	131,072	262,144	262,144	262,144	262,144
1,024	131,072	262,144	393,216	524,288	655,360	786,432	917,504	1,048,576

number of gray levels allowed was 256. With the display area used for each image being the same (a 1024 × 1024 display field), pixels in the lower resolution images were duplicated in order to fill the entire display. This *pixel replication* produced a checkerboard effect, which is particularly visible in the images of lower resolution.

Compare Fig. 2.9(a) with the 512 × 512 image in Fig. 2.9(b) and note that it is virtually impossible to tell these two images apart. If we compared the two original photographs at this scale, we would see an almost imperceptible increase in graininess and a slight decrease in sharpness in the 512 × 512 image, especially toward the center of the bud. Generally, this type of detail is lost in most printing processes and is often difficult to discern even in original displays or photographs depending, of course, on the relative size of the objects. For instance, enlarging Fig. 2.9(b) eventually would render visible the pixel replication used to generate this image. Next, the 256 × 256 image shows a fine checkerboard pattern in the edges and a more pronounced graininess throughout the image. This effect is much more visible in the 128 × 128 image, and it becomes quite pronounced in the 64 × 64 and 32 × 32 images.

Figure 2.10 illustrates the effects produced by decreasing the number of bits used to represent the number of gray levels in an image. Figure 2.10(a) shows the same 1024 × 1024, 8-bit image used in the preceding discussion. Figures 2.10(b)–(h) were obtained by reducing the number of bits from $m = 7$ to $m = 1$ (see Eq. 2.3-3), while keeping the spatial resolution constant at 1024 × 1024 pixels. The 256-, 128-, and 64-level images are visually identical for all practical purposes. The 32-level image shown in Fig. 2.10(d), however, has developed an almost imperceptible set of very fine ridgelike structures in areas of smooth gray levels. This effect, caused by the use of an insufficient number of gray levels in smooth areas of a digital image, is called *false contouring*. It generally is quite visible in images displayed using 16 or less uniformly spaced gray levels, as the images in Figs. 2.10(e)–(h) show clearly.

The preceding results illustrate the effects produced on image quality by varying N and m independently. However, these results only partially answer the question posed earlier, because we have not yet said anything about the relation between these parameters. Huang [1965] considered this problem in an attempt to quantify experimentally the effects on image quality produced by varying N and m. The experiment consisted of a set of subjective tests. Three of the images used are shown in Fig. 2.11. The woman's face is representative of an image with relatively little detail; the picture of the cameraman contains an intermediate amount of detail; and the crowd picture contains, by comparison, a large amount of detail.

Sets of these three images were generated by varying N and m, and observers were then asked to rank them according to their subjective quality. The results are summarized in Fig. 2.12 in the form of *isopreference curves* in the Nm plane. Each point in this plane represents an image having values of N

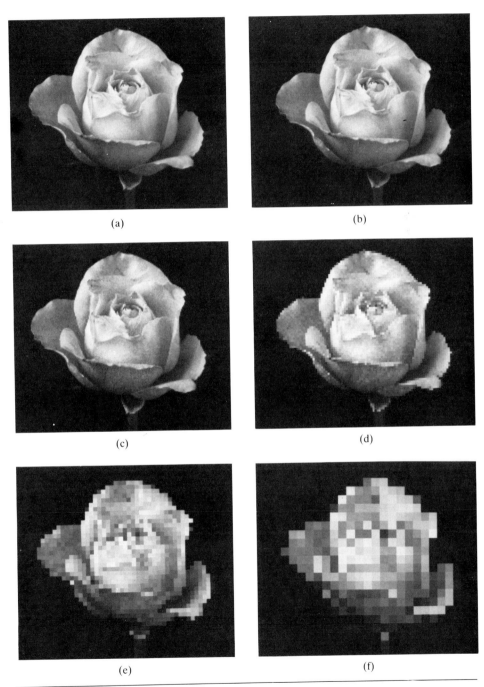

Figure 2.9 Effects of reducing spatial resolution.

(a)   (b)

(c)   (d)

Figure 2.10 *A 1024 × 1024 image displayed in 256, 128, 64, 32, 16, 8, 4, and 2 levels, respectively.*

and *m* equal to the coordinates of that point. Points lying on an isopreference curve correspond to images of equal subjective quality.

The isopreference curves of Fig. 2.12 are arranged, from left to right, in order of increasing subjective quality. These results suggest several empirical conclusions. (1) As expected, the quality of the images tends to increase as *N* and *m* are increased. In a few cases, for fixed *N*, the quality improved by decreasing *m*. The most likely reason for this result is that a decrease in *m*

(e)

(f)

(g)

(h)

Figure 2.10   *(Continued)*

generally increases the apparent contrast of an image. (2) The curves tend to become more vertical as the detail in the image increases. This result suggests that for images with a large amount of detail only a few gray levels are needed. For example, Fig. 2.12(c) shows that, for $N = 64$ or 128, image quality is not improved by an increase in m. The same is not true for the curves in the other two figures. (3) The isopreference curves depart markedly from the curves of constant b (see Eq. 2.3-5), which are shown as dashed lines in Fig. 2.12.

(a)

(b)   (c)

Figure 2.11   *Test images used in evaluating subjective image quality. (From Huang [1965].)*

2.3.2 Nonuniform Sampling and Quantization

For a fixed value of spatial resolution, the appearance of an image can be improved in many cases by using an adaptive scheme where the sampling process depends on the characteristics of the image. In general, fine sampling is required in the neighborhood of sharp gray-level transitions, whereas coarse sampling may be utilized in relatively smooth regions. Consider, for example, a simple image consisting of a face superimposed on a uniform background. Clearly, the background carries little detailed information and can be quite adequately represented by coarse sampling. The face, however, contains considerably more detail. If the additional samples not used in the background are used in this region of the image, the overall result would tend to improve. In

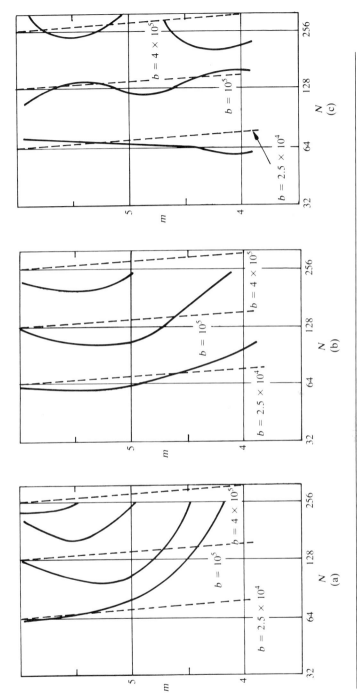

Figure 2.12 *Isopreference curves for (a) face, (b) cameraman, and (c) crowd. (From Huang [1965].)*

distributing the samples, greater sample concentration should be used in gray-level transition boundaries, such as the boundary between the face and the background in this example.

The necessity of having to identify boundaries, even if only roughly, is a definite drawback of the nonuniform sampling approach. This method also is not practical for images containing relatively small uniform regions. For instance, nonuniform sampling would be difficult to justify for an image of a dense crowd of people.

When the number of gray levels must be kept small, the use of unequally spaced levels in the quantization process usually is desirable. A method similar to the nonuniform sampling technique discussed earlier may be used for the distribution of gray levels in an image. However, as the eye is relatively poor at estimating shades of gray near abrupt level changes, the approach in this case is to use few gray levels in the neighborhood of boundaries. The remaining levels can then be used in regions where gray-level variations are smooth, thus avoiding or reducing the false contours that often appear in these regions if they are too coarsely quantized.

This method is subject to the preceding observations about boundary detection and detail content. An alternative technique that is particularly attractive for distributing gray levels consists of computing the frequency of occurrence of all allowed levels. If gray levels in a certain range occur frequently, while others occur rarely, the quantization levels are finely spaced in this range and coarsely spaced outside of it. This method is sometimes called *tapered quantization*. We discuss these topics further in Chapter 6.

2.4 SOME BASIC RELATIONSHIPS BETWEEN PIXELS

In this section we consider several primitive, yet important relationships between pixels in a digital image. As mentioned before, an image is denoted by $f(x, y)$. When referring to a particular pixel, we use lowercase letters, such as p and q. A subset of pixels of $f(x, y)$ is denoted by S.

2.4.1 Neighbors of a Pixel

A pixel p at coordinates (x, y) has four *horizontal* and *vertical* neighbors whose coordinates are given by

$$(x + 1, y), (x - 1, y), (x, y + 1), (x, y - 1).$$

This set of pixels, called the 4-*neighbors* of p, is denoted by $N_4(p)$. Each pixel is a unit distance from (x, y), and some of the neighbors of p lie outside the digital image if (x, y) is on the border of the image.

The four *diagonal* neighbors of p have coordinates

$$(x + 1, y + 1), (x + 1, y - 1), (x - 1, y + 1), (x - 1, y - 1)$$

and are denoted by $N_D(p)$. These points, together with the 4-neighbors, are called the 8-*neighbors* of p, denoted by $N_8(p)$. As before, some of the points in $N_D(p)$ and $N_8(p)$ fall outside the image if (x, y) is on the border of the image.

2.4.2 Connectivity

Connectivity between pixels is an important concept used in establishing boundaries of objects and components of regions in an image. To establish whether two pixels are connected, it must be determined if they are adjacent in some sense (say, if they are 4-neighbors) and if their gray levels satisfy a specified criterion of similarity (say, if they are equal). For instance, in a binary image with values 0 and 1, two pixels may be 4-neighbors, but they are not said to be connected unless they have the same value.

Let V be the set of gray-level values used to define connectivity; for example, in a binary image, $V = \{1\}$ for the connectivity of pixels with value 1. In a gray-scale image, for the connectivity of pixels with a range of intensity values of, say, 32 to 64, it follows that $V = \{32, 33, \ldots, 63, 64\}$. We consider three types of connectivity:

(a) 4-*connectivity*. Two pixels p and q with values from V are 4-connected if q is in the set $N_4(p)$.

(b) 8-*connectivity*. Two pixels p and q with values from V are 8-connected if q is in the set $N_8(p)$.

(c) m-*connectivity* (mixed connectivity). Two pixels p and q with values from V are m-connected if

    (i) q is in $N_4(p)$, *or*

    (ii) q is in $N_D(p)$ *and* the set $N_4(p) \cap N_4(q)$ is empty. (This is the set of pixels that are 4-neighbors of both p and q and whose values are from V.)

Mixed connectivity is a modification of 8-connectivity and is introduced to eliminate the multiple path connections that often arise when 8-connectivity is used. For example, consider the pixel arrangement shown in Fig. 2.13(a). For $V = \{1\}$, the paths between 8-neighbors of the center pixel are shown by dashed lines in Fig. 2.13(b). Note the ambiguity in path connections that results from allowing 8-connectivity. This ambiguity is removed by using m-connectivity, as shown in Fig. 2.13(c).

A pixel p is *adjacent* to a pixel q if they are connected. We can define 4-, 8-, or m-adjacency depending on the type of connectivity specified. Two image subsets S_1 and S_2 are adjacent if some pixel in S_1 is adjacent to some pixel in S_2.

A *path* from pixel p with coordinates (x, y) to pixel q with coordinates (s, t) is a sequence of distinct pixels with coordinates

$$(x_0, y_0), (x_1, y_1), \ldots, (x_n, y_n)$$

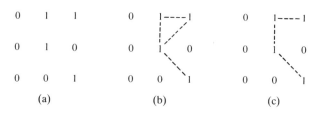

Figure 2.13 *(a) Arrangement of pixels; (b) 8-neighbors of the center pixel; (c) m-neighbors of the same pixel. The dashed lines are paths between that pixel and its neighbors.*

where $(x_0, y_0) = (x, y)$ and $(x_n, y_n) = (s, t)$, (x_i, y_i) is adjacent to (x_{i-1}, y_{i-1}), $1 \leq i \leq n$, and n is the *length* of the path. We can define 4-, 8-, or m-paths depending on the type of adjacency specified.

If p and q are pixels of an image subset S, then p is *connected* to q in S if there is a path from p to q consisting entirely of pixels in S. For any pixel p in S, the set of pixels in S that are connected to p is called a *connected component* of S. Hence any two pixels of a connected component are connected to each other, and distinct connected components are disjoint.

The ability to assign different labels to various disjoint, connected components of an image is of fundamental importance in automated image analysis. In the following section we develop a simple sequential connected component labeling procedure that operates on two rows of a binary image at a time. We develop a different approach based on morphology in Section 8.4.

2.4.3 Labeling of Connected Components

Imagine scanning an image pixel by pixel, from left to right and from top to bottom and assume for the moment that we are interested in 4-connected components. Let p denote the pixel at any step in the scanning process and let r and t denote the upper and left-hand neighbors of p, respectively. The nature of the scanning sequence ensures that when we get to p, points r and t have already been encountered (and labeled if they were 1's).

With the preceding concepts established, let us consider the following procedure. If the value of p is 0, simply move on to the next scanning position. If the value of p is 1, examine r and t. If they are both 0, assign a new label to p (as far as we know, based on the current information, this is the first time that this connected component has been encountered). If only one of the two neighbors is 1, assign its label to p. If they are both 1 and have the same label, assign that label to p. If they are both 1 and have different labels, assign one of the labels to p and make a note that the two labels are equivalent (that is, points r and t are connected through p). At the end of the scan, all points with value 1 have been labeled, but some of these labels may be equivalent. All we need to do now is sort all pairs of equivalent labels into equivalence classes (see Section 2.4.4), assign a different label to each class, and then do a second pass through the image, replacing each label by the label assigned to its equivalence class.

To label 8-connected components we proceed in the same way, but the two upper diagonal neighbors of p, denoted by q and s, also have to be examined. The nature of the scanning sequence ensures that these neighbors have already been processed by the time the procedure gets to p. If p is 0, move on to the next scanning position. If p is 1 and all four neighbors are 0, assign a new label to p. If only one of the neighbors is 1, assign its label to p. If two or more neighbors are 1, assign one of the labels to p and make a note of the appropriate equivalences. After completing the scan of the image sort the equivalent label pairs into equivalence classes, assign a unique label to each class, and do a second scan through the image, replacing each label by the label assigned to its equivalence class.

2.4.4 Relations, Equivalence, and Transitive Closure

The labeling algorithm discussed in the previous section suggests the usefulness of formal tools for handling relationships and equivalences in pixel processing. Let us consider briefly some important concepts that are the bases of such relationships and equivalences.

A *binary relation*† R on a set A is a set of pairs of elements from A. If the pair (a, b) is in R, the notation often used is aRb which, in words, is interpreted to mean "a is related to b." Take for example, the set of points $A = \{p_1, p_2, p_3, p_4\}$ arranged as

$$p_1 \quad p_2$$
$$p_3$$
$$p_4$$

and define the relation "4-connected." In this case, R is the set of pairs of points from A that are 4-connected; that is, $R = \{(p_1, p_2), (p_2, p_1), (p_1, p_3), (p_3, p_1)\}$. Thus p_1 is related to p_2, and p_1 is related to p_3, and vice versa, but p_4 is not related to any other point under the relation "4-connected".

A binary relation R over set A is said to be

(a) *reflexive* if for each a in A, aRa;

(b) *symmetric* if for each a and b in A, aRb implies bRa; and

(c) *transitive* if for a, b, and c in A, aRb and bRc implies aRc.

A relation satisfying these three properties is called an *equivalence relation*.

---

† In this context, the word *binary* refers to "two," and has nothing to do with binary images.

An important property of equivalence relations is that, if R is an equivalence relation on a set A, then A can be divided into k disjoint subsets, called *equivalence classes*, for some k between 1 and ∞, inclusive, such that aRb if and only if a and b are in the same subset.

Expressing a relation in terms of a binary matrix is useful. For example, letting $R = \{(a, a), (a, b), (b, d), (d, b), (c, e)\}$ yields the matrix

$$
\mathbf{B} = \begin{array}{c} \\ a \\ b \\ c \\ d \\ e \end{array}
\begin{array}{ccccc}
a & b & c & d & e \\
\left[\begin{array}{ccccc}
1 & 1 & 0 & 0 & 0 \\
0 & 0 & 0 & 1 & 0 \\
0 & 0 & 0 & 0 & 1 \\
0 & 1 & 0 & 0 & 0 \\
0 & 0 & 0 & 0 & 0
\end{array}\right]
\end{array}
$$

if a 1 is inserted in the locations corresponding to elements that are related and 0's are inserted elsewhere. If the relation in question were reflexive, all the main diagonal terms would be 1; if R were symmetric, $\mathbf{B}$ would be a symmetric matrix.

As indicated above, transitivity implies if aRb and bRc then aRc. In the example just given, a is related to b and b is related to d because (a, b) and (b, d) are in R. However, we note that (a, d) is not in the set R. The set containing these "implied" relations is called the *transitive closure* of R and is denoted by R^+. Here, $R^+ = \{(a, a), (a, b), (a, d), (b, b), (b, d), (d, b), (d, d), (c, e)\}$. The fact that the set includes the pairs (b, b) and (d, d) follows from the definition of transitivity (that is, bRd and dRb, so bRb; and dRb and bRd, so dRd). Expressed in matrix form,

$$
\mathbf{B}^+ = \begin{array}{c} \\ a \\ b \\ c \\ d \\ e \end{array}
\begin{array}{ccccc}
a & b & c & d & e \\
\left[\begin{array}{ccccc}
1 & 1 & 0 & 1 & 0 \\
0 & 1 & 0 & 1 & 0 \\
0 & 0 & 0 & 0 & 1 \\
0 & 1 & 0 & 1 & 0 \\
0 & 0 & 0 & 0 & 0
\end{array}\right]
\end{array}
$$

where the 1-valued elements determine the members of the transitive closure R^+. A straightforward procedure for computing matrix $\mathbf{B}^+$ from a given matrix $\mathbf{B}$ is as follows.

Let $\mathbf{B}$ be an $n \times n$ binary matrix representing a relation R over an alphabet

A of *n* symbols and compute the matrix

$$\mathbf{B}^+ = \mathbf{B} + \mathbf{BB} + \mathbf{BBB} + \cdots + (\mathbf{B})^n \qquad (2.4\text{-}1)$$

where $(\mathbf{B})^n = \mathbf{BBB} \ldots \mathbf{B}$ (*n* times). The 1-valued elements of the matrix $\mathbf{B}^+$ represent the transitive closure, R^+, of relation R (Gries [1971]). The matrix operations are carried out in the usual manner, except that all multiplications are replaced by logical ANDs and all additions (including those shown in Eq. 2.4-1) are replaced by logical ORs. The order of operations in Eq. (2.4-1) is $\mathbf{B}$, $\mathbf{B(B)}$, $\mathbf{B(BB)}$, $\mathbf{B(BBB)}$, . . . so that, at each step, we simply multiply the result up to that point by $\mathbf{B}$. We leave it as an exercise to show that Eq. (2.4-1) gives the same result for $\mathbf{B}^+$ as in the example above.

Implementation of Eq. (2.4-1) requires on the order of n^3 AND and OR operations. Warshall [1962] developed a more efficient algorithm that requires only OR operations involving the elements of $\mathbf{B}$ that have value 1:

Step 1. Set $j = 1$.

Step 2. For $i = 1, 2, \ldots, n$, if $b(i, j) = 1$, then, for $k = 1, 2, \ldots, n$, set $b(i, k) = b(i, k) + b(j, k)$.

Step 3. Increment j by 1.

Step 4. If $j \leq n$, go to *Step* 2; otherwise go to *Step* 5.

Step 5. Stop. The result is $\mathbf{B}^+$ in place of $\mathbf{B}$.

It is instructive to verify that this procedure yields the same result as Eq. (2.4-1) for the example earlier in this section.

In practice (as in the algorithm presented at the end of Section 2.4.3) the assumption typically is that the relations are equivalence relations, in which case matrix $\mathbf{B}$ is symmetric and all the main diagonal terms are set to 1 prior to use of either Eq. (2.4-1) or Warshall's algorithm to compute the transitive closure. The equivalence classes of the various symbols in the alphabet leading to matrix $\mathbf{B}^+$ can then be determined by scanning this matrix from left to right and from top to bottom. When a 1 is encountered in, say, row i and column j, we set the symbol associated with the jth column equal to the symbol associated with the ith row (they are equivalent), zero out the jth column, and continue the scan of matrix $\mathbf{B}^+$.

2.4.5 Distance Measures

For pixels p, q, and z, with coordinates (x, y), (s, t), and (u, v) respectively, D is a *distance function* or *metric* if

(a) $D(p, q) \geq 0$ $(D(p, q) = 0$ iff $p = q)$,

(b) $D(p, q) = D(q, p)$, and

(c) $D(p, z) \leq D(p, q) + D(q, z)$.

The *Euclidean distance* between p and q is defined as

$$D_e(p, q) = [(x - s)^2 + (y - t)^2]^{1/2}$$ (2.4-2)

For this distance measure, the pixels having a distance less than or equal to some value r from (x, y) are the points contained in a disk of radius r centered at (x, y).

The D_4 *distance* (also called *city-block distance*) between p and q is defined as

$$D_4(p, q) = |x - s| + |y - t|$$ (2.4-3)

In this case the pixels having a D_4 distance from (x, y) less than or equal to some value r form a diamond centered at (x, y). For example, the pixels with D_4 distance ≤ 2 from (x, y) (the center point) form the following contours of constant distance:

```
          2
        2 1 2
      2 1 0 1 2
        2 1 2
          2
```

The pixels with $D_4 = 1$ are the 4-neighbors of (x, y).

The D_8 *distance* (also called *chessboard distance*) between p and q is defined as

$$D_8(p, q) = \max(|x - s|, |y - t|).$$ (2.4-4)

In this case the pixels with D_8 distance from (x, y) less than or equal to some value r form a square centered at (x, y). For example, the pixels with D_8 distance ≤ 2 from (x, y) (the center point) form the following contours of constant distance:

```
      2 2 2 2 2
      2 1 1 1 2
      2 1 0 1 2
      2 1 1 1 2
      2 2 2 2 2
```

The pixels with $D_8 = 1$ are the 8-neighbors of (x, y).

The D_4 distance between two points p and q is equal to the length of the shortest 4-path between these two points. The same applies to the D_8 distance. In fact, we can consider both the D_4 and D_8 distances between p and q regardless of whether a connected path exists between them because the definitions of these distances involve only the coordinates of these points. For m-connectivity, however, the value of the distance (length of the path) between two pixels depends on the values of the pixels along the path and those of their neighbors. For instance, consider the following arrangement of pixels and assume that p, p_2, and p_4 have a value of 1 and that p_1 and p_3 can have a value of 0 or 1:

$$p_3 \quad p_4$$
$$p_1 \quad p_2$$
$$p$$

If only connectivity of pixels valued 1 is allowed, and p_1 and p_3 are 0, the m distance between p and p_4 is 2. If either p_1 or p_3 is 1, the distance is 3. If both p_1 and p_3 are 1, the distance is 4.

2.4.6 Arithmetic/Logic Operations

Arithmetic and logic operations between pixels are used extensively in most branches of image processing. The arithmetic operations between two pixels p and q are denoted as follows:

$$\text{Addition:} \quad p + q$$
$$\text{Subtraction:} \quad p - q$$
$$\text{Multiplication:} \quad p*q \text{ (also, } pq \text{ and } p \times q)$$
$$\text{Division:} \quad p \div q$$

Arithmetic operations on entire images are carried out pixel by pixel. The principal use of image addition is for image averaging to reduce noise. Image subtraction is a basic tool in medical imaging, where it is used to remove static background information. One of the principal uses of image multiplication (or division) is to correct gray-level shading resulting from nonuniformities in illumination or in the sensor used to acquire the image. Arithmetic operations involve only one spatial pixel location at a time, so they can be done "in place," in the sense that the result of performing an arithmetic operation at location (x, y) can be stored in that location in one of the existing images, as that location will not be visited again.

The principal logic operations used in image processing are AND, OR, and COMPLEMENT, denoted as follows:

$$\text{AND:} \quad p\text{AND}q \text{ (also, } p \cdot q)$$
$$\text{OR:} \quad p\text{OR}q \text{ (also, } p + q)$$
$$\text{COMPLEMENT:} \quad \text{NOT}q \text{ (also, } \bar{q})$$

These operations are *functionally complete* in the sense that they can be combined to form any other logic operation. Logic operations apply only to binary images, whereas arithmetic operations apply to multivalued pixels. Logic operations are basic tools in binary image processing, where they are used for tasks such as masking, feature detection, and shape analysis. Logic operations on entire images are performed pixel by pixel. Because the AND operation of two binary variables is 1 only when both variables are 1, the result at any location in a resulting AND image is 1 only if the corresponding pixels in the two input images are 1. As logic operations involve only one pixel location at a time, they can be done in place, as in the case of arithmetic operations. Figure 2.14 shows various examples of logic operations, where black indicates 1 and white indicates 0. The XOR (exclusive OR) operation yields a 1 when one or the other pixel (but *not* both) is 1, and it yields a 0 otherwise. This operation is unlike the OR operation, which is 1 when one or the other pixel is 1, or both pixels are 1.

In addition to pixel-by-pixel processing on entire images, arithmetic and logic operations are used in neighborhood-oriented operations. Neighborhood processing typically is formulated in the context of so-called *mask* operations (the terms *template*, *window*, and *filter* also are often used to denote a mask). The idea behind mask operations is to let the value assigned to a pixel be a function of its gray level and the gray level of its neighbors. For instance, consider the subimage area shown in Fig. 2.15(a), and suppose that we want to replace the value of z_5 with the average value of the pixels in a 3×3 region centered at the pixel with value z_5. To do so entails performing an arithmetic operation of the form

$$z = \frac{1}{9} (z_1 + z_2 + \cdots + z_9) = \frac{1}{9} \sum_{i=1}^{9} z_i$$

and assigning to z_5 the value of z.

With reference to the mask shown in Fig. 2.15(b), the same operation can be obtained in more general terms by centering the mask at z_5 multiplying each pixel under the mask by the corresponding coefficient, and adding the results; that is,

$$z = w_1 z_1 + w_2 z_2 + \cdots + w_9 z_9 = \sum_{i=1}^{9} w_i z_i \tag{2.4-5}$$

If we let $w_i = 1/9$, $i = 1, 2, \ldots, 9$, this operation yields the same result as the averaging procedure just discussed.

Equation (2.4-5) is used widely in image processing. Proper selection of the coefficients and application of the mask at each pixel position in an image makes possible a variety of useful image operations, such as noise reduction, region thinning, and edge detection. However, applying a mask at each pixel location in an image is a computationally expensive task. For example, applying a 3×3 mask to a 512×512 image requires nine multiplications and eight

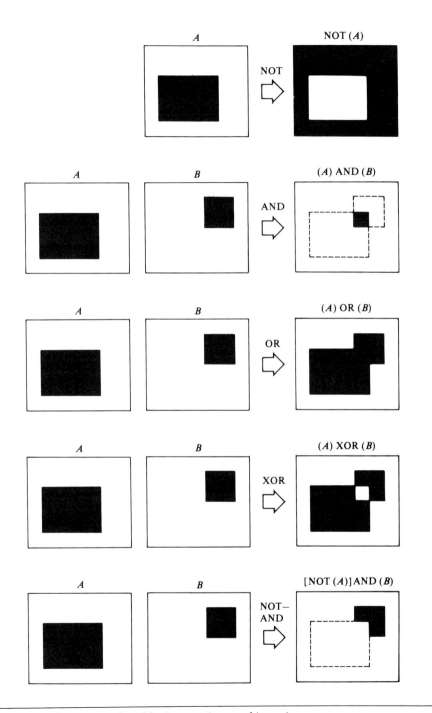

Figure 2.14   *Some examples of logic operations on binary images.*

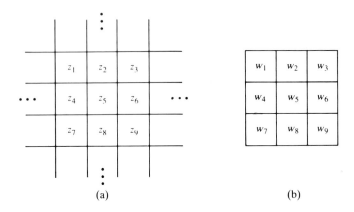

Figure 2.15   *(a) Subarea of an image showing pixel values; (b) a 3 × 3 mask with general coefficients.*

additions at each pixel location, for a total of 2,359,296 multiplications and 2,097,152 additions.

As indicated in Section 1.4.3, most modern image processors are equipped with an Arithmetic–Logic Unit (ALU), whose function is to perform arithmetic and logic operations in parallel, typically at video-frame rates. For U.S. standard video, an ALU can perform an arithmetic or logic operation between two 512×512 images in 1/30 sec. (This time interval is often called one *frame* or one *frame time*.) Given the importance of mask operations in image processing it is of interest to consider in some detail how to use an ALU to accelerate mask processing. For the purpose of illustration, we consider the 3×3 mask shown in Fig. 2.15(b) and the implementation expressed by Eq. (2.4-5). However, the method is easily extendible to an $n \times m$ mask and other arithmetic or logic operations.

The algorithm given here requires two image frame buffers with the capability to scroll and pan by one pixel location (see Section 1.4.2). Let frame buffer A contain the image to which the mask is to be applied. At the end of the process, frame buffer B will contain the result of the operation. Recall that ALU operations are performed on all pixels in one frame time, whereas all buffer shifts are performed virtually instantaneously. We assume that all shifts are by one pixel. Letting $B = A$ initially, and using a dash to indicate no operation, we follow the procedure shown in Table 2.3. The last two shifts are required because, at the end of the last operation on B, the image is in a position equivalent to having the mask with its w_7 coefficient over the z_5 position. The two shifts correct this misalignment.

The key to understanding the procedure in Table 2.3 is to examine what

Table 2.3 ALU Operations

Operations on A	Operations on B
—	Multiply by w_5
Shift right	—
—	Add $w_4{}^*A$
Shift down	—
—	Add $w_1{}^*A$
Shift left	—
—	Add $w_2{}^*A$
Shift left	—
—	Add $w_3{}^*A$
Shift up	—
—	Add $w_6{}^*A$
Shift up	—
—	Add $w_9{}^*A$
Shift right	—
—	Add $w_8{}^*A$
Shift right	—
—	Add $w_7{}^*A$
Shift left	—
Shift down	—

happens in a single pixel of B by considering how a mask would have to be shifted in order to produce the result of Eq. (2.4-5) in that location. The first operation on B produces w_5 multiplied by the pixel value at that location. Since that value is z_5, we have $w_5 z_5$ after this operation. The first shift to the right brings the neighbor with value z_4 (see Fig. 2.15a) over that location. The next operation multiplies z_4 by w_4 and adds the result to the location of the first step. So at this point the result is $w_4 z_4 + w_5 z_5$ at the location in question. The next shift on A and ALU operation on B produce $w_1 z_1 + w_4 z_4 + w_5 z_5$ at that location, and so on. The operations are done in parallel for all locations in B, so this procedure takes place simultaneously at the other locations in that frame buffer. In most ALUs, the operation of multiplying an image by a constant (say, $w_i{}^*A$) followed by an ADD is done in one frame time. Thus the ALU implementation of Eq. (2.4-5) for an entire image takes on the order of nine frame times (9/30 sec). For an $n \times m$ mask it would take on the order of nm frame times.

2.5 IMAGING GEOMETRY

In the following discussion we present several important transformations used in imaging, derive a camera model, and treat the stereo imaging problem in some detail.

2.5.1 Some Basic Transformations

The material in this section deals with development of a unified representation for problems such as image rotation, scaling, and translation. All transformations are expressed in a three-dimensional (3-D) Cartesian coordinate system in which a point has coordinates denoted (X, Y, Z). In cases involving 2-D images, we adhere to our previous convention of lowercase representation (x, y) to denote the coordinates of a pixel. Referring to (X, Y, Z) as the *world coordinates* of a point is common terminology.

Translation

Suppose that the task is to translate a point with coordinates (X, Y, Z) to a new location by using displacements (X_0, Y_0, Z_0). The translation is easily accomplished by using the equations:

$$X^* = X + X_0$$
$$Y^* = Y + Y_0 \qquad (2.5\text{-}1)$$
$$Z^* = Z + Z_0$$

where (X^*, Y^*, Z^*) are the coordinates of the new point. Equation (2.5-1) may be expressed in matrix form by writing

$$
\begin{bmatrix} X^* \\ Y^* \\ Z^* \end{bmatrix} =
\begin{bmatrix} 1 & 0 & 0 & X_0 \\ 0 & 1 & 0 & Y_0 \\ 0 & 0 & 1 & Z_0 \end{bmatrix}
\begin{bmatrix} X \\ Y \\ Z \\ 1 \end{bmatrix} \qquad (2.5\text{-}2)
$$

It is often useful to concatenate several transformations to produce a composite result, such as translation, followed by scaling and then rotation. The use of square matrices simplifies the notational representation of this process considerably. With this in mind, Eq. (2.5-2) can be written as follows:

$$
\begin{bmatrix} X^* \\ Y^* \\ Z^* \\ 1 \end{bmatrix} =
\begin{bmatrix} 1 & 0 & 0 & X_0 \\ 0 & 1 & 0 & Y_0 \\ 0 & 0 & 1 & Z_0 \\ 0 & 0 & 0 & 1 \end{bmatrix}
\begin{bmatrix} X \\ Y \\ Z \\ 1 \end{bmatrix} \qquad (2.5\text{-}3)
$$

In terms of the values of X^*, Y^*, and Z^*, Eqs. (2.5-2) and (2.5-3) are equivalent. Throughout this section, we use the unified matrix representation

$$\mathbf{v}^* = \mathbf{A}\mathbf{v} \qquad (2.5\text{-}4)$$

where $\mathbf{A}$ is a 4×4 transformation matrix, $\mathbf{v}$ is the column vector containing the original coordinates,

$$\mathbf{v} = \begin{bmatrix} X \\ Y \\ Z \\ 1 \end{bmatrix} \tag{2.5-5}$$

and $\mathbf{v}^*$ is a column vector whose components are the transformed coordinates

$$\mathbf{v}^* = \begin{bmatrix} X^* \\ Y^* \\ Z^* \\ 1 \end{bmatrix} \tag{2.5-6}$$

With this notation, the matrix used for translation is

$$\mathbf{T} = \begin{bmatrix} 1 & 0 & 0 & X_0 \\ 0 & 1 & 0 & Y_0 \\ 0 & 0 & 1 & Z_0 \\ 0 & 0 & 0 & 1 \end{bmatrix} \tag{2.5-7}$$

and the translation process is accomplished by using Eq. (2.5-4), so that $\mathbf{v}^* = \mathbf{Tv}$.

Scaling
Scaling by factors S_x, S_y, and S_z along the X, Y, and Z axes is given by the transformation matrix

$$\mathbf{S} = \begin{bmatrix} S_x & 0 & 0 & 0 \\ 0 & S_y & 0 & 0 \\ 0 & 0 & S_z & 0 \\ 0 & 0 & 0 & 1 \end{bmatrix} \tag{2.5-8}$$

Rotation
The transformations used for 3-D rotation are inherently more complex than the transformations discussed thus far. The simplest form of these transformations is for rotation of a point about the coordinate axes. To rotate a point about another arbitrary point in space requires three transformations: the first

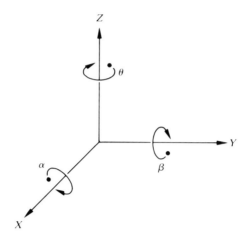

Figure 2.16 *Rotation of a point about each of the coordinate axes. Angles are measured clockwise when looking along the rotation axis toward the origin.*

translates the arbitrary point to the origin, the second performs the rotation, and the third translates the point back to its original position.

With reference to Fig. 2.16, rotation of a point about the Z coordinate axis by an angle θ is achieved by using the transformation

$$
\mathbf{R}_\theta = \begin{bmatrix} \cos\theta & \sin\theta & 0 & 0 \\ -\sin\theta & \cos\theta & 0 & 0 \\ 0 & 0 & 1 & 0 \\ 0 & 0 & 0 & 1 \end{bmatrix}
\tag{2.5-9}
$$

The rotation angle θ is measured clockwise when looking at the origin from a point on the $+Z$ axis. This transformation affects only the values of X and Y coordinates.

Rotation of a point about the X axis by an angle α is performed by using the transformation

$$
\mathbf{R}_\alpha = \begin{bmatrix} 1 & 0 & 0 & 0 \\ 0 & \cos\alpha & \sin\alpha & 0 \\ 0 & -\sin\alpha & \cos\alpha & 0 \\ 0 & 0 & 0 & 1 \end{bmatrix}
\tag{2.5-10}
$$

Finally, rotation of a point about the Y axis by an angle β is achieved by using the transformation

$$\mathbf{R}_\beta = \begin{bmatrix} \cos\beta & 0 & -\sin\beta & 0 \\ 0 & 1 & 0 & 0 \\ \sin\beta & 0 & \cos\beta & 0 \\ 0 & 0 & 0 & 1 \end{bmatrix} \tag{2.5-11}$$

Concatenation and inverse transformations
The application of several transformations can be represented by a single 4 × 4 transformation matrix. For example, translation, scaling, and rotation about the Z axis of a point $\mathbf{v}$ is given by

$$\mathbf{v}^* = \mathbf{R}_\theta(\mathbf{S}(\mathbf{Tv})) \tag{2.5-12}$$
$$= \mathbf{Av}$$

where $\mathbf{A}$ is the 4 × 4 matrix $\mathbf{A} = \mathbf{R}_\theta\mathbf{ST}$. These matrices generally do not commute, so the order of application is important.

Although the discussion thus far has been limited to transformations of a single point, the same ideas extend to transforming a set of m points simultaneously by using a single transformation. With reference to Eq. (2.5-5), let $\mathbf{v}_1, \mathbf{v}_2, \ldots, \mathbf{v}_m$ represent the coordinates of m points. For a 4 × m matrix $\mathbf{V}$ whose columns are these column vectors, the simultaneous transformation of all these points by a 4 × 4 transformation matrix $\mathbf{A}$ is given by

$$\mathbf{V}^* = \mathbf{AV}. \tag{2.5-13}$$

The resulting matrix $\mathbf{V}^*$ is 4 × m. Its ith column, $\mathbf{v}_i^*$, contains the coordinates of the transformed point corresponding to $\mathbf{v}_i$.

Many of the transformations discussed above have inverse matrices that perform the opposite transformation and can be obtained by inspection. For example, the inverse translation matrix is

$$\mathbf{T}^{-1} = \begin{bmatrix} 1 & 0 & 0 & -X_0 \\ 0 & 1 & 0 & -Y_0 \\ 0 & 0 & 1 & -Z_0 \\ 0 & 0 & 0 & 1 \end{bmatrix} \tag{2.5-14}$$

Similarly, the inverse rotation matrix $\mathbf{R}_\theta^{-1}$ is

$$\mathbf{R}_\theta^{-1} = \begin{bmatrix} \cos(-\theta) & \sin(-\theta) & 0 & 0 \\ -\sin(-\theta) & \cos(-\theta) & 0 & 0 \\ 0 & 0 & 1 & 0 \\ 0 & 0 & 0 & 1 \end{bmatrix} \tag{2.5-15}$$

The inverses of more complex transformation matrices are usually obtained by numerical techniques.

2.5.2 Perspective Transformations

A perspective transformation (also called an imaging transformation) projects 3-D points onto a plane. Perspective transformations play a central role in image processing because they provide an approximation to the manner in which an image is formed by viewing a 3-D world. These transformations are fundamentally different from those discussed in Section 2.5.1 because they are nonlinear in that they involve division by coordinate values.

Figure 2.17 shows a model of the image formation process. The camera coordinate system (x, y, z) has the image plane coincident with the xy plane and the optical axis (established by the center of the lens) along the z axis. Thus the center of the image plane is at the origin, and the center of the lens is at coordinates $(0, 0, \lambda)$. If the camera is in focus for distant objects, λ is the *focal length* of the lens. Here the assumption is that the camera coordinate system is aligned with the world coordinate system (X, Y, Z). We remove this restriction in Section 2.5.3.

Let (X, Y, Z) be the world coordinates of any point in a 3-D scene, as shown in Fig. 2.17. We assume throughout the following discussion that $Z > \lambda$; that is, all points of interest lie in front of the lens. The first step is to obtain a relationship that gives the coordinates (x, y) of the projection of the point (X, Y, Z) onto the image plane. This is easily accomplished by the use of similar triangles. With reference to Fig. 2.17,

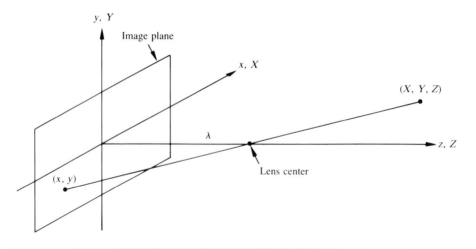

Figure 2.17 *Basic model of the imaging process. The camera coordinate system (x, y, z) is aligned with the world coordinate system (X, Y, Z).*

of similar triangles. With reference to Fig. 2.17,

$$\frac{x}{\lambda} = -\frac{X}{Z - \lambda} \tag{2.5-16}$$

$$= \frac{X}{\lambda - Z}$$

and

$$\frac{y}{\lambda} = -\frac{Y}{Z - \lambda} \tag{2.5-17}$$

$$= \frac{Y}{\lambda - Z}$$

where the negative signs in front of X and Y indicate that image points are actually inverted, as the geometry of Fig. 2.17 shows.

The image-plane coordinates of the projected 3-D point follow directly from Eqs. (2.5-16) and (2.5-17):

$$x = \frac{\lambda X}{\lambda - Z} \tag{2.5-18}$$

and

$$y = \frac{\lambda Y}{\lambda - Z} \tag{2.5-19}$$

These equations are nonlinear because they involve division by the variable Z. Although we could use them directly as shown, it is often convenient to express them in linear matrix form, as in Section 2.5.1 for rotation, translation, and scaling. This is easily accomplished by using homogeneous coordinates.

The homogeneous coordinates of a point with Cartesian coordinates (X, Y, Z) are defined as (kX, kY, kZ, k), where k is an arbitrary, nonzero constant. Clearly, conversion of homogeneous coordinates back to Cartesian coordinates is accomplished by dividing the first three homogeneous coordinates by the fourth. A point in the Cartesian world coordinate system may be expressed in vector form as

$$\mathbf{w} = \begin{bmatrix} X \\ Y \\ Z \end{bmatrix} \tag{2.5-20}$$

and its homogeneous counterpart is given by

$$\mathbf{w}_h = \begin{bmatrix} kX \\ kY \\ kZ \\ k \end{bmatrix} \tag{2.5-21}$$

If we define the *perspective transformation matrix* as

$$
P = \begin{bmatrix} 1 & 0 & 0 & 0 \\ 0 & 1 & 0 & 0 \\ 0 & 0 & 1 & 0 \\ 0 & 0 & -\dfrac{1}{\lambda} & 1 \end{bmatrix}
\tag{2.5-22}
$$

the product Pw_h yields a vector denoted c_h:

$$
c_h = Pw_h
$$

$$
= \begin{bmatrix} 1 & 0 & 0 & 0 \\ 0 & 1 & 0 & 0 \\ 0 & 0 & 1 & 0 \\ 0 & 0 & -\dfrac{1}{\lambda} & 1 \end{bmatrix} \begin{bmatrix} kX \\ kY \\ kZ \\ k \end{bmatrix}
\tag{2.5-23}
$$

$$
= \begin{bmatrix} kX \\ kY \\ kZ \\ \dfrac{-kZ}{\lambda} + k \end{bmatrix}
$$

The elements of c_h are the camera coordinates in homogeneous form. As indicated, these coordinates can be converted to Cartesian form by dividing each of the first three components of c_h by the fourth. Thus the Cartesian coordinates of any point in the camera coordinate system are given in vector form by

$$
c = \begin{bmatrix} x \\ y \\ z \end{bmatrix} = \begin{bmatrix} \dfrac{\lambda X}{\lambda - Z} \\ \dfrac{\lambda Y}{\lambda - Z} \\ \dfrac{\lambda Z}{\lambda - Z} \end{bmatrix}
\tag{2.5-24}
$$

The first two components of c are the (x, y) coordinates in the image plane of a projected 3-D point (X, Y, Z), as shown earlier in Eqs. (2.5-18) and (2.5-19). The third component is of no interest in terms of the model in Fig. 2.17. As shown next, this component acts as a free variable in the inverse perspective transformation.

The inverse perspective transformation maps an image point back into 3-D. Thus from Eq. (2.5-23),

$$\mathbf{w}_h = \mathbf{P}^{-1}\mathbf{c}_h \qquad (2.5\text{-}25)$$

where $\mathbf{P}^{-1}$ is

$$\mathbf{P}^{-1} = \begin{bmatrix} 1 & 0 & 0 & 0 \\ 0 & 1 & 0 & 0 \\ 0 & 0 & 1 & 0 \\ 0 & 0 & \dfrac{1}{\lambda} & 1 \end{bmatrix} \qquad (2.5\text{-}26)$$

Suppose that an image point has coordinates $(x_0, y_0, 0)$, where the 0 in the z location simply indicates that the image plane is located at $z = 0$. This point may be expressed in homogeneous vector form as

$$\mathbf{c}_h = \begin{bmatrix} kx_0 \\ ky_0 \\ 0 \\ k \end{bmatrix} \qquad (2.5\text{-}27)$$

Application of Eq. (2.5-25) then yields the homogeneous world coordinate vector

$$\mathbf{w}_h = \begin{bmatrix} kx_0 \\ ky_0 \\ 0 \\ k \end{bmatrix} \qquad (2.5\text{-}28)$$

or, in Cartesian coordinates,

$$\mathbf{w} = \begin{bmatrix} X \\ Y \\ Z \end{bmatrix} = \begin{bmatrix} x_0 \\ y_0 \\ 0 \end{bmatrix} \qquad (2.5\text{-}29)$$

This result obviously is unexpected because it gives $Z = 0$ for *any* 3-D point. The problem here is caused by mapping a 3-D scene onto the image plane, which is a many-to-one transformation. The image point (x_0, y_0) corresponds to the set of collinear 3-D points that lie on the line passing through $(x_0, y_0, 0)$

and $(0, 0, \lambda)$. The equations of this line in the world coordinate system come from Eqs. (2.5-18) and (2.5-19); that is,

$$X = \frac{x_0}{\lambda} (\lambda - Z) \tag{2.5-30}$$

and

$$Y = \frac{y_0}{\lambda} (\lambda - Z). \tag{2.5-31}$$

Equations (2.5-30) and (2.5-31) show that unless something is known about the 3-D point that generated an image point (for example, its Z coordinate), it is not possible to completely recover the 3-D point from its image. This observation, which certainly is not unexpected, can be used to formulate the inverse perspective transformation by using the z component of $\mathbf{c}_h$ as a free variable, instead of 0. Thus, by letting

$$\mathbf{c}_h = \begin{bmatrix} kx_0 \\ ky_0 \\ kz \\ k \end{bmatrix} \tag{2.5-32}$$

it follows from Eq. (2.5-25) that

$$\mathbf{w}_h = \begin{bmatrix} kx_0 \\ ky_0 \\ kz \\ \dfrac{kz}{\lambda} + k \end{bmatrix} \tag{2.5-33}$$

which, upon conversion to Cartesian coordinates gives

$$\mathbf{w} = \begin{bmatrix} X \\ Y \\ Z \end{bmatrix} = \begin{bmatrix} \dfrac{\lambda x_0}{\lambda + z} \\ \dfrac{\lambda y_0}{\lambda + z} \\ \dfrac{\lambda z}{\lambda + z} \end{bmatrix} \tag{2.5-34}$$

In other words, treating z as a free variable yields the equations

$$X = \frac{\lambda x_0}{\lambda + z}$$

$$Y = \frac{\lambda y_0}{\lambda + z} \qquad (2.5\text{-}35)$$

$$Z = \frac{\lambda z}{\lambda + z}$$

Solving for z in terms of Z in the last equation and substituting in the first two expressions yields

$$X = \frac{x_0}{\lambda}(\lambda - Z) \qquad (2.5\text{-}36)$$

and

$$Y = \frac{y_0}{\lambda}(\lambda - Z) \qquad (2.5\text{-}37)$$

which agrees with the observation that recovering a 3-D point from its image by means of the inverse perspective transformation requires knowledge of at least one of the world coordinates of the point. We address this problem again in Section 2.5.5.

2.5.3 Camera Model

Equations (2.5-23) and (2.5-24) characterize the formation of an image by projection of 3-D points onto an image plane. These two equations thus constitute a basic mathematical model of an imaging camera. This model is based on the assumption that the camera and world coordinate systems are coincident. In this section we consider a more general problem in which the two coordinate systems are allowed to be separate. However, the basic objective of obtaining the image-plane coordinates of any particular world point remains the same.

Figure 2.18 shows a world coordinate system (X, Y, Z) used to locate both the camera and 3-D points (denoted by $\mathbf{w}$). Figure 2.18 also shows the camera coordinate system (x, y, z) and image points (denoted by $\mathbf{c}$). The assumption is that the camera is mounted on a gimbal, which allows pan through an angle θ and tilt through an angle α. Here, *pan* is the angle between the x and X axes, and *tilt* is the angle between the z and Z axes. The offset of the center of the gimbal from the origin of the world coordinate system is denoted by $\mathbf{w}_0$, and the offset of the center of the imaging plane with respect to the gimbal center is denoted by vector $\mathbf{r}$, with components (r_1, r_2, r_3).

The concepts developed in Sections 2.5.1 and 2.5.2 provide all the necessary tools to derive a camera model based on the geometric arrangement of Fig. 2.18. The approach is to bring the camera and world coordinate systems into

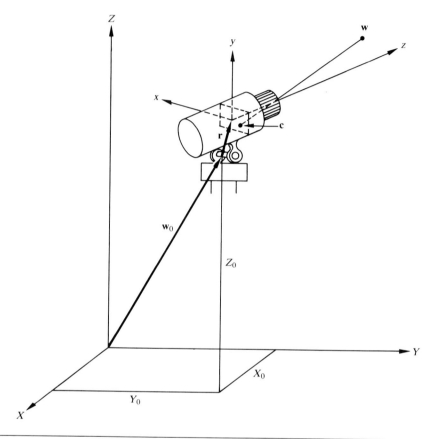

Figure 2.18 *Imaging geometry with two coordinate systems. (From Fu, Gonzalez, and Lee [1987].)*

alignment by applying a set of transformations. After doing so, we simply apply the perspective transformation of Eq. (2.5-22) to obtain the image-plane coordinates for any world point. In other words, we first reduce the problem to the geometric arrangement shown in Fig. 2.17 before applying the perspective transformation.

Suppose that, initially, the camera was in *normal position*, in the sense that the gimbal center and origin of the image plane were at the origin of the world coordinate system, and all axes were aligned. The geometric arrangement of Fig. 2.18 may then be achieved in several ways. Let us assume the following sequence of steps: (1) displacement of the gimbal center from the origin, (2) pan of the x axis, (3) tilt of the z axis, and (4) displacement of the image plane with respect to the gimbal center.

Obviously, the sequence of these mechanical steps does not affect the world points because the set of points seen by the camera after it was moved from normal position is quite different. However, applying exactly the same sequence of steps to all world points can achieve normal position again. A camera in normal position satisfies the arrangement of Fig. 2.17 for application of the perspective transformation. Thus the problem is reduced to applying to every world point a set of transformations that correspond to the steps listed earlier.

Translation of the origin of the world coordinate system to the location of the gimbal center is accomplished by using the transformation matrix

$$\mathbf{G} = \begin{bmatrix} 1 & 0 & 0 & -X_0 \\ 0 & 1 & 0 & -Y_0 \\ 0 & 0 & 1 & -Z_0 \\ 0 & 0 & 0 & 1 \end{bmatrix}. \tag{2.5-38}$$

In other words, a homogeneous world point $\mathbf{w}_h$ that was at coordinates (X_0, Y_0, Z_0) is at the origin of the new coordinate system after the transformation $\mathbf{Gw}_h$.

As indicated earlier, the pan angle is measured between the x and X axes. In normal position, these two axes are aligned. In order to pan the x axis through the desired angle, we simply rotate it by θ. The rotation is with respect to the z axis and is accomplished by using the transformation matrix $\mathbf{R}_\theta$ of Eq. (2.5-9). In other words, application of this matrix to all points (including the point $\mathbf{Gw}_h$) effectively rotates the x axis to the desired location. When using Eq. (2.5-9) it is important to keep clearly in mind the convention established in Fig. 2.16. That is, angles are considered positive when points are rotated clockwise, which implies a counterclockwise rotation of the camera about the z axis. The unrotated (0°) position corresponds to the case when the x and X axes are aligned.

At this point the z and Z axes are still aligned. Since tilt is the angle between these two axes, we tilt the camera an angle α by rotating the z axis by α. The rotation is with respect to the x axis and is accomplished by applying the transformation matrix $\mathbf{R}_\alpha$ of Eq. (2.5-10) to all points (including the point $\mathbf{R}_\theta\mathbf{Gw}_h$). Again, a counterclockwise rotation of the camera implies positive angles, and the 0° mark is when the z and Z axes are aligned.[†]

According to the discussion in Section 2.5.4, the two rotation matrices can be concatenated into a single matrix, $\mathbf{R} = \mathbf{R}_\alpha \mathbf{R}_\theta$. Then, from Eqs. (2.5-9) and

---

[†] A useful way to visualize these transformations is to construct an axis system (for example, with pipe cleaners), label the axes x, y, and z, and perform the rotations manually, one axis at a time.

(2.5-10),

$$\mathbf{R} = \begin{bmatrix} \cos\theta & \sin\theta & 0 & 0 \\ -\sin\theta\cos\alpha & \cos\theta\cos\alpha & \sin\alpha & 0 \\ \sin\theta\sin\alpha & -\cos\theta\sin\alpha & \cos\alpha & 0 \\ 0 & 0 & 0 & 1 \end{bmatrix}$$

(2.5-39)

Finally, displacement of the origin of the image plane by vector $\mathbf{r}$ is achieved by the transformation matrix

$$\mathbf{C} = \begin{bmatrix} 1 & 0 & 0 & -r_1 \\ 0 & 1 & 0 & -r_2 \\ 0 & 0 & 1 & -r_3 \\ 0 & 0 & 0 & 1 \end{bmatrix}$$

(2.5-40)

Thus applying to $\mathbf{w}_h$ the series of transformations $\mathbf{CRGw}_h$ brings the world and camera coordinate systems into coincidence. The image-plane coordinates of a point $\mathbf{w}_h$ are finally obtained by using Eq. (2.5-23). In other words, a homogeneous world point that is being viewed by a camera satisfying the geometric arrangement shown in Fig. 2.18 has the following homogeneous representation in the camera coordinate system:

$$\mathbf{c}_h = \mathbf{PCRGw}_h$$

(2.5-41)

Equation (2.5-41) represents a perspective transformation involving two coordinate systems.

As indicated in Section 2.5.2, we obtain the Cartesian coordinates (x, y) of the imaged point by dividing the first and second components of $\mathbf{c}_h$ by the fourth. Expanding Eq. (2.5-41) and converting to Cartesian coordinates yields

$$x = \lambda \frac{(X - X_0)\cos\theta + (Y - Y_0)\sin\theta - r_1}{-(X - X_0)\sin\theta\sin\alpha + (Y - Y_0)\cos\theta\sin\alpha - (Z - Z_0)\cos\alpha + r_3 + \lambda}$$

(2.5-42)

and

$$y = \lambda \frac{-(X - X_0)\sin\theta\cos\alpha + (Y - Y_0)\cos\theta\cos\alpha + (Z - Z_0)\sin\alpha - r_2}{-(X - X_0)\sin\theta\sin\alpha + (Y - Y_0)\cos\theta\sin\alpha - (Z - Z_0)\cos\alpha + r_3 + \lambda}$$

(2.5-43)

which are the image coordinates of a point $\mathbf{w}$ whose world coordinates are $(X,$

Y, Z). These equations reduce to Eqs. (2.5-18) and (2.5-19) when $X_0 = Y_0 = Z_0 = 0$, $r_1 = r_2 = r_3 = 0$, and $\alpha = \theta = 0°$.

Example: As an illustration of the concepts just discussed, suppose that we want to find the image coordinates of the corner of the block shown in Fig. 2.19. The camera is offset from the origin and is viewing the scene with a pan of 135° and a tilt of 135°. We will follow the convention that transformation angles are positive when the camera rotates counterclockwise, viewing the origin along the axis of rotation.

Let us examine in detail the steps required to move the camera from normal position to the geometry shown in Fig. 2.19. The camera is in normal position in Fig. 2.20(a) and displaced from the origin in Fig. 2.20(b). Note that, after this step, the world coordinate axes are used only to establish angle references. That is, after displacement of the world coordinate origin, all rotations take place about the new (camera) axes. Figure 2.20(c) shows a view along the z axis of the camera to establish pan. In this case the rotation of the camera about the z axis is counterclockwise, so world points are rotated about this axis in the opposite direction, which makes θ a positive angle. Figure 2.20(d) shows a view, after pan, along the x axis of the camera to establish tilt. The rotation about this axis is counterclockwise, which makes α a positive angle. The world coordinate axes are shown as dashed lines in the latter two figures to emphasize that their only use is to establish the zero reference for the pan and tilt angles. We do not show the final step of displacing the image plane from the center of the gimbal.

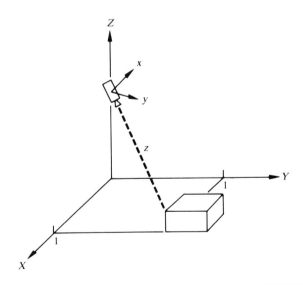

Figure 2.19   *Camera viewing a 3-D scene. (From Fu, Gonzalez, and Lee [1987].)*

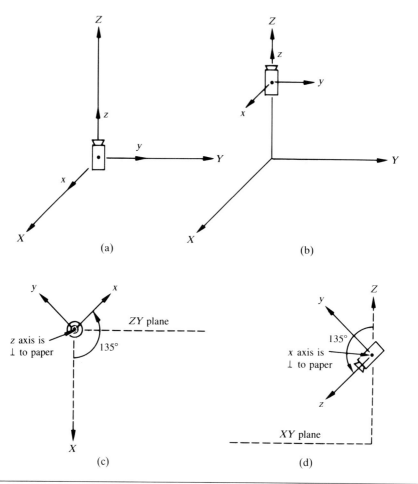

Figure 2.20 (a) Camera in normal position; (b) gimbal center displaced from origin; (c) observer view of rotation about z axis to determine pan angle; (d) observer view of rotation about x axis for tilt. (From Fu, Gonzalez, and Lee [1987].)

The following parameter values apply to this problem:

$$X_0 = 0 \text{ m} \qquad Y_0 = 0 \text{ m} \qquad Z_0 = 1 \text{ m};$$

$$\alpha = 135° \qquad \theta = 135°;$$

$$r_1 = 0.03 \text{ m} \qquad r_2 = r_3 = 0.02 \text{ m} \qquad \lambda = 35 \text{ mm} = 0.035 \text{ m}$$

The corner in question is at coordinates $(X, Y, Z) = (1, 1, 0.2)$.

To compute the image coordinates of the block corner, we simply substitute the parameter values into Eqs. (2.5-42) and (2.5-43); that is,

$$x = \lambda \frac{-0.03}{-1.53 + \lambda}$$

Similarly,

$$y = \lambda \frac{+0.42}{-1.53 + \lambda}$$

Substituting $\lambda = 0.035$ yields the image coordinates

$$x = 0.0007 \text{ m} \quad \text{and} \quad y = -0.009 \text{ m}.$$

Note that these coordinates are well within a 1×1 in. (0.025×0.025 m) imaging plane. It is easily verified that use of a lens with a 200-mm focal length, for example, would have imaged the corner of the block outside the boundary of a plane with these dimensions (that is, outside the effective field of view of the camera).

Finally, note that all coordinates obtained with Eqs. (2.5-42) and (2.5-43) are with respect to the center of the image plane. A change of coordinates is required to use the convention established earlier that the origin of an image is at its top left corner.   ❏

2.5.4 Camera Calibration

In Section 2.5.3 we developed explicit equations for the image coordinates (x, y), of a world point **w**. As shown in Eqs. (2.5-42) and (2.5-43), implementation of these equations requires knowledge of the focal length, offsets, and angles of pan and tilt. Although these parameters could be measured directly, determining one or more of the parameters using the camera itself as a measuring device often is more convenient (especially when the camera moves frequently). This requires a set of image points whose world coordinates are known, and the computational procedure used to obtain the camera parameters using these known points often is referred to as *camera calibration*.

With reference to Eq. (2.5-41), let $\mathbf{A} = \mathbf{PCRG}$. The elements of $\mathbf{A}$ contain all the camera parameters and, from Eq. (2.5-41), $\mathbf{c}_h = \mathbf{A}\mathbf{w}_h$. Letting $k = 1$ in the homogeneous representation yields

$$\begin{bmatrix} c_{h1} \\ c_{h2} \\ c_{h3} \\ c_{h4} \end{bmatrix} = \begin{bmatrix} a_{11} & a_{12} & a_{13} & a_{14} \\ a_{21} & a_{22} & a_{23} & a_{24} \\ a_{31} & a_{32} & a_{33} & a_{34} \\ a_{41} & a_{42} & a_{43} & a_{44} \end{bmatrix} \begin{bmatrix} X \\ Y \\ Z \\ 1 \end{bmatrix} \tag{2.5-44}$$

Based on the discussion in Sections 2.5.2 and 2.5.3, the camera coordinates in

Cartesian form are

$$x = c_{h1}/c_{h4} \tag{2.5-45}$$

and

$$y = c_{h2}/c_{h4}. \tag{2.5-46}$$

Substituting $c_{h1} = xc_{h4}$ and $c_{h2} = yc_{h4}$ in Eq. (2.5-44) and expanding the matrix product yields

$$
\begin{aligned}
xc_{h4} &= a_{11}X + a_{12}Y + a_{13}Z + a_{14} \\
yc_{h4} &= a_{21}X + a_{22}Y + a_{23}Z + a_{24} \\
c_{h4} &= a_{41}X + a_{42}Y + a_{43}Z + a_{44},
\end{aligned} \tag{2.5-47}
$$

where expansion of c_{h3} was ignored because it is related to z.

Substitution of c_{h4} in the first two equations of (2.5-47) yields two equations with 12 unknown coefficients:

$$a_{11}X + a_{12}Y + a_{13}Z - a_{41}xX - a_{42}xY - a_{43}xZ - a_{44}x + a_{14} = 0 \tag{2.5-48}$$

$$a_{21}X + a_{22}Y + a_{23}Z - a_{41}yX - a_{42}yY - a_{43}yZ - a_{44}y + a_{24} = 0. \tag{2.5-49}$$

The calibration procedure then consists of (1) obtaining $m \geq 6$ world points (there are *two* equations) with known coordinates (X_i, Y_i, Z_i), $i = 1, 2, \ldots, m$; (2) imaging these points with the camera in a given position to obtain the corresponding image points (x_i, y_i), $i = 1, 2, \ldots, m$; and (3) using these results in Eqs. (2.5-48) and (2.5-49) to solve for the unknown coefficients. Many numerical techniques exist for finding an optimal solution to a linear system of equations, such as the one given by these equations (see, for example, Noble [1969]).

2.5.5 Stereo Imaging

Recall that mapping a 3-D scene onto an image plane is a many-to-one transformation. That is, an image point does not uniquely determine the location of a corresponding world point. However, the missing *depth* information can be obtained by using stereoscopic (*stereo* for short) imaging techniques.

As Fig. 2.21 shows, stereo imaging involves obtaining two separate image views of an object (a single world point **w** in this discussion). The distance between the centers of the two lenses is called the *baseline*, and the objective is to find the coordinates (X, Y, Z) of the point **w** having image points (x_1, y_1) and (x_2, y_2). The assumption is that the cameras are identical and that the coordinate systems of both cameras are perfectly aligned, differing only in the location of their origins, a condition usually met in practice. Recall that, after

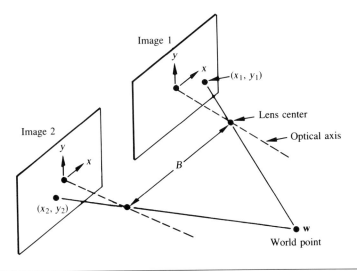

Figure 2.21 *Model of the stereo imaging process. (From Fu, Gonzalez, and Lee [1987].)*

the camera and world coordinate systems have been brought into coincidence, the xy plane of the image is aligned with the XY plane of the world coordinate system. Then, under the above assumption, the Z coordinate of **w** is exactly the same for both camera coordinate systems.

Let us bring the first camera into coincidence with the world coordinate system, as shown in Fig. 2.22. Then, from Eq. (2.5-30), **w** lies on the line with (partial) coordinates

$$X_1 = \frac{x_1}{\lambda} (\lambda - Z_1) \qquad (2.5\text{-}50)$$

where the subscripts on X and Z indicate that the first camera was moved to the origin of the world coordinate system, with the second camera and **w** following, but keeping the relative arrangement shown in Fig. 2.21. If, instead, the second camera is brought to the origin of the world coordinate system, **w** lies on the line with (partial) coordinates

$$X_2 = \frac{x_2}{\lambda} (\lambda - Z_2). \qquad (2.5\text{-}51)$$

However, because of the separation between cameras and because the Z coordinate of **w** is the same for both camera coordinate systems, it follows that

$$X_2 = X_1 + B \qquad (2.5\text{-}52)$$

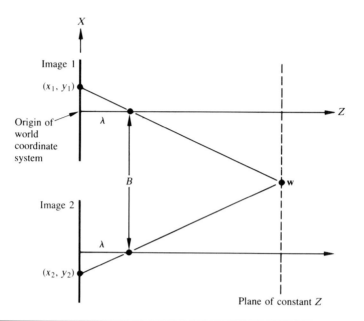

Figure 2.22 *Top view of Fig. 2.21 with the first camera brought into coincidence with the world coordinate system. (From Fu, Gonzalez, and Lee [1987].)*

and

$$Z_2 = Z_1 = Z \tag{2.5-53}$$

where B is the baseline distance.

Substituting Eqs. (2.5-52) and (2.5-53) into Eq. (2.5-50) and (2.5-51) gives

$$X_1 = \frac{x_1}{\lambda}(\lambda - Z) \tag{2.5-54}$$

and

$$X_1 + B = \frac{x_2}{\lambda}(\lambda - Z). \tag{2.5-55}$$

Subtracting Eq. (2.5-54) from (2.5-55) and solving for Z yields

$$Z = \lambda - \frac{\lambda B}{x_2 - x_1} \tag{2.5-56}$$

which indicates that if the difference between the corresponding image coordinates x_2 and x_1 can be determined, and the baseline and focal length are known, calculating the Z coordinate of $\mathbf{w}$ is a simple matter. The X and Y

world coordinates then follow directly from Eqs. (2.5-30) and (2.5-31) using either (x_1, y_1) or (x_2, y_2).

The most difficult task in using Eq. (2.5-56) to obtain Z is to actually find two corresponding points in different images of the same scene. As these points generally are in the same vicinity, a frequently used approach is to select a point within a small region in one of the image views and then attempt to find the best matching region in the other view by using correlation techniques, as discussed in Chapter 9. When the scene contains distinct features, such as prominent corners, a feature-matching approach generally yields a faster solution for establishing correspondence. The calibration procedure developed in Section 2.5.4 is directly applicable to stereo imaging by simply treating the cameras independently.

2.6 PHOTOGRAPHIC FILM

Photographic film is an important element of image processing systems. It often is used as the recording medium for input images, and it is by far the most popular medium for recording output results. For these reasons, we conclude this chapter with a discussion of some basic properties of monochrome photographic film and their relation to image processing applications.

2.6.1 Film Structure and Exposure

Figure 2.23 shows a cross section of a typical photographic film as it would appear under magnification. It consists of the following layers and components: (1) a supercoat of gelatin used for protection against scratches and abrasion marks; (2) an emulsion layer of minute silver halide crystals; (3) a substrate layer to promote adhesion of the emulsion to the film base; (4) the film base or support, made of cellulose triacetate or a related polymer; and (5) a backing layer to prevent curling.

When the film is exposed to light, the silver halide grains absorb optical

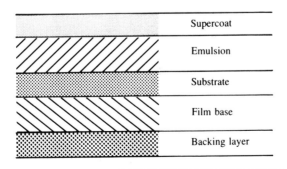

Figure 2.23 *Structure of modern black-and-white film.*

energy and undergo a complex physical change. The grains that have absorbed a sufficient amount of energy contain tiny patches of metallic silver, called *development centers.* When the exposed film is developed, the existence of a single development center in a silver halide grain can precipitate the change of the entire grain to metallic silver. The grains that do not contain development centers do not undergo such a change. After development, the film is "fixed" by chemical removal of the remaining silver halide grains. The more light that reaches an area of the film, the more silver halide is rendered developable and the denser the silver deposit that is formed there. Since the silver grains are largely opaque at optical frequencies, an image of gray tones is obtained where the brightness levels are reversed, thus producing the familiar film negative.

The process is repeated to obtain a positive picture. The negative is projected onto a sensitive paper carrying a silver halide emulsion similar to that used for the film. Exposure by a light source yields a latent image of the negative. After development, the paper bears a positive silver image.

2.6.2   Film Characteristics

Of practical interest to the photographer are contrast, speed, graininess, and resolving power. An understanding of the effect of these parameters is particularly important in specialized applications, such as photographing the results obtained in an image processing system.

Contrast

High-contrast films reproduce tone differences in the subject as large density differences in the photograph; low-contrast films translate tone differences as small density differences. The exposure E to which a film is subjected is defined as *energy per unit area* at each point on the photosensitive area. Exposure depends on the incident intensity I and the duration of the exposure T. These quantities are related by the expression

$$E = IT. \tag{2.6-1}$$

The most widely used description of the photosensitive properties of photographic film is a plot of the density of the silver deposit on a film versus the logarithm of E. These curves are called characteristic curves, D-log-E curves (density versus log exposure), and H & D curves (after Hurter and Driffield, who developed the method). Figure 2.24 shows a typical H & D curve for a photographic negative. When the exposure is below a certain level, the density is independent of exposure and equal to a minimum value called the *gross fog.* In the *toe* of the curve, density begins to increase with increasing exposure. Next is a region of the curve in which density is linearly proportional to logarithmic exposure. The slope of this linear region is referred to as the film *gamma* (γ). Finally, the curve saturates in a region called the *shoulder,* and again density does not change with increasing exposure. The value of γ is a measure of film contrast: the steeper the slope, the higher the contrast rendered.

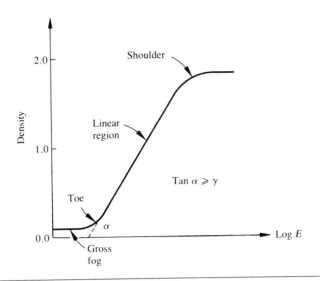

Figure 2.24   *A typical H & D curve.*

General purpose films of medium contrast have gammas in the range of 0.7 to 1.0. High-contrast films have gammas on the order of 1.5 to 10. As a rule, films with relatively low gammas are used for continuous-tone reproduction; high-contrast films are used for copying line originals and other specialized purposes.

Speed

The speed of a film determines how much light is needed to produce a certain amount of silver on development. The lower the speed, the longer the film must be exposed to record a given image. The most widely used standard of speed is the ASA scale. This scale is arithmetic, with the speed number being directly proportional to the film's sensitivity. A film of ASA 200 is twice as fast (and for a given subject requires half as much exposure) as a film of ASA 100. Some speed scales, such as the DIN system used in Europe, are logarithmic. Every increase of three in the DIN speed number doubles the actual speed. An ASA 50 film is equivalent to a DIN 18, an ASA 100 to a DIN 21, and so on.

General purpose films for outdoor and some indoor photography have speeds between ASA 80 and ASA 160; fine-grain films for maximum image definition between ASA 20 and ASA 64; high-speed films for poor light and indoor photography between ASA 200 and ASA 500; and ultraspeed films for very low light levels from ASA 650 and up.

Graininess

The image derived from the silver halide crystals is discontinuous in structure, which gives a grainy appearance in big enlargements. The effect is most prominent in fast films, which have comparatively large crystals; slower, fine-grain emulsions are therefore preferable in applications where fine detail is desired or where enlargement of the negatives is necessary.

Resolving power

The fineness of detail that a film can resolve depends not only on its graininess, but also on the light-scattering properties of the emulsion and on the contrast with which the film reproduces fine detail. Fine-grain films with thin emulsions yield the highest resolving power.

2.6.3   Diaphragm and Shutter Settings

Regardless of the type of film used, proper camera settings are essential in obtaining acceptable pictures. The principal settings are the lens diaphragm and shutter speed.

In the lens diaphragm, a series of leaves increase or decrease the size of the opening to control the amount of light passing through the lens to the film. The diaphragm control ring is calibrated with a scale of so-called *f*-numbers, or stop numbers, in a series such as 1.4, 2, 2.8, 4, 5.6, 8, 11, 16, 22, and 32. The *f*-numbers are inversely proportional to the amount of light admitted. In the preceding series, each setting admits twice as much light as the next higher *f*-number (thus giving twice as much exposure) and half as much light as the next lower value. Shutter speed settings on present-day cameras also follow a standard double-or-half sequence. Typical speeds are 1, ½, ¼, ⅛, 1/15, 1/30, 1/60, 1/125, 1/250, 1/500, and 1/1000 sec. The faster the shutter speed, the shorter the exposure time obtained.

The diaphragm and shutter control the amount of light reaching the film by adjusting the light intensity and the time during which it acts. Different aperture–shutter speed combinations can thus yield the same exposure. For example, diaphragm *f*/2.8 with 1/250 sec, *f*/4 with 1/125 sec, and *f*/5.6 with 1/60 sec, all yield the same exposure. However, the combination chosen for these two settings is not independent of the conditions under which a picture is taken or the characteristics of the film itself.[†] For example, when photographing a scene where depth of focus is of interest, the photographer should select an *f*-stop as high as possible to give the lens a "pin-hole" characteristic. For a given film, this requirement limits the range of shutter speeds that yield adequate exposures. In other applications, the shutter speed is the essential consideration. An example having image processing implications is the problem of photographing a television screen. In this case, the shutter speed must be set below the refreshing rate of the TV (1/30 sec per frame) to compensate for the fact that the shutter is not synchronized with the refresh control signals. Typically,

---

[†] When *T* is long (e.g., greater than 1 sec.), we have to take into account a phenomenon called "reciprocity failure," in which Eq. (2.6-1) no longer holds, and specific film tables have to be used to obtain the proper exposure settings.

¹⁄₈ sec is adequate, although slower speeds are often used in order to achieve frame integration. Many of the images in this book, for example, were photographed at ¹⁄₄ sec with Kodak Panatomic-X fine-grain film (ASA 32). The diaphragm settings were determined by using an exposure meter to measure the light intensity of each image.

2.7 CONCLUDING REMARKS

The material in this chapter is primarily background information for subsequent discussions. Our treatment of the human visual system, although brief, provides a basic idea of the capabilities of the eye in perceiving pictorial information. Similarly, the image model developed in Section 2.2 is used in Chapter 4 as the basis for an image enhancement technique called *homomorphic filtering*.

We consider the sampling ideas introduced in Section 2.3 again in Section 3.3.9, after developing the necessary mathematical tools for a deeper analytical study of this problem. Sampling and quantization considerations also play a central role in Chapter 6 in the context of image encoding applications, where the problem is one of compressing the large quantities of data that result from image digitization.

The material in Section 2.4 is basic to an understanding of numerous image processing techniques discussed in the following chapters. The imaging geometry concepts developed in Section 2.5 play an important role in situations where 3-D scene information must be correlated with images acquired by a camera and subsequently processed by a computer.

REFERENCES

The material presented in Sections 2.1.1 and 2.1.2 is based primarily on the books by Cornsweet [1970] and by Graham [1965]. Additional reading for Section 2.1.3 may be found in Sheppard [1968]; Sheppard, Stratton, and Gazley [1969]; and Stevens [1951]. The image model presented in Section 2.2 has been investigated by Oppenheim, Schafer, and Stockham [1968] in connection with image enhancement applications. References for the illumination and reflectance values used in that section are Moon [1961] and the *IES Lighting Handbook* [1972]. Some of the material presented in Section 2.3 is based on the work of Huang [1965]. The papers by Scoville [1965] and by Gaven, Tavitian, and Harabedian [1970] also are of interest. Additional reading for the material in Section 2.4 may be found in Toriwaki et al. [1979] and in Rosenfeld and Kak [1982]. See also Jain [1989] and Schalkoff [1989]. Section 2.5 is from the book by Fu, Gonzalez, and Lee [1987]. References for Section 2.6 are Mees [1966], Perrin [1960], Nelson [1971], *Kodak Plates and Films for Scientific Photography* [1973], and Langford [1984].

PROBLEMS

2.1 Using the background information provided in Section 2.1, and thinking purely in geometric terms, estimate the diameter of the smallest printed dot that the eye can discern if the page on which the dot is printed is 0.2 m away from the eyes. Assume for simplicity that the visual system ceases to detect the dot when the image of the dot on the fovea becomes smaller than the diameter of one receptor (cone) in that area of the retina. Assume further that the fovea can be modeled as a square array of dimension 1.5×1.5 mm and that the cones and the spaces between them are uniformly distributed throughout this array.

2.2 Suppose that a flat area with center at (x_0, y_0) is illuminated by a light source with intensity distribution

$$i(x, y) = Ke^{-[(x-x_0)^2 + (y-y_0)^2]}.$$

Assume that the reflectance of the area is 1, and let $K = 255$. If the resulting image is digitized with m bits of intensity resolution, and the eye can detect an abrupt change of eight shades of intensity between adjacent pixels, what value of m will cause visible false contouring?

2.3 Sketch the image in Problem 2.2 for $m = 2$.

2.4 A common measure of transmission for digital data is the *baud rate*, defined as the number of bits transmitted per second. Generally, transmission is accomplished in packets consisting of a start bit, a byte (8 bits) of information, and a stop bit. Using this approach, answer the following:

a) How many minutes would it take to transmit a 512×512 image with 256 gray levels at 300 baud?

b) What would the time be at 9600 baud?

c) Repeat (a) and (b) for a 1024×1024 image with 256 gray levels.

2.5 Consider the two image subsets S_1 and S_2 shown below.

	S_1					S_2			
0	0	0	0	0	0	0	1	1	0
1	0	0	1	0	0	1	0	0	1
1	0	0	1	0	1	1	0	0	0
0	0	1	1	1	0	0	0	0	0
0	0	1	1	1	0	0	1	1	1

For $V = \{1\}$, determine whether S_1 and S_2 are (a) 4-connected, (b) 8-connected, or (c) m-connected.

2.6 Develop an algorithm for converting a one-pixel-thick, 8-connected path to a 4-connected path.

2.7 Develop an algorithm for converting a one-pixel-thick, m-connected path to a 4-connected path.

2.8 Suppose that the relation R in a particular application means "4-connected," so that sRt means that s is 4-connected to t. Sketch all the geometric arrangements implied by the matrix.

$$
\mathbf{B}^+ =
\begin{array}{c}
\\ a \\ b \\ c
\end{array}
\begin{array}{ccc}
a & b & c \\
\left[\begin{array}{ccc}
1 & 0 & 1 \\
0 & 1 & 1 \\
1 & 1 & 1
\end{array}\right]
\end{array}
$$

2.9 Prove that the algorithm in Section 2.4.4 for computing matrix $\mathbf{B}^+$ actually gives the same result as Eq. (2.4-1).

2.10 Consider the image segment shown below.
   a) Let $V = \{0, 1\}$ and compute the D_4, D_8, and D_m distances between p and q.
   b) Repeat for $V = \{1, 2\}$.

$$
\begin{array}{cccc}
3 & 1 & 2 & 1(q) \\
2 & 2 & 0 & 2 \\
1 & 2 & 1 & 1 \\
(p)1 & 0 & 1 & 2
\end{array}
$$

2.11 a) Show that the D_4 distance between two points p and q is equal to the shortest 4-path between these points.

   b) Is this path unique?

2.12 The 3×3 mask shown below is frequently used to compute the derivative in the x direction at each point in an image.

$$
\begin{array}{ccc}
-1 & -2 & -1 \\
0 & 0 & 0 \\
1 & 2 & 1
\end{array}
$$

Give an ALU procedure to implement this operation.

2.13 A biotechnology application yields binary images of blobs of the general form shown below.

Develop a method for (a) determining whether an image contains any blobs and, if the answer is yes, (b) classifying each blob as type A if it has no holes in it or as type B if it does. Your method should be able to detect and ignore blobs that touch the boundary of the image.

2.14 A high-technology manufacturing plant wins a government contract to manufacture high-precision washers of the form shown below.

The contract requires that the shape of all washers be inspected by an imaging system. You are hired as a consultant to help specify this system. Propose a solution based on logic operations. Assume that you can easily obtain a binary image of a washer and that someone else will handle any mechanisms needed to move the washers, accurately position them for inspection, and so on.

2.15 A manufacturer who produces the two types of door hinges shown below is having a serious problem. The hinges are identical, except for the number of holes. Workers in the packaging line sometimes make errors by packing hinges with different numbers of holes in the same package. They also sometimes fail to reject hinges that have not been manufactured properly and do not have the correct number of holes.

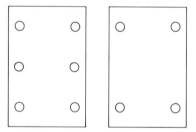

The owner of this small company decides to automate the process fully, and having heard of your success in solving the washer problem, he hires you as a consultant to design an inspection system based on imaging. Someone else will design a robotic system capable, among other things, of accurately positioning a hinge for viewing by a TV camera. All the imaging system has to do is acquire an image, determine whether it is of type A (six holes), type B (four holes), or type C (reject because of an incorrect number of holes), and send the robot one of these three signals. The robot will proceed from there to package or reject the hinge. Propose a solution based on what you have learned so far in this book. Your recommendation to the company owner should be in the form of a block diagram, with a brief explanation detailing the function of each block in the diagram.

2.16 a) Give the transformation matrix used to rotate an *image* by 45° clockwise.

b) How would this transformation be used to achieve the desired image rotation?

c) Use the matrix obtained in (a) to rotate the image point $(x, y) = (1, 0)$.

2.17 Determine whether the world point with coordinates $(1/2, 1/2, \sqrt{2}/2)$ is on the optical axis of a camera located at $(0, 0, \sqrt{2})$, panned 135°, and tilted 135°. Assume a 50-mm lens and let $r_1 = r_2 = r_3 = 0$.

2.18 Start with Eq. (2.5-41) and derive Eqs. (2.5-42) and (2.5-43).

2.19 Modify the ALU procedure in Section 2.4.6 to replace each pixel in an image by the average of its 4-neighbors. Do not include the pixel itself in computing the average.

2.20 A plant produces a line of translucent miniature polymer squares. Stringent quality requirements dictate 100 percent visual inspection, and the plant manager finds the use of human inspectors increasingly expensive. Inspection is semiautomated. At each inspection station, a mechanism places each polymer square over a light located under an optical system that produces a magnified image of the square. The image completely fills a nonreflective viewing screen measuring 80 × 80 mm. Defects appear as dark circular blobs, and the inspector's job is to look at the screen and reject any sample that has one or more such dark blobs with a diameter of 0.8 mm or larger, as measured on the scale of the screen. The manager believes that, if she can find a way to automate the process completely, she will increase profits by 50 percent. She also believes that success will aid her climb up the corporate ladder. After much investigation, the manager decides that the way to solve the problem is to view each inspection screen with a CCD TV camera and feed the output of the camera into an image processing system capable of detecting the blobs, measuring their diameter, and activating the accept/reject buttons previously operated by the inspector. She is able to find a system that can do the job, so long as the smallest defect occupies an area of, at least 2 × 2 pixels in the digital image. The manager hires you to help her specify the camera and lens system, but requires that you use off-the-shelf components. For the lenses, assume that this constraint means any integer multiple of 25 mm or 35 mm, up to 200 mm. For the cameras, it means resolutions of 512 × 512, 1024 × 1024, or 2048 × 2048 pixels. The imaging elements in these cameras are squares measuring 8 × 8 microns, and the spaces between imaging elements are squares of the same size. The cameras cost much more than the lenses, so the problem should be solved with the lowest resolution camera possible, based on the choice of lenses. As a consultant, you are to provide a written recommendation, showing in reasonable detail the analysis that led to your conclusion.

CHAPTER 3

IMAGE TRANSFORMS

And be not conformed to this world: but be ye
transformed by the renewing of your mind. . . .
Romans 12:2

The material in this chapter deals primarily with the development of two-dimensional (2-D) transforms and their properties. Transform theory has played a key role in image processing for many years, and it continues to be a topic of interest in theoretical as well as applied work in this field. In the following chapters, we apply 2-D transforms to image enhancement, restoration, encoding, and description.

Although we discuss other transforms in some detail in this chapter, we emphasize the Fourier transform because of its wide range of applications in image processing problems. Section 3.1 introduces the Fourier transform of one and two continuous variables. Section 3.2 then expresses these concepts in discrete form. Section 3.3 develops and illustrates several important properties of the 2-D Fourier transform. Section 3.4 develops a fast Fourier transform algorithm, which can be used to reduce the number of calculations to a fraction of that required to implement the discrete Fourier transform by direct methods. Section 3.5 deals with the Walsh, Hadamard, discrete cosine, Haar, and Slant transforms. Finally, Section 3.6 introduces the Hotelling transform and some of its applications.

3.1 INTRODUCTION TO THE FOURIER TRANSFORM

Let $f(x)$ be a continuous function of a real variable x. The *Fourier transform* of $f(x)$, denoted $\mathfrak{F}\{f(x)\}$, is defined by the equation

$$\mathfrak{F}\{f(x)\} = F(u) = \int_{-\infty}^{\infty} f(x)\exp[-j2\pi ux]\, dx \qquad (3.1\text{-}1)$$

where $j = \sqrt{-1}$.

Given $F(u)$, $f(x)$ can be obtained by using the *inverse Fourier transform*

$$\mathfrak{F}^{-1}\{F(u)\} = f(x) \qquad (3.1\text{-}2)$$
$$= \int_{-\infty}^{\infty} F(u)\exp[j2\pi ux]\, du.$$

Equations (3.1-1) and (3.1-2), called the *Fourier transform pair*, exist if $f(x)$ is continuous and integrable and $F(u)$ is integrable. These conditions are almost always satisfied in practice.

We are concerned throughout this book with functions $f(x)$ that are real. The Fourier transform of a real function, however, is generally complex; that is,

$$F(u) = R(u) + jI(u) \qquad (3.1\text{-}3)$$

where $R(u)$ and $I(u)$ are the real and imaginary components of $F(u)$, respectively. It is often convenient to express Eq. (3.1-3) in exponential form, that is,

$$F(u) = |F(u)|e^{j\phi(u)} \qquad (3.1\text{-}4)$$

where

$$|F(u)| = [R^2(u) + I^2(u)]^{1/2} \qquad (3.1\text{-}5)$$

and

$$\phi(u) = \tan^{-1}\left[\frac{I(u)}{R(u)}\right]. \qquad (3.1\text{-}6)$$

The magnitude function $|F(u)|$ is called the *Fourier spectrum* of $f(x)$ and $\phi(u)$ its *phase angle*. The square of the spectrum,

$$P(u) = |F(u)|^2 \qquad (3.1\text{-}7)$$
$$= R^2(u) + I^2(u)$$

is commonly referred to as the *power spectrum* of $f(x)$. The term *spectral density* also is commonly used to denote the power spectrum.

The variable u appearing in the Fourier transform often is called the *frequency variable*. This name arises from expression of the exponential term,

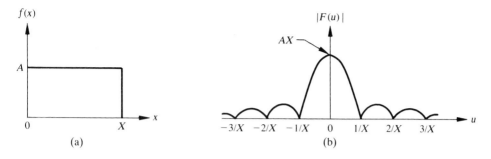

Figure 3.1   *A simple function and its Fourier spectrum.*

$\exp[-j2\pi ux]$—using Euler's formula—in the form:

$$\exp[-j2\pi ux] = \cos 2\pi ux - j \sin 2\pi ux. \tag{3.1-8}$$

Interpreting the integral in Eq. (3.1-1) as a limit summation of discrete terms makes evident that $F(u)$ is composed of an infinite sum of sine and cosine terms and that each value of u determines the *frequency* of its corresponding sine–cosine pair.

Example: Consider the simple function shown in Fig. 3.1(a). Its Fourier transform is obtained from Eq. (3.1-1) as follows:

$$F(u) = \int_{-\infty}^{\infty} f(x) \exp[-j2\pi ux] \, dx$$

$$= \int_{0}^{X} A \exp[-j2\pi ux] \, dx$$

$$= \frac{-A}{j2\pi u} [e^{-j2\pi ux}]_{0}^{X} = \frac{-A}{j2\pi u} [e^{-j2\pi uX} - 1]$$

$$= \frac{A}{j2\pi u} [e^{j\pi uX} - e^{-j\pi uX}] e^{-j\pi uX}$$

$$= \frac{A}{\pi u} \sin(\pi uX) \, e^{-j\pi uX}$$

which is a complex function. The Fourier spectrum is

$$|F(u)| = \left|\frac{A}{\pi u}\right| |\sin(\pi uX)| |e^{-j\pi uX}|$$

$$= AX \left|\frac{\sin(\pi uX)}{(\pi uX)}\right|.$$

Figure 3.1(b) shows a plot of $|F(u)|$.   ❏

The Fourier transform can be easily extended to a function $f(x, y)$ of two variables. If $f(x, y)$ is continuous and integrable and $F(u, v)$ is integrable, the following Fourier transform pair exists:

$$\mathfrak{F}\{f(x, y)\} = F(u, v) = \int\int_{-\infty}^{\infty} f(x, y) \exp[-j2\pi(ux + vy)] \, dx \, dy \qquad (3.1\text{-}9)$$

and

$$\mathfrak{F}^{-1}\{F(u, v)\} = f(x, y) = \int\int_{-\infty}^{\infty} F(u, v) \exp[j2\pi(ux + vy)] \, du \, dv \qquad (3.1\text{-}10)$$

where u and v are the frequency variables.

As in the one-dimensional (1-D) case, the Fourier spectrum, phase, and power spectrum, respectively, are:

$$|F(u, v)| = [R^2(u, v) + I^2(u, v)]^{1/2} \qquad (3.1\text{-}11)$$

$$\phi(u, v) = \tan^{-1}\left[\frac{I(u, v)}{R(u, v)}\right] \qquad (3.1\text{-}12)$$

and

$$P(u, v) = |F(u, v)|^2 = R^2(u, v) + I^2(u, v). \qquad (3.1\text{-}13)$$

Example: The Fourier transform of the function shown in Fig. 3.2(a) is

$$F(u, v) = \int\int_{-\infty}^{\infty} f(x, y) \exp[-j2\pi(ux + vy)] \, dx \, dy$$

$$= A \int_0^X \exp[-j2\pi ux] \, dx \int_0^Y \exp[-j2\pi vy] \, dy$$

$$= A\left[\frac{e^{-j2\pi ux}}{-j2\pi u}\right]_0^X \left[\frac{e^{-j2\pi vy}}{-j2\pi v}\right]_0^Y$$

$$= \frac{A}{-j2\pi u}[e^{-j2\pi uX} - 1]\frac{1}{-j2\pi v}[e^{-j2\pi vY} - 1]$$

$$= AXY\left[\frac{\sin(\pi uX) \, e^{-j\pi uX}}{(\pi uX)}\right]\left[\frac{\sin(\pi vY) \, e^{-j\pi vY}}{(\pi vY)}\right].$$

The spectrum is

$$|F(u, v)| = AXY\left|\frac{\sin(\pi uX)}{(\pi uX)}\right|\left|\frac{\sin(\pi vY)}{(\pi vY)}\right|.$$

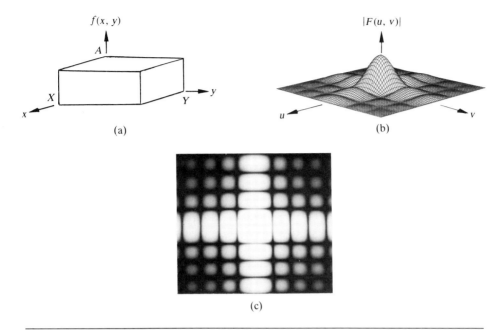

$f(x, y)$

A

X

Y

x y

(a)

$|F(u, v)|$

u v

(b)

(c)

Figure 3.2 (a) A 2-D function; (b) its Fourier spectrum; and (c) the spectrum displayed as an intensity function.

Figure 3.2(b) shows a plot of this function in 3-D perspective. Figure 3.2(c) shows the spectrum as an intensity function, where brightness is proportional to the amplitude of $|F(u, v)|$. Figure 3.3 shows other examples of 2-D functions and their spectra. In this case, both $f(x, y)$ and $|F(u, v)|$ are shown as images. ❑

3.2 THE DISCRETE FOURIER TRANSFORM

Suppose that a continuous function $f(x)$ is discretized into a sequence

$$\{f(x_0), f(x_0 + \Delta x), f(x_0 + 2\Delta x), \dots, f(x_0 + [N - 1]\Delta x)\}$$

by taking N samples Δx units apart, as shown in Fig. 3.4. It will be convenient in subsequent developments to use x as either a discrete or continuous variable, depending on the context of the discussion. To do so requires defining

$$f(x) = f(x_0 + x \, \Delta x) \tag{3.2-1}$$

where x now assumes the discrete values $0, 1, 2, \dots, N - 1$. In other words, the sequence $\{f(0), f(1), f(2), \dots, f(N - 1)\}$ denotes *any* N uniformly spaced samples from a corresponding continuous function.

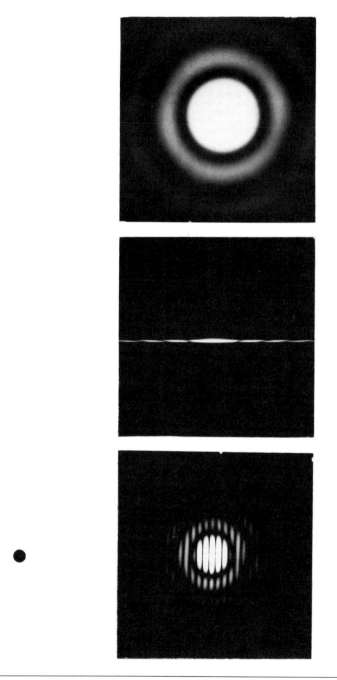

Figure 3.3   *Some 2-D functions and their Fourier spectra.*

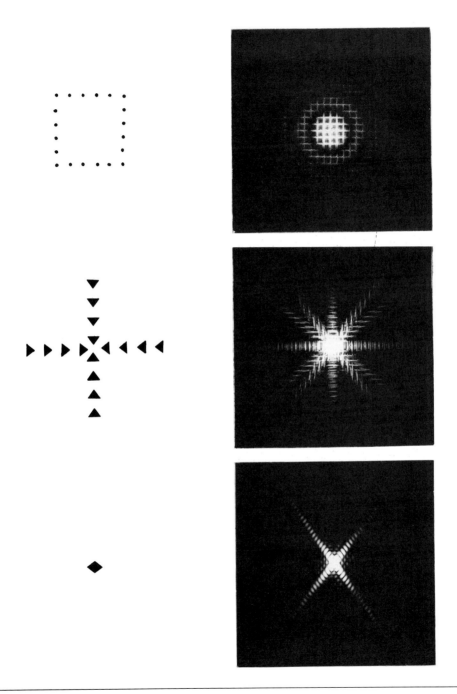

Figure 3.3   *(Continued)*

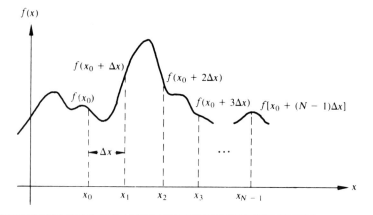

Figure 3.4 *Sampling a continuous function.*

With the above notation in mind, the *discrete* Fourier transform pair that applies to sampled functions is given by[†]

$$F(u) = \frac{1}{N} \sum_{x=0}^{N-1} f(x) \exp[-j2\pi ux/N] \qquad (3.2\text{-}2)$$

for $u = 0, 1, 2, \ldots, N - 1$, and

$$f(x) = \sum_{u=0}^{N-1} F(u) \exp[j2\pi ux/N] \qquad (3.2\text{-}3)$$

for $x = 0, 1, 2, \ldots, N - 1$.

The values $u = 0, 1, 2, \ldots, N - 1$ in the discrete Fourier transform (Eq. 3.2-2) correspond to samples of the continuous transform at values $0, \Delta u, 2\Delta u, \ldots, (N - 1)\Delta u$. In other words, $F(u)$ represents $F(u\Delta u)$. This notation is similar to that used for the discrete $f(x)$, except that the samples of $F(u)$ start at the origin of the frequency axis. The terms Δu and Δx are related by the expression

$$\Delta u = \frac{1}{N\,\Delta x} \qquad (3.2\text{-}4)$$

[†] A proof of these results is outside the scope of this discussion. For proofs relating the continuous and discrete Fourier transforms, see Blackman and Tukey [1958]; Cooley, Lewis, and Welch [1967]; and Brigham [1974].

In the two-variable case the discrete Fourier transform pair is

$$F(u, v) = \frac{1}{MN} \sum_{x=0}^{M-1} \sum_{y=0}^{N-1} f(x, y) \exp[-j2\pi(ux/M + vy/N)] \tag{3.2-5}$$

for $u = 0, 1, 2, \ldots, M - 1, v = 0, 1, 2, \ldots, N - 1$, and

$$f(x, y) = \sum_{u=0}^{M-1} \sum_{v=0}^{N-1} F(u, v) \exp[j2\pi(ux/M + vy/N)] \tag{3.2-6}$$

for $x = 0, 1, 2, \ldots, M - 1$ and $y = 0, 1, 2, \ldots, N - 1$.

Sampling of a continuous function is now in a 2-D grid, with divisions of width Δx and Δy in the x and y axis, respectively. As in the 1-D case, the discrete function $f(x, y)$ represents samples of the function $f(x_0 + x\Delta x, y_0 + y\Delta y)$ for $x = 0, 1, 2, \ldots, M - 1$ and $y = 0, 1, 2, \ldots, N - 1$. Similar comments apply to $F(u, v)$. The sampling increments in the spatial and frequency domains are related by

$$\Delta u = \frac{1}{M\Delta x} \tag{3.2-7}$$

and

$$\Delta v = \frac{1}{N\Delta y} \tag{3.2-8}$$

When images are sampled in a square array, $M = N$ and

$$F(u, v) = \frac{1}{N} \sum_{x=0}^{N-1} \sum_{y=0}^{N-1} f(x, y) \exp[-j2\pi(ux + vy)/N] \tag{3.2-9}$$

for $u, v = 0, 1, 2, \ldots, N - 1$, and

$$f(x, y) = \frac{1}{N} \sum_{u=0}^{N-1} \sum_{v=0}^{N-1} F(u, v) \exp[j2\pi(ux + vy)/N] \tag{3.2-10}$$

for $x, y = 0, 1, 2, \ldots, N - 1$. Note the inclusion of a $1/N$ term in both Eqs. (3.2-9) and (3.2-10). Because $F(u, v)$ and $f(x, y)$ are a Fourier transform pair, the grouping of these constant multiplicative terms is arbitrary. In practice, images typically are digitized in square arrays, so we will be concerned mostly with the Fourier transform pair in Eqs. (3.2-9) and (3.2-10). The formulation in Eqs. (3.2-5) and (3.2-6) is used from time to time when stressing generality of the image size is important.

The Fourier spectrum, phase, and energy spectrum of 1-D and 2-D discrete functions also are given by Eqs. (3.1-5)–(3.1-7) and Eqs. (3.1-11)–(3.1-13), respectively. The only difference is that the independent variables are discrete.

Unlike the continuous case, existence of the discrete Fourier transform is of no concern, because both $F(u)$ and $F(u, v)$ always exist. In the 1-D case, for example, this can be shown by direct substitution of Eq. (3.2-3) into Eq. (3.2-2):

$$F(u) = \frac{1}{N} \sum_{x=0}^{N-1} \left[\sum_{r=0}^{N-1} F(r) \exp[j2\pi rx/N] \right] \exp[-j2\pi ux/N]$$

$$= \frac{1}{N} \sum_{r=0}^{N-1} F(r) \left[\sum_{x=0}^{N-1} \exp[j2\pi rx/N] \exp[-j2\pi ux/N] \right] \qquad (3.2\text{-}11)$$

$$= F(u).$$

Identity (3.2-11) follows from the orthogonality condition

$$\sum_{x=0}^{N-1} \exp[j2\pi rx/N] \exp[-j2\pi ux/N] = \begin{cases} N & \text{if } r = u \\ 0 & \text{otherwise.} \end{cases} \qquad (3.2\text{-}12)$$

Note that changing the variable from u to r in Eq. (3.2-3) clarifies the notation.

Substitution of Eq. (3.2-2) into Eq. (3.2-3) also would yield an identity on $f(x)$, indicating that the Fourier transform pair given by these equations always exists. A similar argument holds for the discrete, 2-D Fourier transform pair.

Example: To illustrate Eqs. (3.2-2) and (3.2-3), consider the function shown in Fig. 3.5(a). Sampling at the argument values $x_0 = 0.5$, $x_1 = 0.75$, $x_2 = 1.0$, and $x_3 = 1.25$—and redefining the argument as discussed above—produces the discrete function shown in Fig. 3.5(b).

Application of Eq. (3.2-2) to the resulting four samples yields the following sequence of steps:

$$F(0) = \frac{1}{4} \sum_{x=0}^{3} f(x) \exp[0]$$

$$= \frac{1}{4} [f(0) + f(1) + f(2) + f(3)]$$

$$= \frac{1}{4} (2 + 3 + 4 + 4)$$

$$= 3.25$$

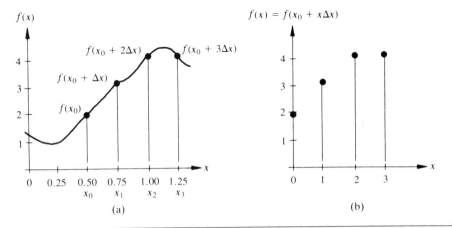

Figure 3.5 *A simple function and samples in the x domain. In (a) x is a continuous variable; in (b) x is discrete.*

and

$$F(1) = \frac{1}{4} \sum_{x=0}^{3} f(x)\exp[-j2\pi x/4]$$

$$= \frac{1}{4}(2e^0 + 3e^{-j\pi/2} + 4e^{-j\pi} + 4e^{-j3\pi/2})$$

$$= \frac{1}{4}(-2 + j)$$

where the last step follows from Euler's formula. Continuing with this procedure gives

$$F(2) = -\frac{1}{4}[1 + j0]$$

and

$$F(3) = -\frac{1}{4}[2 + j].$$

All values of $f(x)$ contribute to *each* of the four terms of the discrete Fourier transform. Conversely, all terms of the transform contribute in forming the inverse transform via Eq. (3.2-3). The procedure for obtaining the inverse is analogous to the one just described for computing $F(u)$.

The Fourier spectrum is obtained from the magnitude of each of the transform terms; that is,

$$|F(0)| = 3.25$$

$$|F(1)| = \left[\left(\frac{2}{4}\right)^2 + \left(\frac{1}{4}\right)^2 \right]^{1/2} = \frac{\sqrt{5}}{4}$$

$$|F(2)| = \left[\left(\frac{1}{4}\right)^2 + \left(\frac{0}{4}\right)^2 \right]^{1/2} = \frac{1}{4}$$

and

$$|F(3)| = \left[\left(\frac{2}{4}\right)^2 + \left(\frac{1}{4}\right)^2 \right]^{1/2} = \frac{\sqrt{5}}{4}.$$

❏

3.3   SOME PROPERTIES OF THE TWO-DIMENSIONAL FOURIER TRANSFORM

This section focuses on properties of the Fourier transform that are of value in subsequent discussions. Although our primary interest is in 2-D, discrete transforms, the underlying concepts of some of these properties are much easier to grasp when they are presented first in their 1-D, continuous form.

Several of the topics considered in this section are illustrated by images and their Fourier spectra displayed as intensity functions. Hence some comments concerning these displays are in order before we begin a discussion of Fourier transform properties. The dynamic range of Fourier spectra usually is much higher than the typical display device is able to reproduce faithfully, in which case only the brightest parts of the image are visible on the display screen. The same often holds for attempts to record such an image on film. A useful technique that compensates for this difficulty consists of displaying the function

$$D(u, v) = c \log[1 + |F(u, v)|] \tag{3.3-1}$$

instead of $|F(u, v)|$, where c is a scaling constant and the logarithm function performs the desired compression. Use of Eq. (3.3-1) greatly facilitates visual analysis of Fourier spectra, as Fig. 3.6 indicates. Figure 3.6(a) shows a digital

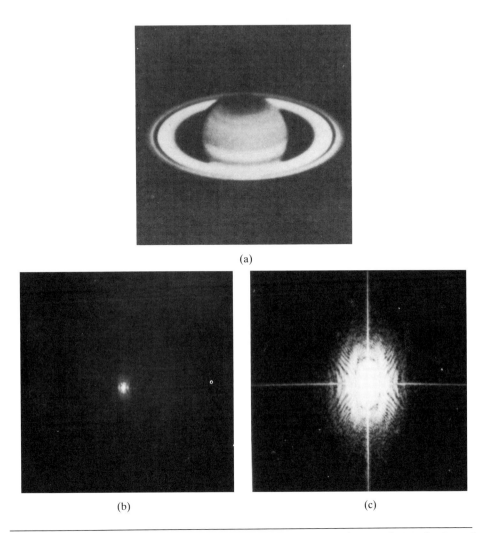

(a)

(b)   (c)

Figure 3.6 *(a) A picture of the planet Saturn; (b) display of /F(u, v)/; (c) display of log[1 + /F(u, v)/] scaled to 8 bits (i.e., 0 to 255 gray levels).*

image of the planet Saturn, and Fig. 3.6(b) shows the normal Fourier spectrum displayed as an intensity image. This particular spectrum had values in the range $[0, 2.5 \times 10^6]$. When this function is scaled linearly for display on an 8-bit system, the brightest values dominate the display, as expected for such a large dynamic range. In this case, the values of $\log[1 + |F(u, v)|]$ range from 0 to 6.4, which, when scaled for display on the same 8-bit system, yield the result shown in Fig. 3.6(c). The increase in visible detail is obvious.

3.3.1 Separability

The discrete Fourier transform pair in Eqs. (3.2-9) and (3.2-10) can be expressed in the separable forms

$$F(u, v) = \frac{1}{N} \sum_{x=0}^{N-1} \exp[-j2\pi ux/N] \sum_{y=0}^{N-1} f(x, y)\exp[-j2\pi vy/N] \qquad (3.3\text{-}2)$$

for $u, v = 0, 1, \ldots, N - 1$, and

$$f(x, y) = \frac{1}{N} \sum_{u=0}^{N-1} \exp[j2\pi ux/N] \sum_{v=0}^{N-1} F(u, v)\exp[j2\pi vy/N] \qquad (3.3\text{-}3)$$

for $x, y = 0, 1, \ldots, N - 1$.

The principal advantage of the separability property is that $F(u, v)$ or $f(x, y)$ can be obtained in two steps by successive applications of the 1-D Fourier transform or its inverse. This advantage becomes evident if Eq. (3.3-2) is expressed in the form

$$F(u, v) = \frac{1}{N} \sum_{x=0}^{N-1} F(x, v)\exp[-j2\pi ux/N] \qquad (3.3\text{-}4)$$

where

$$F(x, v) = N\left[\frac{1}{N} \sum_{y=0}^{N-1} f(x, y)\exp[-j2\pi vy/N]\right]. \qquad (3.3\text{-}5)$$

For *each* value of x, the expression inside the brackets in Eq. (3.3-5) is a 1-D transform, with frequency values $v = 0, 1, \ldots, N - 1$. Therefore the 2-D function $F(x, v)$ is obtained by taking a transform along *each* row of $f(x, y)$ and multiplying the result by N. The desired result, $F(u, v)$, is then obtained by taking a transform along each column of $F(x, v)$, as indicated by Eq. (3.3-4). The procedure is summarized in Fig. 3.7. The same results may be obtained

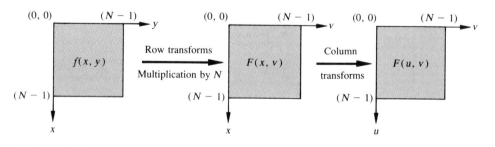

Figure 3.7 *Computation of the 2-D Fourier transform as a series of 1-D transforms.*

by first taking transforms along the columns of $f(x, y)$ and then along the rows of that result. This is easily verified by reversing the order of the summations of Eq. (3.3-2). Identical comments apply to the implementation of Eq. (3.3-3).

3.3.2 Translation

The translation properties of the Fourier transform pair are

$$f(x, y)\exp[j2\pi(u_0x + v_0y)/N] \Leftrightarrow F(u - u_0, v - v_0) \qquad (3.3\text{-}6)$$

and

$$f(x - x_0, y - y_0) \Leftrightarrow F(u, v)\exp[-j2\pi(ux_0 + vy_0)/N] \qquad (3.3\text{-}7)$$

where the double arrow indicates the correspondence between a function and its Fourier transform (and vice versa), as in Eqs. (3.1-9) and (3.1-10) or Eqs. (3.2-9) and (3.2-10).

Equation (3.3-6) shows that multiplying $f(x, y)$ by the indicated exponential term and taking the transform of the product results in a shift of the origin of the frequency plane to the point (u_0, v_0). Similarly, multiplying $F(u, v)$ by the exponential term shown and taking the inverse transform moves the origin of the spatial plane to (x_0, y_0).

In this chapter and Chapter 4, we make considerable use of Eq. (3.3-6), with $u_0 = v_0 = N/2$, or

$$\exp[j2\pi(u_0x + v_0y)/N] = e^{j\pi(x+y)}$$
$$= (-1)^{x+y}$$

and

$$f(x, y)(-1)^{x+y} \Leftrightarrow F(u - N/2, v - N/2). \qquad (3.3\text{-}8)$$

Thus the origin of the Fourier transform of $f(x, y)$ can be moved to the center of its corresponding $N \times N$ frequency square simply by multiplying $f(x, y)$ by $(-1)^{x+y}$. In the one-variable case this shift reduces to multiplication of $f(x)$ by the term $(-1)^x$.

Note from Eq. (3.3-7) that a shift in $f(x, y)$ does not affect the magnitude of its Fourier transform, as

$$|F(u, v)\exp[-j2\pi(ux_0 + vy_0)/N]| = |F(u, v)|. \qquad (3.3\text{-}9)$$

It is important to keep this in mind, because visual examination of the transform is usually limited to a display of its magnitude.

3.3.3 Periodicity and Conjugate Symmetry

The discrete Fourier transform and its inverse are *periodic* with period N; that is,

$$F(u, v) = F(u + N, v) = F(u, v + N) = F(u + N, v + N). \qquad (3.3\text{-}10)$$

The validity of this property can be demonstrated by direct substitution of the variables $(u + N)$ and $(v + N)$ in Eq. (3.2-9). Although Eq. (3.3-10) indicates that $F(u, v)$ repeats itself for infinitely many values of u and v, only the N values of each variable in any one period are required to obtain $f(x, y)$ from $F(u, v)$. In other words, only one period of the transform is necessary to specify $F(u, v)$ completely in the frequency domain. Similar comments apply to $f(x, y)$ in the spatial domain.

If $f(x, y)$ is real, the Fourier transform also exhibits conjugate symmetry:

$$F(u, v) = F^*(-u, -v) \qquad (3.3\text{-}11)$$

or, more interestingly,

$$|F(u, v)| = |F(-u, -v)| \qquad (3.3\text{-}12)$$

where $F^*(u, v)$ is the complex conjugate of $F(u, v)$. As mentioned earlier, displaying the magnitude of the Fourier transform for interpretative purposes often is of interest. In order to examine the implications of Eqs. (3.3-10) and (3.3-12) on a display of the transform magnitude, let us first consider the one-variable case, where

$$F(u) = F(u + N) \quad \text{and}$$
$$|F(u)| = |F(-u)|.$$

The periodicity property indicates that $F(u)$ has a period of length N, and the symmetry property shows that the magnitude of the transform is centered on the origin, as Fig. 3.8(a) shows. Figure 3.8(a) and the preceding comments demonstrate that the magnitudes of the transform values from $(N/2) + 1$ to $N - 1$ are reflections of the values in the half period to the left of the origin. Because the discrete Fourier transform has been formulated for values of u in the interval $[0, N - 1]$, the result of this formulation yields two back-to-back half periods in this interval. To display one full period, all that is necessary is to move the origin of the transform to the point $u = N/2$, as Fig. 3.8(b) shows. To do so, we simply multiply $f(x)$ by $(-1)^x$ prior to taking the transform, as indicated earlier.

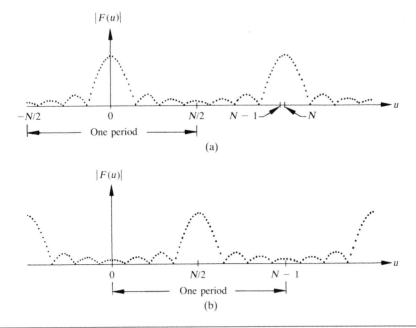

Figure 3.8   *Illustration of the periodicity properties of the Fourier transform: (a) Fourier spectrum showing back-to-back half periods in the interval [0, N − 1]; (b) Shifted spectrum showing a full period in the same interval.*

The same observations hold for the magnitude of the 2-D Fourier transform, with the exception that the results are considerably more difficult to interpret if the origin of the transform is not shifted to the frequency point $(N/2, N/2)$. Figures 3.9(b) and (c) show this difference; the latter image was obtained by using the centering property of expression (3.3-8).

3.3.4   Rotation

If we introduce the polar coordinates

$$x = r \cos \theta \qquad y = r \sin \theta \qquad u = \omega \cos \phi \qquad v = \omega \sin \phi$$

then $f(x, y)$ and $F(u, v)$ become $f(r, \theta)$ and $F(\omega, \phi)$, respectively. Direct substitution in either the continuous or discrete Fourier transform pair yields

$$f(r, \theta + \theta_0) \Leftrightarrow F(\omega, \phi + \theta_0). \tag{3.3-13}$$

In other words, rotating $f(x, y)$ by an angle θ_0 rotates $F(u, v)$ by the same angle. Similarly, rotating $F(u, v)$ rotates $f(x, y)$ by the same angle. Figure 3.10 illustrates this property.

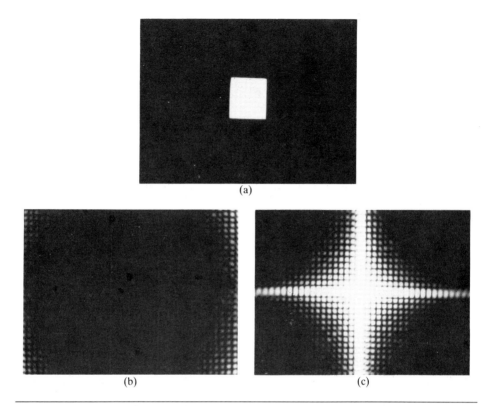

(a)

(b)   (c)

Figure 3.9   *(a) A simple image; (b) Fourier spectrum without shifting; (c) Fourier spectrum shifted to the center of the frequency square.*

3.3.5   Distributivity and Scaling

From the definition of the continuous or discrete transform pair,

$$\Im\{f_1(x, y) + f_2(x, y)\} = \Im\{f_1(x, y)\} + \Im\{f_2(x, y)\} \qquad (3.3\text{-}14)$$

and, in general,

$$\Im\{f_1(x, y) \cdot f_2(x, y)\} \neq \Im\{f_1(x, y)\} \cdot \Im\{f_2(x, y)\}. \qquad (3.3\text{-}15)$$

In other words, the Fourier transform and its inverse are distributive over addition but not over multiplication.

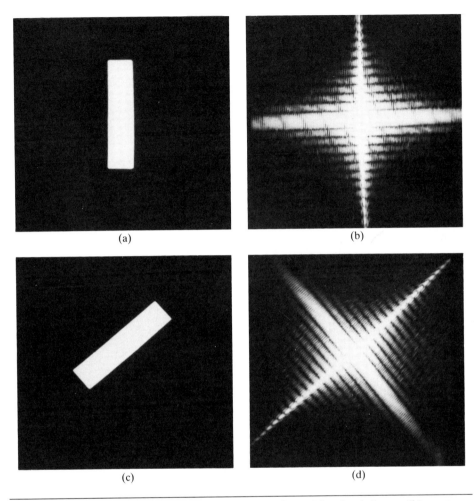

(a)   (b)

(c)   (d)

Figure 3.10 *Rotational properties of the Fourier transform: (a) a simple image; (b) spectrum; (c) rotated image; (d) resulting spectrum.*

For two scalars a and b,

$$af(x, y) \Leftrightarrow aF(u, v) \qquad (3.3\text{-}16)$$

and

$$f(ax, by) \Leftrightarrow \frac{1}{|ab|} F(u/a, v/b). \qquad (3.3\text{-}17)$$

3.3.6 Average Value

A widely used definition of the average value of a 2-D discrete function is the expression:

$$\overline{f}(x, y) = \frac{1}{N^2} \sum_{x=0}^{N-1} \sum_{y=0}^{N-1} f(x, y). \tag{3.3-18}$$

Substituting $u = v = 0$ in Eq. (3.2-9) yields

$$F(0, 0) = \frac{1}{N} \sum_{x=0}^{N-1} \sum_{y=0}^{N-1} f(x, y). \tag{3.3-19}$$

Therefore $\overline{f}(x, y)$ is related to the Fourier transform of $f(x, y)$ by

$$\overline{f}(x, y) = \frac{1}{N} F(0, 0). \tag{3.3-20}$$

3.3.7 Laplacian

The Laplacian of a two-variable function $f(x, y)$ is defined as

$$\nabla^2 f(x, y) = \frac{\partial^2 f}{\partial x^2} + \frac{\partial^2 f}{\partial y^2}. \tag{3.3-21}$$

From the definition of the 2-D Fourier transform,

$$\Im\{\nabla^2 f(x, y)\} \Leftrightarrow -(2\pi)^2 (u^2 + v^2) F(u, v). \tag{3.3-22}$$

The Laplacian operator is useful for outlining edges in an image as shown in Section 7.1.3.

3.3.8 Convolution and Correlation

In this section we consider two Fourier transform relationships that constitute a basic link between the spatial and frequency domains. These relationships, called *convolution* and *correlation*, are of fundamental importance to an understanding of image processing techniques based on the Fourier transform. In order to clarify the concepts involved, we begin the discussion by considering convolution in one dimension and with continuous arguments. We then extend the development to the discrete case and, finally, to the 2-D continuous and discrete cases. We develop the concept of correlation in the same manner.

Convolution

The convolution of two functions $f(x)$ and $g(x)$, denoted by $f(x)*g(x)$, is defined by the integral

$$f(x)*g(x) = \int_{-\infty}^{\infty} f(\alpha)g(x - \alpha) \, d\alpha \tag{3.3-23}$$

where α is a dummy variable of integration. The mechanics of the convolution integral are not particularly easy to visualize, so we begin the discussion with two examples that illustrate graphically the use of Eq. (3.3-23).

Example: The first example demonstrates convolution of the functions $f(x)$ and $g(x)$ shown in Figs. 3.11(a) and (b), respectively. Before the integration can be carried out, the function $g(x - \alpha)$ must be formed. To do so requires the two steps shown in Figs. 3.11(c) and (d). This operation is simply one of folding $g(\alpha)$ about the origin to give $g(-\alpha)$ and then displacing this function by x. Then, for any value of x, we multiply $f(\alpha)$ by the corresponding $g(x - \alpha)$ and integrate the product from $-\infty$ to ∞. The product of $f(\alpha)$ and $g(x - \alpha)$ is the shaded portion of Fig. 3.11(e). This figure is valid for $0 \leqslant x \leqslant 1$. The product is 0 for values of α outside the interval $[0, x]$, so $f(x)*g(x) = x/2$, which is simply the area of the shaded region in Fig. 3.11(e). For x in the interval $[1, 2]$, Fig. 3.11(f) applies, and $f(x)*g(x) = (1 - x/2)$. Thus because $f(\alpha)g(x - \alpha)$ is zero for values of x outside the interval $[0, 2]$, we have finally

$$f(x)*g(x) = \begin{cases} x/2 & 0 \leqslant x \leqslant 1 \\ 1 - x/2 & 1 \leqslant x \leqslant 2 \\ 0 & \text{elsewhere.} \end{cases}$$

Figure 3.11(g) shows the result. ❏

One aspect of Eq. (3.3-23) that is of use later in this section involves the convolution of a function $f(x)$ with the impulse function $\delta(x - x_0)$, which is defined by the relation

$$\int_{-\infty}^{\infty} f(x)\delta(x - x_0)\, dx = f(x_0). \qquad (3.3\text{-}24)$$

The function $\delta(x - x_0)$ may by viewed as having an area of unity in an infinitesimal neighborhood about x_0 and being 0 everywhere else; that is,

$$\int_{-\infty}^{\infty} \delta(x - x_0)\, dx = \int_{x_0^-}^{x_0^+} \delta(x - x_0)\, dx = 1. \qquad (3.3\text{-}25)$$

For most purposes we can say that $\delta(x - x_0)$ is located at $x = x_0$, and that the *strength* of the impulse is determined by the value of $f(x)$ at $x = x_0$. If $f(x) = A$, for instance, $A\delta(x - x_0)$ is an impulse of strength A located at $x = x_0$. Common practice is to represent impulses graphically by an arrow at x_0 with a height equal to the impulse strength. Figure 3.12 shows this representation for $A\delta(x - x_0)$.

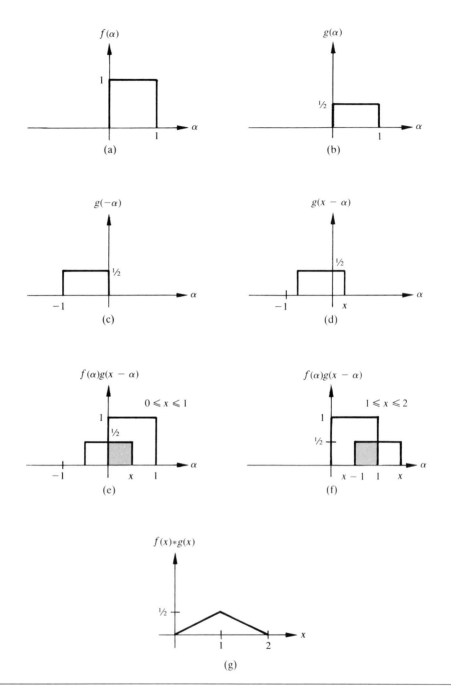

Figure 3.11 *Graphic illustration of convolution. The shaded areas indicate regions where the product is not zero.*

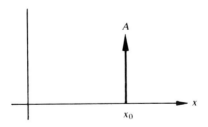

Figure 3.12 *Graphic representation of $A\delta(x - x_0)$.*

Example: In the second illustration of the use of Eq. (3.3-23), the function $f(x)$ shown in Fig. 3.13(a) is convolved with the function $g(x) = \delta(x + T) + \delta(x) + \delta(x - T)$ shown in Fig. 3.13(b). Folding $g(x)$, sliding it past $f(x)$, and making use of Eqs. (3.3-23) and (3.3-24), produce the result shown in Fig. 3.13(c). Convolution in this case amounts merely to "copying" $f(x)$ at the location of each impulse. ❑

The importance of convolution in frequency domain analysis lies in the fact that $f(x)*g(x)$ and $F(u)G(u)$ constitute a Fourier transform pair. In other words, if $f(x)$ has the Fourier transform $F(u)$ and $g(x)$ has the Fourier transform $G(u)$, then $f(x)*g(x)$ has the Fourier transform $F(u)G(u)$. This result, formally stated as

$$f(x)*g(x) \Leftrightarrow F(u)G(u) \qquad (3.3\text{-}26)$$

indicates that convolution in the x domain can also be obtained by taking the inverse Fourier transform of the product $F(u)G(u)$. An analogous result is that convolution in the frequency domain reduces to multiplication in the x domain; that is,

$$f(x)g(x) \Leftrightarrow F(u)*G(u). \qquad (3.3\text{-}27)$$

These two results are commonly referred to as the *convolution theorem.*

Suppose that, instead of being continuous, $f(x)$ and $g(x)$ are discretized into sampled arrays of size A and B, respectively: $\{f(0), f(1), f(2), \ldots, f(A - 1)\}$, and $\{g(0), g(1), g(2), \ldots, g(B - 1)\}$. As pointed out in Section 3.3.3, the discrete Fourier transform and its inverse are periodic functions. Formulating a discrete convolution theorem to be consistent with periodicity involves assuming that the discrete functions $f(x)$ and $g(x)$ are periodic with some period M. The resulting convolution then is periodic with the same period. The problem is how to select a value for M. It can be shown (Brigham [1974]) that unless

$$M \geq A + B - 1 \qquad (3.3\text{-}28)$$

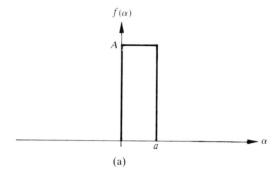

(a)

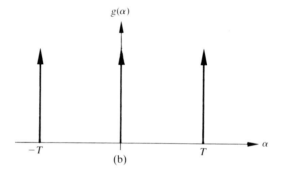

(b)

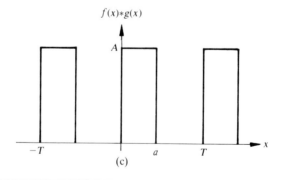

(c)

Figure 3.13   *Convolution involving impulse functions.*

is chosen, the individual periods of the convolution will overlap, a phenomenon commonly referred to as *wraparound error*. If $M = A + B - 1$, the periods will be adjacent; if $M > A + B - 1$, the periods will be separated, with the degree of separation being equal to the difference between M and $A + B - 1$. Because the assumed period must be greater than either A or B, the length of the sampled sequences must be increased so that both are of length M. Appending zeros to the samples forms the *extended* sequences

$$f_e(x) = \begin{cases} f(x) & 0 \leqslant x \leqslant A - 1 \\ 0 & A \leqslant x \leqslant M - 1 \end{cases}$$

and

$$g_e(x) = \begin{cases} g(x) & 0 \leqslant x \leqslant B - 1 \\ 0 & B \leqslant x \leqslant M - 1. \end{cases}$$

Based on these extensions, the discrete convolution of $f_e(x)$ and $g_e(x)$ is defined by the expression

$$f_e(x)*g_e(x) = \frac{1}{M} \sum_{m=0}^{M-1} f_e(m)g_e(x - m) \qquad (3.3\text{-}29)$$

for $x = 0, 1, 2, \ldots, M - 1$. The convolution function is a discrete, periodic array of length M, with the values $x = 0, 1, 2, \ldots, M - 1$ describing a full period of $f_e(x)*g_e(x)$.

The mechanics of discrete convolution are basically the same as for continuous convolution. The only differences are that displacements take place in discrete increments corresponding to the separation between samples, and that a summation replaces integration. Similarly, Eqs. (3.3-26) and (3.3-27) also hold in the discrete case where we use $f_e(x)$ and $g_e(x)$ to avoid wraparound error. The discrete variables x and u take on values in the range $0, 1, 2, \ldots, M - 1$.

Example: Figure 3.14 illustrates graphically the preceding considerations for continuous and discrete convolution. The diagrams for the discrete case show A samples for both $f(x)$ and $g(x)$ in the interval $[0, 1]$ and an assumed period of $M = A + B - 1 = 2A - 1$.

Note that the convolution function is periodic and that, since $M = 2A - 1$, the periods are adjacent. Choosing $M > 2A - 1$ would have produced a larger separation between these periods. Note also that M samples completely describe a period. ❏

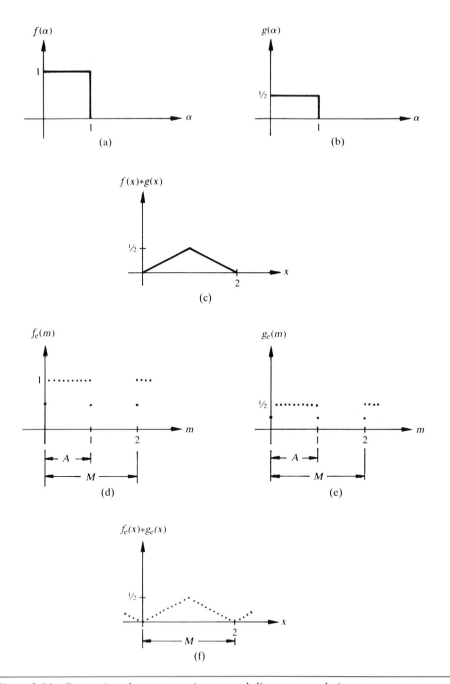

Figure 3.14 *Comparison between continuous and discrete convolution.*

Two-dimensional convolution is analogous in form to Eq. (3.3-23). Thus for two functions $f(x, y)$ and $g(x, y)$,

$$f(x, y)*g(x, y) = \int\int_{-\infty}^{\infty} f(\alpha, \beta)g(x - \alpha, y - \beta) \, d\alpha \, d\beta. \qquad (3.3\text{-}30)$$

The convolution theorem in two dimensions, then, is expressed by the relations

$$f(x, y)*g(x, y) \Leftrightarrow F(u, v)G(u, v) \qquad (3.3\text{-}31)$$

and

$$f(x, y)g(x, y) \Leftrightarrow F(u, v)*G(u, v). \qquad (3.3\text{-}32)$$

Equation (3.3-30) is more difficult to illustrate graphically than Eq. (3.3-23). Figure 3.15 shows the basic folding, displacement, and multiplication operations required for 2-D convolution. The result of varying the displacement variables, x and y, would be a 2-D convolution surface with a shape dependent on the nature of the functions involved in the process.

The 2-D, discrete convolution is formulated by letting $f(x, y)$ and $g(x, y)$ be discrete arrays of size $A \times B$ and $C \times D$, respectively. As in the 1-D case, these arrays must be assumed periodic with some period M and N in the x and y directions, respectively. Wraparound error in the individual convolution periods is avoided by choosing

$$M \geqslant A + C - 1 \qquad (3.3\text{-}33)$$

and

$$N \geqslant B + D - 1. \qquad (3.3\text{-}34)$$

The periodic sequences are formed by extending $f(x, y)$ and $g(x, y)$ as follows:

$$f_e(x, y) = \begin{cases} f(x, y) & 0 \leqslant x \leqslant A - 1 \quad \text{and} \quad 0 \leqslant y \leqslant B - 1 \\ 0 & A \leqslant x \leqslant M - 1 \quad \text{or} \quad B \leqslant y \leqslant N - 1 \end{cases}$$

and

$$g_e(x, y) = \begin{cases} g(x, y) & 0 \leqslant x \leqslant C - 1 \quad \text{and} \quad 0 \leqslant y \leqslant D - 1 \\ 0 & C \leqslant x \leqslant M - 1 \quad \text{or} \quad D \leqslant y \leqslant N - 1. \end{cases}$$

The 2-D convolution of $f_e(x, y)$ and $g_e(x, y)$ is defined by the relation

$$f_e(x, y)*g_e(x, y) = \frac{1}{MN} \sum_{m=0}^{M-1} \sum_{n=0}^{N-1} f_e(m, n)g_e(x - m, y - n) \qquad (3.3\text{-}35)$$

for $x = 0, 1, 2, \ldots , M - 1$ and $y = 0, 1, 2, \ldots , N - 1$. The $M \times N$ array of Eq. (3.3-35) is one period of the discrete, 2-D convolution. If M and N are chosen according to Eqs. (3.3-33) and (3.3-34), this array is guaranteed to be free from interference from other adjacent periods. As in the 1-D case, the continuous convolution theorem, Eqs. (3.3-31) and (3.3-32), also applies to the

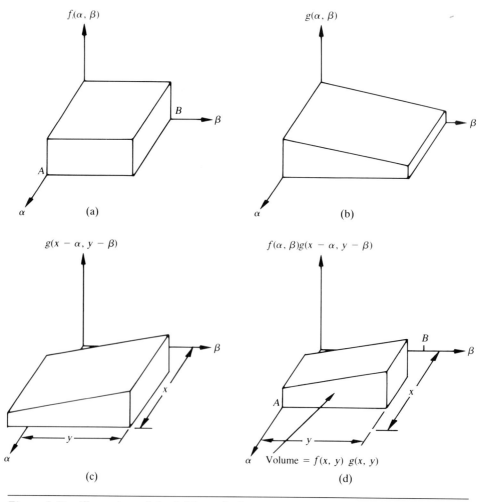

Figure 3.15 *Illustration of the folding, displacement, and multiplication steps needed to perform two-dimensional convolution.*

discrete case with $u = 0, 1, 2, \ldots, M - 1$ and $v = 0, 1, 2, \ldots, N - 1$. All computations involve the extended functions $f_e(x, y)$ and $g_e(x, y)$.

The theoretical power of the convolution theorem will become evident in Section 3.3.9, when we discuss the sampling theorem. Practically, computing the discrete convolution in the frequency domain often is more efficient than using Eq. (3.3-35) directly. The procedure is to compute the Fourier transforms of $f_e(x, y)$ and $g_e(x, y)$ by using a fast Fourier transform (FFT) algorithm (see Section 3.4). The two transforms are then multiplied and the inverse Fourier transform of the product yields the convolution function. A comparison by Brigham [1974] shows that, for 1-D arrays, the FFT approach is faster if the number of points is greater than 32. Although this number depends on the particular machine and algorithms used, it is well below the number of points in a row or column of a typical image.

Correlation

The correlation[†] of two continuous functions $f(x)$ and $g(x)$, denoted $f(x) \circ g(x)$, is defined by the relation

$$f(x) \circ g(x) = \int_{-\infty}^{\infty} f^*(\alpha) g(x + \alpha) \, d\alpha \tag{3.3-36}$$

where * is the complex conjugate. The forms of Eqs. (3.3-36) and (3.3-23) are similar, with the only difference being that the function $g(x)$ is not folded about the origin. Thus, to perform correlation, we simply slide $g(x)$ by $f(x)$ and integrate the product from $-\infty$ to ∞ for each value of displacement x. Figure 3.16 illustrates the procedure. Compare Figs. 3.16 and 3.11.

The discrete equivalent of Eq. (3.3-36) is defined as

$$f_e(x) \circ g_e(x) = \frac{1}{M} \sum_{m=0}^{M-1} f_e^*(m) g_e(x + m) \tag{3.3-37}$$

for $x = 0, 1, 2, \ldots, M - 1$. The comments made earlier regarding $f_e(x)$ and $g_e(x)$, the assumed periodicity of these functions, and the choice of values for M, also apply to Eq. (3.3-37).

Similar expressions hold for two dimensions. Thus if $f(x, y)$ and $g(x, y)$ are functions of continuous variables, their correlation is defined as

$$f(x, y) \circ g(x, y) = \int\int_{-\infty}^{\infty} f^*(\alpha, \beta) g(x + \alpha, y + \beta) \, d\alpha \, d\beta. \tag{3.3-38}$$

[†] If $f(x)$ and $g(x)$ are the same function, Eq. (3.3-36) is usually called the *autocorrelation* function; if $f(x)$ and $g(x)$ are different, the term *cross correlation* is normally used.

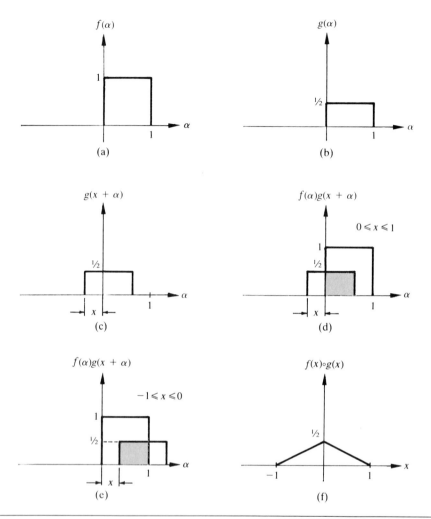

Figure 3.16 *Graphic illustration of correlation. The shaded areas indicate regions where the product is not zero.*

For the discrete case,

$$f_e(x, y) \circ g_e(x, y) = \frac{1}{MN} \sum_{m=0}^{M-1} \sum_{n=0}^{N-1} f_e^*(m, n)g_e(x + m, y + n) \qquad (3.3\text{-}39)$$

for $x = 0, 1, 2, \ldots, M - 1$ and $y = 0, 1, 2, \ldots, N - 1$. As in the case of discrete convolution, $f_e(x, y)$ and $g_e(x, y)$ are extended functions, and M and

N are chosen according to Eqs. (3.3-33) and (3.3-34) in order to avoid wrap-around error in the periods of the correlation function.

For both the continuous and discrete cases, the following *correlation theorem* holds:

$$f(x, y)\circ g(x, y) \Leftrightarrow F^*(u, v)G(u, v) \qquad (3.3\text{-}40)$$

and

$$f^*(x, y)g(x, y) \Leftrightarrow F(u, v)\circ G(u, v). \qquad (3.3\text{-}41)$$

When interpreted for discrete variables, all functions are assumed to be extended and periodic.

One of the principal applications of correlation in image processing is in the area of *template* or *prototype matching*, where the problem is to find the closest match between an unknown image and a set of known images, as discussed in Chapter 9. One approach is to compute the correlation between the unknown and each of the known images. The closest match can then be found by selecting the image that yields the correlation function with the largest value. Because the resultant correlations are 2-D functions, this task involves searching for the largest amplitude of each function. As in the case of discrete convolution, the computation of $f_e(x, y)\circ g_e(x, y)$ often is more efficiently done in the frequency domain using an FFT algorithm to obtain the forward and inverse transforms.

When comparing the results of discrete versus continuous convolution or correlation, it should be noted that the way we defined the discrete cases amounts to evaluation of the continuous forms by rectangular integration. Thus to compare discrete and continuous results on an absolute basis, we have to multiply Eqs. (3.3-29) and (3.3-37) by Δx and Eqs. (3.3-35) and (3.3-39) by $\Delta x \Delta y$, where Δx and Δy are the separations between samples, as defined in Section 3.2. In Fig. 3.14, for example, the continuous and discrete convolution functions have the same amplitude because the discrete result was multiplied by Δx. In computing and evaluating only the discrete forms, however, inclusion of these scale factors is a matter of preference. Moreover, all convolution and correlation expressions hold if $f(x)$ and $g(x)$—along with their corresponding transforms—are interchanged. This condition also is true if the functions are two dimensional.

3.3.9   Sampling

We introduced the basic idea of image sampling in Section 2.3 on an intuitive basis. The Fourier transform and the convolution theorem provide the tools for a deeper analytic study of this problem. In particular, we want to look at the question of how many samples should be taken so that no information is lost in the sampling process. Expressed differently, the problem is one of establishing the sampling conditions under which a continuous image can be recovered fully from a set of sampled values. We begin the analysis with the 1-D case.

One-dimensional functions

Consider the function shown in Fig. 3.17(a), which is assumed to extend from $-\infty$ to ∞. Suppose that the Fourier transform of $f(x)$ vanishes for values of u outside the interval $[-W, W]$. The transform might appear as shown in Fig. 3.17(b).[†] A function whose transform has this property for any finite value of W is called a *band-limited* function.

To obtain a sampled version of $f(x)$ simply involves multiplying this function by a sampling function $s(x)$, which consists of a train of impulses Δx units apart, as shown in Fig. 3.17(c). By the convolution theorem, multiplication in the x domain is equivalent to convolution in the frequency domain. Thus the Fourier transform shown in Fig. 3.17(f) is obtained for the product $s(x)f(x)$. The transform is periodic, with period $1/\Delta x$, and the individual repetitions of $F(u)$ can overlap. In the first period, for example, the center of the overlapped region occurs at $u = 1/2\Delta x$ if the quantity $1/2\Delta x$ is less than W. Therefore to avoid this problem we select the sampling interval Δx so that $1/2\Delta x \geq W$, or

$$\Delta x \leq \frac{1}{2W} \qquad (3.3\text{-}42)$$

The result of decreasing Δx is shown in Figs. 3.17(g) and (h). The net effect is to separate the periods so that no overlap occurs. The importance of this operation is that multiplication of the transform of Fig. 3.17(h) by the function

$$G(u) = \begin{cases} 1 & -W \leq u \leq W \\ 0 & \text{elsewhere} \end{cases} \qquad (3.3\text{-}43)$$

makes possible the complete isolation of $F(u)$, as shown in Fig. 3.17(k). The inverse Fourier transform then yields the original *continuous* function $f(x)$. Complete recovery of a band-limited function from samples whose spacing satisfies Eq. (3.3-42) is known as the *Whittaker–Shannon sampling theorem*.

All the frequency domain information of a band-limited function is contained in the interval $[-W, W]$. However, if Eq. (3.3-42) is not satisfied, the transform in this interval is corrupted by contributions from adjacent periods. This phenomenon, frequently referred to as *aliasing*, precludes complete recovery of an undersampled function.

The preceding results apply to functions that are of unlimited duration in the x domain. This implies an infinite sampling interval, so examining the

---

[†] Recall that the Fourier transform is a complex function. For simplicity, in the following graphic illustrations we show only the magnitude of the transforms. The ordinate axis, however, is labeled $F(u)$, $G(u)$, etc., to indicate that the concepts involved are valid for the complete transform, and not just its magnitude.

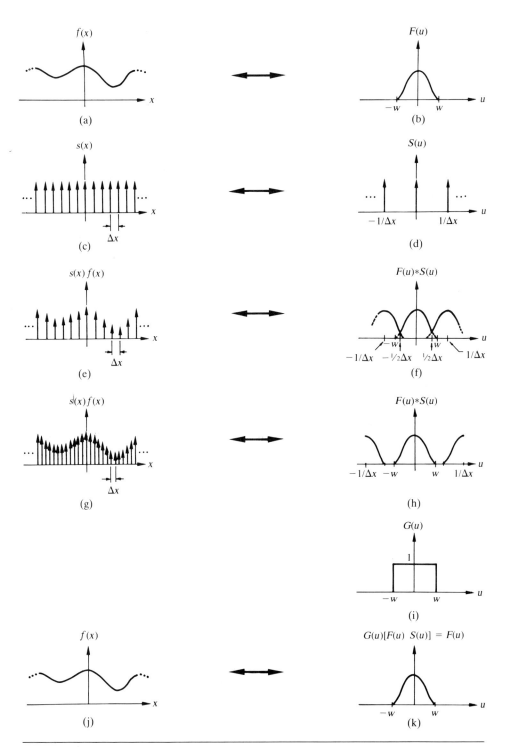

Figure 3.17 *Graphic development of sampling concepts.*

practical case of a function sampled only over a finite region is of interest. The situation is shown graphically in Fig. 3.18. Parts (a)–(f) are the same as in Fig. 3.17, except that the separation between samples is assumed to satisfy the sampling theorem so that no aliasing is present. A finite sampling interval $[0, X]$ can be represented mathematically by multiplying the sampled result shown in Fig. 3.18(e) by the function

$$h(x) = \begin{cases} 1 & 0 \le x \le X \\ 0 & \text{elsewhere.} \end{cases} \tag{3.3-44}$$

This function, often called a *window*, and its Fourier transform are shown in Figs. 3.18(g) and (h), respectively. The results of multiplication are illustrated in Figs. 3.18(i) and (j). The final frequency domain result is obtained by convolving the function $S(u)*F(u)$ with $H(u)$, which is the Fourier transform of the window function $h(x)$. Because $H(u)$ has frequency components that extend to infinity, the convolution of these functions introduces a distortion in the frequency domain representation of a function that has been sampled and limited to a finite region by $h(x)$, as Fig. 3.18(j) shows. Thus even if the separation between samples satisfies the sampling theorem, recovering completely a function that has been sampled only in a finite region of the x domain generally is impossible. Under these conditions the original Fourier transform can be isolated only when $f(x)$ is band limited and periodic, with a period equal to X. In this case the corruptions caused by $H(u)$ cancel out, allowing complete recovery of $f(x)$ if the sampling theorem is satisfied. The recovered function still extends from $-\infty$ to ∞ and is *not* zero outside the range in which $h(x)$ is zero. These considerations lead to the important conclusion that no function $f(x)$ of finite duration can be band limited. Conversely, a function that is band limited must extend from $-\infty$ to ∞ in the x domain. This is an important practical result because it establishes a fundamental limitation in the treatment of digital functions.

Before leaving the discussion of 1-D functions, let us use the preceding results to develop an alternative reason for the periodicity of the discrete Fourier transform. So far, all results in the frequency domain have been of a continuous nature. To obtain a discrete Fourier transform simply requires "sampling" the continuous transform with a train of impulses that are Δu units apart. Figure 3.19 depicts the situation, based on Figs. 3.18(i) and (j). The notation $f(x)$ and $F(u)$ used in Fig. 3.19 facilitates comparison with the discussion in Section 3.2. Keep in mind, however, that Figs. 3.19(a) and (b) are assumed to be the result of the sequence of operations shown in Fig. 3.18.

As previously pointed out, sampling can be represented by multiplying an impulse train with the function of interest. In this case, multiplying $F(u)$ by

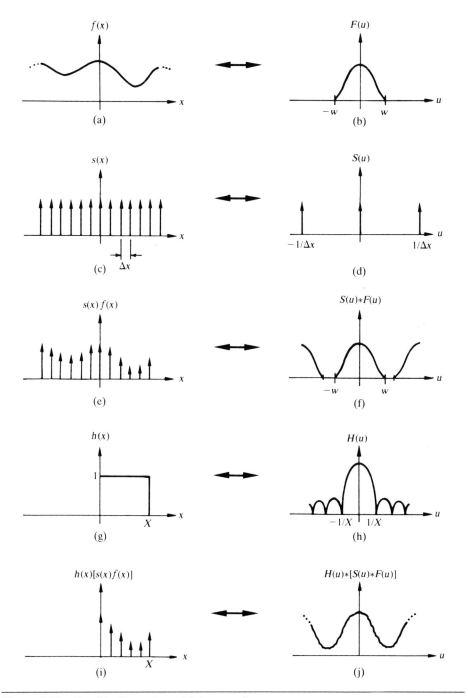

Figure 3.18   *Graphic illustration of finite-sampling concepts.*

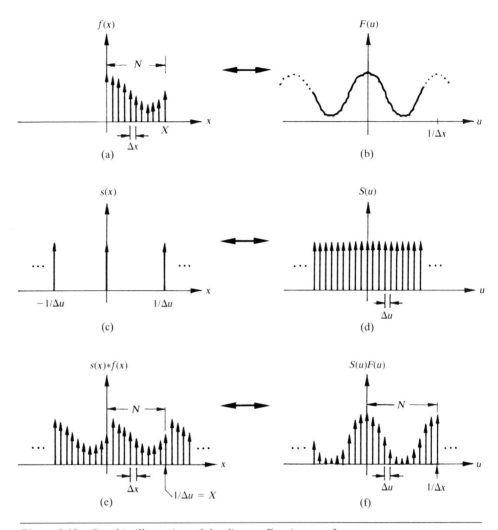

Figure 3.19 *Graphic illustration of the discrete Fourier transform.*

$S(u)$ gives the result shown in Fig. 3.19(f). The equivalent operation in the x domain is convolution, which yields the function shown in Fig. 3.19(e). This function is periodic, with period $1/\Delta u$. If N samples of $f(x)$ and $F(u)$ are taken and the spacings between samples are selected so that a period in each domain is covered by N uniformly spaced samples, then $N\Delta x = X$ in the x domain and $N\Delta u = 1/\Delta x$ in the frequency domain. The latter equation is based on the periodic property of the Fourier transform of a sampled function, with period

$1/\Delta x$, as shown earlier. Hence

$$\Delta u = \frac{1}{N\Delta x} \qquad (3.3\text{-}45)$$

which agrees with Eq. (3.2-4). Choosing this spacing yields the function in Fig. 3.19(e), which is periodic with period $1/\Delta u$. From Eq. (3.3-45), $1/\Delta u = N\Delta x = X$, which is the overall sampling interval in Fig. 3.19(a).

Two-dimensional functions
The preceding sampling concepts, after some modifications in notation, are directly applicable to 2-D functions. The sampling process for these functions can be formulated mathematically by making use of the 2-D impulse function $\delta(x, y)$, which is defined as

$$\int\!\!\!\int_{-\infty}^{\infty} f(x, y)\delta(x - x_0, y - y_0)\, dx\, dy = f(x_0, y_0). \qquad (3.3\text{-}46)$$

The interpretation of Eq. (3.3-46) is analogous to that given in connection with Eqs. (3.3-24) and (3.3-25). A 2-D sampling function consisting of a train of impulses separated Δx units in the x direction and Δy units in the y direction is shown in Fig. 3.20.

For a function $f(x, y)$, where x and y are continuous, a sampled function is obtained by forming the product $s(x, y)f(x, y)$. The equivalent operation in

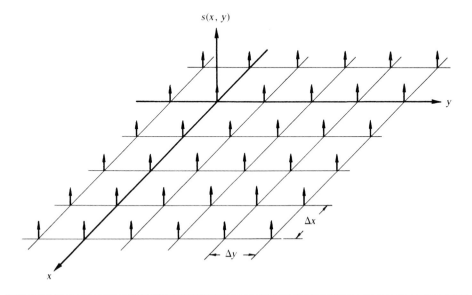

Figure 3.20 *A 2-D sampling function.*

the frequency domain is convolution of $S(u, v)$ and $F(u, v)$, where $S(u, v)$ is a train of impulses with separation $1/\Delta x$ and $1/\Delta y$ in the u and v directions, respectively. If $f(x, y)$ is band limited (that is, its Fourier transform vanishes outside some finite region R) the result of convolving $S(u, v)$ and $F(u, v)$ might look like the case shown in Fig. 3.21. The function shown is periodic in two dimensions.

Let $2W_u$ and $2W_v$ represent the widths in the u and v directions, respectively, of the smallest rectangle that completely encloses the region R. Then, from Fig. 3.21, if $1/\Delta x > 2W_u$ and $1/\Delta y > 2W_v$ (no aliasing), one of the periods can be recovered completely by multiplying $S(u, v)*F(u, v)$ by the function

$$G(u, v) = \begin{cases} 1 & (u, v) \text{ inside one of the} \\ & \text{rectangles enclosing } R \\ 0 & \text{elsewhere.} \end{cases} \tag{3.3-47}$$

The inverse Fourier transform of $G(u, v)[S(u, v)*F(u, v)]$ yields $f(x, y)$.

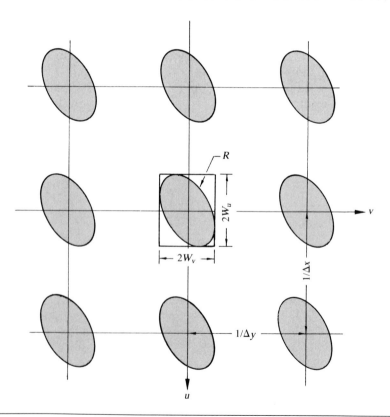

Figure 3.21   *Frequency domain representation of a sampled 2-D, band-limited function.*

The foregoing considerations lead to a form of the 2-D sampling theorem, which states that a band-limited function $f(x, y)$ can be recovered completely from samples whose separation is

$$\Delta x \leq \frac{1}{2W_u} \tag{3.3-48a}$$

and

$$\Delta y \leq \frac{1}{2W_v}. \tag{3.3-48b}$$

When $f(x, y)$ is spatially limited by using a 2-D window $h(x, y)$ analogous to the function $h(x)$ used in Fig. 3.18, the transform of the sampled function is distorted by the convolution of $H(u, v)$ and $S(u, v)*F(u, v)$. This distortion, which is due to the spatially limited nature of digital images, precludes complete recovery of $f(x, y)$ from its samples. As in the 1-D case, periodic functions are an exception, but images satisfying this condition rarely occur in practice.

An argument similar to the one developed for the 1-D case can be made to show how periodicity arises in the 2-D, discrete Fourier transform. For an $N \times N$ image, this analysis also would yield

$$\Delta u = \frac{1}{N\Delta x} \tag{3.3-49a}$$

and

$$\Delta v = \frac{1}{N\Delta y}. \tag{3.3-49b}$$

These relationships between the sample separations guarantee that a complete (2-D) period will be covered by $N \times N$ uniformly spaced values in both the spatial and frequency domains.

3.4 THE FAST FOURIER TRANSFORM

The number of complex multiplications and additions required to implement Eq. (3.2-2) is proportional to N^2. That is, for each of the N values of u, expansion of the summation requires N complex multiplications of $f(x)$ by $\exp[-j2\pi ux/N]$ and $N - 1$ additions of the results. The terms of $\exp[-j2\pi ux/N]$ can be computed once and stored in a table for all subsequent applications. For this reason, the multiplication of u by x in these terms is usually not considered a direct part of the implementation.

Proper decomposition of Eq. (3.2-2) can make the number of multiplication and addition operations proportional to $N \log_2 N$. The decomposition procedure is called the *fast Fourier transform* (FFT) *algorithm.* The reduction in proportionality from N^2 to $N \log_2 N$ operations represents a significant saving in computational effort, as shown in Table 3.1. Obviously, the FFT approach offers a considerable computational advantage over direct implementation of the Fourier transform, particularly when N is relatively large. For example, suppose that the FFT of an 8192-point array requires 5 sec of computation time on a general-purpose computer. The same machine would take about 600 times longer (50 min) to compute the Fourier transform of the same array using Eq. (3.2-2).

In the following discussion, we develop an FFT algorithm of one variable. As indicated in Section 3.3.1, a 2-D Fourier transform can be obtained by successive passes of the 1-D transform.

3.4.1   FFT Algorithm

The FFT algorithm developed in this section is based on the so-called successive doubling method. For convenience we express Eq. (3.2-2) in the form

$$F(u) = \frac{1}{N} \sum_{x=0}^{N-1} f(x) W_N^{ux} \qquad (3.4\text{-}1)$$

where

$$W_N = \exp[-j2\pi/N] \qquad (3.4\text{-}2)$$

Table 3.1   A Comparison of N^2 versus N Log$_2 N$ for Various Values of N

N	N^2 (*Direct* FT)	$N \log_2 N$ (FFT)	*Computational Advantage* ($N/\log_2 N$)
2	4	2	2.00
4	16	8	2.00
8	64	24	2.67
16	256	64	4.00
32	1,024	160	6.40
64	4,096	384	10.67
128	16,384	896	18.29
256	65,536	2,048	32.00
512	262,144	4,608	56.89
1024	1,048,576	10,240	102.40
2048	4,194,304	22,528	186.18
4096	16,777,216	49,152	341.33
8192	67,108,864	106,496	630.15

and N is assumed to be of the form

$$N = 2^n \tag{3.4-3}$$

where n is a positive integer. Hence N can be expressed as

$$N = 2M \tag{3.4-4}$$

where M is also a positive integer. Substitution of Eq. (3.4-4) into Eq. (3.4-1) yields

$$
\begin{aligned}
F(u) &= \frac{1}{2M} \sum_{x=0}^{2M-1} f(x) W_{2M}^{ux} \\
&= \frac{1}{2} \left[\frac{1}{M} \sum_{x=0}^{M-1} f(2x) W_{2M}^{u(2x)} + \frac{1}{M} \sum_{x=0}^{M-1} f(2x+1) W_{2M}^{u(2x+1)} \right].
\end{aligned}
\tag{3.4-5}
$$

From Eq. (3.4-2), $W_{2M}^{2ux} = W_M^{ux}$, so Eq. (3.4-5) may be expressed in the form

$$F(u) = \frac{1}{2} \left[\frac{1}{M} \sum_{x=0}^{M-1} f(2x) W_M^{ux} + \frac{1}{M} \sum_{x=0}^{M-1} f(2x+1) W_M^{ux} W_{2M}^{u} \right]. \tag{3.4-6}$$

Defining

$$F_{even}(u) = \frac{1}{M} \sum_{x=0}^{M-1} f(2x) W_M^{ux} \tag{3.4-7}$$

for $u = 0, 1, 2, \ldots, M - 1$, and

$$F_{odd}(u) = \frac{1}{M} \sum_{x=0}^{M-1} f(2x+1) W_M^{ux} \tag{3.4-8}$$

for $u = 0, 1, 2, \ldots, M - 1$, reduces Eq. (3.4-6) to

$$F(u) = \frac{1}{2} [F_{even}(u) + F_{odd}(u) W_{2M}^{u}]. \tag{3.4-9}$$

Also, since $W_M^{u+M} = W_M^{u}$ and $W_{2M}^{u+M} = -W_{2M}^{u}$, Eqs. (3.4-7)–(3.4-9) give

$$F(u + M) = \frac{1}{2} [F_{even}(u) - F_{odd}(u) W_{2M}^{u}]. \tag{3.4-10}$$

Careful analysis of Eqs. (3.4-7)–(3.4-10) reveals some interesting properties of these expressions. An N-point transform can be computed by dividing the original expression into two parts, as indicated in Eqs. (3.4-9) and (3.4-10). Computation of the first half of $F(u)$ requires evaluation of the two $(N/2)$-point transforms given in Eqs. (3.4-7) and (3.4-8). The resulting values of $F_{even}(u)$

and $F_{odd}(u)$ are then substituted into Eq. (3.4-9) to obtain $F(u)$ for $u = 0, 1, 2, \ldots, (N/2 - 1)$. The other half then follows directly from Eq. (3.4-10) without additional transform evaluations.

In order to examine the computational implications of this procedure, let $m(n)$ and $a(n)$ represent the number of complex multiplications and additions, respectively, required to implement it. As before, the number of samples is 2^n, where n is a positive integer. Suppose first that $n = 1$. A two-point transform requires the evaluation of $F(0)$; then $F(1)$ follows from Eq. (3.4-10). To obtain $F(0)$ first requires computing $F_{even}(0)$ and $F_{odd}(0)$. In this case $M = 1$ and Eqs. (3.4-7) and (3.4-8) are one-point transforms. Because the Fourier transform of a single point is the sample itself, however, no multiplications or additions are required to obtain $F_{even}(0)$ and $F_{odd}(0)$. One multiplication of $F_{odd}(0)$ by W_2^0 and one addition yield $F(0)$ from Eq. (3.4-9). Then $F(1)$ follows from Eq. (3.4-10) with one more addition (subtraction is considered to be the same as addition). As $F_{odd}(0)W_2^0$ had already been computed, the total number of operations required for a two-point transform consists of $m(1) = 1$ multiplication and $a(1) = 2$ additions.

The next allowed value for n is 2. According to the above development, a four-point transform can be divided into two parts. The first half of $F(u)$ requires evaluation of two, two-point transforms, as in Eqs. (3.4-7) and (3.4-8) for $M = 2$. A two-point transform requires $m(1)$ multiplications and $a(1)$ additions, so evaluation of these two equations requires a total of $2m(1)$ multiplications and $2a(1)$ additions. Two further multiplications and additions are necessary to obtain $F(0)$ and $F(1)$ from Eq. (3.4-9). Because $F_{odd}(u)W_{2M}^u$ already had been computed for $u = \{0, 1\}$, two more additions give $F(2)$ and $F(3)$. The total is then $m(2) = 2m(1) + 2$ and $a(2) = 2a(1) + 4$.

When n is equal to 3, two four-point transforms are considered in the evaluation of $F_{even}(u)$ and $F_{odd}(u)$. They require $2m(2)$ multiplications and $2a(2)$ additions. Four more multiplications and eight more additions yield the complete transform. The total then is $m(3) = 2m(2) + 4$ and $a(3) = 2a(2) + 8$.

Continuing this argument for any positive integer value of n leads to recursive expressions for the number of multiplications and additions required to implement the FFT:

$$m(n) = 2m(n - 1) + 2^{n-1} \qquad n \geq 1 \tag{3.4-11}$$

and

$$a(n) = 2a(n - 1) + 2^n \qquad n \geq 1 \tag{3.4-12}$$

where $m(0) = 0$ and $a(0) = 0$ because the transform of a single point does not require any additions or multiplications.

Implementation of Eqs. (3.4-7)–(3.4-10) constitutes the successive doubling FFT algorithm. This name comes from the method of computing a two-point transform from two one-point transforms, a four-point transform from two two-point transforms, and so on, for any N that is equal to an integer power of 2.

3.4.2 Number of Operations

By induction, the number of complex multiplications and additions required to implement the FFT algorithm is

$$
\begin{align}
m(n) &= \frac{1}{2} 2^n \log_2 2^n \\
&= \frac{1}{2} N \log_2 N \qquad (3.4\text{-}13) \\
&= \frac{1}{2} Nn \qquad n \geqslant 1
\end{align}
$$

and

$$
\begin{align}
a(n) &= 2^n \log_2 2^n \\
&= N \log_2 N \qquad (3.4\text{-}14) \\
&= Nn \qquad n \geqslant 1
\end{align}
$$

respectively.

Proof by induction begins with showing that Eqs. (3.4-13) and (3.4-14) hold for $n = 1$. Recall that

$$
m(1) = \tfrac{1}{2}(2)(1) = 1 \quad \text{and} \quad a(1) = (2)(1) = 2.
$$

Next, the assumption is made that the expressions hold for n. Then, we are required to prove that they also are true for $n + 1$.

From Eq. (3.4-11),

$$
m(n + 1) = 2m(n) + 2^n.
$$

Substituting Eq. (3.4-13) for $m(n)$, assumed to be valid for n, yields

$$
\begin{align}
m(n + 1) &= 2(\tfrac{1}{2}Nn) + 2^n \\
&= 2(\tfrac{1}{2}2^n n) + 2^n \\
&= 2^n(n + 1) \\
&= \tfrac{1}{2}(2^{n+1})(n + 1).
\end{align}
$$

Equation (3.4-13) is therefore valid for all positive integer values of n.

From Eq. (3.4-12),

$$
a(n + 1) = 2a(n) + 2^{n+1}.
$$

Substituting Eq. (3.4-14) for $a(n)$ yields

$$a(n + 1) = 2Nn + 2^{n+1}$$
$$= 2(2^n n) + 2^{n+1}$$
$$= 2^{n+1}(n + 1)$$

which completes the proof.

3.4.3   The Inverse FFT

Thus far, we have said little concerning the inverse Fourier transform. The reason is that any algorithm for implementing the discrete forward transform also may be used (with minor modifications in the input) to compute the inverse. To show this, let us return to Eqs. (3.2-2) and (3.2-3), repeated as

$$F(u) = \frac{1}{N} \sum_{x=0}^{N-1} f(x) \exp[-j2\pi ux/N] \tag{3.4-15}$$

and

$$f(x) = \sum_{u=0}^{N-1} F(u) \exp[j2\pi ux/N]. \tag{3.4-16}$$

Taking the complex conjugate of Eq. (3.4-16) and dividing both sides by N yields

$$\frac{1}{N} f^*(x) = \frac{1}{N} \sum_{u=0}^{N-1} F^*(u) \exp[-j2\pi ux/N]. \tag{3.4-17}$$

Comparing this result with Eq. (3.4-15) shows that the right-hand side of Eq. (3.4-17) is in the form of the forward Fourier transform. Thus inputting $F^*(u)$ into an algorithm designed to compute the forward transform gives the quantity $f^*(x)/N$. Taking the complex conjugate and multiplying by N yields the desired inverse $f(x)$.

For 2-D square arrays we take the complex conjugate of Eq. (3.2-10), that is,

$$f^*(x, y) = \frac{1}{N} \sum_{u=0}^{N-1} \sum_{v=0}^{N-1} F^*(u, v) \exp[-j2\pi(ux + vy)/N] \tag{3.4-18}$$

which is in the form of the 2-D forward transform of Eq. (3.2-9). Therefore, inputting $F^*(u, v)$ into an algorithm designed to compute the forward transform gives $f^*(x, y)$. Taking the complex conjugate of this result yields $f(x, y)$. When $f(x)$ or $f(x, y)$ is real, the complex conjugate operation is unnecessary, because $f(x) = f^*(x)$ and $f(x, y) = f^*(x, y)$ for real functions.

Computation of the 2-D transform by successive passes of the 1-D transform is a frequent source of confusion when the preceding technique is used to obtain the inverse. Keep in mind the procedure outlined in Section 3.3.1 and avoid being misled by Eq. (3.4-17). In other words, when a 1-D algorithm is used to compute the 2-D inverse, we do not compute the complex conjugate after processing each row or column. Instead, the function $F^*(u, v)$ is treated as if it were $f(x, y)$ in the forward, 2-D transform procedure summarized in Fig. 3.7. The complex conjugate of the result (if necessary) yields the proper inverse $f(x, y)$.

3.4.4   Implementation

A computer implementation of the FFT algorithm developed in Section 3.4.1 is straightforward. The principal point to keep in mind is that the input data must be arranged in the order required for successive applications of Eqs. (3.4-7) and (3.4-8). The ordering procedure can be illustrated by a simple example. Suppose that we want to use the successive doubling algorithm to compute the FFT of an eight-point function $\{f(0), f(1), \ldots, f(7)\}$. Equation (3.4-7) uses the samples with even arguments, $\{f(0), f(2), f(4), f(6)\}$, and Eq. (3.4-8) uses the samples with odd arguments, $\{f(1), f(3), f(5), f(7)\}$. However, each four-point transform is computed as two two-point transforms, which also requires the use of Eqs. (3.4-7) and (3.4-8). Thus to compute the FFT of the first set above, we must divide it into its even part $\{f(0), f(4)\}$ and odd part $\{f(2), f(6)\}$. Similarly, the second set is subdivided into $\{f(1), f(5)\}$ for Eq. (3.4-7) and $\{f(3), f(7)\}$ for Eq. (3.4-8). No further rearrangement is required, because each two-element set is considered as having one even and one odd element. Combining these results requires that the input array be expressed in the form $\{f(0), f(4), f(2), f(6), f(1), f(5), f(3), f(7)\}$. The successive doubling algorithm operates on this array in the manner shown in Fig. 3.22. At the first level of computation are four two-point transforms involving $\{f(0), f(4)\}$, $\{f(2), f(6)\}$, $\{f(1), f(5)\}$, and $\{f(3), f(7)\}$. The next level uses these results to form two four-point transforms, and the last level uses these two results to produce the desired transform.

Fortunately, the general procedure for reordering an input array follows a simple *bit-reversal* rule. If x represents any valid argument value in $f(x)$, the corresponding argument in the reordered array is obtained by expressing x in binary and reversing the bits. For example, if $N = 2^3$, the seventh element in the original array, $f(6)$, becomes the fourth element in the reordered array, because $6 = 110_2$ becomes $011_2 = 3$ when the bits are reversed. This is a left-to-right reversal of the binary number and should not be confused with the binary complement. Table 3.2 summarizes the procedure for $N = 8$. If the reordered array is used in computing the FFT, the answer will be the elements of the Fourier transform in the correct order. Conversely, if the array is used

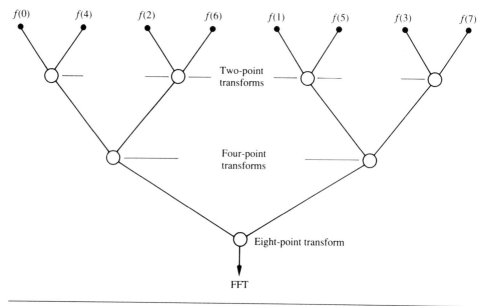

$f(0)$ $f(4)$ $f(2)$ $f(6)$ $f(1)$ $f(5)$ $f(3)$ $f(7)$

Two-point
transforms

Four-point
transforms

Eight-point transform

FFT

Figure 3.22   *Ordered input array and its use in the successive-doubling method.*

in its natural order, the answer will be bit-reversed. Identical comments apply to computing the inverse transform.

Figure 3.23 shows a FORTRAN subroutine for computing the FFT by the successive doubling method. The parameters in the subroutine argument are as follows. On input, F is an array whose transform is desired and LN is equal to n. On output, the array F contains the Fourier transform. Because F is a

Table 3.2   Example of Bit Reversal and Reordering of Array for Input into FFT Algorithm

Original Argument			Original Array	Bit-Reversed Argument			Reordered Array
0	0	0	$f(0)$	0	0	0	$f(0)$
0	0	1	$f(1)$	1	0	0	$f(4)$
0	1	0	$f(2)$	0	1	0	$f(2)$
0	1	1	$f(3)$	1	1	0	$f(6)$
1	0	0	$f(4)$	0	0	1	$f(1)$
1	0	1	$f(5)$	1	0	1	$f(5)$
1	1	0	$f(6)$	0	1	1	$f(3)$
1	1	1	$f(7)$	1	1	1	$f(7)$

```
        SUBROUTINE FFT(F,LN)
        COMPLEX F(1024),U,W,T,CMPLX
        PI=3.141593
        N=2**LN
        NV2=N/2
        NM1=N-1
        J=1
        DO 3 I=1,NM1
            IF(I.GE.J) GO TO 1
            T=F(J)
            F(J)=F(I)
            F(I)=T
    1       K=NV2
    2       IF(K.GE.J) GO TO 3
            J=J-K
            K=K/2
            GO TO 2
    3   J=J+K
        DO 5 L=1,LN
            LE=2**L
            LE1=LE/2
            U=(1.0,0.0)
            W=CMPLX(COS(PI/LE1),-SIN(PI/LE1))
            DO 5 J=1,LE1
                DO 4 I=J,N,LE
                    IP=I+LE1
                    T=F(IP)*U
                    F(IP)=F(I)-T
    4               F(I)=F(I)+T
    5   U=U*W
        DO 6 I=1,N
    6   F(I)=F(I)/FLOAT(N)
        RETURN
        END
```

Figure 3.23 *A FORTRAN implementation of the successive-doubling FFT algorithm. (Adapted from Cooley* et al. *[1969].)*

complex array, if the input is a real function, the imaginary part of F must be set to zero before calling the subroutine.

The first part of the program, including the "DO 3" loop, reorders the input data. The second part, including the "DO 5" loop, does the successive doubling calculations. The "DO 6" loop divides the results by N. For $N = 1024$, this simple program is only about 12 percent less efficient than a more optimally written FORTRAN program that uses a table for storing values of W_{2M}^u.

Equations (3.3-3)–(3.3-6), along with Figs. 3.7 and 3.23, provide the necessary information for implementing the 2-D, forward FFT. The same concepts apply to the inverse transform if the complex conjugate of the Fourier transform is used as the input to the FFT subroutine, as indicated in Section 3.4.3.

Integer bases greater than 2 may be used to formulate the FFT. In fact, a base-3 formulation requires slightly fewer operations than any other base (Cooley, Lewis, and Welch [1969]), but its disadvantage in terms of programming makes it an unattractive choice. A base-4 is equal to a base-2 implementation in terms of required operations. All other bases are less efficient, requiring a progressively larger number of operations. Fast Fourier transform algorithms usually are formulated in a base-2 format because it is easier to implement in assembly language.

3.5 OTHER SEPARABLE IMAGE TRANSFORMS

The 1-D, discrete Fourier transform is one of a class of important transforms that can be expressed in terms of the general relation

$$T(u) = \sum_{x=0}^{N-1} f(x)g(x, u) \tag{3.5-1}$$

where $T(u)$ is the transform of $f(x)$, $g(x, u)$ is the *forward transformation kernel*, and u has values in the range $0, 1, \ldots, N - 1$. Similarly, the inverse transform is the relation

$$f(x) = \sum_{u=0}^{N-1} T(u)h(x, u) \tag{3.5-2}$$

where $h(x, u)$ is the *inverse transformation kernel* and x has values in the range $0, 1, \ldots, N - 1$. The properties of its transformation kernel determine the nature of a transform.

For 2-D square arrays the forward and inverse transforms are

$$T(u, v) = \sum_{x=0}^{N-1} \sum_{y=0}^{N-1} f(x, y)g(x, y, u, v) \tag{3.5-3}$$

and

$$f(x, y) = \sum_{u=0}^{N-1} \sum_{v=0}^{N-1} T(u, v)h(x, y, u, v) \tag{3.5-4}$$

where, again, $g(x, y, u, v)$ and $h(x, y, u, v)$ are called the *forward* and *inverse transformation kernels*, respectively. The kernels depend only on the indexes x, y, u, v, not on the values of $f(x, y)$ or $T(u, v)$, so $g(x, y, u, v)$ and $h(x, y, u, v)$ can be viewed as the basis functions of a series expansion via Eq. (3.5-3) or (3.5-4). We discuss this point in more detail later in this section.

The forward kernel is said to be *separable* if

$$g(x, y, u, v) = g_1(x, u)g_2(y, v). \tag{3.5-5}$$

In addition, the kernel is *symmetric* if g_1 is functionally equal to g_2. In this case, Eq. (3.5-5) can be expressed in the form

$$g(x, y, u, v) = g_1(x, u)g_1(y, v). \qquad (3.5\text{-}6)$$

Identical comments apply to the inverse kernel if $g(x, y, u, v)$ is replaced by $h(x, y, u, v)$ in Eqs. (3.5-5) and (3.5-6).

The 2-D Fourier transform is a special case of Eq. (3.5-3). It has the kernel

$$g(x, y, u, v) = \frac{1}{N} \exp[-j2\pi(ux + vy)/N]$$

which is separable and symmetric, because

$$g(x, y, u, v) = g_1(x, u)g_1(y, v) \qquad (3.5\text{-}7)$$
$$= \frac{1}{\sqrt{N}} \exp[-j2\pi ux/N] \frac{1}{\sqrt{N}} \exp[-j2\pi vy/N].$$

The inverse Fourier kernel also is separable and symmetric.

A transform with a separable kernel can be computed in two steps, each requiring a 1-D transform. First, taking the 1-D transform along each row of $f(x, y)$ yields

$$T(x, v) = \sum_{y=0}^{N-1} f(x, y)g_2(y, v) \qquad (3.5\text{-}8)$$

for $x, v = 0, 1, 2, \ldots, N - 1$. Next, taking the 1-D transform along each column of $T(x, v)$ results in the expression

$$T(u, v) = \sum_{x=0}^{N-1} T(x, v)g_1(x, u) \qquad (3.5\text{-}9)$$

for $u, v = 0, 1, 2, \ldots, N - 1$. This procedure agrees with the method given in Section 3.3.1 for the Fourier transform. The same final results are obtained by taking the transform first along each column of $f(x, y)$ to obtain $T(y, u)$ and then along each row of the latter function to obtain $T(u, v)$. Similar comments apply to the inverse transform if $h(x, y, u, v)$ is separable.

If the kernel $g(x, y, u, v)$ is separable and symmetric, Eq. (3.5-3) also may be expressed in matrix form:

$$\mathbf{T} = \mathbf{AFA} \qquad (3.5\text{-}10)$$

where $\mathbf{F}$ is the $N \times N$ image matrix, $\mathbf{A}$ is an $N \times N$ symmetric transformation matrix with elements $a_{ij} = g_1(i, j)$, and $\mathbf{T}$ is the resulting $N \times N$ transform for values of u and v in the range $0, 1, 2, \ldots, N - 1$.

To obtain the inverse transform, we premultiply and postmultiply Eq. (3.5-10) by an inverse transformation matrix **B**:

$$\mathbf{BTB} = \mathbf{BAFAB}. \tag{3.5-11}$$

If $\mathbf{B} = \mathbf{A}^{-1}$,

$$\mathbf{F} = \mathbf{BTB} \tag{3.5-12}$$

indicating that the digital image **F** can be recovered completely from its transform. If **B** is not equal to $\mathbf{A}^{-1}$, use of Eq. (3.5-11) yields an approximation to **F**:

$$\hat{\mathbf{F}} = \mathbf{BAFAB}. \tag{3.5-13}$$

Several transforms—including the Fourier, Walsh, Hadamard, discrete cosine, Haar, and Slant transforms—may be expressed in the forms of Eqs. (3.5-10) and (3.5-12). An important property of the resulting transformation matrices is that they can be decomposed into products of matrices with fewer nonzero entries than the original matrix. This result, first formulated by Good [1958] for the Fourier transform, reduces redundancy and, consequently, the number of operations required to implement a 2-D transform. The degree of reduction is equivalent to that achieved by an FFT algorithm: on the order of $N \log_2 N$ operations for each row or column of an $N \times N$ image. Although we stress computational procedures based on successive applications of 1-D algorithms to obtain the forward and inverse transforms of an image, equivalent computational results can be obtained via a matrix formulation of the problem. See Andrews [1970] for additional details on this topic.

3.5.1 Walsh Transform

When $N = 2^n$, the discrete Walsh transform of a function $f(x)$, denoted $W(u)$, is obtained by substituting the kernel

$$g(x, u) = \frac{1}{N} \prod_{i=0}^{n-1} (-1)^{b_i(x)b_{n-1-i}(u)} \tag{3.5-14}$$

into Eq. (3.5-1). In other words,

$$W(u) = \frac{1}{N} \sum_{x=0}^{N-1} f(x) \prod_{i=0}^{n-1} (-1)^{b_i(x)b_{n-1-i}(u)} \tag{3.5-15}$$

where $b_k(z)$ is the kth bit in the binary representation of z. For example, if $n = 3$ and $z = 6$ (110 in binary), $b_0(z) = 0$, $b_1(z) = 1$, and $b_2(z) = 1$.

The values of $g(x, u)$, excluding the $1/N$ constant term, are listed in Table 3.3 for $N = 8$. The array formed by the Walsh transformation kernel is a

Table 3.3   Values of the 1-D Walsh Transformation Kernel for N = 8

u \ x	0	1	2	3	4	5	6	7
0	+	+	+	+	+	+	+	+
1	+	+	+	+	−	−	−	−
2	+	+	−	−	+	+	−	−
3	+	+	−	−	−	−	+	+
4	+	−	+	−	+	−	+	−
5	+	−	+	−	−	+	−	+
6	+	−	−	+	+	−	−	+
7	+	−	−	+	−	+	+	−

symmetric matrix having orthogonal rows and columns. These properties, which hold in general, lead to an inverse kernel identical to the forward kernel except for a constant multiplicative factor of $1/N$; that is,

$$h(x, u) = \prod_{i=0}^{n-1} (-1)^{b_i(x)b_{n-1-i}(u)}. \tag{3.5-16}$$

Thus the inverse Walsh transform is

$$f(x) = \sum_{u=0}^{N-1} W(u) \prod_{i=0}^{n-1} (-1)^{b_i(x)b_{n-1-i}(u)}. \tag{3.5-17}$$

Unlike the Fourier transform, which is based on trigonometric terms, the Walsh transform consists of a series expansion of basis functions whose values are $+1$ or -1.

The validity of Eq. (3.5-17) is easily established by substituting Eq. (3.5-15) for $W(u)$ and making use of the orthogonality condition mentioned previously. Note in Eqs. (3.5-15) and (3.5-17) that the forward and inverse Walsh transforms differ only by the $1/N$ term. Thus any algorithm for computing the forward transform may be used directly to obtain the inverse transform simply by multiplying the result of the algorithm by N.

The 2-D forward and inverse Walsh kernels are given by the relations

$$g(x, y, u, v) = \frac{1}{N} \prod_{i=0}^{n-1} (-1)^{[b_i(x)b_{n-1-i}(u) + b_i(y)b_{n-1-i}(v)]} \tag{3.5-18}$$

and

$$h(x, y, u, v) = \frac{1}{N} \prod_{i=0}^{n-1} (-1)^{[b_i(x)b_{n-1-i}(u) + b_i(y)b_{n-1-i}(v)]}. \tag{3.5-19}$$

Although grouping both $1/N$ terms in front of $g(x, y, u, v)$ or $h(x, y, u, v)$ is valid, the forms of Eqs. (3.5-18) and (3.5-19) are preferable in image processing applications, where there is equal interest in taking the forward and inverse transforms. As the formulation in these equations yields identical kernels, Eqs. (3.5-3) and (3.5-4) also lead to forward and inverse Walsh transforms that are equal in form; that is,

$$W(u, v) = \frac{1}{N} \sum_{x=0}^{N-1} \sum_{y=0}^{N-1} f(x, y) \prod_{i=0}^{n-1} (-1)^{[b_i(x)b_{n-1-i}(u) + b_i(y)b_{n-1-i}(v)]} \qquad (3.5\text{-}20)$$

and

$$f(x, y) = \frac{1}{N} \sum_{u=0}^{N-1} \sum_{v=0}^{N-1} W(u, v) \prod_{i=0}^{n-1} (-1)^{[b_i(x)b_{n-1-i}(u) + b_i(y)b_{n-1-i}(v)]}. \qquad (3.5\text{-}21)$$

Thus any algorithm used to compute the 2-D forward Walsh transform may also be used without modification to compute the inverse transform.

The Walsh transform kernels are separable and symmetric, because

$$
\begin{aligned}
g(x, y, u, v) &= g_1(x, u)g_1(y, v) \\
&= h_1(x, u)h_1(y, v) \\
&= \left[\frac{1}{\sqrt{N}} \prod_{i=0}^{n-1} (-1)^{b_i(x)b_{n-1-i}(u)} \right]\left[\frac{1}{\sqrt{N}} \prod_{i=0}^{n-1} (-1)^{b_i(y)b_{n-1-i}(v)} \right].
\end{aligned}
\qquad (3.5\text{-}22)
$$

Hence $W(u, v)$ and its inverse may be computed by successive applications of the 1-D Walsh transform in Eq. (3.5-15). The procedure followed in the computation is the same as that in Section 3.3.1 and Fig. 3.7 for the Fourier transform.

The Walsh transform may be computed by a fast algorithm nearly identical in form to the successive doubling method in Section 3.4.1 for the FFT. The only difference is that all exponential terms W_N are set equal to 1 in the case of the fast Walsh transform (FWT).[†] Equations (3.4-9) and (3.4-10), the basic relations leading to the FFT, then become

$$W(u) = \tfrac{1}{2}[W_{\text{even}}(u) + W_{\text{odd}}(u)] \qquad (3.5\text{-}23)$$

and

$$W(u + M) = \tfrac{1}{2}[W_{\text{even}}(u) - W_{\text{odd}}(u)] \qquad (3.5\text{-}24)$$

[†] The use of W in this section to denote the Walsh transform should not be confused with our use of the same symbol in Section 3.4.1 to denote exponential terms.

where $M = N/2$, $u = 0, 1, \ldots, M - 1$, and $W(u)$ denotes the 1-D Walsh transform. Rather than giving a general proof of this result, we can illustrate the use of Eq. (3.5-15) and the validity of Eqs. (3.5-23) and (3.5-24) by means of an example. For further details on this subject, see Shanks [1969].

Example: If $N = 4$, use of Eq. (3.5-15) results in the following sequence of steps:

$$W(0) = \frac{1}{4} \sum_{x=0}^{3} \left[f(x) \prod_{i=0}^{1} (-1)^{b_i(x)b_{1-i}(0)} \right]$$

$$= \frac{1}{4} [f(0) + f(1) + f(2) + f(3)]$$

$$W(1) = \frac{1}{4} \sum_{x=0}^{3} \left[f(x) \prod_{i=0}^{1} (-1)^{b_i(x)b_{1-i}(1)} \right]$$

$$= \frac{1}{4} [f(0) + f(1) - f(2) - f(3)]$$

$$W(2) = \frac{1}{4} \sum_{x=0}^{3} \left[f(x) \prod_{i=0}^{1} (-1)^{b_i(x)b_{1-i}(2)} \right]$$

$$= \frac{1}{4} [f(0) - f(1) + f(2) - f(3)]$$

$$W(3) = \frac{1}{4} \sum_{x=0}^{3} \left[f(x) \prod_{i=0}^{1} (-1)^{b_i(x)b_{1-i}(3)} \right]$$

$$= \frac{1}{4} [f(0) - f(1) - f(2) + f(3)].$$

Subdividing these results into two groups shows the validity of Eqs. (3.5-23) and (3.5-24):

$$W_{even}(0) = \frac{1}{2} [f(0) + f(2)] \quad \text{and} \quad W_{odd}(0) = \frac{1}{2} [f(1) + f(3)]$$

$$W_{even}(1) = \frac{1}{2} [f(0) - f(2)] \quad \text{and} \quad W_{odd}(1) = \frac{1}{2} [f(1) - f(3)].$$

From Eq. (3.5-23),

$$W(0) = \frac{1}{2} [W_{even}(0) + W_{odd}(0)]$$

$$= \frac{1}{4} [f(0) + f(1) + f(2) + f(3)]$$

and

$$W(1) = \frac{1}{2}[W_{even}(1) + W_{odd}(1)]$$

$$= \frac{1}{4}[f(0) + f(1) - f(2) - f(3)].$$

Computing the next two terms from these results, using Eq. (3.5-24), gives

$$W(2) = \frac{1}{2}[W_{even}(0) - W_{odd}(0)]$$

$$= \frac{1}{4}[f(0) - f(1) + f(2) - f(3)]$$

and

$$W(3) = \frac{1}{2}[W_{even}(1) - W_{odd}(1)]$$

$$= \frac{1}{4}[f(0) - f(1) - f(2) + f(3)].$$

Thus computation of $W(u)$ by Eq. (3.5-15) or by Eqs. (3.5-23) and (3.5-24) yields identical results.   ❏

As mentioned earlier an algorithm used to compute the FFT by the successive doubling method may be easily modified for computing a fast Walsh transform simply by setting all trigonometric terms equal to 1. Figure 3.24 illustrates the required modifications of the FFT program in Fig. 3.23. The Walsh transform is real, thus requiring less computer storage for a problem than the Fourier transform, which is generally complex.

As indicated in connection with Eqs. (3.5-3) and (3.5-4), a transform and its inverse may be expressed in terms of a series expansion involving the appropriate kernels. The kernels depend only on the indexes u, v, x, and y—not on the values of the image or its transform—so the kernels serve as a set of basis functions whose nature is completely fixed once the dimensions of the image have been fixed. For example, Fig. 3.25 shows the basis functions (kernels) as a function of u and v (excluding the $1/N$ constant term) for computing the Walsh transform when $N = 4$. Each block corresponds to varying x and y from 0 to 3 (that is, 0 to $N - 1$), while keeping u and v fixed at the values

```
        SUBROUTINE FWT(F,LN)
        REAL F(1024),T
        N=2**LN
        NV2=N/2
        NM1=N-1
        J=1
        DO 3 I=1,NM1
            IF(I.GE.J) GO TO 1
            T=F(J)
            F(J)=F(I)
            F(I)=T
1       K=NV2
2       IF(K.GE.J) GO TO 3
        J=J-K
        K=K/2
        GO TO 2
3       J=J+K
        DO 5 L=1,LN
            LE=2**L
            LE1=LE/2
            DO 5 J=1,LE1
                DO 4 I=J,N,LE
                    IP=I+LE1
                    T=F(IP)
                    F(IP)=F(I)-T
4                   F(I)=F(I)+T
5       CONTINUE
        DO 6 I=1,N
6       F(I)=F(I)/FLOAT(N)
        RETURN
        END
```

Figure 3.24 *Modification of the successive doubling FFT algorithm for computing the fast Walsh transform.*

corresponding to that block. Thus each block consists of an array of 4×4 binary elements. In the block for $u = v = 0$, all values of the kernel are 1 (shown in white). The maximum variability occurs when $u = v = 2$, where alternating 1's and -1's (shown in black) form a checkerboard pattern in the 4×4 block. To use the basis functions shown in Fig. 3.25 to compute the Walsh transform of an image of size 4×4 simply requires obtaining $W(0, 0)$ by multiplying the image array point-by-point with the 4×4 basis block corresponding to $u = v = 0$, adding the results, and dividing by 4. To obtain $W(0, 1)$ requires using the block corresponding to $u = 0$ and $v = 1$, and so on for all 16 blocks. Because the inverse kernel for the Walsh transform is identical to the forward kernel, the functions in Fig. 3.25 also apply to the inverse transform, except that now x and y are fixed for each block, and u and v vary from 0 to $N - 1$ within that block.

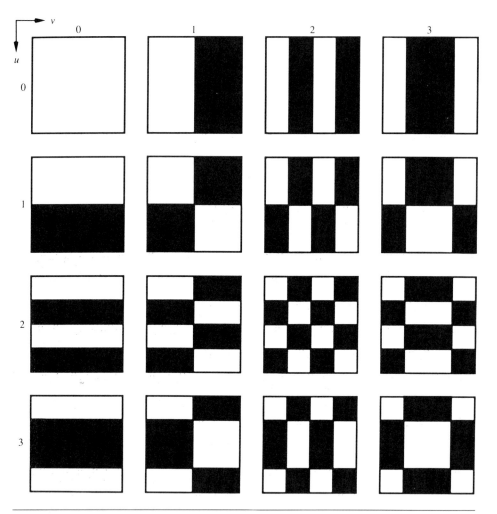

Figure 3.25 *Walsh basis functions for N = 4. Each block consists of 4 × 4 elements, corresponding to x and y varying from 0 to 3. The origin of each block is at its top left. White and black denote +1 and −1, respectively.*

3.5.2 Hadamard Transform

One of several known formulations for the 1-D, forward Hadamard kernel is the relation

$$g(x, u) = \frac{1}{N}(-1)^{\sum_{i=0}^{n-1} b_i(x)b_i(u)} \tag{3.5-25}$$

where the summation in the exponent is performed in modulo 2 arithmetic and, as in Eq. (3.5-14), $b_k(z)$ is the kth bit in the binary representation of z. Substitution of Eq. (3.5-25) into Eq. (3.5-1) yields the following expression for the 1-D Hadamard transform:

$$H(u) = \frac{1}{N} \sum_{x=0}^{N-1} f(x)(-1)^{\sum_{i=0}^{n-1} b_i(x)b_i(u)} \qquad (3.5\text{-}26)$$

where $N = 2^n$, and u has values in the range 0, 1, 2, . . . , $N - 1$.

As in the case of the Walsh transform, the Hadamard kernel forms a matrix having orthogonal rows and columns. This condition again leads to an inverse kernel that, except for the $1/N$ term, is equal to the forward Hadamard kernel; that is,

$$h(x, u) = (-1)^{\sum_{i=0}^{n-1} b_i(x)b_i(u)} \qquad (3.5\text{-}27)$$

Substitution of this kernel into Eq. (3.5-2) yields the following expression for the inverse Hadamard transform:

$$f(x) = \sum_{u=0}^{N-1} H(u)(-1)^{\sum_{i=0}^{n-1} b_i(x)b_i(u)} \qquad (3.5\text{-}28)$$

for $x = 0, 1, 2, . . . , N - 1$.

Similarly, the 2-D kernels are given by the relations

$$g(x, y, u, v) = \frac{1}{N} (-1)^{\sum_{i=0}^{n-1} [b_i(x)b_i(u) + b_i(y)b_i(v)]} \qquad (3.5\text{-}29)$$

and

$$h(x, y, u, v) = \frac{1}{N} (-1)^{\sum_{i=0}^{n-1} [b_i(x)b_i(u) + b_i(y)b_i(v)]} \qquad (3.5\text{-}30)$$

where the summation in the exponent again is carried out in modulo 2 arithmetic. As in the case of the Walsh transform, the 2-D Hadamard kernels are identical.

Substitution of Eqs. (3.5-29) and (3.5-30) into Eqs. (3.5-3) and (3.5-4) yields the following 2-D Hadamard transform pair:

$$H(u, v) = \frac{1}{N} \sum_{x=0}^{N-1} \sum_{y=0}^{N-1} f(x, y)(-1)^{\sum_{i=0}^{n-1} [b_i(x)b_i(u) + b_i(y)b_i(v)]} \qquad (3.5\text{-}31)$$

and

$$f(x, y) = \frac{1}{N} \sum_{u=0}^{N-1} \sum_{v=0}^{N-1} H(u, v)(-1)^{\sum_{i=0}^{n-1} [b_i(x)b_i(u) + b_i(y)b_i(v)]}$$

(3.5-32)

Because the forward and inverse transforms are identical, an algorithm used for computing $H(u, v)$ may be used without modification to obtain $f(x, y)$, and vice versa. Keeping in mind the modulo 2 summation, it can be shown that the Hadamard kernels are separable and symmetric. Hence

$$g(x, y, u, v) = g_1(x, u)g_1(y, v)$$
$$= h_1(x, u)h_1(y, v)$$

(3.5-33)

$$= \left[\frac{1}{\sqrt{N}} (-1)^{\sum_{i=0}^{n-1} b_i(x)b_i(u)} \right] \left[\frac{1}{\sqrt{N}} (-1)^{\sum_{i=0}^{n-1} b_i(y)b_i(v)} \right].$$

With the exception of the $1/\sqrt{N}$ term, g_1 and h_1 are identical to Eq. (3.5-25). Moreover, as the 2-D Hadamard kernels are separable, the 2-D transform pair may be obtained by successive applications of a 1-D Hadamard transform algorithm.

Table 3.4 shows the matrix of values produced by the 1-D Hadamard kernel in Eq. (3.5-25) for $N = 8$, where the constant $1/N$ term has been omitted for simplicity. Although the entries are the same as for the Walsh transform, the order of the rows and columns is different. In fact, when $N = 2^n$, that is the only difference between these two transforms. When N is not equal to an integer power of 2, the difference is more important. The Walsh transform can be formulated for any positive integer value of N, but existence of the Hadamard transform for values of N other than integer powers of 2 has been shown only up to $N = 200$.

Table 3.4   Values of the 1-D Hadamard Transformation Kernel for $N = 8$

u \ x	0	1	2	3	4	5	6	7
0	+	+	+	+	+	+	+	+
1	+	−	+	−	+	−	+	−
2	+	+	−	−	+	+	−	−
3	+	−	−	+	+	−	−	+
4	+	+	+	+	−	−	−	−
5	+	−	+	−	−	+	−	+
6	+	+	−	−	−	−	+	+
7	+	−	−	+	−	+	+	−

Because most of the applications of transforms in image processing are based on $N = 2^n$ samples per row or column of an image, use (and terminology) of the Walsh and Hadamard transforms is intermixed in the image processing literature. The term Walsh–Hadamard transform often is used to denote either transform.

Two important features that might influence the choice of one of these transforms over the other are worth noting. As indicated in Section 3.5.2, an advantage of the formulation in Eq. (3.5-15) is that it can be expressed directly in a successive doubling format. This property allows computation of the FWT by a straightforward modification of the FFT algorithm developed in Section 3.4.1. Further modifications of this algorithm would be required to compute the fast Hadamard transform (FHT) to take into account the difference in ordering. An alternative approach is to use the FWT algorithm of Fig. 3.24 and then reorder the results to obtain the Hadamard transform.

Although the Hadamard ordering has disadvantages in terms of a successive doubling, it leads to a simple recursive relationship for generating the transformation matrices needed to implement Eqs. (3.5-10) and (3.5-12). The Hadamard matrix of lowest order ($N = 2$) is

$$\mathbf{H}_2 = \begin{bmatrix} 1 & 1 \\ 1 & -1 \end{bmatrix} \qquad (3.5\text{-}34)$$

Then, letting $\mathbf{H}_N$ represent the matrix of order N, the recursive relationship is given by the expression

$$\mathbf{H}_{2N} = \begin{bmatrix} \mathbf{H}_N & \mathbf{H}_N \\ \mathbf{H}_N & -\mathbf{H}_N \end{bmatrix} \qquad (3.5\text{-}35)$$

where $\mathbf{H}_{2N}$ is the Hadamard matrix of order $2N$ and $N = 2^n$ is assumed.

The transformation matrix for use in Eq. (3.5-10) is obtained by normalizing the corresponding Hadamard matrix by the square root of the matrix order. Thus in the $N \times N$ case, these two matrixes are related by

$$\mathbf{A} = \frac{1}{\sqrt{N}} \mathbf{H}_N. \qquad (3.5\text{-}36)$$

The expressions for the inverse Hadamard matrix are identical to Eqs. (3.5-34)–(3.5-36).

Example: Use of Eqs. (3.5-34) and (3.5-35) leads to the following Hadamard matrices of order four and eight:

$$
\mathbf{H}_4 = \begin{bmatrix} \mathbf{H}_2 & \mathbf{H}_2 \\ \mathbf{H}_2 & -\mathbf{H}_2 \end{bmatrix}
$$

$$
= \begin{bmatrix}
+ & + & + & + \\
+ & - & + & - \\
+ & + & - & - \\
+ & - & - & +
\end{bmatrix}
$$

and

$$
\mathbf{H}_8 = \begin{bmatrix} \mathbf{H}_4 & \mathbf{H}_4 \\ \mathbf{H}_4 & -\mathbf{H}_4 \end{bmatrix}
$$

$$
= \begin{bmatrix}
+ & + & + & + & + & + & + & + \\
+ & - & + & - & + & - & + & - \\
+ & + & - & - & + & + & - & - \\
+ & - & - & + & + & - & - & + \\
+ & + & + & + & - & - & - & - \\
+ & - & + & - & - & + & - & + \\
+ & + & - & - & - & - & + & + \\
+ & - & - & + & - & + & + & -
\end{bmatrix}
$$

where + and − indicate +1 and −1, respectively.

As Eqs. (3.5-25) and (3.5-33) show, $g(x, u)$ and $g_1(x, u)$ differ only by a constant multiplier term. Because $a_{ij} = g_1(i, j)$, the entries in the **A** matrix have the same form as the expansion of $g(x, u)$. This statement is easily verified in this example by comparing Table 3.4 and the expression for

$$
\mathbf{A} = \frac{1}{\sqrt{8}} \mathbf{H}_8. \qquad \square
$$

The number of sign changes along a column of the Hadamard matrix often is called the *sequency* of that column.[†] As the elements of this matrix are derived from the kernel values, the sequency concept applies to the expansion of $g_1(x,$

[†] As in the case of the Fourier transform, where u is a frequency variable, the concept of sequency normally is restricted to this variable. Thus the association of sequency with the columns of the Hadamard matrix is based on the assumption that the columns vary as a function of u and the rows as a function of x. This convention is used in Table 3.4.

Table 3.5   Values of the 1-D Ordered Hadamard Kernel for $N = 8$

u \ x	0	1	2	3	4	5	6	7
0	+	+	+	+	+	+	+	+
1	+	+	+	+	−	−	−	−
2	+	+	−	−	−	−	+	+
3	+	+	−	−	+	+	−	−
4	+	−	−	+	+	−	−	+
5	+	−	−	+	−	+	+	−
6	+	−	+	−	−	+	−	+
7	+	−	+	−	+	−	+	−

u) for $x, u = 0, 1, \ldots, N - 1$. For instance, the sequencies of the eight columns of $\mathbf{H}_8$ and Table 3.4 are 0, 7, 3, 4, 1, 6, 2, and 5.

Expressing the Hadamard kernels so that the sequency increases as a function of increasing u is analogous to the Fourier transform, where frequency also increases as a function of increasing u. The 1-D Hadamard kernel that achieves this particular ordering is the relation

$$g(x, u) = \frac{1}{N} (-1)^{\sum_{i=0}^{n-1} b_i(x)p_i(u)}$$

(3.5-37)

where

$$p_0(u) = b_{n-1}(u)$$
$$p_1(u) = b_{n-1}(u) + b_{n-2}(u)$$
$$p_2(u) = b_{n-2}(u) + b_{n-3}(u)$$
$$\cdot$$
$$\cdot$$
$$\cdot$$
$$p_{n-1}(u) = b_1(u) + b_0(u).$$

(3.5-38)

As before, the summations in Eqs. (3.5-37) and (3.5-38) are performed in modulo 2 arithmetic. The expansion of Eq. (3.5-37) is shown in Table 3.5 for $N = 8$, where the constant multiplier term has been omitted for simplicity and the $+$ and $-$ entries indicate $+1$ and -1, respectively. The columns and, by symmetry, the rows are in order of increasing sequency.

The inverse, ordered Hadamard kernel is

$$h(x, u) = (-1)^{\sum_{i=0}^{n-1} b_i(x)p_i(u)}$$

(3.5-39)

where $p_i(u)$ is computed by using Eq. (3.5-38). Substituting the forward and inverse kernels into Eqs. (3.5-1) and (3.5-2) yields the following ordered Hadamard transform pair:

$$H(u) = \frac{1}{N} \sum_{x=0}^{N-1} f(x)(-1)^{\sum_{i=0}^{n-1} b_i(x)p_i(u)} \tag{3.5-40}$$

and

$$f(x) = \sum_{u=0}^{N-1} H(u)(-1)^{\sum_{i=0}^{n-1} b_i(x)p_i(u)} \tag{3.5-41}$$

As in the unordered case, the 2-D kernels are separable and identical:

$$g(x, y, u, v) = h(x, y, u, v) \tag{3.5-42}$$
$$= \frac{1}{N}(-1)^{\sum_{i=0}^{n-1} [b_i(x)p_i(u) + b_i(y)p_i(v)]}$$

Substitution of these kernels into Eqs. (3.5-3) and (3.5-4) yields the following 2-D, ordered Hadamard transform pair:

$$H(u, v) = \frac{1}{N} \sum_{x=0}^{N-1} \sum_{y=0}^{N-1} f(x, y)(-1)^{\sum_{i=0}^{n-1} [b_i(x)p_i(u) + b_i(y)p_i(v)]} \tag{3.5-43}$$

and

$$f(x, y) = \frac{1}{N} \sum_{u=0}^{N-1} \sum_{v=0}^{N-1} H(u, v)(-1)^{\sum_{i=0}^{n-1} [b_i(x)p_i(u) + b_i(y)p_i(v)]} \tag{3.5-44}$$

Figure 3.26 shows the 2-D, ordered Hadamard basis functions (kernels) for $N = 4$. The basis functions in Figs. 3.26 and 3.25 differ only in the sense that the functions in Fig. 3.26 are ordered in increasing sequency and thus are more "natural" to interpret. Figure 3.27 shows a simple image and the log magnitude of its ordered Hadamard transform. Unlike the Fourier spectrum, in which the concept of frequency plays a significant role, Fig. 3.27(b) does not have such a useful physical interpretation. However, sequency does increase as a function of u and v. Moreover, Fig. 3.27(b) is a decomposition of the original image function, based on basis functions that are simply $+1$ or -1 instead of the more complex sine and cosine functions used in the Fourier transform.

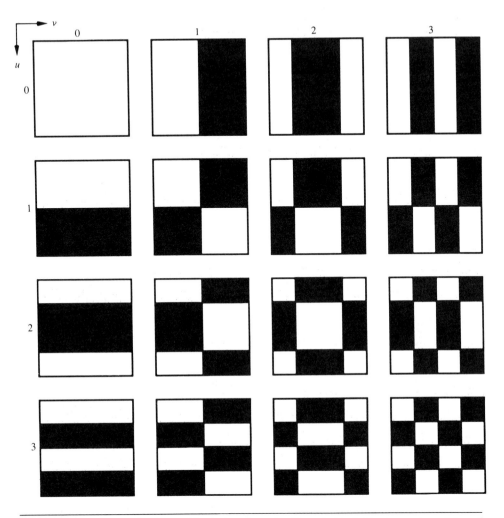

Figure 3.26   *Ordered Hadamard basis functions for N = 4. Each block consists of 4 × 4 elements, corresponding to x and y varying from 0 to 3. The origin of each block is at its top left. White and black denote +1 and −1, respectively.*

3.5.3   Discrete Cosine Transform

The 1-D discrete cosine transform (DCT) is defined as

$$C(u) = \alpha(u) \sum_{x=0}^{N-1} f(x)\cos\left[\frac{(2x + 1)u\pi}{2N}\right] \tag{3.5-45}$$

for $u = 0, 1, 2, \ldots, N - 1$. Similarly, the inverse DCT is defined as

$$f(x) = \sum_{u=0}^{N-1} \alpha(u)C(u)\cos\left[\frac{(2x + 1)u\pi}{2N}\right] \tag{3.5-46}$$

for $x = 0, 1, 2, \ldots, N - 1$. In both Eqs. (3.5-45) and (3.5-46), α is

$$\alpha(u) = \begin{cases} \sqrt{\dfrac{1}{N}} & \text{for } u = 0 \\[3mm] \sqrt{\dfrac{2}{N}} & \text{for } u = 1, 2, \ldots, N - 1. \end{cases} \tag{3.5-47}$$

The corresponding 2-D DCT pair is

$$C(u, v) = \alpha(u)\alpha(v) \sum_{x=0}^{N-1} \sum_{y=0}^{N-1} f(x, y) \cos\left[\frac{(2x + 1)u\pi}{2N}\right] \cos\left[\frac{(2y + 1)v\pi}{2N}\right] \tag{3.5-48}$$

for $u, v = 0, 1, 2, \ldots, N - 1$, and

$$f(x, y) = \sum_{u=0}^{N-1} \sum_{v=0}^{N-1} \alpha(u)\alpha(v) C(u, v) \cos\left[\frac{(2x + 1)u\pi}{2N}\right] \cos\left[\frac{(2y + 1)v\pi}{2N}\right] \tag{3.5-49}$$

for $x, y = 0, 1, 2, \ldots, N - 1$, where α is given in Eq. (3.5-47).

In recent years the discrete cosine transform has become the method of choice for image data compression, for reasons that are discussed in Chapter 6. Figure 3.28 shows the DCT basis functions for $N = 4$, and Fig. 3.29 shows a simple image and the log magnitude of its discrete cosine transform.

(a)   (b)

Figure 3.27 *A simple image and the log magnitude of its Hadamard transform.*

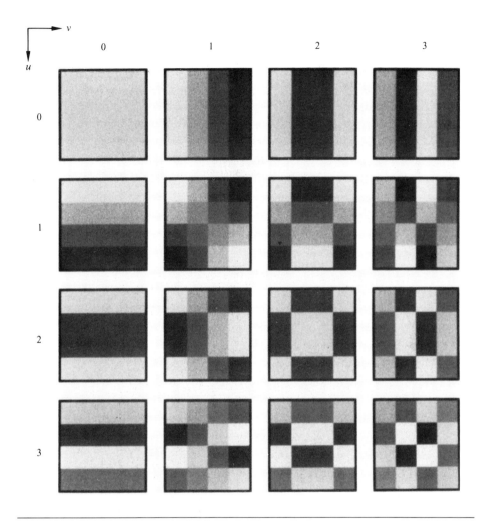

Figure 3.28 *Discrete cosine transform basis functions for N = 4. Each block consists of 4 × 4 elements, corresponding to x and y varying from 0 to 3. The origin of each block is at its top left. The highest value is shown in white. Other values are shown in grays, with darker meaning smaller.*

3.5.4   The Haar Transform

The transforms discussed so far are well-known, useful tools of signal and image processing. The transforms discussed in this section and Section 3.5.5 are considerably less well-known and are not as useful in practice. We include them here for completeness.

The Haar transform is based on the Haar functions, $h_k(z)$, which are defined over the continuous, closed interval $z \in [0, 1]$, and for $k = 0, 1, 2, \ldots,$ $N - 1$, where $N = 2^n$. The first step in generating the Haar transform is to note that the integer k can be decomposed uniquely as

$$k = 2^p + q - 1 \qquad (3.5\text{-}50)$$

where $0 \le p \le n - 1$, $q = 0$ or 1 for $p = 0$, and $1 \le q \le 2^p$ for $p \neq 0$. For example, if $N = 4$, k, q, and p have the following values:

k	p	q
0	0	0
1	0	1
2	1	1
3	1	2

With this background, the Haar functions are defined as

$$h_0(z) \triangleq h_{00}(z) = \frac{1}{\sqrt{N}} \qquad \text{for } z \in [0, 1] \qquad (3.5\text{-}51a)$$

and

$$h_k(z) \triangleq h_{pq}(z) = \frac{1}{\sqrt{N}} \begin{cases} 2^{p/2} & \dfrac{q-1}{2^p} \le z < \dfrac{q-1/2}{2^p} \\[2ex] -2^{p/2} & \dfrac{q-1/2}{2^p} \le z < \dfrac{q}{2^p} \\[2ex] 0 & \text{otherwise for } z \in [0, 1]. \end{cases} \qquad (3.5\text{-}51b)$$

(a)   (b)

Figure 3.29   *A simple image and the log magnitude of its discrete cosine transform.*

These results allow derivation of Haar transformation matrices of order $N \times N$ by formation of the ith row of a Haar matrix from elements of $h_i(z)$ for $z = 0/N, 1/N, 2/N, \ldots, (N - 1)/N$. For instance, when $N = 2$, the first row of the 2×2 Haar matrix is computed by using $h_0(z)$ with $z = 0/2, 1/2$. From Eq. (3.5-51a), $h_0(z)$ is equal to $1/\sqrt{2}$, independent of z, so the first row of the matrix has two identical $1/\sqrt{2}$ elements. The second row is obtained by computing $h_1(z)$ for $z = 0/2, 1/2$. When $k = 1, p = 0$ and $q = 1$ (from Eq. 3.5-50). Thus, from Eq. (3.5-51b), $h_1(0) = 2^0/\sqrt{2} = 1/\sqrt{2}$, and $h_1(1/2) = -2^0/\sqrt{2} = -1/\sqrt{2}$. The 2×2 Haar matrix then is

$$\mathbf{A}_2 = \frac{1}{\sqrt{2}} \begin{bmatrix} 1 & 1 \\ 1 & -1 \end{bmatrix}.$$

Following a similar procedure yields the matrix for $N = 4$:

$$\mathbf{A}_4 = \frac{1}{\sqrt{4}} \begin{bmatrix} 1 & 1 & 1 & 1 \\ 1 & 1 & -1 & -1 \\ \sqrt{2} & -\sqrt{2} & 0 & 0 \\ 0 & 0 & \sqrt{2} & -\sqrt{2} \end{bmatrix}$$

The Haar matrixes are orthogonal and have the necessary properties to allow implementation of a fast Haar algorithm based on the matrix formulation discussed in connection with Eqs. (3.5-10) and (3.5-12).

3.5.5 The Slant Transform

The Slant transform matrix of order $N \times N$ is the recursive expression

$$\mathbf{S}_N = \frac{1}{\sqrt{2}} \begin{bmatrix} \begin{array}{cc|c} 1 & 0 & \\ a_N & b_N & \mathbf{0} \\ \hline 0 & & \mathbf{I}_{(N/2)-2} \\ 0 & 1 & \\ -b_N & a_N & \mathbf{0} \\ \hline 0 & & \mathbf{I}_{(N/2)-2} \end{array} \middle| \begin{array}{cc|c} 1 & 0 & \\ -a_N & b_N & \mathbf{0} \\ \hline 0 & & \mathbf{I}_{(N/2)-2} \\ 0 & -1 & \\ b_N & a_N & \mathbf{0} \\ \hline 0 & & -\mathbf{I}_{(N/2)-2} \end{array} \end{bmatrix} \begin{bmatrix} \mathbf{S}_{N/2} & \mathbf{0} \\ \hline \mathbf{0} & \mathbf{S}_{N/2} \end{bmatrix} \quad (3.5\text{-}52)$$

where $\mathbf{I}_M$ is the identity matrix of order $M \times M$, and

$$\mathbf{S}_2 = \frac{1}{\sqrt{2}} \begin{bmatrix} 1 & 1 \\ 1 & -1 \end{bmatrix} \tag{3.5-53}$$

The coefficients are

$$a_N = \left[\frac{3N^2}{4(N^2 - 1)} \right]^{1/2} \tag{3.5-54}$$

and

$$b_N = \left[\frac{N^2 - 4}{4(N^2 - 1)} \right]^{1/2} \tag{3.5-55}$$

for $N > 1$. An example of the use of Eqs. (3.5-52)–(3.5-55) is Slant matrix $\mathbf{S}_4$:

$$\mathbf{S}_4 = \frac{1}{\sqrt{4}} \begin{bmatrix} 1 & 1 & 1 & 1 \\ \dfrac{3}{\sqrt{5}} & \dfrac{1}{\sqrt{5}} & \dfrac{-1}{\sqrt{5}} & \dfrac{-3}{\sqrt{5}} \\ 1 & -1 & -1 & 1 \\ \dfrac{1}{\sqrt{5}} & \dfrac{-3}{\sqrt{5}} & \dfrac{3}{\sqrt{5}} & \dfrac{-1}{\sqrt{5}} \end{bmatrix}$$

The Slant matrixes are orthogonal and have the necessary properties to allow implementation of a fast Slant transform algorithm based on the matrix formulation discussed in connection with Eqs. (3.5-10) and (3.5-12).

3.6   THE HOTELLING TRANSFORM

Unlike the transforms discussed so far, the Hotelling[†] transform developed in this section is based on statistical properties of vector representations. The Hotelling transform has several useful properties that make it an important tool for image processing.

[†] This transform also is commonly referred to as the *eigenvector, principal component*, or *discrete Karhunen–Loève transform.*

Consider a population of random vectors of the form

$$\mathbf{x} = \begin{bmatrix} x_1 \\ x_2 \\ \vdots \\ x_n \end{bmatrix} \tag{3.6-1}$$

The *mean vector* of the population is defined as

$$\mathbf{m_x} = E\{\mathbf{x}\} \tag{3.6-2}$$

where $E\{arg\}$ is the expected value of the argument, and the subscript denotes that $\mathbf{m}$ is associated with the population of $\mathbf{x}$ vectors. Recall that the expected value of a vector or matrix is obtained by taking the expected value of each element.

The *covariance matrix* of the vector population is defined as

$$\mathbf{C_x} = E\{(\mathbf{x} - \mathbf{m_x})(\mathbf{x} - \mathbf{m_x})^T\} \tag{3.6-3}$$

where T indicates vector transposition. Because $\mathbf{x}$ is n dimensional, $\mathbf{C_x}$ and $(\mathbf{x} - \mathbf{m_x})(\mathbf{x} - \mathbf{m_x})^T$ are matrices of order $n \times n$. Element c_{ii} of $\mathbf{C_x}$ is the variance of x_i, the ith component of the $\mathbf{x}$ vectors in the population, and element c_{ij} of $\mathbf{C_x}$ is the covariance between elements x_i and x_j of these vectors. The matrix $\mathbf{C_x}$ is real and symmetric. If elements x_i and x_j are uncorrelated, their covariance is zero and, therefore, $c_{ij} = c_{ji} = 0$.

For M vector samples from a random population, the mean vector and covariance matrix can be approximated from the samples by

$$\mathbf{m_x} = \frac{1}{M} \sum_{k=1}^{M} \mathbf{x}_k \tag{3.6-4}$$

and

$$\mathbf{C_x} = \frac{1}{M} \sum_{k=1}^{M} \mathbf{x}_k \mathbf{x}_k^T - \mathbf{m_x}\mathbf{m_x}^T. \tag{3.6-5}$$

Example: As an example illustrating the mechanics of Eqs. (3.6-4) and (3.6-5), consider the four column vectors $\mathbf{x}_1 = (0,0,0)^T$, $\mathbf{x}_2 = (1,0,0)^T$, $\mathbf{x}_3 = (1,1,0)^T$, and $\mathbf{x}_4 = (1,0,1)^T$, where the transpose is used so that column vectors may be conveniently written horizontally on a line of text. Applying Eq. (3.6-4) yields the following mean vector:

$$\mathbf{m}_x = \frac{1}{4}\begin{bmatrix} 3 \\ 1 \\ 1 \end{bmatrix}$$

Similarly, applying Eq. (3.6-5) yields the following covariance matrix:

$$\mathbf{C}_x = \frac{1}{16}\begin{bmatrix} 3 & 1 & 1 \\ 1 & 3 & -1 \\ 1 & -1 & 3 \end{bmatrix}$$

All the elements along the main diagonal are equal, which indicates that the three components of the vectors in the population have the same variance. Also, elements x_1 and x_2, as well as x_1 and x_3, are positively correlated; elements x_2 and x_3 are negatively correlated. ❏

Because $\mathbf{C}_x$ is real and symmetric, finding a set of n orthonormal eigenvectors always is possible (Noble [1969]). Let $\mathbf{e}_i$ and λ_i, $i = 1, 2, \ldots, n$, be the eigenvectors and corresponding eigenvalues of $\mathbf{C}_x$,[†] arranged (for convenience) in descending order so that $\lambda_j \geq \lambda_{j+1}$ for $j = 1, 2, \ldots, n - 1$. Let $\mathbf{A}$ be a matrix whose rows are formed from the eigenvectors of $\mathbf{C}_x$, ordered so that the first row of $\mathbf{A}$ is the eigenvector corresponding to the largest eigenvalue, and the last row is the eigenvector corresponding to the smallest eigenvalue.

Suppose that $\mathbf{A}$ is a transformation matrix that maps the $\mathbf{x}$'s into vectors denoted by $\mathbf{y}$'s, as follows:

$$\mathbf{y} = \mathbf{A}(\mathbf{x} - \mathbf{m}_x). \tag{3.6-6}$$

Equation (3.6-6) is called the *Hotelling transform*. The mean of the $\mathbf{y}$ vectors resulting from this transformation is zero; that is,

$$\mathbf{m}_y = \mathbf{0} \tag{3.6-7}$$

and the covariance matrix of the $\mathbf{y}$'s can be obtained in terms of $\mathbf{A}$ and $\mathbf{C}_x$ by

$$\mathbf{C}_y = \mathbf{A}\mathbf{C}_x\mathbf{A}^T. \tag{3.6-8}$$

[†] By definition, the eigenvectors and eigenvalues of an $n \times n$ matrix, $\mathbf{C}$, satisfy the relation $\mathbf{C}\mathbf{e}_i = \lambda_i\mathbf{e}_i$, for $i = 1, 2, \ldots, n$.

Furthermore, $\mathbf{C}_y$ is a diagonal matrix whose elements along the main diagonal are the eigenvalues of $\mathbf{C}_x$; that is,

$$\mathbf{C}_y = \begin{bmatrix} \lambda_1 & & & 0 \\ & \lambda_2 & & \\ & & \cdot & \\ 0 & & & \lambda_n \end{bmatrix} \tag{3.6-9}$$

The off-diagonal elements of the covariance matrix are 0, so the elements of the $\mathbf{y}$ vectors are uncorrelated. Keep in mind that the λ_j's are the eigenvalues of $\mathbf{C}_x$ and that the elements along the main diagonal of a diagonal matrix are its eigenvalues (Noble [1969]). Thus $\mathbf{C}_x$ and $\mathbf{C}_y$ have the same eigenvalues. In fact, the same is true for the eigenvectors.

Example: Figure 3.30 illustrates the concepts just discussed. The binary object shown is treated as a 2-D population. In other words, each pixel in the object

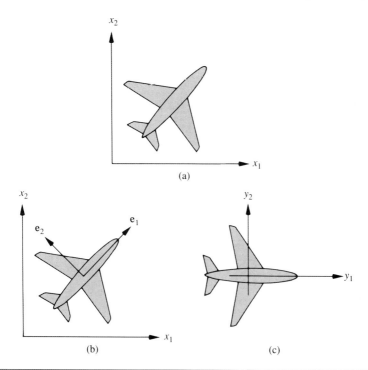

(a)

(b)   (c)

Figure 3.30   *(a) A binary object; (b) its principal axes (eigenvectors); (c) object rotated by using Eq. (3.6-6).*

is treated as a 2-D vector $\mathbf{x} = (a, b)^T$, where a and b are the coordinate values of that pixel with respect to the x_1 and x_2 axes. These vectors are used to compute the mean vector and covariance matrix of the population (object).

The net effect of using Eq. (3.6-6) is to establish a new coordinate system whose origin is at the centroid of the population and whose axes are in the direction of the eigenvectors of $\mathbf{C}_x$, as shown in Fig. 3.30(b). This coordinate system clearly shows that the transformation in Eq. (3.6-6) is a rotation transformation that aligns the data with the eigenvectors, as shown in Fig. 3.30(c). In fact, this alignment is precisely the mechanism that decorrelates the data. Furthermore, as the eigenvalues appear along the main diagonal of $\mathbf{C}_y$, λ_i is the variance of component y_i along eigenvector $\mathbf{e}_i$.

The concept of aligning a 2-D object with its principal eigenvector plays an important role in image analysis. As we show in Chapters 8 and 9, after an object has been extracted from an image, computer techniques for recognizing the object are generally sensitive to object rotation. Because the identity of the object obviously would not be known prior to recognition, the ability to align the object with its principal axes provides a reliable means for removing the effects of rotation from the image analysis process.   ❑

Another important property of the Hotelling transform deals with the reconstruction of $\mathbf{x}$ from $\mathbf{y}$. Because the rows of $\mathbf{A}$ are orthonormal vectors, $\mathbf{A}^{-1} = \mathbf{A}^T$, and any vector $\mathbf{x}$ can be recovered from its corresponding $\mathbf{y}$ by using the relation

$$\mathbf{x} = \mathbf{A}^T\mathbf{y} + \mathbf{m}_x. \tag{3.6-10}$$

Suppose, however, that instead of using all the eigenvectors of $\mathbf{C}_x$ we form matrix $\mathbf{A}_K$ from the K eigenvectors corresponding to the K largest eigenvalues, yielding a transformation matrix of order $K \times n$. The $\mathbf{y}$ vectors would then be K dimensional, and the reconstruction given in Eq. (3.6-10) would no longer be exact. The vector reconstructed by using $\mathbf{A}_K$ is

$$\hat{\mathbf{x}} = \mathbf{A}_K^T\mathbf{y} + \mathbf{m}_x. \tag{3.6-11}$$

It can be shown that the mean square error between $\mathbf{x}$ and $\hat{\mathbf{x}}$ is given by the expression

$$e_{ms} = \sum_{j=1}^{n} \lambda_j - \sum_{j=1}^{K} \lambda_j \tag{3.6-12}$$

$$= \sum_{j=K+1}^{n} \lambda_j$$

The first part of Eq. (3.6-12) indicates that the error is zero if $K = n$ (that is, if all the eigenvectors are used in the transformation). Because the λ_j's decrease monotonically, Eq. (3.6-12) also shows that the error can be minimized by selecting the K eigenvectors associated with the largest eigenvalues. Thus the Hotelling transform is optimal in the sense that it minimizes the mean square error between the vectors $\mathbf{x}$ and their approximations $\hat{\mathbf{x}}$.

Example: We conclude this section with another example of the versatility of the Hotelling transform for image processing. Figure 3.31 shows six images generated by a 6-band multispectral scanner operating in the wavelengths shown in Table 3.6. Viewing the images as shown in Fig. 3.32 allows formation of a 6-dimensional vector $\mathbf{x} = (x_1, x_2, \ldots, x_6)^T$ from each set of corresponding pixels in the images. The images in this particular application were of resolution 384×239, so the population consisted of 91,776 vectors from which to compute the mean vector and covariance matrix. Table 3.7 shows the eigenvalues of $\mathbf{C}_x$; note the dominance of the first two components.

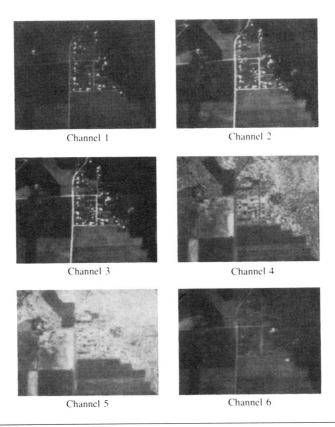

Channel 1

Channel 2

Channel 3

Channel 4

Channel 5

Channel 6

Figure 3.31 *Six spectral images from an airborne scanner. (Courtesy of the Laboratory for Applications of Remote Sensing, Purdue University.)*

Table 3.6   Channel Numbers and Wavelengths

Channel	Wavelength Band (μm)
1	0.40–0.44
2	0.62–0.66
3	0.66–0.72
4	0.80–1.00
5	1.00–1.40
6	2.00–2.60

Use of Equation (3.6-6) generated a set of transformed **y** vectors corresponding to the **x** vectors. From them, six principal component images were assembled by reversing the process shown in Fig. 3.32. Figure 3.33 shows the results. Component 1 denotes the image formed from all the y_1 components of the transformed vectors, and so on for the other five images. Recall from basic matrix theory that y_1 is obtained by performing the inner (dot) product of the first row of **A** with the column vector $(\mathbf{x} - \mathbf{m}_x)^T$. The first row of **A** is the eigenvector corresponding to the largest eigenvalue of the covariance matrix

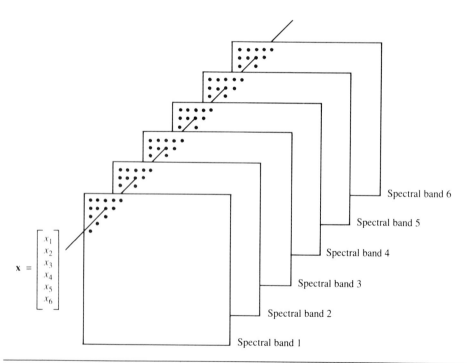

Figure 3.32 *Formation of a vector from corresponding pixels in six images.*

Table 3.7   Eigenvalues of the Covariance Matrix of the Images Shown in Fig. 3.31

λ_1	λ_2	λ_3	λ_4	λ_5	λ_6
3210	931.4	118.5	83.88	64.00	13.40

of the population, and this eigenvalue gives the variance of the gray levels of the first transformed image. Thus based on the numbers shown in Table 3.7, this image should have the highest contrast. That such is the case is quite evident in Fig. 3.33. Because the first two images account for about 94 percent of the total variance, the fact that the other four principal-component images have low contrast is not unexpected. Thus if instead of storing all six images for posterity, only the first two transformed images, along with $\mathbf{m}_x$ and the first two rows of $\mathbf{A}$, were stored, a credible job of reconstructing an approximation

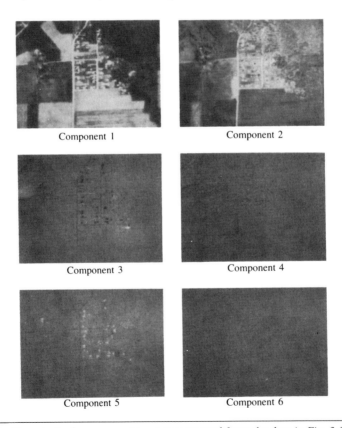

Component 1   Component 2

Component 3   Component 4

Component 5   Component 6

Figure 3.33   *Six principal-component images computed from the data in Fig. 3.31. (Courtesy of the Laboratory for Applications of Remote Sensing, Purdue University.)*

to the six original images could be done at a later date. This capability for performing *data compression*, although not impressive by today's standards (see Chapter 6) is a useful by-product of the Hotelling transform.   □

3.7 CONCLUDING REMARKS

The principal purpose of this chapter was to present a theoretical foundation of image transforms and their properties. Within this framework, the essential points necessary for a basic understanding of these concepts were developed and illustrated.

The emphasis placed on the Fourier transform reflects its wide scope of application in image processing problems. The material on the fast Fourier transform is of particular importance because of its computational implications. The separability, centralization, and convolution properties of the Fourier transform also are used extensively in the following chapters.

Transform theory has played a central role in the development of image processing as a formal discipline, as will be evident in subsequent discussions. In the next several chapters, we consider some uses of the Fourier transform for image enhancement and restoration. Further discussion of the other transforms discussed in Section 3.5 is deferred until Chapter 6, where their usefulness for data compression is considered in some detail. The Hotelling transform is mentioned again in Chapters 8 and 9 in connection with normalization of object rotation.

REFERENCES

Our treatment of the Fourier transform is introductory in nature. The classic texts by Titchmarsh [1948] and Papoulis [1962] offer comprehensive theoretical treatments of the continuous Fourier transform and its properties. Most engineering circuits and communications books offer a variety of developments and explanations of the Fourier transform. The books by Van Valkenburg [1955], Carlson [1968], and Thomas [1969] are representative.

The derivation of the discrete Fourier transform from its continuous form is also covered extensively in the literature. Three good references on this topic are Blackman and Tukey [1958], Cooley, Lewis, and Welch [1967], and Brigham [1974]. The first and last references are particularly suited for introductory reading.

Formulation of the fast Fourier transform is often credited to Cooley and Tukey [1965]. The FFT, however, has an interesting history worth sketching here. In response to the Cooley–Tukey paper, Rudnick [1966] reported that he was using a similar technique, whose number of operations also was proportional to $N \log_2 N$ and which was based on a method published by Danielson and Lanczos [1942]. These authors, in turn, referenced Runge [1903, 1905] as the source of their technique. The latter two papers, together with the lecture notes of Runge and König [1924], contain the essential computational advantages of present FFT algorithms. Similar techniques also were published by Yates [1937], Stumpff [1939], Good [1958], and Thomas [1963]. A paper by Cooley, Lewis, and Welch [1967a] presents a historical summary and an interesting comparison of results prior to the 1965 Cooley–Tukey paper.

The FFT algorithm presented in this chapter is by no means a unique formulation. For example, the so-called Sande–Tukey algorithm (Gentleman and Sande [1966]) is based on an alternative decomposition of the input data. The book by Brigham [1974] contains a comprehensive discussion of this algorithm as well as numerous other formulations of the FFT, including procedures for bases other than 2.

Although we have focused exclusively on digital techniques, we point out that 2-D Fourier transforms can also be obtained by optical methods (see Problem 3.7). The books by Papoulis [1968], Goodman [1968], and Hech and Zajac [1975] span the theoretical and applied aspects of optics and optical transforms at an introductory level.

For further reading on the matrix formulation of image transforms, see the book by Andrews [1970], which also develops the concept of matrix decomposition and discusses other image transforms in addition to the ones covered in this chapter. The papers by Good [1958], Gentleman [1968], Kahaner [1970], and the book by Elliott and Rao [1983] also are of interest.

The original paper on the Walsh transform (Walsh [1923]) is worth reading from a historical point of view. Additional references on the transform are Fine [1949, 1950], Hammond and Johnson [1962], Henderson [1964], Shanks [1969], and Andrews [1970].

For further reading on the Hadamard transform, see the original paper by Hadamard [1893]. Also see Williamson [1944], Whelchel [1968], and Andrews [1970]. Two interesting notes dealing with the search for Hadamard matrices based on other than integer powers of 2 are Baumert [1962] and Golomb [1963]. The concept of sequency appears to have been introduced by Harmuth [1968]. References for the discrete cosine transform are Ahmed *et al.* [1974] and Ahmed and Rao [1975]. The latter reference also contains an extensive discussion of other orthogonal transforms. References on the Haar and Slant transforms are Harmuth [1970], Shore [1973], Jain [1989], and Pratt [1991].

Hotelling [1933] was the first to derive and publish the transformation that transforms discrete variables into uncorrelated coefficients. He referred to this technique as *the method of principal components*. His paper gives considerable insight into the method and is worth reading. Hotelling's transformation was rediscovered by Kramer and Mathews [1956] and Huang and Schultheiss [1963]. See Lawley and Maxwell [1963] for a general discussion of this topic. The analogous transformation for transforming continuous data into a set of uncorrelated coefficients was discovered by Karhunen [1947] and Loève [1948] and is called the *Karhunen–Loève expansion*. See Selin [1965] for an excellent discussion. The result that the Karhunen–Loève expansion minimizes the mean square truncation error was first published by Koschman [1954] and rediscovered by Brown [1960].

PROBLEMS

3.1 a) Assume continuous variables and show that the Fourier transform of the constant function $f(x, y) = 1$ is the unit impulse function $\delta(u, v)$, defined as $\delta(u, v) = \infty$, if $u = v = 0$ and $\delta(u, v) = 0$ otherwise. (With reference to Eq. (3.3-46), the integral of the unit impulse function is 1.)

   b) What is the result if $f(x, y) = 1$ is now a digital image of size $N \times N$?

3.2 a) Starting with Eq. (3.1-9), show that the Fourier transform of the 2-D sinusoidal function $n(x, y) = A \sin (u_0 x + v_0 y)$ is

$$N(u, v) = -jA/2[\delta(u - u_0/2\pi, v - v_0/2\pi) - \delta(u + u_0/2\pi, v + v_0/2\pi)].$$

b) Obtain the spectrum of $N(u, v)$.

3.3 A real function $f(x)$ can be decomposed as the sum of an even function and an odd function.

a) Show that $f_{\text{even}}(x) = \frac{1}{2}[f(x) + f(-x)]$ and $f_{\text{odd}}(x) = \frac{1}{2}[f(x) - f(-x)]$.

b) Show that $\Im[f_{\text{even}}(x)] = \text{Re}\{\Im[f(x)]\}$ and $\Im[f_{\text{odd}}(x)] = j \, \text{Im} \{\Im[f(x)]\}$.

3.4 Show that the Fourier transform of the autocorrelation function of $f(x)$ is the power spectrum (spectral density) $|F(u)|^2$.

3.5 Show the validity of Eqs. (3.3-7a) and (3.3-7b).

3.6 Obtain the Fourier transforms of (a) $df(x)/dx$, (b) $[\partial f(x, y)/\partial x + \partial f(x, y)/\partial y]$, and (c) $[\partial^2 f(x, y)/\partial x^2 + \partial^2 f(x, y)/\partial y^2]$. Assume that x and y are continuous variables.

3.7 In the References section of this chapter, the statement is made that the Fourier transform can be computed optically. The basic process consists of obtaining a transparency of the image in question, putting it in front of a convex lens, and shining a collimated beam of coherent light (say, from a laser) through the transparency and lens. A fundamental result from optics is that the 2-D Fourier transform of the image is formed on the focal plane of the lens. In essence, it forms an unbounded transform on that plane. Actually, the Fourier spectra shown in Fig. 3.3 were obtained using this method by inserting a film plate at the focal plane of the lens. With reference to Fig. 3.3, the spectrum of a small black circle is a set of concentric circles. What would the equivalent result look like if the spectrum were obtained by taking the discrete Fourier transform a digital image consisting of a small black circle on a white background? Sketch the spectrum and explain your reasoning.

3.8 Show that the discrete Fourier transform and its inverse are periodic functions. For simplicity, assume 1-D functions.

3.9 Show that the Fourier transform of the convolution of two functions is the product of their Fourier transforms. For simplicity, assume functions of one variable.

3.10 As indicated in Section 3.4.2, $N \log_2 N$ additions and $\frac{1}{2} N \log_2 N$ multiplications are needed to compute the FFT of N points. How many additions and multiplications would computing the 2-D FFT of an $N \times N$ image require?

3.11 With reference to the discussion in Section 3.4.1, show that

a) $W_{2M}^{2ux} = W_M^{ux}$,

b) $W_M^{u+M} = W_M^u$, and

c) $W_{2M}^{u+M} = -W_{2M}^u$.

3.12 Numerous available FFT computer programs are restricted to 1-D, *real* data inputs.

a) Show how such a program could be used to compute the FFT of 1-D *complex* data.

b) What would be the procedure for using the program to compute the 2-D FFT of an image whose pixels are real numbers?

3.13 With reference to Table 3.2, how would you order a 16-point array for use with a successive doubling FFT algorithm?

3.14 Show that Eqs. (3.5-15) and (3.5-17) constitute a transform pair. That is, prove that these two equations are inverses of each other.

3.15 A manufacturer of hypodermic needles is having a manufacturing problem that results in some needles having deformed tips. Although the percentage of bad needles is quite small, a bad needle causes so much pain in a patient that the reputation of this manufacturer is beginning to be affected. The manufacturer hires you to design a system capable of inspecting all needles so that the bad ones can be rejected. Propose a solution using the Fourier transform. The problem is so urgent to the manufacturer that you may assume that any equipment you need for a solution will be made available to you.

3.16 Show that Eqs. (3.5-45) and (3.5-46) for the discrete cosine transform constitute a transform pair. That is, prove that these two equations are inverses of each other.

3.17 Because the 2-D discrete cosine transform kernel is separable, the 2-D DCT of an image can be computed by row and column passes with a 1-D DCT algorithm. In fact, an interesting property of the 1-D DCT is that it can be computed by using an FFT algorithm. Show in detail how this computation can be made.

3.18 With reference to the basis functions for the discrete cosine transform for $N = 4$ (Fig. 3.28), work out by hand the values that make up the block corresponding to $u = v = 1$. Ignore $\alpha(u)$.

3.19 Obtain the Haar transform matrix for $N = 8$.

3.20 Obtain the Slant transform matrix for $N = 8$.

3.21 Prove the validity of Eqs. (3.6-7), (3.6-8), and (3.6-9).

3.22 A statement at the end of the last example in Section 3.6 indicates that a credible job could be done of reconstructing approximations to the six original images by using only the two principal-component images associated with the largest eigenvalues. What would be the mean square error incurred in doing so? Express your answer as a percentage of the maximum possible error.

3.23 For a set of images of size 64×64, assume that the covariance matrix given in Eq. (3.6-9) turns out to be the identity matrix. What would be the mean square error between the original images and images reconstructed using Eq. (3.6-11) with only half of the original eigenvectors?

CHAPTER 4

IMAGE ENHANCEMENT

*It makes all the difference whether one sees
darkness through the light or brightness through
the shadows.*
David Lindsay

The principal objective of enhancement techniques is to process an image so that the result is more suitable than the original image for a specific application. The word *specific* is important, because it establishes at the outset that the techniques discussed in this chapter are very much problem-oriented. Thus, for example, a method that is quite useful for enhancing x-ray images may not necessarily be the best approach for enhancing pictures of Mars transmitted by a space probe.

The approaches discussed in this chapter fall into two broad categories: spatial domain methods and frequency domain methods. The *spatial domain* refers to the image plane itself, and approaches in this category are based on direct manipulation of pixels in an image. *Frequency domain* processing techniques are based on modifying the Fourier transform of an image. Enhancement techniques based on various combinations of methods from these two categories are not unusual.

The basic methodology underlying this chapter's material is presented in Section 4.1. Section 4.2 deals with enhancement techniques based on point processing, which modify the gray level of a pixel independently of the nature of its neighbors. Section 4.3 covers enhancement methods based on mask processing. Masks, defined as small subimages, are used in local processing to modify each pixel in the image to be enhanced. Section 4.4 covers various techniques for carrying out image enhancement in the frequency domain via the Fourier transform. Section 4.5 shows how to generate small spatial masks from a frequency domain specification, providing a useful conceptual link between Sections 4.3 and 4.4. Finally, Section 4.6 deals with the enhancement of color images. This section develops the fundamentals of color generation and perception, introduces various color models, and covers various color image enhancement techniques in some detail.

4.1 BACKGROUND

The image enhancement methods presented in this chapter are based on either spatial or frequency domain techniques. The purpose of this section is to de-velop the fundamental ideas underlying and relating these two approaches.

4.1.1 Spatial Domain Methods

The term *spatial domain* refers to the aggregate of pixels composing an image, and spatial domain methods are procedures that operate directly on these pixels. Image processing functions in the spatial domain may be expressed as

$$g(x, y) = T[f(x, y)] \qquad (4.1\text{-}1)$$

where $f(x, y)$ is the input image, $g(x, y)$ is the processed image, and T is an operator on f, defined over some neighborhood of (x, y). In addition T can also operate on a *set* of input images, such as performing the pixel-by-pixel sum of M images for noise reduction, as discussed in Section 4.2.4.

The principal approach to defining a neighborhood about (x, y) is to use a square or rectangular subimage area centered at (x, y), as Fig. 4.1 shows.

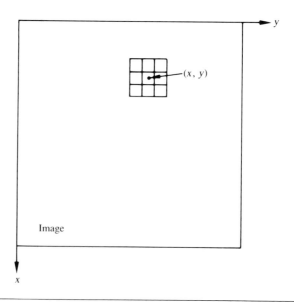

Figure 4.1   *A 3 × 3 neighborhood about a point (x, y) in an image.*

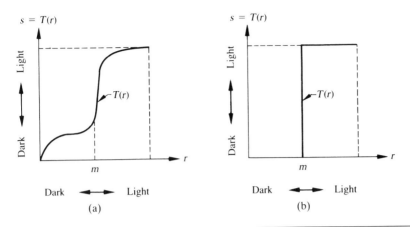

Figure 4.2   *Gray-level transformation functions for contrast enhancement.*

The center of the subimage is moved from pixel to pixel starting, say, at the top left corner and applying the operator at each location (x, y) to yield g at that location. Although other neighborhood shapes, such as approximations to a circle, sometimes are used, square and rectangular arrays are by far the most predominant because of their ease of implementation.

The simplest form of T is when the neighborhood is 1×1. In this case, g depends only on the value of f at (x, y), and T becomes a *gray-level transformation* (also called *mapping*) *function* of the form

$$s = T(r) \tag{4.1-2}$$

where, for simplicity in notation, r and s are variables denoting the gray level of $f(x, y)$ and $g(x, y)$ at any point (x, y). For example, if $T(r)$ has the form shown in Fig. 4.2(a), the effect of this transformation is to produce an image of higher contrast than the original by darkening the levels below m and brightening the levels above m in the original image. In this technique, known as *contrast stretching*, the values of r below m are compressed by the transformation function into a narrow range of s toward black; the opposite effect takes place for values of r above m. In the limiting case shown in Fig. 4.2(b), $T(r)$ produces a two-level (binary) image. Some fairly simple, yet powerful, processing approaches can be formulated with gray-level transformations. Because enhancement at any point in an image depends only on the gray level at that point, techniques in this category often are referred to as *point processing*.

Larger neighborhoods allow a variety of processing functions that go beyond just image enhancement. Regardless of the specific application, however, the general approach is to let the values of f in a predefined neighborhood of (x, y) determine the value of g at (x, y). One of the principal approaches in this formulation is based on the use of so-called *masks* (also referred to as *templates, windows,* or *filters*). Basically, a mask is a small (say, 3 × 3) 2-D array, such as the one shown in Fig. 4.1, in which the values of the coefficients determine the nature of the process, such as image sharpening. Enhancement techniques based on this type of approach often are referred to as *mask processing* or *filtering.*

4.1.2 Frequency Domain Methods

The foundation of frequency domain techniques is the convolution theorem. Let $g(x, y)$ be an image formed by the convolution of an image $f(x, y)$ and a linear, position invariant operator $h(x, y),^†$ that is,

$$g(x, y) = h(x, y)*f(x, y). \qquad (4.1\text{-}3)$$

Then, from the convolution theorem (Section 3.3.8), the following frequency domain relation holds:

$$G(u, v) = H(u, v)F(u, v) \qquad (4.1\text{-}4)$$

where G, H, and F are the Fourier transforms of g, h, and f, respectively. In the terminology of linear system theory, the transform $H(u, v)$ is called the *transfer function* of the process. In optics, $H(u, v)$ is called the *optical transfer function,* and its magnitude is called the *modulation transfer function.*

Numerous image enhancement problems can be expressed in the form of Eq. (4.1-4). In a typical image enhancement application, $f(x, y)$ is given and the goal, after computation of $F(u, v)$, is to select $H(u, v)$ so that the desired image,

$$g(x, y) = \mathfrak{F}^{-1}[H(u, v)F(u, v)] \qquad (4.1\text{-}5)$$

exhibits some highlighted feature of $f(x, y)$. For instance, edges in $f(x, y)$ can be accentuated by using a function $H(u, v)$ that emphasizes the high-frequency components of $F(u, v)$. We discuss this topic further in Section 4.4.

In Fig. 4.3(a), $h(x, y)$ characterizes a system whose function is to produce an output image $g(x, y)$ from an input image $f(x, y)$. The system performs the convolution of $h(x, y)$ with the input image and outputs the result. The convolution theorem allows a different view of the process in the sense that the same result can be achieved by multiplying $F(u, v)$ by $H(u, v)$ to yield $G(u, v)$. Taking the inverse Fourier transform of the output then gives the desired image.

---

† A position-invariant operator is one whose result depends only on the value of $f(x, y)$ at a point in the image and not on the position of the point. Position invariance is an implicit requirement in the definition of the convolution integrals given in Eqs. (3.3-23) and (3.3-30). We discuss the concepts of linearity and position invariance in more detail in Section 5.1.

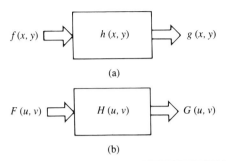

Figure 4.3 *Operation of a linear system. In (a), the system output is the convolution of* $h(x, y)$ *with the input. In (b), the output is the product of* $H(u, v)$ *with the input.*

Suppose for a moment that $h(x, y)$ is unknown and that we apply a unit impulse function (that is, a point of light) to the system. The Fourier transform of a unit impulse is simply 1 so, from Eq. (4.1-4), $G(u, v) = H(u, v)$. The inverse transform of the output $G(u, v)$ then is $h(x, y)$. This result is well known in linear system theory: A linear, position invariant system is completely spec-ified by its response to an impulse. That is, when the Fourier transform of a unit impulse is applied to such a system, its output is precisely the system transfer function $H(u, v)$. Alternatively, applying the impulse directly yields $h(x, y)$ at the output. For this reason, $h(x, y)$, the inverse transform of the system transfer function, is called the *impulse response* in the terminology of linear system theory. In optics, $h(x, y)$, the inverse of the optical transfer function, is called the *point spread function*. This name is based on the optical phenomenon that the impulse corresponds to a point of light and that an optical system responds by blurring (spreading) the point, with the degree of blurring being determined by the quality of the optical components. Thus the optical transfer function and the point spread function of a linear system are Fourier transforms of each other. This relationship is of considerable use in Sec-tion 4.3.

Equation (4.1-3) describes a spatial process that is analogous to the use of the masks discussed in Section 4.1.1. In fact, the discrete convolution expression given in Eq. (3.3-35) basically is a mathematical representation of the mechanics involved in implementing the mask-shifting process explained in Fig. 4.1. For this reason, $h(x, y)$ is often referred to as a *spatial convolution mask*. The same term is often used in connection with the spatial masks discussed in Section 4.1.1. Strictly speaking, this term is not correct in general because convolution involves flipping one of the images about the origin, as discussed in Section 3.3.8. Use of this name in connection with the masks discussed in Section 4.1.1 is correct only when the mask is symmetric about its origin.

Although it may already be obvious, we note that there is no general theory of image enhancement. When an image is processed for visual interpretation, the viewer is the ultimate judge of how well a particular method works. Visual evaluation of image quality is a highly subjective process, thus making the definition of a "good image" an elusive standard by which to compare algorithm performance. When the problem is one of processing images for machine perception, the evaluation task is somewhat easier. For example, in dealing with a character recognition application, the best image processing method would be the one yielding the best machine recognition results. However, even in situations when a clear-cut criterion of performance can be imposed on the problem, the analyst usually is still faced with a certain amount of trial and error before being able to settle on a particular image processing approach.

4.2   ENHANCEMENT BY POINT PROCESSING

We begin the study of image enhancement techniques by considering processing methods that are based only on the intensity of single pixels. As indicated in Section 4.1, single-point processes are among the simplest of all image enhancement techniques. In what follows, we denote the intensity of pixels before and after processing by r and s, respectively.

4.2.1   Some Simple Intensity Transformations

Image negatives

Negatives of digital images are useful in numerous applications, such as displaying medical images and photographing a screen with monochrome positive film with the idea of using the resulting negatives as normal slides. The negative of a digital image is obtained by using the transformation function $s = T(r)$ shown in Fig. 4.4(a), where L is the number of gray levels. The idea is to reverse the order from black to white so that the intensity of the output image decreases as the intensity of the input increases. Figures 4.4(b) and (c) illustrate the use of this simple transformation.

Contrast stretching

Low-contrast images can result from poor illumination, lack of dynamic range in the imaging sensor, or even wrong setting of a lens aperture during image acquisition. The idea behind contrast stretching is to increase the dynamic range of the gray levels in the image being processed. Figure 4.5(a) shows a typical transformation used for contrast stretching. The locations of points (r_1, s_1) and (r_2, s_2) control the shape of the transformation function. For instance, if $r_1 = s_1$ and $r_2 = s_2$, the transformation is a linear function that produces no changes in gray levels. If $r_1 = r_2$, $s_1 = 0$ and $s_2 = L - 1$, the transformation becomes a *thresholding function* that creates a binary image. Intermediate values of (r_1, s_1) and (r_2, s_2) produce various degrees of spread in the gray levels of the output image, thus affecting its contrast. In general, $r_1 \leq r_2$ and $s_1 \leq s_2$ is assumed so that the function is single valued and monotonically increasing. This condition preserves the order of gray levels, thus preventing the creation

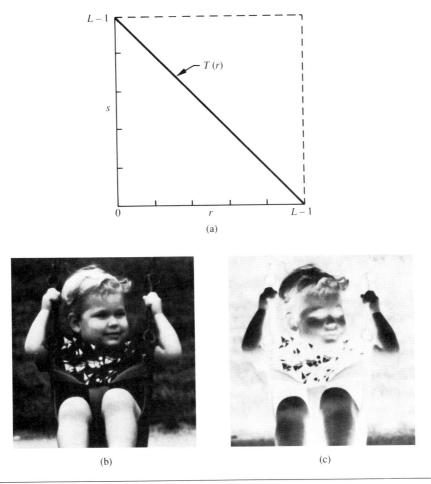

Figure 4.4 *Obtaining the negative of an image: (a) gray-level transformation function; (b) an image; and (c) its negative. In (a), r and s denote the input and output gray levels, respectively.*

of intensity artifacts in the processed image. Figure 4.5(b) shows an 8-bit image with low contrast, Fig. 4.5(c) shows the result of contrast stretching, and Fig. 4.5(d) shows the result of thresholding this image. The thresholding level is $r = 128$, with the output set at 255 (white) for any gray level in the input image of 128 or higher and at 0 (black) for all other values.

Compression of dynamic range
Sometimes the dynamic range of a processed image far exceeds the capability of the display device, in which case only the brightest parts of the image are visible on the display screen. The same often holds for attempts to record such

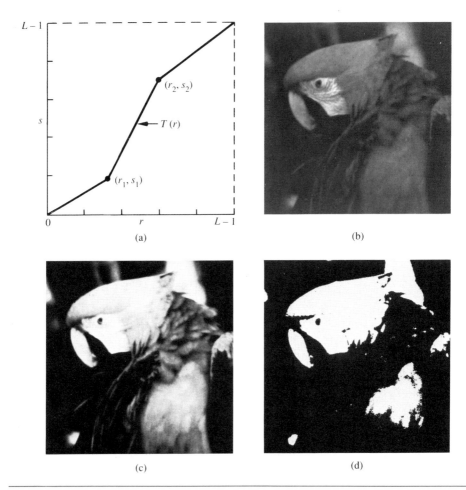

Figure 4.5 *Contrast stretching: (a) form of transformation function; (b) a low-contrast image; (c) result of contrast stretching; (d) result of thresholding.*

an image on film. One of the classic illustrations of this problem is in the display of the Fourier spectrum of an image, as discussed in Section 3.3. An effective way to compress the dynamic range of pixel values is to perform the following intensity transformation:

$$s = c \log(1 + |r|) \tag{4.2-1}$$

where c is a scaling constant, and the logarithm function performs the desired compression. Figure 4.6(a) shows the shape of this transformation function. Figure 4.6(b) shows a Fourier spectrum with values in the range $[0, R] = [0, 2.5 \times 10^6]$. When this function is scaled linearly for display on an 8-bit system, the brightest values dominate the display, as expected from such a large dynamic range. In this case, the values of $\log(1 + |r|)$ ranged from 0 to 6.4. We wanted to scale this range up to $[0, L - 1] = [0, 255]$ for display on the same 8-bit system. Thus we selected the scaling factor $c = 255/6.4$. Figure 4.6(c) shows the result after transformation and scaling. Note the significant increase in visible detail.

Gray-level slicing
Highlighting a specific range of gray levels in an image often is desired. Applications include enhancing features such as masses of water in satellite imagery and enhancing flaws in x-ray images. There are several ways of doing level slicing, but most of them are variations of two basic themes. One approach is

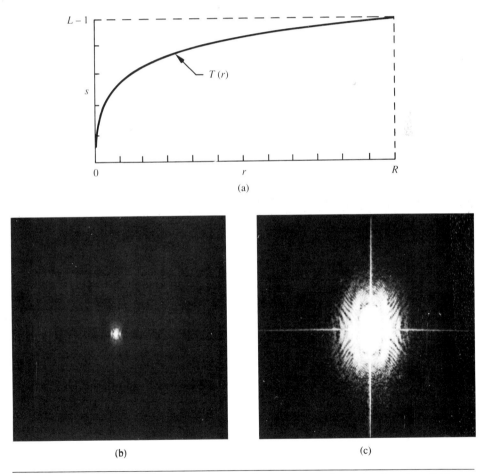

Figure 4.6 *Compression of dynamic range: (a) logarithm transformation function; (b) image with large dynamic range (pixel values ranging from 0 to 2.5×10^6); (c) result after transformation.*

to display a high value for all gray levels in the range of interest and a low value for all other gray levels. This transformation, shown in Fig. 4.7(a), produces a binary image. The second approach, based on the transformation shown in Fig. 4.7(b), brightens the desired range of gray levels but preserves the background and gray-level tonalities in the image. Figure 4.7(c) shows a gray-scale image, and Fig. 4.7(d) shows the result of using the transformation in Fig. 4.7(a). Variants of the two intensity transformations shown in Fig. 4.7 are easy to formulate.

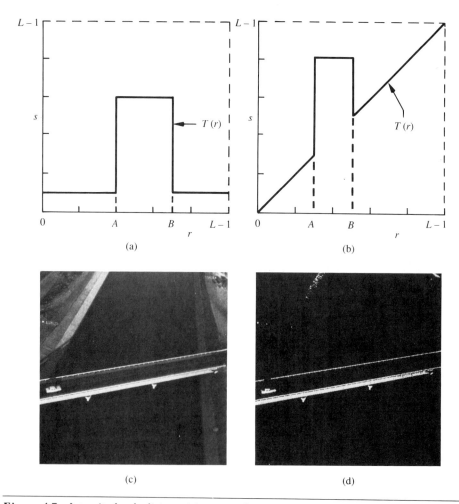

Figure 4.7 *Intensity-level slicing: (a) a transformation function that highlights a range [A, B] of intensities while diminishing all others to a constant, low level; (b) a transformation that highlights a range [A, B] of intensities but preserves all others; (c) an image; (d) result of using the transformation in (a).*

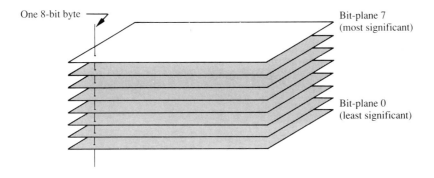

One 8-bit byte

Bit-plane 7
(most significant)

Bit-plane 0
(least significant)

Figure 4.8   *Bit-plane representation of an 8-bit digital image.*

Bit-plane slicing

Instead of highlighting intensity ranges, highlighting the contribution made to total image appearance by specific bits might be desired. Suppose that each pixel in an image is represented by 8 bits. Imagine that the image is composed of eight 1-bit planes, ranging from plane 0 for the least significant bit to plane 7 for the most significant bit. In terms of 8-bit bytes, plane 0 contains all the lowest order bits in the bytes comprising the pixels in the image and plane 7 contains all the high-order bits. Figure 4.8 illustrates these ideas, whereas Fig. 4.9 shows the various bit planes for the image shown in Fig. 4.5(c). Note that only the five highest order bits contain visually significant data. The other bit planes contribute to more subtle details in the image. Also note by comparing plane 7 in Fig. 4.9 with Fig. 4.5(d), that plane 7 corresponds exactly with an image thresholded at gray level 128. We leave it as an exercise to specify the gray-level ranges covered by the other bit planes.

4.2.2   Histogram Processing

The histogram of a digital image with gray levels in the range $[0, L - 1]$ is a discrete function $p(r_k) = n_k/n$, where r_k is the kth gray level, n_k is the number of pixels in the image with that gray level, n is the total number of pixels in the image, and $k = 0, 1, 2, \ldots, L - 1$.

Loosely speaking, $p(r_k)$ gives an estimate of the probability of occurrence of gray-level r_k. A plot of this function for all values of k provides a global description of the appearance of an image. For example, Fig. 4.10 shows the histograms of four basic types of images. The histogram shown in Fig. 4.10(a) shows that the gray levels are concentrated toward the dark end of the gray-scale range. Thus this histogram corresponds to an image with overall dark characteristics. Just the opposite is true in Fig. 4.10(b). The histogram shown in Fig. 4.10(c) has a narrow shape, which indicates little dynamic range and thus corresponds to an image having low contrast. As all gray levels occur toward the middle of the gray scale, the image would appear a murky gray.

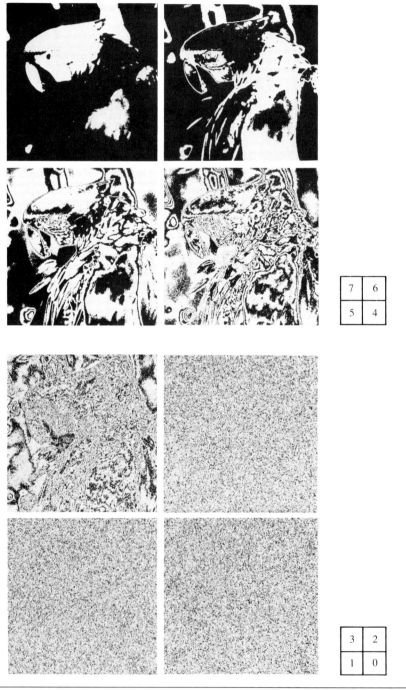

Figure 4.9 *Bit planes for the image in Fig. 4.5(c). The numbers in the small squares identify individual planes. Plane 7 contains the most significant bits, and plane 0 contains the least significant bits of the pixels in the original image.*

Finally, Fig. 4.10(d) shows a histogram with significant spread, corresponding to an image with high contrast.

Although the properties just discussed are global descriptions that say nothing specific about image content, the shape of the histogram of an image does give us useful information about the possibility for contrast enhancement. The following discussion develops methods for manipulating histograms in a consistent and meaningful manner.

Histogram equalization

Let the variable r represent the gray levels in the image to be enhanced. In the initial part of our discussion, the assumption is that pixel values are continuous quantities that have been normalized so that they lie in the interval $[0, 1]$, with $r = 0$ representing black and $r = 1$ representing white. Later, we consider a discrete formulation and allow pixel values to be in the interval $[0, L - 1]$.

For any r in the interval $[0, 1]$, we focus attention on transformations of the form

$$s = T(r) \tag{4.2-2}$$

which produce a level s for every pixel value r in the original image. It is assumed that the transformation function given in Eq. (4.2-2) satisfies the conditions:

(a) $T(r)$ is single-valued and monotonically increasing in the interval $0 \leqslant r \leqslant 1$; and

(b) $0 \leqslant T(r) \leqslant 1$ for $0 \leqslant r \leqslant 1$.

Condition (a) preserves the order from black to white in the gray scale, whereas condition (b) guarantees a mapping that is consistent with the allowed range of pixel values. Figure 4.11 illustrates a transformation function satisfying these conditions.

The inverse transformation from s back to r is denoted

$$r = T^{-1}(s) \qquad 0 \leqslant s \leqslant 1 \tag{4.2-3}$$

where the assumption is that $T^{-1}(s)$ also satisfies conditions (a) and (b) with respect to the variable s.

The gray levels in an image may be viewed as random quantities in the interval $[0, 1]$. If they are continuous variables, the original and transformed gray levels can be characterized by their probability density functions $p_r(r)$ and $p_s(s)$, respectively, where the subscripts on p are used to indicate that p_r and p_s are different functions.

From elementary probability theory, if $p_r(r)$ and $T(r)$ are known and $T^{-1}(s)$ satisfies condition (a), the probability density function of the transformed gray

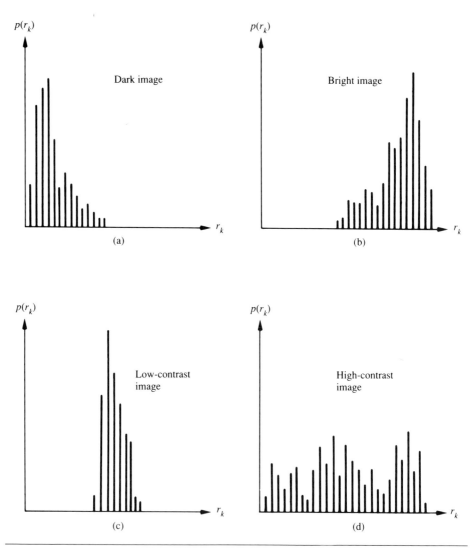

Figure 4.10 *Histograms corresponding to four basic image types.*

levels is

$$p_s(s) = \left[p_r(r) \frac{dr}{ds} \right]_{r = T^{-1}(s)} \tag{4.2-4}$$

The following enhancement techniques are based on modifying the appearance of an image by controlling the probability density function of its gray levels via the transformation function $T(r)$.

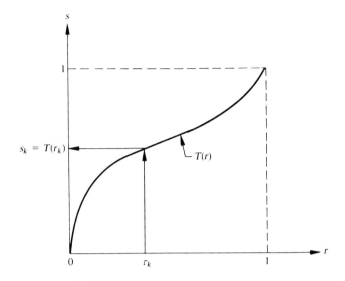

Figure 4.11 *A gray-level transformation function.*

Consider the transformation function

$$s = T(r) = \int_0^r p_r(w)\,dw \qquad 0 \leqslant r \leqslant 1 \tag{4.2-5}$$

where w is a dummy variable of integration. The rightmost side of Eq. (4.2-5) is recognized as the cumulative distribution function (CDF) of r. Conditions (a) and (b) presented earlier are satisfied by this transformation function, because the CDF increases monotonically from 0 to 1 as a function of r.

From Eq. (4.2-5), the derivative of s with respect to r is

$$\frac{ds}{dr} = p_r(r). \tag{4.2-6}$$

Substituting dr/ds into Eq. (4.2-4) yields

$$
\begin{aligned}
p_s(s) &= \left[p_r(r)\, \frac{1}{p_r(r)} \right]_{r = T^{-1}(s)} \\
&= [1]_{r = T^{-1}(s)} \\
&= 1 \qquad 0 \leqslant s \leqslant 1
\end{aligned}
\tag{4.2-7}
$$

which is a uniform density in the interval of definition of the transformed variable s. This result is independent of the inverse transformation function, which is important, because obtaining $T^{-1}(s)$ analytically is not always easy.

The foregoing development indicates that using a transformation function equal to the cumulative distribution of r produces an image whose gray levels have a uniform density. In terms of enhancement, this result implies an increase in the dynamic range of the pixels, which can have a considerable effect in the appearance of an image.

Example: Before proceeding with a discussion of discrete variables, let us consider a simple illustration of the use of Eqs. (4.2-4) and (4.2-5). Assume that the levels r have the probability density function shown in Fig. 4.12(a). In

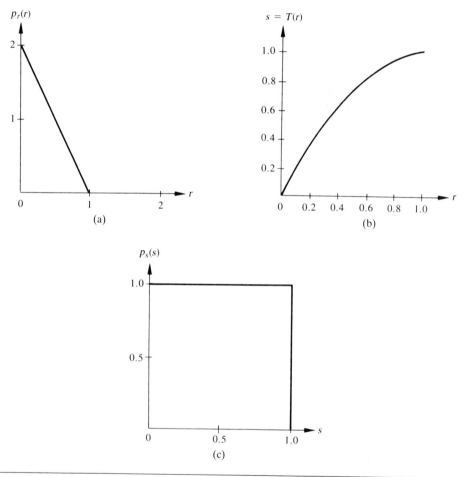

Figure 4.12 *Illustration of the uniform density transformation method: (a) original probability density function; (b) transformation function; (c) resulting uniform density.*

this case $p_r(r)$ is

$$p_r(r) = \begin{cases} -2r + 2 & 0 \leq r \leq 1 \\ 0 & \text{elsewhere.} \end{cases}$$

Substitution of this expression in Eq. (4.2-5) yields the transformation function

$$s = T(r) = \int_0^r (-2w + 2)dw$$
$$= -r^2 + 2r.$$

Although $T(r)$ is all that is needed for histogram equalization, it will be instructive to show that the resulting density $p_s(s)$ is in fact uniform. In practice this step is not required, because Eq. (4.2-7) is independent of the inverse transformation function. Solving for r in terms of s yields

$$r = T^{-1}(s) = 1 \pm \sqrt{1 - s}.$$

Since r lies in the interval $[0, 1]$, only the solution

$$r = T^{-1}(s) = 1 - \sqrt{1 - s}$$

is valid.

The probability density function of s is obtained by using Eq. (4.2-4):

$$p_s(s) = \left[p_r(r) \frac{dr}{ds} \right]_{r=T^{-1}(s)}$$
$$= \left[(-2r + 2) \frac{dr}{ds} \right]_{r=1-\sqrt{1-s}}$$
$$= \left[(2\sqrt{1-s}) \frac{d}{ds} (1 - \sqrt{1-s}) \right]$$
$$= 1 \qquad 0 \leq s \leq 1$$

which is a uniform density in the desired range. Figure 4.12(b) shows the transformation function $T(r)$, and Fig. 4.12(c) shows $p_s(s)$. ❏

In order to be useful for digital image processing, the concepts previously developed must be formulated in discrete form. For gray levels that take on discrete values, we deal with probabilities:

$$p_r(r_k) = \frac{n_k}{n} \qquad 0 \leq r_k \leq 1 \quad \text{and} \quad k = 0, 1, \ldots, L - 1 \qquad (4.2\text{-}8)$$

where, as indicated at the beginning of this section, L is the number of levels, $p_r(r_k)$ is the probability of the kth gray level, n_k is the number of times this level appears in the image, and n is the total number of pixels in the image. A plot of $p_r(r_k)$ versus r_k is called a *histogram*, and the technique used for obtaining a uniform histogram is known as *histogram equalization* or *histogram linearization*.

The discrete form of Eq. (4.2-5) is given by the relation

$$s_k = T(r_k) = \sum_{j=0}^{k} \frac{n_j}{n}$$

$$= \sum_{j=0}^{k} p_r(r_j) \qquad 0 \leq r_k \leq 1 \quad \text{and} \quad k = 0, 1, \ldots, L - 1.$$

(4.2-9)

The inverse transformation is denoted

$$r_k = T^{-1}(s_k) \qquad 0 \leq s_k \leq 1$$

where both $T(r_k)$ and $T^{-1}(s_k)$ are assumed to satisfy conditions (a) and (b) stated previously in this section. The transformation function $T(r_k)$ may be computed directly from the image by using Eq. (4.2-9). Although the inverse function $T^{-1}(s_k)$ is not used in histogram equalization, it plays a central role in the method discussed in the next section.

Example: To illustrate the usefulness of histogram equalization, consider Fig. 4.13(a), which shows a 512×512, 8-bit image (of a welding) that is dark and has very poor dynamic range. Based on the preceding discussion, the histogram of this image should be relatively narrow and be located toward the dark end of the gray scale. This, in fact, is the case, as the histogram in Fig. 4.13(b) shows. The horizontal axis of the histogram encompasses the range [0, 255], which is the possible range of gray-level values for an 8-bit image. The vertical axis shows the number of pixels for each gray level instead of probabilities, as discussed earlier. The representation shown in Fig. 4.13(b) is common in practice because it is more natural and easier to interpret. Converting the vertical axis to probabilities would be easy: we simply divide the values by $(512)^2$. Similarly, the horizontal axis can be normalized to [0, 1] by dividing all values by 255. The key to all of this is that we are talking mostly about interpretation. The shape and meaning of the histogram are not affected by the axis readings.

Figure 4.13(c) shows the result of histogram equalization. The improvement over the original image is quite evident. Figure 4.13(d) shows the histogram of the equalized image. Note that the histogram is not flat—a result that should not be a surprise because nothing in the discrete approximation of the continuous result previously derived says that it should be flat (see Problem 4.2). Note, however, that the gray levels of an image that has been subjected to

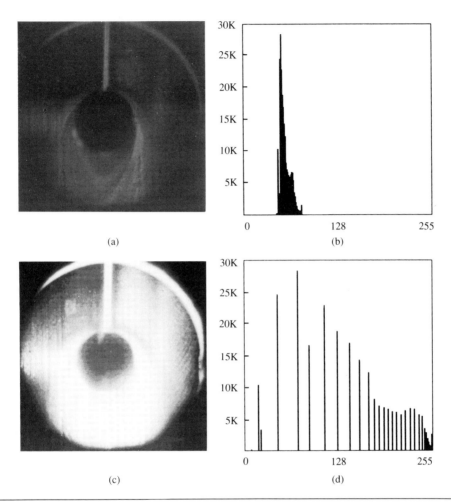

Figure 4.13 *(a) Original image and (b) its histogram; (c) image subjected to histogram equalization and (d) its histogram.*

histogram equalization are spread out and always reach white. This process increases the dynamic range of gray levels and, consequently, produces an increase in image contrast. In images with narrow histograms and relatively few gray levels, the increase in dynamic range normally has the adverse effect of increasing visual graininess and "patchiness," both of which are apparent in Fig. 4.13(c). Horizontal stripes associated with faulty digitization also have been enhanced. Overall, however, histogram equalization significantly improved the visual appearance of this image. Similar enhancement results could have been achieved by using the contrast stretching approach discussed in the preceding section. Of course, the advantage of histogram equalization over manual contrast manipulation techniques is that the former is fully automatic.   ❑

Histogram specification

Although the histogram equalization method is quite useful, it does not lend itself to interactive image enhancement applications. The reason is that this method is capable of generating only one result: an approximation to a uniform histogram.

Sometimes the ability to specify particular histogram shapes capable of highlighting certain gray-level ranges in an image is desirable. To see how this can be accomplished, let us return for a moment to continuous gray levels. Let $p_r(r)$ and $p_z(z)$ be the original and desired probability density functions, respectively. Suppose that histogram equalization is first utilized on the original image by applying Eq. (4.2-5); that is,

$$s = T(r) = \int_0^r p_r(w)dw. \qquad (4.2\text{-}10)$$

If the desired image were available, its levels could also be equalized by using the transformation function

$$v = G(z) = \int_0^z p_z(w)dw. \qquad (4.2\text{-}11)$$

The inverse process, $z = G^{-1}(v)$, would then give us back the levels, z, of the desired image . This formulation, of course, is hypothetical because the z levels are precisely what is being sought. However, $p_s(s)$ and $p_v(v)$ would be identical uniform densities because the final result of Eq. (4.2-5) is independent of the density inside the integral. Thus, if instead of using v in the inverse process we use the uniform levels s obtained from the original image, the resulting levels, $z = G^{-1}(s)$, would have the desired probability density function. Assuming that $G^{-1}(s)$ is single-valued, the procedure can be summarized as follows.

(1) Equalize the levels of the original image using Eq. (4.2-5).

(2) Specify the desired density function and obtain the transformation function $G(z)$ using Eq. (4.2-11).

(3) Apply the inverse transformation function, $z = G^{-1}(s)$, to the levels obtained in step (1).

This procedure yields a processed version of the original image, with the new gray levels characterized by the specified density $p_z(z)$.

Although the method of histogram specification involves two transformation functions, $T(r)$ followed by $G^{-1}(s)$, combining both enhancement steps
into one function that yields the desired levels starting with the original pixels
is a simple matter. From the preceding discussion,

$$z = G^{-1}(s). \qquad (4.2\text{-}12)$$

Substitution of Eq. (4.2-5) in Eq. (4.2-12) results in the combined transformation function

$$z = G^{-1}[T(r)] \qquad (4.2\text{-}13)$$

which relates r to z. When $G^{-1}[T(r)] = T(r)$, Eq. (4.2-13) reduces to histogram
equalization.

The implication of Eq. (4.2-13) is simply that an image need not be his-
togram-equalized explicitly. All that is required is that $T(r)$ be determined and
combined with the inverse transformation function G^{-1}. The problem with using
the preceding method for continuous variables lies in obtaining the inverse
function analytically. In the discrete case this problem is circumvented by the
fact that the number of distinct gray levels is usually relatively small, and
calculating and storing a mapping for each possible pixel value becomes feasible.
The discrete formulation of the histogram specification technique parallels Eqs.
(4.2-8) and (4.2-9).

In practice the inverse transformation from s to z often is not single valued.
This situation arises when there are unfilled levels in the specified histogram
(which makes the CDF remain constant over the unfilled intervals), or in the
process of rounding off $G^{-1}(s)$ to the nearest allowable gray level. Generally,
the easiest solution to this problem is to assign the levels in such a way as to
match the histogram as closely as possible.

The principal difficulty in applying the histogram specification method to
image enhancement lies in being able to construct a meaningful histogram.
Two solutions to this problem are as follows. The first is to specify a particular
probability density function (such as a Gaussian density) and then form a
histogram by digitizing the given function. The second approach consists of
specifying a histogram shape by means of a graphic device (say, an interactive
screen or drawing tablet) whose output is fed into the processor executing the
histogram specification algorithm.

Example: Consider Fig. 4.14(a) which shows a semidark room viewed from a
doorway. Figure 4.14(b) shows the image after histogram equalization and Fig.
4.14(c) is the result of interactive histogram specification. Figure 4.14(d) shows
the histograms: from bottom to top, the original, equalized, specified, and
resulting histograms, respectively.

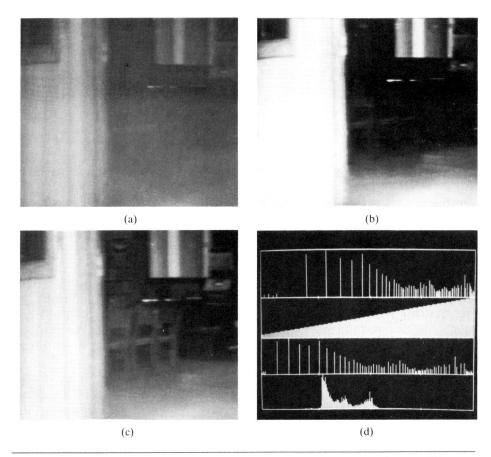

(a)   (b)

(c)   (d)

Figure 4.14   *Illustration of the histogram specification method: (a) original image; (b) image after histogram equalization; (c) image enhanced by histogram specification; (d) histograms.*

Note that histogram equalization produced an image whose contrast was somewhat high, whereas the result shown in Fig. 4.14(c) has a much more balanced appearance. Because of its flexibility, the histogram specification method generally yields results that are superior to histogram equalization. ☐

Local enhancement
The two histogram processing methods discussed in the previous two sections are global in the sense that pixels are modified by a transformation function based on the gray-level distribution over an entire image. Although this global approach is suitable for overall enhancement, it is often necessary to enhance details over small areas. The number of pixels in these areas may have negligible influence on the computation of a global transformation, so the use of this type

of transformation does not necessarily guarantee the desired local enhancement. The solution is to devise transformation functions based on the gray-level distribution—or other properties—in the neighborhood of every pixel in the image. Although processing methods based on neighborhoods are the topic of Section 4.3, we discuss local histogram processing here for the sake of clarity and continuity.

The histogram processing techniques previously described are easily adaptable to local enhancement. The procedure is to define a square or rectangular neighborhood and move the center of this area from pixel to pixel. At each location, the histogram of the points in the neighborhood is computed and either a histogram equalization or histogram specification transformation function is obtained. This function is finally used to map the gray level of the pixel centered in the neighborhood. The center of the neighborhood region is then moved to an adjacent pixel location and the procedure is repeated. Since only one new row or column of the neighborhood changes during a pixel-to-pixel translation of the region, updating the histogram obtained in the previous location with the new data introduced at each motion step is possible (see Problem 4.5). This approach has obvious advantages over repeatedly computing the histogram over all pixels in the neighborhood region each time the region is moved one pixel location. Another approach often used to reduce computation is to utilize nonoverlapping regions, but this method usually produces an undesirable checkerboard effect.

Example: Figure 4.15 illustrates local histogram equalization with the neighborhood moved from pixel to pixel. Figure 4.15(a) shows an image that has been slightly blurred to reduce its noise content (see Section 4.3.2). Figure 4.15(b) shows the result of global histogram equalization. As is often the case when this technique is applied to smooth, noisy areas, Fig. 4.15(b) shows considerable enhancement of the noise, with a slight increase in contrast. Note, however, that no new structural details were brought out by this method. However, local histogram equalization using a 7×7 neighborhood revealed the presence of small squares inside the larger dark squares. The small squares were too close in gray level and their sizes too small to influence global histogram equalization significantly. Note also the finer noise texture in Fig. 4.15(c), a result of local processing in relatively small neighborhoods. ❑

Instead of using histograms, local enhancement can be based on other properties of the pixel intensities in a neighborhood. The intensity mean and variance (or standard deviation) are two such properties frequently used because of their relevance to the appearance of an image. That is, the mean is a measure of average brightness and the variance is a measure of contrast.

A typical local transformation based on these concepts maps the intensity of an input image $f(x, y)$ into a new image $g(x, y)$ by performing the following

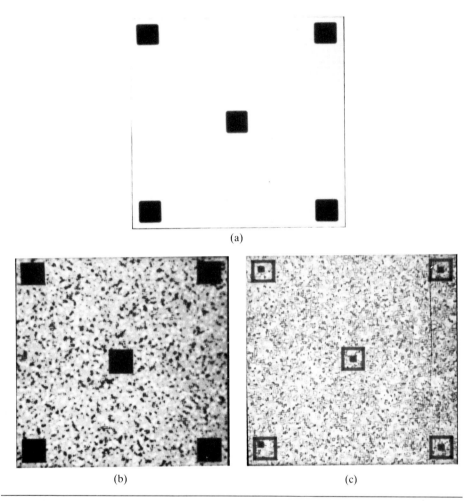

Figure 4.15 *(a) Original image; (b) result of global histogram equalization; (c) result of local histogram equalization using a 7 × 7 neighborhood about each pixel. (From Fu, Gonzalez, and Lee [1987].)*

transformation at each pixel location (x, y):

$$g(x, y) = A(x, y) \cdot [f(x, y) - m(x, y)] + m(x, y) \qquad (4.2\text{-}14)$$

where

$$A(x, y) = k\,\frac{M}{\sigma(x, y)} \qquad 0 < k < 1. \qquad (4.2\text{-}15)$$

In this formulation $m(x, y)$ and $\sigma(x, y)$ are the gray-level mean and standard deviation computed in a neighborhood centered at (x, y), M is the global mean of $f(x, y)$, and k is a constant in the range indicated in Eq. (4.2-15).

The values of the variable quantities A, m, and σ depend on a predefined neighborhood of (x, y). Application of the local gain factor $A(x, y)$ to the difference between $f(x, y)$ and the local mean amplifies local variations. Because $A(x, y)$ is inversely proportional to the standard deviation of the intensity, areas with low contrast receive larger gain. The mean is added back in Eq. (4.2-14) to restore the average intensity level of the image in the local region. In practice adding back a fraction of the local mean and restricting the variations of $A(x, y)$ between two limits (A_{min}, A_{max}) often is desirable in order to balance large excursions of intensity in isolated regions.

Example: An example of the capabilities of Eqs. (4.2-14) and (4.2-15) using a local region of 15×15 pixels is shown in Fig. 4.16. Note the enhancement of detail at the boundary between two regions of different overall gray levels and the rendition of gray-level details in each region. ❑

4.2.3 Image Subtraction

The difference between two images $f(x, y)$ and $h(x, y)$, expressed as

$$g(x, y) = f(x, y) - h(x, y) \tag{4.2-16}$$

is obtained by computing the difference between all pairs of corresponding pixels from f and h. Image subtraction has numerous important applications in segmentation (Chapter 7) and enhancement.

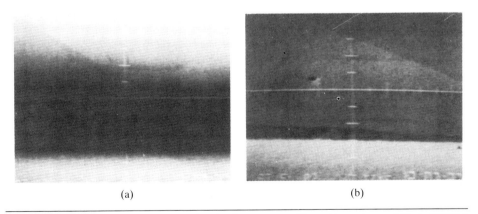

(a)   (b)

Figure 4.16 *Images before and after local enhancement. (From Narendra and Fitch [1981].)*

A classic application of Eq. (4.2-16) for enhancement is in an area of medical imaging called *mask mode radiography*. In this case $h(x, y)$, the *mask*, is an x-ray image of a region of a patient's body captured by an intensifier and TV camera (instead of traditional x-ray film) located opposite an x-ray source. The image $f(x, y)$ is one sample of a series of similar TV images of the same anatomical region but acquired after injection of a dye into the bloodstream. The net effect of subtracting the mask from each sample in the incoming stream of TV images is that only the areas that are different between $f(x, y)$ and $h(x, y)$ appear in the output image as enhanced detail. Because images can be captured at TV rates, this procedure in essence gives a movie showing how the dye propagates through the various arteries.

Example: Figure 4.17(a) shows an x-ray image of the top of a patient's head prior to injection of an iodine dye into the bloodstream. The camera yielding this image was positioned above the patient's head, looking down. As a reference point, the bright spot in the lower one-third of the image is the core of the spinal column. Figure 4.17(b) shows the difference between the mask (Fig. 4.17a) and an image taken sometime after the dye was introduced into the bloodstream. The bright arterial paths carrying the dye are unmistakably enhanced in Fig. 4.17(b). These arteries appear quite bright because they are not subtracted out (that is, they are not part of the mask image). The overall background is much darker than that in Fig. 4.17(a) because differences between areas of little change yield low values, which in turn appear as dark

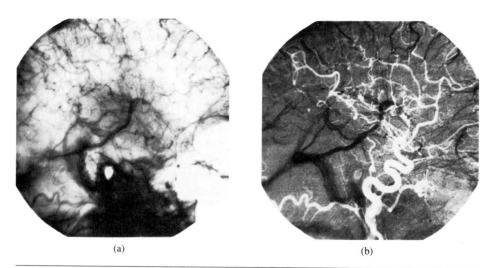

(a)   (b)

Figure 4.17   *Enhancement by image subtraction: (a) mask image; (b) image (after injection of dye into the bloodstream) with mask subtracted out.*

shades of gray in the difference image. Note, for instance, that the spinal cord, which is bright in Fig. 4.17(a), appears quite dark in Fig. 4.17(b) as a result of subtraction. ❏

4.2.4 Image Averaging

Consider a noisy image $g(x, y)$ formed by the addition of noise $\eta(x, y)$ to an original image $f(x, y)$; that is,

$$g(x, y) = f(x, y) + \eta(x, y) \tag{4.2-17}$$

where the assumption is that at every pair of coordinates (x, y) the noise is uncorrelated and has zero average value. The objective of the following procedure is to reduce the noise effects by adding a set of noisy images, $\{g_i(x, y)\}$.

 If the noise satisfies the constraints just stated, it is a simple problem to show (see Papoulis [1965]) that if an image $\bar{g}(x, y)$ is formed by averaging M different noisy images,

$$\bar{g}(x, y) = \frac{1}{M} \sum_{i=1}^{M} g_i(x, y) \tag{4.2-18}$$

then it follows that

$$E\{\bar{g}(x, y)\} = f(x, y) \tag{4.2-19}$$

and

$$\sigma^2_{\bar{g}(x, y)} = \frac{1}{M} \sigma^2_{\eta(x, y)} \tag{4.2-20}$$

where $E\{\bar{g}(x, y)\}$ is the expected value of $\bar{g}$, and $\sigma^2_{\bar{g}(x, y)}$ and $\sigma^2_{\eta(x, y)}$ are the variances of $\bar{g}$ and η, all at coordinates (x, y). The standard deviation at any point in the average image is

$$\sigma_{\bar{g}(x, y)} = \frac{1}{\sqrt{M}} \sigma_{\eta(x, y)}. \tag{4.2-21}$$

 Equations (4.2-20) and (4.2-21) indicate that, as M increases, the variability of the pixel values at each location (x, y) decreases. Because $E\{\bar{g}(x, y)\} = f(x, y)$, this condition means that $\bar{g}(x, y)$ approaches $f(x, y)$ as the number of noisy images used in the averaging process increases. In practice the images $g_i(x, y)$ must be registered in order to avoid blurring in the output image.

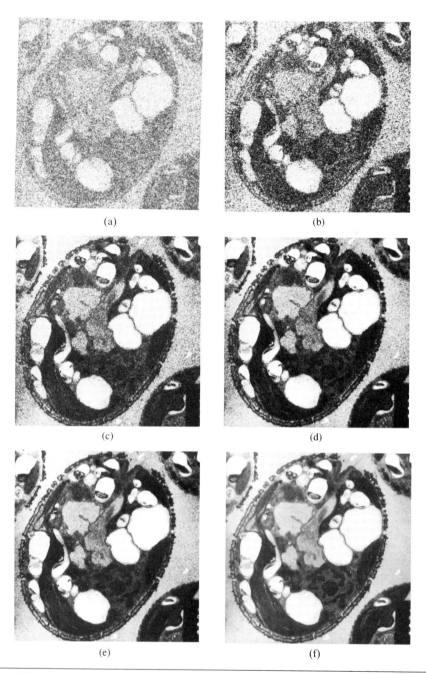

Figure 4.18   *Example of noise reduction by averaging: (a) a typical noisy image; (b)–(f) results of averaging 2, 8, 16, 32, and 128 noisy images.*

Example: Figure 4.18(a) shows a noisy microscope image of a cell, and Figs. 4.18(b)–(f) show the results of averaging 2, 8, 16, 32, and 128 such noisy images. For purposes of visual analysis, the image obtained with $M = 32$ is reasonably clean and, for all practical purposes, the result obtained with $M = 128$ is essentially noise free.   ❏

4.3 SPATIAL FILTERING

4.3.1 Background

The use of spatial masks for image processing usually is called *spatial filtering* (as opposed to *frequency domain filtering* using the Fourier transform), and the masks themselves are called *spatial filters*. In this section we consider linear and nonlinear spatial filters for image enhancement.

Linear filters are based on the concepts introduced in Section 4.1, which state that the transfer function and the impulse or point spread function of a linear system are inverse Fourier transforms of each other. So-called *lowpass* filters attenuate or eliminate high-frequency components in the Fourier domain while leaving low frequencies untouched (that is, the filter "passes" low frequencies). High-frequency components characterize edges and other sharp details in an image, so the net effect of lowpass filtering is image blurring. Similarly, *highpass* filters attenuate or eliminate low-frequency components. Because these components are responsible for the slowly varying characteristics of an image, such as overall contrast and average intensity, the net result of highpass filtering is a reduction of these features and a correspondingly apparent sharpening of edges and other sharp details. A third type of filtering, called *bandpass filtering*, removes selected frequency regions between low and high frequencies. These filters are used for image restoration (Section 5.8) and are seldom of interest in image enhancement.

Figure 4.19 shows cross sections of circularly symmetric lowpass, highpass, and bandpass filters in the frequency domain and their corresponding spatial filters. The horizontal axes for the figures in the top row correspond to frequency, and their counterparts in the bottom row are spatial coordinates. The shapes in the bottom row are used as guidelines for specifying linear spatial filters. Regardless of the type of linear filter used, however, the basic approach is to sum products between the mask coefficients and the intensities of the pixels under the mask at a specific location in the image. Figure 4.20 shows a general 3×3 mask. Denoting the gray levels of pixels under the mask at any location by $z_1, z_2, \ldots, z_9$, the response of a linear mask is

$$R = w_1 z_1 + w_2 z_2 + \cdots + w_9 z_9. \tag{4.3-1}$$

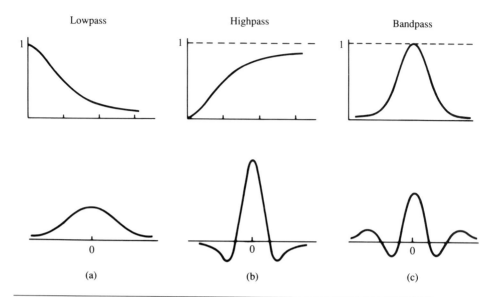

Figure 4.19   *Top: cross sections of basic shapes for circularly symmetric frequency domain filters. Bottom: cross sections of corresponding spatial domain filters.*

With reference to Fig. 4.1, if the center of the mask is at location (x, y) in the image, the gray level of the pixel located at (x, y) is replaced by R. The mask is then moved to the next pixel location in the image and the process is repeated. This continues until all pixel locations have been covered. The value of R is computed by using partial neighborhoods for pixels that are located in the border of the image. Also, usual practice is to create a new image to store the values of R, instead of changing pixel values in place. This practice avoids using gray levels in Eq. (4.3-1) that have been altered as a result of an earlier application of this equation.

Nonlinear spatial filters also operate on neighborhoods. In general, however, their operation is based directly on the values of the pixels in the neighborhood under consideration, and they do not explicitly use coefficients in the manner described in Eq. (4.3-1). As shown in the next section, noise

w_1	w_2	w_3
w_4	w_5	w_6
w_7	w_8	w_9

Figure 4.20   *A 3 × 3 mask with arbitrary coefficients (weights).*

reduction can be achieved effectively with a nonlinear filter whose basic function is to compute the median gray-level value in the neighborhood in which the filter is located. Other examples include the *max* filter (with a response $R = \max\{z_k \mid k = 1, 2, \ldots, 9\}$), which is used to find the brightest points in an image, and the *min* filter, which is used for the opposite purpose.

4.3.2 Smoothing Filters

Smoothing filters are used for blurring and for noise reduction. Blurring is used in preprocessing steps, such as removal of small details from an image prior to (large) object extraction, and bridging of small gaps in lines or curves. Noise reduction can be accomplished by blurring with a linear filter and also by nonlinear filtering.

Lowpass spatial filtering

The shape of the impulse response needed to implement a lowpass (smoothing) spatial filter indicates that the filter has to have all positive coefficients (see Fig. 4.19a). Although the spatial filter shape shown in Fig. 4.19(a) could be modeled by, say, a sampled Gaussian function, the key requirement is that all the coefficients be positive. For a 3×3 spatial filter, the simplest arrangement would be a mask in which all coefficients have a value of 1. However, from Eq. (4.3-1), the response would then be the sum of gray levels for nine pixels, which could cause R to be out of the valid gray-level range. The solution is to scale the sum by dividing R by 9. Figure 4.21(a) shows the resulting mask. Larger masks follow the same concept, as Figs. 4.21(b) and (c) show. Note that, in all these cases, the response R would simply be the average of all the pixels in the area of the mask. For this reason, the use of masks of the form shown in Fig. 4.21 is often referred to as *neighborhood averaging*. Figure 4.22 shows an example of blurring by successively larger smoothing masks. Note in particular the loss of sharpness in the filament of the bulb as the smoothing mask becomes larger.

Median filtering

One of the principal difficulties of the smoothing method discussed in the preceding section is that it blurs edges and other sharp details. If the objective is to achieve noise reduction rather than blurring, an alternative approach is to use *median filters*. That is, the gray level of each pixel is replaced by the median of the gray levels in a neighborhood of that pixel, instead of by the average. This method is particularly effective when the noise pattern consists of strong, spikelike components and the characteristic to be preserved is edge sharpness. As indicated earlier, median filters are nonlinear.

The median m of a set of values is such that half the values in the set are less than m and half are greater than m. In order to perform median filtering in a neighborhood of a pixel, we first sort the values of the pixel and its neighbors, determine the median, and assign this value to the pixel. For example,

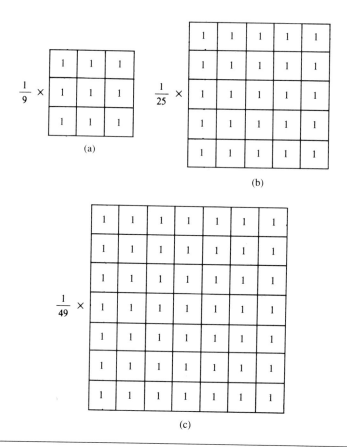

Figure 4.21 *Spatial lowpass filters of various sizes.*

in a 3 × 3 neighborhood the median is the 5th largest value, in a 5 × 5 neighborhood the 13th largest value, and so on. When several values in a neighborhood are the same, all equal values have to be grouped. For example, suppose that a 3 × 3 neighborhood has values (10, 20, 20, 20, 15, 20, 20, 25, 100). These values are sorted as (10, 15, 20, 20, 20, 20, 20, 25, 100), which results in a median of 20. Thus the principal function of median filtering is to force points with distinct intensities to be more like their neighbors, actually eliminating intensity spikes that appear isolated in the area of the filter mask.

Example: Figure 4.23(a) shows an original image, and Fig. 4.23(b) shows the same image but with approximately 20 percent of the pixels corrupted by impulse noise. Figure 4.23(c) shows the result of neighborhood averaging over a 5 × 5 area, and Fig. 4.23(d) shows the result of a 5 × 5 median filter. The superiority in this case of the median filter over neighborhood averaging needs

(a)

(b)

(c)

(d)

(e)

(f)

Figure 4.22 *(a) Original image; (b)–(f) results of spatial lowpass filtering with a mask of size n × n, n = 3, 5, 7, 15, 25.*

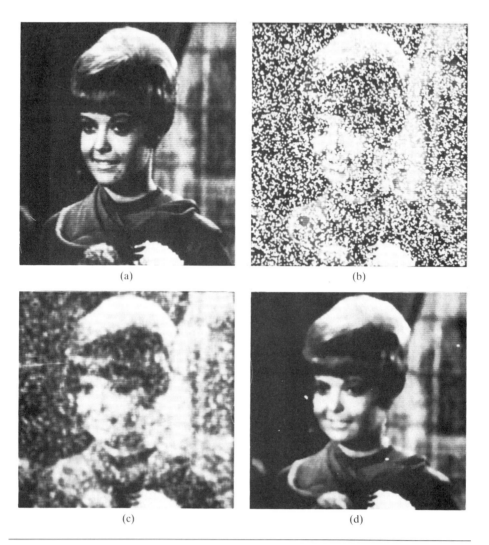

(a)

(b)

(c)

(d)

Figure 4.23 *(a) Original image; (b) image corrupted by impulse noise; (c) result of 5 × 5 neighborhood averaging; (d) result of 5 × 5 median filtering. (Courtesy of Martin Connor, Texas Instruments, Inc., Lewisville, Tex.)*

no explanation. The bright dots remaining in Fig. 4.23(d) resulted from a large concentration of noise at those points, thus biasing the median calculation. Two or more passes with a median filter would eliminate those points.   ❏

4.3.3 Sharpening Filters

The principal objective of sharpening is to highlight fine detail in an image or to enhance detail that has been blurred, either in error or as a natural effect of a particular method of image acquisition. Uses of image sharpening vary and include applications ranging from electronic printing and medical imaging to industrial inspection and autonomous target detection in smart weapons.

Basic highpass spatial filtering
The shape of the impulse response needed to implement a highpass (sharpening) spatial filter indicates that the filter should have positive coefficients near its center, and negative coefficients in the outer periphery (see Fig. 4.19b). For a 3 × 3 mask, choosing a positive value in the center location with negative coefficients in the rest of the mask meets this condition.

Figure 4.24 shows the classic implementation of a 3 × 3 sharpening filter. Note that the sum of the coefficients is 0. Thus when the mask is over an area of constant or slowly varying gray level, the output of the mask is zero or very small (see Eq. 4.3-1). This result is consistent with what is expected from the corresponding frequency domain filter shown in Fig. 4.19(b). Note also that this filter eliminates the zero-frequency term. From the discussion in Section 3.3.6, recall that eliminating this term reduces the average gray-level value in the image to zero, reducing significantly the global contrast of the image. Figure 4.25(b) shows the result of using the filter of Fig. 4.24 on the image of Fig. 4.25(a). The original image consists of fairly fine detail over a significant portion of slowly varying background levels. As expected, the result is characterized by somewhat enhanced edges over a rather dark background. Significantly better results can be obtained by using high-boost filtering which is discussed in the next section.

Reducing the average value of an image to zero implies that the image must have some negative gray levels. As we deal only with positive levels, the results

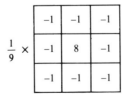

Figure 4.24   *A basic highpass spatial filter.*

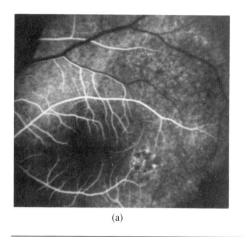
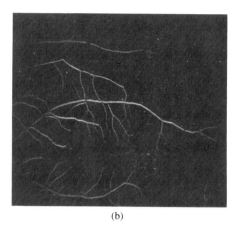

(a)   (b)

Figure 4.25   *(a) Image of a human retina; (b) highpass filtered result using the mask in Fig. 4.24.*

of highpass filtering involve some form of scaling and/or clipping so that the gray levels of the final result span the range $[0, L - 1]$. Taking the absolute value of the filtered image to make all values positive is usually not a good idea because large negative values would appear brightly in the image.

High-boost filtering

A highpass filtered image may be computed as the difference between the original image and a lowpass filtered version of that image; that is,

$$\text{Highpass} = \text{Original} - \text{Lowpass}. \tag{4.3-2}$$

As an exercise, it is instructive to verify the validity of this equation by using Eq. (4.3-1) in conjunction with Figs. 4.21(a) and 4.24. Multiplying the original image by an amplification factor, denoted by A, yields the definition of a *high-boost* or *high-frequency-emphasis* filter:

$$
\begin{aligned}
\text{High boost} &= (A)(\text{Original}) - \text{Lowpass} \\
&= (A - 1)(\text{Original}) + \text{Original} - \text{Lowpass} \\
&= (A - 1)(\text{Original}) + \text{Highpass}.
\end{aligned}
\tag{4.3-3}
$$

An $A = 1$ value yields the standard highpass result. When $A > 1$, part of the original is added back to the highpass result, which restores partially the low-frequency components lost in the highpass filtering operation. The result is that the high-boost image looks more like the original image, with a relative degree of edge enhancement that depends on the value of A. The general process of subtracting a blurred image from an original, as given in the first line of Eq.

(4.3-3), is called *unsharp masking*. This method is one of the basic tools for image processing applications in the printing and publishing industry.

In terms of implementation, the preceding results can be combined by letting the center weight of the mask shown in Fig. 4.26 be

$$w = 9A - 1 \qquad (4.3\text{-}4)$$

with $A \geq 1$. The value of A determines the nature of the filter.

Example: Figure 4.27 shows the original image of Fig. 4.25(a) and high-boost filtering results for $A = 1.1, 1.15$, and 1.2. The advantage of using high-boost filtering over classical highpass filtering is vividly demonstrated by comparing the results in Figs. 4.27 with those of Fig. 4.25. Note, in particular, that the result with $A = 1.1$ which, as previously indicated, is the same as adding 0.1 of the original to the basic highpass result, is a considerable improvement over the result shown in Fig. 4.25(b). As A increases, the background of the high-boost result becomes brighter. In fact, the result for $A = 1.2$ is on the verge of being unacceptable. Note also that noise plays a significant role in the visual appearance of the image that has been high-boost filtered. This result is not unexpected, because highpass filtering enhances noise, along with other sharp intensity transitions in an image. High-boost filtering simply increases that effect. ❏

As in the case of lowpass spatial filters, specifying highpass spatial filters of sizes greater than those discussed so far is possible. For instance, a basic 7×7 highpass filter would have a center weight of 48, the rest of the coefficients would be -1, and the normalizing factor would be 1/49. In practice, however, highpass filters larger than 3×3 seldom are needed.

Derivative filters

Averaging of pixels over a region tends to blur detail in an image. As averaging is analogous to integration, differentiation can be expected to have the opposite effect and thus sharpen an image.

$$\frac{1}{9} \times \begin{array}{|c|c|c|} \hline -1 & -1 & -1 \\ \hline -1 & w & -1 \\ \hline -1 & -1 & -1 \\ \hline \end{array}$$

Figure 4.26 *Mask used for high-boost spatial filtering. The value of the center weight is w = 9A − 1, with A ≥ 1.*

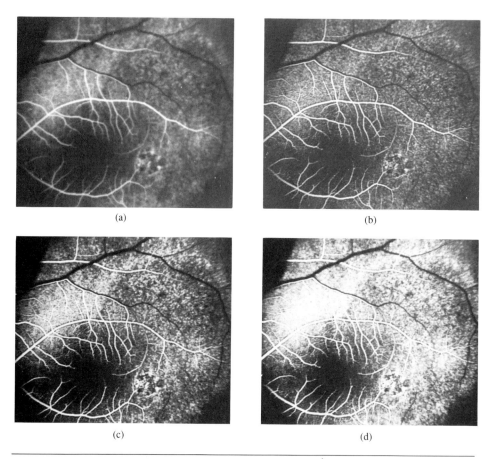

(a)

(b)

(c)

(d)

Figure 4.27   *(a) Original image; (b)–(d) result of high-boost filtering using the mask in Fig. 4.26, with A = 1.1, 1.15, and 1.2, respectively. Compare these results with those shown in Fig. 4.25.*

The most common method of differentiation in image processing applications is the gradient. For a function $f(x, y)$, the gradient of f at coordinates (x, y) is defined as the vector

$$\nabla \mathbf{f} = \begin{bmatrix} \dfrac{\partial f}{\partial x} \\[2mm] \dfrac{\partial f}{\partial y} \end{bmatrix}$$

(4.3-5)

The magnitude of this vector,

$$\nabla f = \mathrm{mag}(\nabla \mathbf{f}) = \left[\left(\frac{\partial f}{\partial x}\right)^2 + \left(\frac{\partial f}{\partial y}\right)^2\right]^{1/2} \tag{4.3-6}$$

is the basis for various approaches to image differentiation. Consider the image region shown in Fig. 4.28(a), where the z's denote the values of gray levels. Equation (4.3-6) can be approximated *at point* z_5 in a number of ways. The simplest is to use the difference $(z_5 - z_8)$ in the x direction and $(z_5 - z_6)$ in the y direction, combined as

$$\nabla f \approx [(z_5 - z_8)^2 + (z_5 - z_6)^2]^{1/2}. \tag{4.3-7a}$$

Instead of using squares and square roots, we can obtain similar results by using absolute values:

$$\nabla f \approx |z_5 - z_8| + |z_5 - z_6| \tag{4.3-7b}$$

Another approach for approximating Eq. (4.3-6) is to use cross differences:

$$\nabla f \approx [(z_5 - z_9)^2 + (z_6 - z_8)^2]^{1/2} \tag{4.3-8a}$$

or, using absolute values,

$$\nabla f \approx |z_5 - z_9| + |z_6 - z_8|. \tag{4.3-8b}$$

Equations (4.3-7) and (4.3-8) can be implemented by using masks of size 2×2. For example, Eq. (4.3-8b) can be implemented by taking the absolute value of the response of the two masks shown in Fig. 4.28(b) and summing the results. These masks are called the *Roberts cross-gradient operators*.

Masks of even sizes are awkward to implement. An approximation to Eq. (4.3-6), still at point z_5 but now using a 3×3 neighborhood, is

$$\nabla f \approx |(z_7 + z_8 + z_9) - (z_1 + z_2 + z_3)|$$
$$+ |(z_3 + z_6 + z_9) - (z_1 + z_4 + z_7)|. \tag{4.3-9}$$

The difference between the third and first row of the 3×3 region approximates the derivative in the x direction, and the difference between the third and first column approximates the derivative in the y direction. The masks shown in Fig. 4.28(c), called the *Prewitt operators*, can be used to implement Eq. (4.3-9). Finally, Fig. 4.28(d) shows yet another pair of masks (called the *Sobel operators*) for approximating the magnitude of the gradient. We discuss Sobel operators further in Section 7.1.

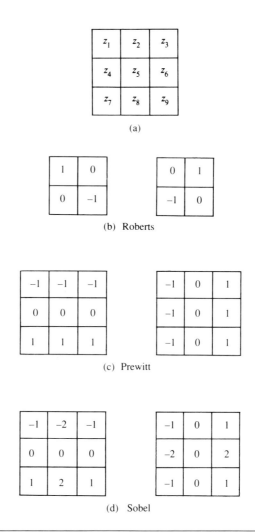

Figure 4.28   *A 3 × 3 region of an image (the z's are gray-level values) and various masks used to compute the derivative at point labeled z_5. Note that all mask coefficients sum to 0, indicating a response of 0 in constant areas, as expected of a derivative operator.*

Example: Figure 4.29(a) shows an original image, and Fig. 4.29(b) shows the result of computing the magnitude of the gradient by using the Prewitt masks (Eq. 4.3-9). Figure 4.29(c) was obtained by setting to maximum white (255) any gradient value greater than 25 (that is, approximately 10 percent or higher of the highest possible gray-level value in the image). Any point for which the gradient value did not meet this criterion was set equal to its original value in the image, thus restoring the background while, at the same time, enhancing

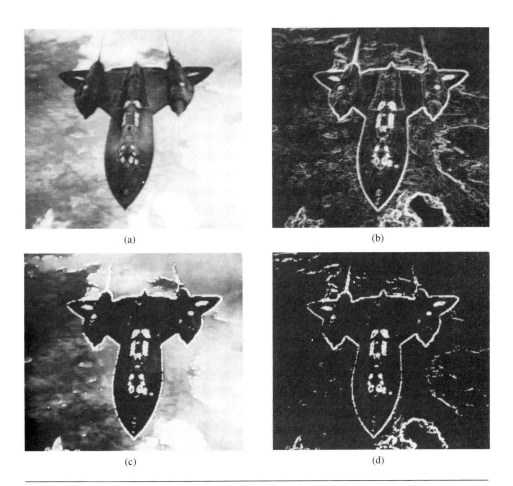

(a)

(b)

(c)

(d)

Figure 4.29   *Edge enhancement by gradient techniques (see text).*

prominent edges. Finally, Fig. 4.29(d) was obtained in the same way as Fig. 4.29(c), except that points for which the gradient did not exceed 25 were set to zero (black). Clearly, this last result produced a binary image. In all cases, the principal edges are enhanced considerably.   ❏

4.4   ENHANCEMENT IN THE FREQUENCY DOMAIN

In terms of the discussion in Section 4.1.2, enhancement in the frequency domain in principle is straightforward. We simply compute the Fourier transform of the image to be enhanced, multiply the result by a filter transfer function, and take the inverse transform to produce the enhanced image.

The ideas of blurring by reduction of high-frequency content or of sharpening by increasing the magnitude of high-frequency components relative to low-frequency components come from concepts directly related to the Fourier transform. In fact, the whole idea of linear filtering is considerably more appealing and intuitive in the frequency domain. In practice, small spatial masks are used considerably more than the Fourier transform because of their simplicity of implementation and speed of operation. However, an understanding of frequency domain concepts is essential to the solution of many problems not easily addressable by spatial techniques. The homomorphic filtering approach discussed in this section, and several image restoration techniques discussed in Chapter 5, are examples of this.

4.4.1 Lowpass Filtering

As indicated earlier, edges and other sharp transitions (such as noise) in the gray levels of an image contribute significantly to the high-frequency content of its Fourier transform. Hence blurring (smoothing) is achieved in the frequency domain by attenuating a specified range of high-frequency components in the transform of a given image.

From Eq. (4.1-4),

$$G(u, v) = H(u, v)F(u, v) \qquad (4.4\text{-}1)$$

where $F(u, v)$ is the Fourier transform of an image to be smoothed. The problem is to select a filter transfer function $H(u, v)$ that yields $G(u, v)$ by attenuating the high-frequency components of $F(u, v)$. The inverse transform then will yield the desired smoothed image $g(x, y)$. In the following discussion we consider filter transfer functions that affect the real and imaginary parts of $F(u, v)$ in exactly the same manner. Such filters are referred to as *zero-phase-shift filters* because they do not alter the phase of the transform.

Ideal filter

A 2-D ideal lowpass filter (ILPF) is one whose transfer function satisfies the relation

$$H(u, v) = \begin{cases} 1 & \text{if } D(u, v) \leqslant D_0 \\ 0 & \text{if } D(u, v) > D_0 \end{cases} \qquad (4.4\text{-}2)$$

where D_0 is a specified nonnegative quantity, and $D(u, v)$ is the distance from point (u, v) to the origin of the frequency plane; that is,

$$D(u, v) = (u^2 + v^2)^{1/2}. \qquad (4.4\text{-}3)$$

Figure 4.30(a) shows a 3-D perspective plot of $H(u, v)$ as a function of u and v. The name *ideal* filter indicates that *all* frequencies inside a circle of radius

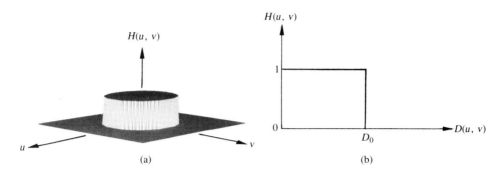

Figure 4.30 (a) Perspective plot of an ideal lowpass filter transfer function; (b) filter cross section.

D_0 are passed with no attenuation, whereas *all* frequencies outside this circle are completely attenuated.

The lowpass filters considered in this chapter are radially symmetric about the origin. For this type of filter, specifying a cross section extending as a function of distance from the origin along a radial line is sufficient, as Fig. 4.30(b) shows. The complete filter transfer function can then be generated by rotating the cross section 360° about the origin. Specification of radially symmetric filters centered on the $N \times N$ frequency square is based on the assumption that the origin of the Fourier transform has been centered on the square, as discussed in Section 3.3.2.

For an ideal lowpass filter cross section, the point of transition between $H(u, v) = 1$ and $H(u, v) = 0$ is often called the *cutoff frequency*. In the case of Fig. 4.30(b), for example, the cutoff frequency is D_0. As the cross section is rotated about the origin, the point D_0 traces a circle giving a locus of cutoff frequencies, all of which are a distance D_0 from the origin. The cutoff frequency concept is quite useful in specifying filter characteristics. It also serves as a common base for comparing the behavior of different types of filters.

The sharp cutoff frequencies of an ideal lowpass filter cannot be realized with electronic components, although they can certainly be simulated in a computer. The effects of using these "nonphysical" filters on a digital image are discussed after the following example.

Example: Figure 4.31(a) shows an image of a European hornet eating the pulp of a ripe plum. This figure was chosen to illustrate the lowpass filters discussed in this section because of its variety of detail, from fine (the hairs surrounding the head) to coarse (the antennas and other similar dark structures around the head). Note in particular the white dot in the middle top part of the head, the reflections off the antennas, and the small indentations in the frontal part of the head.

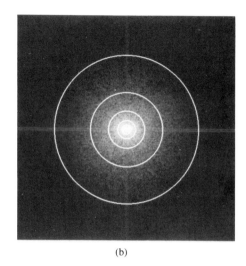

(a)   (b)

Figure 4.31   (a) 512 × 512 image and (b) its Fourier spectrum. The superimposed circles, which have radii equal to 8, 18, 43, 78, and 152, enclose 90, 93, 95, 99, and 99.5 percent of the image power, respectively.

The performance of all lowpass filters introduced in this section are compared by using the same cutoff frequency loci. One way to establish a set of standard loci is to compute circles that enclose various amounts of the total signal power P_T. This quantity is obtained by summing the power at each point (u, v) for $u, v = 0, 1, \ldots, N - 1$; that is,

$$P_T = \sum_{u=0}^{N-1} \sum_{v=0}^{N-1} P(u, v)$$

where $P(u, v)$ is given by Eq. (3.1-13). If the transform has been centered, a circle of radius r with origin at the center of the frequency square encloses β percent of the power, where

$$\beta = 100\left[\sum_{u} \sum_{v} P(u, v)/P_T\right]$$

and the summation is taken over values of (u, v) which lie inside the circle or on its boundary.

Figure 4.31(b) shows the Fourier spectrum of Fig. 4.31(a). The circles superimposed on the spectrum have radii of 8, 18, 43, 78, and 152. These circles enclose β percent of the power for $\beta = 90, 93, 95, 99$, and 99.5, respectively.

The spectrum falls off rapidly, with 90 percent of the total power being enclosed by a relatively small circle of radius 8.

Figure 4.32 shows the results of applying ideal lowpass filters with cutoff frequencies at the radii given earlier. Figure 4.32(a) is useless for all practical purposes. The severe blurring in this image is a clear indication that most of the sharp detail information in the picture is contained in the 10 percent power removed by the filter. As the filter radius increases, less and less high-frequency energy is removed, resulting in less severe blurring. However, even with only 5 percent of the energy removed, the blurred image is still characterized by severe *ringing,* a property of ideal filters. The image with only 1 percent of the energy removed by the filter exhibits a mild degree of blurring, as is evident by comparing the reflection off the antennas and the dot in the top of the head with the same features in Fig. 4.32(a). Finally, the result for $\beta = 99.5$ is essentially the same as the original, indicating that little edge and other sharp detail information is contained in the upper 0.5 percent power of the spectrum in this particular case. ◻

The blurring and ringing properties of the ILPF can be easily explained by reference to the convolution theorem. Because the Fourier transforms of the original and blurred images are related in the frequency domain by the equation

$$G(u, v) = H(u, v)F(u, v)$$

use of the convolution theorem leads to the following expression in the spatial domain:

$$g(x, y) = h(x, y)*f(x, y)$$

where $h(x, y)$ is the inverse Fourier transform of the filter transfer function $H(u, v)$.

The key to understanding blurring as a convolution process in the spatial domain lies in the nature of $h(x, y)$. For an ILPF, $h(x, y)$ has the general form shown in Fig. 4.33(a).[†] Suppose that $f(x, y)$ is a simple image composed of two bright pixels on a black background, as Fig. 4.33(b) shows. The two bright points may be viewed as approximations of two impulses whose strength depends on the brightness of these points. Then, the convolution of $h(x, y)$ and $f(x, y)$ is simply a process of "copying" $h(x, y)$ at the location of each impulse, as explained in Section 3.3.8. The result of this operation, shown in Fig. 4.33(c), explains how the two original points are blurred as a consequence of convolving

---

[†] This general form is easily verified by taking the inverse Fourier transform of Eq. (4.4-2).

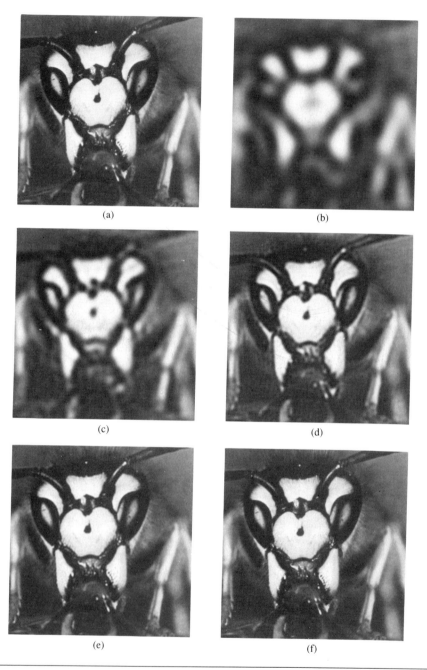

(a)

(b)

(c)

(d)

(e)

(f)

Figure 4.32 (a) Original image; (b)–(f) results of ideal lowpass filtering with the cutoff frequency set at the radii shown in Fig. 4.31(b).

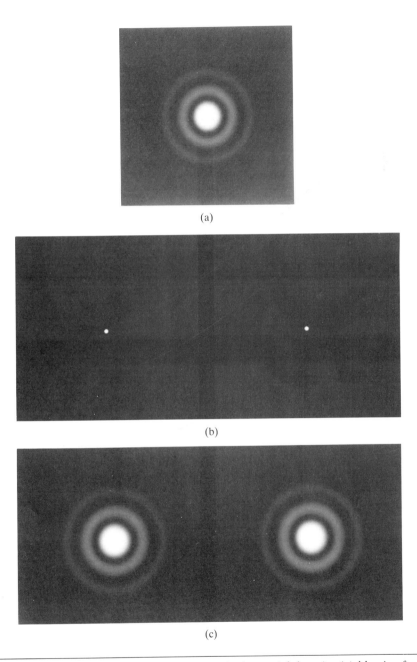

Figure 4.33 *Illustration of the blurring process in the spatial domain: (a) blurring function h(x, y) for an ideal lowpass filter; (b) a simple image composed of two bright dots; (c) convolution of h(x, y) and f(x, y).*

$f(x, y)$ with the blurring function $h(x, y)$. These concepts are extended to more complex images by considering each pixel as an impulse with a strength proportional to the gray level of the pixel.

The shape of $h(x, y)$ depends on the radius of the filter function in the frequency domain. Computing the inverse transform of $H(u, v)$ for an ILPF shows that the radii of the concentric rings in $h(x, y)$ are inversely proportional to the value of D_0 in Eq. (4.4-2). Thus severe filtering in the frequency domain (that is, choice of a small D_0) produces a relatively small number of broad rings in $h(x, y)$ and, consequently, pronounced blurring in $g(x, y)$. As D_0 increases, the number of rings in a region increases, thus producing more finely spaced rings and less blurring. This effect can be observed by comparing Figs. 4.32(d) and (e). If D_0 is outside the domain of definition of $F(u, v)$, $h(x, y)$ becomes 1 in its corresponding spatial region, and the convolution of $h(x, y)$ and $f(x, y)$ is simply $f(x, y)$. This situation, of course, corresponds to no filtering at all. The spatial domain effect of the Butterworth filter discussed in the following section can be explained in a similar manner.

Butterworth filter

The transfer function of the Butterworth lowpass filter (BLPF) of order n and with cutoff frequency locus at a distance D_0 from the origin is defined by the relation

$$H(u, v) = \frac{1}{1 + [D(u, v)/D_0]^{2n}} \tag{4.4-4}$$

where $D(u, v)$ is given by Eq. (4.4-3). A perspective plot and cross section of the BLPF function are shown in Fig. 4.34.

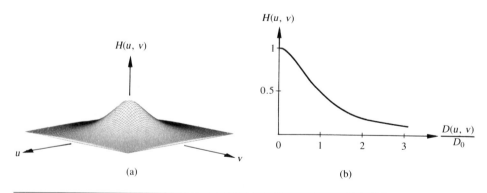

(a)   (b)

Figure 4.34   *(a) A Butterworth lowpass filter; (b) radial cross section for $n = 1$.*

Unlike the ILPF, the BLPF transfer function does not have a sharp discontinuity that establishes a clear cutoff between passed and filtered frequencies. For filters with smooth transfer functions, defining a cutoff frequency locus at points for which $H(u, v)$ is down to a certain fraction of its maximum value is customary. In the case of Eq. (4.4-4), $H(u, v) = 0.5$ (down 50 percent from its maximum value of 1) when $D(u, v) = D_0$. Another value commonly used is $1/\sqrt{2}$ of the maximum value of $H(u, v)$. For Eq. (4.4-4), the following simple modification yields the desired value when $D(u, v) = D_0$:

$$H(u, v) = \frac{1}{1 + [\sqrt{2} - 1][D(u, v)/D_0]^{2n}}$$

$$= \frac{1}{1 + 0.414[D(u, v)/D_0]^{2n}}. \qquad (4.4\text{-}5)$$

Example: Figure 4.35 shows the results of applying BLPFs (Eq. 4.4-5) to Fig. 4.31(a), with $n = 1$ and D_0 equal to the five radii shown in Fig. 4.31(b). Unlike the results shown in Fig. 4.32, we note here a smooth transition in blurring as a function of the amount of power removed from the spectrum. Moreover, no ringing is evident in any of the images processed with the BLPF, a fact attributed to the filter's smooth transition between low and high frequencies. ❑

The lowpass filtering results given thus far have been with images of good quality in order to illustrate and compare filter effects. Figure 4.36 shows two practical applications of lowpass filtering for image smoothing. The image shown in Fig. 4.36(a) was digitized with only 16 gray levels and, as a consequence, exhibits a considerable amount of false contouring. Figure 4.36(b) is the result of smoothing this image with a lowpass Butterworth filter of order 1. Similarly, Fig. 4.36(d) shows the effect of applying a BLPF to the noisy image of Fig. 4.36(c). We see from these examples that lowpass filtering is a cosmetic process that reduces spurious effects at the expense of image sharpness.

4.4.2 Highpass Filtering

In Section 4.4.1 we showed that an image can be blurred by attenuating the high-frequency components of its Fourier transform. Because edges and other abrupt changes in gray levels are associated with high-frequency components, image sharpening can be achieved in the frequency domain by a *highpass filtering* process, which attenuates the low-frequency components without disturbing high-frequency information in the Fourier transform. In discussing the high-frequency counterparts of the filters developed in Section 4.4.1, we

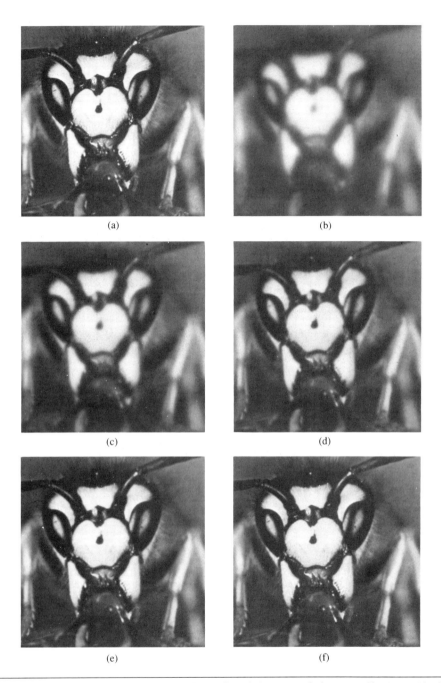

(a)

(b)

(c)

(d)

(e)

(f)

Figure 4.35 *(a) Original image; (b)–(f) results of Butterworth lowpass filtering with the cutoff point set at the radii shown in Fig. 4.31(b).*

(a)

(b)

(c)

(d)

Figure 4.36 *Two examples of image smoothing by lowpass filtering (see text).*

consider only zero-phase-shift filters that are radially symmetric and can be completely specified by a cross section extending as a function of distance from the origin of the centered Fourier transform.

Ideal filter

A 2-D ideal highpass filter (IHPF) is one whose transfer function satisfies the relation

$$H(u, v) = \begin{cases} 0 & \text{if } D(u, v) \leq D_0 \\ 1 & \text{if } D(u, v) > D_0 \end{cases} \qquad (4.4\text{-}6)$$

where D_0 is the cutoff distance measured from the origin of the frequency plane, and $D(u, v)$ is given by Eq. (4.4-3). Figure 4.37 shows a perspective plot and cross section of the IHPF function. This filter is the opposite of the ideal lowpass filter discussed in Section 4.4.1 because it completely attenuates all frequencies inside a circle of radius D_0 while passing, without attenuation, all frequencies outside the circle. As in the case of the ideal lowpass filter, the IHPF is not physically realizable.

Butterworth filter

The transfer function of the Butterworth highpass filter (BHPF) of order n and with cutoff frequency locus at a distance D_0 from the origin is defined by the relation

$$H(u, v) = \frac{1}{1 + [D_0/D(u, v)]^{2n}} \qquad (4.4\text{-}7)$$

where $D(u, v)$ is given by Eq. (4.4-3). Figure 4.38 shows a perspective plot and cross section of the BHPF function.

Note that when $D(u, v) = D_0$, $H(u, v)$ is down to $\frac{1}{2}$ of its maximum value. As in the case of the Butterworth lowpass filter, common practice is to select the cutoff frequency locus at points for which $H(u, v)$ is down to $1/\sqrt{2}$ of its maximum value. Equation (4.4-7) is easily modified to satisfy this constraint by using the following scaling:

$$\begin{aligned} H(u, v) &= \frac{1}{1 + [\sqrt{2} - 1][D_0/D(u, v)]^{2n}} \\ &= \frac{1}{1 + 0.414[D_0/D(u, v)]^{2n}}. \end{aligned} \qquad (4.4\text{-}8)$$

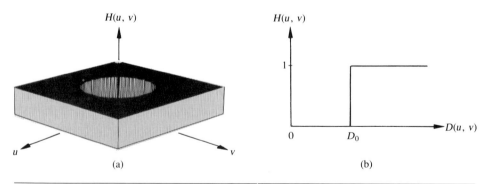

Figure 4.37 *Perspective plot and radial cross section of ideal highpass filter.*

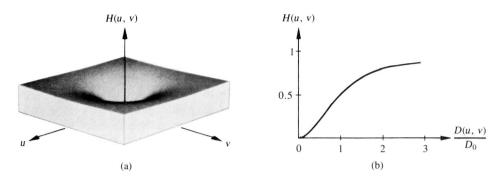

$H(u, v)$

$H(u, v)$

1

0.5

0   1   2   3

$\dfrac{D(u, v)}{D_0}$

(a)

(b)

Figure 4.38 *Perspective plot and radial cross section of Butterworth highpass filter for n =*
1.

Example: Figure 4.39(a) shows a chest x-ray that was poorly developed, and
Fig. 4.39(b) shows the image after it was processed with a highpass Butterworth
filter of order 1. Only the edges are predominant in this image because the
low-frequency components were severely attenuated, thus making different (but
smooth) gray-level regions appear essentially the same.

A technique often used to alleviate this problem consists of adding a constant to a highpass filter transfer function in order to preserve the low-frequency
components. This addition, of course, amplifies the high-frequency components
to values that are higher than in the original transform. This technique, called
high-frequency emphasis, is illustrated in Fig. 4.39(c). Note that the image in
this case has a little better tonality, particularly in the lower left part of the
photograph. This process is analogous to the high-boost filter discussed in
Section 4.3.3.

Although high-frequency emphasis preserves the low-frequency components, the proportionally larger high-frequency terms tend to obscure the result,
as shown by the small gain in quality from Fig. 4.39(b) to Fig. 4.39(c). A
technique often used to compensate for this problem is postfiltering processing
to redistribute the gray levels. Histogram equalization is ideally suited for this
purpose because of its ability to increase contrast. Figure 4.39(d) shows the
significant improvement that can be obtained by histogram equalization of an
image that has been processed by high-frequency emphasis.   ❏

4.4.3 Homomorphic Filtering

The illumination–reflectance model introduced in Section 2.2 can be used as
the basis for a frequency domain procedure that is useful for improving the
appearance of an image by simultaneous brightness range compression and

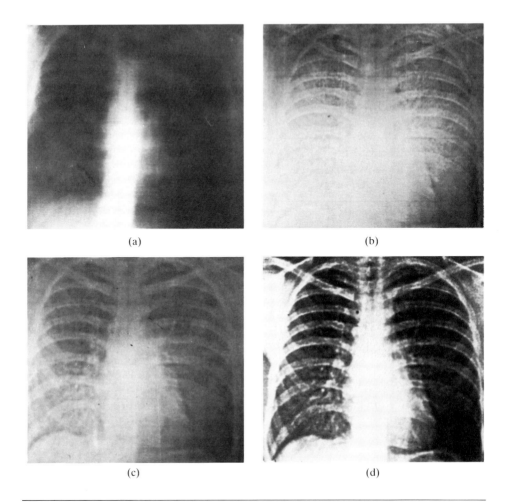

(a)   (b)

(c)   (d)

Figure 4.39 *Example of highpass filtering: (a) original image; (b) image processed with a highpass Butterworth filter; (c) result of high-frequency emphasis; (d) high-frequency emphasis and histogram equalization. (From Hall et al. [1971].)*

contrast enhancement. From the discussion in Section 2.2, an image $f(x, y)$ can be expressed in terms of its illumination and reflectance components by means of the relation

$$f(x, y) = i(x, y)r(x, y). \tag{4.4-9}$$

Equation (4.4-9) cannot be used directly in order to operate separately on the frequency components of illumination and reflectance because the Fourier transform of the product of two functions is not separable; in other words,

$$\mathfrak{F}\{f(x, y)\} \neq \mathfrak{F}\{i(x, y)\}\mathfrak{F}\{r(x, y)\}.$$

Suppose, however, that we define

$$z(x, y) = \ln f(x, y) \tag{4.4-10}$$
$$= \ln i(x, y) + \ln r(x, y).$$

Then,

$$\mathfrak{F}\{z(x, y)\} = \mathfrak{F}\{\ln f(x, y)\} \tag{4.4-11}$$
$$= \mathfrak{F}\{\ln i(x, y)\} + \mathfrak{F}\{\ln r(x, y)\}$$

or

$$Z(u, v) = I(u, v) + R(u, v) \tag{4.4-12}$$

where $I(u, v)$ and $R(u, v)$ are the Fourier transforms of $\ln i(x, y)$ and $\ln r(x, y)$, respectively.

If we process $Z(u, v)$ by means of a filter function $H(u, v)$ then, from Eq. (4.1-4),

$$S(u, v) = H(u, v)Z(u, v) \tag{4.4-13}$$
$$= H(u, v)I(u, v) + H(u, v)R(u, v)$$

where $S(u, v)$ is the Fourier transform of the result. In the spatial domain,

$$s(x, y) = \mathfrak{F}^{-1}\{S(u, v)\} \tag{4.4-14}$$
$$= \mathfrak{F}^{-1}\{H(u, v)I(u, v)\} + \mathfrak{F}^{-1}\{H(u, v)R(u, v)\}.$$

By letting

$$i'(x, y) = \mathfrak{F}^{-1}\{H(u, v)I(u, v)\} \tag{4.4-15}$$

and

$$r'(x, y) = \mathfrak{F}^{-1}\{H(u, v)R(u, v)\} \tag{4.4-16}$$

Eq. (4.4-14) can be expressed in the form

$$s(x, y) = i'(x, y) + r'(x, y). \tag{4.4-17}$$

Finally, as $z(x, y)$ was formed by taking the logarithm of the original image $f(x, y)$, the inverse operation yields the desired enhanced image $g(x, y)$; that is,

$$g(x, y) = \exp[s(x, y)]$$
$$= \exp[i'(x, y)] \cdot \exp[r'(x, y)] \qquad (4.4\text{-}18)$$
$$= i_0(x, y)r_0(x, y)$$

where

$$i_0(x, y) = \exp[i'(x, y)] \qquad (4.4\text{-}19)$$

and

$$r_0(x, y) = \exp[r'(x, y)] \qquad (4.4\text{-}20)$$

are the illumination and reflectance components of the output image.

The enhancement approach using the foregoing concepts is summarized in Fig. 4.40. This method is based on a special case of a class of systems known as *homomorphic systems*. In this particular application, the key to the approach is that separation of the illumination and reflectance components is achieved in the form shown in Eq. (4.4-12). The *homomorphic filter function* $H(u, v)$ can then operate on these components separately, as indicated in Eq. (4.4-13).

The illumination component of an image is generally characterized by slow spatial variations, while the reflectance component tends to vary abruptly, particularly at the junctions of dissimilar objects. These characteristics lead to associating the low frequencies of the Fourier transform of the logarithm of an image with illumination and the high frequencies with reflectance. Although these associations are rough approximations, they can be used to advantage in image enhancement.

A good deal of control can be gained over the illumination and reflectance components with a homomorphic filter. This control requires specification of a filter function $H(u, v)$ that affects the low- and high-frequency components of the Fourier transform in different ways. Figure 4.41 shows a cross section of such a function. A complete specification of $H(u, v)$ is obtained by rotating the cross section 360° about the vertical axis. If the parameters γ_L and γ_H are chosen so that $\gamma_L < 1$ and $\gamma_H > 1$, the filter function shown in Fig. 4.41 tends

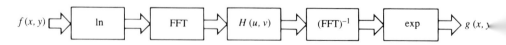

Figure 4.40 *Homomorphic filtering approach for image enhancement.*

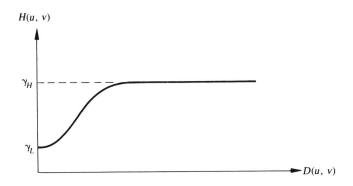

Figure 4.41 *Cross section of a circularly symmetric filter function for use in homomorphic filtering. D(u, v) is the distance from the origin.*

to decrease the low frequencies and amplify the high frequencies. The net result is simultaneous dynamic range compression and contrast enhancement.

Example: Figure 4.42 is typical of the results that can be obtained with the homomorphic filter function shown in Fig. 4.41. In the original image, Fig. 4.42(a), the details inside the room are obscured by the glare from the outside walls. Figure 4.42(b) shows the result of processing this image by homomorphic

(a)   (b)

Figure 4.42 *(a) Original image; (b) image processed by homomorphic filtering to achieve simultaneous dynamic range compression and contrast enhancement. (From Stockham [1972].)*

filtering, with $\gamma_L = 0.5$ and $\gamma_H = 2.0$ in the above filter function. A reduction of dynamic range in the brightness, together with an increase in contrast, brought out the details of objects inside the room and balanced the gray levels of the outside wall.   ❏

4.5 GENERATION OF SPATIAL MASKS FROM FREQUENCY DOMAIN SPECIFICATIONS

As indicated in Section 4.1, speed and simplicity of implementation are important features of spatial masks in image processing. In this section we develop a method for generating spatial masks that approximate (in a least square error sense) a given frequency domain filter.

Recall from Section 4.1 that the filtering process in the frequency domain is based on the equation

$$G(u, v) = H(u, v)F(u, v) \tag{4.5-1}$$

where $F(u, v)$ and $G(u, v)$ are the Fourier transforms of the input and output images, respectively, and $H(u, v)$ is the filter transfer function. From the convolution theorem (Section 3.3.8), we know that Eq. (4.5-1) can be implemented in the spatial domain by the expression

$$g(x, y) = \sum_{i=0}^{N-1} \sum_{k=0}^{N-1} h(x - i, y - k)f(i, k) \tag{4.5-2}$$

with $x, y = 0, 1, 2, \ldots, N - 1$. For simplicity in notation, the use of square image arrays is assumed. Moreover, we assume that all functions have been properly extended, as discussed in Section 3.3.8 regarding convolution.

In Eq. (4.5-2), h is the spatial representation of the filter (that is, the inverse Fourier transform of $H(u, v)$), f is the input image, and g is the filtered image. As discussed in Section 4.1.2, the term h often is referred to as a *spatial convolution mask*. If this mask is of size $N \times N$, the result given in Eq. (4.5-2) is identical to taking the inverse Fourier transform of $G(u, v)$ in Eq. (4.5-1).

As H is the Fourier transform of h, it follows from Eq. (3.2-9) that

$$H(u, v) = \frac{1}{N} \sum_{x=0}^{N-1} \sum_{y=0}^{N-1} h(x, y)\exp[-j2\pi(ux + vy)/N] \tag{4.5-3}$$

for $u, v = 0, 1, 2, \ldots, N - 1$. Suppose, however, that $h(x, y)$ is restricted to zero for values of $x > n$ and $y > n$, with $n < N$. This restriction in effect creates an $n \times n$ convolution mask $\hat{h}$ with Fourier transform

$$\hat{H}(u, v) = \frac{1}{N} \sum_{x=0}^{n-1} \sum_{y=0}^{n-1} \hat{h}(x, y) \exp[-j2\pi(ux + vy)/N] \tag{4.5-4}$$

for $u, v = 0, 1, 2, \ldots, N - 1$. The objective in the following discussion is to find the coefficients of $\hat{h}(x, y)$ so that the error quantity

$$e^2 = \sum_{u=0}^{N-1} \sum_{v=0}^{N-1} |\hat{H}(u, v) - H(u, v)|^2 \tag{4.5-5}$$

is minimized, where $|\cdot|$ designates the complex magnitude.

Equation (4.5-4) can be expressed in matrix form:

$$\hat{\mathbf{H}} = \mathbf{C}\hat{\mathbf{h}} \tag{4.5-6}$$

where $\hat{\mathbf{H}}$ is a column vector of order N^2 containing the elements of $\hat{H}(u, v)$ in some order, $\hat{\mathbf{h}}$ is a column vector of order n^2 containing the elements of $\hat{h}(x, y)$ in some order, and $\mathbf{C}$ is an $N^2 \times n^2$ matrix of exponential terms whose positions are determined by the ordering in $\hat{\mathbf{H}}$ and $\hat{\mathbf{h}}$. A simple procedure for generating the elements $\hat{H}(i)$, $i = 0, 1, 2, \ldots, N^2 - 1$, of the vector $\hat{\mathbf{H}}$ from $\hat{H}(u, v)$ is

$$\hat{H}(u, v) \Rightarrow \hat{H}(i) \tag{4.5-7}$$

for $i = uN + v$, with $u, v = 0, 1, 2, \ldots, N - 1$. Stepping through the rows of $\hat{H}(u, v)$ by letting $u = 0, v = 0, 1, 2, \ldots, N - 1; u = 1, v = 0, 1, 2, \ldots, N - 1$; and so on, corresponds to forming the first N elements of $\hat{\mathbf{H}}$ from the first row of $\hat{H}(u, v)$, the next N elements from the second row, and so on. The elements of $\hat{\mathbf{h}}$, denoted $\hat{h}(k)$, $k = 0, 1, 2, \ldots, n^2 - 1$, are similarly formed by letting

$$\hat{h}(x, y) \Rightarrow \hat{h}(k) \tag{4.5-8}$$

for $k = xn + y$, with $x, y = 0, 1, 2, \ldots, n - 1$. Finally, the corresponding elements of the matrix $\mathbf{C}$, denoted $C(i, k)$, are generated from the exponential terms

$$\frac{1}{N} \exp[-j2\pi(ux + vy)/N] \Rightarrow C(i, k) \tag{4.5-9}$$

for $i = uN + v$ and $k = xn + y$, with $u, v = 0, 1, 2, \ldots, N - 1$, and $x, y = 0, 1, 2, \ldots, n - 1$.

In matrix notation, Eq. (4.5-5) becomes

$$
\begin{aligned}
e^2 &= (\hat{\mathbf{H}} - \mathbf{H})^*(\hat{\mathbf{H}} - \mathbf{H}) \\
&= \|\hat{\mathbf{H}} - \mathbf{H}\|^2 \\
&= \|\mathbf{C}\hat{\mathbf{h}} - \mathbf{H}\|^2
\end{aligned}
\qquad (4.5\text{-}10)
$$

where $*$ is the conjugate transpose, $\|\cdot\|$ is the complex Euclidean norm, and $\mathbf{H}$ is a vector formed from $H(u, v)$, as previously explained. Taking the partial derivative and equating it to the zero vector yields the minimum of e^2 with

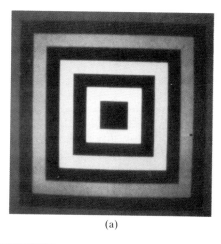

(a)

(b)

(c)

Figure 4.43   *(a) Original image; (b) blurred image obtained with a Butterworth lowpass filter of order 1 in the frequency domain; (c) image blurred spatially by a 9 × 9 convolution mask obtained using Eq. (4.5-12). (From Meyer and Gonzalez [1983].)*

respect to $\hat{\mathbf{h}}$:

$$\frac{\partial e^2}{\partial \hat{\mathbf{h}}} = 2\mathbf{C}^*(\mathbf{C}\hat{\mathbf{h}} - \mathbf{H}) = \mathbf{0} \qquad (4.5\text{-}11)$$

or

$$\hat{\mathbf{h}} = (\mathbf{C}^*\mathbf{C})^{-1}\mathbf{C}^*\mathbf{H} \qquad (4.5\text{-}12)$$
$$= \mathbf{C}^{\#}\mathbf{H}$$

where the matrix $\mathbf{C}^{\#} = (\mathbf{C}^*\mathbf{C})^{-1}\mathbf{C}^*$ often is called the *Moore–Penrose generalized inverse* (Noble [1969]).

Equation (4.5-12) yields the necessary minimum-error coefficients to construct an $n \times n$ convolution mask $\hat{h}(x, y)$ from a specified $N \times N$ filter function $H(u, v)$ in the frequency domain. In general, the elements of $\hat{h}(x, y)$ are complex quantities. However, if the frequency domain filter function is real and symmetric (like all the filters discussed in this chapter), $\hat{h}(x, y)$ also is real and symmetric.

Example: As an illustration of the method just developed, the test pattern shown in Fig. 4.43(a) was filtered using a Butterworth lowpass filter to produce the blurred image shown in Fig. 4.43(b). A 9×9 convolution mask was generated using Eq. (4.5-12) and applied to the original image. The result, shown in Fig. 4.43(c), is slightly less blurred than that obtained by using the complete filter in the frequency domain. This result is expected, because the spatial domain process with $n < N$ is only an approximation in the least square error sense. Other examples of this technique are given in Section 5.8. ❑

4.6 COLOR IMAGE PROCESSING

The use of color in image processing is motivated by two principal factors. First, in automated image analysis, color is a powerful descriptor that often simplifies object identification and extraction from a scene. Second, in image analysis performed by human beings, the motivation for color is that the human eye can discern thousands of color shades and intensities, compared to about only two-dozen shades of gray.

Color image processing is divided into two major areas: *full color* and *pseudo-color* processing. In the first category, the images in question typically are acquired with a full-color sensor, such as a color TV camera or color scanner. In the second category, the problem is one of assigning a shade of color to a particular monochrome intensity or range of intensities. Until relatively recently, most color image processing was done at the pseudo-color level. The significant progress made in the 1980's has made color sensors and hardware for processing color images available at reasonable prices. As a result of these advances, full-color image processing techniques are becoming significant in a broad range of applications.

4.6.1   Color Fundamentals

Although the process followed by the human brain in perceiving color is a physiopsychological phenomenon that is not yet fully understood, the physical nature of color can be expressed on a formal basis supported by experimental and theoretical results.

In 1666, Sir Isaac Newton discovered that when a beam of sunlight is passed through a glass prism the emerging beam of light is not white, but consists instead of a continuous spectrum of colors ranging from violet at one end to red at the other. As Plate I shows, the color spectrum may be divided into six broad regions: violet, blue, green, yellow, orange, and red. When viewed in full color (Plate II) no color in the spectrum ends abruptly, but rather each color blends smoothly into the next.

Basically, the colors that human beings perceive in an object are determined by the nature of the light reflected from the object. As illustrated in Plate II, visible light is composed of a relatively narrow band of frequencies in the electromagnetic energy spectrum. A body that reflects light that is relatively balanced in all visible wavelengths appears white to the observer. However, a body that favors reflectance in a limited range of the visible spectrum exhibits some shades of color. For example, green objects reflect light with wavelengths primarily in the 500 to 570 nm (10^{-9} m) range, while absorbing most of the energy at other wavelengths.

Characterization of light is central to the science of color. If the light is achromatic (void of color), its only attribute is its *intensity*, or amount. Achromatic light is what viewers see on a black and white television set, and it has been an implicit component of our discussion of image processing so far. Thus the term *gray level* refers to a scalar measure of intensity that ranges from black, to grays, and finally to white.

Chromatic light spans the electromagnetic energy spectrum from approximately 400 to 700 nm. Three basic quantities are used to describe the quality of a chromatic light source: radiance, luminance, and brightness. *Radiance* is the total amount of energy that flows from the light source, and it is usually measured in watts (W). *Luminance*, measured in lumens (lm), gives a measure of the amount of energy an observer *perceives* from a light source. For example, light emitted from a source operating in the far infrared region of the spectrum could have significant energy (radiance), but an observer would hardly perceive it; its luminance would be almost zero. Finally, *brightness* is a subjective descriptor that is practically impossible to measure. It embodies the achromatic notion of intensity and is one of the key factors in describing color sensation.

Owing to the structure of the human eye, all colors are seen as variable combinations of the three so-called *primary colors* red (R), green (G), and blue (B). For the purpose of standardization, the CIE (Commission Internationale de l'Eclairage—the International Commission on Illumination) designated in 1931 the following specific wavelength values to the three primary colors: blue = 435.8 nm, green = 546.1 nm, and red = 700 nm. Note from Plate II, however, that no single color may be called red, green, or blue. Thus, having three specific color wavelengths for the purpose of standardization does not mean that these three fixed RGB components acting alone can generate all spectrum colors. This realization is important, because use of the word *primary* has been widely misinterpreted to mean that the three standard primaries, when mixed in various intensity proportions, can produce all visible colors. This interpretation is not correct, unless the wavelength is also allowed to vary.

The primary colors can be added to produce the *secondary* colors of light— magenta (red plus blue), cyan (green plus blue), and yellow (red plus green). Mixing the three primaries, or a secondary with its opposite primary color, in the right intensities produces white light. This result is shown in Plate III(a), which also illustrates the three primary colors and their combinations to produce the secondary colors.

Differentiating between the primary colors of light and the primary colors of pigments or colorants is important. In the latter, a primary color is defined as one that subtracts or absorbs a primary color of light and reflects or transmits the other two. Therefore the primary colors of pigments are magenta, cyan, and yellow, and the secondary colors are red, green, and blue. These colors are shown in Plate III(b). A proper combination of the three pigment primaries, or a secondary with its opposite primary, produces black.

Color television reception is an example of the additive nature of light colors. The interior of many color TV tubes is composed of a large array of triangular dot patterns of electron-sensitive phosphor. When excited, each dot in a triad is capable of producing light in one of the primary colors. The intensity of the red-emitting phosphor dots is modulated by an electron gun inside the tube, which generates pulses corresponding to the "red energy" seen by the TV camera. The green and blue phosphor dots in each triad are modulated in the same manner. The effect, viewed on the television receiver, is that the three primary colors from each phosphor triad are "added" together and received by the color-sensitive cones in the eye, and a full-color image is perceived. Thirty successive image changes per second in all three colors complete the illusion of a continuous image display on the screen.

The characteristics generally used to distinguish one color from another are *brightness, hue,* and *saturation.* As already indicated, brightness embodies the chromatic notion of intensity. Hue is an attribute associated with the dominant wavelength in a mixture of light waves. Thus hue represents dominant color as perceived by an observer; when we call an object red, orange, or yellow we are specifying its hue. Saturation refers to relative purity or the amount of white light mixed with a hue. The pure spectrum colors are fully saturated. Colors such as pink (red and white) and lavender (violet and white) are less saturated, with the degree of saturation being inversely proportional to the amount of white light added.

Hue and saturation taken together are called *chromaticity,* and therefore, a color may be characterized by its brightness and chromaticity. The amounts of red, green, and blue needed to form any particular color are called the *tristimulus* values and are denoted, X, Y, and Z, respectively. A color is then specified by its *trichromatic coefficients,* defined as

$$x = \frac{X}{X + Y + Z} \qquad (4.6\text{-}1)$$

$$y = \frac{Y}{X + Y + Z} \qquad (4.6\text{-}2)$$

and

$$z = \frac{Z}{X + Y + Z}. \qquad (4.6\text{-}3)$$

Obviously, from these equations,

$$x + y + z = 1. \qquad (4.6\text{-}4)$$

For any wavelength of light in the visible spectrum, the tristimulus values needed to produce the color corresponding to that wavelength can be obtained directly from curves or tables that have been compiled from extensive experimental results (Walsh [1958], Kiver [1965]).

Another approach for specifying colors is the *chromaticity diagram* (Plate IV), which shows color composition as a function of x (red) and y (green). For any value of x and y, the corresponding value of z (blue) is obtained from Eq. (4.6-4) by noting that $z = 1 - (x + y)$. The point marked green in Plate IV, for example, has approximately 62 percent green and 25 percent red content. From Eq. (4.6-4) then, the composition of blue is approximately 13 percent.

The positions of the various spectrum colors—from violet at 380 nm to red at 780 nm—are indicated around the boundary of the tongue-shaped chromaticity diagram. These are the pure colors shown in the spectrum of Plate II. Any point not actually on the boundary but within the diagram represents some mixture of spectrum colors. The point of equal energy shown in Plate IV corresponds to equal fractions of the three primary colors; it represents the CIE standard for white light. Any point located on the boundary of the chromaticity chart is said to be completely saturated. As a point leaves the boundary and approaches the point of equal energy, more white light is added to the color and it becomes less saturated. The saturation at the point of equal energy is zero.

The chromaticity diagram is useful for color mixing because a straight-line segment joining any two points in the diagram defines all the different color variations that can be obtained by combining these two colors additively. Consider, for example, a straight line drawn from the red to the green points shown in Plate IV. If there is more red light than green light, the exact point representing the new color will be on the line segment, but it will be closer to the red point than to the green point. Similarly, a line drawn from the point of equal energy to any point on the boundary of the chart will define all the shades of that particular spectrum color.

Extension of this procedure to three colors is straightforward. To determine the range of colors that can be obtained from any three given colors in the chromaticity diagram, we simply draw connecting lines to each of the three color points. The result is a triangle, and any color inside the triangle can be produced by various combinations of the three initial colors. A triangle with vertices at any three *fixed* colors does not enclose the entire color region in Plate IV. This observation supports graphically the remark made earlier that not all colors can be obtained with three single primaries.

4.6.2 Color Models

The purpose of a color model is to facilitate the specification of colors in some standard, generally accepted way. In essence, a color model is a specification of a 3-D coordinate system and a subspace within that system where each color is represented by a single point.

Most color models in use today are oriented either toward hardware (such as for color monitors and printers) or toward applications where color manipulation is a goal (such as in the creation of color graphics for animation). The hardware-oriented models most commonly used in practice are the RGB (red, green, blue) model for color monitors and a broad class of color video cameras; the CMY (cyan, magenta, yellow) model for color printers; and the YIQ model, which is the standard for color TV broadcast. In the third model the Y corresponds to luminance, and I and Q are two chromatic components called *inphase,* and *quadrature,* respectively. Among the models frequently used for color image manipulation are the HSI (hue, saturation, intensity) model and the HSV (hue, saturation, value) model.

The color models most often used for image processing are the RGB, the YIQ, and the HSI[†] models. In the following sections we introduce the basic

---

[†] Although we use I in both the YIQ and HSI models for consistency with most of the published literature, keep in mind that this symbol means something very different in these two models.

features of these three models and discuss their differences and usefulness in digital image processing applications. Although the CMY model is used for printing, rather than for actual image processing, we also cover it here because of its importance in obtaining hard-copy outputs.

The RGB color model

In the RGB model, each color appears in its primary spectral components of red, green, and blue. This model is based on a Cartesian coordinate system. The color subspace of interest is the cube shown in Fig. 4.44, in which RGB values are at three corners; cyan, magenta, and yellow are at three other corners; black is at the origin; and white is at the corner farthest from the origin. In this model, the gray scale extends from black to white along the line joining these two points, and colors are points on or inside the cube, defined by vectors extending from the origin. For convenience, the assumption is that all color values have been normalized so that the cube shown in Fig. 4.44 is the unit cube. That is, all values of R, G, and B are assumed to be in the range [0, 1].

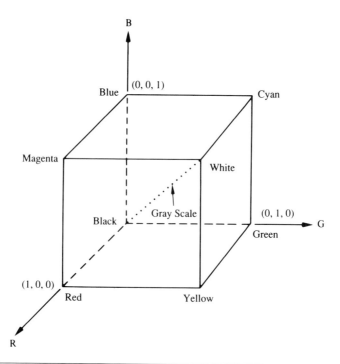

Figure 4.44 *RGB color cube. Points along the main diagonal have gray values, from black at the origin to white at point (1, 1, 1).*

Images in the RGB color model consist of three independent image planes, one for each primary color. When fed into an RGB monitor, these three images combine on the phosphor screen to produce a composite color image. Thus the use of the RGB model for image processing makes sense when the images themselves are naturally expressed in terms of three color planes. Alternatively, most color cameras used for acquiring digital images utilize the RGB format, which alone makes this an important model in image processing.

One of the best examples of the usefulness of the RGB model is in the processing of aerial and satellite multispectral image data. Images are obtained by imaging sensors operating in different spectral ranges. For instance, one frame of LANDSAT[†] imagery consists of four digital images. Each image is of the same scene, but taken through a different spectral range or *window*. Two of the windows are in the visible section of the spectrum, corresponding roughly to green and red; the other two windows are in the infrared section of the spectrum. Thus each image plane has physical meaning, and color combinations obtained using the RGB model for processing and display usually make sense when viewed on a color screen or, as in Chapter 7, when segmenting a color image based on its spectral components.

Suppose, though, that the problem is one of enhancing a color image of a human face, part of which is hidden in a shadow. As discussed in Section 4.2, histogram equalization is an ideal tool for this type of problem. Because of the presence of three images and because histogram equalization deals only with intensity values, the obvious approach is to subject each image plane to histogram equalization independently. The part of the image hidden by the shadow in all likelihood will be enhanced. However, the intensities in all three image planes will be altered differently, resulting in a change of the relative intensities between them. The net result will be that important color properties in the image, such as flesh tones, will not appear natural when viewed on an RGB monitor. Some of the color models discussed in the following sections are better suited for problems such as this.

The CMY color model

As indicated previously, cyan, magenta, and yellow are the secondary colors of light or, alternatively, the primary colors of pigments. For example, when a surface coated with cyan pigment is illuminated with white light, no red light is reflected from the surface. That is, cyan subtracts red light from reflected white light, which itself is composed of equal amounts of red, green, and blue light.

[†] LANDSAT is the abbreviation for *Land Satellite*, a name given by NASA to satellites designed to monitor the Earth's surface.

Most devices that deposit colored pigments on paper, such as color printers and copiers, require CMY data input or perform an RGB to CMY conversion internally. This conversion is performed using the simple operation:

$$\begin{bmatrix} C \\ M \\ Y \end{bmatrix} = \begin{bmatrix} 1 \\ 1 \\ 1 \end{bmatrix} - \begin{bmatrix} R \\ G \\ B \end{bmatrix} \qquad (4.6\text{-}5)$$

where, again, the assumption is that all color values have been normalized to the range [0, 1]. Equation (4.6-5) demonstrates that light reflected from a surface coated with pure cyan does not contain red (that is, $C = 1 - R$ in the equation); similarly, pure magenta does not reflect green, and pure yellow does not reflect blue. Equation (4.6-5) also reveals that RGB values can be obtained easily from a set of CMY values by subtracting the individual CMY values from 1. As indicated earlier, in image processing this color model is used in connection with generating hardcopy output, so the inverse operation from CMY to RGB is generally of no practical interest.

The YIQ color model
The YIQ model is used in commercial color TV broadcasting. Basically, YIQ is a recoding of RGB for transmission efficiency and for maintaining compatibility with monochrome TV standards. In fact, the Y component of the YIQ system provides all the video information required by a monochrome television set. The RGB to YIQ conversion is defined as

$$\begin{bmatrix} Y \\ I \\ Q \end{bmatrix} = \begin{bmatrix} 0.299 & 0.587 & 0.114 \\ 0.596 & -0.275 & -0.321 \\ 0.212 & -0.523 & 0.311 \end{bmatrix} \begin{bmatrix} R \\ G \\ B \end{bmatrix} \qquad (4.6\text{-}6)$$

In order to obtain the RGB values from a set of YIQ values, we simply perform the inverse matrix operation.

The YIQ model was designed to take advantage of the human visual system's greater sensitivity to changes in luminance than to changes in hue or saturation. Thus the YIQ standards call for more bandwidth (or bits in the case of digital color) to be used in representing Y, and less bandwidth (bits) in representing I and Q. For further details on this important property, see Pritchard [1977] and Smith [1978].

In addition to its being a widely supported standard, the principal advantage of the YIQ model in image processing is that the luminance (Y) and color information (I and Q) are decoupled. Keep in mind that luminance is proportional to the amount of light perceived by the eye. Thus the importance of this decoupling is that the luminance component of an image can be processed without affecting its color content. For instance, as opposed to the problem with the RGB model mentioned earlier, we can apply histogram equalization to a color image represented in YIQ format simply by applying histogram equalization to its Y component. The relative colors in the image are not affected by this process.

The HSI color model

Recall from the discussion in Section 4.6.1 that hue is a color attribute that describes a pure color (pure yellow, orange, or red), whereas saturation gives a measure of the degree to which a pure color is diluted by white light. The HSI color model owes its usefulness to two principal facts. First, the intensity component, I, is decoupled from the color information in the image. Second, the hue and saturation components are intimately related to the way in which human beings perceive color. These features make the HSI model an ideal tool for developing image processing algorithms based on some of the color sensing properties of the human visual system.

Examples of the usefulness of the HSI model range from the design of imaging systems for automatically determining the ripeness of fruits and vegetables, to systems for matching color samples or inspecting the quality of finished color goods. In these and similar applications, the key is to base system operation on color properties the way a person might use those properties for performing the task in question.

The conversion formulas to go from RGB to HSI and back are considerably more complicated than in the preceding models. Rather than just stating these formulas, however, we take the time to derive them here in order to give the reader a deeper understanding of color manipulation.

Conversion from RGB to HSI. As discussed earlier, the RGB model is defined with respect to a unit cube. However, the color components of the HSI model (hue and saturation) are defined with respect to the color triangle shown in Fig. 4.45(a). (Recall from the discussion of the chromaticity diagram in Section 4.6.1 that all the colors obtainable by combining three given colors lie inside a triangle whose vertices are defined by the three initial colors.) In Fig. 4.45(a), note that the hue, H, of color point P is the angle of the vector shown with respect to the red axis. Thus when $H = 0°$, the color is red, when H is $60°$ the color is yellow, and so on. The saturation, S, of color point P is the degree to which the color is undiluted by white and is proportional to the distance from P to the center of the triangle. The farther P is from the center of the triangle, the more saturated its color is.

Intensity in the HSI model is measured with respect to a line perpendicular to the triangle and passing through its center. Intensities along this line lying below the triangle tend from dark down to black. Conversely, intensities above the triangle tend from light up to white.

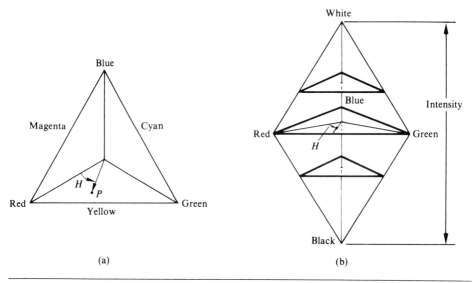

Figure 4.45 (a) HSI color triangle; (b) HSI color solid.

Combining hue, saturation, and intensity in a 3-D color space yields the three-sided, pyramidlike structure shown in Fig. 4.45(b). Any point on the surface of this structure represents a purely saturated color. The hue of that color is determined by its angle with respect to the red axis and its intensity by its perpendicular distance from the black point (that is, the greater the distance from black, the greater is the intensity of the color). Similar comments apply to points inside the structure, the only difference being that colors become less saturated as they approach the vertical axis.

Colors in the HSI model are defined with respect to normalized red, green, and blue values, given in terms of RGB primaries by

$$r = \frac{R}{(R + G + B)} \tag{4.6-7}$$

$$g = \frac{G}{(R + G + B)} \tag{4.6-8}$$

and

$$b = \frac{B}{(R + G + B)} \tag{4.6-9}$$

where, as before, the assumption is that R, G, and B, have been normalized so that they are in the range [0, 1]. Equations (4.6-7)–(4.6-9) show that r, g, and b also are in the interval $[0, 1]$ and that

$$r + g + b = 1. \qquad (4.6\text{-}10)$$

Note that, whereas R, G, and B can all be 1 simultaneously, the normalized variables have to satisfy Eq. (4.6-10). In fact, this is the equation of the plane that contains the HSI triangle.

For any three R, G, and B color components, each in the range $[0, 1]$, the intensity component in the HSI model is defined as

$$I = \frac{1}{3}(R + G + B) \qquad (4.6\text{-}11)$$

which yields values in the range $[0, 1]$.

The next step is to obtain H and S. To obtain H requires the geometric construction of the HSI triangle shown in Figs. 4.46(a), (b), and (c), from which we note the following conditions.

(a) The point W has coordinates $(1/3, 1/3, 1/3)$.

(b) An arbitrary color point P has coordinates (r, g, b).

(c) The vector extending from the origin to W is denoted $\mathbf{w}$. Similarly, the vectors extending from the origin to P_R and to P are denoted $\mathbf{p}_R$ and $\mathbf{p}$, respectively.

(d) The lines $P_i Q_i$, $i = R, G, B$, intersect at W by construction.

(e) Letting $r_0 = R/I$, $g_0 = G/I$, and $b_0 = B/I$, where I is given in Eq. (4.6-11), we see from Fig. 4.46(a) that $P_R Q_R$ is the locus of points (r_0, g_0, b_0) for which $g_0 = b_0$. Similarly, $r_0 = g_0$ along $P_B Q_B$, and $r_0 = b_0$ along $P_G Q_G$.

(f) Any point in the planar region bounded by triangle $P_R Q_R P_G$ has $g_0 \geq b_0$. Any point in the region bounded by triangle $P_R Q_R P_B$ has $b_0 \geq g_0$. Thus line $P_R Q_R$ separates the $g_0 > b_0$ region from the $g_0 < b_0$ region. Similarly, $P_G Q_G$ separates the $b_0 > r_0$ region from the $b_0 < r_0$ region, and $P_B Q_B$ separates the $g_0 > r_0$ region from the $g_0 < r_0$ region.

(g) For $i = R, G$, or B, $|WQ_i|/|P_iQ_i| = 1/3$ and $|WP_i|/|P_iQ_i| = 2/3$, where $|\text{arg}|$ denotes the length of the argument.

(h) By definition the *RG sector* is the region bounded by $WP_R P_G$, the *GB sector* is the region bounded $WP_G P_B$, and the *BR sector* is the region bounded by $WP_B P_R$.

With reference to Fig. 4.46(a), the hue of an arbitrary color is defined by the angle between the line segments WP_R and WP or, in vector form (Fig. 4.46c), by the angle between vectors $(\mathbf{p}_R - \mathbf{w})$ and $(\mathbf{p} - \mathbf{w})$. For example, as

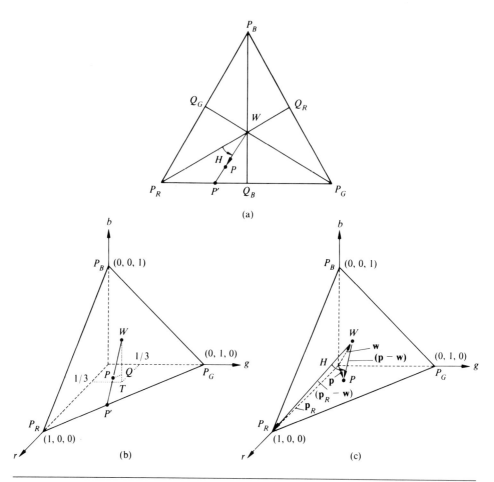

Figure 4.46 Details of the HSI color triangle needed to obtain expressions for hue and saturation.

stated earlier, $H = 0°$ corresponds to red, $H = 120°$ corresponds to green, and so on. Although the angle H could be measured with respect to any line passing through W, measuring hue with respect to red is a convention. In general, the following equation holds for $0° \le H \le 180°$:

$$(\mathbf{p} - \mathbf{w}) \cdot (\mathbf{p}_R - \mathbf{w}) = \|\mathbf{p} - \mathbf{w}\| \|\mathbf{p}_R - \mathbf{w}\| \cos H \qquad (4.6\text{-}12)$$

where $(\mathbf{x}) \cdot (\mathbf{y}) = \mathbf{x}^T \mathbf{y} = \|\mathbf{x}\| \|\mathbf{y}\| \cos H$ denotes the dot or inner product of the two vectors, and the double bars denote the norm (length) of the vector argument. The problem now is to express this result in terms of a set of RGB primaries.

From conditions (a) and (b),

$$\|\mathbf{p} - \mathbf{w}\| = \left[\left(r - \frac{1}{3} \right)^2 + \left(g - \frac{1}{3} \right)^2 + \left(b - \frac{1}{3} \right)^2 \right]^{1/2} \qquad (4.6\text{-}13)$$

because the length of a vector $\mathbf{a}$ with components a_1, a_2, and a_3 is $\|\mathbf{a}\| = [a_1^2 + a_2^2 + a_3^2]^{1/2}$. Substituting Eqs. (4.6-7)–(4.6-9) for r, g, and b in Eq. (4.6-13) and simplifying yields

$$\|\mathbf{p} - \mathbf{w}\| = \left[\frac{9(R^2 + G^2 + B^2) - 3(R + G + B)^2}{9(R + G + B)^2} \right]^{1/2}. \qquad (4.6\text{-}14)$$

As vectors $\mathbf{p}_R$ and $\mathbf{w}$ extend from the origin to points $(1, 0, 0)$ and $(1/3, 1/3, 1/3)$, respectively,

$$\|\mathbf{p}_R - \mathbf{w}\| = \left(\frac{2}{3} \right)^{1/2}. \qquad (4.6\text{-}15)$$

Keep in mind that, for two vectors $\mathbf{a}$ and $\mathbf{b}$, $\mathbf{a} \cdot \mathbf{b} = \mathbf{a}^T \mathbf{b} = a_1 b_1 + a_2 b_2 + a_3 b_3$. Then

$$(\mathbf{p} - \mathbf{w}) \cdot (\mathbf{p}_R - \mathbf{w}) = \frac{2}{3} \left(r - \frac{1}{3} \right) - \frac{1}{3} \left(g - \frac{1}{3} \right) + \frac{1}{3} \left(b - \frac{1}{3} \right) \qquad (4.6\text{-}16)$$

$$= \frac{2R - G - B}{3(R + G + B)}.$$

From Eq. (4.6-12),

$$H = \cos^{-1} \left[\frac{(\mathbf{p} - \mathbf{w}) \cdot (\mathbf{p}_R - \mathbf{w})}{\|\mathbf{p} - \mathbf{w}\| \|\mathbf{p}_R - \mathbf{w}\|} \right]. \qquad (4.6\text{-}17)$$

Substituting Eqs. (4.6-14)–(4.6-16) into Eq. (4.6-17) and simplifying yields the following expression for H in terms of R, G, and B:

$$H = \cos^{-1} \left\{ \frac{\frac{1}{2}[(R - G) + (R - B)]}{[(R - G)^2 + (R - B)(G - B)]^{1/2}} \right\}. \qquad (4.6\text{-}18)$$

Equation (4.6-18) yields values of H in the interval $0° \le H \le 180°$. If $b_0 > g_0$, then H has to be greater than $180°$. So, whenever $b_0 > g_0$, we simply let $H = 360° - H$. Sometimes the equation for hue is expressed in terms of the tangent by using the trigonometric identity $\cos^{-1}(x) = 90° - \tan^{-1}(x/\sqrt{1 - x^2})$. However, Eq. (4.6-18) not only is simpler to visualize, but it also is superior in terms of hardware implementation.

The next step is to derive an expression for S in terms of a set of RGB primary values. To do so again requires Figs. 4.46(a) and (b). Because the saturation of a color is the degree to which that color is undiluted by white, from Fig. 4.46(a) the saturation, S, of color point P is given by the ratio $|WP|/|WP'|$, where P' is obtained by extending line WP until it intersects the nearest side of the triangle.

With reference to Fig. 4.46(b), let T be the projection of W onto the rg plane, parallel to the b axis and let Q be the projection of P onto WT, parallel to the rg plane. Then

$$S = \frac{|WP|}{|WP'|} = \frac{|WQ|}{|WT|} = \frac{|WT| - |QT|}{|WT|} \tag{4.6-19}$$

where the second step follows from similar triangles. Since $|WT| = 1/3$ and $|QT| = b$ in the sector shown,

$$S = 3\left(\frac{1}{3} - b\right)$$
$$= 1 - 3b \tag{4.6-20}$$
$$= 1 - b_0$$

where the last step follows from Eq. (4.6-10) and condition (e). Also, we note that $b_0 = \min(r_0, g_0, b_0)$ in the RG sector. In fact, an argument similar to the one just given would show that the relationship

$$S = 1 - \min(r_0, g_0, b_0)$$
$$= 1 - \frac{3}{(R + G + B)}[\min(R, G, B)] \tag{4.6-21}$$

is true in general for any point lying on the HSI triangle.

The results obtained thus far give the following expressions for obtaining HSI values in the range [0, 1] from a set of RGB values in the same range:

$$I = \frac{1}{3}(R + G + B) \tag{4.6-22}$$

$$S = 1 - \frac{3}{(R + G + B)}[\min(R, G, B)] \tag{4.6-23}$$

and

$$H = \cos^{-1}\left\{\frac{\frac{1}{2}[(R - G) + (R - B)]}{[(R - G)^2 + (R - B)(G - B)]^{1/2}}\right\} \tag{4.6-24}$$

where, as indicated earlier, we let $H = 360° - H$, if $(B/I) > (G/I)$. In order to normalize hue to the range $[0, 1]$, we let $H = H/360°$. Finally, if $S = 0$, it follows from Eq. (4.6-19) that $|WP|$ must be zero, which means that W and P have become the same point, making it meaningless to define angle H. Thus hue is not defined when the saturation is zero. Similarly, from Eqs. (4.6-22) and (4.6-23), saturation is undefined if $I = 0$.

Conversion from HSI to RGB. For values of HSI in $[0, 1]$, we now want to find the corresponding RGB values in the same range. The analysis depends on which of the sectors defined in condition (h) contains the given value of H. We begin by letting $H = 360°(H)$, which returns the hue to the range $[0°, 360°]$.

For the *RG Sector* $(0° < H \leq 120°)$, from Eq. (4.6-20),

$$b = \frac{1}{3}(1 - S).$$ (4.6-25)

Next, we find r by noting from Fig. 4.46(a) that the value of r is the projection of P onto the red axis. Consider the triangle $P_R O Q_R$ shown in Fig. 4.47, where O is the origin of the *rgb* coordinate system. The hypotenuse of this triangle is the line segment $P_R Q_R$ in Fig. 4.46(a), and the line extending from O to P_R is the red axis containing r. The dashed line is the intersection of triangle $P_R O Q_R$ with the plane that contains P and is perpendicular to the red axis. These two conditions imply that the plane also contains r. Furthermore, the point at which $P_R Q_R$ intersects the plane contains the projection of P onto line $P_R Q_R$, which, from Fig. 4.46(a), is $|WP| \cos H$. From similar triangles,

$$\frac{|P_R Q_R|}{|P_R O|} = \frac{a}{d}.$$ (4.6-26)

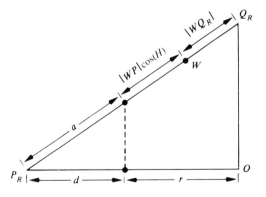

Figure 4.47 *Arrangement used to derive equations for converting from HSI to RGB.*

But $|P_R O| = 1$, $d = 1 - r$, and $a = |P_R Q_R| - (|WP| \cos H + |WQ_R|)$. Substituting these results into Eq. (4.6-26) and simplifying yields

$$r = \frac{|WQ_R|}{|P_R Q_R|} + \frac{|WP|}{|P_R Q_R|} \cos H$$

$$= \frac{1}{3} + \frac{|WP|}{|P_R Q_R|} \cos H \qquad (4.6\text{-}27)$$

where we used $|P_R Q_R| = 3|WQ_R|$ from Fig. 4.46(a). The only unknown in this equation is $|WP|$, which, from Eq. (4.6-19), is $|WP| = S|WP'|$. In Fig. 4.46(a), the angle formed at W by line segments $P_R Q_R$ and WQ_B is 60°; therefore $|WQ_B| = |WP'| \cos(60° - H)$, or $|WP'| = |WQ_B|/\cos(60° - H)$. Noting that $|WQ_B| = |WQ_R|$ and substituting these results into Eq. (4.6-27) yields

$$r = \frac{1}{3} + \frac{S|WQ_R| \cos H}{|P_R Q_R| \cos(60° - H)}$$

$$= \frac{1}{3}\left[1 + \frac{S \cos H}{\cos(60° - H)}\right] \qquad (4.6\text{-}28)$$

where we used $|P_R Q_R| = 3|WQ_R|$ again. Finally, $g = 1 - (r + b)$ from Eq. (4.6-10). Hence the results for $0° < H \le 120°$ are

$$b = \frac{1}{3}(1 - S) \qquad (4.6\text{-}29)$$

$$r = \frac{1}{3}\left[1 + \frac{S \cos H}{\cos(60° - H)}\right] \qquad (4.6\text{-}30)$$

and

$$g = 1 - (r + b). \qquad (4.6\text{-}31)$$

The color components just obtained are normalized in the sense of Eq. (4.6-10). We recover the RGB components by noting from Eqs. (4.6-7)–(4.6-11) that $R = 3Ir$, $G = 3Ig$, and $B = 3Ib$.

For the *GB sector* ($120° < H \le 240°$), a development similar to the one just completed yields

$$H = H - 120° \qquad (4.6\text{-}32)$$

$$r = \frac{1}{3}(1 - S) \qquad (4.6\text{-}33)$$

$$g = \frac{1}{3}\left[1 + \frac{S \cos H}{\cos(60° - H)}\right] \qquad (4.6\text{-}34)$$

and

$$b = 1 - (r + g). \tag{4.6-35}$$

The values of R, G, and B, are obtained from r, g, and b in the manner previously described.

For the *BR sector* $(240° < H \le 360°)$,

$$H = H - 240° \tag{4.6-36}$$

$$g = \frac{1}{3}(1 - S) \tag{4.6-37}$$

$$b = \frac{1}{3}\left[1 + \frac{S \cos H}{\cos(60° - H)}\right] \tag{4.6-38}$$

and

$$r = 1 - (g + b). \tag{4.6-39}$$

The values of R, G, and B, are obtained from r, g, and b in the manner previously described.

Image processing examples using the HSI model are presented in Section 4.6.4.

4.6.3 Pseudo-color Image Processing

In this section we present several approaches for assigning color to monochrome images based on various properties of their gray-level content.

Intensity slicing

The technique of *intensity* (sometimes called *density*) *slicing* and color coding is one of the simplest examples of pseudo-color image processing. If an image is viewed as a 2-D intensity function (see Section 1.2), the method can be interpreted as one of placing planes parallel to the coordinate plane of the image; each plane then "slices" the function in the area of intersection. Figure 4.48 shows an example of using a plane at $f(x, y) = l_i$ to "slice" a function into two levels.

If a different color is assigned to each side of the plane shown in Fig. 4.48, any pixel whose gray level is above the plane will be coded with one color, and any pixel below the plane will be coded with the other. Levels that lie on the plane itself may be arbitrarily assigned one of the two colors. The result is a two-color image whose relative appearance can be controlled by moving the slicing plane up and down the gray-level axis.

In general, the technique may be summarized as follows. Suppose that M planes are defined at levels $l_1, l_2, \ldots, l_M$ and let l_0 represent black $[f(x, y) = 0]$ and l_L represent white $[f(x, y) = L]$. Then, assuming that $0 < M < L$, the

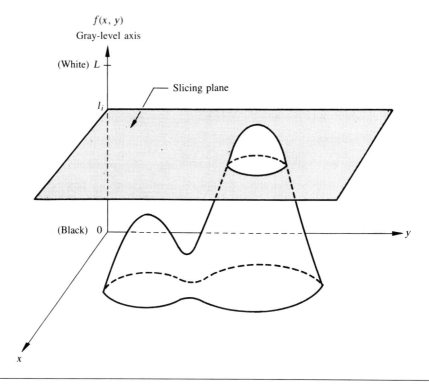

Figure 4.48   *Geometric interpretation of the intensity-slicing technique.*

M planes partition the gray scale into $M + 1$ regions and color assignments are made according to the relation,

$$f(x, y) = c_k \quad \text{if } f(x, y) \in R_k, \tag{4.6-40}$$

where c_k is the color associated with the kth region R_k defined by the partitioning planes.

The idea of planes is useful primarily for a geometric interpretation of the intensity-slicing technique. Figure 4.49 shows an alternative representation that defines the same mapping as Fig. 4.48. According to the mapping function shown in Fig. 4.49, any input gray level is assigned one of two colors, depending on whether it is above or below the value of l_i. When more levels are used, the mapping function takes on a staircase form. This type of mapping is a special case of the approach discussed in the next section.

Example: An example of intensity slicing is shown in Plate V. Part (a) is a monochrome image of the Picker Thyroid Phantom (a radiation test pattern), and Plate V(b) is the result of intensity slicing this image into eight color regions.

Regions that appear of constant intensity in the monochrome image are really quite variable, as shown by the various colors in the sliced image. The left lobe, for instance, is a dull gray in the monochrome image, and picking out variations in intensity is difficult. By contrast, the color image clearly shows eight different regions of constant intensity, one for each of the colors used.   ❑

Gray level to color transformations

Other types of transformations are more general and thus are capable of achieving a wider range of pseudo-color enhancement results than the simple slicing technique discussed in the preceding section. An approach that is particularly attractive is shown in Fig. 4.50. Basically, the idea underlying this approach is to perform three independent transformations on the gray level of any input pixel. The three results are then fed separately into the red, green, and blue guns of a color television monitor. This method produces a composite image whose color content is modulated by the nature of the transformation functions. Note that these are transformations on the gray-level values of an image and are not functions of position.

As indicated in the preceding section, the method shown in Fig. 4.49 is a special case of the technique just described. There, piecewise linear functions of the gray levels generate colors. However, the method discussed in this section can be based on smooth, nonlinear functions which, as might be expected, gives the technique considerably more flexibility.

Example: Plate VI(a) shows a composite monochrome image consisting of two images of luggage obtained from an airport x-ray scanning system. The image on the left contains ordinary articles. The image on the right contains the same

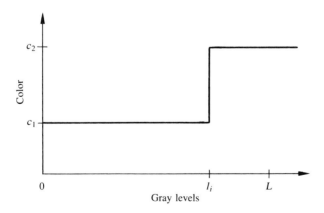

Figure 4.49 *An alternative representation of the intensity-slicing method.*

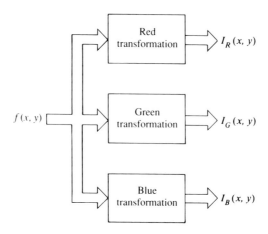

Figure 4.50 *Functional block diagram for pseudo-color image processing.* I_R, I_G, *and* I_B *are fed into the red, green, and blue inputs, respectively, of an RGB color monitor.*

articles, as well as a block of simulated plastic explosives. The purpose of this example is to illustrate the use of gray level to color transformations to obtain various degrees of enhancement.

Figure 4.51 shows the transformation functions used. These sinusoidal functions contain regions of relatively constant value around the peaks as well as regions that change rapidly near the valleys. Changing the phase and frequency of each sinusoid can emphasize (in color) ranges in the gray scale. For instance, if all three transformations have the same phase and frequency, the output image will be monochrome. A small change in the phase between the three transformations produces little change in pixels whose gray levels correspond to peaks in the sinusoids, especially if the sinusoids have broad profiles (low frequencies). Pixels with gray-level values in the steep section of the sinusoids are assigned a much stronger color content as a result of significant differences between the amplitudes of the three sinusoids caused by the phase displacement between them.

The image shown in Plate VI(b) was obtained with the transformation functions in Fig. 4.51(a), which shows the gray-level bands corresponding to the explosive, garment bag, and background, respectively. Note that the explosive and background have quite different gray levels, but they were both coded with approximately the same color as a result of the periodicity of the sine waves. The image shown in Plate VI(c) was obtained with the transformation functions in Fig. 4.51(b). In this case the explosive and garment bag intensity bands were mapped by similar transformations and thus received essentially the same color assignments. Note that this mapping allows an ob-

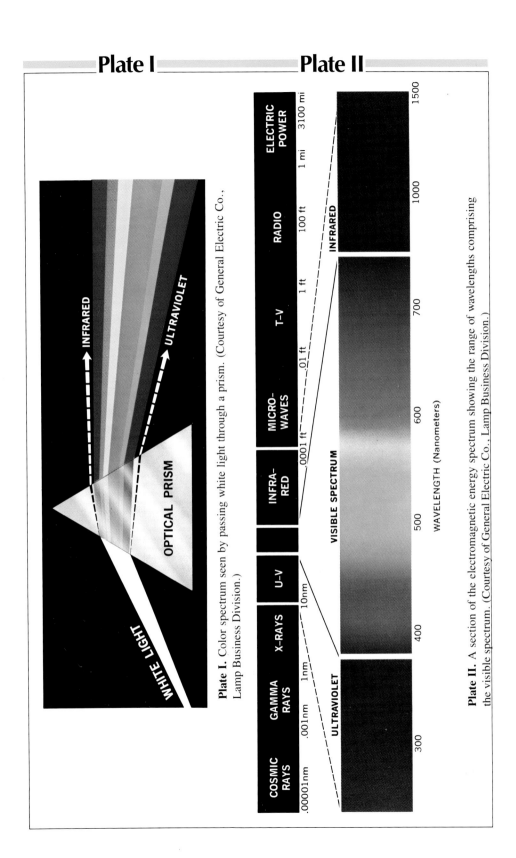

Plate I **Plate II**

Plate I. Color spectrum seen by passing white light through a prism. (Courtesy of General Electric Co., Lamp Business Division.)

Plate II. A section of the electromagnetic energy spectrum showing the range of wavelengths comprising the visible spectrum. (Courtesy of General Electric Co., Lamp Business Division.)

Plate III

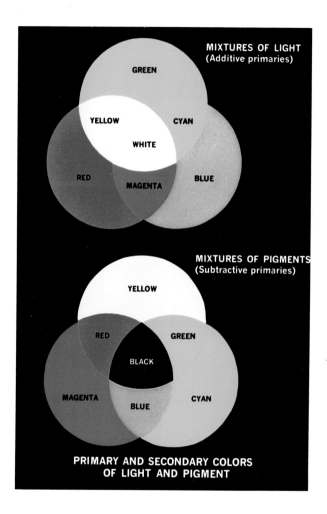

Plate III. Primary and secondary colors of light and pigments. (Courtesy of General Electric Co., Lamp Business Division.)

Plate IV

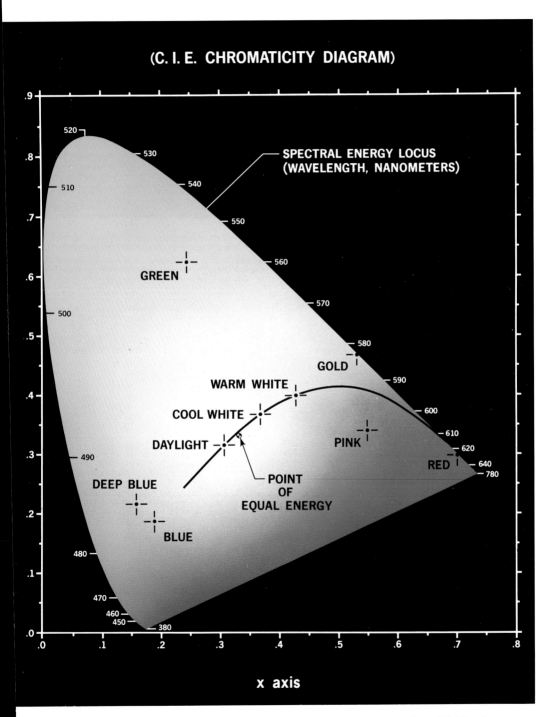

Plate IV. Chromaticity diagram. (Courtesy of General Electric Co., Lamp Business Division.)

Plate V

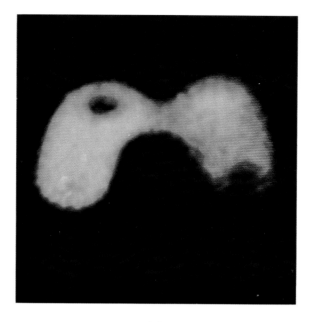

(a)

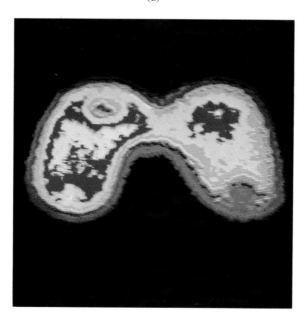

(b)

Plate V. (a) Monochrome image of the Picker Thyroid Phantom. (b) Result of density slicing into eight color regions. (Courtesy of Dr. J.L. Blankenship, Instrumentation and Controls Division, Oak Ridge National Laboratory.)

Plate VI

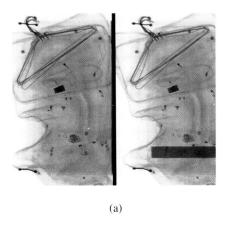

(a)

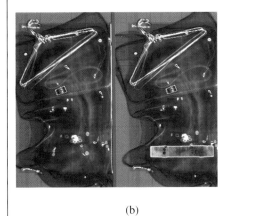

(b)

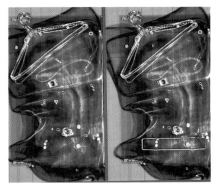

(c)

Plate VI. Pseudo-color enhancement by using the gray-level to color transformations in Fig. 4.38. Original image courtesy of Dr. Mike Hurwitz, Research and Development Center, Westinghouse Electric Corporation.

Plate VII

(a)

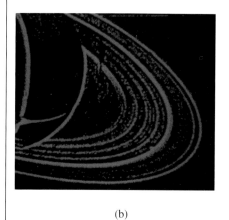

(b)

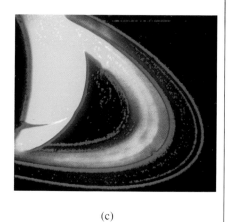

(c)

Plate VII. (a) Monochrome image. (b) Result of highpass Butterworth filter displayed on the red gun of a color monitor. (c) Composite image with the lowpass, bandpass, and highpass images displayed on the blue, green, and red guns, respectively.

Plate VIII ——————— Plate IX

(a)

(b)

(c)

(d)

Plate VIII. (a) Original RGB image. (b)–(d) Hue, saturation, and intensity images.

(a)

(b)

Plate IX. (a) Original RGB image. (b) Result of histogram equalization (see text).

Plate X

(a)

66:1

(b)

Plate X. (a) An original 24-bit color image. (b) Result of compressing and reconstructing the image of (a) using the Joint Photographic Experts Group (JPEG) coding standard. (Courtesy of C-Cube Microsystems, Inc. of San Jose, CA.)

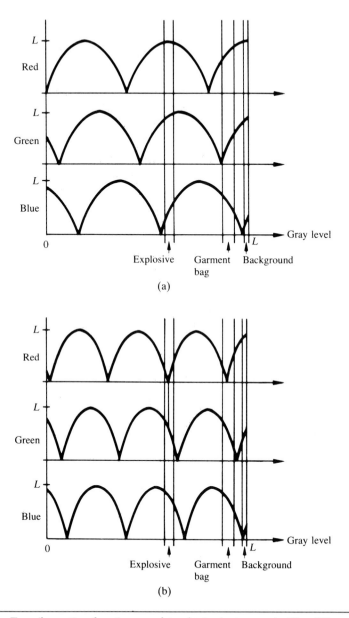

Figure 4.51 *Transformation functions used to obtain the images in Plate VI.*

server to "see" through the explosives. The background mappings were about the same as those used for Plate VI(b), producing almost identical color assignments.   ❏

A filtering approach

Figure 4.52 shows a color-coding scheme based on frequency domain operations. The idea depicted is the same as that of the basic filtering approach discussed earlier in this chapter, except that the Fourier transform of an image is modified independently by three filter functions to produce three images that can be fed into the red, green, and blue inputs of a color monitor. Consider, for example, the sequence of steps followed in obtaining the image for the red channel. The Fourier transform of the input image is altered by using a specified filter function. The processed image is then obtained by using the inverse Fourier transform. These steps can then be followed by additional processing (such as histogram equalization) before the image is fed into the red input of the monitor. Similar comments apply to the other two paths in Fig. 4.52.

The objective of this color-processing technique is to color code regions of an image based on frequency content. A typical filtering approach is to use lowpass, bandpass (or bandreject), and highpass filters to obtain three ranges of frequency components. Bandreject and bandpass filters are extensions of the lowpass and highpass filter concepts already discussed. A simple approach for generating filters that reject or attenuate frequencies about a circular neighborhood of a point (u_0, v_0) is to perform a translation of coordinates for the highpass filters discussed in Section 4.4.2. The procedure for the ideal filter is as follows.

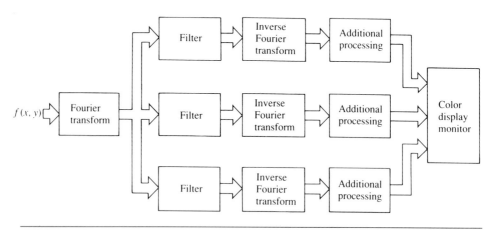

Figure 4.52   *A filtering model for pseudo-color image processing.*

An ideal bandreject filter (IBRF) suppresses all frequencies in a neighborhood of radius D_0 about a point (u_0, v_0) and is given by the relation

$$H(u, v) = \begin{cases} 0 & \text{if } D(u, v) \leq D_0 \\ 1 & \text{if } D(u, v) > D_0 \end{cases} \qquad (4.6\text{-}41)$$

where

$$D(u, v) = [(u - u_0)^2 + (v - v_0)^2]^{1/2}. \qquad (4.6\text{-}42)$$

Note that Eq. (4.6-41) is identical in form to Eq. (4.4-6), but the distance function $D(u, v)$ is computed about the point (u_0, v_0) instead of the origin.

Owing to the symmetry of the Fourier transform, band rejection that is not about the origin must be carried out in symmetric *pairs* in order to obtain meaningful results. In the case of the ideal filter, Eq. (4.6-41) becomes

$$H(u, v) = \begin{cases} 0 & \text{if } D_1(u, v) \leq D_0 \quad \text{or} \quad D_2(u, v) \leq D_0 \\ 1 & \text{otherwise} \end{cases} \qquad (4.6\text{-}43)$$

where

$$D_1(u, v) = [(u - u_0)^2 + (v - v_0)^2]^{1/2} \qquad (4.6\text{-}44)$$

and

$$D_2(u, v) = [(u + u_0)^2 + (v + v_0)^2]^{1/2}. \qquad (4.6\text{-}45)$$

The procedure can be extended similarly to four or more regions. The Butterworth filter discussed in Section 4.4.2 can also be applied directly to band rejection by following the technique just described for the ideal filter. Figure 4.53 shows a perspective plot of a typical IBRF transfer function.

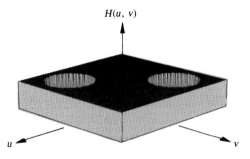

Figure 4.53 *Ideal bandreject filter.*

The filter discussed above is localized about some point off the origin of the Fourier transform. To remove a band of frequencies centered on the origin, symmetric filters similar to the low and highpass filters discussed earlier can be considered. The procedure for the ideal and Butterworth filters is as follows.

A radially symmetric ideal bandreject filter, which removes a band of frequencies about the origin, is given by the relation

$$H(u, v) = \begin{cases} 1 & \text{if } D(u, v) < D_0 - \dfrac{W}{2} \\ 0 & \text{if } D_0 - \dfrac{W}{2} \leq D(u, v) \leq D_0 + \dfrac{W}{2} \\ 1 & \text{if } D(u, v) > D_0 + \dfrac{W}{2} \end{cases} \qquad (4.6\text{-}46)$$

where W is the width of the band and D_0 is its radial center. As is the case with all radially symmetric filters, this filter can be specified completely by a cross section. For example, a radially symmetric Butterworth bandreject filter (BBRF) of order n has the transfer function

$$H(u, v) = \dfrac{1}{1 + \left[\dfrac{D(u, v)W}{D^2(u, v) - D_0^2} \right]^{2n}} \qquad (4.6\text{-}47)$$

where W is the width of the band and D_0 is its center.

Bandpass filters pass frequencies in a specified band or region while attenuating, or completely suppressing, all other frequencies. Therefore they are exactly the opposite of bandreject filters. Thus, if $H_R(u, v)$ is the transfer function of any of the bandreject filters just discussed, the corresponding bandpass function, $H(u, v)$ can be obtained simply by "flipping" $H_R(u, v)$; that is,

$$H(u, v) = -[H_R(u, v) - 1]. \qquad (4.6\text{-}48)$$

Example: Plate VII(a) shows a monochrome image and Plates VII(b) and (c) show the results of using Butterworth filters. Plate VII(b) shows (in the red gun of a color monitor) the result of applying a highpass filter with the cutoff point at the circle enclosing 90 percent of the image energy (see Section 4.4.1). Plate VII(c) shows the highpass filtered image on the red gun, as well as a lowpass (blue gun) and bandpass (green gun) filtered version of Plate VII(a). The lowpass image was obtained with the cutoff point at the circle enclosing

98 percent of the image energy; the bandpass range was between the circles enclosing 20 percent and 95 percent of the energy. The principal enhancement resulting from this process was the increased visibility of the outer ring, which is almost invisible in the original image. ❏

4.6.4 Full-color Image Processing

We conclude the discussion of color image processing by presenting in some detail the role of full-color techniques for image enhancement. In particular, we are interested in the HSI model for the reasons stated in Section 4.6.2: (1) the intensity and color information in this model are decoupled; and (2) hue and saturation are closely related to the way in which human beings describe color perception.

HSI component images from an RGB image

Because of the importance of the RGB model in the display of color images, we begin the discussion of full-color processing by illustrating the differences and correspondences between images expressed in the RGB and HSI modes. This development also serves the purpose of deepening our understanding of the HSI model itself. Recall that an image processed in HSI space must be converted back to RGB for display.

Plate VIII(a) shows an RGB color test pattern consisting, at the top, of eight thin bands that contain black, followed by the pure primaries and secondaries (the order shown has no particular significance), and finally ending in white. These eight bands are followed by a broad multicolor band that ranges across from blue, to green, to red. This band is followed by two gray-scale wedges in opposite directions. The color patterns then repeat themselves going the other way to form a square image. Figure 4.54 shows the mixture of red, green, and blue used to produce the band of varying color in Plate VIII(a). Note that pure blue is achieved on the extreme left, pure red on the extreme right, and equal parts of red and blue with twice the amount of green give the color at the center of the band.

The terminology used to refer to a full-color image commonly gives all the bits used in the color's representation. Thus a 24-bit color image indicates that 24 bits are used to render it. Generally (but not always), the bits are equally distributed among the three color component images. This distribution is the case for the image shown in Plate VIII(a), in which 8 bits per color component were used. Thus each pixel in a component image has values in the range [0, 255]. In Section 4.6.2 we mentioned the assumption that RGB pixels have values in the range [0, 1]. These two ranges are not inconsistent, because an 8-bit representation can be thought of as giving values between 0 and 255 in

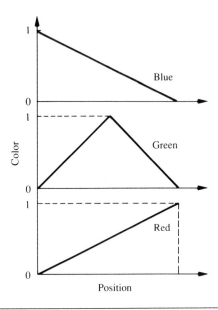

Figure 4.54 *Color functions used to generate the band of varying color in the RGB image of Plate VIII.*

increments of 1 or, equivalently, as giving values between 0 to 1 in increments of $\frac{1}{255}$.

The situation with HSI component images is slightly different. The intensity image is just like any of the three RGB images just discussed. Each pixel in the hue image has values expressed in degrees. With 8 bits, 256 such values can be represented in the range $[0°, 360°]$ in increments of $n(360/255)°$, for $n = 0, 1, 2, \ldots, 255$. Similarly, pixels in the saturation image may be viewed as having values from 0 (no saturation) to 1 (full saturation) in increments of $\frac{1}{255}$.

Consider Plate VIII(b), which shows the hue image obtained from the RGB image in Plate VIII(a) by using Eq. (4.6-24). As the monochrome components shown in the RGB image have zero saturation, hue is not defined (see the discussion following Eq. 4.6-24) for those regions; they are arbitrarily shown in black in Plate VIII(b). With hue values in degrees, the grays in Plate VIII(b) must be interpreted as angles (measured from red, according to Fig. 4.45). Thus lighter shades of gray in Plate VIII(b) correspond to increasingly larger angle values. Because reds have the smallest angle values (see Fig. 4.45), we expect that the reds in Plate VIII(a) will appear as the darkest grays in Plate VIII(b), that yellow will appear the next lighter shade of gray, and so on for green, cyan, blue, and magenta, in that order. This result, in fact, is the case, as we can see by comparing the colors in Plate VIII(a) with the grays in Plate

VIII(b). Note in particular the variations in gray corresponding to the varying color band.

Plate VIII(c) shows the saturation image obtained from the RGB image using Eq. (4.6-23). The maximally saturated pure primary and secondary colors appear as white (maximum) in the saturation image. As saturation is not defined when the intensity is zero (see the discussion following Eq. 4.6-24), all black components of the RGB image are shown (arbitrarily) in white in Plate VIII(c). Note also that whites in Plate VIII(a) appear as black in Plate VIII(c), because white corresponds to zero saturation. The grays corresponding to the varying color band are lighter toward both ends of the band, indicating greater color saturation there. The grays corresponding to the center (green) portion of the band are darker than in the extreme portions of the band, indicating less saturation in the green region. This condition is consistent with the way in which the dominant green part of the test pattern was generated (see Fig. 4.54).

Finally, Plate VIII(d) shows the intensity component of the HSI image obtained from Eq. (4.6-22). As expected, black, white, and grays appear as in the RGB image. The components corresponding to the pure primary colors all have the same value and thus appear in constant gray in Plate VIII(d). The pure secondary colors also yield constant values of intensity, but they are double the value of the intensity corresponding to the primaries and thus appear a lighter gray. This result also is expected, because a secondary of light is obtained by adding two primaries. The intensities corresponding to the varying color band also are as expected and vary from dark, to bright, and back to dark.

Enhancement using the HSI model

As previously indicated, the HSI model is ideally suited for image enhancement, because the intensity component is decoupled from the color information in an image. Therefore any monochrome enhancement technique discussed in this chapter can be carried over as a tool for enhancing full-color images. It simply calls for converting the image to the HSI format, processing the intensity component, and converting the result to RGB for display. The color content of the image is not affected.

Plate IX illustrates this approach. Plate IX(a) shows an RGB color image whose background detail is obscured significantly. The image was converted to HSI and its intensity component was subjected to histogram equalization by using the approach developed in Section 4.2.2. The image was then converted back to RGB, yielding the result shown in Plate IX(b). The improvements in visible detail are apparent. Because histogram equalization has a tendency to brighten images significantly, the color components appear somewhat different than in the original image. Although the hue and saturation are the same, the colors appear lighter because of the increase in intensity. Applying this enhancement technique to each component of the RGB image would increase visible detail and brightness, but the resulting colors would have nonsensical hues as a result of changes of relative values between corresponding pixels in the three RGB component images.

4.7 CONCLUDING REMARKS

The material presented in this chapter is representative of techniques commonly used in practice for digital image enhancement. However, this area of image processing is a dynamic field and reports of new techniques and applications in the literature are common. For this reason, the topics included in this chapter were selected mostly for their value as fundamental material that would serve as a foundation for further study in this field.

REFERENCES

The material in Section 4.1 is from Gonzalez [1986]. Complementary reading for the material in Section 4.2.1 may be found in Schowengerdt [1983] and in Jain [1989]. The discussion on histogram processing techniques (Section 4.2.2) is based on the papers by Hall et al. [1971], Hall [.1974], Hummel [1974], Gonzalez and Fittes [1977], and Woods and Gonzalez [1981]. For further details on local enhancement, see Ketcham [1976], and Narendra and Fitch [1981]. Image subtraction (Section 4.2.3) is a generic image processing tool widely used in medical instrumentation. Additional uses of this technique for change detection are presented in Schalkoff [1989]. The method of noise reduction by image averaging (Section 4.2.4) was first proposed by Kohler and Howell [1963].

A comprehensive discussion of spatial filtering (Section 4.3) is given by Levine [1985]. The books by Rosenfeld and Kak [1982] and by Schowengerdt [1983] also are of interest in this regard. For more details on implementing median filters, see Huang et al. [1979], Wolfe and Mannos [1979], and Chaudhuri [1983]. The book by Pitas and Venetsanopoulos [1990] also deals with median and other nonlinear spatial filters. The material on high-boost filtering is from Schowengerdt [1983].

Early references on image sharpening by differentiation are Goldmard and Hollywood [1951] and Kovasznay and Joseph [1953, 1955]. The Roberts gradient was first proposed by Roberts [1965]. A survey of techniques used in this area a decade later is given by Davis [1975]. The articles by Prewitt [1970] and Frei and Chen [1977] also are of interest. More recent work in this field emphasizes computational speed, as exemplified by Lee [1983] and Chaudhuri [1983].

The frequency domain filtering concepts introduced in Section 4.4 are based on direct extensions of 1-D filters where, instead of using a single variable, we used the distance from the origin of the frequency plane in order to obtain circularly symmetric filter functions. For extensive discussions of 1-D filters, see, for example, the books by Weinberg [1962] and by Budak [1974]. The discussion of high-frequency emphasis is from Hall et al. [1971]. The material on homomorphic filtering is based on a paper by Stockham [1972]; see also the books by Oppenheim and Schafer [1975] and Pitas and Venetsanopoulos [1990].

The material in Section 4.5 is from Schutten and Vermeij [1980] and Meyer and Gonzalez [1983]. Basic material on color fundamentals (Section 4.6) is included in the books by Walsh [1958] and by Kiver [1965]. See also the paper by Pritchard [1977]. The derivation of the HSI model in Section 4.6 is based on a paper by Smith [1978]. Additional references for color fundamentals and color models are Foley and Van Dam [1982] and Pokorny and

Gerald [1989]. The pseudo-color processing techniques in Section 4.6.3 are based on the papers by Smith [1963], Roth [1968], Billingsley et al. [1970], and Andrews et al. [1972]. The book by Green [1983] is also of interest.

PROBLEMS

4.1 Propose a set of gray-level-slicing transformations capable of producing all the individual bit planes of an 8-bit monochrome image. (For example, a transformation function with the property $T(r) = 0$ for r in the range $[0, 127]$, and $T(r) = 255$ for r in the range $[128, 255]$ produces an image of the 7th bit plane in an 8-bit image.)

4.2 Explain why the discrete histogram equalization technique will not, in general, yield a flat histogram.

4.3 Suppose that a digital image is subjected to histogram equalization. Show that a second pass of histogram equalization will produce exactly the same result as the first pass.

4.4 An image has the gray level *PDF* $p_r(r)$ shown in the following diagram. It is desired to transform the gray levels of this image so that they will have the specified $p_z(z)$ shown. Assume continuous quantities and find the transformation (in terms of r and z) that will accomplish this.

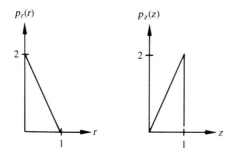

4.5 Propose a method for updating the local histogram for use in the local enhancement technique discussed in Section 4.2.2.

4.6 Prove the validity of Eqs. (4.2-19) and (4.2-20).

4.7 In an industrial application, x-ray imaging is to be used to inspect the inside of certain iron castings. The objective is to look for voids in the castings, which typically appear as small blobs in the image. However, high noise content often makes inspection difficult, so the decision is made to use image averaging to reduce the noise and thus improve visible contrast. In computing the average, it is important to keep the number of images as small as possible in order to reduce the time the parts have to remain stationary during imaging. After numerous experiments, it is concluded that decreasing the noise variance by a factor of 10 is sufficient. If the imaging device can produce 30 frames/sec, how long would the castings have to remain stationary during imaging to achieve the desired decrease in variance? Assume that the noise is uncorrelated and has zero mean.

4.8 Discuss the limiting effect of repeatedly applying a 3×3 lowpass spatial filter to a digital image. You may ignore border effects.

4.9 The implementation of spatial filters requires moving the center of a mask throughout an image and, at each location, computing the sum of products of the mask coefficients with the corresponding pixels at that location (see Eq. 4.3-1). In the case of lowpass filtering, all coefficients are 1, allowing use of the so-called *box-filter* or *moving-average* algorithm, which consists of updating only the part of the computation that changes from one location to the next.

a) Formulate such an algorithm for an $n \times n$ filter, showing not only the nature of the computations involved, but also the scanning sequence used for moving the mask around the image.

b) The ratio of the number of computations performed by a brute-force implementation to the number of computations performed by the box-filter algorithm is called the *computational advantage*. Obtain the computational advantage in this case and plot it as a function of n for $n > 1$. The $1/n^2$ scaling factor is common to both approaches, so you need not consider it in obtaining the computational advantage. Assume that the image has an outer border of zeros that is thick enough to allow you to ignore border effects in your analysis.

4.10 a) Develop a procedure for computing the median of an $n \times n$ neighborhood.

b) Propose a technique for updating the median as the center of the neighborhood is moved from pixel to pixel.

4.11 Show that a highpass-filtered image can be obtained in the spatial domain as Highpass = Original − Lowpass, as indicated in Section 4.3.3. For simplicity, assume 3×3 filters.

4.12 The second column in Fig. 4.19 shows cross sections of the transfer function for a highpass filter and the corresponding impulse response function. What would the transfer function and impulse response look like for a high-boost filter?

4.13 Suppose that you form a lowpass spatial filter that averages the 4-neighbors (see Section 2.4.1) of a point (x, y), but excludes the point (x, y) itself.

a) Find the equivalent filter $H(u, v)$ in the frequency domain.

b) Show that your result is a lowpass filter.

4.14 The basic approach used to compute the digital gradient (Section 4.3.3) involves taking differences of the form $f(x, y) - f(x + 1, y)$.

a) Obtain the filter transfer function, $H(u, v)$, for performing the equivalent process in the frequency domain.

b) Show that this is a highpass filter.

4.15 Under what condition does the Butterworth lowpass filter given in Eq. (4.4-4) become an ideal lowpass filter?

4.16 a) Show that a highpass-filtered image in the frequency domain can be obtained by using the method of subtracting a lowpass-filtered image from the original.

b) As a specific example, start with the equation of the Butterworth lowpass filter and use the concept in (a) to generate its highpass counterpart.

4.17 A popular procedure for image enhancement combines high-frequency emphasis and histogram equalization to achieve edge sharpening and contrast enhancement.

a) Prove whether or not it matters which process is applied first.

b) If the order does matter, give a rationale for using one or the other method first.

4.18 Suppose that you are given a set of images generated by an experiment dealing with the analysis of stellar events. Each image contains a set of bright, widely scattered dots corresponding to stars in a sparsely occupied section of the universe. The problem is that the stars are barely visible, owing to superimposed illumination resulting from atmospheric dispersion. If these images are modeled as the product of a constant illumination component with a set of impulses, give an enhancement procedure based on homomorphic filtering designed to bring out the image components due to the stars themselves.

4.19 With reference to the discussion in Section 4.5, show that if $H(u, v)$ is real and symmetric, $h(x, y)$ also must be real and symmetric.

4.20 In an automatic assembly application, three classes of parts are to be color coded to simplify detection. However, only a monochrome TV camera is available. Propose a technique for using this camera to detect the three different colors.

4.21 Show that Eq. (4.6-21) is valid for any point P lying on the HSI color triangle.

4.22 A skilled medical technician is charged with the job of inspecting a certain class of images generated by an electron microscope. In order to simplify the inspection task, the technician decides to use digital image enhancement and, to this end, examines a set of representative images and finds the following problems: (1) bright, isolated dots that are of no interest; (2) lack of sharpness; (3) not enough contrast in some images; and (4) shifts in the average gray-level value, when this value should be K to perform correctly certain intensity measurements. The technician wants to correct these problems and then color in constant red all gray levels in the band between I_1 and I_2, while keeping normal tonality in the remaining gray levels. Propose a sequence of processing steps that the technician can follow to achieve the desired goal.

4.23 Explain the reason why the midpoint of the multicolor band in Plate VIII(a) appears to be pure green, when, according to Fig. 4.54, that point is composed of red and blue components in equal amounts and green in twice the amount of red or blue.

4.24 You are to design an image processing system capable of discriminating between automobile body panels of identical shape but of different colors. The panels move down an assembly line conveyor, and the objective is to identify each panel according to color so that robots can pick them up for subsequent placement on other assembly lines in the manufacturing process. The colors of the various panels flowing through the assembly line are red, yellow, green, and blue. You have the following equipment at your disposal: a color video camera with RGB outputs, a color digitizer that accepts these RGB analog video signals and is capable of outputting either RGB or HSI digital images at frame rates (that is, one complete color image every $1/30$ sec), three frame buffers capable of accepting images at frame rates, and a hardware histogram module capable of computing the histogram of a single digital image at frame rates. All this image processing hardware is integrated into a suitably equipped PC. The objective is to design a software system that will work as fast as possible, using the available hardware, and whose function is to output the color of the panels. How would you design the system using only the concepts developed in this chapter? You may assume that the panels are moving slowly enough so that blur in the digitized images is negligible. Give your design in terms of a flowchart, discussing in detail the purpose of each function and your rationale for selecting that function.

IMAGE
RESTORATION

> Things which we see are not by themselves
> what we see. . . . It remains completely
> unknown to us what the objects may be by
> themselves and apart from the receptivity of our
> senses. We know nothing but our manner of
> perceiving them. . . .
> *Immanuel Kant*

As in image enhancement, the ultimate goal of restoration techniques is to improve an image in some sense. For the purpose of differentiation, we consider restoration to be a process that attempts to reconstruct or recover an image that has been degraded by using some a priori knowledge of the degradation phenomenon. Thus restoration techniques are oriented toward modeling the degradation and applying the inverse process in order to recover the original image. This approach usually involves formulating a criterion of goodness that will yield some optimal estimate of the desired result. By contrast, enhancement techniques basically are heuristic procedures designed to manipulate an image in order to take advantage of the psychophysical aspects of the human visual system. For example, contrast stretching is considered an enhancement technique because it is based primarily on the pleasing aspects it might present to the viewer, whereas removal of image blur by applying a deblurring function is considered a restoration technique.

Early techniques for digital image restoration were derived mostly from frequency domain concepts. However, this chapter focuses on a more modern, algebraic approach, which has the advantage of allowing the derivation of numerous restoration techniques from the same basic principles. Although a direct solution by algebraic methods generally involves the manipulation of large systems of simultaneous equations, we show that, under certain conditions, computational complexity can be reduced to the same level as that required by traditional frequency domain restoration techniques.

The material developed in this chapter is strictly introductory. We consider the restoration problem only from the point where a degraded, *digital* image is given; thus we do not consider topics dealing with sensor, digitizer, and display degradations. These subjects, although of importance in the overall treatment of image restoration applications, are beyond the present discussion. The references cited at the end of the chapter provide a guide to the voluminous literature on these and related topics.

5.1 DEGRADATION MODEL

As Fig. 5.1 shows, the degradation process is modeled in this chapter as an operator (or system) H, which together with an additive noise term $\eta(x, y)$ operates on an input image $f(x, y)$ to produce a degraded image $g(x, y)$. Digital image restoration may be viewed as the process of obtaining an approximation to $f(x, y)$, given $g(x, y)$ and a knowledge of the degradation in the form of the operator H. We assume that knowledge of $\eta(x, y)$ is limited to information of a statistical nature.

5.1.1 Some Definitions

The input–output relationship in Fig. 5.1 is expressed as

$$g(x, y) = H[f(x, y)] + \eta(x, y). \qquad (5.1\text{-}1)$$

For the moment, let us assume that $\eta(x, y) = 0$ so that $g(x, y) = H[f(x, y)]$. Then H is *linear* if

$$H[k_1 f_1(x, y) + k_2 f_2(x, y)] = k_1 H[f_1(x, y)] + k_2 H[f_2(x, y)] \qquad (5.1\text{-}2)$$

where k_1 and k_2 are constants and $f_1(x, y)$ and $f_2(x, y)$ are any two input images. If $k_1 = k_2 = 1$, Eq. (5.1-2) becomes

$$H[f_1(x, y) + f_2(x, y)] = H[f_1(x, y)] + H[f_2(x, y)] \qquad (5.1\text{-}3)$$

which is called the property of *additivity*; this property simply says that, if H is a linear operator, the response to a sum of two inputs is equal to the sum of the two responses.

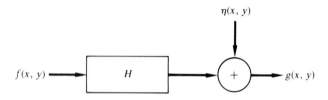

Figure 5.1   *A model of the image degradation process.*

With $f_2(x, y) = 0$, Eq. (5.1-2) becomes

$$H[k_1f_1(x, y)] = k_1H[f_1(x, y)] \qquad (5.1\text{-}4)$$

which is called the property of *homogeneity*. It says that the response to a constant multiple of any input is equal to the response to that input multiplied by the same constant. Thus a linear operator possesses both the property of additivity and the property of homogeneity.

An operator having the input–output relationship $g(x, y) = H[f(x, y)]$ is said to be *position* (or *space*) *invariant* if

$$H[f(x - \alpha, y - \beta)] = g(x - \alpha, y - \beta) \qquad (5.1\text{-}5)$$

for any $f(x, y)$ and any α and β. This definition indicates that the response at any point in the image depends only on the value of the input at that point and not on the position of the point.

5.1.2 Degradation Model for Continuous Functions

With a slight (but equivalent) change in notation in the definition of the impulse function, Eq. (3.3-46), $f(x, y)$ can be expressed in the form

$$f(x, y) = \int\limits_{-\infty}^{\infty}\!\!\int f(\alpha, \beta)\delta(x - \alpha, y - \beta)\, d\alpha\, d\beta. \qquad (5.1\text{-}6)$$

Then, if $\eta(x, y) = 0$ in Eq. (5.1-1),

$$g(x, y) = H[f(x, y)] = H\left[\int\limits_{-\infty}^{\infty}\!\!\int f(\alpha, \beta)\delta(x - \alpha, y - \beta)\, d\alpha\, d\beta\right]. \qquad (5.1\text{-}7)$$

If H is a linear operator and we extend the additivity property to integrals, then

$$g(x, y) = \int\limits_{-\infty}^{\infty}\!\!\int H[f(\alpha, \beta)\delta(x - \alpha, y - \beta)]\, d\alpha\, d\beta. \qquad (5.1\text{-}8)$$

Since $f(\alpha, \beta)$ is independent of x and y, and from the homogeneity property,

$$g(x, y) = \int\limits_{-\infty}^{\infty}\!\!\int f(\alpha, \beta)H[\delta(x - \alpha, y - \beta)]\, d\alpha\, d\beta. \qquad (5.1\text{-}9)$$

The term

$$h(x, \alpha, y, \beta) = H[\delta(x - \alpha, y - \beta)] \qquad (5.1\text{-}10)$$

is called the *impulse response* of H. In other words, if $\eta(x, y) = 0$ in Eq. (5.1-1), then $h(x, \alpha, y, \beta)$ is the response of H to an impulse of strength 1 at coordinates (α, β). In optics, the impulse becomes a point of light and $h(x, \alpha, y, \beta)$ is commonly referred to in this case as the *point spread function* (PSF), as discussed in Section 4.1.2.

Substituting Eq. (5.1-10) into Eq. (5.1-9) yields the expression

$$g(x, y) = \int\int_{-\infty}^{\infty} f(\alpha, \beta) h(x, \alpha, y, \beta) \, d\alpha \, d\beta \qquad (5.1\text{-}11)$$

which is called the *superposition* (or *Fredholm*) *integral of the first kind*. This expression is of fundamental importance in linear system theory. It states that if the response of H to an impulse is known, the response to any input $f(\alpha, \beta)$ can be calculated by means of Eq. (5.1-11). In other words, a linear system H is completely characterized by its impulse response.

If H is position invariant, from Eq. (5.1-5),

$$H[\delta(x - \alpha, y - \beta)] = h(x - \alpha, y - \beta). \qquad (5.1\text{-}12)$$

Equation (5.1-11) reduces in this case to

$$g(x, y) = \int\int_{-\infty}^{\infty} f(\alpha, \beta) h(x - \alpha, y - \beta) \, d\alpha \, d\beta \qquad (5.1\text{-}13)$$

which is the convolution integral defined in Eq. (3.3-30).

In the presence of additive noise the expression describing a linear degradation model becomes

$$g(x, y) = \int\int_{-\infty}^{\infty} f(\alpha, \beta) h(x, \alpha, y, \beta) \, d\alpha \, d\beta + \eta(x, y). \qquad (5.1\text{-}14)$$

If H is position invariant, Eq. (5.1-14) becomes

$$g(x, y) = \int\int_{-\infty}^{\infty} f(\alpha, \beta) h(x - \alpha, y - \beta) \, d\alpha \, d\beta + \eta(x, y). \qquad (5.1\text{-}15)$$

The noise, of course, is assumed in both cases to be independent of position in the image.

Many types of degradations can be approximated by linear, position invariant processes. The advantage of this approach is that the extensive tools of linear system theory then become available for the solution of image restoration problems. Nonlinear and space variant techniques, although more general (and usually more accurate), introduce difficulties that often have no known solution or are very difficult to solve computationally. This chapter focuses on linear, space invariant restoration techniques. However, even this simplification can result in computational problems that, if attacked directly, are beyond the practical capabilities of most present-day computers.

5.1.3 Discrete Formulation

The development of a discrete, space invariant degradation model is simplified by starting with the 1-D case and temporarily neglecting the noise term. Suppose that two functions $f(x)$ and $h(x)$ are sampled uniformly to form arrays of dimensions A and B, respectively. In this case, x is a discrete variable in the ranges, $0, 1, 2, \ldots, A - 1$ for $f(x)$ and $0, 1, 2, \ldots, B - 1$ for $h(x)$.

The discrete convolution formulation given in Section 3.3.8 is based on the assumption that the sampled functions are periodic, with a period M. Overlap in the individual periods of the resulting convolution is avoided by choosing $M \geq A + B - 1$ and extending the functions with zeros so that their length is equal to M. Letting $f_e(x)$ and $h_e(x)$ represent the extended functions yields, from Eq. (3.3-29), their convolution:

$$g_e(x) = \sum_{m=0}^{M-1} f_e(m) h_e(x - m) \tag{5.1-16}$$

for $x = 0, 1, 2, \ldots, M - 1$. As both $f_e(x)$ and $h_e(x)$ are assumed to have a period equal to M, $g_e(x)$ also has this period.

Using matrix notation, Eq. (5.1-16) can be expressed in the form

$$\mathbf{g} = \mathbf{Hf} \tag{5.1-17}$$

where $\mathbf{f}$ and $\mathbf{g}$ are M-dimensional column vectors:

$$\mathbf{f} = \begin{bmatrix} f_e(0) \\ f_e(1) \\ \vdots \\ f_e(M - 1) \end{bmatrix} \tag{5.1-18}$$

and

$$\mathbf{g} = \begin{bmatrix} g_e(0) \\ g_e(1) \\ \vdots \\ g_e(M-1) \end{bmatrix} \tag{5.1-19}$$

and **H** is the $M \times M$ matrix

$$\mathbf{H} = \begin{bmatrix} h_e(0) & h_e(-1) & h_e(-2) & \cdots & h_e(-M+1) \\ h_e(1) & h_e(0) & h_e(-1) & \cdots & h_e(-M+2) \\ h_e(2) & h_e(1) & h_e(0) & \cdots & h_e(-M+3) \\ \vdots & & & & \\ h_e(M-1) & h_e(M-2) & h_e(M-3) & \cdots & h_e(0) \end{bmatrix} \tag{5.1-20}$$

Because of the periodicity assumption on $h_e(x)$, it follows that $h_e(x) = h_e(M + x)$. This property allows Eq. (5.1-20) to be written in the form

$$\mathbf{H} = \begin{bmatrix} h_e(0) & h_e(M-1) & h_e(M-2) & \cdots & h_e(1) \\ h_e(1) & h_e(0) & h_e(M-1) & \cdots & h_e(2) \\ h_e(2) & h_e(1) & h_e(0) & \cdots & h_e(3) \\ \vdots & & & & \\ h_e(M-1) & h_e(M-2) & h_e(M-3) & \cdots & h_e(0) \end{bmatrix} \tag{5.1-21}$$

The structure of this matrix plays a fundamental role throughout the remainder of this chapter. In Eq. (5.1-21) the rows are related by a *circular shift* to the right; that is, the right-most element in one row is equal to the left-most element in the row immediately below. The shift is called circular because an element shifted off the right end of a row reappears at the left end of the next row. Moreover, in Eq. (5.1-21) the circularity of **H** is complete in the sense that it extends from the last row back to the first row. A square matrix in which each row is a circular shift of the preceding row, and the first row is a circular shift of the last row, is called a *circulant matrix*. Keep in mind that the circular behavior of **H** is a direct consequence of the assumed periodicity of $h_e(x)$.

Example: Suppose that $A = 4$ and $B = 3$. We may choose $M = 6$ and then append two zeros to the samples of $f(x)$ and three zeros to samples of $h(x)$.

In this case **f** and **g** are 6-D vectors and **H** is the 6 × 6 matrix

$$\mathbf{H} = \begin{bmatrix} h_e(0) & h_e(5) & h_e(4) & \cdots & h_e(1) \\ h_e(1) & h_e(0) & h_e(5) & \cdots & h_e(2) \\ h_e(2) & h_e(1) & h_e(0) & \cdots & h_e(3) \\ \vdots & & & & \\ h_e(5) & h_e(4) & h_e(3) & \cdots & h_e(0) \end{bmatrix}$$

However, as $h_e(x) = 0$ for $x = 3, 4, 5$, and $h_e(x) = h(x)$ for $x = 0, 1, 2,$

$$\mathbf{H} = \begin{bmatrix} h(0) & & & & & h(2) & h(1) \\ h(1) & h(0) & & & & & h(2) \\ h(2) & h(1) & h(0) & & & & \\ & h(2) & h(1) & h(0) & & & \\ & & h(2) & h(1) & h(0) & & \\ & & & h(2) & h(1)) & h(0) \end{bmatrix}$$

where all elements not indicated in the matrix are zero. ❑

Extension of the discussion to a 2-D, discrete degradation model is straight-forward. For two digitized images $f(x, y)$ and $h(x, y)$ of sizes $A \times B$ and $C \times D$, respectively, extended images of size $M \times N$ may be formed by padding the above functions with zeros. As indicated in Section 3.3.8, one procedure for doing this is to let

$$f_e(x, y) = \begin{cases} f(x, y) & 0 \leq x \leq A - 1 \quad \text{and} \quad 0 \leq y \leq B - 1 \\ 0 & A \leq x \leq M - 1 \quad \text{or} \quad B \leq y \leq N - 1 \end{cases}$$

and

$$h_e(x, y) = \begin{cases} h(x, y) & 0 \leq x \leq C - 1 \quad \text{and} \quad 0 \leq y \leq D - 1 \\ 0 & C \leq x \leq M - 1 \quad \text{or} \quad D \leq y \leq N - 1. \end{cases}$$

Treating the extended functions $f_e(x, y)$ and $h_e(x, y)$ as periodic in two dimensions, with periods M and N in the x and y directions, respectively, yields, from Eq. (3.3-35), the convolution of these two functions:

$$g_e(x, y) = \sum_{m=0}^{M-1} \sum_{n=0}^{N-1} f_e(m, n) h_e(x - m, y - n) \tag{5.1-22}$$

for $x = 0, 1, 2, \ldots, M - 1$ and $y = 0, 1, 2, \ldots, N - 1$. The convolution function $g_e(x, y)$ is periodic with the same period of $f_e(x, y)$ and $h_e(x, y)$. Overlap of the individual convolution periods is avoided by choosing $M \geq A + C - 1$ and $N \geq B + D - 1$. To complete the discrete degradation model requires adding an $M \times N$ extended discrete noise term $\eta_e(x, y)$ to Eq. (5.1-22) so that

$$g_e(x, y) = \sum_{m=0}^{M-1} \sum_{n=0}^{N-1} f_e(m, n) h_e(x - m, y - n) + \eta_e(x, y) \qquad (5.1-23)$$

for $x = 0, 1, 2, \ldots, M - 1$ and $y = 0, 1, 2, \ldots, N - 1$.

Let **f**, **g**, and **n** represent MN-dimensional column vectors formed by stacking the rows of the $M \times N$ functions $f_e(x, y)$, $g_e(x, y)$, and $\eta_e(x, y)$. The first N elements of **f**, for example, are the elements in the first row of $f_e(x, y)$, the next N elements are from the second row, and so on for all M rows of $f_e(x, y)$. This convention allows Eq. (5.1-23) to be expressed in vector-matrix form:

$$\mathbf{g} = \mathbf{Hf} + \mathbf{n} \qquad (5.1-24)$$

where **f**, **g**, and **n** are of dimension $(MN) \times 1$ and **H** is of dimension $MN \times MN$. This matrix consists of M^2 partitions, each partition being of size $N \times N$ and ordered according to

$$\mathbf{H} = \begin{bmatrix} \mathbf{H}_0 & \mathbf{H}_{M-1} & \mathbf{H}_{M-2} & \cdots & \mathbf{H}_1 \\ \mathbf{H}_1 & \mathbf{H}_0 & \mathbf{H}_{M-1} & \cdots & \mathbf{H}_2 \\ \mathbf{H}_2 & \mathbf{H}_1 & \mathbf{H}_0 & \cdots & \mathbf{H}_3 \\ \vdots & & & & \\ \mathbf{H}_{M-1} & \mathbf{H}_{M-2} & \mathbf{H}_{M-3} & \cdots & \mathbf{H}_0 \end{bmatrix} \qquad (5.1-25)$$

Each partition $\mathbf{H}_j$ is constructed from the jth row of the extended function $h_e(x, y)$, as follows:

$$\mathbf{H}_j = \begin{bmatrix} h_e(j,0) & h_e(j,N-1) & h_e(j,N-2) & \cdots & h_e(j,1) \\ h_e(j,1) & h_e(j,0) & h_e(j,N-1) & \cdots & h_e(j,2) \\ h_e(j,2) & h_e(j,1) & h_e(j,0) & \cdots & h_e(j,3) \\ \vdots & & & & \\ h_e(j,N-1) & h_e(j,N-2) & h_e(j,N-3) & \cdots & h_e(j,0) \end{bmatrix} \qquad (5.1-26)$$

where, as in Eq. (5.1-21), use was made of the periodicity of $h_e(x, y)$. Here, $\mathbf{H}_j$ is a circulant matrix, and the blocks of **H** are subscripted in a circular manner.

For these reasons, the matrix **H** in Eq. (5.1-25) is often called a *block-circulant* matrix.

Most of the discussion in the following sections centers on the discrete degradation model given in Eq. (5.1-24). Keep in mind that derivation of this expression was based on the assumption of a linear, space invariant degradation process. As indicated earlier, the objective is to estimate the image $f(x, y)$ given $g(x, y)$ and a knowledge of $h(x, y)$ and $\eta(x, y)$. In terms of Eq. (5.1-24), this objective requires estimating **f**, given **g** and some knowledge about **H** and **n**.

Although Eq. (5.1-24) seems deceptively simple, a direct solution of this expression to obtain the elements of **f** is a monumental processing task for images of practical size. If, for example, $M = N = 512$, **H** is of size 262,144 × 262,144. Thus to obtain **f** directly would require the solution of a system of 262,144 simultaneous linear equations. Fortunately, the complexity of this problem can be reduced considerably by taking advantage of the circulant properties of **H**.

5.2 DIAGONALIZATION OF CIRCULANT AND BLOCK-CIRCULANT MATRICES

We show in this section that solutions that are computationally feasible may be obtained from the model in Eq. (5.1-24) by diagonalizing the **H** matrix. In order to simplify the explanation we begin the discussion by considering circulant matrices and then extend the procedure to block-circulant matrices.

5.2.1 Circulant Matrices

Consider an $M \times M$ circulant matrix **H** of the form

$$\mathbf{H} = \begin{bmatrix} h_e(0) & h_e(M-1) & h_e(M-2) & \cdots & h_e(1) \\ h_e(1) & h_e(0) & h_e(M-1) & \cdots & h_e(2) \\ h_e(2) & h_e(1) & h_e(0) & \cdots & h_e(3) \\ \vdots & & & & \\ h_e(M-1) & h_e(M-2) & h_e(M-3) & \cdots & h_e(0) \end{bmatrix} \quad (5.2\text{-}1)$$

Let us define a scalar function $\lambda(k)$ and a vector $\mathbf{w}(k)$ as

$$\lambda(k) = h_e(0) + h_e(M-1)\exp\left[j\frac{2\pi}{M}k\right] + h_e(M-2)\exp\left[j\frac{2\pi}{M}2k\right]$$
$$+ \cdots + h_e(1)\exp\left[j\frac{2\pi}{M}(M-1)k\right] \quad (5.2\text{-}2)$$

where $j = \sqrt{-1}$, and

$$
\mathbf{w}(k) = \begin{bmatrix} 1 \\ \exp\left[j\dfrac{2\pi}{M}k\right] \\ \exp\left[j\dfrac{2\pi}{M}2k\right] \\ \vdots \\ \exp\left[j\dfrac{2\pi}{M}(M-1)k\right] \end{bmatrix}
\tag{5.2-3}
$$

for $k = 0, 1, 2, \ldots, M - 1$. It can be shown by matrix multiplication that

$$
\mathbf{Hw}(k) = \lambda(k)\mathbf{w}(k).
\tag{5.2-4}
$$

This expression indicates that $\mathbf{w}(k)$ is an eigenvector of the circulant matrix $\mathbf{H}$ and that $\lambda(k)$ is its corresponding eigenvalue (see Section 3.6).

Next, let us form an $M \times M$ matrix $\mathbf{W}$ by using the M eigenvectors of $\mathbf{H}$ as columns:

$$
\mathbf{W} = [\mathbf{w}(0) \quad \mathbf{w}(1) \quad \mathbf{w}(2) \quad \cdots \quad \mathbf{w}(M-1)].
\tag{5.2-5}
$$

The kith element of $\mathbf{W}$, denoted by $W(k, i)$, is given by

$$
W(k, i) = \exp\left[j\frac{2\pi}{M}ki\right]
\tag{5.2-6}
$$

for $k, i = 0, 1, 2, \ldots, M - 1$. The orthogonality properties of the complex exponential allows writing the inverse matrix, $\mathbf{W}^{-1}$, by inspection; its kith element, symbolized as $W^{-1}(k, i)$, is

$$
W^{-1}(k, i) = \frac{1}{M}\exp\left[-j\frac{2\pi}{M}ki\right].
\tag{5.2-7}
$$

From Eqs. (5.2-6) and (5.2-7),

$$
\mathbf{WW}^{-1} = \mathbf{W}^{-1}\mathbf{W} = \mathbf{I}
\tag{5.2-8}
$$

where $\mathbf{I}$ is the $M \times M$ identity matrix.

The importance of the existence of the inverse matrix $\mathbf{W}^{-1}$ is that it guarantees that the columns of $\mathbf{W}$ (the eigenvectors of $\mathbf{H}$) are *linearly independent*.

From elementary matrix theory (Noble [1969]) **H** then may be expressed in the form

$$\mathbf{H} = \mathbf{WDW}^{-1} \tag{5.2-9}$$

or

$$\mathbf{D} = \mathbf{W}^{-1}\mathbf{HW} \tag{5.2-10}$$

where **D** is a diagonal matrix whose elements $D(k, k)$ are the eigenvalues of **H**; that is,

$$D(k, k) = \lambda(k). \tag{5.2-11}$$

Equation (5.2-10) indicates that **H** is diagonalized by using $\mathbf{W}^{-1}$ and **W** in the order indicated.

5.2.2 Block-Circulant Matrices

The transformation matrix for diagonalizing block circulants is constructed as follows. Let

$$w_M(i, m) = \exp\left[j\,\frac{2\pi}{M}\,im\right] \tag{5.2-12}$$

and

$$w_N(k, n) = \exp\left[j\,\frac{2\pi}{N}\,kn\right]. \tag{5.2-13}$$

Based on this notation, we define a matrix **W** of size $MN \times MN$ and containing M^2 partitions of size $N \times N$. The imth partition of **W** is

$$\mathbf{W}(i, m) = w_M(i, m)\mathbf{W}_N \tag{5.2-14}$$

for $i, m = 0, 1, 2, \ldots, M - 1$. Then $\mathbf{W}_N$ is an $N \times N$ matrix with elements

$$W_N(k, n) = w_N(k, n) \tag{5.2-15}$$

for $k, n = 0, 1, 2, \ldots, N - 1$.

The inverse matrix $\mathbf{W}^{-1}$ is also of size $MN \times MN$ with M^2 partitions of size $N \times N$. The imth partition of $\mathbf{W}^{-1}$, symbolized as $\mathbf{W}^{-1}(i, m)$, is

$$\mathbf{W}^{-1}(i, m) = \frac{1}{M}\,w_M^{-1}(i, m)\mathbf{W}_N^{-1} \tag{5.2-16}$$

where $w_M^{-1}(i, m)$ is

$$w_M^{-1}(i, m) = \exp\left[-j\frac{2\pi}{M}im\right] \tag{5.2-17}$$

for $i, m = 0, 1, 2, \ldots, M - 1$. The matrix $\mathbf{W}_N^{-1}$ has elements

$$W_N^{-1}(k, n) = \frac{1}{N} w_N^{-1}(k, n) \tag{5.2-18}$$

where

$$w_N^{-1}(k, n) = \exp\left[-j\frac{2\pi}{N}kn\right] \tag{5.2-19}$$

for $k, n = 0, 1, 2, \ldots, N - 1$. It can be verified by direct substitution of the elements of $\mathbf{W}$ and $\mathbf{W}^{-1}$ that

$$\mathbf{WW}^{-1} = \mathbf{W}^{-1}\mathbf{W} = \mathbf{I} \tag{5.2-20}$$

where $\mathbf{I}$ is the $MN \times MN$ identity matrix.

From the results in Section 5.2.1, and if $\mathbf{H}$ is a block-circulant matrix, it can be shown (Hunt [1973]) that

$$\mathbf{H} = \mathbf{WDW}^{-1} \tag{5.2-21}$$

or

$$\mathbf{D} = \mathbf{W}^{-1}\mathbf{HW} \tag{5.2-22}$$

where $\mathbf{D}$ is a diagonal matrix whose elements $D(k, k)$ are related to the discrete Fourier transform of the extended function $h_e(x, y)$ discussed in Section 5.1.3. Moreover, the transpose of $\mathbf{H}$, denoted $\mathbf{H}^T$, is

$$\mathbf{H}^T = \mathbf{WD}^*\mathbf{W}^{-1} \tag{5.2-23}$$

where $\mathbf{D}^*$ is the complex conjugate of $\mathbf{D}$.

5.2.3 Effects of Diagonalization on the Degradation Model

The matrix $\mathbf{H}$ in the discrete, 1-D model of Eq. (5.1-17) is circulant, so it may be expressed in the form of Eq. (5.2-9). Equation (5.1-17) then becomes

$$\mathbf{g} = \mathbf{WDW}^{-1}\mathbf{f}. \tag{5.2-24}$$

Rearranging this equation yields

$$\mathbf{W}^{-1}\mathbf{g} = \mathbf{DW}^{-1}\mathbf{f}. \tag{5.2-25}$$

The product $\mathbf{W}^{-1}\mathbf{f}$ is an M-dimensional column vector. From Eq. (5.2-7) and the definition of $\mathbf{f}$ in Section 5.1.3, the kth element of the product $\mathbf{W}^{-1}\mathbf{f}$, denoted $F(k)$, is

$$F(k) = \frac{1}{M} \sum_{i=0}^{M-1} f_e(i)\exp\left[-j\frac{2\pi}{M}ki\right] \tag{5.2-26}$$

for $k = 0, 1, 2, \ldots, M - 1$. This expression is recognized as the discrete Fourier transform of the extended sequence $f_e(x)$. In other words, multiplication of $\mathbf{f}$ by $\mathbf{W}^{-1}$ yields a vector whose elements are the Fourier transforms of the elements of $\mathbf{f}$. Similarly, $\mathbf{W}^{-1}\mathbf{g}$ yields the Fourier transform of the elements of $\mathbf{g}$, denoted $G(k)$, $k = 0, 1, 2, \ldots, M - 1$.

Next, we examine the matrix $\mathbf{D}$ in Eq. (5.2-25). The discussion in Section 5.2.1 showed that the main diagonal elements of $\mathbf{D}$ are the eigenvalues of the circulant matrix $\mathbf{H}$. The eigenvalues are given in Eq. (5.2-2) which, using the fact that

$$\exp\left[j\frac{2\pi}{M}(M-i)k\right] = \exp\left[-j\frac{2\pi}{M}ik\right] \tag{5.2-27}$$

may be written in the form

$$\lambda(k) = h_e(0) + h_e(1)\exp\left[-j\frac{2\pi}{M}k\right] + h_e(2)\exp\left[-j\frac{2\pi}{M}2k\right]$$
$$+ \cdots + h_e(M-1)\exp\left[-j\frac{2\pi}{M}(M-1)k\right]. \tag{5.2-28}$$

From Eqs. (5.2-11) and (5.2-28),

$$D(k, k) = \lambda(k) = \sum_{i=0}^{M-1} h_e(i)\exp\left[-j\frac{2\pi}{M}ki\right] \tag{5.2-29}$$

for $k = 0, 1, 2, \ldots, M - 1$. The right-hand side of this equation is $MH(k)$, where $H(k)$ is the discrete Fourier transform of the extended sequence $h_e(x)$. Thus

$$D(k, k) = MH(k). \tag{5.2-30}$$

These transforms can be combined into one result. Since $\mathbf{D}$ is a diagonal matrix, the product of $\mathbf{D}$ with any vector multiplies each element of that vector by a single diagonal element of $\mathbf{D}$. Consequently, the matrix formulation given in Eq. (5.2-25) can be reduced to a term-by-term product of 1-D Fourier transform sequences. In other words,

$$G(k) = MH(k)F(k) \tag{5.2-31}$$

for $k = 0, 1, 2, \ldots, M - 1$, where $G(k)$ are the elements of the vector $\mathbf{W}^{-1}\mathbf{g}$ and $MH(k)F(k)$ the elements of vector $\mathbf{DW}^{-1}\mathbf{f}$. The right-hand side of Eq. (5.2-31) is the convolution of $f_e(x)$ and $h_e(x)$ in the frequency domain (see Section 3.3.8). Computationally, this result implies considerable simplification, because $G(k)$, $H(k)$, and $F(k)$ are M-sample discrete transforms, which can be obtained by using a fast Fourier transform algorithm.

A procedure similar to the preceding development yields equivalent results for the 2-D degradation model. Multiplying both sides of Eq. (5.1-24) by $\mathbf{W}^{-1}$ and using Eqs. (5.2-20) and (5.2-21) yields

$$\mathbf{W}^{-1}\mathbf{g} = \mathbf{DW}^{-1}\mathbf{f} + \mathbf{W}^{-1}\mathbf{n} \tag{5.2-32}$$

where $\mathbf{W}^{-1}$ is an $MN \times MN$ matrix whose elements are given in Eq. (5.2-16), $\mathbf{D}$ is an $MN \times MN$ diagonal matrix, $\mathbf{H}$ is the $MN \times MN$ block-circulant matrix defined in Eq. (5.1-25), and $\mathbf{f}$ and $\mathbf{g}$ are vectors of dimension MN formed by stacking the rows of the extended images $f_e(x, y)$ and $g_e(x, y)$, respectively.

The left-hand side of Eq. (5.2-32) is a vector of dimension $MN \times 1$. Let us denote its elements $G(0, 0)$, $G(0, 1)$, $\ldots$, $G(0, N - 1)$; $G(1, 0)$, $G(1, 1)$, $\ldots$, $G(1, N - 1)$; $\ldots$; $G(M - 1, 0)$, $G(M - 1, 1)$, $\ldots$, $G(M - 1, N - 1)$. It can be shown (Hunt [1973]) that

$$G(u, v) = \frac{1}{MN} \sum_{x=0}^{M-1} \sum_{y=0}^{N-1} g_e(x, y) \exp\left[-j2\pi\left(\frac{ux}{M} + \frac{vy}{N}\right)\right] \tag{5.2-33}$$

for $u = 0, 1, 2, \ldots, M - 1$, and $v = 0, 1, 2, \ldots, N - 1$. Equation (5.2-33) is the 2-D Fourier transform of $g_e(x, y)$. In other words, the elements of $\mathbf{W}^{-1}\mathbf{g}$ correspond to the stacked rows of the Fourier transform matrix with elements $G(u, v)$ for $u = 0, 1, 2, \ldots, M - 1$ and $v = 0, 1, 2, \ldots, N - 1$. Similarly, the vectors $\mathbf{W}^{-1}\mathbf{f}$ and $\mathbf{W}^{-1}\mathbf{n}$ are MN-dimensional and contain elements $F(u, v)$ and $N(u, v)$, where

$$F(u, v) = \frac{1}{MN} \sum_{x=0}^{M-1} \sum_{y=0}^{N-1} f_e(x, y) \exp\left[-j2\pi\left(\frac{ux}{M} + \frac{vy}{N}\right)\right] \tag{5.2-34}$$

and

$$N(u, v) = \frac{1}{MN} \sum_{x=0}^{M-1} \sum_{y=0}^{N-1} \eta_e(x, y) \exp\left[-j2\pi\left(\frac{ux}{M} + \frac{vy}{N}\right)\right] \tag{5.2-35}$$

for $u = 0, 1, 2, \ldots, M - 1$ and $v = 0, 1, 2, \ldots, N - 1$.

Finally, the elements of the diagonal matrix $\mathbf{D}$ are related to the Fourier transform of the extended impulse response function $h_e(x, y)$; that is,

$$H(u, v) = \frac{1}{MN} \sum_{x=0}^{M-1} \sum_{y=0}^{N-1} h_e(x, y) \exp\left[-j2\pi\left(\frac{ux}{M} + \frac{vy}{N}\right)\right] \tag{5.2-36}$$

for $u = 0, 1, 2, \ldots , M - 1$, and $v = 0, 1, 2, \ldots , N - 1$. The MN diagonal elements of **D** are formed as follows. The first N elements are $H(0, 0)$, $H(0, 1), \ldots , H(0, N - 1)$; the next, $H(1, 0), H(1, 1), \ldots , H(1, N - 1)$; and so on, with the last N diagonal elements being $H(M - 1, 0), H(M - 1, 1), \ldots , H(M - 1, N - 1)$. The off-diagonal elements, of course, are zero. The entire matrix formed from the preceding elements is then multiplied by MN to obtain **D**. A more concise way of expressing this construction is as

$$D(k, i) = \begin{cases} MNH\left(\left[\dfrac{k}{N}\right], k \bmod N\right) & \text{if } i = k \\ 0 & \text{if } i \neq k \end{cases}$$

(5.2-37)

where $[c]$ is used to denote the greatest integer not exceeding c, and $k \bmod N$ is the remainder obtained by dividing k by N.

Equations (5.2-33)–(5.2-36) can be used to show that the individual elements of Eq. (5.2-32) are related by the expression

$$G(u, v) = MNH(u, v)F(u, v) + N(u, v)$$

(5.2-38)

for $u = 0, 1, 2, \ldots , M - 1$, and $v = 0, 1, 2, \ldots , N - 1$.

The term MN is simply a scale factor, which for notational purposes can be absorbed conveniently in $H(u, v)$. With this notation, Eqs. (5.2-37) and (5.2-38) may be expressed as

$$D(k, i) = \begin{cases} H\left(\left[\dfrac{k}{N}\right], k \bmod N\right) & \text{if } i = k \\ 0 & \text{if } i \neq k \end{cases}$$

(5.2-39)

for $k, i = 0, 1, 2, \ldots , MN - 1$, and

$$G(u, v) = H(u, v)F(u, v) + N(u, v)$$

(5.2-40)

for $u = 0, 1, 2, \ldots , M - 1$, and $v = 0, 1, 2, \ldots , N - 1$, with $H(u, v)$ now scaled by the factor MN.

The significance of Eq. (5.2-38) or (5.2-40) is that the large system of equations implicit in the model in Eq. (5.1-24) can be reduced to computation of a few discrete Fourier transforms of size $M \times N$. If M and N are integer powers of 2, for example, this is a simple problem if we use an FFT algorithm. As mentioned earlier, however, the problem becomes an almost impossible computational task if approached directly from the model in Eq. (5.1-24).

We use the model in Eq. (5.1-24) in the following sections as the basis for deriving several image restoration approaches. We then simplify the results, which are in matrix form, by using the concepts introduced in this section. Keep in mind that the simplifications achieved are the result of assuming that (1) the degradation is a linear, space invariant process, and (2) all images are treated as extended, periodic functions.

Equation (5.2-40) could have been written directly from Eq. (5.1-15) via the convolution theorem. However, our objective was to show that the same result could be achieved by a matrix formulation. In so doing, we established a number of important matrix properties for use in Section 5.3 to develop a unified approach to restoration.

5.3 ALGEBRAIC APPROACH TO RESTORATION

As indicated in Section 5.1.3, the objective of image restoration is to estimate an original image $\mathbf{f}$ from a degraded image $\mathbf{g}$ and some knowledge or assumptions about $\mathbf{H}$ and $\mathbf{n}$. Assuming that these quantities are related according to the model in Eq. (5.1-24) allows formulation of a class of image restoration problems in a unified linear algebraic framework.

Central to the algebraic approach is the concept of seeking an estimate of $\mathbf{f}$, denoted $\hat{\mathbf{f}}$, that minimizes a predefined criterion of performance. Because of their simplicity, this chapter focuses on least squares criterion functions. This choice has the added advantage of yielding a central approach for the derivation of several well-known restoration methods. These methods are the result of considering either an unconstrained or a constrained approach to the least squares restoration problem.

5.3.1 Unconstrained Restoration

From Eq. (5.1-24), the noise term in the degradation model is

$$\mathbf{n} = \mathbf{g} - \mathbf{Hf}. \tag{5.3-1}$$

In the absence of any knowledge about $\mathbf{n}$, a meaningful criterion function is to seek an $\hat{\mathbf{f}}$ such that $\mathbf{H}\hat{\mathbf{f}}$ approximates $\mathbf{g}$ in a least squares sense by assuming that the norm of the noise term is as small as possible. In other words, we want to find an $\hat{\mathbf{f}}$ such that

$$\|\mathbf{n}\|^2 = \|\mathbf{g} - \mathbf{H}\hat{\mathbf{f}}\|^2 \tag{5.3-2}$$

is minimum, where, by definition,

$$\|\mathbf{n}\|^2 = \mathbf{n}^T\mathbf{n} \quad \text{and} \quad \|\mathbf{g} - \mathbf{H}\hat{\mathbf{f}}\|^2 = (\mathbf{g} - \mathbf{H}\hat{\mathbf{f}})^T(\mathbf{g} - \mathbf{H}\hat{\mathbf{f}})$$

are the squared norms of $\mathbf{n}$ and $(\mathbf{g} - \mathbf{H}\hat{\mathbf{f}})$, respectively. Equation (5.3-2) allows the equivalent view of this problem as one of minimizing the criterion function

$$J(\hat{\mathbf{f}}) = \|\mathbf{g} - \mathbf{H}\hat{\mathbf{f}}\|^2 \qquad (5.3\text{-}3)$$

with respect to $\hat{\mathbf{f}}$. Aside from the requirement that it minimize Eq. (5.3-3), $\hat{\mathbf{f}}$ is not constrained in any other way.

Minimization of Eq. (5.3-3) is straightforward. We simply differentiate J with respect to $\hat{\mathbf{f}}$ and set the result equal to the zero vector; that is,

$$\frac{\partial J(\hat{\mathbf{f}})}{\partial \hat{\mathbf{f}}} = \mathbf{0} = -2\mathbf{H}^T(\mathbf{g} - \mathbf{H}\hat{\mathbf{f}}). \qquad (5.3\text{-}4)$$

Solving Eq. (5.3-4) for $\hat{\mathbf{f}}$ yields

$$\hat{\mathbf{f}} = (\mathbf{H}^T\mathbf{H})^{-1}\mathbf{H}^T\mathbf{g}. \qquad (5.3\text{-}5)$$

Letting $M = N$ so that $\mathbf{H}$ is a square matrix and assuming that $\mathbf{H}^{-1}$ exists reduces Eq. (5.3-5) to

$$\hat{\mathbf{f}} = \mathbf{H}^{-1}(\mathbf{H}^T)^{-1}\mathbf{H}^T\mathbf{g} \qquad (5.3\text{-}6)$$
$$= \mathbf{H}^{-1}\mathbf{g}.$$

5.3.2   Constrained Restoration

In this section, we consider the least squares restoration problem as one of minimizing functions of the form $\|\mathbf{Q}\hat{\mathbf{f}}\|^2$, where $\mathbf{Q}$ is a linear operator on $\mathbf{f}$, subject to the constraint $\|\mathbf{g} - \mathbf{H}\hat{\mathbf{f}}\|^2 = \|\mathbf{n}\|^2$. This approach introduces considerable flexibility in the restoration process because it yields different solutions for different choices of $\mathbf{Q}$. The constraint imposed on a solution is consistent with the model in Eq. (5.1-24).

The addition of an equality constraint in the minimization problem can be handled without difficulty by using the method of *Lagrange multipliers* (Elsgolc [1961]). The procedure calls for expressing the constraint in the form $\alpha(\|\mathbf{g} - \mathbf{H}\hat{\mathbf{f}}\|^2 - \|\mathbf{n}\|^2)$ and then appending it to the function $\|\mathbf{Q}\hat{\mathbf{f}}\|^2$. In other words, we seek an $\hat{\mathbf{f}}$ that minimizes the criterion function

$$J(\hat{\mathbf{f}}) = \|\mathbf{Q}\hat{\mathbf{f}}\|^2 + \alpha(\|\mathbf{g} - \mathbf{H}\hat{\mathbf{f}}\|^2 - \|\mathbf{n}\|^2) \qquad (5.3\text{-}7)$$

where α is a constant called the *Lagrange multiplier*. After the constraint has been appended, minimization is carried out in the usual way.

Differentiating Eq. (5.3-7) with respect to $\hat{\mathbf{f}}$ and setting the result equal to the zero vector yields

$$\frac{\partial J(\hat{\mathbf{f}})}{\partial \hat{\mathbf{f}}} = \mathbf{0} = 2\mathbf{Q}^T\mathbf{Q}\hat{\mathbf{f}} - 2\alpha\mathbf{H}^T(\mathbf{g} - \mathbf{H}\hat{\mathbf{f}}). \qquad (5.3\text{-}8)$$

The solution is obtained by solving Eq. (5.3-8) for $\hat{\mathbf{f}}$; that is,

$$\hat{\mathbf{f}} = (\mathbf{H}^T\mathbf{H} + \gamma\mathbf{Q}^T\mathbf{Q})^{-1}\mathbf{H}^T\mathbf{g} \qquad (5.3\text{-}9)$$

where $\gamma = 1/\alpha$. This quantity must be adjusted so that the constraint is satisfied, a problem considered later in this chapter. Equations (5.3-6) and (5.3-9) are the bases for all the restoration procedures discussed in the following sections. In Section 5.4, for example, we show that Eq. (5.3-6) leads to the traditional inverse-filter restoration method. Similarly, the general formulation in Eq. (5.3-9) can be used to derive results such as the classical Wiener filter, as well as other restoration techniques. To do so simply requires selecting an appropriate transformation matrix $\mathbf{Q}$ and using the simplifications derived in Section 5.2.

5.4 INVERSE FILTERING

5.4.1 Formulation

We begin the derivation of image restoration techniques by considering the unconstrained result in Eq. (5.3-6). If we assume that $M = N$ and use Eq. (5.2-21), Eq. (5.3-6) becomes

$$\begin{aligned}\hat{\mathbf{f}} &= \mathbf{H}^{-1}\mathbf{g} \\ &= (\mathbf{W}\mathbf{D}\mathbf{W}^{-1})^{-1}\mathbf{g} \\ &= \mathbf{W}\mathbf{D}^{-1}\mathbf{W}^{-1}\mathbf{g}.\end{aligned} \qquad (5.4\text{-}1)$$

Premultiplying both sides of Eq. (5.4-1) by $\mathbf{W}^{-1}$ yields

$$\mathbf{W}^{-1}\hat{\mathbf{f}} = \mathbf{D}^{-1}\mathbf{W}^{-1}\mathbf{g}. \qquad (5.4\text{-}2)$$

From the discussion in Section 5.2.3, the elements comprising Eq. (5.4-2) may be written in the form

$$\hat{F}(u, v) = \frac{G(u, v)}{H(u, v)} \qquad (5.4\text{-}3)$$

for $u, v = 0, 1, 2, \ldots, N - 1$. According to Eq. (5.2-39), $H(u, v)$ is assumed to be scaled by N^2 and, because $\mathbf{D}$ is a diagonal matrix, its inverse is easily obtained by inspection.

The image restoration approach given by Eq. (5.4-3) is commonly referred to as the *inverse filter* method. This terminology arises from considering $H(u, v)$ as a "filter" function that multiplies $F(u, v)$ to produce the transform of the degraded image $g(x, y)$. The division of $G(u, v)$ by $H(u, v)$ indicated in Eq. (5.4-3) then constitutes an inverse filtering operation in this context. The restored image, of course, is obtained by using the relation

$$\hat{f}(x, y) = \mathfrak{F}^{-1}[\hat{F}(u, v)] \qquad (5.4\text{-}4)$$
$$= \mathfrak{F}^{-1}[G(u, v)/H(u, v)]$$

for $x, y = 0, 1, 2, \ldots, N - 1$. This procedure is normally implemented by means of an FFT algorithm.

Note in Eq. (5.4-4) that computational difficulties will be encountered in the restoration process if $H(u, v)$ vanishes or becomes very small in any region of interest in the uv plane. If the zeros of $H(u, v)$ are located at a few known points in the uv plane, they generally can be neglected in the computation of $\hat{F}(u, v)$ without noticeably affecting the restored result.

A more serious difficulty arises in the presence of noise. Substituting Eq. (5.2-40) into Eq. (5.4-3) yields

$$\hat{F}(u, v) = F(u, v) + \frac{N(u, v)}{H(u, v)}. \qquad (5.4\text{-}5)$$

This expression clearly indicates that if $H(u, v)$ is zero or becomes very small, the term $N(u, v)/H(u, v)$ could dominate the restoration result $\mathfrak{F}^{-1}[\hat{F}(u, v)]$. In practice $H(u, v)$ often drops off rapidly as a function of distance from the origin of the uv plane. The noise term, however, usually falls off at a much slower rate. In such situations, reasonable results often can be obtained by carrying out the restoration in a limited neighborhood about the origin in order to avoid small values of $H(u, v)$.

Example: Figure 5.2(a) shows a point image $f(x, y)$, and Fig. 5.2(b) shows a degraded image $g(x, y)$ obtained by blurring $f(x, y)$. Considering the point source to be an approximation to a unit impulse function gives

$$G(u, v) = H(u, v)F(u, v)$$
$$\approx H(u, v)$$

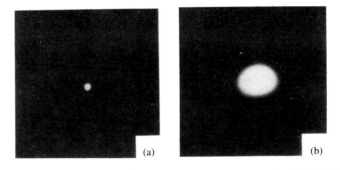
(a)   (b)

Figure 5.2   *Blurring of a point source to obtain $H(u, v)$.*

because $\mathcal{F}[\delta(x, y)] = 1$. This expression indicates that the transfer function $H(u, v)$ can be approximated by the Fourier transform of the degraded image. The procedure of blurring a known function to obtain an approximation to $H(u, v)$ is a useful one in practice because it can often be used in a trial-and-error approach to restore images for which the blurring function $H(u, v)$ is not known a priori.

The result of applying the same blurring function as above to the ideal image shown in Fig. 5.3(a) is shown in Fig. 5.3(b). The restored image shown in Fig. 5.3(c) was obtained by using Eq. (5.4-4) for values of u and v near enough to the origin of the uv plane to avoid excessively small values of $H(u, v)$. The result of carrying out the restoration for a larger neighborhood is shown in Fig. 5.3(d). These results clearly point out the difficulties introduced by a vanishing function $H(u, v)$.   ❏

If $H(u, v)$, $G(u, v)$, and $N(u, v)$ all are known, an exact inverse filtering expression can be obtained directly from Eq. (5.2-40); that is,

$$F(u, v) = \frac{G(u, v)}{H(u, v)} - \frac{N(u, v)}{H(u, v)}. \qquad (5.4\text{-}6)$$

In addition to the potential difficulties with $H(u, v)$ outlined in the preceding example, a problem with this formulation is that the noise is seldom known well enough to allow computation of $N(u, v)$.

5.4.2   Removal of Blur Caused by Uniform Linear Motion

There are practical applications in which $H(u, v)$ can be obtained analytically, but the solution has zero values in the frequency range of interest. In Section 5.4.1, we gave an example of the difficulties caused by a vanishing $H(u, v)$. In the following discussion we consider the problem of restoring an image that has been blurred by uniform linear motion. We singled out this problem because of its practical implications and also because it lends itself well to an analytical formulation. Solution of the uniform blurring case also demonstrates how zeros of $H(u, v)$ can be handled computationally. These considerations are important, because they often arise in practice in other contexts of image restoration by inverse filtering.

Suppose that an image $f(x, y)$ undergoes planar motion and that $x_0(t)$ and $y_0(t)$ are the time varying components of motion in the x and y directions, respectively. The total exposure at any point of the recording medium (say, film) is obtained in this case by integrating the instantaneous exposure over the time interval during which the shutter is open. Assuming that shutter opening and closing takes place instantaneously and that the optical imaging process is perfect isolates the effect of image motion. Then, if T is the duration of the

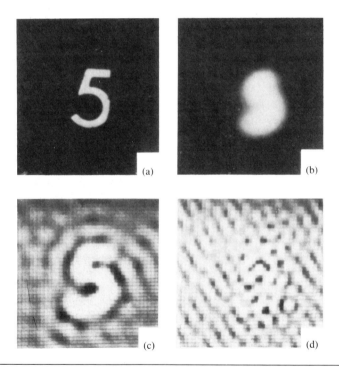

Figure 5.3 *Example of image restoration by inverse filtering: (a) original image $f(x, y)$; (b) degraded (blurred) image $g(x, y)$; (c) result of restoration by considering a neighborhood about the origin of the uv plane that does not include excessively small values of $H(u, v)$; (d) result of using a larger neighborhood in which this condition does not hold. (From McGlamery [1967].)*

exposure, it follows that

$$g(x, y) = \int_0^T f[x - x_0(t), y - y_0(t)] \, dt \qquad (5.4\text{-}7)$$

where $g(x, y)$ is the blurred image.

From Eq. (3.1-9), the Fourier transform of Eq. (5.4-7) is

$$G(u, v) = \int\int_{-\infty}^{\infty} g(x, y) \exp[-j2\pi(ux + vy)] \, dx \, dy$$

$$= \int\int_{-\infty}^{\infty} \left[\int_0^T f[x - x_0(t), y - y_0(t)] \, dt \right] \exp[-j2\pi(ux + vy)] \, dx \, dy. \qquad (5.4\text{-}8)$$

Reversing the order of integration allows Eq. (5.4-8) to be expressed in the form

$$G(u, v) = \int_0^T \left[\int\int_{-\infty}^{\infty} f[x - x_0(t), y - y_0(t)] \exp[-j2\pi(ux + vy)] \, dx \, dy \right] dt. \qquad (5.4\text{-}9)$$

The term inside the outer brackets is the Fourier transform of the displaced function $f[x - x_0(t), y - y_0(t)]$. Using Eq. (3.3-7b) then yields the relation

$$G(u, v) = \int_0^T F(u, v) \exp\{-j2\pi[ux_0(t) + vy_0(t)]\} \, dt$$

$$= F(u, v) \int_0^T \exp\{-j2\pi[ux_0(t) + vy_0(t)]\} \, dt \qquad (5.4\text{-}10)$$

where the last step follows from the fact that $F(u, v)$ is independent of t.

By defining

$$H(u, v) = \int_0^T \exp\{-j2\pi[ux_0(t) + vy_0(t)]\} \, dt \qquad (5.4\text{-}11)$$

Eq. (5.4-10) may be expressed in the familiar form

$$G(u, v) = H(u, v) F(u, v). \qquad (5.4\text{-}12)$$

If the nature of the motion variables $x_0(t)$ and $y_0(t)$ is known, the transfer function $H(u, v)$ can be obtained directly from Eq. (5.4-11). As an illustration, suppose that the image in question undergoes uniform linear motion in the x direction only, at a rate given by $x_0(t) = at/T$. When $t = T$, the image has been displaced by a total distance a. With $y_0(t) = 0$, Eq. (5.4-11) yields

$$H(u, v) = \int_0^T \exp[-j2\pi u x_0(t)] \, dt$$

$$= \int_0^T \exp[-j2\pi u a t / T] \, dt \qquad (5.4\text{-}13)$$

$$= \frac{T}{\pi u a} \sin(\pi u a) e^{-j\pi u a}.$$

Obviously, H vanishes at values of u given by $u = n/a$, where n is an integer. When $f(x, y)$ is zero (or known) outside an interval $0 \leqslant x \leqslant L$, the problem presented by Eq. (5.4-13) can be avoided and the image completely reconstructed from a knowledge of $g(x, y)$ in this interval. Because y is time invariant, suppressing this variable temporarily allows Eq. (5.4-7) to be written as

$$g(x) = \int_0^T f[x - x_0(t)] \, dt$$

$$= \int_0^T f\left(x - \frac{at}{T}\right) dt \qquad 0 \leqslant x \leqslant L. \qquad (5.4\text{-}14)$$

Substituting $\tau = x - at/T$ in this expression and ignoring a scale factor yields

$$g(x) = \int_{x-a}^x f(\tau) \, d\tau \qquad 0 \leqslant x \leqslant L. \qquad (5.4\text{-}15)$$

Then, by differentiation with respect to x (using Liebnitz's rule),

$$g'(x) = f(x) - f(x - a) \qquad 0 \leqslant x \leqslant L \qquad (5.4\text{-}16)$$

or

$$f(x) = g'(x) + f(x - a) \qquad 0 \leqslant x \leqslant L. \qquad (5.4\text{-}17)$$

In the following development a convenient assumption is that $L = Ka$, where K is an integer. Then the variable x may be expressed in the form

$$x = z + ma \qquad (5.4\text{-}18)$$

where z takes on values in the interval $[0, a]$ and m is the integral part of (x/a). For example, if $a = 2$ and $x = 3.5$, then $m = 1$ (the integral part of $3.5/2$), and $z = 1.5$. Clearly, $z + ma = 3.5$, as required. Note also that, for $L = Ka$, the index m can assume any of the integer values $0, 1, \ldots, K - 1$. For instance, when $x = L$, then $z = a$ and $m = K - 1$.

Substitution of Eq. (5.4-18) into Eq. (5.4-17) yields

$$f(z + ma) = g'(z + ma) + f[z + (m - 1)a]. \qquad (5.4\text{-}19)$$

Next, denoting $\phi(z)$ as the portion of the scene that moves into the range $0 \leqslant z < a$ during exposure gives

$$\phi(z) = f(z - a) \qquad 0 \leqslant z < a. \qquad (5.4\text{-}20)$$

Equation (5.4-19) can be solved recursively in terms of $\phi(z)$. Thus for $m = 0$,

$$\begin{aligned} f(z) &= g'(z) + f(z - a) \\ &= g'(z) + \phi(z). \end{aligned} \qquad (5.4\text{-}21)$$

For $m = 1$, Eq. (5.4-19) becomes

$$f(z + a) = g'(z + a) + f(z). \qquad (5.4\text{-}22)$$

Substituting Eq. (5.4-21) into Eq. (5.4-22) yields

$$f(z + a) = g'(z + a) + g'(z) + \phi(z). \qquad (5.4\text{-}23)$$

In the next step, letting $m = 2$ results in the expression

$$f(z + 2a) = g'(z + 2a) + f(z + a) \qquad (5.4\text{-}24)$$

or, substituting Eq. (5.4-23) for $f(z + a)$,

$$f(z + 2a) = g'(z + 2a) + g'(z + a) + g'(z) + \phi(z). \qquad (5.4\text{-}25)$$

Continuing with this procedure finally yields

$$f(z + ma) = \sum_{k=0}^{m} g'(z + ka) + \phi(z). \qquad (5.4\text{-}26)$$

However, as $x = z + ma$, Eq. (5.4-26) may be expressed in the form

$$f(x) = \sum_{k=0}^{m} g'(x - ka) + \phi(x - ma) \qquad 0 \leqslant x \leqslant L. \qquad (5.4\text{-}27)$$

Because $g(x)$ is known, the problem is reduced to that of estimating $\phi(x)$.

One way to estimate this function directly from the blurred image is as follows. First note that, as x varies from 0 to L, m ranges from 0 to $K - 1$. The argument of ϕ is $(x - ma)$, which is always in the range $0 \leqslant x - ma <$

a, so ϕ is repeated K times during the evaluation of $f(x)$ for $0 \leqslant x \leqslant L$. Next, defining

$$\bar{f}(x) = \sum_{j=0}^{m} g'(x - ja) \tag{5.4-28}$$

allows rewriting Eq. (5.4-27) as

$$\phi(x - ma) = f(x) - \bar{f}(x). \tag{5.4-29}$$

Evaluating the left-hand and right-hand sides of Eq. (5.4-29) for $ka \leqslant x < (k + 1)a$, and adding the results for $k = 0, 1, \ldots, K - 1$ gives

$$K\phi(x) = \sum_{k=0}^{K-1} f(x + ka) - \sum_{k=0}^{K-1} \bar{f}(x + ka) \qquad 0 \leqslant x < a \tag{5.4-30}$$

where $m = 0$ because $0 \leqslant x < a$. Dividing through by K yields

$$\phi(x) = \frac{1}{K} \sum_{k=0}^{K-1} f(x + ka) - \frac{1}{K} \sum_{k=0}^{K-1} \bar{f}(x + ka). \tag{5.4-31}$$

The first sum on the right-hand side of this expression is, of course, unknown. However, for large values of K it approaches the average value of f. Thus this sum may be taken as a constant A, giving the approximation

$$\phi(x) \approx A - \frac{1}{K} \sum_{k=0}^{K-1} \bar{f}(x + ka) \qquad 0 \leqslant x < a \tag{5.4-32}$$

or

$$\phi(x - ma) \approx A - \frac{1}{K} \sum_{k=0}^{K-1} \bar{f}(x + ka - ma) \qquad 0 \leqslant x \leqslant L. \tag{5.4-33}$$

Substituting Eq. (5.4-28) for $\bar{f}$ yields[†]

$$\phi(x - ma) \approx A - \frac{1}{K} \sum_{k=0}^{K-1} \sum_{j=0}^{k} g'(x + ka - ma - ja)$$

$$\approx A - \frac{1}{K} \sum_{k=0}^{K-1} \sum_{j=0}^{k} g'[x - ma + (k - j)a]. \tag{5.4-34}$$

[†] Note that the limit on the second summation is k instead of m. If we had started from Eq. (5.4-18) with $x + ka - ma$ instead of x, the limit in the summation of Eq. (5.4-28) would have been k because, from Eq. (5.4-18), $x + (ka - ma) = z + ma + (ka - ma) = z + ka$.

From Eqs. (5.4-28) and (5.4-29), we have the final result:

$$f(x) \approx A - \frac{1}{K} \sum_{k=0}^{K-1} \sum_{j=0}^{k} g'[x - ma + (k - j)a] + \sum_{j=0}^{m} g'(x - ja) \quad (5.4\text{-}35)$$

for $0 \le x \le L$. Reintroducing the suppressed variable y yields

$$f(x, y) \approx A - \frac{1}{K} \sum_{k=0}^{K-1} \sum_{j=0}^{k} g'[x - ma + (k - j)a, y] + \sum_{j=0}^{m} g'(x - ja, y) \quad (5.4\text{-}36)$$

for $0 \le x, y \le L$. As before, $f(x, y)$ is assumed to be a square image. Interchanging x and y in the right-hand side of Eq. (5.4-36) would give the reconstruction of an image that moves only in the y direction during exposure. The concepts presented can also be used to derive a deblurring expression that takes into account simultaneous uniform motion in both directions.

Example: The image shown in Fig. 5.4(a) was blurred by uniform linear motion in one direction during exposure, with the total distance traveled being approximately equal to $\frac{1}{8}$ the width of the photograph. Figure 5.4(b) shows the deblurred result obtained by using Eq. (5.4-36) with x and y interchanged because motion is in the y direction. The error in the approximation given by this equation is not objectionable. ❏

(a)   (b)

Figure 5.4 *(a) Image blurred by uniform linear motion; (b) image restored by using Eq. (5.4-36). (From Sondhi [1972].)*

5.5   LEAST MEAN SQUARE (WIENER) FILTER

Let $\mathbf{R_f}$ and $\mathbf{R_n}$ be the correlation matrices of $\mathbf{f}$ and $\mathbf{n}$, defined respectively by the equations

$$\mathbf{R_f} = E\{\mathbf{ff}^T\} \tag{5.5-1}$$

and

$$\mathbf{R_n} = E\{\mathbf{nn}^T\} \tag{5.5-2}$$

where $E\{\cdot\}$ denotes the expected value operation, and $\mathbf{f}$ and $\mathbf{n}$ are as defined in Section 5.1.3. The ijth element of $\mathbf{R_f}$ is given by $E\{f_i f_j\}$, which is the correlation between the ith and the jth elements of $\mathbf{f}$. Similarly, the ijth element of $\mathbf{R_n}$ gives the correlation between the two corresponding elements in $\mathbf{n}$. Since the elements of $\mathbf{f}$ and $\mathbf{n}$ are real, $E\{f_i f_j\} = E\{f_j f_i\}$, $E\{n_i n_j\} = E\{n_j n_i\}$, and it follows that $\mathbf{R_f}$ and $\mathbf{R_n}$ are real symmetric matrices. For most image functions the correlation between pixels (that is, elements of $\mathbf{f}$ or $\mathbf{n}$) does not extend beyond a distance of 20 to 30 pixels in the image, so a typical correlation matrix has a band of nonzero elements about the main diagonal and zeros in the right upper and left lower corner regions. Based on the assumption that the correlation between any two pixels is a function of the distance between the pixels and not their position, $\mathbf{R_f}$ and $\mathbf{R_n}$ can be made to approximate block-circulant matrices and therefore can be diagonalized by the matrix $\mathbf{W}$ with the procedure described in Section 5.2.2 (Andrews and Hunt [1977]). Using $\mathbf{A}$ and $\mathbf{B}$ to denote matrices gives

$$\mathbf{R_f} = \mathbf{WAW}^{-1} \tag{5.5-3}$$

and

$$\mathbf{R_n} = \mathbf{WBW}^{-1}. \tag{5.5-4}$$

Just as the elements of the diagonal matrix $\mathbf{D}$ in the relation $\mathbf{H} = \mathbf{WDW}^{-1}$ correspond to the Fourier transform of the block elements of $\mathbf{H}$, the elements of $\mathbf{A}$ and $\mathbf{B}$ are the transforms of the correlation elements in $\mathbf{R_f}$ and $\mathbf{R_n}$, respectively. As indicated in Problem 3.4, the Fourier transform of these correlations is called the *power spectrum* (or *spectral density*) of $f_e(x, y)$ and $\eta_e(x, y)$, respectively and is denoted $S_f(u, v)$ and $S_\eta(u, v)$ in the following discussion.

Defining

$$\mathbf{Q}^T\mathbf{Q} = \mathbf{R_f}^{-1}\mathbf{R_n} \tag{5.5-5}$$

and substituting this expression in Eq. (5.3-9) gives

$$\hat{\mathbf{f}} = (\mathbf{H}^T\mathbf{H} + \gamma\mathbf{R}_f^{-1}\mathbf{R}_n)^{-1}\mathbf{H}^T\mathbf{g}. \tag{5.5-6}$$

Using Eqs. (5.2-21), (5.2-23), (5.5-3), and (5.5-4) yields

$$\hat{\mathbf{f}} = (\mathbf{W}\mathbf{D}^*\mathbf{D}\mathbf{W}^{-1} + \gamma\mathbf{W}\mathbf{A}^{-1}\mathbf{B}\mathbf{W}^{-1})^{-1}\mathbf{W}\mathbf{D}^*\mathbf{W}^{-1}\mathbf{g}. \tag{5.5-7}$$

Multiplying both sides by $\mathbf{W}^{-1}$ and performing some matrix manipulations reduces Eq. (5.5-7) to

$$\mathbf{W}^{-1}\hat{\mathbf{f}} = (\mathbf{D}^*\mathbf{D} + \gamma\mathbf{A}^{-1}\mathbf{B})^{-1}\mathbf{D}^*\mathbf{W}^{-1}\mathbf{g}. \tag{5.5-8}$$

Keeping in mind the meaning of the elements of $\mathbf{A}$ and $\mathbf{B}$, recognizing that the matrices inside the parentheses are diagonal, and making use of the concepts developed in Section 5.2.3, allows writing the elements of Eq. (5.5-8) in the form

$$\begin{aligned}
\hat{F}(u, v) &= \left[\frac{H^*(u, v)}{|H(u, v)|^2 + \gamma[S_\eta(u, v)/S_f(u, v)]}\right]G(u, v) \\
&= \left[\frac{1}{H(u, v)}\frac{|H(u, v)|^2}{|H(u, v)|^2 + \gamma[S_\eta(u, v)/S_f(u, v)]}\right]G(u, v)
\end{aligned} \tag{5.5-9}$$

for $u, v = 0, 1, 2, \ldots, N - 1$, where $|H(u, v)|^2 = H^*(u, v)H(u, v)$ and it is assumed that $M = N$.

When $\gamma = 1$, the term inside the outer brackets in Eq. (5.5-9) reduces to the so-called *Wiener filter*. If γ is variable this expression is called the *parametric Wiener filter*. In the absence of noise, $S_\eta(u, v) = 0$ and the Wiener filter reduces to the ideal inverse filter discussed in Section 5.4. However, when $\gamma = 1$, the use of Eq. (5.5-9) no longer yields an optimal solution in the sense defined in Section 5.3.2 because, as pointed out in that section, γ must be adjusted to satisfy the constraint $\|\mathbf{g} - \mathbf{H}\hat{\mathbf{f}}\|^2 = \|\mathbf{n}\|^2$. It can be shown however, that the solution obtained with $\gamma = 1$ *is* optimal in the sense that it minimizes the quantity $E\{[f(x, y) - \hat{f}(x, y)]^2\}$. Clearly, this is a statistical criterion that treats f and $\hat{f}$ as random variables.

When $S_\eta(u, v)$ and $S_f(u, v)$ are unknown (a problem often encountered in practice) approximating Eq. (5.5-9) by the relation

$$\hat{F}(u, v) \approx \left[\frac{1}{H(u, v)}\frac{|H(u, v)|^2}{|H(u, v)|^2 + K}\right]G(u, v) \tag{5.5-10}$$

where K is a constant, sometimes is useful. An example of results obtained with (5.5-10) follows. The problem of selecting the optimal γ for image restoration is discussed in some detail in Section 5.6.

Example: The first column in Fig. 5.5 shows three pictures of a domino corrupted by linear motion (at $-45°$ with respect to the horizontal) and noise whose variance at any point in the image was proportional to the brightness of the point. The three images were generated by varying the constant of proportionality so that the ratios of maximum brightness to noise amplitude were 1, 10, and 100, respectively, as shown on the left in Fig. 5.5. The Fourier spectra of the degraded images are shown in Fig. 5.5(b).

Since the effects of uniform linear motion can be expressed analytically, an equation describing $H(u, v)$ can be obtained without difficulty, as shown in Section 5.4.2. Figure 5.5(c) was obtained by direct inverse filtering following the procedure described in Section 5.4.1. The results are dominated by noise, but as the third image shows, the inverse filter successfully removed the degradation (blur) caused by motion. By contrast, Fig. 5.5(d) shows the results

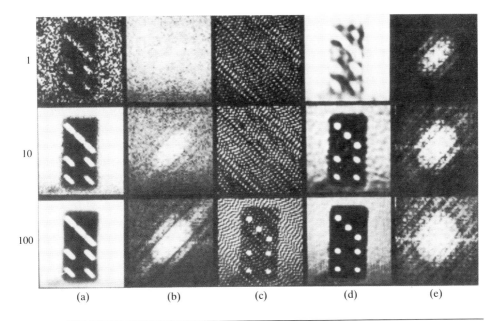

Figure 5.5 *Example of image restoration by inverse and Wiener filters: (a) degraded images and (b) their Fourier spectra; (c) images restored by inverse filtering; (d) images restored by Wiener filtering; (e) Fourier spectra of images in (d). (From Harris [1968].)*

obtained using Eq. (5.5-10) with $K = 2\sigma^2$, where σ^2 is the noise variance. The improvements over the direct inverse filtering approach are obvious, particularly for the third image. Figure 5.5(e) shows the Fourier spectra of the restored images.   ❏

5.6   CONSTRAINED LEAST SQUARES RESTORATION

The least mean squares approach derived in Section 5.5 is a statistical procedure because the criterion for optimality is based on the correlation matrices of the image and noise functions. This implies that the results obtained by using a Wiener filter are optimal in an average sense. The restoration procedure developed in this section, however, is optimal for *each* given image and requires knowledge only of the noise mean and variance. Also considered is the problem of adjusting γ to satisfy the constraint leading to Eq. (5.3-9).

As indicated in Section 5.3.2, the restoration solution obtained by using Eq. (5.3-9) depends on the choice of the matrix $\mathbf{Q}$. Owing to ill-conditioning, that equation sometimes yields solutions that are obscured by large oscillating values. Therefore the feasibility of choosing $\mathbf{Q}$ so that these adverse effects are minimized is of interest. One possibility, suggested by Phillips [1962], is to formulate a criterion of optimality based on a measure of smoothness such as, for example, minimizing some function of the second derivative. In order to see how this criterion can be expressed in a form compatible with Eq. (5.3-9), let us first consider the 1-D case.

For a discrete function $f(x)$, $x = 0, 1, 2, \ldots$, the second derivative at a point x may be approximated by the expression

$$\frac{\partial^2 f(x)}{\partial x^2} \approx f(x + 1) - 2f(x) + f(x - 1). \tag{5.6-1}$$

A criterion based on this expression, then, might be to minimize $(\partial^2 f/\partial x^2)^2$ over x; that is,

$$\text{minimize} \left\{ \sum_x [f(x + 1) - 2f(x) + f(x - 1)]^2 \right\} \tag{5.6-2}$$

or, in matrix notation,

$$\text{minimize} \{ \mathbf{f}^T \mathbf{C}^T \mathbf{C} \mathbf{f} \} \tag{5.6-3}$$

where

$$
\mathbf{C} =
\begin{bmatrix}
1 & & & & & & & \\
-2 & 1 & & & & & & \\
1 & -2 & 1 & & & & & \\
& 1 & -2 & 1 & & & & \\
& & & \ddots & & & & \\
& & & & 1 & -2 & 1 & \\
& & & & & 1 & -2 & \\
& & & & & & 1 &
\end{bmatrix}
\tag{5.6-4}
$$

is a "smoothing" matrix, and $\mathbf{f}$ is a vector whose elements are the samples of $f(x)$.

In the 2-D case we consider a direct extension of Eq. (5.6-1). In this case the criterion is to

$$
\text{minimize} \left[\frac{\partial^2 f(x, y)}{\partial x^2} + \frac{\partial^2 f(x, y)}{\partial y^2} \right]^2
\tag{5.6-5}
$$

where the derivative function is approximated by the expression

$$
\begin{aligned}
\frac{\partial^2 f}{\partial x^2} + \frac{\partial^2 f}{\partial y^2} &\approx [2f(x, y) - f(x + 1, y) - f(x - 1, y)] \\
&\quad + [2f(x, y) - f(x, y + 1) - f(x, y - 1)] \\
&\approx 4f(x, y) - [f(x + 1, y) + f(x - 1, y) + f(x, y + 1) \\
&\quad + f(x, y - 1)].
\end{aligned}
\tag{5.6-6}
$$

The derivative function given in Eq. (5.6-5) is the Laplacian operator discussed in Section 3.3.7.

Equation (5.6-6) can be implemented directly in a computer. However, the same operation can be carried out by convolving $f(x, y)$ with the operator

$$
p(x, y) =
\begin{bmatrix}
0 & -1 & 0 \\
-1 & 4 & -1 \\
0 & -1 & 0
\end{bmatrix}
\tag{5.6-7}
$$

As indicated in Section 5.1.3, wraparound error in the discrete convolution process is avoided by extending $f(x, y)$ and $p(x, y)$. Having already considered the formation of $f_e(x, y)$, we form $p_e(x, y)$ in the same manner:

$$p_e(x, y) = \begin{cases} p(x, y) & 0 \le x \le 2 \quad\quad \text{and} \quad 0 \le y \le 2 \\ 0 & 3 \le x \le M - 1 \quad \text{or} \quad 3 \le y \le N - 1. \end{cases}$$

If $f(x, y)$ is of size $A \times B$, we choose $M \ge A + 3 - 1$ and $N \ge B + 3 - 1$, because $p(x, y)$ is of size 3×3.

The convolution of the extended functions then is

$$g_e(x, y) = \sum_{m=0}^{M-1} \sum_{n=0}^{N-1} f_e(m, n) p_e(x - m, y - n) \tag{5.6-8}$$

which agrees with Eq. (5.1-23).

Following an argument similar to the one given in Section 5.1.3 allows expression of the smoothness criterion in matrix form. First, we construct a block-circulant matrix of the form

$$\mathbf{C} = \begin{bmatrix} \mathbf{C}_0 & \mathbf{C}_{M-1} & \mathbf{C}_{M-2} & \cdots & \mathbf{C}_1 \\ \mathbf{C}_1 & \mathbf{C}_0 & \mathbf{C}_{M-1} & \cdots & \mathbf{C}_2 \\ \mathbf{C}_2 & \mathbf{C}_1 & \mathbf{C}_0 & \cdots & \mathbf{C}_3 \\ \vdots & & & & \\ \mathbf{C}_{M-1} & \mathbf{C}_{M-2} & \mathbf{C}_{M-3} & \cdots & \mathbf{C}_0 \end{bmatrix} \tag{5.6-9}$$

where each submatrix $\mathbf{C}_j$ is an $N \times N$ circulant constructed from the jth row of $p_e(x, y)$; that is,

$$\mathbf{C}_j = \begin{bmatrix} p_e(j, 0) & p_e(j, N - 1) & \cdots & p_e(j, 1) \\ p_e(j, 1) & p_e(j, 0) & \cdots & p_e(j, 2) \\ \vdots & & & \\ p_e(j, N - 1) & p_e(j, N - 2) & \cdots & p_e(j, 0) \end{bmatrix} \tag{5.6-10}$$

Since $\mathbf{C}$ is block circulant, it is diagonalized by the matrix $\mathbf{W}$ defined in Section 5.2.2. In other words,

$$\mathbf{E} = \mathbf{W}^{-1} \mathbf{C} \mathbf{W} \tag{5.6-11}$$

where $\mathbf{E}$ is a diagonal matrix whose elements are given by

$$
E(k, i) = \begin{cases} P\left(\left[\dfrac{k}{N}\right], k \bmod N\right) & \text{if } i = k \\ 0 & \text{if } i \neq k \end{cases}
\tag{5.6-12}
$$

as in Eq. (5.2-39). In this case $P(u, v)$ is the 2-D Fourier transform of $p_e(x, y)$. As with Eqs. (5.2-37) and (5.2-39), the assumption is that Eq. (5.6-12) has been scaled by the factor MN.

The convolution operation described above is equivalent to implementing Eq. (5.6-6), so the smoothness criterion of Eq. (5.6-5) takes the same form as Eq. (5.6-3):

$$
\text{minimize}\{\mathbf{f}^T\mathbf{C}^T\mathbf{Cf}\}
\tag{5.6-13}
$$

where $\mathbf{f}$ is an MN-dimensional vector and $\mathbf{C}$ is of size $MN \times MN$. By letting $\mathbf{Q} = \mathbf{C}$, and recalling that $\|\mathbf{Qf}\|^2 = (\mathbf{Qf})^T(\mathbf{Qf}) = \mathbf{f}^T\mathbf{Q}^T\mathbf{Qf}$, this criterion may be expressed as

$$
\text{minimize}\,\|\mathbf{Qf}\|^2
\tag{5.6-14}
$$

which is the same form used in Section 5.3.2. In fact, if we require that the constraint $\|\mathbf{g} - \mathbf{H\hat{f}}\|^2 = \|\mathbf{n}\|^2$ be satisfied, the optimal solution is given by Eq. (5.3-9) with $\mathbf{Q} = \mathbf{C}$:

$$
\mathbf{\hat{f}} = (\mathbf{H}^T\mathbf{H} + \gamma\mathbf{C}^T\mathbf{C})^{-1}\mathbf{H}^T\mathbf{g}.
\tag{5.6-15}
$$

Using Eqs. (5.2-21), (5.2-23), and (5.6-11), allows Eq. (5.6-15) to be expressed as

$$
\mathbf{\hat{f}} = (\mathbf{WD}^*\mathbf{DW}^{-1} + \gamma\mathbf{WE}^*\mathbf{EW}^{-1})^{-1}\mathbf{WD}^*\mathbf{W}^{-1}\mathbf{g}.
\tag{5.6-16}
$$

Multiplying both sides by $\mathbf{W}^{-1}$ and performing some matrix manipulations reduces Eq. (5.6-16) to

$$
\mathbf{W}^{-1}\mathbf{\hat{f}} = (\mathbf{D}^*\mathbf{D} + \gamma\mathbf{E}^*\mathbf{E})^{-1}\mathbf{D}^*\mathbf{W}^{-1}\mathbf{g}.
\tag{5.6-17}
$$

Keeping in mind that the elements inside the parentheses are diagonal and making use of the concepts developed in Section 5.2.3, allows expressing the elements of Eq. (5.6-17) in the form

$$
\hat{F}(u, v) = \left[\frac{H^*(u, v)}{|H(u, v)|^2 + \gamma|P(u, v)|^2}\right]G(u, v)
\tag{5.6-18}
$$

for $u, v = 0, 1, 2, \ldots, N - 1$, where $|H(u, v)|^2 = H^*(u, v)H(u, v)$, and we have assumed that $M = N$. Note that Eq. (5.6-18) resembles the parametric Wiener filter derived in Section 5.5. The principal difference between Eqs. (5.5-9) and (5.6-18) is that the latter does not require explicit knowledge of statistical parameters other than an estimate of the noise mean and variance.

The general formulation given in Eq. (5.3-9) requires that γ be adjusted to satisfy the constraint $\|\mathbf{g} - \mathbf{H}\mathbf{f}\|^2 = \|\mathbf{n}\|^2$. Thus the solution given in Eq. (5.6-18) can be optimal only when γ satisfies this condition. An iterative procedure for estimating this parameter follows.

Define a residual vector $\mathbf{r}$ as

$$\mathbf{r} = \mathbf{g} - \mathbf{H}\hat{\mathbf{f}}. \tag{5.6-19}$$

Substituting Eq. (5.6-15) for $\hat{\mathbf{f}}$ yields

$$\mathbf{r} = \mathbf{g} - \mathbf{H}(\mathbf{H}^T\mathbf{H} + \gamma\mathbf{C}^T\mathbf{C})^{-1}\mathbf{H}^T\mathbf{g}. \tag{5.6-20}$$

Equation (5.6.20) indicates that $\mathbf{r}$ is a function of γ. In fact, it can be shown (Hunt [1973]) that

$$\begin{aligned} \phi(\gamma) &= \mathbf{r}^T\mathbf{r} \\ &= \|\mathbf{r}\|^2 \end{aligned} \tag{5.6-21}$$

is a monotonically increasing function of γ. What we want to do is adjust γ so that

$$\|\mathbf{r}\|^2 = \|\mathbf{n}\|^2 \pm a, \tag{5.6-22}$$

where a is an accuracy factor. Clearly, if $\|\mathbf{r}\|^2 = \|\mathbf{n}\|^2$ the constraint $\|\mathbf{g} - \mathbf{H}\hat{\mathbf{f}}\|^2 = \|\mathbf{n}\|^2$ will be strictly satisfied, in view of Eq. (5.6-19).

Because $\phi(\gamma)$ is monotonic, finding a γ that satisfies Eq. (5.6-17) is not difficult. One simple approach is to

(1) specify an initial value of γ;

(2) compute $\hat{\mathbf{f}}$ and $\|\mathbf{r}\|^2$; and

(3) stop if Eq. (5.6-22) is satisfied; otherwise return to step 2 after increasing γ if $\|\mathbf{r}\|^2 < \|\mathbf{n}\|^2 - a$ or decreasing γ if $\|\mathbf{r}\|^2 > \|\mathbf{n}\|^2 + a$.

Other procedures such as a Newton–Raphson algorithm can be used to improve speed of convergence.

Implementation of these concepts requires some knowledge about $\|\mathbf{n}\|^2$. The variance of $\eta_e(x, y)$ is

$$\begin{aligned} \sigma_\eta^2 &= E\{[\eta_e(x, y) - \bar{\eta}_e]^2\} \\ &= E[\eta_e^2(x, y)] - \bar{\eta}_e^2 \end{aligned} \tag{5.6-23}$$

where

$$\bar{\eta}_e = \frac{1}{(M-1)(N-1)} \sum_x \sum_y \eta_e(x, y) \qquad (5.6\text{-}24)$$

is the mean value of $\eta_e(x, y)$. If a sample average is used to approximate the expected value of $\eta_e^2(x, y)$, Eq. (5.6-23) becomes

$$\sigma_\eta^2 = \frac{1}{(M-1)(N-1)} \sum_x \sum_y \eta_e^2(x, y) - \bar{\eta}_e^2. \qquad (5.6\text{-}25)$$

The summation term simply indicates squaring and adding all values in the array $\eta_e(x, y)$, $x = 0, 1, 2, \ldots, M - 1$, and $y = 0, 1, 2, \ldots, N - 1$. This manipulation is simply the product $\mathbf{n}^T \mathbf{n}$, which, by definition, equals $\|\mathbf{n}\|^2$. Thus Eq. (5.6-25) reduces to

$$\sigma_\eta^2 = \frac{\|\mathbf{n}\|^2}{(M-1)(N-1)} - \bar{\eta}_e^2 \qquad (5.6\text{-}26)$$

or

$$\|\mathbf{n}\|^2 = (M-1)(N-1)[\sigma_\eta^2 + \bar{\eta}_e^2]. \qquad (5.6\text{-}27)$$

The importance of this equation is that it allows determination of a value for the constraint in terms of the noise mean and variance, quantities that, if not known, can often be approximated or measured in practice.

The constrained least squares restoration procedure can be summarized as follows.

Step 1. Choose an initial value of γ and obtain an estimate of $\|\mathbf{n}\|^2$ by using Eq. (5.6-27).

Step 2. Compute $\hat{F}(u, v)$ using Eq. (5.6-18). Obtain $\hat{\mathbf{f}}$ by taking the inverse Fourier transform of $\hat{F}(u, v)$.

Step 3. Form the residual vector $\mathbf{r}$ according to Eq. (5.6-19) and compute $\phi(\gamma) = \|\mathbf{r}\|^2$.

Step 4. Increment or decrement γ.

(a) $\phi(\gamma) < \|\mathbf{n}\|^2 - a$. Increment γ according to the algorithm given above or other appropriate method (such as a Newton–Raphson procedure).

(b) $\phi(\gamma) > \|\mathbf{n}\|^2 + a$. Decrement γ according to an appropriate algorithm.

Step 5. Return to step 2 and continue unless step 6 is true.

Step 6. $\phi(\gamma) = \|\mathbf{n}\|^2 \pm a$, where a determines the accuracy with which the constraint is satisfied. Stop the estimation procedure, with $\hat{\mathbf{f}}$ for the present value of γ being the restored image.

Example: Figure 5.6(b) was obtained by convolving the Gaussian-shaped point spread function

$$h(x, y) = \exp\left(-\frac{x^2 + y^2}{2400}\right)$$

with the original image shown in Fig. 5.6(a) and adding noise drawn from a uniform distribution in the interval $[0, 0.5]$. Figure 5.6(c) shows the result of

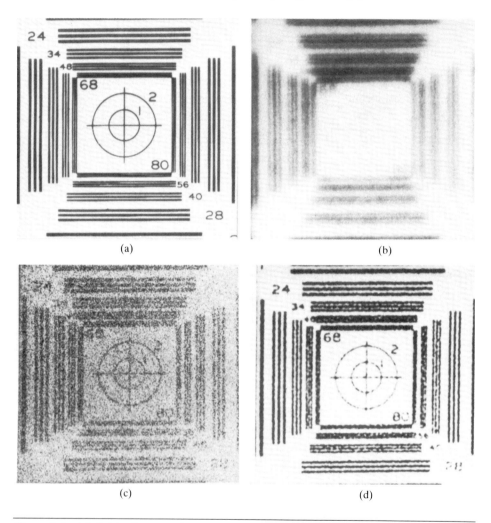

(a)   (b)

(c)   (d)

Figure 5.6 *(a) Original image; (b) image blurred and corrupted by additive noise; (c) image restored by inverse filtering; (d) image restored by the method of constrained least squares. (From Hunt [1973].)*

using the algorithm with $\gamma = 0$ (inverse filter). The ill-conditioned nature of the solution is evident by the dominance of the noise on the restored image. Figure 5.6(d) was obtained by using the preceding algorithm to seek a γ that would satisfy the constraint. The variance and mean of the uniform density in the interval $[0, 0.5]$ were used to estimate $\|\mathbf{n}\|^2$, and the accuracy factor a was chosen so that $a = 0.025\|\mathbf{n}\|^2$. The improvement of the constrained solution over direct inverse filtering is clearly visible. ❏

5.7 INTERACTIVE RESTORATION

So far, we have focused on a strictly analytical approach to restoration. In many applications, the practical approach is to take advantage of human intuition, coupled with the versatility of a digital computer, to restore images interactively. In this case, the observer controls the restoration process and, by "tuning" the available parameters, is able to obtain a final result that may be quite adequate for a specific purpose.

One of the simplest cases of image corruption that lends itself well to interactive restoration is the occurrence of a 2-D sinusoidal interference pattern (often called *coherent noise*) superimposed on an image. Let $\eta(x, y)$ denote a sinusoidal interference pattern of amplitude A and frequency components (u_0, v_0); that is,

$$\eta(x, y) = A \sin(u_0 x + v_0 y). \tag{5.7-1}$$

Direct substitution of Eq. (5.7-1) into Eq. (3.1-9) yields the Fourier transform of $\eta(x, y)$:

$$N(u, v) = \frac{-jA}{2}\left[\delta\left(u - \frac{u_0}{2\pi}, v - \frac{v_0}{2\pi}\right) - \delta\left(u + \frac{u_0}{2\pi}, v + \frac{v_0}{2\pi}\right)\right]. \tag{5.7-2}$$

In other words, the Fourier transform of a 2-D sine function is a pair of impulses of strength $-A/2$ and $A/2$ located at coordinates $(u_0/2\pi, v_0/2\pi)$ and $(-u_0/2\pi, -v_0/2\pi)$, respectively, of the frequency plane. In this case the transform has only imaginary components.

With the only degradation considered being additive noise, it follows from Eq. (5.2-40) that

$$G(u, v) = F(u, v) + N(u, v). \tag{5.7-3}$$

A display of the magnitude of $G(u, v)$ contains the magnitude of the sum of $F(u, v)$ and $N(u, v)$. If A is large enough, the two impulses of $N(u, v)$ usually appear as bright dots on the display, especially if they are located relatively far from the origin so that the contribution of the components of $F(u, v)$ is small.

If $\eta(x, y)$ were known completely, the original image, of course, could be recovered by subtracting the interference from $g(x, y)$. As this situation is seldom the case, a useful approach is to identify visually the location of impulse components in the frequency domain and use a bandreject filter (see Section 4.6.3) at these locations.

Example: The image shown in Fig. 5.7(a) was corrupted by a sinusoidal pattern of the form shown in Eq. (5.7-1). The Fourier spectrum of this image, shown

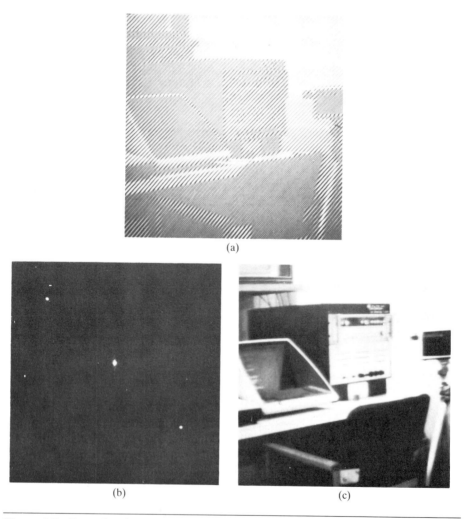

(a)

(b)   (c)

Figure 5.7 *Example of sinusoidal interference removal: (a) corrupted image; (b) Fourier spectrum showing impulses due to sinusoidal pattern; (c) image restored by using a bandreject filter with a radius of 1.*

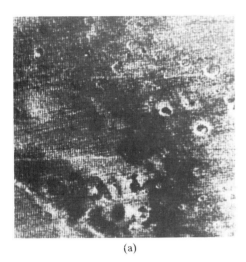

(a)   (b)

Figure 5.8   *(a) Picture of the Martian terrain taken by Mariner 6; (b) Fourier spectrum. Note the periodic interference in the image and the corresponding spikes in the spectrum. (Courtesy of NASA, Jet Propulsion Laboratory.)*

in Fig. 5.7(b), clearly exhibits a pair of symmetric impulses resulting from sinusoidal interference. Figure 5.7(c) was obtained by manually placing (from a computer console) two bandreject filters of radius 1 at the location of the impulses and then taking the inverse Fourier transform of the result. For all practical purposes, the restored image is free of interference.   ❏

The presence of a single, clearly defined interference pattern, such as the one just illustrated, seldom occurs in practice. Notable examples are images derived from electro-optical scanners, such as those commonly used in space missions. A common problem with these sensors is interference caused by coupling and amplification of low-level signals in the electronic circuitry. As a result, images reconstructed from the scanner output tend to contain a pronounced, 2-D periodic structure superimposed on the scene data.

Figure 5.8(a), an example of this type of periodic image degradation, shows a digital image of the Martian terrain taken by the *Mariner 6* spacecraft. The interference pattern is quite similar to the one shown in Fig. 5.7(a), but the former pattern is considerably more subtle and, consequently, harder to detect in the frequency plane.

Figure 5.8(b) shows the Fourier spectrum of the image in question. The starlike components were caused by the interference, and several pairs of components are present, indicating that the pattern was composed of more than just one sinusoidal component. When several interference components are present, the method discussed above is not always acceptable because it may remove too much image information in the filtering process. In addition, these components generally are not single-frequency bursts. Instead, they tend to have broad skirts that carry information about the interference pattern. These skirts are not always easily detectable from the normal transform background.

A procedure that has found acceptance in processing space-related scenes consists of first isolating the principal contributions of the interference pattern and then subtracting a variable, weighted portion of the pattern from the corrupted image. Although we develop the procedure in the context of a specific application, the basic approach is quite general and can be applied to other restoration tasks when multiple periodic interference is a problem.

The first step is to extract the principal frequency components of the interference pattern. This extraction can be done by placing a bandpass filter $H(u, v)$ at the location of each spike (see Section 4.6.3). If $H(u, v)$ is constructed to pass only components associated with the interference pattern, it follows that the Fourier transform of the pattern is given by the relation

$$P(u, v) = H(u, v)G(u, v) \tag{5.7-4}$$

where $G(u, v)$ is the Fourier transform of the corrupted image $g(x, y)$ and, for $N \times N$ digitization, u and v take on values in the range $0, 1, \ldots, N - 1$.

Formation of $H(u, v)$ requires considerable judgment about what is or is not an interference spike. For this reason, the bandpass filter generally is constructed interactively by observing the spectrum of $G(u, v)$ on a display. After a particular filter has been selected, the corresponding pattern in the spatial domain is obtained from the expression

$$p(x, y) = \mathfrak{F}^{-1}\{H(u, v)G(u, v)\}. \tag{5.7-5}$$

Because the corrupted image is formed by the addition of $f(x, y)$ and the interference, if $p(x, y)$ were known completely, subtracting the pattern from $g(x, y)$ to obtain $f(x, y)$ would be a simple matter. The problem, of course, is that this filtering procedure usually yields only an approximation of the true pattern. The effects of components not present in the estimate of $p(x, y)$ can be minimized by instead subtracting from $g(x, y)$ a weighted portion of $p(x, y)$ to obtain an estimate of $f(x, y)$:

$$\hat{f}(x, y) = g(x, y) - w(x, y)p(x, y) \tag{5.7-6}$$

where $\hat{f}(x, y)$ is the estimate of $f(x, y)$ and $w(x, y)$ is to be determined. The function $w(x, y)$ is called a *weighting* or *modulation* function, and the objective of the procedure is to select this function so that the result is optimized in some meaningful way. One approach is to select $w(x, y)$ so that the variance of $\hat{f}(x, y)$ is minimized over a specified neighborhood of every point (x, y).

Consider a neighborhood of size $(2X + 1)$ by $(2Y + 1)$ about a point (x, y). The "local" variance of $\hat{f}(x, y)$ at coordinates (x, y) is

$$\sigma^2(x, y) = \frac{1}{(2X + 1)(2Y + 1)} \sum_{m=-X}^{X} \sum_{n=-Y}^{Y} [\hat{f}(x + m, y + n) - \bar{\hat{f}}(x, y)]^2$$

(5.7-7)

where $\bar{\hat{f}}(x, y)$ is the average value of $\hat{f}(x, y)$ in the neighborhood; that is,

$$\bar{\hat{f}}(x, y) = \frac{1}{(2X + 1)(2Y + 1)} \sum_{m=-X}^{X} \sum_{n=-Y}^{Y} \hat{f}(x + m, y + n).$$

(5.7-8)

Points on or near the edge of the image can be treated by considering partial neighborhoods.

Substituting Eq. (5.7-6) into Eq. (5.7-7) yields

$$\sigma^2(x,y) = \frac{1}{(2X + 1)(2Y + 1)} \sum_{m=-X}^{X} \sum_{n=-Y}^{Y} \{[g(x + m, y + n)$$
$$- w(x + m, y + n)p(x + m, y + n)] - [\bar{g}(x, y) - \overline{w(x, y)p(x, y)}]\}^2.$$

(5.7-9)

Assuming that $w(x, y)$ remains essentially constant over the neighborhood gives the approximations

$$w(x + m, y + n) = w(x, y)$$

(5.7-10)

for $-X \leqslant m \leqslant X$ and $-Y \leqslant n \leqslant Y$; also

$$\overline{w(x, y)p(x, y)} = w(x, y)\bar{p}(x, y)$$

(5.7-11)

in the neighborhood. With these approximations, Eq. (5.7-9) becomes

$$\sigma^2(x, y) = \frac{1}{(2X + 1)(2Y + 1)} \sum_{m=-X}^{X} \sum_{n=-Y}^{Y} \{[g(x + m, y + n)$$
$$- w(x, y)p(x + m, y + n)] - [\bar{g}(x, y) - w(x, y)\bar{p}(x,y)]\}^2.$$

(5.7-12)

To minimize $\sigma^2(x, y)$ we solve

$$\frac{\partial \sigma^2(x, y)}{\partial w(x, y)} = 0$$

(5.7-13)

for $w(x, y)$. The result is

$$w(x, y) = \frac{\overline{g(x, y)p(x, y)} - \overline{g}(x, y)\overline{p}(x, y)}{\overline{p^2}(x, y) - \overline{p}^2(x, y)}. \qquad (5.7\text{-}14)$$

To obtain the restored image $\hat{f}(x, y)$ we compute $w(x, y)$ from Eq. (5.7-14) and then make use of Eq. (5.7-6). As $w(x, y)$ is assumed to be constant in a neighborhood, computing this function for every value of x and y in the image is unnecessary. Instead, $w(x, y)$ is computed for *one* point in each nonoverlapping neighborhood (preferably the center point) and then used to process all the image points contained in that neighborhood.

Example: Figures 5.9 through 5.11 show the result of applying the above technique to the image shown in Fig. 5.8(a). In this case $N = 512$ and a neighborhood with $X = Y = 15$ was selected. Figure 5.9 shows the Fourier spectrum of the corrupted image, but the origin was not shifted to the center of the frequency plane. Figure 5.10(a) shows the spectrum of $P(u, v)$, where only the noise spikes are present. Figure 5.10(b) shows the interference pattern $p(x, y)$ obtained by taking the inverse Fourier transform of $P(u, v)$. Note the similarity between this pattern and the structure of the noise present in Fig. 5.8(a). Finally, Fig. 5.11 shows the processed image obtained by using Eq. (5.7-6). The periodic

Figure 5.9 *Fourier spectrum (without shifting) of the image shown in Fig. 5.8(a). (Courtesy of NASA, Jet Propulsion Laboratory.)*

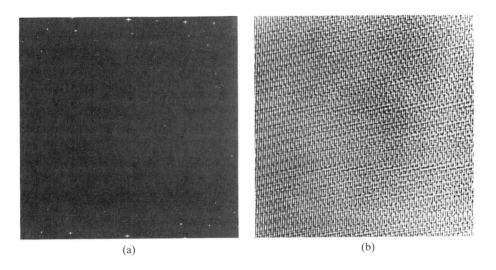

(a)   (b)

Figure 5.10   *(a) Fourier spectrum of P(u, v); (b) corresponding interference pattern p(x, y). (Courtesy of NASA, Jet Propulsion Laboratory.)*

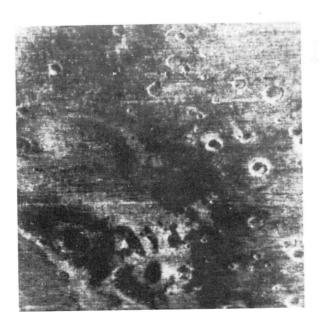

Figure 5.11   *Processed image. (Courtesy of NASA, Jet Propulsion Laboratory.)*

interference, for all practical purposes, has been removed, leaving only spotty noise that is not periodic. This noise can be processed by other methods, such as median filtering.   ❑

5.8 RESTORATION IN THE SPATIAL DOMAIN

After a suitable frequency domain restoration filter has been obtained by any of the methods discussed earlier, implementing the solution in the spatial domain via a convolution mask in order to expedite processing (see Section 4.1) often is desirable. As indicated in Section 4.5, the coefficients of a convolution mask can be obtained directly from a given filter function via Eq. (4.5-12). Although the discussion in Section 4.5 deals with enhancement, the concepts developed there are equally applicable to restoration; the difference lies in the nature of the filter.

Example: Figure 5.12(a) shows an infrared image of a set of military targets in a field. The image is corrupted by nearly periodic scanner interference, visible as a "ripple" effect in the vertical direction. Because of its periodic nature, the interference produces bursts of concentrated energy in the vertical axis of the Fourier spectrum of the image, as shown in Fig. 5.13(a).

A simple approach for reducing the effect of the interference is to use a notch filter, $H(u, v)$, which attenuates the values of the Fourier transform in the vertical axis and multiplies all other values of the transform by 1, in a manner analogous to the procedure discussed in Section 5.7. Figure 5.13(b) shows such a filter superimposed on the spectrum, where the dark bands are the attenuated regions.

Figure 5.12(b) shows the result of using the notch filter and taking the inverse Fourier transform. Note that, for all practical purposes, the interference was eliminated from the image. The image shown in Fig. 5.12(c) was obtained by applying a 9×9 convolution mask (see Section 4.1) to the original, corrupted image. The coefficients of this mask were generated from the notch filter by using Eq. (4.5-12). This small mask is only an approximation of the Fourier filtering process, so some vertical lines are still visible in the processed image. A second pass of the mask further reduced the interference (at the cost of some noticeable blurring), as Fig. 5.12(d) shows.   ❑

5.9 GEOMETRIC TRANSFORMATIONS

We conclude this chapter with an introductory discussion on the use of geometric transformations for image restoration. Unlike the techniques discussed so far, geometric transformations generally modify the spatial relationships

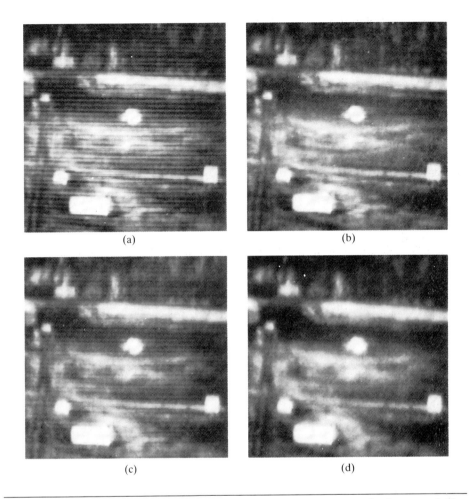

(a)   (b)

(c)   (d)

Figure 5.12   *(a) Infrared image showing interference; (b) image restored using a notch filter in the frequency domain; (c) image restored using a 9 × 9 convolution mask; (d) result of applying the mask a second time. (From Meyer and Gonzalez [1983].)*

between pixels in an image. Geometric transformations often are called *rubber-sheet transformations*, because they may be viewed as the process of "printing" an image on a sheet of rubber and then stretching this sheet according to some predefined set of rules.

In terms of digital image processing, a geometric transformation consists of two basic operations: (1) a *spatial transformation*, which defines the "re-arrangement" of pixels on the image plane; and (2) a *gray-level interpolation*, which deals with the assignment of gray levels to pixels in the spatially trans-

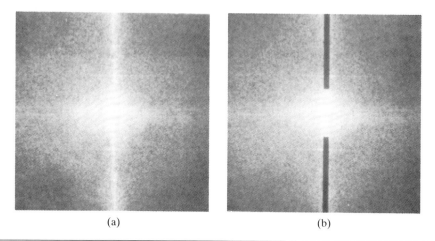

| (a) | (b) |

Figure 5.13   *(a) Fourier spectrum of the image in Fig. 5.12(a); (b) Notch filter superimposed on the spectrum. (From Meyer and Gonzalez [1983].)*

formed image. We discuss the fundamental ideas underlying these concepts, and their use in the context of image restoration, in the following sections.

5.9.1   Spatial Transformations

Suppose that an image f with pixel coordinates (x, y) undergoes geometric distortion to produce an image g with coordinates $(\hat{x}, \hat{y})$. This transformation may be expressed as

$$\hat{x} = r(x, y) \tag{5.9-1}$$

and

$$\hat{y} = s(x, y) \tag{5.9-2}$$

where $r(x, y)$ and $s(x, y)$ represent the spatial transformations that produced the geometrically distorted image $g(\hat{x}, \hat{y})$. For example, if $r(x, y) = x/2$ and $s(x, y) = y/2$, the "distortion" is simply a shrinking of the size of $f(x, y)$ by one-half in both spatial directions.

If $r(x, y)$ and $s(x, y)$ were known analytically, recovering $f(x, y)$ from the distorted image $g(\hat{x}, \hat{y})$ by applying the transformations in reverse might be possible theoretically. In practice, however, formulating analytically a single set of functions $r(x, y)$ and $s(x, y)$ that describe the geometric distortion process over the entire image plane generally is not possible. The method used most frequently to overcome this difficulty is to formulate the spatial relocation of pixels by the use of *tiepoints*, which are a subset of pixels whose location in the input (distorted) and output (corrected) images is known precisely.

Figure 5.14 shows quadrilateral regions in a distorted and corresponding corrected image. The vertices of the quadrilaterals are corresponding tiepoints. Suppose that the geometric distortion process within the quadrilateral regions is modeled by a pair of bilinear equations so that

$$r(x, y) = c_1x + c_2y + c_3xy + c_4 \qquad (5.9\text{-}3)$$

and

$$s(x, y) = c_5x + c_6y + c_7xy + c_8. \qquad (5.9\text{-}4)$$

Then, from Eqs. (5.9-1) and (5.9-2),

$$\hat{x} = c_1x + c_2y + c_3xy + c_4 \qquad (5.9\text{-}5)$$

and

$$\hat{y} = c_5x + c_6y + c_7xy + c_8. \qquad (5.9\text{-}6)$$

Since there are a total of eight known tiepoints, these equations can be easily solved for the eight coefficients c_i, $i = 1, 2, \ldots , 8$. The coefficients constitute the model used to transform *all* pixels within the quadrilateral region characterized by the tiepoints used to obtain the coefficients. In general, enough tiepoints are needed to generate a set of quadrilaterals that cover the entire image, with each quadrilateral having its own set of coefficients.

The procedure used to generate the corrected image is straightforward. For example, to generate $f(0, 0)$, substitute $(x, y) = (0, 0)$ into Eqs. (5.9-5) and (5.9-6) and obtain a pair of coordinates $(\hat{x}, \hat{y})$ from those equations. Then, let $f(0, 0) = g(\hat{x}, \hat{y})$, where $\hat{x}$ and $\hat{y}$ are the coordinate values just obtained. Next, substitute $(x, y) = (0, 1)$ into Eqs. (5.9-5) and (5.9-6), obtain another pair of values $(\hat{x}, \hat{y})$, and let $f(0, 1) = g(\hat{x}, \hat{y})$ for those coordinate values. The procedure continues pixel by pixel and row by row until an array whose size does

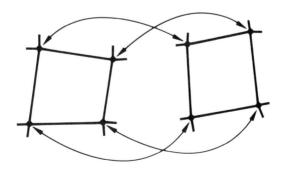

Figure 5.14   *Corresponding tiepoints in two image segments.*

not exceed the size of image g is obtained. A column (rather than a row) scan would yield identical results. Also, a bookkeeping procedure is essential to keep track of which quadrilaterals apply at a given pixel location in order to use the proper coefficients.

5.9.2 Gray-Level Interpolation

The method just discussed steps through integer values of the coordinates (x, y) to yield the corrected image $f(x, y)$. However, depending on the coefficients c_i, Eqs. (5.9-5) and (5.9-6) can yield noninteger values for $\hat{x}$ and $\hat{y}$. Because the distorted image g is digital, its pixel values are defined only at integer coordinates. Thus using noninteger values for $\hat{x}$ and $\hat{y}$ causes a mapping into locations of g for which no gray levels are defined. Inferring what the gray-level values at those locations should be, based only on the pixel values at integer coordinate locations, then becomes necessary. The technique used to accomplish this is called *gray-level interpolation*.

The simplest scheme for gray-level interpolation is based on a nearest neighbor approach. This method, also called *zero-order interpolation*, is illustrated in Fig. 5.15. This figure shows: (1) the mapping of integer coordinates (x, y) into fractional coordinates $(\hat{x}, \hat{y})$ by means of Eqs. (5.9-5) and (5.9-6); (2) the selection of the closest integer coordinate neighbor to $(\hat{x}, \hat{y})$; and (3) the assignment of the gray level of this nearest neighbor to the pixel located at (x, y).

Although nearest neighbor interpolation is simple to implement, this method often has the drawback of producing undesirable artifacts, such as distortion of straight edges in images of fine resolution. Smoother results can be obtained by using more sophisticated techniques, such as *cubic convolution interpolation* (Bernstein [1976]), which fits a surface of the $(\sin x)/x$ type through a much larger number of neighbors (say, 16) in order to obtain a smooth estimate of the gray level at any desired point. However, from a computational point of view this technique is costly, and a reasonable compromise is to use

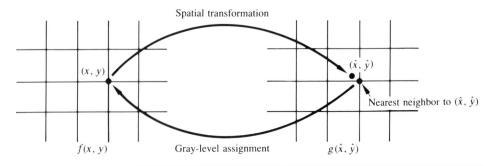

Figure 5.15 *Gray-level interpolation based on the nearest neighbor concept.*

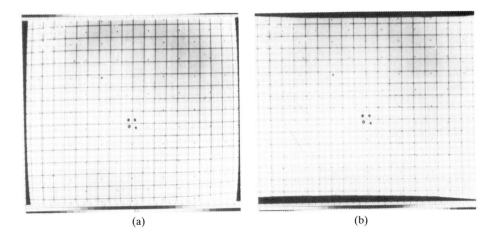

(a)   (b)

Figure 5.16 (a) Distorted image; (b) image after geometric correction. (From O'Handley and Green [1972].)

a *bilinear interpolation* approach that uses the gray levels of the four nearest neighbors. In other words, the idea is that the gray level of each of the four integral nearest neighbors of a nonintegral pair of coordinates $(\hat{x}, \hat{y})$ is known. The gray-level value of $(\hat{x}, \hat{y})$, denoted $v(\hat{x}, \hat{y})$, can then be interpolated from the values of its neighbors by using the relationship

$$v(\hat{x}, \hat{y}) = a\hat{x} + b\hat{y} + c\hat{x}\hat{y} + d \qquad (5.9\text{-}7)$$

where the four coefficients are easily determined from the four equations in four unknowns that can be written using the four known neighbors of $(\hat{x}, \hat{y})$. When these coefficients have been determined, $v(\hat{x}, \hat{y})$ is computed and this value is assigned to the location in $f(x, y)$ which yielded the spatial mapping into location $(\hat{x}, \hat{y})$. It is easy to visualize this procedure with the aid of Fig. 5.15. The exception is that, instead of using the gray-level value of the nearest neighbor to $(\hat{x}, \hat{y})$, we actually interpolate a value at location $(\hat{x}, \hat{y})$ and use this value for the gray-level assignment at (x, y).

Example: The methods developed in this section and Section (5.9.1) can be illustrated by applying these techniques to the problem of correcting an image that has been distorted geometrically. The image in question is shown in Fig. 5.16(a). This image exhibits the "barrel" distortion found in many vidicon-based imaging cameras. The rectilinear grid shown in Fig. 5.16(a) is severely distorted, particularly near the edges of the image. Note also that the distortion is not uniform and that the degree of distortion increases nonlinearly as a function of distance from the center of the image.

As indicated in Section 5.9.1, the use of Eqs. (5.9-5) and (5.9-6) requires knowledge of tiepoints in both the distorted and corrected images. In this particular case, tiepoints are the *reseau marks* visible in Fig. 5.16(a) as small dark dots scattered throughout the image. (Reseau marks are small metallic squares embedded directly on the surface of the imaging tube.) As the locations of these marks are known precisely, they serve as ideal tiepoints. Figure 5.16(b) shows the result of using Eqs. (5.9-5) and (5.9-6) for spatial mappings and Eq. (5.9-7) for gray-level interpolation. Note the significant degree of geometric correction achieved by using these equations.   ❏

The preceding example indicates but one of the many possible uses of geometric transformations for image restoration. Another important application is *image registration*, or finding correspondence between two images. The procedure for image registration is the same as the method just illustrated for geometric correction. However, the emphasis is on transforming an image so that it will correspond with another image of the same scene but viewed perhaps from another perspective. Other applications of the techniques discussed in this section include rectification of display distortions, map projections, and cartographic projections. The books by Castleman [1979] and Green [1983] contain numerous examples of these applications.

Establishing corresponding tiepoints in two images in many cases can be a rather difficult task. Not every situation is characterized by the availability of controlled artifacts such as reseau marks. When marks are not known a priori, tiepoints are usually established by using correlation techniques (see Chapter 9) to find corresponding features in two images. However, correlation measures are affected by factors such as noise and image rotation and thus generally yield less precise spatial correspondences between tiepoints.

5.10 CONCLUDING REMARKS

The principal concepts developed in this chapter are a formulation of the image restoration problem in the framework of linear algebra and the subsequent simplification of algebraic solutions based on the properties of circulant and block-circulant matrices.

Most of the restoration techniques derived in preceding sections are based on a least squares criterion of optimality. The use of the word *optimal* in this context refers strictly to a mathematical concept, not to optimal response of the human visual system. In fact, the present lack of knowledge about visual perception precludes a general formulation of the image restoration problem that takes into account observer preferences and capabilities. In view of these limitations, the advantage of the procedures followed in this chapter is the development of a basic approach from which a set of previously known (but not unified) results can be derived. Thus the power of the algebraic approach is evident in the simplicity by which methods such as the Wiener and constrained least squares filters can be obtained, starting from the same basic principles.

The key points leading to the results in the first eight sections of this chapter are based on the assumption of linear, space invariant degradations. This assumption leads immediately to the convolution integral, whose discrete formulation can be expressed in terms of the basic degradation model given in Eq. (5.1-24). The assumed periodicity of the input functions further simplified the problem by producing circulant and block-circulant matrices. In terms of implementation, these matrices allow all the derived restoration techniques to be carried out in the frequency domain by means of a 2-D FFT algorithm, thus greatly reducing the computational complexity posed by the original matrix formulation of the degradation process.

The material in Section 5.8 provides a convenient way to implement in the spatial domain an approximation of the results in Sections 5.2–5.7. Finally, the discussion in Section 5.9 introduces the problem of restoring images that have been distorted geometrically.

REFERENCES

The definitions given in Section 5.1 were adapted from Schwarz and Friedland [1965]. Background for most of the basic matrix operations used in this chapter is contained in Deutsch [1965], Noble [1969], and Bellman [1970]. Development of the discrete degradation model in terms of circulant and block-circulant matrices is based on two papers by Hunt [1971, 1973]. These papers and the book by Bellman [1970] also consider the diagonalization properties discussed in Section 5.2. For additional information on the material of Section 5.3, as well as the algebraic derivation of the various restoration techniques used in this chapter, see Andrews and Hunt [1977]. That book, devoted entirely to the topic of image restoration, treats in detail other restoration techniques in addition to those developed here.

Numerous investigators have considered the inverse filtering approach. References for the material in Section 5.4 are McGlamery [1967], Sondhi [1972], Cutrona and Hall [1968], and Slepian [1967]. Additional references on the least squares restoration approach discussed in Section 5.5 are Helstrom [1967], Slepian [1967], Harris [1968], Rino [1969], Horner [1969], and Rosenfeld and Kak [1982]. Comparison of the classical derivations in these references with the algebraic approach in Section 5.5 is interesting. The material in Section 5.6 is based on a paper by Hunt [1973]. Other references related to the topics discussed in Sections 5.1–5.7 are Slepian and Pollak [1961], Phillips [1962], Twomey [1963], Shack [1964], Lohman and Paris [1965], Harris [1966], Mueller and Reynolds [1967], Blackman [1968], Huang [1968], Rushforth and Harris [1968], MacAdam [1970], Falconer [1970], Som [1971], Frieden [1972, 1974], Habibi [1972], Sawchuck [1972], Robbins and Huang [1972], Andrews [1974], Jain and Angel [1974], and Anderson and Netravali [1976]. The material in Section 5.8 is from Meyer and Gonzalez [1983]. Additional reading for the topics in Section 5.9 may be found in O'Handley and Green [1972], Bernstein [1976], Castleman [1979], and Green [1983].

For further reading on the general topic of image restoration, see Bates and McDonnell [1986], Stark [1987], Jain [1989], and Kak and Slaney [1988]. The latter reference deals almost exclusively with computerized tomographic imaging, a topic that although beyond our discussion, is of considerable interest in medical imaging.

PROBLEMS

5.1 Consider a linear, position invariant image degradation system with impulse response $h(x - \alpha, y - \beta) = e^{-[(x-\alpha)^2 + (y-\beta)^2]}$. Suppose that the input to the system is an image consisting of a line of infinitesimal width located at $x = a$, and modeled by $f(x, y) = \delta(x - a)$. Assuming no noise, what is the output image $g(x, y)$?

5.2 Show the validity of Eq. (5.2-8).

5.3 A professor of archeology doing research on currency exchange practices during the Roman empire recently became aware that four Roman coins crucial to his research are listed in the holdings of the British Museum in London. Unfortunately, he was told after arriving there that the coins recently had been stolen. Further research on his part revealed that the museum keeps photographs of every item for which it is responsible. Unfortunately, the photos of the coins in question are blurred to the point where the date and other small markings are not readable. The blurring was caused by the camera being out of focus when the pictures were taken. You are hired as a consultant to determine whether computer processing can be utilized to restore the images to the point where the professor can read the markings. You are told that the original camera used to take the photos is still available, as are other representative coins of the same era. Propose a step-by-step solution to this problem.

5.4 Derive an equation analogous to Eq. (5.4-13), but for arbitrary uniform velocity in both the x and y directions.

5.5 Consider the problem of image blurring caused by uniform acceleration in the x direction. If the image is at rest at time $t = 0$ and accelerates with a uniform acceleration $x_0(t) = at^2/2$ for a time T, find the transfer function $H(u, v)$.

5.6 A space probe is designed to transmit images from a planet as it approaches it for landing. During the last stages of landing, one of the control thrusters fails, resulting in rapid rotation of the craft about its vertical axis. The images sent during the last two seconds prior to landing are blurred as a consequence of this circular motion. The camera is located in the bottom of the probe, along its vertical axis, and pointing down. Fortunately, the rotation of the craft is also about its vertical axis, so the images are blurred by uniform rotational motion. In addition, during the acquisition time of each image the craft rotation was limited to $\pi/8$ radians. The image acquisition process can be modeled as an ideal shutter that is open only during the time the craft rotated the $\pi/8$ radians. You may assume that vertical motion was negligible during image acquisition. How would you use the concepts you have learned in this chapter to restore the images? You are not being asked to provide a specific solution. Rather, you are asked to provide a basic approach to the solution.

5.7 Provide a specific solution (in the form of equations) to Problem 5.6, listing any assumptions that you made in arriving at that solution.

5.8 a) Show how Eq. (5.5-8) follows from Eq. (5.5-7).

b) Show how Eq. (5.5-9) follows from Eq. (5.5-8).

5.9 Image blurring caused by long-term exposure to atmospheric turbulence can be modeled by the transfer function $H(u, v) = \exp[-(u^2 + v^2)/2\sigma^2]$. Assume negligible noise. What is the equation of the Wiener filter you would use to restore an image blurred by this type of degradation?

5.10 Assume that the model in Fig. 5.1 is linear and position-invariant and show that the power spectrum of the output is given by $|G(u, v)|^2 = |H(u, v)|^2|F(u, v)|^2 + |N(u, v)|^2$. Refer to Eq. (5.2-40).

5.11 Cannon [1974] suggested a restoration filter $R(u, v)$ satisfying the condition $|\hat{F}(u, v)|^2 = |R(u, v)|^2|G(u, v)|^2$ and based on the premise of forcing the power spectrum of the restored image, $|\hat{F}(u, v)|^2$, to equal the power spectrum of the original image, $|F(u, v)|^2$.

a) Find $R(u, v)$ in terms of $|F(u, v)|^2$, $|H(u, v)|^2$, and $|N(u, v)|^2$. (*Hint:* Refer to Fig. 5.1, Eq. (5.2-40), and Problem 5.10.)

b) Use your result in (a) to state a result in the form of Eq. (5.5-9).

5.12 Suppose that each element of an image is normalized to the range [0, 1]. Then it is possible to interpret each such element as the probability of a certain number of photons hitting that particular element location in the image. Entropy is defined as $E = -p \ln p$, where p is a probability, and $\ln$ is the natural logarithm (see Chapter 6). We define $E = -\mathbf{f}^T \ln \mathbf{f}$ to be the entropy of an image that has been normalized and has been expressed in vector form. In this notation, the vector $\ln \mathbf{f}$ is formed by taking the natural logarithm of each component of $\mathbf{f}$. A useful filter for addressing degradations based on a random grain model (similar to modeling film grain) is obtained by performing a constrained least squares minimization of the negative of the entropy. Show that the resulting restored image is given by the transcendental equation $\hat{\mathbf{f}} = \exp[-1 - 2\alpha \mathbf{H}^T(\mathbf{g} - \mathbf{H}\hat{\mathbf{f}})]$.

5.13 A linear approximation to the maximum entropy solution given in Problem 5.12 can be obtained by expanding the exponential in a Taylor series and then keeping only the linear part of the expansion. Show that this approach results in the constrained least squares formulation in Eq. (5.3-9) but with $\mathbf{Q} = \mathbf{I}$.

5.14 A certain x-ray imaging geometry produces a blurring degradation that can be modeled as the convolution of the sensed image with the spatial, circularly symmetric function $h(r) = [(r^2 - 2\sigma^2)/\sigma^4]\exp[-r^2/2\sigma^2]$, where $r^2 = x^2 + y^2$. Obtain the transfer function of a constrained least squares filter you could use to deblur the images produced by this x-ray system. You may assume that the images are square.

5.15 Start with Eq. (5.7-12) and derive Eq. (5.7-14).

5.16 Suppose that, instead of using quadrilaterals, you used triangular regions in Section 5.9 to establish a spatial transformation and gray-level interpolation. What would be the equations analogous to Eqs. (5.9-5), (5.9-6), and (5.9-7) for triangular regions?

CHAPTER 6

IMAGE COMPRESSION

But life is short and information endless. . .
Abbreviation is a necessary evil and the
abbreviator's business is to make the best of a
job which, although intrinsically bad, is still
better than nothing.
Aldous Huxley

An enormous amount of data is produced when a 2-D light intensity function is sampled and quantized to create a digital image. In fact, the amount of data generated may be so great that it results in impractical storage, processing, and communications requirements. In such cases, representations beyond the simple 2-D sampling and gray-level quantization of Section 2.3 are needed. For instance, more than 25 gigabytes (25×10^9 bytes) of data are required to represent the *Encyclopaedia Britannica* in digital form.[†]

Image compression addresses the problem of reducing the amount of data required to represent a digital image. The underlying basis of the reduction process is the removal of redundant data. From a mathematical viewpoint, this amounts to transforming a 2-D pixel array into a statistically uncorrelated data set. The transformation is applied prior to storage or transmission of the image. At some later time, the compressed image is decompressed to reconstruct the original image or an approximation to it.

Interest in image compression dates back more than 25 years. The initial focus of research efforts in this field was on the development of analog methods for reducing video transmission bandwidth, a process called *bandwidth compression*. The advent of the digital computer and subsequent development of ad-

---

[†] The *Encyclopaedia Britannica* contains about 25,000 pages. A single page scanned at 300 dots per inch and quantized to two levels generates more than 8,000,000 bits (1,000,000 bytes) of data.

vanced integrated circuits, however, caused interest to shift from analog to digital compression approaches. With the recent adoption of several key international image compression standards, the field is now poised for significant growth through the practical application of the theoretic work that began in the 1940s, when C. E. Shannon and others first formulated the probabilistic view of information and its representation, transmission, and compression.

Over the years, the need for image compression has grown steadily. Currently, it is recognized as an "enabling technology." For example, image compression has been and continues to be crucial to the growth of multimedia computing (that is, the use of digital computers in printing and publishing and video production and dissemination). In addition, it is the natural technology for handling the increased spatial resolutions of today's imaging sensors and evolving broadcast television standards. Furthermore, image compression plays a crucial role in many important and diverse applications, including televideoconferencing, remote sensing (the use of satellite imagery for weather and other earth-resource applications), document and medical imaging, facsimile transmission (FAX), and the control of remotely piloted vehicles in military, space, and hazardous waste control applications. In short, an ever-expanding number of applications depend on the efficient manipulation, storage, and transmission of binary, gray-scale, or color images.

In this chapter, we examine both the theoretic and practical aspects of the image compression process. Sections 6.1–6.3 constitute an introduction to the fundamentals that collectively form the theory of this discipline. Section 6.1 describes the data redundancies that may be exploited by image compression algorithms, Section 6.2 presents a model-based paradigm for the general compression–decompression process, and Section 6.3 examines in some detail a number of basic concepts from information theory and their role in establishing fundamental limits on the representation of information.

Sections 6.4–6.6 cover the practical aspects of image compression, including both the principal techniques in use, and the standards that have been instrumental in increasing the scope and acceptance of this discipline. Compression techniques fall into two broad categories: *information preserving* and *lossy*. Section 6.4 addresses methods in the first category, which are particularly useful in image archiving (as in the storage of legal or medical records). These methods allow an image to be compressed and decompressed without losing information. Section 6.5 describes methods in the second category, which provide higher levels of data reduction but result in a less than perfect reproduction of the original image. Lossy image compression is useful in applications such as broadcast television, videoconferencing, and facsimile transmission, in which a certain amount of error is an acceptable trade-off for increased compression performance. Finally, Section 6.6 deals with existing and proposed image compression standards.

6.1 FUNDAMENTALS

The term *data compression* refers to the process of reducing the amount of data required to represent a given quantity of information. A clear distinction must be made between *data* and *information*. They are not synonymous. In fact, data are the means by which information is conveyed. Various amounts of data may be used to represent the same amount of information. Such might be the case, for example, if a long-winded individual and someone who is short and to the point were to relate the same story. Here, the information of interest is the story; words are the data used to relate the information. If the two individuals use a different number of words to tell the same basic story, two different versions of the story are created, and at least one includes nonessential data. That is, it contains data (or words) that either provide no relevant information or simply restate that which is already known. It is thus said to contain *data redundancy*.

Data redundancy is a central issue in digital image compression. It is not an abstract concept but a mathematically quantifiable entity. If n_1 and n_2 denote the number of information carrying units in two data sets that represent the same information, the *relative data redundancy* R_D of the first data set (the one characterized by n_1) can be defined as

$$R_D = 1 - \frac{1}{C_R} \tag{6.1-1}$$

where C_R, commonly called the *compression ratio*, is

$$C_R = \frac{n_1}{n_2}. \tag{6.1-2}$$

For the case $n_2 = n_1$, $C_R = 1$ and $R_D = 0$, indicating that (relative to the second data set) the first representation of the information contains no redundant data. When $n_2 \ll n_1$, $C_R \to \infty$ and $R_D \to 1$, implying significant compression and highly redundant data. In the final case, $n_2 \gg n_1$, $C_R \to 0$ and $R_D \to -\infty$, indicating that the second data set contains much more data than the original representation. This, of course, is the normally undesirable case of data expansion. In general, C_R and R_D lie in the open intervals $(0, \infty)$ and $(-\infty, 1)$, respectively. A practical compression ratio, such as 10 (or 10:1) means that the first data set has 10 information carrying units (say, bits) for every 1 unit in the second or compressed data set. The corresponding redundancy of 0.9 implies that 90 percent of the data in the first data set is redundant.

In digital image compression, three basic data redundancies can be identified and exploited: *coding* redundancy, *interpixel* redundancy, and *psycho-*

visual redundancy. Data compression is achieved when one or more of these redundancies are reduced or eliminated.

6.1.1 Coding Redundancy

In Chapter 4 we formulated the material on image enhancement by histogram modification on the assumption that the gray levels of an image are random quantities. We showed that a great deal of information about the appearance of an image could be obtained from a histogram of its gray levels. In this section, we utilize a similar formulation to show how the gray-level histogram of an image also can provide a great deal of insight into the construction of codes[†] to reduce the amount of data used to represent it.

Let us assume, once again, that a discrete random variable r_k in the interval $[0, 1]$ represents the gray levels of an image and that each r_k occurs with probability $p_r(r_k)$. As in Chapter 4,

$$p_r(r_k) = \frac{n_k}{n} \quad k = 0, 1, 2, \ldots, L - 1 \tag{6.1-3}$$

where L is the number of gray levels, n_k is the number of times that the kth gray level appears in the image, and n is the total number of pixels in the image. If the number of bits used to represent each value of r_k is $l(r_k)$, the average number of bits required to represent each pixel is

$$L_{\text{avg}} = \sum_{k=0}^{L-1} l(r_k) \, p_r(r_k). \tag{6.1-4}$$

That is, the average length of the code words assigned to the various gray-level values is found by summing the product of the number of bits used to represent each gray level and the probability that the gray level occurs. Thus the total number of bits required to code an $M \times N$ image is MNL_{avg}.

Representing the gray levels of an image with a natural m-bit binary code[‡] reduces the right-hand side of Eq. (6.1-4) to m bits. That is, $L_{\text{avg}} = m$ when m is substituted for $l(r_k)$. Then the constant m may be taken outside the sum-

---

[†] A code is a system of symbols (letters, numbers, bits, and the like) used to represent a body of information or set of events. Each piece of information or event is assigned a sequence of *code symbols*, called a *code word*. The number of symbols in each code word is its *length*. One of the most famous codes was used by Paul Revere on April 18th, 1775. The phrase "one if by land, two if by sea" is often used to describe that code, in which one or two lights were used to indicate whether the British were traveling by land or sea.

[‡] A natural (or straight) binary code is one in which each event or piece of information to be encoded (such as gray-level value) is assigned one of 2^m m-bit binary codes from an m-bit binary counting sequence.

mation, leaving only the sum of the $p_r(r_k)$ for $0 \le k \le L - 1$, which, of course, equals 1.

Example: An 8-level image has the gray-level distribution shown in Table 6.1. If a natural 3-bit binary code [see code 1 and $l_1(r_k)$ in Table 6.1] is used to represent the 8 possible gray levels, L_{avg} is 3 bits, because $l_1(r_k) = 3$ bits for all r_k. If code 2 in Table 6.1 is used, however, the average number of bits required to code the image is reduced to

$$L_{avg} = \sum_{k=0}^{7} l_2(r_k) \, p_r(r_k)$$

$$= 2(0.19) + 2(0.25) + 2(0.21) + 3(0.16) + 4(0.08)$$
$$+ 5(0.06) + 6(0.03) + 6(0.02)$$
$$= 2.7 \text{ bits.}$$

From Eq. (6.1-1), the resulting compression ratio C_R is 3/2.7 or 1.11. Thus approximately 10 percent of the data resulting from the use of code 1 is redundant. The exact level of redundancy can be determined from Eq. (6.1-2):

$$R_D = 1 - \frac{1}{1.11} = 0.099.$$

Figure 6.1 illustrates the underlying basis for the compression achieved by code 2. It shows both the histogram of the image [a plot of $p_r(r_k)$ versus r_k] and $l_2(r_k)$. Because these two functions are inversely proportional, that is, $l_2(r_k)$ increases as $p_r(r_k)$ decreases, the shortest code words in code 2 are assigned to the gray levels that occur most frequently in an image. ❑

In the preceding example, assigning fewer bits to the more probable gray levels than to the less probable ones achieves data compression. This process

Table 6.1 Variable-Length Coding Example

r_k	$p_r(r_k)$	Code 1	$l_1(r_k)$	Code 2	$l_2(r_k)$
$r_0 = 0$	0.19	000	3	11	2
$r_1 = 1/7$	0.25	001	3	01	2
$r_2 = 2/7$	0.21	010	3	10	2
$r_3 = 3/7$	0.16	011	3	001	3
$r_4 = 4/7$	0.08	100	3	0001	4
$r_5 = 5/7$	0.06	101	3	00001	5
$r_6 = 6/7$	0.03	110	3	000001	6
$r_7 = 1$	0.02	111	3	000000	6

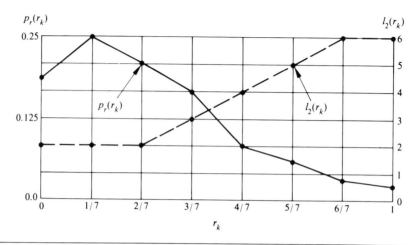

Figure 6.1 *Graphic representation of the fundamental basis of data compression through variable-length coding.*

commonly is referred to as *variable-length coding.* If the gray levels of an image are coded in a way that uses more code symbols than absolutely necessary to represent each gray level (that is, the code fails to minimize Eq. 6.1-4), the resulting image is said to contain *coding redundancy.* In general, coding redundancy is present when the codes assigned to a set of events (such as gray-level values) have not been selected to take full advantage of the probabilities of the events. It is almost always present when an image's gray levels are represented with a straight or natural binary code. In this case, the underlying basis for the coding redundancy is that images are typically composed of objects that have a regular and somewhat predictable morphology (shape) and reflectance, and are generally sampled so that the objects being depicted are much larger than the picture elements. The natural consequence is that, in most images, certain gray levels are more probable than others (that is, the histograms of most images are not uniform). A natural binary coding of their gray levels assigns the same number of bits to both the most and least probable values, thus failing to minimize Eq. (6.1-4) and resulting in coding redundancy.

6.1.2 Interpixel Redundancy

Consider the images shown in Figs. 6.2(a) and (b). As Figs. 6.2(c) and (d) show, these images have virtually identical histograms. Note also that both histograms are trimodal, indicating the presence of three dominant ranges of gray-level values. Because the gray levels in these images are not equally probable, variable-length coding can be used to reduce the coding redundancy that would result from a straight or natural binary encoding of their pixels. The coding process, however, would not alter the level of correlation between the pixels within the images. In other words, the codes used to represent the gray levels of each image have nothing to do with the correlation between pixels. These correlations result from the structural or geometric relationships between the objects in the image.

Figures 6.2(e) and (f) show the respective autocorrelation coefficients computed along one line of each image. These coefficients were computed using a normalized version of Eq. (3.3-37) in which

$$\gamma(\Delta n) = \frac{A(\Delta n)}{A(0)} \tag{6.1-5}$$

where

$$A(\Delta n) = \frac{1}{N - \Delta n} \sum_{y=0}^{N-1-\Delta n} f(x, y)f(x, y + \Delta n). \tag{6.1-6}$$

The scaling factor in Eq. (6.1-6) accounts for the varying number of sum terms that arise for each integer value of Δn. Of course, Δn must be strictly less than N, the number of pixels on a line. The variable x is the coordinate of the line used in the computation. Note the dramatic difference between the shape of the functions shown in Figs. 6.2(e) and (f). Their shapes can be qualitatively related to the structure in the images in Figs. 6.2(a) and (b). This relationship is particularly noticeable in Fig. 6.2(f), where the high correlation between pixels separated by 45 and 90 samples can be directly related to the spacing between the vertically oriented matches of Fig. 6.2(b). In addition, the adjacent pixels of both images are highly correlated. When Δn is 1, γ is 0.9922 and 0.9928 for the images of Figs. 6.2(a) and (b), respectively. These values are typical of most properly sampled television images.

These illustrations reflect another important form of data redundancy— one directly related to the interpixel correlations within an image. Because the value of any given pixel can be reasonably predicted from the value of its neighbors, the information carried by individual pixels is relatively small. Much of the visual contribution of a single pixel to an image is redundant; it could have been guessed on the basis of its neighbors' values. A variety of names, including *spatial redundancy*, *geometric redundancy*, and *interframe redundancy*, have been coined to refer to these interpixel dependencies. We use the term *interpixel redundancy* to encompass them all.

In order to reduce the interpixel redundancies in an image, the 2-D pixel array normally used for human viewing and interpretation must be transformed into a more efficient (but usually "nonvisual") format. For example, the differences between adjacent pixels can be used to represent an image. Transformations of this type (that is, those that remove interpixel redundancy) are referred to as *mappings*. They are called *reversible* if the original image elements can be reconstructed from the transformed data set.

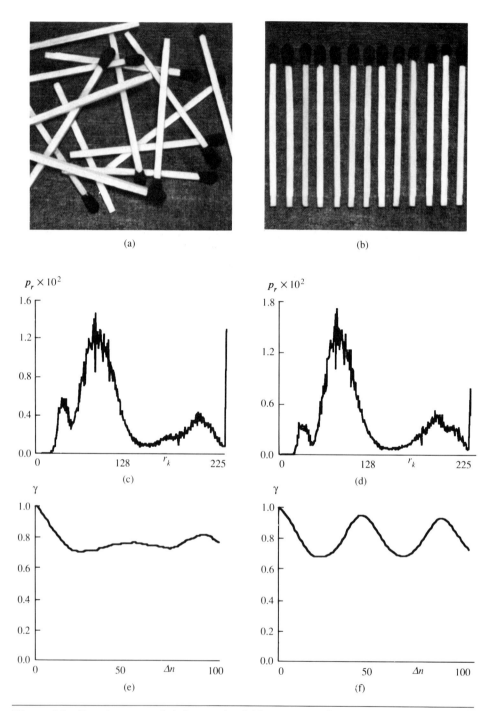

Figure 6.2 *Two images and their gray-level histograms and normalized autocorrelation coefficients along one line.*

Example: Figure 6.3 illustrates a simple mapping procedure. Figure 6.3(a) depicts a 1-in. × 3-in. section of an electrical assembly drawing that has been sampled at about 330 dpi (dots per inch). Figure 6.3(b) shows a binary version of this drawing. In addition, Fig. 6.3(c) depicts the gray-level profile of one line of the image and the threshold used to obtain the binary version. Because the binary image contains many regions of constant intensity, a more efficient representation can be constructed by mapping the pixels along each scan line $f(x, 0), f(x, 1), \ldots, f(x, N - 1)$ into a sequence of pairs $(g_1, r_1), (g_2, r_2), \ldots,$ in which g_i denotes the ith gray level encountered along the line and r_i the run length of the ith run. In other words, the thresholded image can be more efficiently represented by the value and length of its constant gray-level runs (a nonvisual representation) than by a 2-D array of binary pixels.

Figure 6.3(d) shows the run-length encoded data corresponding to the thresholded line profile of Fig. 6.3(c). Only 88 bits are needed to represent the 1024 bits of binary data. In fact, the entire 1024 × 343 section shown in Fig. 6.3(b) can be reduced to 12,166 runs. As 11 bits are required to represent each run-length pair, the resulting compression ratio and corresponding relative redundancy are

$$C_R = \frac{(1024)(343)(1)}{(12166)(11)} = 2.63$$

and

$$R_D = 1 - \frac{1}{2.63} = 0.62.$$

❏

6.1.3 Psychovisual Redundancy

We noted in Chapter 2 that the brightness of a region, as perceived by the eye, depends on factors other than simply the light reflected by the region. For example, intensity variations (Mach bands) can be perceived in an area of constant intensity. Such phenomena result from the fact that the eye does not respond with equal sensitivity to all visual information. Certain information simply has less relative importance than other information in normal visual processing. This information is said to be *psychovisually redundant.* It can be eliminated without significantly impairing the quality of image perception.

That psychovisual redundancies exist should not come as a surprise, because human perception of the information in an image normally does not involve quantitative analysis of every pixel or luminance value in the image. In general, an observer searches for distinguishing features such as edges or textural regions and mentally combines them into recognizable groupings. The brain then cor-

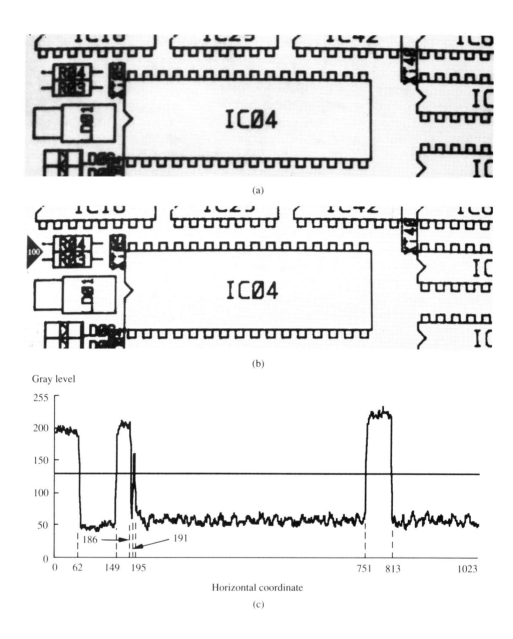

(a)

(b)

Gray level

(c)

Line 100: (1, 63) (0, 87) (1, 37) (0, 5) (1, 4) (0, 556) (1, 62) (0, 210)

(d)

Figure 6.3 *Illustration of run-length coding: (a) original image; (b) binary image with line 100 marked; (c) line profile and binarization threshold; (d) run-length code.*

relates these groupings with prior knowledge in order to complete the image interpretation process.

Psychovisual redundancy is fundamentally different from the redundancies discussed earlier. Unlike coding and interpixel redundancy, psychovisual redundancy is associated with real or quantifiable visual information. Its elimination is possible only because the information itself is not essential for normal visual processing. Since the elimination of psychovisually redundant data results in a loss of quantitative information, it is commonly referred to as *quantization*. This terminology is consistent with normal usage of the word, which generally means the mapping of a broad range of input values to a limited number of output values. As it is an irreversible operation (visual information is lost), quantization results in lossy data compression.

Example: Consider the images in Fig. 6.4. Figure 6.4(a) shows a monochrome image with 256 possible gray levels. Figure 6.4(b) shows the same image after uniform quantization to four bits or 16 possible levels. The resulting compression ratio is 2:1. Note, as discussed in Section 2.3, that false contouring is present in the previously smooth regions of the original image. This is the natural visual effect of more coarsely representing the gray levels of the image.

(a)   (b)   (c)

Figure 6.4   (a) Original image; (b) uniform quantization to 16 levels; (c) IGS quantization to 16 levels.

Figure 6.4(c) illustrates the significant improvements possible with quantization that takes advantage of the peculiarities of the human visual system. Although the compression ratio resulting from this second quantization procedure also is 2:1, false contouring is greatly reduced at the expense of some additional but less objectionable graininess. The method used to produce this result is known as *improved gray-scale* (IGS) *quantization.* It recognizes the eye's inherent sensitivity to edges and breaks them up by adding to each pixel a pseudo-random number, which is generated from the low-order bits of neighboring pixels, before quantizing the result. Because the low-order bits are fairly random (see the bit planes in Section 4.2.1), this amounts to adding a level of randomness, which depends on the local characteristics of the image, to the artificial edges normally associated with false contouring.

Table 6.2 illustrates this method. A sum—initially set to zero—is first formed from the current 8-bit gray-level value and the four least significant bits of a previously generated sum. If the four most significant bits of the current value are 1111_2, however, 0000_2 is added instead. The four most significant bits of the resulting sum are used as the coded pixel value.   ☐

Improved gray-scale quantization is typical of a large group of quantization procedures that operate directly on the gray levels of the image to be compressed. They usually entail a decrease in the image's spatial, gray-scale, or temporal resolution. The resulting false contouring or other related effects (jerky motion, blurring, and so on) necessitates the use of heuristic techniques to compensate for the visual impact of quantization. The normal 2:1 line interlacing approach used in commercial broadcast television, for example, is a form of quantization in which interleaving portions of adjacent frames allows reduced video scanning rates with little decrease in perceived image quality.

6.1.4   Fidelity Criteria

As noted previously, removal of psychovisually redundant data results in a loss of real or quantitative visual information. Because information of interest may be lost, a repeatable or reproducible means of quantifying the nature and extent of information loss is highly desirable. Two general classes of criteria are used

Table 6.2   IGS Quantization Procedure

Pixel	Gray Level	Sum	IGS Code
$i - 1$	N/A	0000 0000	N/A
i	0110 1100	0110 1100	0110
$i + 1$	1000 1011	1001 0111	1001
$i + 2$	1000 0111	1000 1110	1000
$i + 3$	1111 0100	1111 0100	1111

as the basis for such an assessment: (1) objective fidelity criteria and (2) subjective fidelity criteria.

When the level of information loss can be expressed as a function of the original or input image and the compressed and subsequently decompressed output image, it is said to be based on an *objective fidelity criterion*. A good example is the root-mean-square (rms) error between an input and output image. Let $f(x, y)$ represent an input image and let $\hat{f}(x, y)$ denote an estimate or approximation of $f(x, y)$ that results from compressing and subsequently decompressing the input. For any value of x and y, the error $e(x, y)$ between $f(x, y)$ and $\hat{f}(x, y)$ can be defined as

$$e(x, y) = \hat{f}(x, y) - f(x, y) \tag{6.1-7}$$

so that the total error between the two images is

$$\sum_{x=0}^{M-1} \sum_{y=0}^{N-1} [\hat{f}(x, y) - f(x, y)]$$

where the images are of size $M \times N$. The *root-mean-square error*, e_{rms}, between $f(x, y)$ and $\hat{f}(x, y)$ then is the square root of the squared error averaged over the $M \times N$ array, or

$$e_{rms} = \left[\frac{1}{MN} \sum_{x=0}^{M-1} \sum_{y=0}^{N-1} [\hat{f}(x, y) - f(x, y)]^2 \right]^{1/2} \tag{6.1-8}$$

A closely related objective fidelity criterion is the mean-square signal-to-noise ratio of the compressed–decompressed image. If $\hat{f}(x, y)$ is considered (by a simple rearrangement of the terms in Eq. (6.1-7)) to be the sum of the original image $f(x, y)$ and a noise signal $e(x, y)$, the *mean-square signal-to-noise ratio* of the output image, denoted SNR_{ms}, is

$$SNR_{ms} = \frac{\displaystyle\sum_{x=0}^{M-1} \sum_{y=0}^{N-1} \hat{f}(x, y)^2}{\displaystyle\sum_{x=0}^{M-1} \sum_{y=0}^{N-1} [\hat{f}(x, y) - f(x, y)]^2} . \tag{6.1-9}$$

The rms value of the signal-to-noise ratio, denoted SNR_{rms}, is obtained by taking the square root of Eq. (6.1-9).

Although objective fidelity criteria offer a simple and convenient mechanism for evaluating information loss, most decompressed images ultimately are viewed by human beings. Consequently, measuring image quality by the subjective evaluations of a human observer often is more appropriate. This can be accomplished by showing a "typical" decompressed image to an appropriate cross section of viewers and averaging their evaluations. The evaluations may

**Table 6.3   Television Allocations Study Organization Rating Scale
(From Frendendall and Behrend [1960])**

Value	Rating	Description
1	Excellent	An image of extremely high quality, as good as you could desire.
2	Fine	An image of high quality, providing enjoyable viewing. Interference is not objectionable.
3	Passable	An image of acceptable quality. Interference is not objectionable.
4	Marginal	An image of poor quality; you wish you could improve it. Interference is somewhat objectionable.
5	Inferior	A very poor image, but you could watch it. Objectionable interference is definitely present.
6	Unusable	An image so bad that you could not watch it.

be made using an absolute rating scale or by means of side-by-side comparisons of $f(x, y)$ and $\hat{f}(x, y)$. Table 6.3 shows one possible absolute rating scale. Side-by-side comparisons can be done with a scale such as $\{-3, -2, -1, 0, 1, 2, 3\}$ to represent the subjective evaluations {*much worse, worse, slightly worse, the same, slightly better, better, much better*}, respectively. In either case, the evaluations are said to be based on *subjective fidelity criteria*.

Example: The rms errors in the quantized images of Fig. 6.4(b) and (c) are 6.93 and 6.78 gray levels, respectively. The corresponding rms signal-to-noise ratios are 10.25 and 10.39. Although these values are quite similar, a subjective evaluation of the visual quality of the two coded images might result in a *marginal* rating for the image in Fig. 6.4(b) and a *passable* rating for that in Fig. 6.4(c).   ❏

6.2   IMAGE COMPRESSION MODELS

In Section 6.1 we discussed individually three general techniques for reducing or compressing the amount of data required to represent an image. However, these techniques typically are combined to form practical image compression systems. In this section, we examine the overall characteristics of such a system and develop a general model to represent it.

As Fig. 6.5 shows, a compression system consists of two distinct structural blocks: an *encoder* and a *decoder*.[†] An input image $f(x, y)$ is fed into the encoder, which creates a set of symbols from the input data. After transmission over

---

[†] It would be reasonable to expect these blocks to be called the "compressor" and "decompressor." The terms *encoder* and *decoder* reflect the influence of information theory (to be discussed in Section 6.3) on the field of image compression.

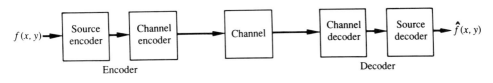

Figure 6.5 *A general compression system model.*

the *channel*, the encoded representation is fed to the decoder, where a reconstructed output image $\hat{f}(x, y)$ is generated. In general, $\hat{f}(x, y)$ may or may not
be an exact replica of $f(x, y)$. If it is, the system is error free or information
preserving; if not, some level of distortion is present in the reconstructed image.

Both the encoder and decoder shown in Fig. 6.5 consist of two relatively
independent functions or subblocks. The encoder is made up of a *source
encoder*, which removes input redundancies, and a *channel encoder*, which
increases the noise immunity of the source encoder's output. As would be
expected, the decoder includes a *channel decoder* followed by a *source decoder*.
If the channel between the encoder and decoder is noise free (not prone to
error), the channel encoder and decoder are omitted, and the general encoder
and decoder become the source encoder and decoder, respectively.

6.2.1 The Source Encoder and Decoder

The source encoder is responsible for reducing or eliminating any coding,
interpixel, or psychovisual redundancies in the input image. The specific application and associated fidelity requirements dictate the best encoding approach to use in any given situation. Normally, the approach can be modeled
by a series of three independent operations. As Fig. 6.6(a) shows, each operation is designed to reduce one of the three redundancies described in Section
6.1. Figure 6.6(b) depicts the corresponding source decoder.

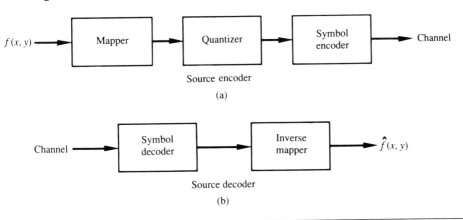

Figure 6.6 *(a) Source encoder and (b) source decoder model.*

In the first stage of the source encoding process, the *mapper* transforms the input data into a (usually nonvisual) format designed to reduce interpixel redundancies in the input image. This operation generally is reversible and may or may not reduce directly the amount of data required to represent the image. Run-length coding (Sections 6.1.2 and 6.4.2) is an example of a mapping that directly results in data compression in this initial stage of the overall source encoding process. The representation of an image by a set of transform coefficients (Section 6.5.2) is an example of the opposite case. Here, the mapper transforms the image into an array of coefficients, making its interpixel redundancies more accessible for compression in later stages of the encoding process.

The second stage, or *quantizer* block in Fig. 6.6(a), reduces the accuracy of the mapper's output in accordance with some preestablished fidelity criterion. This stage reduces the psychovisual redundancies of the input image. As noted in Section 6.1.3, this operation is irreversible. Thus it must be omitted when error-free compression is desired.

In the third and final stage of the source encoding process, the *symbol coder* creates a fixed- or variable-length code to represent the quantizer output and maps the output in accordance with the code. The term symbol coder distinguishes this coding operation from the overall source encoding process. In most cases, a variable-length code is used to represent the mapped and quantized data set. It assigns the shortest code words to the most frequently occurring output values and thus reduces coding redundancy. The operation, of course, is reversible. Upon completion of the symbol coding step, the input image has been processed to remove each of the three redundancies described in Section 6.1.

Figure 6.6(a) shows the source encoding process as three successive operations, but all three operations are not necessarily included in every compression system. Recall, for example, that the quantizer must be omitted when error-free compression is desired. In addition, some compression techniques normally are modeled by merging blocks that are physically separate in Fig. 6.6(a). In the predictive compression systems of Section 6.5.1, for instance, the mapper and quantizer are often represented by a single block, which simultaneously performs both operations.

The source decoder shown in Fig. 6.6(b) contains only two components: a *symbol decoder* and an *inverse mapper*. These blocks perform, in reverse order, the inverse operations of the source encoder's symbol encoder and mapper blocks. Because quantization results in irreversible information loss, an inverse quantizer block is not included in the general source decoder model shown in Fig. 6.6(b).

6.2.2 The Channel Encoder and Decoder

The channel encoder and decoder play an important role in the overall encoding–decoding process when the channel of Fig. 6.5 is noisy or prone to error. They are designed to reduce the impact of channel noise by inserting a controlled form of redundancy into the source encoded data. As the output of the source encoder contains little redundancy, it would be highly sensitive to transmission noise without the addition of this "controlled redundancy."

One of the most useful channel encoding techniques was devised by R. W. Hamming (Hamming [1950]). It is based on appending enough bits to the data being encoded to ensure that some minimum number of bits must change between valid code words. Hamming showed, for example, that if 3 bits of redundancy are added to a 4-bit word, so that the *distance*[†] between any two valid code words is 3, all single-bit errors can be detected *and* corrected. (By appending additional bits of redundancy, multiple-bit errors can be detected and/or corrected.) The 7-bit *Hamming (7,4) code* word $h_1 \ldots h_5 h_6 h_7$ associated with a 4-bit binary number $b_3 b_2 b_1 b_0$ is

$$
\begin{aligned}
h_1 &= b_3 \oplus b_2 \oplus b_0 & h_3 &= b_3 \\
h_2 &= b_3 \oplus b_1 \oplus b_0 & h_5 &= b_2 \\
h_4 &= b_2 \oplus b_1 \oplus b_0 & h_6 &= b_1 \\
& & h_7 &= b_0
\end{aligned}
\tag{6.2-1}
$$

where $\oplus$ denotes the exclusive OR operation. Note that bits h_1, h_2, and h_4 are even-parity bits for the bit fields $b_3 b_2 b_0$, $b_3 b_1 b_0$, and $b_2 b_1 b_0$, respectively.

To decode a Hamming encoded result, the channel decoder must check the encoded value for odd parity over the bit fields in which even parity was previously established. A single-bit error is indicated by a nonzero parity word $c_4 c_2 c_1$, where

$$
\begin{aligned}
c_1 &= h_1 \oplus h_3 \oplus h_5 \oplus h_7 \\
c_2 &= h_2 \oplus h_3 \oplus h_6 \oplus h_7 \\
c_4 &= h_4 \oplus h_5 \oplus h_6 \oplus h_7.
\end{aligned}
\tag{6.2-2}
$$

If a nonzero value is found, the decoder simply complements the code word bit position indicated by the parity word. The decoded binary value is then extracted from the corrected code word as $h_3 h_5 h_6 h_7$.

Example: Consider the transmission of the 4-bit IGS data of Table 6.2 over a noisy communication channel. A single-bit error could cause a decompressed pixel to deviate from its correct value by as many as 128 gray levels.[‡] A Hamming

---

[†] The *distance* between two code words is defined as the number of digits that must change in one word so that the other word results. For example, the distance between 101101 and 011101 is 2. The *minimum distance* of a code is the smallest number of digits by which any two code words differ.

[‡] A simple procedure for decompressing 4-bit IGS data is to multiply the decimal equivalent of the IGS value by 16. For example, if the IGS value is 1110, the decompressed gray level is (14)(16) or 224. If the most significant bit of this IGS value was incorrectly transmitted as a 0, the decompressed gray level becomes 96. The resulting error is 128 gray levels.

channel encoder can be utilized to increase the noise immunity of this source encoded IGS data by inserting enough redundancy to allow the detection and correction of single-bit errors. From Eq. (6.2-1), the Hamming encoded value for the first IGS value in Table 6.2 is 1100110_2. Because the Hamming channel encoder increases the number of bits required to represent the IGS value from 4 to 7, the 2:1 compression ratio noted in the IGS example is reduced to 8/7 or 1.14:1. This reduction in compression is the price paid for increased noise immunity.   ❏

6.3 ELEMENTS OF INFORMATION THEORY

In Section 6.1 we introduced several ways to reduce the amount of data used to represent an image. The question that naturally arises is: How few data actually are needed to represent the image? That is, is there a minimum amount of data that is sufficient to describe completely the image without loss of information? Information theory provides the mathematical framework to answer this and related questions.

6.3.1 Measuring Information

The fundamental premise of information theory is that the generation of information can be modeled as a probabilistic process that can be measured in a manner that agrees with intuition. In accordance with this supposition, a random event E that occurs with probability $P(E)$ is said to contain

$$I(E) = \log \frac{1}{P(E)} = -\log P(E) \qquad (6.3\text{-}1)$$

units of information. The quantity $I(E)$ often is called the *self-information* of E. Generally speaking, the amount of self-information attributed to event E is inversely related to the probability of E. If $P(E) = 1$ (that is, the event always occurs), $I(E) = 0$ and no information is attributed to it. That is, because no uncertainty is associated with the event, no information would be transferred by communicating that the event has occurred. However, if $P(E) = 0.99$, communicating that E has occurred conveys some small amount of information. Communicating that E has not occurred conveys more information, because this outcome is less likely.

The base of the logarithm in Eq. (6.3-1) determines the unit used to measure information.[†] If the base r logarithm is used, the measurement is said to be in

---

[†] When we do not explicitly specify the base of the log used in an expression, the result may be interpreted in any base and corresponding information unit.

r-ary units. If the base 2 is selected, the resulting unit of information is called a *bit*. Note that if $P(E) = \frac{1}{2}$, $I(E) = -\log_2 \frac{1}{2}$, or 1 bit. That is, 1 bit is the amount of information conveyed when one of two possible equally likely events occurs. A simple example of such a situation is flipping a coin and communicating the result.

6.3.2   The Information Channel

When self-information is transferred between an information source and a user of the information, the source of information is said to be connected to the user of information by an *information channel*. The information channel is the physical medium that links the source to the user. It may be a telephone line, an electromagnetic energy propagation path, or a wire in a digital computer. Figure 6.7 shows a simple mathematical model for a discrete information system. Here, the parameter of particular interest is the system's *capacity*, defined as its ability to transfer information.

Let us assume that the information source in Fig. 6.7 generates a random sequence of symbols from a finite or countably infinite set of possible symbols. That is, the output of the source is a discrete random variable. The set of source symbols $\{a_1, a_2, \dots, a_J\}$ is referred to as the *source alphabet A*, and the elements of the set, denoted a_j, are called *symbols* or *letters*. The probability of the event that the source will produce symbol a_j is $P(a_j)$, and

$$\sum_{j=1}^{J} P(a_j) = 1. \tag{6.3-2}$$

The $J \times 1$ vector $\mathbf{z} = [P(a_1), P(a_2), \dots, P(a_J)]^T$ customarily represents the set of all source symbol probabilities $\{P(a_1), P(a_2), \dots, P(a_J)\}$. The finite *ensemble* $(A, \mathbf{z})$ describes the information source completely.

The probability that the discrete source will emit symbol a_j is $P(a_j)$, so the self-information generated by the production of a single source symbol is, in accordance with Eq. (6.3-1), $I(a_j) = -\log P(a_j)$. If k source symbols are generated, the law of large numbers stipulates that, for a sufficiently large value

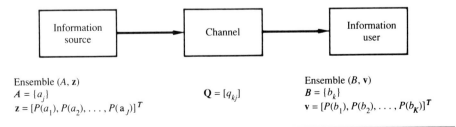

Ensemble $(A, \mathbf{z})$
$A = \{a_j\}$
$\mathbf{z} = [P(a_1), P(a_2), \dots, P(a_J)]^T$

$Q = [q_{kj}]$

Ensemble $(B, \mathbf{v})$
$B = \{b_k\}$
$\mathbf{v} = [P(b_1), P(b_2), \dots, P(b_K)]^T$

Figure 6.7   *A simple information system.*

of k, symbol a_j will (on average) be output $kP(a_j)$ times. Thus the average self-information obtained from k outputs is

$$-kP(a_1) \log P(a_1) - kP(a_2) \log P(a_2) - \ldots - kP(a_J) \log P(a_J)$$

or

$$-k \sum_{j=1}^{J} P(a_j) \log P(a_j).$$

The average information per source output, denoted $H(\mathbf{z})$, is

$$H(\mathbf{z}) = -\sum_{j=1}^{J} P(a_j) \log P(a_j) \qquad (6.3\text{-}3)$$

and is called the *uncertainty* or *entropy* of the source. It defines the average amount of information (in r-ary units per symbol) obtained by observing a single source output. As its magnitude increases, more uncertainty and thus more information is associated with the source. If the source symbols are equally probable, the entropy or uncertainty of Eq. (6.3-3) is maximized and the source provides the greatest possible average information per source symbol.

Having modeled the information source, we can develop the transfer function of the information channel rather easily. Because we modeled the input to the channel in Fig. 6.7 as a discrete random variable, the information transferred to the output of the channel is also a discrete random variable. Like the source random variable, it takes on values from a finite or countably infinite set of symbols $\{b_1, b_2, \ldots, b_K\}$ called the *channel alphabet B*. The probability of the event that symbol b_k is presented to the *information user* is $P(b_k)$. The finite ensemble $(B, \mathbf{v})$, where $\mathbf{v} = [P(b_1), P(b_2), \ldots, P(b_K)]^T$, describes the channel output completely and thus the information received by the user.

The probability of a given channel output $P(b_k)$ and the probability distribution of the source $\mathbf{z}$ are related by the expression[†]

$$P(b_k) = \sum_{j=1}^{J} P(b_k|a_j)P(a_j) \qquad (6.3\text{-}4)$$

where $P(b_k|a_j)$ is the conditional probability that output symbol b_k is received, given that source symbol a_j was generated. If the conditional probabilities

---

[†] One of the fundamental laws of probability theory is that, for an arbitrary event D and t mutually exclusive events $C_1, C_2, \ldots, C_t$, the total probability of D is $P(D) = P(D|C_1)P(C_1) + \cdots + P(D|C_t)P(C_t)$.

referenced in Eq. (6.3-4) are arranged in a $K \times J$ matrix $\mathbf{Q}$, such that

$$
\mathbf{Q} = \begin{bmatrix}
P(b_1|a_1) & P(b_1|a_2) & \cdots & P(b_1|a_J) \\
P(b_2|a_1) & \cdot & \cdots & \cdot \\
\cdot & \cdot & & \cdot \\
\cdot & \cdot & \cdots & \cdot \\
\cdot & & & \\
P(b_K|a_1) & P(b_K|a_2) & \cdots & P(b_K|a_J)
\end{bmatrix}
\tag{6.3-5}
$$

the probability distribution of the complete output alphabet can be computed from

$$
\mathbf{v} = \mathbf{Qz}.
\tag{6.3-6}
$$

Matrix $\mathbf{Q}$, with elements $q_{kj} = P(b_k|a_j)$, is referred to as the *forward channel transition matrix* or by the abbreviated term *channel matrix*.

To determine the capacity of an information channel with forward channel transition matrix $\mathbf{Q}$, the entropy of the information source must first be computed under the assumption that the information user observes a particular output b_k. Equation (6.3-4) defines a distribution of source symbols for any observed b_k, so each b_k has one *conditional entropy function*. Based on the steps leading to Eq. (6.3-3), this conditional entropy function, denoted $H(\mathbf{z}|b_k)$, can be written as

$$
H(\mathbf{z}|b_k) = -\sum_{j=1}^{J} P(a_j|b_k) \log P(a_j|b_k)
\tag{6.3-7}
$$

where $P(a_j|b_k)$ is the probability that symbol a_j was transmitted by the source, given that the user received b_k. The expected value or average of this expression over all b_k is

$$
H(\mathbf{z}|\mathbf{v}) = \sum_{k=1}^{K} H(\mathbf{z}|b_k)P(b_k)
\tag{6.3-8}
$$

which, after substitution of Eq. (6.3-7) for $H(\mathbf{z}|b_k)$ and some minor rearrangement,[†] can be written as

$$
H(\mathbf{z}|\mathbf{v}) = -\sum_{j=1}^{J} \sum_{k=1}^{K} P(a_j, b_k) \log P(a_j|b_k).
\tag{6.3-9}
$$

[†] Use is made of the fact that the joint probability of two events, C and D, is $P(C, D) = P(C)P(D|C) = P(D)P(C|D)$.

Here, $P(a_j, b_k)$ is the joint probability of a_j and b_k. That is, $P(a_j, b_k)$ is the probability that a_j is transmitted *and* b_k is received.

The term $H(\mathbf{z}|\mathbf{v})$ is called the *equivocation* of $\mathbf{z}$ with respect to $\mathbf{v}$. It represents the average information of one source symbol, assuming observation of the output symbol that resulted from its generation. Because $H(\mathbf{z})$ is the average information of one source symbol, assuming no knowledge of the resulting output symbol, the difference between $H(\mathbf{z})$ and $H(\mathbf{z}|\mathbf{v})$ is the average information received upon observing a single output symbol. This difference, denoted $I(\mathbf{z}, \mathbf{v})$ and called the *mutual information* of $\mathbf{z}$ and $\mathbf{v}$, is

$$I(\mathbf{z}, \mathbf{v}) = H(\mathbf{z}) - H(\mathbf{z}|\mathbf{v}). \tag{6.3-10}$$

Substituting Eqs. (6.3-3) and (6.3-9) for $H(\mathbf{z})$ and $H(\mathbf{z}|\mathbf{v})$ and recalling that $P(a_j) = P(a_j, b_1) + P(a_j, b_2) + \cdots + P(a_j, b_K)$ yields

$$I(\mathbf{z}, \mathbf{v}) = \sum_{j=1}^{J} \sum_{k=1}^{K} P(a_j, b_k) \log \frac{P(a_j, b_k)}{P(a_j)P(b_k)} \tag{6.3-11}$$

which, after further manipulation, can be written as

$$I(\mathbf{z}, \mathbf{v}) = \sum_{j=1}^{J} \sum_{k=1}^{K} P(a_j) \, q_{kj} \log \frac{q_{kj}}{\sum_{i=1}^{J} P(a_i) q_{ki}}. \tag{6.3-12}$$

Thus the average information received upon observing a single output of the information channel is a function of the input or source symbol probability distribution $\mathbf{z}$ and channel matrix $\mathbf{Q}$. The minimum possible value of $I(\mathbf{z}, \mathbf{v})$ is zero and occurs when the input and output symbols are statistically independent. Then, $P(a_j, b_k) = P(a_j)P(b_k)$ and the log term in Eq. (6.3-11) is 0 for all j and k. The maximum value of $I(\mathbf{z}, \mathbf{v})$ over all possible choices of source distribution $\mathbf{z}$ is the *capacity*, C, of the channel described by channel matrix $\mathbf{Q}$. That is,

$$C = \max_{\mathbf{z}} [I(\mathbf{z}, \mathbf{v})] \tag{6.3-13}$$

where the maximum is taken over all possible input distributions. The capacity of the channel defines the maximum rate (in r-ary information units per source symbol) that information can be transmitted reliably through the channel. Moreover, the capacity of a channel does not depend on the input probabilities of the source (that is, on how the channel is used) but is a function of the conditional probabilities defining the channel alone.

Example: Consider a binary information source with source alphabet $A = \{a_1, a_2\} = \{0, 1\}$. The probabilities that the source will produce symbols a_1 and a_2

are $P(a_1) = p_{bs}$ and $P(a_2) = 1 - p_{bs} = \overline{p}_{bs}$, respectively. From Eq. (6.3-3), the entropy of the source is

$$H(\mathbf{z}) = - p_{bs} \log_2 p_{bs} - \overline{p}_{bs} \log_2 \overline{p}_{bs}.$$

Because $\mathbf{z} = [P(a_1), P(a_2)]^T = [p_{bs}, 1 - p_{bs}]^T$, $H(\mathbf{z})$ is dependent on the single parameter p_{bs}, and the right-hand side of the equation is called the *binary entropy function*, denoted $H_{bs}(\cdot)$. Thus, for example, $H_{bs}(t)$ is the function $-t \log_2 t - \overline{t} \log_2 \overline{t}$. Figure 6.8(a) shows a plot of $H_{bs}(p_{bs})$ for $0 \le p_{bs} \le 1$. Note that H_{bs} obtains its maximum value (of 1 bit) when p_{bs} is ½. For all other values of p_{bs}, the source provides less than 1 bit of information.

Now assume that the information is to be transmitted over a noisy binary information channel and let the probability of an error during the transmission of any symbol be p_e. Such a channel is called a *binary symmetric channel* (BSC) and is defined by the channel matrix

$$\mathbf{Q} = \begin{bmatrix} 1 - p_e & p_e \\ p_e & 1 - p_e \end{bmatrix} = \begin{bmatrix} \overline{p}_e & p_e \\ p_e & \overline{p}_e \end{bmatrix}$$

For each input or source symbol, the BSC produces one output b_j from the output alphabet $B = \{b_1, b_2\} = \{0, 1\}$. The probabilities of receiving output symbols b_1 and b_2 can be determined from Eq. (6.3-6):

$$\mathbf{v} = \mathbf{Qz} = \begin{bmatrix} \overline{p}_e & p_e \\ p_e & \overline{p}_e \end{bmatrix} \begin{bmatrix} p_{bs} \\ \overline{p}_{bs} \end{bmatrix} = \begin{bmatrix} \overline{p}_e p_{bs} + p_e \overline{p}_{bs} \\ p_e p_{bs} + \overline{p}_e \overline{p}_{bs} \end{bmatrix}$$

Consequently, the probability that the output is a 0 is $\overline{p}_e p_{bs} + p_e \overline{p}_{bs}$, and the probability that it is a 1 is $p_e p_{bs} + \overline{p}_e \overline{p}_{bs}$. These probabilities can be extracted from the preceding expression for $\mathbf{v}$, because $\mathbf{v} = [P(b_1), P(b_2)]^T = [P(0), P(1)]^T$.

The mutual information of the BSC can now be computed from Eq. (6.3-12). Expanding the summations of this equation and collecting the appropriate terms gives

$$I(\mathbf{z}, \mathbf{v}) = H_{bs}(p_{bs} p_e + \overline{p}_{bs} \overline{p}_e) - H_{bs}(p_e)$$

where $H_{bs}(\cdot)$ is the binary entropy function of Fig. 6.8(a). For a fixed value of p_e, $I(\mathbf{z}, \mathbf{v})$ is 0 when p_{bs} is 0 or 1. Moreover, it achieves its maximum value when the binary source symbols are equally probable. Figure 6.8(b) shows $I(\mathbf{z}, \mathbf{v})$ for all values of p_{bs} and a given channel error p_e.

In accordance with Eq. (6.3-13), the capacity of the BSC is obtained by taking the maximum of the mutual information over all possible source distributions. From Fig. 6.8(b), which plots $I(\mathbf{z}, \mathbf{v})$ for all possible binary source

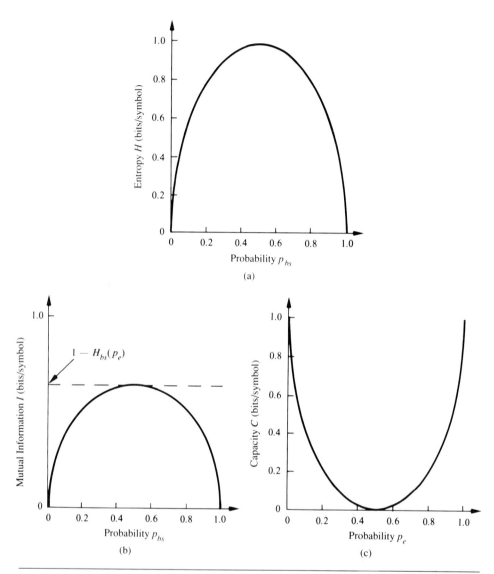

Figure 6.8   *Three binary information functions: (a) the binary entropy function; (b) the mutual information of a binary symmetric channel (BSC); (c) the capacity of the BSC.*

distributions (that is, for $0 \le p_{bs} \le 1$ or for $\mathbf{z} = [0, \ 1]^T$ to $\mathbf{z} = [1, \ 0]^T$), we see that $I(\mathbf{z}, \mathbf{v})$ is maximum (for any p_e) when $p_{bs} = \frac{1}{2}$. This value of p_{bs} corresponds to source distribution $\mathbf{z} = [\frac{1}{2}, \frac{1}{2}]^T$. The corresponding value of $I(\mathbf{z}, \mathbf{v})$ is $1 - H_{bs}(p_e)$. Thus the capacity of the BSC, plotted in Fig. 6.8(c), is

$$C = 1 - H_{bs}(p_e).$$

Note that when there is no possibility of a channel error ($p_e = 0$)—as well as when a channel error is a certainty ($p_e = 1$)—the capacity of the channel obtains its maximum value of 1 bit/symbol. In either case, maximum information transfer is possible because the channel's output is completely predictable. However, when $p_e = \frac{1}{2}$, the channel's output is completely unpredictable and no information can be transferred through it.   ❏

6.3.3   Fundamental Coding Theorems

The overall mathematical framework introduced in Section 6.3.2 is based on the model shown in Fig. 6.7, which contains an information source, channel, and user. In this section, we add a communication system to the model and examine three basic theorems regarding the coding or representation of information. As Fig. 6.9 shows, the communication system is inserted between the source and the user and consists of an encoder and decoder.

The noiseless coding theorem
When both the information channel and communication system are error free, the principal function of the communication system is to represent the source as compactly as possible. Under these circumstances, the *noiseless coding theorem*, also called *Shannon's first theorem* (Shannon [1948]), defines the minimum average code word length per source symbol that can be achieved.

A source of information with finite ensemble $(A, \mathbf{z})$ and statistically independent source symbols is called a *zero-memory* source. If we consider its

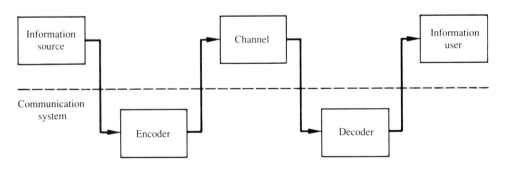

Figure 6.9   *A communication system model.*

output to be an n-tuple of symbols from the source alphabet (rather than a single symbol), the source output is a block random variable. It takes on one of J^n possible values, denoted α_i, from the set of all possible n element sequences $A' = \{\alpha_1, \alpha_2, \ldots, \alpha_{J^n}\}$, where each α_i is composed of n symbols from A. (The notation A' distinguishes the set of block symbols from A, the set of single symbols.) The probability of a given α_i is $P(\alpha_i)$ and is related to the single-symbol probabilities $P(a_j)$ by

$$P(\alpha_i) = P(a_{j_1}) P(a_{j_2}) \cdots P(a_{j_n}) \tag{6.3-14}$$

where the additional subscript is used to index the n symbols from A that make up an α_i. As before the vector $\mathbf{z}'$ (the prime was added to indicate the use of the block random variable) denotes the set of all source probabilities $\{P(\alpha_1), P(\alpha_2), \ldots, P(\alpha_{J^n})\}$, and the entropy of the source is

$$H(\mathbf{z}') = - \sum_{i=1}^{J^n} P(\alpha_i) \log P(\alpha_i).$$

Substituting Eq. (6.3-14) for $P(\alpha_i)$ and simplifying yields

$$H(\mathbf{z}') = n \, H(\mathbf{z}). \tag{6.3-15}$$

Thus the entropy of the zero-memory information source (that produces the block random variable) is n times the entropy of the corresponding single symbol source. Such a source is referred to as the *nth extension* of the single symbol or nonextended source. Note that the first extension of any source is the nonextended source itself.

Because the self-information of source output α_i is $\log [1/P(\alpha_i)]$, it seems reasonable to code α_i with a code word of integer length $l(\alpha_i)$ such that

$$\log \frac{1}{P(\alpha_i)} \le l(\alpha_i) < \log \frac{1}{P(\alpha_i)} + 1. \tag{6.3-16}$$

Intuition suggests that the source output α_i be represented by a code word whose length is the smallest integer exceeding the self-information of α_i.[†] Multiplying this result by $P(\alpha_i)$ and summing over all i gives

$$\sum_{i=1}^{J^n} P(\alpha_i) \log \frac{1}{P(\alpha_i)} \le \sum_{i=1}^{J^n} P(\alpha_i) \, l(\alpha_i) < \sum_{i=1}^{J^n} P(\alpha_i) \log \frac{1}{P(\alpha_i)} + 1$$

or

$$H(\mathbf{z}') \le L'_{\text{avg}} < H(\mathbf{z}') + 1 \tag{6.3-17}$$

[†] A uniquely decodable code can be constructed subject to this constraint.

where L'_{avg} represents the average word length of the code corresponding to the nth extension of the nonextended source. That is,

$$L'_{\text{avg}} = \sum_{i=1}^{J^n} P(\alpha_i)\, l(\alpha_i). \tag{6.3-18}$$

Dividing Eq. (6.3-17) by n and noting that, in accordance with Eq. (6.3-15), $H(\mathbf{z}')/n$ is $H(\mathbf{z})$, yields

$$H(\mathbf{z}) \le \frac{L'_{\text{avg}}}{n} < H(\mathbf{z}) + \frac{1}{n} \tag{6.3-19}$$

which, in the limiting case, becomes

$$\lim_{n \to \infty} \left[\frac{L'_{\text{avg}}}{n} \right] - H(\mathbf{z}). \tag{6.3-20}$$

Equation (6.3-19) states Shannon's first theorem for a zero-memory source. It reveals that it is possible to make L'_{avg}/n arbitrarily close to $H(\mathbf{z})$ by coding infinitely long extensions of the source. Although derived under the assumption of statistically independent source symbols, the result is easily extended to more general sources, like the mth order Markov source, where the occurrence of source symbol a_j may depend on a finite number m of preceding symbols. Markov sources commonly are used to model interpixel correlations in an image. Because $H(\mathbf{z})$ is a lower bound on L'_{avg}/n [that is, the limit of L'_{avg}/n as n becomes large in Eq. (6.3-20) is $H(\mathbf{z})$], the *efficiency* η of any encoding strategy can be defined as

$$\eta = n \frac{H(\mathbf{z})}{L'_{\text{avg}}}. \tag{6.3-21}$$

Example: A zero-memory information source with source alphabet $A = \{a_1, a_2\}$ has symbol probabilities $P(a_1) = \tfrac{2}{3}$ and $P(a_2) = \tfrac{1}{3}$. The entropy of this source (using Eq. 6.3-3) is 0.918 bits/symbol. If symbols a_1 and a_2 are represented by the binary code words 0 and 1, $L_{\text{avg}} = 1$ bit/symbol and the resulting code efficiency is $\eta = (1)(0.918)/1$, or 0.918.

Table 6.4 summarizes the code just described and an alternative encoding based on the second extension of the source. The lower portion of Table 6.4 lists the four block symbols (α_1, α_2, α_3, and α_4) in the second extension of the source. Their probabilities, using Eq. (6.3-14), are $\tfrac{4}{9}$, $\tfrac{2}{9}$, $\tfrac{2}{9}$, and $\tfrac{1}{9}$, respectively. In accordance with Eq. (6.3-18), the average word length of the second encoding is $\tfrac{17}{9}$ or 1.89 bits/symbol. The entropy of the second extension is twice the entropy of the nonextended source, or 1.83 bits/symbol, so the effi-

Table 6.4 Extension Coding Example

α_i	Source Symbols	$P(\alpha_i)$ Eq. (6.3-14)	$I(\alpha_i)$ Eq. (6.3-1)	$l(\alpha_i)$ Eq. (6.3-16)	Code Word	Code Length
First Extension						
α_1	a_1	2/3	0.59	1	0	1
α_2	a_2	1/3	1.58	2	1	1
Second Extension						
α_1	$a_1 a_1$	4/9	1.17	2	0	1
α_2	$a_1 a_2$	2/9	2.17	3	10	2
α_3	$a_2 a_1$	2/9	2.17	3	110	3
α_4	$a_2 a_2$	1/9	3.17	4	111	3

ciency of the second encoding is $\eta = 1.83/1.89 = 0.97$. It is slightly better than the nonextended coding efficiency of 0.92. Encoding the second extension of the source reduces the average number of code bits per source symbol from 1 bit/symbol to 1.89/2 or 0.94 bits/symbol.   ❑

The noisy coding theorem

If the channel of Fig. 6.9 is noisy or prone to error, interest shifts from representing the information as compactly as possible to encoding it so that reliable communication is possible. The question that naturally arises is: How small can the error in communication be made?

Example: A binary symmetric channel (BSC) has a probability of error $p_e = 0.01$ (that is, 99 percent of all source symbols are transmitted through the channel correctly). A simple method for increasing the reliability of the communication is to repeat each message or binary symbol several times. Suppose, for example, that rather than transmitting a 0 or a 1, the coded messages 000 and 111 are used. The probability that no errors will occur during the transmission of a three-symbol message is $(1 - p_e)^3$ or $\bar{p}_e^3$. The probability of a single error is $3p_e\bar{p}_e^2$, the probability of two errors is $3p_e^2\bar{p}_e$, and the probability of three errors is p_e^3. Because the probability of a single symbol transmission error is less than 50 percent, received messages can be decoded by using a majority vote of the three received symbols. Thus the probability of incorrectly decoding a three-symbol code word is the sum of the probabilities of two symbol errors and three symbol errors, or $p_e^3 + 3p_e^2\bar{p}_e$. When no errors or a single error occurs, the majority vote decodes the message correctly. For $p_e = 0.01$, the probability of a communication error is reduced to 0.0003.   ❑

By extending the repetitive coding scheme just described, we can make the overall error in communication as small as desired. In the general case, we do so by encoding the nth extension of the source using K-ary code sequences of length r, where $K^r \geq J^n$. The key to this approach is to select only φ of the K^r possible code sequences as valid code words and devise a decision rule that optimizes the probability of correct decoding. In the preceding example, repeating each source symbol three times is equivalent to block encoding the nonextended binary source using two out of 2^3, or 8, possible binary code words. The two valid code words are 000 and 111. If a nonvalid code word is presented to the decoder, a majority vote of the three code bits determines the output.

A zero-memory information source generates information at a *rate* (in information units per symbol) equal to its entropy $H(\mathbf{z})$. The nth extension of the source provides information at a rate of $H(\mathbf{z}')/n$ information units per symbol. If the information is coded, as in the preceding example, the maximum rate of coded information is $(\log \varphi)/r$ and occurs when the φ valid code words used to code the source are equally probable. Hence, a code of size φ and block length r is said to have rate

$$R = \log \frac{\varphi}{r}. \qquad (6.3\text{-}22)$$

Shannon's second theorem (Shannon [1948]), also called the *noisy coding theorem*, tells us that for any $R < C$, where C is the capacity of the *zero-memory channel* with matrix $\mathbf{Q}$,[†] there exists an integer r, and code of block length r and rate R such that the probability of a block decoding error is less than or equal to ϵ for any $\epsilon > 0$. Thus the probability of error can be made arbitrarily small so long as the coded message rate is less than the capacity of the channel.

The source coding theorem

The theorems described so far establish fundamental limits on error-free communication over both reliable and unreliable channels. In this section, we turn to the case in which the channel is error free but the communication process itself is lossy. Under these circumstances, the principal function of the communication system is "information compression." In most cases, the average error introduced by the compression is constrained to some maximum allowable level D. We want to determine the smallest rate, subject to the given fidelity criterion, at which information about the source can be conveyed to the user. This problem is specifically addressed by a branch of information theory known as *rate distortion theory*.

Let the information source and decoder outputs in Fig. 6.9 be defined by the finite ensembles $(A, \mathbf{z})$, and $(B, \mathbf{v})$, respectively. The assumption now is that the channel of Fig. 6.9 is error free, so a channel matrix $\mathbf{Q}$, which relates $\mathbf{z}$ to $\mathbf{v}$ in accordance with Eq. (6.3-6), can be thought of as modeling the

---

[†] A zero-memory channel is one in which the channel's response to the current input symbol is independent of its response to previous input symbols.

encoding–decoding process alone. Because the encoding–decoding process is deterministic, $\mathbf{Q}$ describes an artificial zero-memory channel that models the effect of the information compression and decompression. Each time the source produces source symbol a_j, it is represented by a code symbol that is then decoded to yield output symbol b_k with probability q_{kj} (see Section 6.3.2).

Addressing the problem of encoding the source so that the average distortion is less than D requires that a rule be formulated to assign quantitatively a distortion value to every possible approximation at the source output. For the simple case of a nonextended source, a nonnegative cost function $\rho(a_j, b_k)$, called a *distortion measure*, can be used to define the penalty associated with reproducing source output a_j with decoder output b_k. The output of the source is random, so the distortion also is a random variable whose average value, denoted $d(\mathbf{Q})$, is

$$
\begin{aligned}
d(\mathbf{Q}) &= \sum_{j=1}^{J} \sum_{k=1}^{K} \rho(a_j, b_k)\, P(a_j, b_k) \\
&= \sum_{j=1}^{J} \sum_{k=1}^{K} \rho(a_j, b_k)\, P(a_j)\, q_{kj}.
\end{aligned}
\tag{6.3-23}
$$

The notation $d(\mathbf{Q})$ emphasizes that the average distortion is a function of the encoding–decoding procedure, which (as noted above) is modeled by $\mathbf{Q}$. A particular encoding–decoding procedure is said to be *D-admissible* if and only if the average distortion associated with $\mathbf{Q}$ is less than or equal to D. The set of all D-admissible encoding–decoding procedures therefore is

$$
\mathbf{Q}_D = \{ q_{kj} \mid d(\mathbf{Q}) \le D \}.
\tag{6.3-24}
$$

Because every encoding–decoding procedure is defined by an artificial channel matrix $\mathbf{Q}$, the average information obtained from observing a single decoder output can be computed in accordance with Eq. (6.3-12). Hence, we can define a *rate distortion function*

$$
R(D) = \min_{\mathbf{Q} \in \mathbf{Q}_D} [I(\mathbf{z}, \mathbf{v})]
\tag{6.3-25}
$$

which assumes the minimum value of Eq. (6.3-12) over all D-admissible codes. Note that the minimum can be taken over $\mathbf{Q}$, because $I(\mathbf{z}, \mathbf{v})$ is a function of the probabilities in vector $\mathbf{z}$ and elements in matrix $\mathbf{Q}$. If $D = 0$, $R(D)$ is less than or equal to the entropy of the source, or $R(0) \le H(\mathbf{z})$.

Equation (6.3-25) defines the minimum rate at which information about the source can be conveyed to the user subject to the constraint that the average distortion be less than or equal to D. To compute this rate [that is, $R(D)$], we simply minimize $I(\mathbf{z}, \mathbf{v})$ (Eq. 6.3-12) by appropriate choice of $\mathbf{Q}$ (or q_{kj}) subject to the constraints

$$q_{kj} \geq 0 \tag{6.3-26}$$

$$\sum_{k=1}^{K} q_{kj} = 1 \tag{6.3-27}$$

and

$$d(\mathbf{Q}) = D. \tag{6.3-28}$$

Equations (6.3-26) and (6.3-27) are fundamental properties of channel matrix $\mathbf{Q}$. The elements of $\mathbf{Q}$ must be positive and, because some output must be received for any input symbol generated, the terms in any one column of $\mathbf{Q}$ must sum to 1. Equation (6.3-28) indicates that the minimum information rate occurs when the maximum possible distortion is allowed.

Example: Consider a zero-memory binary source with equally probable source symbols $\{0, 1\}$ and the simple distortion measure

$$\rho(a_j, b_k) = 1 - \delta_{jk}$$

where δ_{jk} is the impulse or delta function. Because $\rho(a_j, b_k)$ is 1 if $a_j \neq b_k$ but is 0 otherwise, each encoding–decoding error is counted as one unit of distortion. The calculus of variations can be used to compute $R(D)$. Letting $\mu_1, \mu_2,$ $\ldots, \mu_{J+1}$ be Lagrangian multipliers, we form the augmented criterion function

$$J(\mathbf{Q}) = I(\mathbf{z}, \mathbf{v}) - \sum_{j=1}^{J} \mu_j \sum_{k=1}^{K} q_{kj} - \mu_{J+1} \, d(\mathbf{Q})$$

equate its JK derivatives with respect to q_{kj} to 0 (that is, $dJ/dq_{kj} = 0$), and solve the resulting equations, together with the $J + 1$ equations associated with Eqs. (6.3-27) and (6.3-28), for unknowns q_{kj} and $\mu_1, \mu_2, \ldots, \mu_{J+1}$. If the resulting q_{kj} are nonnegative (or satisfy Eq. 6.3-26), a valid solution is found. For the source and distortion pair defined above, we get the following 7 equations (with 7 unknowns):

$$2q_{11} = (q_{11} + q_{12}) \exp [2\mu_1] \qquad\qquad 2q_{22} = (q_{21} + q_{22}) \exp [2\mu_2]$$

$$2q_{12} = (q_{11} + q_{12}) \exp [2\mu_1 + \mu_3] \qquad 2q_{21} = (q_{21} + q_{22}) \exp [2\mu_2 + \mu_3]$$

$$q_{11} + q_{21} = 1 \qquad\qquad\qquad\qquad\qquad q_{12} + q_{22} = 1$$

$$q_{21} + q_{12} = 2D.$$

A series of straightforward algebraic steps then yields

$$q_{12} = q_{21} = D$$
$$q_{11} = q_{22} = 1 - D$$
$$\mu_1 = \mu_2 = \log \sqrt{2(1 - D)}$$
$$\mu_3 = \log \frac{D}{1 - D}$$

so that

$$\mathbf{Q} = \begin{bmatrix} 1 - D & D \\ D & 1 - D \end{bmatrix}$$

Because the source symbols are equally probable, the maximum possible distortion is $\frac{1}{2}$. Thus $0 \le D \le \frac{1}{2}$ and $\mathbf{Q}$ satisfies Eq. (6.3-12) for all D. The mutual information associated with $\mathbf{Q}$ and the previously defined binary source is computed by using Eq. (6.3-12). Noting the similarity between $\mathbf{Q}$ and the binary symmetric channel matrix, however, we can immediately write

$$I(\mathbf{z}, \mathbf{v}) = 1 - H_{bs}(D).$$

This result follows from the example of Section 6.3.2 by substituting $p_{bs} = \frac{1}{2}$ and $p_e = D$ into $I(\mathbf{z}, \mathbf{v}) = H_{bs}(p_{bs}p_e + \bar{p}_{bs}\bar{p}_e) - H_{bs}(p_e)$. The rate distortion function follows immediately from Eq. (6.3-25):

$$R(D) = \min_{\mathbf{Q} \in \mathbf{Q}_D} [1 - H_{bs}(D)] = 1 - H_{bs}(D).$$

The final simplification is based on the fact that, for a given D, $1 - H_{bs}(D)$ assumes a single value, which, by default, is the minimum. The resulting function is plotted in Fig. 6.10. Its shape is typical of most rate distortion functions. Note the maximum value of D, denoted $D_{\max}$, such that $R(D) = 0$ for all $D \ge D_{\max}$. In addition, $R(D)$ is always positive, monotonically decreasing, and convex in the interval $(0, D_{\max})$.   ❑

Rate distortion functions can be computed analytically for simple sources and distortion measures, as in the preceding example. Moreover, convergent iterative algorithms suitable for implementation on digital computers can be used when analytical methods fail or are impractical. After $R(D)$ is computed (for any zero-memory source and *single-letter* distortion measure[†]), the *source*

[†] A single-letter distortion measure is one in which the distortion associated with a block of letters (or symbols) is the sum of the distortions for each letter (or symbol) in the block.

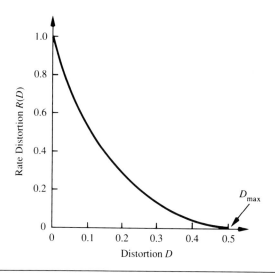

Figure 6.10   *The rate distortion function for a binary symmetric source.*

coding theorem tells us that for any $\epsilon > 0$, there exists an r, and code of blocklength r and rate $R < R(D) + \epsilon$ such that the average per letter distortion $d(\mathbf{Q}) \le D + \epsilon$. An important practical consequence of this theorem and the noisy coding theorem is that the source output can be recovered at the decoder with an arbitrarily small probability of error provided the channel has capacity $C > R(D) + \epsilon$. This latter result is known as the *information transmission theorem*.

6.3.4   Using Information Theory

Information theory provides the basic tools needed to deal with information representation and manipulation directly and quantitatively. In this section we explore the application of these tools to the specific problem of image compression. Because the fundamental premise of information theory is that the generation of information can be modeled as a probabilistic process, we first develop a statistical model of the image generation process.

Example: Consider the problem of estimating the information content (or entropy) of the simple 8-bit image:

$$\begin{array}{cccccccc}
21 & 21 & 21 & 95 & 169 & 243 & 243 & 243 \\
21 & 21 & 21 & 95 & 169 & 243 & 243 & 243 \\
21 & 21 & 21 & 95 & 169 & 243 & 243 & 243 \\
21 & 21 & 21 & 95 & 169 & 243 & 243 & 243
\end{array}$$

One relatively simple approach is to assume a particular source model and compute the entropy of the image based on that model. For example, we can assume that the image was produced by an imaginary "8-bit gray-level source" that sequentially emitted statistically independent pixels in accordance with a predefined probability law. In this case, the source symbols are gray levels, and the source alphabet is composed of 256 possible symbols. If the symbol probabilities are assumed to have a standard form (say, Gaussian), the average information content or entropy of each pixel in the image can be computed by using Eq. (6.3-3). In the case of a uniform distribution, for instance, the source symbols are equally probable, and the source is characterized by an entropy of 8 bits/pixel. That is, the average information per source output (pixel) is 8 bits. Then, the total entropy of the preceding sample 4×8 image is 256 bits. This particular image is but one of $2^{8 \times 4 \times 8}$, or 2^{256} ($\sim 10^{77}$), equally probable 4×8 images that can be produced by the source.

An alternative method of estimating information content is to construct a source model based on the relative frequency of occurrence of the gray levels in the image under consideration. That is, an observed image can be interpreted as a sample of the behavior of the gray-level source that generated it. Because the observed image is the only available indicator of source behavior, modeling the probabilities of the source symbols using the gray-level histogram of the sample image is reasonable:

Gray Level	Count	Probability
21	12	3/8
95	4	1/8
169	4	1/8
243	12	3/8

An estimate, called the *first-order estimate*, of the entropy of the source can be computed with Eq. (6.3-3). The first-order estimate in this example is 1.81 bits/pixel. The entropy of the source and/or image thus is approximately 1.81 bits/pixel, or 58 total bits.

Better estimates of the entropy of the gray-level source that generated the sample image can be computed by examining the relative frequency of pixel blocks in the sample image, where a block is a grouping of adjacent pixels. As block size approaches infinity, the estimate approaches the source's true entropy. (This result can be shown with the procedure utilized to prove the validity of the noiseless coding theorem in Section 6.3.3.) Thus by assuming that the sample image is connected from line to line and end to beginning, we can compute the relative frequency of pairs of pixels (that is, the second extension of the source):

Gray Level Pair	Count	Probability
(21, 21)	8	1/4
(21, 95)	4	1/8
(95, 169)	4	1/8
(169, 243)	4	1/8
(243, 243)	8	1/4
(243, 21)	4	1/8

The resulting entropy estimate (again using Eq. 6.3-3) is 2.5/2, or 1.25 bits/pixel, where division by 2 is a consequence of considering two pixels at a time. This estimate is called the *second-order estimate* of the source entropy, because it was obtained by computing the relative frequencies of 2-pixel blocks. Although the third-, fourth-, and higher-order estimates would provide even better approximations of source entropy, convergence of these estimates to the true source entropy is slow and computationally involved. For instance, a general 8-bit image has $(2^8)^2$, or 65,536, possible symbol pairs whose relative frequency must be computed. If 5-pixel blocks are considered, the number of possible 5-tuples is $(2^8)^5$, or $\sim 10^{12}$.   ❏

Although computing the actual entropy of an image is difficult, estimates such as those in the preceding example provide insight into image compressibility. The first-order estimate of entropy, for example, is a lower bound on the compression that can be achieved through variable-length coding alone. (Recall from Section 6.1.1 that variable-length coding is used to reduce coding redundancies.) In addition, the differences between the higher-order estimates of entropy and the first-order estimate indicate the presence or absence of interpixel redundancies. That is, they reveal whether the pixels in an image are statistically independent. If the pixels are statistically independent (that is, there is no interpixel redundancy), the higher-order estimates are equivalent to the first-order estimate, and variable-length coding provides optimal compression. For the image considered in the preceding example, the numerical difference between the first- and second-order estimates indicates that a mapping can be created that allows an additional 1.81 − 1.25 = 0.56 bits/pixel to be eliminated from the image's representation.

Example: Consider mapping the pixels of the image in the preceding example to create the representation:

$$
\begin{array}{cccccccc}
21 & 0 & 0 & 74 & 74 & 74 & 0 & 0 \\
21 & 0 & 0 & 74 & 74 & 74 & 0 & 0 \\
21 & 0 & 0 & 74 & 74 & 74 & 0 & 0 \\
21 & 0 & 0 & 74 & 74 & 74 & 0 & 0
\end{array}
$$

Here, we construct a difference array by replicating the first column of the original image and using the arithmetic difference between adjacent columns for the remaining elements. For example, the element in the first row, second column of the new representation is $(21 - 21)$, or 0. The resulting difference distribution is:

Gray Level or Difference	Count	Probability
0	12	1/2
21	4	1/8
74	12	3/8

If we now consider the mapped array to be generated by a "difference source," we can again use Eq. (6.3-3) to compute a first-order estimate of the entropy of the array, which is 1.41 bits/pixel. Thus by variable-length coding the mapped difference image, the original image can be represented with only 1.41 bits/pixel or a total of about 46 bits. This value is greater than the 1.25 bits/pixel second-order estimate of entropy computed in the preceding example, so we know that we can find an even better mapping.   ❑

   The preceding examples illustrate that the first-order estimate of the entropy of an image is not necessarily the minimum code rate for the image. The reason is that pixels in an image generally are not statistically independent. The process of minimizing the actual entropy of an image is, as noted in Section 6.2, called source coding. In the error-free case it encompasses the two operations of mapping and symbol coding. If information loss can be tolerated, it also includes the third step of quantization.
   The slightly more complicated problem of lossy image compression can also be approached using the tools of information theory. In this case, however, the principal result is the source coding theorem. As indicated in Section 6.3.3, this theorem reveals that any zero-memory source can be encoded by using a code of rate $R < R(D)$ such that the average per symbol distortion is less than D. To apply this result correctly to lossy image compression requires identifying an appropriate source model, devising a meaningful distortion measure, and computing the resulting rate distortion function $R(D)$. The first step of this process has already been considered. The second step can be conveniently approached through the use of an objective fidelity criterion from Section 6.1.4. The final step involves finding a matrix $\mathbf{Q}$ which minimizes Eq. (6.3-12), subject to the constraints imposed by Eqs. (6.3-24)–(6.3-28). Unfortunately, this task is particularly difficult—and only a few cases of any practical interest have been solved. One is when the images are Gaussian random fields and the

distortion measure is a weighted square error function. In this case, the optimal encoder must expand the image into its Karhunen–Loève components and represent each component with equal mean-square error (Davisson [1972]).

6.4 ERROR-FREE COMPRESSION

In numerous applications error-free compression is the only acceptable means of data reduction. One such application is the archival of medical or business documents, where lossy compression usually is prohibited for legal reasons. Another is the processing of LANDSAT imagery, where both the use and cost of collecting the data makes any loss undesirable. Yet another is digital radiography, where the loss of information can compromise diagnostic accuracy. In these cases, and in others, the need for error-free compression is motivated by the intended use or nature of the images under consideration.

In this section, we focus on the principal error-free compression strategies currently in use. They normally provide compression ratios of 2 to 10. Moreover, they are equally applicable to both binary and gray-scale images. As indicated in Section 6.2, error-free compression techniques generally are composed of two relatively independent operations: (1) devising an alternative representation of the image in which its interpixel redundancies are reduced; and (2) coding the representation to eliminate coding redundancies. These steps correspond to the mapping and symbol coding operations of the source coding model discussed in connection with Fig. 6.6.

6.4.1 Variable-Length Coding

The simplest approach to error-free image compression is to reduce *only* coding redundancy. Coding redundancy normally is present in any natural binary encoding of the gray levels in an image. As we noted in Section 6.1.1, it can be eliminated by coding the gray levels so that Eq. (6.1-4) is minimized. To do so requires construction of a variable-length code that assigns the shortest possible code words to the most probable gray levels. Here, we examine several optimal and near optimal techniques for constructing such a code. These techniques are formulated in the language of information theory. In practice, the source symbols may be either the gray levels of an image or the output of a gray-level mapping operation (pixel differences, run-lengths, and so on).

Huffman coding

The most popular technique for removing coding redundancy is Huffman's (Huffman [1951]). When coding the symbols of an information source individually, *Huffman coding* yields the smallest possible number of code symbols per source symbol. In terms of the noiseless coding theorem (see Section 6.3.3), the resulting code is optimal for a fixed value of n, subject to the constraint that the source symbols be coded *one at a time*.

The first step in Huffman's approach is to create a series of source reductions by ordering the probabilities of the symbols under consideration and combining the lowest probability symbols into a single symbol that replaces them in the next source reduction. Figure 6.11 illustrates this process for binary coding (*K*-ray Huffman codes can also be constructed). At the far left, a hypothetical set of source symbols and their probabilities are ordered from top to bottom in terms of decreasing probability values. To form the first source reduction, the bottom two probabilities, 0.06 and 0.04, are combined to form a "compound symbol" with probability 0.1. This compound symbol and its associated probability are placed in the first source reduction column so that the probabilities of the reduced source are also ordered from the most to the least probable. This process is then repeated until a reduced source with two symbols (at the far right) is reached.

The second step in Huffman's procedure is to code each reduced source, starting with the smallest source and working back to the original source. The minimal length binary code for a two-symbol source, of course, is the symbols 0 and 1. As Fig. 6.12 shows, these symbols are assigned to the two symbols on the right (the assignment is arbitrary; reversing the order of the 0 and 1 would work just as well). As the reduced source symbol with probability 0.6 was generated by combining two symbols in the reduced source to its left, the 0 used to code it is now assigned to *both* of these symbols, and a 0 and 1 are arbitrarily appended to each to distinguish them from each other. This operation is then repeated for each reduced source until the original source is reached. The final code appears at the far left in Fig. 6.12. The average length of this code is

$$L_{avg} = (0.4)(1) + (0.3)(2) + (0.1)(3) + (0.1)(4) + (0.06)(5) + (0.04)(5)$$

$$= 2.2 \text{ bits/symbol}$$

and the entropy of the source is 2.14 bits/symbol. In accordance with Eq. (6.3-20), the resulting Huffman code efficiency is 0.973.

Original source		Source reduction			
Symbol	Probability	1	2	3	4
a_2	0.4	0.4	0.4	0.4	0.6
a_6	0.3	0.3	0.3	0.3	0.4
a_1	0.1	0.1	0.2	0.3	
a_4	0.1	0.1	0.1		
a_3	0.06	0.1			
a_5	0.04				

Figure 6.11 *Huffman source reductions.*

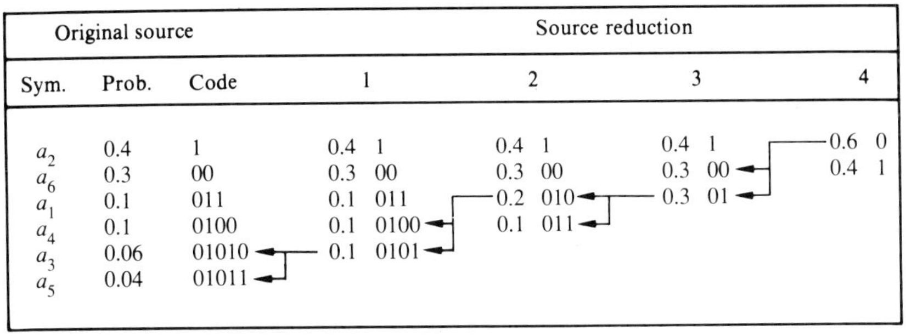

Original source			Source reduction			
Sym.	Prob.	Code	1	2	3	4
a_2	0.4	1	0.4 1	0.4 1	0.4 1	0.6 0
a_6	0.3	00	0.3 00	0.3 00	0.3 00	0.4 1
a_1	0.1	011	0.1 011	0.2 010	0.3 01	
a_4	0.1	0100	0.1 0100	0.1 011		
a_3	0.06	01010	0.1 0101			
a_5	0.04	01011				

Figure 6.12 *Huffman code assignment procedure.*

Huffman's procedure creates the optimal code for a set of symbols and probabilities *subject to* the constraint that the symbols be coded one at a time. After the code has been created, coding and/or decoding is accomplished in a simple look-up table manner. The code itself is an instantaneous uniquely decodable block code. It is called a *block code*, because each source symbol is mapped into a fixed sequence of code symbols. It is *instantaneous*, because each code word in a string of code symbols can be decoded without referencing succeeding symbols. It is *uniquely decodable*, because any string of code symbols can be decoded in only one way. Thus, any string of Huffman encoded symbols can be decoded by examining the individual symbols of the string in a left to right manner. For the binary code of Fig. 6.12, a left-to-right scan of the encoded string 010100111100 reveals that the first valid code word is 01010, which is the code for symbol a_3. The next valid code is 011, which corresponds to symbol a_1. Continuing in this manner reveals the completely decoded message to be $a_3 a_1 a_2 a_2 a_6$.

Other near optimal variable length codes

When a large number of symbols is to be coded, the construction of the optimal binary Huffman code is a nontrivial task. For the general case of J source symbols, $J - 2$ source reductions must be performed (see Fig. 6.11) and $J - 2$ code assignments made (see Fig. 6.12). Thus construction of the optimal Huffman code for an image with 256 gray levels requires 254 source reductions and 254 code assignments. In view of the computational complexity of this task, sacrificing coding efficiency for simplicity in code construction sometimes is necessary.

Table 6.5 illustrates four variable-length codes that provide such a trade-off. Note that the average length of the Huffman code—the last row of the table—is lower than the other codes listed. The natural binary code has the greatest average length. In addition, the 4.05 bits/symbol code rate achieved by Huffman's technique approaches the 4.0 bits/symbol entropy bound of the

Table 6.5   Variable-Length Codes

Source Symbol	Prob- ability	Binary Code	Huffman	Truncated Huffman	B_2-Code	Binary Shift	Huffman Shift
Block 1							
a_1	0.2	00000	10	11	C00	000	10
a_2	0.1	00001	110	011	C01	001	11
a_3	0.1	00010	111	0000	C10	010	110
a_4	0.06	00011	0101	0101	C11	011	100
a_5	0.05	00100	00000	00010	C00C00	100	101
a_6	0.05	00101	00001	00011	C00C01	101	1110
a_7	0.05	00110	00010	00100	C00C10	110	1111
Block 2							
a_8	0.04	00111	00011	00101	C00C11	111 000	00 10
a_9	0.04	01000	00110	00110	C01C00	111 001	00 11
a_{10}	0.04	01001	00111	00111	C01C01	111 010	00 110
a_{11}	0.04	01010	00100	01000	C01C10	111 011	00 100
a_{12}	0.03	01011	01001	01001	C01C11	111 100	00 101
a_{13}	0.03	01100	01110	10 0000	C10C00	111 101	00 1110
a_{14}	0.03	01101	01111	10 0001	C10C01	111 110	00 1111
Block 3							
a_{15}	0.03	01110	01100	10 0010	C10C10	111 111 000	00 00 10
a_{16}	0.02	01111	010000	10 0011	C10C11	111 111 001	00 00 11
a_{17}	0.02	10000	010001	10 0100	C11C00	111 111 010	00 00 110
a_{18}	0.02	10001	001010	10 0101	C11C01	111 111 011	00 00 100
a_{19}	0.02	10010	001011	10 0110	C11C10	111 111 100	00 00 101
a_{20}	0.02	10011	011010	10 0111	C11C11	111 111 101	00 00 1110
a_{21}	0.01	10100	011011	10 1000	C00C00C00	111 111 110	00 00 1111

Entropy	4.0						
Average Length		5.0	4.05	4.24	4.65	4.59	4.13

source, computed by using Eq. (6.3-3) and given at the bottom of the table. Although none of the remaining codes in Table 6.5 achieve the Huffman coding efficiency, all are easier to construct. Like Huffman's technique, they assign the shortest code words to the most likely source symbols.

Column five of Table 6.5 illustrates a simple modification of the basic Huffman coding strategy known as *truncated Huffman coding*. A truncated Huffman code is generated by Huffman coding only the most probable ψ symbols of the source, for some positive integer $\psi < J$. A prefix code followed by a suitable fixed-length code is used to represent all other source symbols. In Table 6.5, ψ arbitrarily was selected as 12 and the prefix code was generated as the 13th Huffman code word. That is, a "prefix symbol" whose probability was the sum of the probabilities of symbols a_{13} through a_{21} was included as a 13th symbol during the Huffman coding of the 12 most probable source symbols.

The remaining 9 symbols were then coded using the prefix code, which turned out to be 10, and a 4-bit binary value equal to the symbol subscript minus 13.

Column six of Table 6.5 illustrates a second, near optimal, and variable-length code known as a B-code. It is close to optimal when the source symbol probabilities obey a power law of the form

$$P(a_j) = cj^{-\beta} \tag{6.4-1}$$

for some positive constant β and normalizing constant $c = 1/\Sigma_{j=0}^{J} j^{-\beta}$. For example, the distribution of run lengths in a binary representation of a typical typewritten text document is nearly exponential. As Table 6.5 shows, each code word is made up of *continuation* bits, denoted C, and *information* bits, which are natural binary numbers. The only purpose of the continuation bits is to seperate individual code words, so they simply alternate between 0 and 1 for each code word in a string. The B-code shown in Table 6.5 is called a B_2-code, because two information bits are used per continuation bit. The sequence of B_2-codes corresponding to the source symbol string $a_{11}a_2a_7$ is 001 010 101 000 010 or 101 110 001 100 110, depending on whether the first continuation bit is assumed to be a 0 or 1.

The two remaining variable-length codes in Table 6.5 are referred to as *shift codes*. A shift code is generated by (1) arranging the source symbols so that their probabilities are monotonically decreasing, (2) dividing the total number of symbols into symbol blocks of equal size, (3) coding the individual elements within all blocks identically, and (4) adding special *shift-up* and/or *shift-down* symbols to identify each block. Each time a shift-up or shift-down symbol is recognized at the decoder, it moves one block up or down with respect to a predefined reference block.

To generate the 3-bit binary shift code in column seven of Table 6.5 the 21 source symbols are first ordered in accordance with their probabilities of occurrence and divided into three blocks of seven symbols. The individual symbols (a_1 through a_7) of the upper block—considered the reference block—are then coded with the binary codes 000 through 110. The eighth binary code (111) is not included in the reference block; instead, it is used as a single shift-up control that identifies the remaining blocks (in this case, a shift-down symbol is not used). The symbols in the remaining two blocks are then coded by one or two shift-up symbols in combination with the binary codes used to code the reference block. For example, source symbol a_{19} is coded as 111 111 100.

The Huffman shift code in column eight of Table 6.5 is generated in a similar manner. The principal difference is in the assignment of a probability to the shift symbol prior to Huffman coding the reference block. Normally, this assignment is accomplished by summing the probabilities of all the source symbols outside the reference block, that is, by using the same concept utilized to define the prefix symbol in the truncated Huffman code. Here, the sum is taken over symbols a_8 through a_{21} and is 0.39. The shift symbol is thus the most probable symbol and is assigned one of the shortest Huffman code words (00).

Arithmetic coding
Unlike the variable-length codes described above, *arithmetic coding* generates nonblock codes. In arithmetic coding, which can be traced to the work of Elias (see Abramson [1963]), a one-to-one correspondence between source symbols and code words does not exist. Instead, an entire sequence of source symbols (or message) is assigned a single arithmetic code word. The code word itself defines an interval of real numbers between 0 and 1. As the number of symbols in the message increases, the interval used to represent it becomes smaller and the number of information units (say, bits) required to represent the interval becomes larger. Each symbol of the message reduces the size of the interval in accordance with its probability of occurrence. Because the technique does not require, as does Huffman's approach, that each source symbol translate into an integral number of code symbols (that is, that the symbols be coded one at a time), it achieves (but only in theory) the bound established by the noiseless coding theorem of Section 6.3.3.

Figure 6.13 illustrates the basic arithmetic coding process. Here, a five-symbol sequence or message, $a_1a_2a_3a_3a_4$, from a four-symbol source is coded. At the start of the coding process, the message is assumed to occupy the entire half-open interval [0, 1). As Table 6.6 shows, this interval is initially subdivided into four regions based on the probabilities of each source symbol. Symbol a_1, for example, is associated with subinterval [0, 0.2). Because it is the first symbol

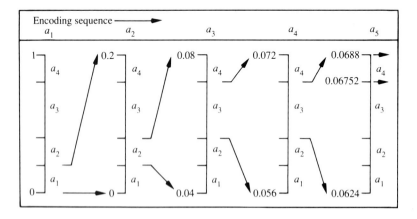

Figure 6.13   *Arithmetic coding procedure.*

Table 6.6   Arithmetic Coding Example

Source Symbol	Probability	Initial Subinterval
a_1	0.2	[0.0, 0.2)
a_2	0.2	[0.2, 0.4)
a_3	0.4	[0.4, 0.8)
a_4	0.2	[0.8, 1.0)

of the message being coded, the message interval is initially narrowed to [0, 0.2). Thus in Fig. 6.13 [0, 0.2) is expanded to the full height of the figure and its end points labeled by the values of the narrowed range. The narrowed range is then subdivided in accordance with the original source symbol probabilities and the process continues with the next message symbol. In this manner, symbol a_2 narrows the subinterval to [0.04, 0.08), a_3 further narrows it to [0.056, 0.072), and so on. The final message symbol, which must be reserved as a special end-of-message indicator, narrows the range to [0.06752, 0.0688). Of course, any number within this subinterval, for example 0.068, can be used to represent the message.

In the arithmetically coded message of Fig. 6.13, three decimal digits are used to represent the five-symbol message. This translates into ⅗ or 0.6 decimal digits per source symbol and compares favorably with the entropy of the source, which, from Eq. (6.3-3), is 0.58 decimal digits or 10-ary units/symbol. As the length of the sequence being coded increases, the resulting arithmetic code approaches the bound established by the noiseless coding theorem. In practice, two factors cause coding performance to fall short of the bound: (1) the addition of the end-of-message indicator that is needed to separate one message from another; and (2) the use of finite precision arithmetic. Practical implementations of arithmetic coding address the latter problem by introducing a scaling strategy and a rounding strategy (Langdon and Rissanen [1981]). The scaling strategy renormalizes each subinterval to the [0,1) range before subdividing it in accordance with the symbol probabilities. The rounding strategy guarantees that the truncations associated with finite precision arithmetic do not prevent the coding subintervals from being represented accurately.

6.4.2   Bit-Plane Coding

Having examined the principal methods for removing coding redundancy, we now consider one of several error-free compression techniques that also attack an image's interpixel redundancies. The technique, called *bit-plane coding*, is based on the concept of decomposing a multilevel (monochrome or color) image into a series of binary images and compressing each binary image via one of several well-known binary compression methods. In this section, we describe the most popular decomposition approaches and review several of the more commonly used compression methods.

Bit-plane decomposition

The gray levels of an m-bit gray-scale image can be represented in the form of the base 2 polynomial

$$a_{m-1} \, 2^{m-1} + a_{m-2} \, 2^{m-2} + \cdots + a_1 \, 2^1 + a_0 \, 2^0. \tag{6.4-2}$$

Based on this property, a simple method of decomposing the image into a collection of binary images is to separate the m coefficients of the polynomial into m 1-bit *bit planes*. As noted in Chapter 4, the zeroth-order bit plane is generated by collecting the a_0 bits of each pixel, while the $(m - 1)$st-order bit plane contains the a_{m-1} bits or coefficients. In general, each bit plane is numbered from 0 to $m - 1$ and is constructed by setting its pixels equal to the values of the appropriate bits or polynomial coefficients from each pixel in the original image. The inherent disadvantage of this approach is that small changes in gray level can have a significant impact on the complexity of the bit planes. If a pixel of intensity 127 (0111111) is adjacent to a pixel of intensity 128 (1000000), for instance, every bit plane will contain a corresponding 0 to 1 (or 1 to 0) transition. For example, as the most significant bits of the two binary codes for 127 and 128 are different, bit plane 7 will contain a zero-valued pixel next to a pixel of value 1, creating a 0 to 1 (or 1 to 0) transition at that point.

An alternative decomposition approach (which reduces the effect of small gray-level variations) is to first represent the image by an m-bit *Gray code*. The m-bit Gray code $g_{m-1} \cdots g_2 g_1 g_0$ that corresponds to polynomial (6.4-2) can be computed from

$$g_i = a_i \oplus a_{i+1} \qquad 0 \le i \le m - 2 \tag{6.4-3}$$
$$g_{m-1} = a_{m-1}.$$

Here, $\oplus$ denotes the exclusive OR operation. This code has the unique property that successive code words differ in only one bit position. Thus, small changes in gray level are less likely to affect all m bit planes. When gray levels 127 and 128 are adjacent, for instance, only the 7th bit plane will contain a 0 to 1 transition, because the Gray codes that correspond to 127 and 128 are 11000000 and 01000000, respectively.

Example: The 1024 × 1024 images shown in Figs. 6.14(a) and (b) are used to illustrate the compression techniques described in the remainder of this section. The 8-bit monochrome image of a child was generated with a high-resolution CCD camera. The binary image of a warranty deed prepared by President

 (image is two-part: photo (a) and handwriting (b))

(a)   (b)

Figure 6.14 *A 1024 × 1024 (a) 8-bit monochrome image and (b) binary image.*

Andrew Jackson in 1796 was produced on a flatbed document scanner. Figures 6.15 and 6.16 show the eight binary and Gray coded bit planes of the image of the child. Note that the high-order bit planes are far less complex than their low-order counterparts. That is, they contain large uniform areas of significantly less detail, busyness, or randomness. In addition, the Gray coded bit planes are less complex than the corresponding binary bit planes.   ❏

Constant area coding

A simple but effective method of compressing a binary image or bit plane is to use special code words to identify large areas of contiguous 1's or 0's. In one such approach, called *constant area coding* (CAC), the image is divided into blocks of size $m \times n$ pixels, which are classified as all white, all black, or mixed intensity. The most probable or frequently occurring category is then assigned the 1-bit code word 0, and the other two categories are assigned the 2-bit codes 10 and 11. Compression is achieved because the mn bits that normally would be used to represent each constant area are replaced by a 1-bit or 2-bit code word. Of course, the code assigned to the mixed intensity category is used as a prefix, which is followed by the mn-bit pattern of the block.

When predominantly white text documents are being compressed, a slightly simpler approach is to code the solid white areas as 0 and all other blocks (including the solid black blocks) by a 1 followed by the bit pattern of the block. This approach, called *white block skipping* (WBS), takes advantage of the anticipated structural tendencies of the image to be compressed. As few

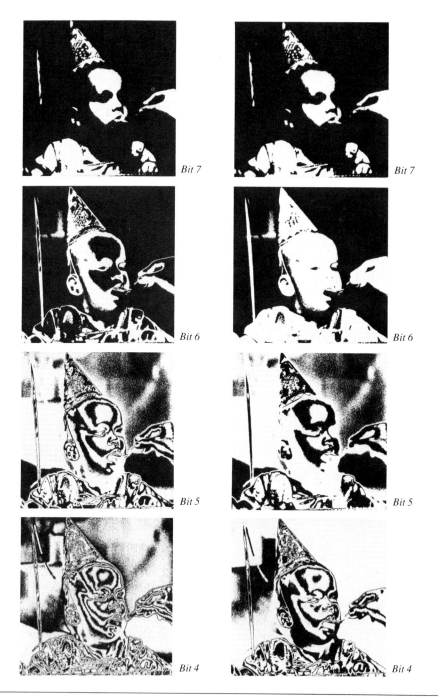

Figure 6.15   *The four most significant binary (left column) and Gray (right column) coded bit planes of the image in Fig. 6.14(a).*

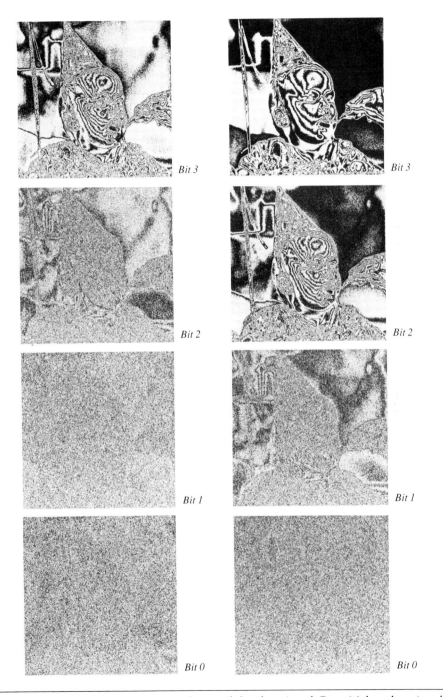

Figure 6.16 *The four least significant binary (left column) and Gray (right column) coded bit planes of the image in Fig. 6.14(a).*

solid black areas are expected, they are grouped with the mixed intensity regions, allowing a 1-bit code word to be used for the highly probable white blocks. A particularly effective modification of this procedure (with blocks of size $1 \times n$) is to code the solid white lines as 0's and all other lines with a 1 followed by the normal WBS code sequence. Another is to employ an iterative approach in which the binary image or bit plane is decomposed into successively smaller and smaller subblocks. For 2-D blocks, a solid white image is coded as a 0, and all other images are divided into subblocks that are assigned a prefix of 1 and similarly coded. That is, if a subblock is all white, it is represented by the prefix 1, indicating that it is a first iteration subblock, followed by a 0, indicating that it is solid white. If the subblock is not solid white, the decomposition process is repeated until a predefined subblock size is reached and coded as either a 0 (if it is all white) or a 1 followed by the block bit pattern.

One-dimensional run-length coding
An effective alternative to constant area coding is to represent each row of an image or bit plane by a sequence of lengths that describe successive runs of black and white pixels. This technique, referred to as *run-length coding*, was developed in the 1950s and has become, along with its 2-D extensions, the standard compression approach in facsimile (FAX) coding. The basic concept is to code each contiguous group of 0's or 1's encountered in a left to right scan of a row by its length and to establish a convention for determining the value of the run. The most common approaches for determining the value of a run are (1) to specify the value of the first run of each row, or (2) to assume that each row begins with a white run, whose run length may in fact be zero.

Although run-length coding is in itself an effective method of compressing an image (see the example in Section 6.1.2), additional compression usually can be realized by variable-length coding the run lengths themselves. In fact, the black and white run lengths may be coded separately using variable-length codes that are specifically tailored to their own statistics. For example, letting symbol a_j represent a black run of length j, we can estimate the probability that symbol a_j was emitted by an imaginary black run-length source by dividing the number of black run lengths of length j in the entire image by the total number of black runs. An estimate of the entropy of this black run-length source, denoted H_0, follows by substituting these probabilities into Eq. (6.3-3). A similar argument holds for the entropy of the white runs, denoted H_1. The approximate run-length entropy of the image is

$$H_{RL} = \frac{H_0 + H_1}{L_0 + L_1} \tag{6.4-4}$$

where the variables L_0 and L_1 denote the average values of black and white run lengths, respectively. Equation (6.4-4) provides an estimate of the average number of bits per pixel required to code the run lengths in a binary image using a variable-length code.

Two-dimensional run-length coding

One-dimensional run-length coding concepts are easily extended to create a variety of 2-D coding procedures. One of the better known results is *relative address coding* (RAC), which is based on the principle of tracking the binary transitions that begin and end each black and white run. Figure 6.17(a) illustrates one implementation of this approach. Note that ec is the distance from the current transition c to the last transition of the current line e, whereas cc' is the distance from c to the first similar (in the same direction) transition past e, denoted c', on the previous line. If $ec \le cc'$, the RAC coded distance d is set equal to ec and used to represent the current transition at c. But if $cc' < ec$, d is set equal to cc'.

Like run-length coding, relative address coding requires the adoption of a convention for determining run values. In addition, imaginary transitions at the start and end of each line, as well as an imaginary starting line (say, an all-white line), must be assumed so that image boundaries can be handled properly. Finally, since the probability distributions of the RAC distances of most images are not uniform in practice (see Section 6.1.1), the final step of the RAC process is to code the RAC distance selected (that is, the shortest) and its distance, d, by using a suitable variable-length code. As Fig. 6.17(b) shows, a code similar to a B_1-code can be utilized. The smallest distances are assigned the shortest

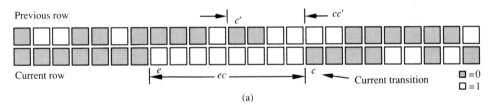

(a)

Distance measured	Distance	Code	Distance range	Code $h(d)$
cc'	0	0	1 – 4	0 ××
ec or cc' (left)	1	100	5 – 20	10 ××××
cc' (right)	1	101	21 – 84	110 ××××××
ec	d ($d>1$)	111 $h(d)$	85 – 340	1110 ××××××××
cc' (c' to left)	d ($d>1$)	1100 $h(d)$	341 – 1364	11110 ××××××××××
cc' (c' to right)	d ($d>1$)	1101 $h(d)$	1365 – 5460	111110 ××××××××××

(b)

Figure 6.17 *A relative address coding (RAC) illustration.*

code words, and all other distances are coded by using a prefix to indicate the shortest RAC distance, a second prefix that assigns d to a specific range of distances, and the binary representation (denoted $\times \times \times \ldots \times$ in Fig. 6.17b) of d minus the base distance of the range itself. If ec and cc' are $+8$ and $+4$, as in Fig. 6.17(a), the proper RAC code word is 1100011. Finally, if $d = 0$, c is directly below c', whereas if $d = 1$, the decoder may have to determine the closest transition point, because the 100 code does not specify whether the measurement is relative to the current row or to the previous row.

Contour tracing and coding

Relative address coding is one approach for representing intensity transitions that make up the contours in a binary image. Another approach is to represent each contour by a set of boundary points or by a single boundary point and a set of directionals. The latter sometimes is referred to as *direct contour tracing*. In this section, we describe yet another method, called *predictive differential quantizing* (PDQ), which demonstrates the essential characteristics of both approaches. It is a scan line-oriented contour tracing procedure.

In predictive differential quantizing, the front and back contours (Fig. 6.18) of each object of an image are traced simultaneously to generate a sequence of pairs (Δ', Δ''). The term Δ' is the difference between the starting coordinates of the front contours on adjacent lines, and Δ'' is the difference between the front-to-back contour lengths. These differences, together with special messages that indicate the start of new contours (the *new start* message) and the end of old contours (the *merge* message), represent each object. If Δ'' is replaced by the difference between the back contour coordinates of adjacent lines, denoted Δ''', the technique is referred to as *double delta coding* (DDC).

The new start and merge messages allow the (Δ', Δ'') or (Δ', Δ''') pairs generated on a scan line basis to be linked properly to the corresponding pairs in the previous and next rows. Without these messages, the decoder would be unable to reference one difference pair to another or to position correctly the

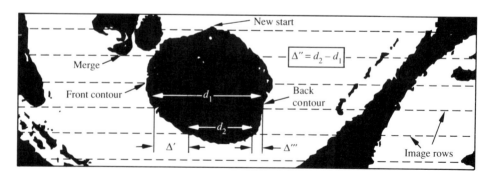

Figure 6.18 *Parameters of the PDQ algorithm.*

Table 6.7 Error-Free Bit-Plane Coding Results for Fig. 6.14(a): $H \approx 6.82$ Bits/Pixel

Method	Bit-Plane Code Rate (Bits/Pixel)								Code Rate	Compression Ratio
	7	6	5	4	3	2	1	0		
Binary Bit-Plane Coding										
CBC (4 × 4)	0.14	0.24	0.60	0.79	0.99	—	—	—	5.75	1.4: 1
RLC	0.09	0.19	0.51	0.68	0.87	1.00	1.00	1.00	5.33	1.5: 1
PDQ	0.07	0.18	0.79	—	—	—	—	—	6.04	1.3: 1
DDC	0.07	0.18	0.79	—	—	—	—	—	6.03	1.3: 1
RAC	0.06	0.15	0.62	0.91	—	—	—	—	5.17	1.4: 1
Gray Bit-Plane Coding										
CBC (4 × 4)	0.14	0.18	0.48	0.40	0.61	0.98	—	—	4.80	1.7: 1
RLC	0.09	0.13	0.40	0.33	0.51	0.85	1.00	1.00	4.29	1.9: 1
PDQ	0.07	0.12	0.61	0.40	0.82	—	—	—	5.02	1.6: 1
DDC	0.07	0.11	0.61	0.40	0.81	—	—	—	5.00	1.6: 1
RAC	0.06	0.10	0.49	0.31	0.62	—	—	—	4.05	1.8: 1

contours within the image. To avoid encoding both the row and column co-ordinates of each new start and merge message, a unique code often is used to identify scan lines that do not contain object pixels. The final step in both PDQ and DDC coding is to represent Δ', Δ'' or Δ''', and the coordinates of the new starts and merges with a suitable variable-length code.

Example: We conclude this section by comparing the binary compression techniques described. Each approach was used to compress the images of Fig. 6.14. The resulting code rates and compression ratios are provided in Tables 6.7 and 6.8. When interpreting these results, note that first-order estimates (see Section 6.3.4) of the entropies of the RLC run lengths and PDQ and DDC distances were computed and used as an approximation of the compression performance that could be achieved under the variable-length coding approaches of Section 6.4.1.

The results contained in Tables 6.7 and 6.8 show that all the techniques were able to eliminate some amount of interpixel redundancy. That is, the

Table 6.8 Error-Free Binary Image Compression Results for Fig. 6.14(b): $H \approx$ 0.55 Bits/Pixel

	WBS (1 × 8)	WBS (4 × 4)	RLC	PDQ	DDC	RAC
Code Rate (bits/pixel)	0.48	0.39	0.32	0.23	0.22	0.23
Compression Ratio	2.1: 1	2.6: 1	3.1: 1	4.4: 1	4.7: 1	4.4: 1

resulting code rates were less than the first-order entropy estimate of each image. Run-length coding proved to be the best coding method for the bit-plane coded images, whereas the 2-D techniques (such as PDQ, DDC, and RAC) performed better when compressing the binary image. Furthermore, the relatively straightforward procedure of Gray coding the image of Fig. 6.14(a) improved the achievable coding performance by about 1 bit/pixel. Finally, note that the five compression methods were able to compress the monochrome image only by a factor of 1 to 2, while compressing the binary image of Fig. 6.14(b) by a factor of 2 to 5. As Table 6.7 shows, the reason for this performance difference is that the algorithms were unable to successfully compress the lower-order bit planes of the bit-plane coded images. In fact, the dashed entries of the table indicate instances in which the algorithms caused data expansion. In these cases, the raw data were used to represent the bit plane, and only 1 bit/pixel was added to the total code rate.   ❏

6.4.3 Lossless Predictive Coding

Let us now turn to an error-free compression approach that does not require decomposition of an image into a collection of bit planes. The approach, commonly referred to as *lossless predictive coding*, is based on eliminating the interpixel redundancies of closely spaced pixels by extracting and coding *only* the new information in each pixel. The *new information* of a pixel is defined as the difference between the actual and predicted value of that pixel.

Figure 6.19 shows the basic components of a lossless predictive coding system. The system consists of an encoder and a decoder, each containing an

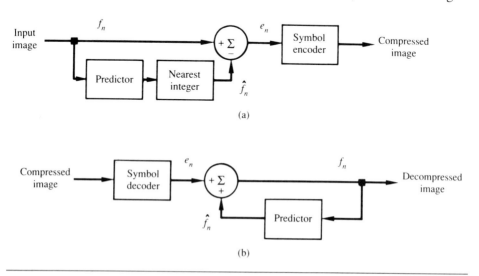

Figure 6.19 *A lossless predictive coding model: (a) encoder; (b) decoder.*

identical *predictor*. As each successive pixel of the input image, denoted f_n, is introduced to the encoder, the predictor generates the anticipated value of that pixel based on some number of past inputs. The output of the predictor is then rounded to the nearest integer, denoted $\hat{f}_n$, and used to form the difference or *prediction error*

$$e_n = f_n - \hat{f}_n \qquad (6.4-5)$$

which is coded using a variable-length code (by the symbol encoder) to generate the next element of the compressed data stream. The decoder of Fig. 6.19(b) reconstructs e_n from the received variable-length code words and performs the inverse operation

$$f_n = e_n + \hat{f}_n. \qquad (6.4-6)$$

Various local, global, and adaptive (see Section 6.5.1) methods can be used to generate $\hat{f}_n$. In most cases, however, the prediction is formed by a linear combination of m previous pixels. That is,

$$\hat{f}_n = \text{round} \left[\sum_{i=1}^{m} \alpha_i f_{n-i} \right] \qquad (6.4-7)$$

where m is the order of the linear predictor, round is a function used to denote the rounding or nearest integer operation, and the α_i for $i = 1, 2, \ldots, m$ are prediction coefficients. In raster scan applications, the subscript n indexes the predictor outputs in accordance with their time of occurrence. That is, f_n, $\hat{f}_n$, and e_n in Eqs. (6.4-5)–(6.4-7) could be replaced with the more explicit notation $f(t)$, $\hat{f}(t)$, and $e(t)$, where t represents time. In other cases, n is used as an index on the spatial coordinates and/or frame number (in a time sequence of images) of an image. In 1-D linear predictive coding, for example, Eq. (6.4-7) can be written

$$\hat{f}_n(x, y) = \text{round} \left[\sum_{i=1}^{m} \alpha_i f(x, y - i) \right] \qquad (6.4-8)$$

where each subscripted variable is now expressed explicitly as a function of spatial coordinates x and y. Note that, in accordance with Eq. (6.4-8), the 1-D linear prediction $\hat{f}(x, y)$ is a function of the previous pixels on the current line alone. In 2-D predictive coding, the prediction is a function of the previous pixels in a left-to-right, top-to-bottom scan of an image. In the 3-D case, it is based on these pixels and the previous pixels of preceding frames. Equation (6.4-8) cannot be evaluated for the first m pixels of each line, so these pixels must be coded by using other means (such as a Huffman code) and considered as an overhead of the predictive coding process. A similar comment applies to the higher dimensional cases.

Example: Consider encoding the monochrome image of Fig. 6.14(a) using the simple first-order linear predictor

$$\hat{f}(x, y) = \text{round}\, [\alpha f(x, y - 1)]. \tag{6.4-9}$$

A predictor of this general form commonly is called a *previous pixel* predictor, and the corresponding predictive coding procedure is referred to as *differential coding* or *previous pixel coding*. Figure 6.20(a) shows the prediction error image that results from Eq. (6.4-9) with $\alpha = 1$. In this image, gray-level 128 represents a prediction error of zero, whereas all nonzero positive and negative prediction errors (under and over estimates) are multiplied by 8 and displayed as lighter and darker shades of gray, respectively. The mean value of the prediction image is 128.02, which corresponds to an average prediction error of only 0.02 bits.

Figures 6.20(b) and (c) show the gray-level histogram of the image in Fig. 6.14(a) and the histogram of the prediction error resulting from Eq. (6.4-9). Note that the variance of the prediction error in Fig. 6.20(c) is much smaller than the variance of the gray levels in the original image. Moreover, the first-order estimate of the entropy of the prediction error image is significantly less than the corresponding first-order estimate for the original image (3.96 bits/pixel as opposed to 6.81 bits/pixel). This decrease in entropy reflects removal of a great deal of redundancy by the predictive coding process, despite the fact that for m-bit images, $(m + 1)$-bit numbers are needed to represent accurately the error sequence that results from Eq. (6.4-5). Although any of the variable-length coding procedures of Section 6.4.1 can be used to code this error sequence, the resulting compression will be limited to approximately 8/3.96, or about 2:1. In general, an estimate of the maximum compression of any lossless predictive coding approach may be obtained by dividing the average number of bits used to represent each pixel in the original image by a first-order estimate of the entropy of the prediction error data. ❑

The preceding example emphasizes that the amount of compression achieved in lossless predictive coding is related directly to the entropy reduction that results from mapping the input image into the prediction error sequence. Because a great deal of interpixel redundancy is removed by the prediction and differencing process, the probability density function of the prediction error is, in general, highly peaked at zero and characterized by a relatively small (in comparison to the input gray level distribution) variance. In fact, the density function of the prediction error often is modeled by the zero mean uncorrelated

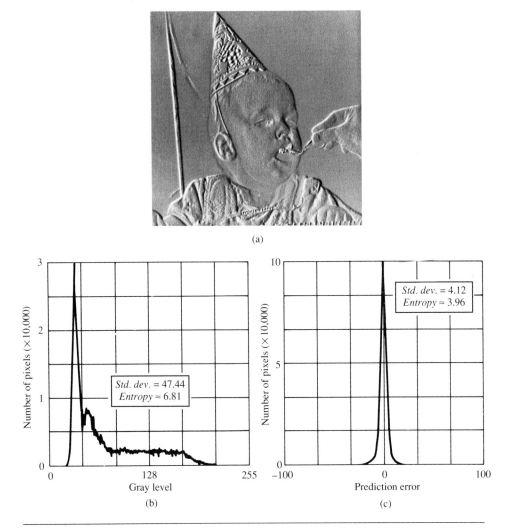

Figure 6.20 (a) The prediction error image resulting from Eq. (6.4-9); (b) the original image's gray-level histogram; (c) the prediction error histogram.

Laplacian pdf

$$p_e(e) = \frac{1}{\sqrt{2}\sigma_e} \exp\left(\frac{-\sqrt{2}\,|e|}{\sigma_e}\right) \tag{6.4-10}$$

where σ_e is the standard deviation of e.

6.5 LOSSY COMPRESSION

Unlike the error-free approaches outlined in the previous section, lossy en-coding is based on the concept of compromising the accuracy of the recon-structed image in exchange for increased compression. If the resulting distortion (which may or may not be visually apparent) can be tolerated, the increase in compression can be significant. In fact, many lossy encoding techniques are capable of reproducing recognizable monochrome images from data that have been compressed by more than 30:1 and images that are virtually indistinguish-able from the originals at 10:1 to 20:1. Error-free encoding of monochrome images, however, seldom results in more than a 3:1 reduction in data. As indicated in Section 6.2, the principal difference between these two approaches is the presence or absence of the quantizer block of Fig. 6.6.

6.5.1 Lossy Predictive Coding

In this section, we add a quantizer to the model introduced in Section 6.4.3 and examine the resulting trade-off between reconstruction accuracy and compression performance. As Fig. 6.21 shows, the quantizer, which absorbs the nearest integer function of the error-free encoder, is inserted between the symbol encoder and the point at which the prediction error is formed. It maps the prediction error into a limited range of outputs, denoted $\dot{e}_n$, which establish the amount of compression and distortion associated with lossy predictive coding.

In order to accommodate the insertion of the quantization step, the error-free encoder of Fig. 6.19(a) must be altered so that the predictions generated by the encoder and decoder are equivalent. As Fig. 6.21(a) shows, this is accomplished by placing the lossy encoder's predictor within a feedback loop, where its input, denoted $\dot{f}_n$, is generated as a function of past predictions and the corresponding quantized errors. That is,

$$\dot{f}_n = \dot{e}_n + \hat{f}_n \tag{6.5-1}$$

where $\hat{f}_n$ is as defined in Section 6.4.3. This closed loop configuration prevents error buildup at the decoder's output. Note from Fig. 6.21(b) that the output of the decoder also is given by Eq. (6.5-1).

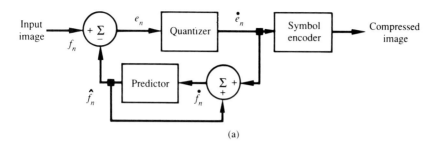

(a)

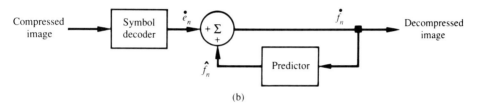

(b)

Figure 6.21 *A lossy predictive coding model: (a) encoder; (b) decoder.*

Example: *Delta modulation* (DM) is a simple but well-known form of lossy predictive coding in which the predictor and quantizer are defined as

$$\hat{f}_n = \alpha \dot{f}_{n-1} \tag{6.5-2}$$

and

$$\dot{e}_n = \begin{cases} +\zeta \text{ for } e_n > 0 \\ -\zeta \text{ otherwise} \end{cases} \tag{6.5-3}$$

where α is a prediction coefficient (normally less than 1) and ζ is a positive constant. The output of the quantizer, $\dot{e}_n$, can be represented by a single bit (Fig. 6.22a), so the symbol encoder of Fig. 6.21(a) can utilize a 1-bit fixed-length code. The resulting DM code rate is 1 bit/pixel.

Figure 6.22(c) illustrates the mechanics of the delta modulation process, where the calculations needed to compress and reconstruct the input sequence $\{14, 15, 14, 15, 13, 15, 15, 14, 20, 26, 27, 28, 27, 27, 29, 37, 47, 62, 75, 77, 78, 79, 80, 81, 81, 82, 82\}$ with $\alpha = 1$ and $\zeta = 6.5$ are tabulated. The process begins with the error-free transfer of the first input pixel to the decoder. With the initial condition $\hat{f}_0 = f_0 = 14$ established at both the encoder and decoder, the remaining outputs can be computed by repeatedly evaluating Eqs. (6.5-2), (6.4-5), (6.5-3), and (6.5-1). Thus, when $n = 1$, for example, $\hat{f}_1 = (1)(14) =$

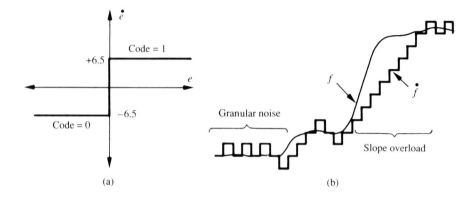

Figure 6.22   *A delta modulation (DM) example.*

14, $e_1 = 15 - 14 = 1$, $\dot{e}_1 = +6.5$ (because $e_1 > 0$), $\dot{f}_1 = 6.5 + 14 = 20.5$, and the resulting reconstruction error is $(15 - 20.5)$, or -5.5 gray levels.

Figure 6.22(b) depicts graphically the tabulated data shown in Fig. 6.22(c). Both the input and completely decoded output (f_n and $\dot{f}_n$) are shown. Note that in the rapidly changing area from $n = 14$ to 19, where ζ was too small to represent the input's largest changes, a distortion known as *slope overload* occurs. Moreover, when ζ was too large to represent the input's smallest changes, as in the relatively smooth region from $n = 0$ to $n = 7$, *granular noise* appears. In most images, these two phenomena lead to blurred object edges and grainy or noisy surfaces (that is, distorted smooth areas).   ∎

The distortions noted in the preceding example are common to all forms of lossy predictive coding. The severity of these distortions depends on a complex set of interactions between the quantization and prediction methods employed. Despite these interactions, the predictor normally is designed under the assumption of no quantization error, and the quantizer is designed to minimize its own error. That is, the predictor and quantizer are designed independently of each other.

Optimal predictors

The optimal predictor used in most predictive coding applications minimizes the encoder's mean-square prediction error[†]

$$E\{e_n^2\} = E\{[f_n - \hat{f}_n]^2\} \tag{6.5-4}$$

subject to the constraint that

$$\dot{f}_n = \dot{e}_n + \hat{f}_n \approx e_n + \hat{f}_n = f_n \tag{6.5-5}$$

and

$$\hat{f}_n = \sum_{i=1}^{m} \alpha_i f_{n-i}. \tag{6.5-6}$$

That is, the optimization criterion is chosen to minimize the mean-square prediction error, the quantization error is assumed to be negligible ($\dot{e}_n \approx e_n$), and the prediction is constrained to a linear combination of m previous pixels.[‡] These restrictions are not essential, but they simplify the analysis considerably and, at the same time, decrease the computational complexity of the predictor. The resulting predictive coding approach is referred to as *differential pulse code modulation* (DPCM).

Under these conditions, the optimal predictor design problem is reduced to the relatively straightforward exercise of selecting the m prediction coefficients that minimize the expression

$$E\{e_n^2\} = E\left\{\left[f_n - \sum_{i=1}^{m} \alpha_i f_{n-1}\right]^2\right\}. \tag{6.5-7}$$

[†] The notation $E\{\cdot\}$ denotes the statistical expectation operator.

[‡] In general, the optimal predictor for a non-Gaussian image is a nonlinear function of the pixels used to form the estimate.

Differentiating Eq. (6.5-7) with respect to each coefficient, equating the derivatives to zero, and solving the resulting set of simultaneous equations under the assumption that f_n has mean zero and variance σ^2 yields

$$\boldsymbol{\alpha} = \mathbf{R}^{-1}\mathbf{r} \tag{6.5-8}$$

where $\mathbf{R}^{-1}$ is the inverse of the $m \times m$ autocorrelation matrix

$$\mathbf{R} = \begin{bmatrix} E\{f_{n-1}f_{n-1}\} & E\{f_{n-1}f_{n-2}\} & \cdots & E\{f_{n-1}f_{n-m}\} \\ E\{f_{n-2}f_{n-1}\} & \cdot & \cdots & \cdot \\ \cdot & \cdot & \cdots & \cdot \\ \cdot & \cdot & \cdots & \cdot \\ E\{f_{n-m}f_{n-1}\} & E\{f_{n-m}f_{n-2}\} & \cdots & E\{f_{n-m}f_{n-m}\} \end{bmatrix} \tag{6.5-9}$$

and $\mathbf{r}$ and $\boldsymbol{\alpha}$ are the m-element vectors

$$\mathbf{r} = \begin{bmatrix} E\{f_n f_{n-1}\} \\ E\{f_n f_{n-2}\} \\ \vdots \\ E\{f_n f_{n-m}\} \end{bmatrix} \quad \text{and} \quad \boldsymbol{\alpha} = \begin{bmatrix} \alpha_1 \\ \alpha_2 \\ \vdots \\ \alpha_m \end{bmatrix} \tag{6.5-10}$$

Thus for any input image, the coefficients that minimize Eq. (6.5-7) can be determined via a series of elementary matrix operations. Moreover, the coefficients depend only on the autocorrelations of the pixels in the original image. The variance of the prediction error that results from the use of these optimal coefficients is

$$\sigma_e^2 = \sigma^2 - \boldsymbol{\alpha}^T\mathbf{r} = \sigma^2 - \sum_{i=1}^{m} E\{f_n f_{n-i}\}\alpha_i. \tag{6.5-11}$$

Although the mechanics of evaluating Eq. (6.5-8) are quite simple, computation of the autocorrelations needed to form $\mathbf{R}$ and $\mathbf{r}$ is so difficult in practice that *local* predictions (those in which the prediction coefficients are computed image by image) are almost never used. In most cases, a set of *global* coefficients is computed by assuming a simple image model and substituting the corresponding autocorrelations into Eqs. (6.5-9) and (6.5-10). For instance, when a 2-D Markov source (see Section 6.3.3) with separable autocorrelation function

$$E\{f(x, y) f(x - i, y - j)\} = \sigma^2 \rho_v^i \rho_h^j \tag{6.5-12}$$

and generalized fourth-order linear predictor

$$\hat{f}(x, y) = \alpha_1 f(x, y - 1) + \alpha_2 f(x - 1, y - 1) \qquad (6.5\text{-}13)$$
$$+ \alpha_3 f(x - 1, y) + \alpha_4 f(x - 1, y + 1)$$

are assumed, the resulting optimal coefficients (Jain [1991]) are

$$\alpha_1 = \rho_h \qquad \alpha_2 = -\rho_v \rho_h \qquad \alpha_3 = \rho_v \qquad \alpha_4 = 0 \qquad (6.5\text{-}14)$$

where ρ_h and ρ_v are the horizontal and vertical correlation coefficients, respectively, of the image under consideration.

Finally, the sum of the prediction coefficients in Eq. (6.5-6) normally is required to be less than or equal to one. That is,

$$\sum_{i=1}^{m} \alpha_i \le 1. \qquad (6.5\text{-}15)$$

This restriction is made to ensure that the predictor's output falls within the allowed range of gray levels and to reduce the impact of transmission noise, which is generally seen as horizontal streaks in the reconstructed image. Reducing the DPCM decoder's susceptibility to input noise is important, because a single error (under the right circumstances) can propagate to all future outputs. That is, the decoder's output may become unstable. Restricting Eq. (6.5-19) to be strictly less than 1 confines the impact of an input error to a small number of outputs.

Example: Consider the prediction error that results from DPCM coding the monochrome image of Fig. 6.23 under the assumption of zero quantization error and with each of four predictors:

$$\hat{f}(x, y) = 0.97 f(x, y - 1) \qquad (6.5\text{-}16)$$

$$\hat{f}(x, y) = 0.5 f(x, y - 1) + 0.5 f(x - 1, y) \qquad (6.5\text{-}17)$$

$$\hat{f}(x, y) = 0.75 f(x, y - 1) + 0.75 f(x - 1, y) - 0.5 f(x - 1, y - 1) \qquad (6.5\text{-}18)$$

$$\hat{f}(x, y) = \begin{cases} 0.97 f(x, y - 1) & \text{if } \Delta h \le \Delta v \\ 0.97 f(x - 1, y) & \text{otherwise} \end{cases} \qquad (6.5\text{-}19)$$

where $\Delta h = |f(x - 1, y) - f(x - 1, y - 1)|$ and $\Delta v = |f(x, y - 1) - f(x - 1, y - 1)|$ denote the horizontal and vertical gradients at point (x, y). Equations (6.5-16)–(6.5-18) define a relatively robust set of α_i, which provide satisfactory performance over a wide range of images. The adaptive predictor of Eq. (6.5-19) is designed to improve edge rendition by computing a local measure

Figure 6.23 *A 512 × 512 8-bit monochrome image.*

of the directional properties of an image (Δh and Δv) and selecting a predictor specifically tailored to the measured behavior.

Figures 6.24(a)–(d) show the prediction error images that result from using the predictors of Eqs. (6.5-16)–(6.5-19). Note that the visually perceptible error decreases as the order of the predictor increases.[†] The standard deviations of the prediction error distributions follow a similar pattern. They are 4.9, 3.7, 3.3 and 4.1 gray levels, respectively. ❏

Optimal quantization
The staircase quantization function $t = q(s)$ shown in Fig. 6.25 is an odd function of s [that is, $q(-s) = -q(s)$] that can be completely described by the $L/2$ s_i and t_i shown in the first quadrant of the graph. These break points define function discontinuities and are called the *decision* and *reconstruction levels* of the quantizer. As a matter of convention, s is considered to be mapped to t_i if it lies in the half-open interval $(s_i, s_{i+1}]$.

The quantizer design problem is to select the best s_i and t_i for a particular optimization criterion and input probability density function $p(s)$. If the optimization criterion, which could be either a statistical or psychovisual measure,[‡] is the minimization of the mean-square quantization error (that is, $E\{(s - t_i)^2\}$)

[†] Predictors that use more than three or four previous pixels provide little compression gain for the added predictor complexity (Habibi [1971]).

[‡] See Netravali [1977] and Limb and Rubinstein [1978] for more on psychovisual measures.

(a)

(b)

(c)

(d)

Figure 6.24 *A comparison of four linear prediction techniques.*

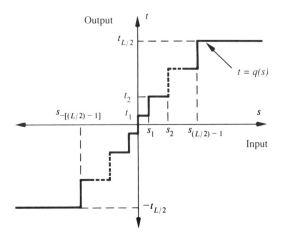

Figure 6.25   *A typical quantization function.*

and $p(s)$ is an even function, the conditions for minimal error (Max [1960]) are

$$\int_{s_{i-1}}^{s_i} (s - t_i)p(s)\ ds = 0 \qquad i = 1, 2, \ldots, \frac{L}{2} \tag{6.5-20}$$

$$
s_i =
\begin{cases}
0 & i = 0 \\[2mm]
\dfrac{t_i + t_{i+1}}{2} & i = 1, 2, \ldots, \dfrac{L}{2} - 1 \\[2mm]
\infty & i = \dfrac{L}{2}
\end{cases}
\tag{6.5-21}
$$

and

$$s_{-i} = -s_i \qquad t_{-i} = -t_i. \tag{6.5-22}$$

Equation (6.5-20) indicates that the reconstruction levels are the centroids of the areas under $p(s)$ over the specified decision intervals, whereas Eq. (6.5-21) indicates that the decision levels are halfway between the reconstruction levels. Equation (6.5-22) is a consequence of the fact that q is an odd function. For any L, the s_i and t_i that satisfy Eqs. (6.5-20)–(6.5-22) are optimal in the mean-square error sense; the corresponding quantizer is called an L-level *Lloyd–Max* quantizer.

Table 6.9 lists the 2-, 4-, and 8-level Lloyd–Max decision and reconstruction levels for a unit variance Laplacian probability density function (see Eq. 6.4-10). Because obtaining an explicit or closed-form solution to Eqs. (6.5-20)–(6.5-22) for most nontrivial $p(s)$ is difficult, these values were generated numerically (Paez and Glisson [1972]). The three quantizers shown provide fixed output rates of 1, 2, and 3 bits/pixel, respectively. As Table 6.9 was constructed for a unit variance distribution, the reconstruction and decision levels for the case of $\sigma \neq 1$ are obtained by multiplying the tabulated values by the standard deviation of the probability density function under consideration. The final row of the table lists the step size, θ, that simultaneously satisfies Eqs. (6.5-20)–(6.5-22) *and* the additional constraint that

$$t_i - t_{i-1} = s_i - s_{i-1} = \theta. \tag{6.5-23}$$

If a symbol encoder that utilizes a variable-length code is used in the general lossy predictive encoder of Fig. 6.21(a), an *optimum uniform quantizer* of step size θ will provide a lower code rate (for a Laplacian pdf) than a fixed-length coded Lloyd–Max quantizer with the same output fidelity (O'Neil [1971]).

Although the Lloyd–Max and optimum uniform quantizers are not adaptive, much can be gained from adjusting the quantization levels based on the local behavior of an image. In theory, slowly changing regions can be finely quantized, while the rapidly changing areas are quantized more coarsely. This approach simultaneously reduces both granular noise and slope overload, while requiring only a minimal increase in code rate. The trade-off is increased quantizer complexity.

Example: Figures 6.26(a), (c), and (e) show the DPCM reconstructed images that resulted from combining the 2-, 4-, and 8-level Lloyd–Max quantizers in Table 6.9 with the planar predictor of Eq. (6.5-18). The quantizers were generated by multiplying the tabulated Lloyd–Max decision and reconstruction levels by the standard deviation of the nonquantized planar prediction error from the preceding example (that is, 3.3 gray levels). Note that the edges of the decoded images are blurred from slope overload. This result is particularly noticeable in Fig. 6.26(a), which was generated using a two-level quantizer, but is less apparent in Figs. 6.26(c) and (e), where four and eight quantization levels were applied. Figures 6.27(a), (c), and (e) show the scaled differences between these decoded images and the original image of Fig. 6.23.

Table 6.9   Lloyd-Max Quantizers for a Laplacian Probability Density Function of Unit Variance

Levels	2		4		8	
i	s_i	t_i	s_i	t_i	s_i	t_i
1	∞	0.707	1.102	0.395	0.504	0.222
2			∞	1.810	1.181	0.785
3					2.285	1.576
4					∞	2.994
θ	1.414			1.087		0.731

(a)

(b)

(c)

(d)

(e)

(f)

Figure 6.26 *DPCM result images: (a) 1.0; (b) 1.125; (c) 2.0; (d) 2.125; (e) 3.0; (f) 3.125 bits/pixel.*

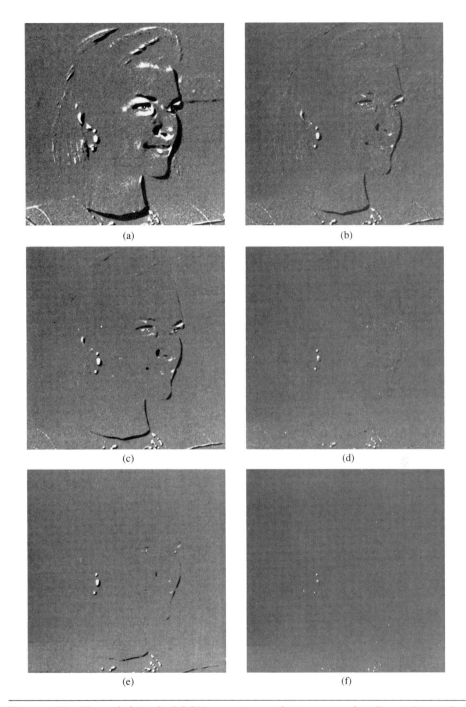

Figure 6.27 *The scaled (× 8) DPCM error images that correspond to Figs. 6.26(a)–(f).*

In order to generate the decoded images in Figs. 6.26(b), (d), and (f), and the resulting error images in Figs. 6.27(b), (d) and (f), we used an adaptive quantization method in which the best (in a mean-square error sense) of four possible quantizers was selected for each block of 16 pixels. The four quantizers were scaled versions of the optimal Lloyd–Max quantizers previously described. The scaling factors were 0.5, 1.0, 1.75, and 2.5. Because a 2-bit code was appended to each block in order to specify the selected quantizer, the overhead associated with the quantizer switching was $^2/_{16}$ or 0.125 bits/pixel. Note the substantial decrease in perceived error that resulted from this relatively small increase in code rate.

Table 6.10 lists the rms errors of the difference images in Figs. 6.27(a)–(f), as well as for a number of other combinations of predictors and quantizers. Note that in a mean-square error sense, the two-level adaptive quantizers performed about as well as the four-level nonadaptive versions. Moreover, the four-level adaptive quantizers outperformed the eight-level nonadaptive approaches. In general, the numerical results indicate that the predictors of Eqs. (6.5-15), (6.5-17), and (6.5-19) exhibit the same overall characteristics as the predictor of Eq. (6.5-18). The compression that resulted under each of the quantization methods is listed in the last row of Table 6.10. Note that the substantial decrease in rms error (Eq. 6.1-8) achieved by the adaptive approaches did not significantly affect compression performance.   ❑

6.5.2   Transform Coding

The predictive coding techniques discussed in Section 6.5.1 operate directly on the pixels of an image and thus are called *spatial domain methods*. In this section, we consider compression techniques that are based on modifying the transform of an image. In *transform coding*, a reversible, linear transform (such as the Fourier transform) is used to map the image into a set of transform coefficients, which are then quantized and coded. For most natural images, a significant number of the coefficients have small magnitudes and can be coarsely quantized (or discarded entirely) with little image distortion. Any of the transformations of Chapter 3 can be used to transform the image data.

Table 6.10   Lossy DPCM RMSE Summary

Predictor	Lloyd-Max Quantizer			Adaptive Quantizer		
	2-level	4-level	8-level	2-level	4-level	8-level
Eq. (6.5-16)	30.88	6.86	4.08	7.49	3.22	1.55
Eq. (6.5-17)	14.59	6.94	4.09	7.53	2.49	1.12
Eq. (6.5-18)	9.90	4.30	2.31	4.61	1.70	0.76
Eq. (6.5-19)	38.18	9.25	3.36	11.46	2.56	1.14
Compression	8.00:1	4.00:1	2.70:1	7.11:1	3.77:1	2.56:1

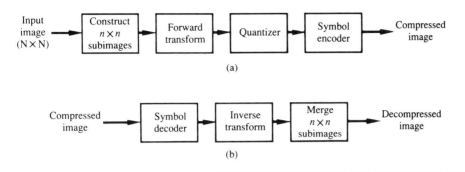

Figure 6.28 *A transform coding system: (a) encoder; (b) decoder.*

Figure 6.28 shows a typical transform coding system. The decoder implements the inverse sequence of steps (with the exception of the quantization function) of the encoder, which performs four relatively straightforward operations: subimage decomposition, transformation, quantization, and coding. An $N \times N$ input image first is subdivided into subimages of size $n \times n$, which are then transformed to generate $(N/n)^2$ $n \times n$ subimage transform arrays. The goal of the transformation process is to decorrelate the pixels of each subimage, or to pack as much information as possible into the smallest number of transform coefficients. The quantization stage then selectively eliminates or more coarsely quantizes the coefficients that carry the least information. These coefficients have the smallest impact on reconstructed subimage quality. The encoding process terminates by coding (normally using a variable-length code) the quantized coefficients. Any or all of the transform encoding steps can be adapted to local image content, called *adaptive transform coding*, or fixed for all subimages, called *nonadaptive transform coding*.

Transform selection
Transform coding systems based on the Karhunen–Loève (KLT), discrete Fourier (DFT), discrete cosine (DCT), Walsh–Hadamard (WHT), and various other transforms have been constructed and/or studied extensively. The choice of a particular transform in a given application depends on the amount of reconstruction error that can be tolerated and the computational resources available. Compression is achieved during the quantization of the transformed coefficients (not during the transformation step).

Example: Figures 6.29(a), (c), and (e) show three approximations to the 512 × 512 monochrome image of Fig. 6.23. These pictures were obtained by dividing the original image into subimages of size 8 × 8, representing each subimage by its DFT, WHT, or DCT transform, truncating 50 percent of the resulting coefficients, and taking the inverse transform of the truncated coefficient arrays.

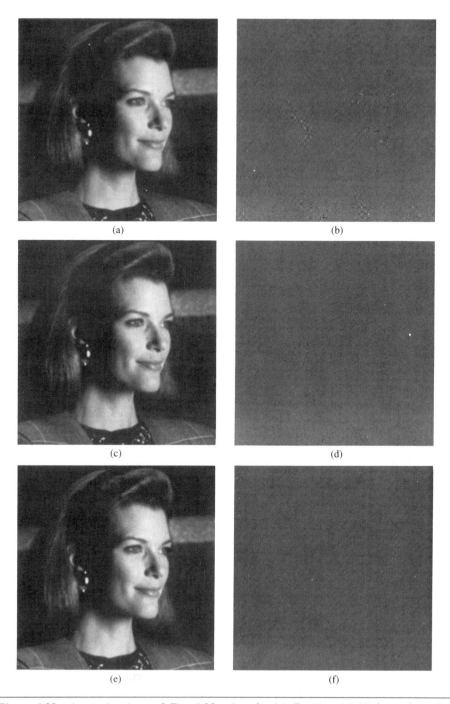

(a)

(b)

(c)

(d)

(e)

(f)

Figure 6.29 *Approximations of Fig. 6.23 using the (a) Fourier, (c) Hadamard, and (e) cosine transforms, together with the corresponding scaled error images.*

In each case, the 32 retained coefficients were selected on the basis of maximum magnitude. When we disregard any quantization or coding issues, this process amounts to compressing the original image by a factor of 2. Note that in all cases, the 32 discarded coefficients had little visual impact on reconstructed image quality. Their elimination, however, was accompanied by some mean-square error, which can be seen in the scaled error images of Figs. 6.29(b), (d), and (f). The actual rms errors were 1.28, 0.86, and 0.68 gray levels, respectively.   ❑

The small differences in mean-square reconstruction error noted in the preceding example are related directly to the energy or information packing properties of the transforms employed. Recall that, in accordance with Eq. (3.5-4), an $n \times n$ image $f(x, y)$ can be expressed as a function of its 2-D transform $T(u, v)$:

$$f(x, y) = \sum_{u=0}^{n-1} \sum_{v=0}^{n-1} T(u, v)h(x, y, u, v) \qquad (6.5\text{-}24)$$

for $x, y = 0, 1, \ldots, n - 1$. Note that we merely replaced N (in Eq. 3.5-4) with n and now consider $f(x, y)$ to represent a subimage of the image being compressed. Since the inverse kernel $h(x, y, u, v)$ in Eq. (6.5-24) depends only on the indices x, y, u, and v—not on the values of $f(x, y)$ or $T(u, v)$—it can be viewed as defining a set of *basis images* for the series defined by Eq. (6.5-24). This interpretation becomes clearer if the notation used in Eq. (6.5-24) is modified to obtain

$$\mathbf{F} = \sum_{u=0}^{n-1} \sum_{v=0}^{n-1} T(u, v) \, \mathbf{H}_{uv} \qquad (6.5\text{-}25)$$

where $\mathbf{F}$ is an $n \times n$ matrix containing the pixels of $f(x, y)$ and

$$\mathbf{H}_{uv} = \begin{bmatrix} h(0, 0, u, v) & h(0, 1, u, v) & \cdots & h(0, n-1, u, v) \\ h(1, 0, u, v) & \cdot & \cdots & \cdot \\ \cdot & \cdot & \cdots & \cdot \\ \cdot & \cdot & \cdots & \cdot \\ \cdot & & & \\ h(n-1, 0, u, v) & h(n-1, 1, u, v) & \cdots & h(n-1, n-1, u, v) \end{bmatrix} \qquad (6.5\text{-}26)$$

Then $\mathbf{F}$, the matrix containing the pixels of the input subimage, is explicitly defined as a linear combination of n^2 $n \times n$ matrices—that is, the $\mathbf{H}_{uv}$ for u, $v = 0, 1, \ldots, n - 1$ of Eq. (6.5-26). These matrices in fact are the basis images of the transform (see Section 3.5) used to compute the series expansion weighting coefficients, $T(u, v)$.

If we now define a transform coefficient *masking function*

$$m(u, v) = \begin{cases} 0 & \text{if } T(u, v) \text{ satisfies a specified truncation criterion} \\ 1 & \text{otherwise} \end{cases} \qquad (6.5\text{-}27)$$

for $u, v = 0, 1, \ldots, n - 1$, an approximation of $\mathbf{F}$ can be obtained from the truncated expansion

$$\hat{\mathbf{F}} = \sum_{u=0}^{n-1} \sum_{v=0}^{n-1} T(u, v) m(u, v) \mathbf{H}_{uv} \qquad (6.5\text{-}28)$$

where $m(u, v)$ is constructed to eliminate the basis images that make the smallest contribution to the total sum in Eq. (6.5-25). The mean-square error between subimage $\mathbf{F}$ and approximation $\hat{\mathbf{F}}$ then is

$$\begin{aligned} e_{ms} &= E\{\|\mathbf{F} - \hat{\mathbf{F}}\|^2\} \\ &= E\left\{\left\|\sum_{u=0}^{n-1} \sum_{v=0}^{n-1} T(u, v)\mathbf{H}_{uv} - \sum_{u=0}^{n-1} \sum_{v=0}^{n-1} T(u, v)m(u, v)\mathbf{H}_{uv}\right\|^2\right\} \\ &= E\left\{\left\|\sum_{u=0}^{n-1} \sum_{v=0}^{n-1} T(u, v)\mathbf{H}_{uv}[1 - m(u, v)]\right\|^2\right\} \\ &= \sum_{u=0}^{n-1} \sum_{v=0}^{n-1} \sigma^2_{T(u,v)}[1 - m(u, v)] \end{aligned} \qquad (6.5\text{-}29)$$

where $\|\mathbf{F} - \hat{\mathbf{F}}\|$ is the matrix norm of $(\mathbf{F} - \hat{\mathbf{F}})$, and $\sigma^2_{T(u,v)}$ is the variance of the coefficient at transform location (u, v). The final simplification is based on the orthonormal nature of the basis images and the assumption that the pixels of $\mathbf{F}$ are generated by a random process with zero mean and known covariance. The total mean-square approximation error thus is the sum of the variances of the discarded transform coefficients [that is, the coefficients for which $m(u, v) = 0$, so that $[1 - m(u, v)]$ in Eq. (6.5-29) is 1]. Transformations that redistribute or pack the most information into the fewest coefficients provide the best subimage approximations and, consequently, the smallest reconstruction errors. Finally, under the assumptions that led to Eq. (6.5-29), the mean-square error of the $(N/n)^2$ subimages of an $N \times N$ image are identical. Thus the mean-square error (being a measure of *average* error) of the $N \times N$ image equals the mean-square error of a single subimage.

The earlier example showed that the information packing ability of the DCT is superior to that of the DFT and WHT. Although this condition usually holds for most natural images, the KLT, not the DCT, is the optimal transform in an information packing sense. That is, the KLT minimizes the mean-square error in Eq. (6.5-29) for any input image and any number of retained coefficients

(Kramer and Mathews [1956]).[†] However, because the KLT is data dependent, obtaining the KLT basis images for each subimage, in general, is a nontrivial computational task. For this reason, the KLT is seldom used in practice. Instead, a transform, such as the DCT, whose basis images are fixed (input independent), normally is selected. Of the possible input independent transforms, the nonsinusoidal transforms (such as the WHT or Haar transform) are the simplest to implement. The sinusoidal transforms (such as the DFT or DCT) more closely approximate the information packing ability of the optimal KLT.

Hence most practical transform coding systems are based on the DCT, which provides a good compromise between information packing ability and computational complexity. In fact, the properties of the DCT have proved to be of such practical value that it has become the international standard for transform coding systems (see Section 6.6). Compared to the other input independent transforms, it has the advantages of having been implemented in a single integrated circuit, packing the most information into the fewest coefficients[‡] (for most natural images), and minimizing the blocklike appearance, called *blocking artifact*, that results when the boundaries between subimages become visible. This last property is particularly important in comparisons with the other sinusoidal transforms. As Fig. 6.30(a) shows, the implicit n-point periodicity of the DFT gives rise to boundary discontinuities that result in substantial high-frequency transform content. When the DFT transform coefficients are truncated or quantized, Gibbs phenomenon[‡‡] causes the boundary points to take on erroneous values, which appear in an image as blocking artifact. That is, the boundaries between adjacent subimages become visible because the boundary pixels of the subimages assume the mean values of discontinuities formed at the boundary points (see Fig. 6.30a). The DCT of Fig. 6.30(b) reduces this effect, because its implicit $2n$-point periodicity does not inherently produce boundary discontinuities.

Subimage size selection
Another significant factor affecting transform coding error and computational complexity is subimage size. In most applications, images are subdivided so that the correlation (redundancy) between adjacent subimages is reduced to

---

[†] An additional condition for optimality is that the masking function of Eq. (6.5-27) select the KLT coefficients of maximum variance.

[‡] Ahmed et al. [1974] first noticed that the KLT basis images of a first-order Markov image source closely resemble the DCT's basis images. As the correlation between adjacent pixels approaches one, the input dependent KLT basis images become identical to the input independent DCT basis images (Clarke [1985]).

[‡‡] The phenomenon, described in most electrical engineering texts on circuit analysis (e.g., Guillemin [1949]), occurs because the Fourier transform fails to converge uniformly at discontinuities. At discontinuities, Fourier expansions take the mean values.

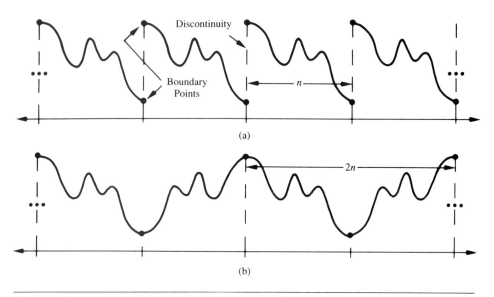

Figure 6.30   *The periodicity implicit in the 1-D (a) DFT and (b) DCT.*

some acceptable level and so that n is an integer power of 2 where, as before, n is the subimage dimension. The latter condition simplifies the computation of the subimage transforms (see the base-2 successive doubling methods discussed in Sections 3.4 and 3.5). In general, both the level of compression and computational complexity increase as the subimage size increases. The most popular subimage sizes are 8×8 and 16×16.

Example: Figure 6.31 illustrates graphically the impact of subimage size on transform coding reconstruction error. The data plotted were obtained by dividing the monochrome image of Fig. 6.23 into subimages of size $n \times n$, for $n = 2, 4, 8, 16$, and 32, computing the transform of each subimage, truncating 75 percent of the resulting coefficients, and taking the inverse transform of the truncated arrays. Note that the Hadamard and cosine curves flatten as the size of the subimage becomes greater than 8×8, whereas the Fourier reconstruction error decreases even more rapidly in this region. Extrapolation of these curves to larger values of n suggests that the Fourier reconstruction error will cross the Hadamard curve and converge to the cosine result. In fact, this result is consistent with the theoretical and experimental findings reported by Netravali and Limb [1980] and by Pratt [1978] for a 2-D Markov image source.

  All three curves intersect when 2×2 subimages are used. In this case, only one of the four coefficients (25 percent) of each transformed array was retained. The coefficient in all cases was the DC component, so the inverse transform simply replaced the four subimage pixels by their average or DC value (for example, see Eq. 3.3-20). This condition is evident in Fig. 6.32(d), which shows a zoomed portion of the 2 × 2 DCT result. Note that the blocking artifact that is prevalent in this result decreases as the subimage size increases to 4 × 4 and 8 × 8 in Figs. 6.32(e) and (f). Figure 6.32(c) shows a zoomed portion of the original image for reference. In addition, Figs. 6.32(a) and (b) facilitate comparison of these results to those of the preceding example. ❏

Bit allocation
The reconstruction error associated with the truncated series expansion of Eq. (6.5-28) is a function of the number and relative importance of the transform coefficients that are discarded, as well as the precision that is used to represent the retained coefficients. In most transform coding systems, the retained coefficients are selected [that is, the sampling function of Eq. (6.5-27) is constructed] on the basis of maximum variance, called *zonal coding*, or on the basis of maximum magnitude, called *threshold coding*. The overall process of truncating, quantizing, and coding the coefficients of a transformed subimage is commonly called *bit allocation*.

Example: Figures 6.33(a) and (b) show two approximations of Fig. 6.23 in which 87.5 percent of the DCT coefficients of each 8 × 8 subimage were discarded. The first result was obtained via threshold coding by keeping the

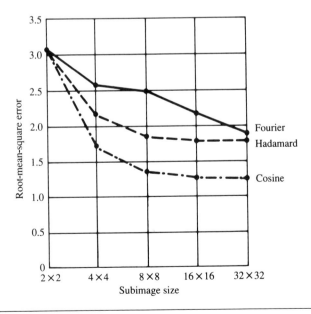

Figure 6.31 *Reconstruction error versus subimage size.*

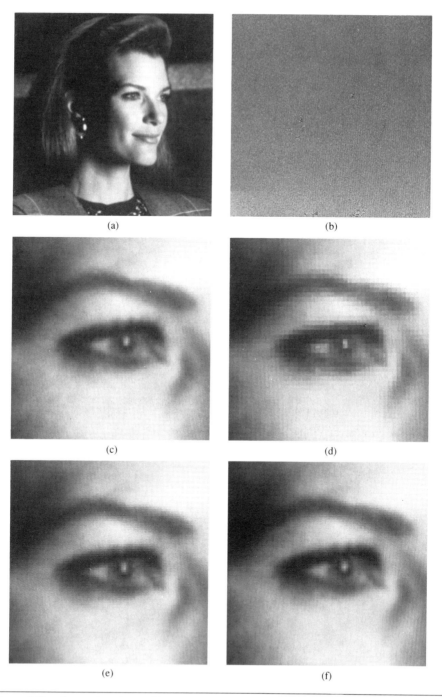

(a)

(b)

(c)

(d)

(e)

(f)

Figure 6.32 *Approximations of Fig. 6.23 using 25 percent of the DCT coefficients: (a) and (b) 8 × 8 subimage results; (c) zoomed original; (d) 2 × 2 result; (e) 4 × 4 result; and (f) 8 × 8 result.*

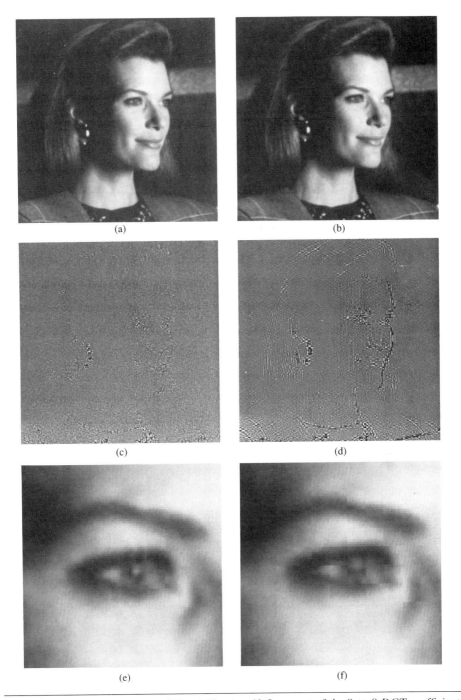

(a)

(b)

(c)

(d)

(e)

(f)

Figure 6.33 *Approximations of Fig. 6.23 using 12.5 percent of the 8 × 8 DCT coefficients: (a), (c), and (e) threshold coding results; (b), (d), and (f) zonal coding results.*

eight largest transform coefficients, and the second image was generated by using a zonal coding approach. In the latter case, each DCT coefficient was considered a random variable whose distribution could be computed over the ensemble of all transformed subimages. The 8 distributions of largest variance (12.5 percent of the 64 coefficients in the transformed 8×8 subimage) were located and used to determine the coordinates, u and v, of the coefficients, $T(u, v)$, that were retained for all subimages. Note that the threshold coding difference image of Fig. 6.33(c) contains far less error than the zonal coding result in Fig. 6.33(d). Figures 6.33(e) and (f) provide a closer view of a small portion of the reconstructed images in (a) and (c).   ☐

Zonal coding: Zonal coding is based on the information theory concept of viewing information as uncertainty. Therefore the transform coefficients of maximum variance carry the most picture information and should be retained in the coding process. The variances themselves can be calculated directly from the ensemble of $(N/n)^2$ transformed subimage arrays, as in the preceding example, or based on an assumed image model (say, a Markov autocorrelation function). In either case, the zonal sampling process can be viewed, in accordance with Eq. (6.5-28), as multiplying each $T(u, v)$ by the corresponding element in a *zonal mask*, which is constructed by placing a 1 in the locations of maximum variance and a 0 in all other locations. Coefficients of maximum variance usually are located around the origin of an image transform, resulting in the typical zonal mask shown in Fig. 6.34(a).

The coefficients retained during the zonal sampling process must be quantized and coded, so zonal masks are sometimes depicted showing the number of bits used to code each coefficient (Fig. 6.34b). In most cases, the coefficients are allocated the same number of bits, or some fixed number of bits is distributed among them unequally. In the first case, the coefficients generally are normalized by their standard deviations and uniformly quantized. In the second case, a quantizer, such as an optimal Lloyd–Max quantizer, is designed for each coefficient. To construct the required quantizers, the zeroth or DC coefficient normally is modeled by a Rayleigh density function, whereas the remaining coefficients are modeled by a Laplacian or Gaussian density.[†] The number of quantization levels (and thus the number of bits) allotted to each quantizer is made proportional to $\log_2 \sigma^2_{T(u,v)}$. This allocation is consistent with rate distortion theory, which indicates that a Gaussian random variable of variance σ^2 cannot be represented by less than $\frac{1}{2} \log_2 (\sigma^2/D)$ bits and be reproduced with mean-square error less than D (see Problem 6.11). The intuitive

---

[†] As each coefficient is a linear combination of the pixels in its subimage (see Eq. 3.5-3), the central limit theorem suggests that, as subimage size increases, the coefficients tend to become Gaussian. This result does not apply to the DC coefficient, however, because nonnegative images always have positive DC coefficients.

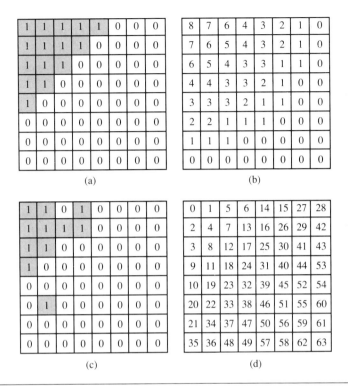

Figure 6.34   *A typical (a) zonal mask, (b) zonal bit allocation, (c) threshold mask, and (d) thresholded coefficient ordering sequence. Shading highlights the coefficients that are retained.*

conclusion is that the information content of a Gaussian random variable is proportional to $\log_2 (\sigma^2/D)$. Thus the retained coefficients in Eq. (6.5-28)— which (in the context of the current discussion) are selected on the basis of maximum variance—should be assigned bits in proportion to the logarithm of the coefficient variances.

Threshold coding: Zonal coding usually is implemented by using a single fixed mask for all subimages. Threshold coding, however, is inherently adaptive in the sense that the location of the transform coefficients retained for each subimage vary from one subimage to another. In fact, threshold coding is the adaptive transform coding approach most often used in practice because of its computational simplicity. The underlying concept is that, for any subimage, the transform coefficients of largest magnitude make the most significant contribution to reconstructed subimage quality, as demonstrated in the last example. Because the locations of the maximum coefficients vary from one subimage to another, the elements of $T(u, v)m(u, v)$ normally are reordered (in a predefined manner) to form a 1-D, run-length coded sequence. Figure 6.34(c) shows a typical *threshold mask* for one subimage of a hypothetical image. This mask provides a convenient way to visualize the threshold coding process for the corresponding subimage, as well as to mathematically describe the process using Eq. (6.5-28). When the mask is applied (via Eq. 6.5-28) to the subimage for which it was derived, and the resulting $n \times n$ array is reordered to form an n^2-element coefficient sequence in accordance with the zigzag ordering pattern of Fig. 6.34(d), the reordered 1-D sequence contains several long runs of 0's. These runs normally are run-length coded. The nonzero or retained coefficients, corresponding to the mask locations that contain a 1, are represented using one of the variable-length codes of Section 6.4.

There are three basic ways to threshold a transformed subimage or, stated differently, to create a subimage threshold masking function of the form given in Eq. (6.5-27): (1) a single global threshold can be applied to all subimages; (2) a different threshold can be used for each subimage; or (3) the threshold can be varied as a function of the location of each coefficient within the subimage. In the first approach, the level of compression differs from image to image, depending on the number of coefficients that exceed the global threshold. In the second, called *N-largest coding*, the same number of coefficients is discarded for each subimage. As a result, the code rate is constant and known in advance. The third technique, like the first, results in a variable code rate, but offers the advantage that thresholding *and* quantization can be combined by replacing $T(u, v)m(u, v)$ in Eq. (6.5-28) with

$$\hat{T}(u, v) = \text{round} \left[\frac{T(u, v)}{Z(u, v)} \right] \tag{6.5-30}$$

where $\hat{T}(u, v)$ is a thresholded and quantized approximation of $T(u, v)$, and $\mathbf{Z}$ is the transform normalization array

$$\mathbf{Z} = [Z(u, v)] = \begin{bmatrix} Z(0, 0) & Z(0, 1) & \cdots & Z(0, n-1) \\ Z(1, 0) & & & \\ \vdots & \vdots & \cdots & \vdots \\ & & \cdots & \\ Z(n-1, 0) & Z(n-1, 1) & \cdots & Z(n-1, n-1) \end{bmatrix} \tag{6.5-31}$$

Before a normalized (thresholded and quantized) subimage transform, $\hat{T}(u,v)$, can be inverse transformed to obtain an approximation of $F(u, v)$, it must be multiplied by $Z(u, v)$. The resulting denormalized array, denoted $\dot{T}(u, v)$, is an approximation of $\hat{T}(u, v)$:

$$\dot{T}(u, v) = \hat{T}(u, v) \, Z(u, v). \tag{6.5-32}$$

The inverse transform of $\dot{T}(u, v)$ yields the decompressed subimage approximation.

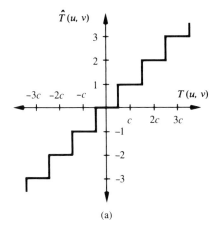

16	11	10	16	24	40	51	61
12	12	14	19	26	58	60	55
14	13	16	24	40	57	69	56
14	17	22	29	51	87	80	62
18	22	37	56	68	109	103	77
24	35	55	64	81	104	113	92
49	64	78	87	103	121	120	101
72	92	95	98	112	100	103	99

(a)   (b)

Figure 6.35 (a) A threshold coding quantization curve (see Eq. 6.5-30); (b) a typical normalization matrix.

Figure 6.35(a) depicts Eq. (6.5-30) graphically for the case in which $Z(u, v)$ is assigned a particular value c. Note that $\hat{T}(u, v)$ assumes integer value k if and only if

$$kc - \frac{c}{2} \le T(u, v) < kc + \frac{c}{2}.$$

If $Z(u, v) > 2T(u, v)$, $\hat{T}(u, v) = 0$, and the transform coefficient is completely truncated or discarded. When $\hat{T}(u, v)$ is represented with a variable-length code that increases in length as the magnitude of k increases, the number of bits used to represent $T(u, v)$ is controlled by the value of c. Thus the elements of **Z** can be scaled to achieve a variety of compression levels. Figure 6.35(b) shows a typical normalization array. This array, which has been used extensively in the JPEG[†] standardization efforts (see Section 6.6.2), weighs each coefficient of a transformed subimage according to heuristically determined perceptual or psychovisual importance.

Example: Figures 6.36(a) and (b) show two threshold coded approximations of the monochrome image in Fig. 6.23. Both images were generated using an 8×8 DCT and the normalization array of Fig. 6.35(b). The first result, which provides a compression ratio of about 34 to 1, was obtained by direct application of that normalization array. The second, which compresses the original image by a ratio of 67 to 1, was generated after multiplying (scaling) the normalization

---

[†] JPEG is an abbreviation for the Joint Photographic Experts Group.

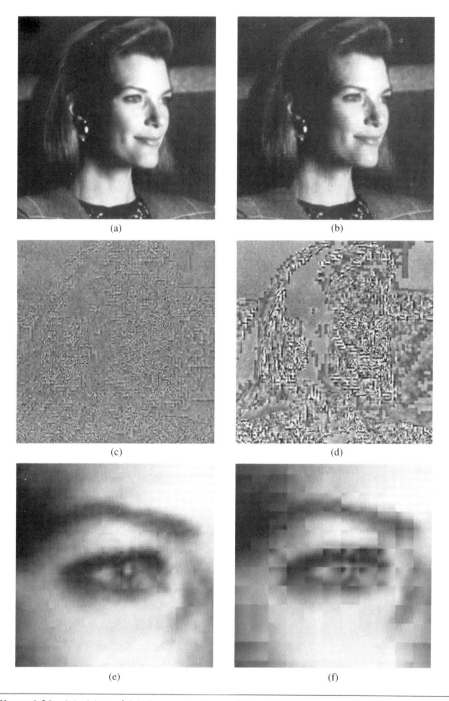

Figure 6.36 (a), (c), and (e) Approximations of Fig. 6.23 using the DCT and normalization array of Fig. 6.35(b); (b), (d), and (f) similar results for 4**Z**.

array by 4. By comparison, the *average* compression ratio obtained by using all the error-free methods discussed in Section 6.4 was only 2.62 to 1.

The differences between the original image of Fig. 6.23 and the reconstructed images of Figs. 6.36(a) and (b) are shown in Figs. 6.36(c) and (d), respectively. The corresponding rms errors (see Eq. 6.1-8) are 3.42 and 6.33 gray levels. The precise nature of the errors are more visible in the zoomed images of Figures 6.36(e) and (f). These images show a magnified section of Figs. 6.36(a) and (b), respectively. They allow a better assessment of the subtle differences between the reconstructed images.   ❏

6.6   IMAGE COMPRESSION STANDARDS

Many of the lossy and error-free compression methods described so far have played important roles in the development and adoption of current principal image compression standards. In this section we examine these standards, which in most cases have been developed and sanctioned under the joint auspices of the International Standardization Organization (ISO) and the Consultative Committee of the International Telephone and Telegraph (CCITT). Taken together, they address both binary and continuous-tone (monochrome and color) image compression, as well as both still-frame and sequential (or motion picture) applications.

6.6.1   Bilevel (Binary) Image Compression Standards

The most widely used image compression standards are the CCITT Group 3 and 4 standards for bilevel image compression. Although they are currently utilized in a wide variety of computer applications, they were originally designed as facsimile (FAX) coding methods for transmitting documents over telephone networks. The Group 3 standard applies a nonadaptive, 1-D run-length coding technique in which the last $K - 1$ lines of each group of K lines (for $K = 2$ or 4) are optionally coded in a 2-D manner. The Group 4 standard is a simplified or streamlined version of the Group 3 standard in which only 2-D coding is allowed. Both standards use the same nonadaptive 2-D coding approach. This approach is quite similar to the relative address coding (RAC) technique described in Section 6.4.2.

During the development of the CCITT standards, eight representative "test" documents were selected and used as a baseline for evaluating various binary compression alternatives. The existing Group 3 and 4 standards compress these documents, which include both typed and handwritten text (in several languages), as well as a few line drawings, by about 15:1. Because the Group 3 and 4 standards are based on nonadaptive techniques and, in some cases, can result in data expansion, the Joint Bilevel Imaging Group (JBIG)—a joint committee of the CCITT and ISO—has been given the task of identifying an adaptive algorithm that will outperform the existing standards. Other committee goals include extending the utility of the selected compression method to other types of images (that is, beyond those characterized by the eight test images); accommodating progressive image transmission and reconstruction applications (see Problem 6.22); and handling digital halftone images, which often are expanded (rather than compressed) by the existing Group 3 and 4 standards.

One-dimensional compression

In the 1-D CCITT Group 3 compression method, each line of an image[†] is encoded as a series of variable-length code words that represent the run lengths of the alternating white and black runs in a left-to-right scan of the line. The code words themselves are of two types. If the run length is less than 63, a terminating code from the modified Huffman code in Table 6.11 is used. If the run length is greater than 63, the largest possible makeup code (not exceeding the run length) from Table 6.12 is used in conjunction with a terminating code that represents the difference between the makeup code and the actual run length. The standard requires that each line begins with a white run-length code word, which may in fact be 00110101, the code for a white run of length zero. Finally, a unique end-of-line (EOL) code word 000000000001 is used to terminate each line, as well as to signal the first line of each new image. The end of a sequence of images is indicated by six consecutive EOLs.

Two-dimensional compression

The 2-D compression approach adopted for both the CCITT Group 3 and 4 standards is a line-by-line method in which the position of each black-to-white or white-to-black run transition is coded with respect to the position of a *reference element* a_0 that is situated on the current *coding line*. The previously coded line is called the *reference line*; the reference line for the first line of each new image is an imaginary white line.

Figure 6.37 shows the basic coding process for a single scan line. Note that the initial steps of the procedure are directed at locating several key transition or *changing elements*: a_0, a_1, a_2, b_1, and b_2. A changing element is defined as a pixel whose value is different from that of the previous pixel on the same line. The most important changing element is a_0 (the reference element), which is either set to the location of an imaginary white changing element to the left of the first pixel of each new coding line or determined from the previous coding mode. After a_0 is located, a_1 is identified as the location of the next changing element to the right of a_0 on the current coding line, a_2 as the next changing element to the right of a_1 on the coding line, b_1 as the changing element of the opposite value (of a_0) and to the right of a_0 on the reference (or previous) line,

---

[†] In the standard, images are referred to as *pages* and sequences of images are referred to as *documents*.

Table 6.11   CCITT Terminating Codes

Run Length	White Code Word	Black Code Word	Run Length	White Code Word	Black Code Word
0	00110101	0000110111	32	00011011	000001101010
1	000111	010	33	00010010	000001101011
2	0111	11	34	00010011	000011010010
3	1000	10	35	00010100	000011010011
4	1011	011	36	00010101	000011010100
5	1100	0011	37	00010110	000011010101
6	1110	0010	38	00010111	000011010110
7	1111	00011	39	00101000	000011010111
8	10011	000101	40	00101001	000001101100
9	10100	000100	41	00101010	000001101101
10	00111	0000100	42	00101011	000011011010
11	01000	0000101	43	00101100	000011011011
12	001000	0000111	44	00101101	000001010100
13	000011	00000100	45	00000100	000001010101
14	110100	00000111	46	00000101	000001010110
15	110101	000011000	47	00001010	000001010111
16	101010	0000010111	48	00001011	000001100100
17	101011	0000011000	49	01010010	000001100101
18	0100111	0000001000	50	01010011	000001010010
19	0001100	00001100111	51	01010100	000001010011
20	0001000	00001101000	52	01010101	000000100100
21	0010111	00001101100	53	00100100	000000110111
22	0000011	00000110111	54	00100101	000000111000
23	0000100	00000101000	55	01011000	000000100111
24	0101000	00000010111	56	01011001	000000101000
25	0101011	00000011000	57	01011010	000001011000
26	0010011	000011001010	58	01011011	000001011001
27	0100100	000011001011	59	01001010	000000101011
28	0011000	000011001100	60	01001011	000000101100
29	00000010	000011001101	61	00110010	000001011010
30	00000011	000001101000	62	00110011	000001100110
31	00011010	000001101001	63	00110100	000001100111

and b_2 as the next changing element to the right of b_1 on the reference line. If any of these changing elements are not detected, they are set to the location of an imaginary pixel to the right of the last pixel on the appropriate line. Figure 6.38 provides two illustrations of the general relationships between the various changing elements.

After identification of the current reference element and associated changing elements, two simple tests are performed to select one of three possible coding modes: *pass mode*, *vertical mode*, or *horizontal mode*. The initial test, which corresponds to the first branch point in the flow chart shown in Fig. 6.37, compares the location of b_2 to that of a_1. The second test, which corresponds

Table 6.12   CCITT Makeup Codes

Run Length	White Code Word	Black Code Word	Run Length	White Code Word	Black Code Word
64	11011	0000001111	960	011010100	0000001110011
128	10010	000011001000	1024	011010101	0000001110100
192	010111	000011001001	1088	011010110	0000001110101
256	0110111	000001011011	1152	011010111	0000001110110
320	00110110	000000110011	1216	011011000	0000001110111
384	00110111	000000110100	1280	011011001	0000001010010
448	01100100	000000110101	1344	011011010	0000001010011
512	01100101	0000001101100	1408	011011011	0000001010100
576	01101000	0000001101101	1472	010011000	0000001010101
640	01100111	0000001001010	1536	010011001	0000001011010
704	011001100	0000001001011	1600	010011010	0000001011011
768	011001101	0000001001100	1664	011000	0000001100100
832	011010010	0000001001101	1728	010011011	0000001100101
896	011010011	0000001110010			

	Code Word			Code Word	
1792	00000001000		2240	000000010110	
1856	00000001100		2304	000000010111	
1920	00000001101		2368	000000011100	
1984	000000010010		2432	000000011101	
2048	000000010011		2496	000000011110	
2112	000000010100		2560	000000011111	
2176	000000010101				

to the second branch point in Fig. 6.37, computes the distance (in pixels) between the locations of a_1 and b_1 and compares it against 3. Depending on the outcome of these tests, one of the three outlined coding blocks of Fig. 6.37 is entered and the appropriate coding procedure is executed. A new reference element is then established, as per the flow chart, in preparation for the next coding iteration.

Table 6.13 defines the specific codes utilized for each of the three possible coding modes. In pass mode, which specifically excludes the case in which b_2 is directly above a_1, only the pass mode code word 0001 is needed. As Fig. 6.38(a) shows, this mode identifies white or black reference line runs that do not overlap the current white or black coding line runs. In horizontal coding mode, the distances from a_0 to a_1 and a_1 to a_2 must be coded in accordance with the termination and makeup codes of Tables 6.11 and 6.12 and then appended to the horizontal mode code word 001. This is indicated in Table 6.13 by the notation $001 + M(a_0a_1) + M(a_1a_2)$, where a_0a_1 and a_1a_2 denote the distances from a_0 to a_1 and a_1 to a_2, respectively. Finally, in vertical coding mode, one of six special variable-length codes is assigned to the distance be-

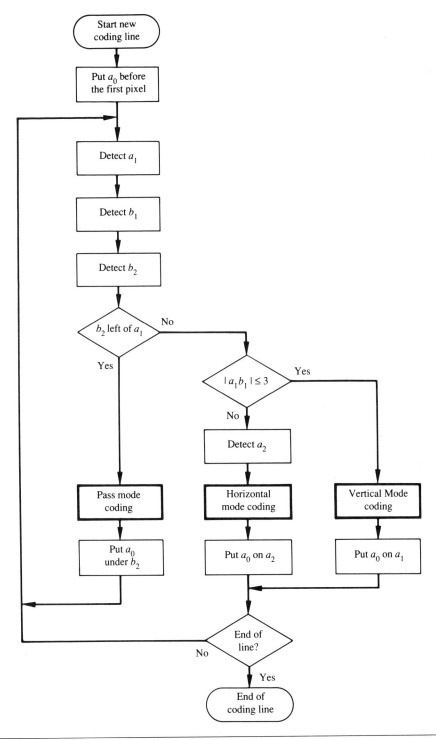

Figure 6.37 *CCITT 2-D coding procedure. The notation $|a_1 b_1|$ denotes the absolute value of the distance between changing elements a_1 and b_1.*

393

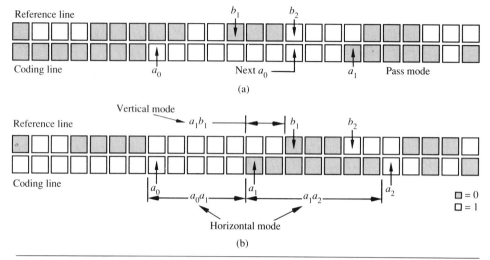

Figure 6.38   *CCITT (a) pass mode and (b) horizontal and vertical mode coding parameters.*

tween a_1 and b_1. Figure 6.38(b) illustrates the parameters involved in both horizontal and vertical mode coding. The *extension mode* code word at the bottom of Table 6.13 is used to enter an optional facsimile coding mode. For example, the 0000001111 code is used to initiate an uncompressed mode of transmission.

Example: Although Fig. 6.38(b) is annotated with the parameters for both horizontal and vertical mode coding, the depicted condition in reality is a case for vertical mode coding. That is, as b_2 is to the right of a_1, the first (or pass mode) test in Fig. 6.37 fails. The second test, which determines whether the vertical or horizontal coding mode is entered, indicates that vertical mode coding should be used, because the distance from a_1 to b_1 is less than 3. In accordance with Table 6.13, the appropriate code word is 000010, implying that a_1 is two pixels left of b_1. In preparation for the next coding iteration, a_0 is moved to the location of a_1.   ❑

6.6.2   Continuous Tone Image Compression Standards

The CCITT and ISO have defined several continuous tone (as opposed to bilevel) image compression standards. These standards, which are in various phases of the adoption process, address both monochrome and color image compression, as well as still-frame and sequential frame applications. In contrast to the bilevel compression standards described in Section 6.6.1, all continuous tone standards are based on the lossy transform coding techniques of Section 6.5.2. To develop the standards, CCITT and ISO committees solicited algorithm recommendations from a large number of companies, universities, and research laboratories. The best of those submitted were selected on the basis of image quality and compression performance. Hence the resulting standards represent the state of the art in continuous tone image compression. They deliver still-frame and sequential frame VHS-compatible[+] image quality with compression ratios of about 25:1 and 100:1, respectively.

Still-frame monochrome and color compression
The CCITT and ISO collaborated to develop the most popular and comprehensive continuous tone, still-frame compression standard, called the JPEG standard. The JPEG standard defines three different coding systems: (1) a lossy *baseline coding system*, which is based on the DCT and is adequate for most compression applications; (2) an *extended coding system* for greater compression, higher precision, or progressive reconstruction applications; and (3) a lossless *independent coding system* for reversible compression. To be JPEG compatible, a product or system must include support for the baseline system. No particular file format, spatial resolution, or color space model is specified.

In the baseline system, often called the *sequential baseline system*, the input and output data precision is limited to 8 bits, whereas the quantized DCT values are restricted to 11 bits. The compression itself is performed in three sequential steps: DCT computation, quantization, and variable-length code assignment.

Table 6.13 CCITT Two-Dimensional Code Table

Mode	Code Word
Pass	0001
Horizontal	$001 + M(a_0a_1) + M(a_1a_2)$
Vertical	
a_1 below b_1	1
a_1 one to the right of b_1	011
a_1 two to the right of b_1	000011
a_1 three to the right of b_1	0000011
a_1 one to the left of b_1	010
a_1 two to the left of b_1	000010
a_1 three to the left of b_1	0000010
Extension	0000001×××

[+] VHS is the most common 1/2-in. home video cassette recorder (VCR) tape format.

Table 6.14 JPEG Coefficient Coding Categories

Range	DC Difference Category	AC Category
0	0	N/A
−1, 1	1	1
−3, −2, 2, 3	2	2
−7, . . . , −4, 4, . . . , 7	3	3
−15, . . . , −8, 8, . . . , 15	4	4
−31, . . . , −16, 16, . . . , 31	5	5
−63, . . . , −32, 32, . . . , 63	6	6
−127, . . . , −64, 64, . . . , 127	7	7
−255, . . . , 128, 128, . . . , 255	8	8
−511, . . . , −256, 256, . . . , 511	9	9
−1023, . . . , −512, 512, . . . , 1023	A	A
−2047, . . . , −1024, 1024, . . . , 2047	B	B
−4095, . . . , −2048, 2048, . . . , 4095	C	C
−8191, . . . , −4096, 4096, . . . , 8191	D	D
−16383, . . . , −8192, 8192, . . . , 16383	E	E
−32767, . . . , −16384, 16384, . . . , 32767	F	N/A

The image is first subdivided into pixel blocks of size 8×8, which are processed left to right, top to bottom. As each 8×8 block or subimage is encountered, its 64 pixels are level shifted by subtracting the quantity 2^{n-1}, where 2^n is the maximum number of gray levels. The 2-D discrete cosine transform of the block is then computed, quantized in accordance with Eq. (6.5-30), and reordered, using the zigzag pattern of Fig. 6.34(d), to form a 1-D sequence of quantized coefficients.

Since the one-dimensionally reordered array generated under the zigzag pattern of Fig. 6.34(d) is qualitatively arranged according to increasing spatial frequency, the JPEG coding procedure is designed to take advantage of the long runs of zeros that normally result from the reordering. In particular, the nonzero $AC^{\dagger}$ coefficients are coded using a variable-length code that defines the coefficient's value and number of preceding zeros. The DC coefficient is difference coded relative to the DC coefficient of the previous subimage. Tables 6.14, 6.15, and 6.16 provide the default JPEG Huffman codes for luminance imagery. The JPEG recommended luminance quantization array is given in Fig. 6.35(b) and can be scaled to provide a variety of compression levels. Although default coding tables and proven quantization arrays are provided for both luminance and chrominance processing, the user is free to construct

---

† In the standard, the term AC denotes all transform coefficients with the exception of the zeroth or DC coefficient.

Table 6.15 JPEG Default DC Code (Luminance)

Category	Base Code	Length	Category	Base Code	Length
0	010	3	6	1110	10
1	011	4	7	11110	12
2	100	5	8	111110	14
3	00	5	9	1111110	16
4	101	7	A	11111110	18
5	110	8	B	111111110	20

custom tables and/or arrays, which may in fact be adapted to the characteristics of the image being compressed.

Example: Consider compression and reconstruction of the following 8×8 subimage with the JPEG baseline standard:

52	55	61	66	70	61	64	73
63	59	66	90	109	85	69	72
62	59	68	113	144	104	66	73
63	58	71	122	154	106	70	69
67	61	68	104	126	88	68	70
79	65	60	70	77	68	58	75
85	71	64	59	55	61	65	83
87	79	69	68	65	76	78	94

The original image consists of 256 or 2^8 possible gray levels, so the coding process begins by level shifting the pixels of the original subimage by -2^7 or -128 gray levels. The resulting shifted array is

-76	-73	-67	-62	-58	-67	-64	-55
-65	-69	-62	-38	-19	-43	-59	-56
-66	-69	-60	-15	16	-24	-62	-55
-65	-70	-57	-6	26	-22	-58	-59
-61	-67	-60	-24	-2	-40	-60	-58
-49	-63	-68	-58	-51	-65	-70	-53
-43	-57	-64	-69	-73	-67	-63	-45
-41	-49	-59	-60	-63	-52	-50	-34

Table 6.16   JPEG Default AC Code (Luminance)

Run/ Category	Base Code	Length	Run/ Category	Base Code	Length
0/0	**1010 (= EOB)**	**4**			
0/1	00	3	8/1	11111010	9
0/2	01	4	8/2	111111111000000	17
0/3	100	6	8/3	1111111110110111	19
0/4	1011	8	8/4	1111111110111000	20
0/5	11010	10	8/5	1111111110111001	21
0/6	111000	12	8/6	1111111110111010	22
0/7	1111000	14	8/7	1111111110111011	23
0/8	1111110110	18	8/8	1111111110111100	24
0/9	1111111110000010	25	8/9	1111111110111101	25
0/A	1111111110000011	26	8/A	1111111110111110	26
1/1	1100	5	9/1	111111000	10
1/2	111001	8	9/2	1111111110111111	18
1/3	1111001	10	9/3	1111111111000000	19
1/4	111110110	13	9/4	1111111111000001	20
1/5	11111110110	16	9/5	1111111111000010	21
1/6	1111111110000100	22	9/6	1111111111000011	22
1/7	1111111110000101	23	9/7	1111111111000100	23
1/8	1111111110000110	24	9/8	1111111111000101	24
1/9	1111111110000111	25	9/9	1111111111000110	25
1/A	1111111110001000	26	9/A	1111111111000111	26
2/1	11011	6	A/1	111111001	10
2/2	11111000	10	A/2	1111111111001000	18
2/3	1111110111	13	A/3	1111111111001001	19
2/4	1111111110001001	20	A/4	1111111111001010	20
2/5	1111111110001010	21	A/5	1111111111001011	21
2/6	1111111110001011	22	A/6	1111111111001100	22
2/7	1111111110001100	23	A/7	1111111111001101	23
2/8	1111111110001101	24	A/8	1111111111001110	24
2/9	1111111110001110	25	A/9	1111111111001111	25
2/A	1111111110001111	26	A/A	1111111111010000	26
3/1	111010	7	B/1	111111010	10
3/2	111110111	11	B/2	1111111111010001	18
3/3	11111110111	14	B/3	1111111111010010	19
3/4	1111111110010000	20	B/4	1111111111010011	20
3/5	1111111110010001	21	B/5	1111111111010100	21
3/6	1111111110010010	22	B/6	1111111111010101	22
3/7	1111111110010011	23	B/7	1111111111010110	23
3/8	1111111110010100	24	B/8	1111111111010111	24
3/9	1111111110010101	25	B/9	1111111111011000	25
3/A	1111111110010110	26	B/A	1111111111011001	26

Table 6.16 **Continued**

Run/Category	Base Code	Length	Run/Category	Base Code	Length
4/1	111011	7	C/1	1111111010	11
4/2	1111111000	12	C/2	1111111111011010	18
4/3	1111111110010111	19	C/3	1111111111011011	19
4/4	1111111110011000	20	C/4	1111111111011100	20
4/5	1111111110011001	21	C/5	1111111111011101	21
4/6	1111111110011010	22	C/6	1111111111011110	22
4/7	1111111110011011	23	C/7	1111111111011111	23
4/8	1111111110011100	24	C/8	1111111111100000	24
4/9	1111111110011101	25	C/9	1111111111100001	25
4/A	1111111110011110	26	C/A	1111111111100010	26
5/1	1111010	8	D/1	11111111010	12
5/2	1111111001	12	D/2	1111111111100011	18
5/3	1111111110011111	19	D/3	1111111111100100	19
5/4	1111111110100000	20	D/4	1111111111100101	20
5/5	1111111110100001	21	D/5	1111111111100110	21
5/6	1111111110100010	22	D/6	1111111111100111	22
5/7	1111111110100011	23	D/7	1111111111101000	23
5/8	1111111110100100	24	D/8	1111111111101001	24
5/9	1111111110100101	25	D/9	1111111111101010	25
5/A	1111111110100110	26	D/A	1111111111101011	26
6/1	1111011	8	E/1	11111110110	13
6/2	11111111000	13	E/2	1111111111101100	18
6/3	1111111110100111	19	E/3	1111111111101101	19
6/4	1111111110101000	20	E/4	1111111111101110	20
6/5	1111111110101001	21	E/5	1111111111101111	21
6/6	1111111110101010	22	E/6	1111111111110000	22
6/7	1111111110101011	23	E/7	1111111111110001	23
6/8	1111111110101100	24	E/8	1111111111110010	24
6/9	1111111110101101	25	E/9	1111111111110011	25
6/A	1111111110101110	26	E/A	1111111111110100	26
7/1	11111001	9	**F/0**	**11111110111**	**12**
7/2	11111111001	13	F/1	1111111111110101	17
7/3	1111111110101111	19	F/2	1111111111110110	18
7/4	1111111110110000	20	F/3	1111111111110111	19
7/5	1111111110110001	21	F/4	1111111111111000	20
7/6	1111111110110010	22	F/5	1111111111111001	21
7/7	1111111110110011	23	F/6	1111111111111010	22
7/8	1111111110110100	24	F/7	1111111111111011	23
7/9	1111111110110101	25	F/8	1111111111111100	24
7/A	1111111110110110	26	F/9	1111111111111101	25
			F/A	1111111111111110	26

which, when transformed in accordance with the forward DCT of Eq. (3.5-48) for $N = 8$, becomes

$$
\begin{array}{rrrrrrrr}
-415 & -29 & -62 & 25 & 55 & -20 & -1 & 3 \\
7 & -21 & -62 & 9 & 11 & -7 & -6 & 6 \\
-46 & 8 & 77 & -25 & -30 & 10 & 7 & -5 \\
-50 & 13 & 35 & -15 & -9 & 6 & 0 & 3 \\
11 & -8 & -13 & -2 & -1 & 1 & -4 & 1 \\
-10 & 1 & 3 & -3 & -1 & 0 & 2 & -1 \\
-4 & -1 & 2 & -1 & 2 & -3 & 1 & -2 \\
-1 & -1 & -1 & -2 & -1 & -1 & 0 & -1
\end{array}
$$

If the JPEG recommended normalization array of Fig. 6.35(b) is used to quantize the transformed array, the scaled and truncated (that is, normalized in accordance with Eq. 6.5-30) coefficients are

$$
\begin{array}{rrrrrrrr}
-26 & -3 & -6 & 2 & 2 & 0 & 0 & 0 \\
1 & -2 & -4 & 0 & 0 & 0 & 0 & 0 \\
-3 & 1 & 5 & -1 & -1 & 0 & 0 & 0 \\
-4 & 1 & 2 & -1 & 0 & 0 & 0 & 0 \\
1 & 0 & 0 & 0 & 0 & 0 & 0 & 0 \\
0 & 0 & 0 & 0 & 0 & 0 & 0 & 0 \\
0 & 0 & 0 & 0 & 0 & 0 & 0 & 0 \\
0 & 0 & 0 & 0 & 0 & 0 & 0 & 0
\end{array}
$$

where, for instance, the DC coefficient is computed as

$$
\hat{T}(0, 0) = \text{round} \left[\frac{T(0, 0)}{Z(0, 0)} \right]
$$

$$
= \text{round} \left[\frac{-415}{16} \right] = -26.
$$

Note that the transformation and normalization process produces a large number of zero-valued coefficients. When the coefficients are reordered in accordance with the zigzag ordering pattern of Fig. 6.34(d), the resulting 1-D coefficient sequence is

$$[-26 \quad -3 \quad 1 \quad -3 \quad -2 \quad -6 \quad 2 \quad -4 \quad 1 \quad -4 \quad 1 \quad 1 \quad 5 \quad 0 \quad 2 \quad 0$$
$$0 \quad -1 \quad 2 \quad 0 \quad 0 \quad 0 \quad 0 \quad 0 \quad -1 \quad -1 \quad \text{EOB}]$$

where the EOB symbol denotes the end-of-block condition. A special EOB Huffman code word (see category 0 and run-length 0 in Table 6.16) is provided to indicate that the remainder of the coefficients in a reordered sequence are zeros.

The construction of the default JPEG code for the reordered coefficient sequence begins with the computation of the difference between the current DC coefficient and that of the previously encoded subimage. As the subimage here was taken from Fig. 6.23 and the DC coefficient of the transformed and quantized subimage to its immediate left was -17, the resulting DPCM difference is $[-26 - (-17)]$ or -9, which lies in DC difference category 4 of Table 6.14. In accordance with the default Huffman difference code of Table 6.15, the proper base code for a category 4 difference is 101 (a 3-bit code), while the total length of a completely encoded category 4 coefficient is 7 bits. The remaining 4 bits must be generated from the least significant bits (LSBs) of the difference value. For a general DC difference category (say, category K), an additional K bits are needed and computed as either the K LSBs of the positive difference or the K LSBs of the negative difference minus 1. For a difference of -9, the appropriate LSBs are $(0111) - 1$ or 0110, and the complete DPCM coded DC code word is 1010110.

The nonzero AC coefficients of the reordered array are coded similarly from Tables 6.14 and 6.16. The principal difference is that each default AC Huffman code word depends on the number of zero-valued coefficients preceding the nonzero coefficient to be coded, as well as the magnitude category of the nonzero coefficient. (See the column labeled Run/Category in Table 6.16.) Thus the first nonzero AC coefficient of the reordered array (-3) is coded as 0100. The first 2 bits of this code indicate that the coefficient was in magnitude category 2 and preceded by no zero-valued coefficients (see Table 6.14); the last 2 bits are generated by the same process used to arrive at the LSBs of the DC difference code. Continuing in this manner, the completely coded (reordered) array is

1010110 0100 001 0100 0101 100001 0110 100011 001 100011 001

001 100101 11100110 110110 0110 11110100 000 1010

where the spaces have been inserted solely for readability. Although it was not needed in this example, the default JPEG code contains a special code word for a run of 15 zeros followed by a zero (see category 0 and run-length F in Table 6.16). The total number of bits in the completely coded reordered array (and thus the number of bits required to represent the entire 8×8, 8-bit subimage of this example) is 92. The resulting compression ratio is 512/92, or about 5.6:1.

To decompress a JPEG compressed subimage, the decoder must first re-create the normalized transform coefficients that led to the compressed bit stream. Because a Huffman coded binary sequence is instantaneous and uniquely decodable, this step is easily accomplished in a simple lookup table manner. Here the regenerated array of quantized coefficients is

-26	-3	-6	2	2	0	0	0
1	-2	-4	0	0	0	0	0
-3	1	5	-1	-1	0	0	0
-4	1	2	-1	0	0	0	0
1	0	0	0	0	0	0	0
0	0	0	0	0	0	0	0
0	0	0	0	0	0	0	0
0	0	0	0	0	0	0	0

After denormalization in accordance with Eq. (6.5-32), the array becomes

-416	-33	-60	32	48	0	0	0
12	-24	-56	0	0	0	0	0
-42	13	80	-24	-40	0	0	0
-56	17	44	-29	0	0	0	0
18	0	0	0	0	0	0	0
0	0	0	0	0	0	0	0
0	0	0	0	0	0	0	0
0	0	0	0	0	0	0	0

where, for example, the DC coefficient is computed as

$$\dot{T}(0, 0) = \hat{T}(0, 0) \, Z(0, 0) = (-26)(16) = -416.$$

The completely reconstructed subimage is obtained by taking the inverse DCT of the denormalized array in accordance with Eq. (3.5-49) to obtain

-70	-64	-61	-64	-69	-66	-58	-50
-72	-73	-61	-39	-30	-40	-54	-59
-68	-78	-58	-9	13	-12	-48	-64
-59	-77	-57	0	22	-13	-51	-60
-54	-75	-64	-23	-13	-44	-63	-56
-52	-71	-72	-54	-54	-71	-71	-54
-45	-59	-70	-68	-67	-67	-61	-50
-35	-47	-61	-66	-60	-48	-44	-44

and level shifting each inverse transformed pixel by $+2^7$ (or $+128$) to yield

58	64	67	64	59	62	70	78
56	55	67	89	98	88	74	69
60	50	70	119	141	116	80	64
69	51	71	128	149	115	77	68
74	53	64	105	115	84	65	72
76	57	56	74	75	57	57	74
83	69	59	60	61	61	67	78
93	81	67	62	69	80	84	84

Any differences between the original and reconstructed subimage are a result of the lossy nature of the JPEG compression and decompression process. In this example, the errors range from -14 to $+11$ and are distributed as follows:

-6	-9	-6	2	11	-1	-6	-5
7	4	-1	1	11	-3	-5	3
2	9	-2	-6	-3	-12	-14	9
-6	7	0	-4	-5	-9	-7	1
-7	8	4	-1	11	4	3	-2
3	8	4	-4	2	11	1	1
2	2	5	-1	-6	0	-2	5
-6	-2	2	6	-4	-4	-6	10

The root-mean-square error of the overall compression and reconstruction process is approximately 5.9 gray levels.   ❏

The reconstructed subimage in the preceding example is located physically at about the center of the woman's right eye in Fig. 6.36(a). Note that both the original subimage and reconstructed result contain a local gray-level peak in the fourth row and fifth column, where a light is reflected in the woman's pupil. This local peak causes the root-mean-square error of the reconstructed subimage to exceed substantially the overall error of the completely decompressed image. In fact, it is approximately twice as great as the error associated with Fig. 6.36(a), which also was compressed with the baseline JPEG algorithm. The reason is that many of the subimages of the original image are nearly constant and can be represented with little distortion. Additional JPEG results are provided in Fig. 6.36(b) and Plate X. In Plate X, a full color original and a 66:1 JPEG compressed result are shown. Note the slight blocking effect in the pink drapes and the ringing in some of the white roses against the black background. These effects are virtually imperceptible when the compression is less than 25:1.

Sequential frame monochrome and color compression
The only formally adopted standard for compression and decompression of sequential frame imagery is the H.261 (also referred to as $P \times 64$) standard of the CCITT. Two additional standards, called MPEG I and MPEG II, are being developed by the Motion Picture Experts Group of the CCITT and ISO.

The H.261 standard is intended for video teleconferencing applications, where full motion video is to be transmitted over T1 lines[†] with transmission delays of less than 150 msec. (Delays exceeding 150 msec do not provide viewers the "feeling" of direct visual feedback.) By contrast, the proposed MPEG I standard is an "entertainment quality" video compression standard for the storage and retrieval of compressed imagery on digital media, such as a compact disk read-only-memory (CD-ROM). Although the transfer rates of today's CD-ROMs are about the same as T1 transmission lines, the MPEG I standard is written to allow higher bit rates and higher quality encoding. It does not, however, specify a particular encoding procedure; it merely defines a standard encoded bit stream and corresponding decoder. The MPEG II standard supports video transfer rates between 5 and 10 Mbit/s, a range which is suitable for cable TV distribution and narrow-channel satellite broadcasting.

Both MPEG standards and H.261 extend the DCT-based compression approach described in the preceding section to include methods for reducing frame-to-frame redundancies. They first compress a starting or reference frame

---

[†] The T1 line was introduced by the Bell System for digital voice communications over short distances of 10 to 50 miles. Twenty-four telephone channels are time-multiplexed, sampled, and coded into a 1.544 Mbit/s PCM (pulse code modulation) signal for transmission over a single T1 line.

using a JPEG-like DCT-based approach, reconstruct the compressed frame, estimate the motion of objects between the reconstructed frame and the next frame, and decide, based on the amount of motion, whether to compress the next frame independently or by using references to the previously coded frame. The motion estimation step typically involves sliding each reconstructed sub-image around its immediate neighborhood in the next frame and computing a measure of correlation (such as the sum of the square of the pixel-by-pixel differences). In fact, this process is often carried out in subpixel increments (such as sliding the subimage $\frac{1}{4}$ pixels at a time), which necessitates interpolating pixel values prior to computing the correlation measure. The overall process can be computationally intense. Because the MPEG standard is intended for applications in which many rapid scene changes may occur, it specifically requires that every 15th frame be encoded without reference to any preceding frames. This requirement also is helpful in video editing applications. The principal difference between MPEG and H.261 is the manner in which motion estimation is handled. The H.261 standard specifies that each frame be compared to a single preceding frame, whereas the proposed MPEG standard does not define the number of frames that may be used in the motion estimation process.

6.7 CONCLUDING REMARKS

The principal objectives of this chapter were to present the theoretic foundation of digital image compression and to describe the most commonly used compression methods that form the core of the technology as it exists currently. Although the level of the presentation is introductory in nature, the depth and breadth of the material covered is sufficient to serve as the basis for independent reading in this subject area. The references provide an entry into the extensive body of literature dealing with image compression and related topics. In addition to extensive uses involving gray-scale imagery, compression methods are playing an increasingly important role in document image storage and transmission, as evidenced by the emergence of the international standards discussed in Section 6.6. In addition to medical imaging, compression is one of the few areas of image processing that has received a sufficiently broad commercial appeal to warrant the adoption of widely accepted standards.

REFERENCES

The introductory material of the chapter, which is generally confined to Sections 6.1 and 6.2, is basic to image compression and may be found in one form or another in most of the general image processing books cited at the end of Chapter 1. The material in Section 6.1.3

on improved gray-scale quantization is based on Bisignani, Richards, and Whelan [1966]. For additional information on the human visual system, see Netravali and Limb [1981], as well as in Huang [1966], Schreiber and Knapp [1958], and the references cited at the end of Chapter 2. Subjective fidelity criteria are discussed in Frendendall and Behrend [1960]. Error detecting and correcting codes are covered in most introductory texts on switching or finite automata theory, as well as in general information theory texts.

The material in Section 6.3 is based on several excellent books on information theory. Noteworthy are Abramson [1963], Blahut [1987], and Berger [1971]. Shannon's classic paper, "A Mathematical Theory of Communication" [1948], lays the foundation for most of the material in the section and is another excellent reference.

The descriptions of the error-free encoding techniques of Section 6.4 are, for the most part, based on the original papers cited in the text or as follows. The algorithms covered are representative of the work in this area, but are by no means exhaustive. Related methods of potential interest include the work of Ziv and Lempel [1977, 1978] and Welch [1984], which are unique in the sense that the code is constructed as the data is being coded. The material on arithmetic coding follows the development in Witten, Neal, and Cleary [1987]. One of the more important implementations of arithmetic coding is summarized in Pennebaker et al. [1988]. For additional information on bit-plane coding, see Schwartz and Barker [1966] and the tutorial by Rabbani and Jones [1991], which also contains a good discussion of lossless predictive coding. Huang and Hussian [1975] first published the details of white-block skipping. Relative address coding and predictive differential quantizing were first reported by Yamazaki, Wakahara, and Teramura [1976] and Huang [1972], respectively. The adaptive predictor of Eq. (6.5-19) is from Graham [1958].

The material in Section 6.5 covers the two principal lossy encoding approaches. Various other methods are directly based on these two techniques. Noteworthy among them are *hybrid encoding* (Habibi [1974]), a scheme that combines 1-D transform coding and DPCM to obtain about the same performance as 2-D transform coding using fewer computations; *subband coding* (Woods and O'Neil [1986]), in which an image is filtered into a set of images (with different spatial frequencies) that may be individually DPCM coded; and *interframe coding* (Roese et al. [1977]), where the redundancy between successive frames in a time sequence of images is reduced by using a predictive or transform coding approach. In addition, a variety of lossy techniques are closely related to the two techniques described. These include, among others, *block truncation coding* (Delp and Mitchell [1979]), in which a 1-bit quantizer is designed for each $n \times n$ block of a subdivided image; *vector quantization* (Linde et al. [1980]), in which an image is decomposed into vectors (containing pixels, transform coefficients, and so on) that are matched against a codebook of possible vectors and coded to indicate the best fit; and *hierarchical coding* (Knowlton [1980]), which usually involves the generation of a pyramid-structured data set that can be progressively accessed to obtain better and better representations of the original image. These references do not necessarily cite the inventor of the techniques; they provide a starting point for additional reading on the methods. Other articles of interest include Tasto and Wintz [1971], Gharavi and Tabatabai [1988], Baylon and Lim [1990], Candy et al. [1971], Jain and Jain [1981], Healy and Mitchell [1981], Lema and Mitchell [1984], Udpikar and Raina [1987], Gray [1984], Equitz [1989], Sezan et al. [1989], Tanimoto [1979], Blume and Fand [1989], and Rabbani and Jones [1991].

Section 6.6 is based on the published drafts and formal standards of the International Standards Organization and the Consultative Committee of International Telephone and Telegraph. These documents are available from these standards organizations or the American National Standards Institute (ANSI). Additional references on compression standards include Hunter and Robinson [1980], Ang et al. [1991], and Fox [1991].

Several survey articles have been devoted to the field of image compression. Noteworthy are Netravali and Limb [1980], Jain [1981], a special issue on picture communication systems in the *IEEE Transactions on Communications* [1981], a special issue on the encoding of graphics in the *Proceedings of IEEE* [1980], and a special issue on visual communication systems in the *Proceedings of the IEEE* [1985]. The papers in *Proceedings of DCC '91* (J. A. Storer, J. H. Reif, Editors) [1991] are representative of the most recent work in the field.

PROBLEMS

6.1 a) Can variable-length coding procedures be used to compress a histogram equalized image with 2^n gray levels? Explain.

b) Can such an image contain interpixel redundancies that could be exploited for data compression?

6.2 One variation of the run-length coding procedure described in Section 6.1.2 involves (1) coding only the runs of 0s or 1s (not both) and (2) assigning a special code to the start of each line to reduce the effect of transmission errors. One possible code pair is (x_k, r_k), where x_k and r_k represent the kth run's starting coordinate and run length, respectively. The code $(0, 0)$ is used to signal each new line.

a) Derive a general expression for the maximum average runs per scan line required to guarantee data compression when run-length coding a $2^n \times 2^n$ binary image.

b) Compute the maximum allowable value for $n = 1024$.

6.3 Consider an 8-pixel line of gray-scale data, {12, 12, 13, 13, 10, 13, 57, 54}, which has been uniformly quantized with 6-bit accuracy. Construct its 3-bit IGS code.

6.4 Compute the rms error and rms signal-to-noise ratios for the decoded IGS data of Problem 6.3.

6.5 a) Use the Hamming (7,4) code to code the IGS quantized data of Table 6.2.

b) Determine which bit, if any, is in error in the Hamming encoded messages 1100111, 1100110, and 1100010. What are the decoded values?

6.6 The base e unit of information is commonly called a *nat*, and the base 10 information unit is called a *Hartley*. Compute the conversion factors needed to relate these units to the base 2 unit of information (the bit).

6.7 Prove that, for a zero-memory source with q symbols, the maximum value of the entropy is log q, which is achieved if and only if all source symbols are equiprobable. *Hint*: Consider the quantity log $q - H(\mathbf{z})$ and note the inequality $\ln x \le x - 1$.

6.8 Calculate the various probabilities associated with the information channel in which
$A = \{0, 1\}$, $B = \{0, 1\}$, $\mathbf{z} = [0.75, 0.25]^T$, and

$$
\mathbf{Q} = \begin{bmatrix} \dfrac{2}{3} & \dfrac{1}{3} \\[2mm] \dfrac{1}{10} & \dfrac{9}{10} \end{bmatrix}
$$

Include $P(a = 0)$, $P(a = 1)$, $P(b = 0)$, $P(b = 1)$, $P(b = 0|a = 0)$, $P(b = 0|a = 1)$, $P(b = 1|a = 0)$, $P(b = 1|a = 1)$, $P(a = 0|b = 0)$, $P(a = 0|b = 1)$, $P(a = 1|b = 0)$, $P(a = 1|b = 1)$, $P(a = 0, b = 0)$, $P(a = 0, b = 1)$, $P(a = 1, b = 0)$, and $P(a = 1, b = 1)$.

6.9 Consider the binary information source and BSC of the example in Section 6.3.2 and let $p_{bs} = \frac{3}{4}$ and $p_e = \frac{1}{3}$.
a) What is the entropy of the source?
b) How much less uncertainty about the input is there when the output has been observed?
c) What is this difference in uncertainty called and how does it compare numerically to the channel's capacity?

6.10 A *binary erasure channel* is one in which there is a finite probability β that a transmitted symbol will not be received. The channel has three possible outputs: a 0, an erasure (no received symbol), and a 1. These three outcomes form the three rows of the binary erasure channel matrix

$$
\mathbf{Q} = \begin{bmatrix} 1\text{-}\beta & 0 \\ \beta & \beta \\ 0 & 1\text{-}\beta \end{bmatrix}
$$

a) Find the capacity of the channel.
b) Would you prefer a binary symmetric channel with a 0.125 probability of error or an erasure channel with probability of erasure $\beta = 0.5$?

6.11 The rate distortion function of a zero-memory Gaussian source of arbitrary mean and variance σ^2 with respect to the mean-square error criterion (Berger [1971]) is

$$
R(D) = \begin{cases} \dfrac{1}{2} \log \dfrac{\sigma^2}{D} & \text{for } 0 \le D \le \sigma^2 \\[3mm] 0 & \text{for } D \ge \sigma^2. \end{cases}
$$

a) Plot this function.

b) What is D_{max}?

c) If a distortion of no more than 75 percent of the source's variance is allowed, what is the maximum compression that can be achieved?

6.12 a) How many unique Huffman codes are there for a three symbol source?

b) Construct them.

6.13 a) Compute the entropy of the source whose symbol probabilities are defined in Table 6.1.

b) Construct a Huffman code for the source symbols and explain any differences between the constructed code and Code 2 of the table.

c) Construct the best B_1-code for this distribution.

d) Construct the best 2-bit binary shift code.

e) Divide the symbols into two blocks of four and construct the best Huffman shift code.

f) Compute the average word lengths for each code and compare them to the entropy from part (a).

6.14 The arithmetic decoding process is the reverse of the encoding procedure. Decode the message 0.23355 given the coding model

Symbol	Probability
a	0.2
e	0.3
i	0.1
o	0.2
u	0.1
!	0.1

6.15 a) Construct the entire 4-bit Gray code.

b) Create a general procedure for converting a Gray coded number to its binary equivalent and use it to decode 0111010100111.

6.16 A 64 × 64 pixel binary image has been coded using 1-D WBS with blocks of four pixels. The WBS code for one line of the image was 01100100000010000010010000000, where a 0 is used to represent a black pixel.

a) Decode the line.

b) Create a 1-D iterative WBS procedure that begins by looking for all white lines (a 64-pixel block) and successively halves nonwhite intervals until four pixel blocks are reached.

c) Use your algorithm to code the previously decoded line. It should require fewer bits.

6.17 a) Explain why the first similar transition past e on the previous line is used as c' in relative address coding.

b) Can you devise an alternate approach?

6.18 An image whose autocorrelation function is of the form of Eq. (6.5-12) with $\rho_h = 0$ is to be DPCM coded using a second-order predictor.

a) Form the autocorrelation matrix $\mathbf{R}$ and vector $\mathbf{r}$.

b) Find the optimal prediction coefficients.

c) Compute the variance of the prediction error that would result from using the optimal coefficients.

6.19 Derive the Lloyd–Max decision and reconstruction levels for $L = 4$ and the uniform probability density function

$$p(s) = \begin{cases} \dfrac{1}{2A} & -A \le s \le A \\ 0 & \text{otherwise.} \end{cases}$$

6.20 Use the CCITT Group 4 compression algorithm to code the second line of the following two-line segment:

```
0 1 1 0 0 1 1 1 0 0 1 1 1 1 1 1 1 1 0 0 0 0 1
1 1 1 1 1 1 1 0 0 0 1 1 1 0 0 0 0 1 1 1 1 1 1
```

Assume that the initial reference element a_0 is located on the first pixel of the second line segment.

6.21 a) List all the members of the JPEG DC coefficient difference category 3.

b) Compute their default Huffman codes using Table 6.15.

6.22 A radiologist from a well-known research hospital recently attended a medical conference at which a system that could transmit 4096×4096 12-bit digitized x-ray images over standard T1 phone lines was exhibited. The system transmitted the images in a compressed form using a *progressive* technique in which a reasonably good approximation of the x-ray was first reconstructed at the viewing station and then refined gradually to produce an error-free display. The transmission of the data needed to generate the first approximation took approximately 5 or 6 sec. Refinements were made every 5 or 6 sec (on the average) for the next 1 min, with the first and last refinements having the most and least significant impact on the reconstructed x-ray, respectively. The physician was favorably impressed with the system, because she could begin her diagnosis by using the first approximation of the x-ray and complete it as the error-free reconstruction of the x-ray was being generated. Upon returning to her office, she submitted a purchase request to the hospital administrator. Unfortunately, the hospital was on a relatively tight budget, which recently had been stretched thinner by the hiring of an aspiring young electrical engineering graduate. To appease the radiologist, the administrator gave the young engineer the task of designing such a system. (He thought it might be cheaper to design and build a similar system in-house. The hospital currently owned some of the elements of such a system, but the transmission of the raw x-ray data took more than 2 min.) The administrator asked the engineer to have an initial block diagram by the afternoon staff meeting. With little time and only a copy of *Digital Image Processing* (this text, of course) from his recent school days in hand, the engineer was able to devise conceptually a system to satisfy the transmission and associated compression requirements. Construct a conceptual block diagram of such a system, specifying the compression techniques you would recommend.

CHAPTER 7

IMAGE SEGMENTATION

The whole is equal to the sum of its parts.
Euclid

The whole is greater than the sum of its parts.
Max Wertheimer

In the first six chapters we proceeded from background material in Chapters 1–3 to a detailed accounting of image processing techniques in Chapters 4–6, which we classified as preprocessing methods. The final group of chapters in this book deals with techniques for extracting information from an image. We refer to this area of processing as *image analysis.*

The first step in image analysis generally is to segment the image. Segmentation subdivides an image into its constituent parts or objects. The level to which this subdivision is carried depends on the problem being solved. That is, segmentation should stop when the objects of interest in an application have been isolated. For example, in autonomous air-to-ground target acquisition applications, interest lies, among other things, in identifying vehicles on a road. The first step is to segment the road from the image and then to segment the contents of the road down to objects of a range of sizes that correspond to potential vehicles. There is no point in carrying segmentation below this scale, nor is there any need to attempt segmentation of image components that lie outside the boundaries of the road.

In general, autonomous segmentation is one of the most difficult tasks in image processing. This step in the process determines the eventual success or failure of the analysis. In fact, effective segmentation rarely fails to lead to a successful solution. For this reason, considerable care should be taken to improve the probability of rugged segmentation. In some situations, such as industrial inspection applications, at least some measure of control over the environment is possible at times. The experienced image processing system designer invariably pays considerable attention to such opportunities. In other applications, such as target acquisition, the system designer has no control of the environment. Then, the usual approach is to focus on selecting the types of sensors most likely to enhance the objects of interest while diminishing the contribution of irrelevant image components. A good example is the use of infrared imaging to detect objects with a strong heat signature, such as tanks in motion.

Segmentation algorithms for monochrome images generally are based on one of two basic properties of gray-level values: discontinuity and similarity. In the first category, the approach is to partition an image based on abrupt changes in gray level. The principal areas of interest within this category are detection of isolated points and detection of lines and edges in an image. The principal approaches in the second category are based on thresholding, region growing, and region splitting and merging. The concept of segmenting an image based on discontinuity or similarity of the gray-level values of its pixels is applicable to both static and dynamic (time varying) images. In the latter case, however, motion can often be used as a powerful cue to improve the performance of segmentation algorithms.

7.1 DETECTION OF DISCONTINUITIES

In this section we present several techniques for detecting the three basic types of discontinuities in a digital image: points, lines, and edges. In practice, the most common way to look for discontinuities is to run a mask through the image in the manner described in Section 4.1. For the 3×3 mask shown in Fig. 7.1, this procedure involves computing the sum of products of the coefficients with the gray levels contained in the region encompassed by the mask. That is, the response of the mask at any point in the image is

$$R = w_1 z_1 + w_2 z_2 + \cdots + w_9 z_9 \qquad (7.1\text{-}1)$$

$$= \sum_{i=1}^{9} w_i z_i$$

w_1'	w_2'	w_3'
w_4'	w_5'	w_6'
w_7'	w_8'	w_9'

Figure 7.1   *A general 3 × 3 mask.*

-1	-1	-1
-1	8	-1
-1	-1	-1

Figure 7.2 *A mask used for detecting isolated points different from a constant background.*

where z_i is the gray level of the pixel associated with mask coefficient w_i. As usual, the response of the mask is defined with respect to its center location. When the mask is centered on a boundary pixel, the response is computed by using the appropriate partial neighborhood.

7.1.1 Point Detection

The detection of isolated points in an image is straightforward. Using the mask shown in Fig. 7.2, we say that a point has been detected at the location on which the mask is centered if

$$|R| > T \tag{7.1-2}$$

where T is a nonnegative threshold, and R is given by Eq. (7.1-1). Basically, all that this formulation does is measure the weighted differences between the center point and its neighbors. The idea is that the gray level of an isolated point will be quite different from the gray level of its neighbors.

The mask in Fig. 7.2 is the same as the mask used for high-frequency spatial filtering (see Fig. 4.24). The emphasis here, however, is strictly on the detection of points. That is, only differences that are large enough (as determined by T) to be considered isolated points in an image are of interest.

7.1.2 Line Detection

The next level of complexity involves the detection of lines in an image. Consider the masks shown in Fig. 7.3. If the first mask were moved around an image, it would respond more strongly to lines (one pixel thick) oriented horizontally. With constant background, the maximum response would result when the line passed through the middle row of the mask. This is easily verified by sketching a simple array of 1's with a line of a different gray level (say, 5's) running horizontally through the array. A similar experiment would reveal that the second mask in Fig. 7.3 responds best to lines oriented at 45°; the third mask to vertical lines; and the fourth mask to lines in the $-45°$ direction. These directions can also be established by noting that the preferred direction of each

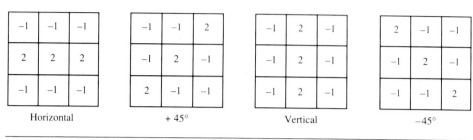

-1	-1	-1
2	2	2
-1	-1	-1

Horizontal

-1	-1	2
-1	2	-1
2	-1	-1

+ 45°

-1	2	-1
-1	2	-1
-1	2	-1

Vertical

2	-1	-1
-1	2	-1
-1	-1	2

-45°

Figure 7.3   *Line masks.*

mask is weighted with a larger coefficient (that is, 2) than other possible directions.

Let R_1, R_2, R_3, and R_4 denote the responses of the masks in Fig. 7.3, from left to right, where the R's are given by Eq. (7.1-1). Suppose that all masks are run through an image. If, at a certain point in the image, $|R_i| > |R_j|$, for all $j \neq i$, that point is said to be more likely associated with a line in the direction of mask i. For example, if at a point in the image, $|R_1| > |R_j|$, for $j = 2, 3, 4$, that particular point is said to be more likely associated with a horizontal line.

7.1.3   Edge Detection

Although point and line detection certainly are elements of any discussion on segmentation, edge detection is by far the most common approach for detecting meaningful discontinuities in gray level. The reason is that isolated points and thin lines are not frequent occurrences in most practical applications.

Basic formulation

An edge is the boundary between two regions with relatively distinct gray-level properties. In the following discussion, the assumption is that the regions in question are sufficiently homogeneous so that the transition between two regions can be determined on the basis of gray-level discontinuities alone. When this assumption is not valid, the segmentation techniques discussed in Section 7.3 or 7.4 generally are more applicable than edge detection.

Basically, the idea underlying most edge-detection techniques is the computation of a local derivative operator. Figure 7.4 illustrates this concept. Figure 7.4(a) shows an image of a light stripe on a dark background, the gray-level profile along a horizontal scan line of the image, and the first and second derivatives of the profile. Note from the profile that an edge (transition from dark to light) is modeled as a smooth, rather than as an abrupt, change of gray level. This model reflects the fact that edges in digital images are generally slightly blurred as a result of sampling.

Figure 7.4(a) shows that the first derivative of the gray-level profile is positive at the leading edge of a transition, negative at the trailing edge, and, as expected, zero in areas of constant gray level. The second derivative is

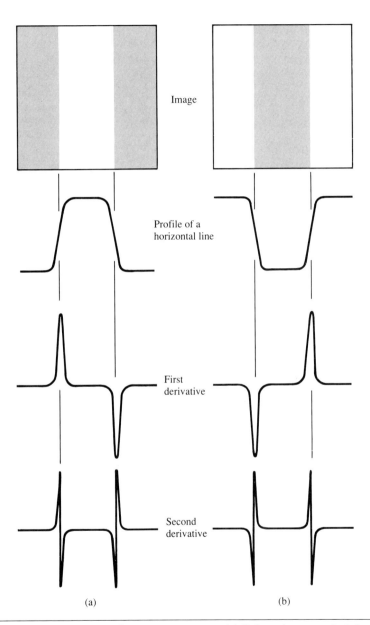

Figure 7.4 *Edge detection by derivative operators: (a) light stripe on a dark background; (b) dark stripe on a light background. Note that the second derivative has a zero crossing at the location of each edge.*

positive for that part of the transition associated with the dark side of the edge, negative for that part of the transition associated with the light side of the edge, and zero in areas of constant gray level. Hence the magnitude of the first derivative can be used to detect the presence of an edge in an image, and the sign of the second derivative can be used to determine whether an edge pixel lies on the dark or light side of an edge. Note that the second derivative has a zero crossing at the midpoint of a transition in gray level. As shown later in this section zero crossings provide a powerful approach for locating edges in an image.

Although the discussion so far has been limited to a 1-D horizontal profile, a similar argument applies to an edge of any orientation in an image. We simply define a profile perpendicular to the edge direction at any desired point and interpret the results as in the preceding discussion. The first derivative at any point in an image is obtained by using the magnitude of the gradient at that point. The second derivative is similarly obtained by using the Laplacian.

Gradient operators

In Section 4.3.3 we introduced briefly the concept of using the gradient for image differentiation. From Eq. (4.3-5), the gradient of an image $f(x, y)$ at location (x, y) is the vector

$$\nabla \mathbf{f} = \begin{bmatrix} G_x \\ G_y \end{bmatrix} = \begin{bmatrix} \dfrac{\partial f}{\partial x} \\ \dfrac{\partial f}{\partial y} \end{bmatrix} \tag{7.1-3}$$

It is well known from vector analysis that the gradient vector points in the direction of maximum rate of change of f at (x, y). In edge detection an important quantity is the magnitude of this vector, generally referred to simply as the *gradient* and denoted ∇f, where:

$$\nabla f = \text{mag}(\nabla \mathbf{f}) = [G_x^2 + G_y^2]^{1/2}. \tag{7.1-4}$$

This quantity equals the maximum rate of increase of $f(x, y)$ per unit distance in the direction of $\nabla \mathbf{f}$. Common practice is to approximate the gradient with absolute values:

$$\nabla f \approx |G_x| + |G_y| \tag{7.1-5}$$

which is much simpler to implement, particularly with dedicated hardware.

The *direction* of the gradient vector also is an important quantity. Let $\alpha(x, y)$ represent the direction angle of the vector $\nabla \mathbf{f}$ at (x, y). Then, from vector analysis,

$$\alpha(x, y) = \tan^{-1}\left(\frac{G_y}{G_x}\right) \tag{7.1-6}$$

where the angle is measured with respect to the x axis.

Note from Eqs. (7.1-3) and (7.1-4) that computation of the gradient of an image is based on obtaining the partial derivatives $\partial f/\partial x$ and $\partial f/\partial y$ at every pixel location. As discussed in Section 4.3.3 (see Fig. 4.28), derivatives may be implemented in digital form in several ways. However, the Sobel operators have the advantage of providing both a differencing and a smoothing effect (see Problem 7.3). Because derivatives enhance noise, the smoothing effect is a particularly attractive feature of the Sobel operators. From Fig. 7.5, derivatives based on the Sobel operator masks are

$$G_x = (z_7 + 2z_8 + z_9) - (z_1 + 2z_2 + z_3) \tag{7.1-7}$$

and

$$G_y = (z_3 + 2z_6 + z_9) - (z_1 + 2z_4 + z_7) \tag{7.1-8}$$

where, as before, the z's are the gray levels of the pixels overlapped by the masks at any location in an image. Computation of the gradient at the location

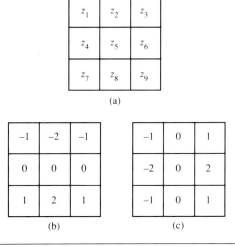

(a)

(b)

(c)

Figure 7.5   (a) 3 × 3 image region; (b) mask used to compute G_x at center point of the 3 × 3 region; (c) mask used to compute G_y at that point. These masks are often referred to as the Sobel operators.

of the center of the masks then utilizes Eq. (7.1-4) or (7.1-5), which gives one value of the gradient. To get the next value, the masks are moved to the next pixel location and the procedure is repeated. Thus, after the procedure has been completed for all possible locations, the result is a gradient image of the same size as the original image. As usual, mask operations on the border of an image are implemented by using the appropriate partial neighborhoods.

Example: Figure 7.6(a) shows an original image, and Fig. 7.6(b) shows the result of computing $|G_x|$ with the mask shown in Fig. 7.5(b). Recall that we defined the x axis to be in the vertical direction (see Fig. 1.5). Thus the strongest response produced by $|G_x|$ is expected to be on edges perpendicular to the x axis. This result is obvious in Fig. 7.6(b), which shows strong responses along horizontal edges, such as the river bank. Note also the relative lack of response along vertical edges. The reverse situation occurs upon computation of $|G_y|$, as Fig. 7.6(c) shows. Combining these two results via Eq. (7.1-5) yielded the gradient image shown in Fig. 7.6(d).   ❑

Laplacian
The Laplacian of a 2-D function $f(x, y)$ is a second-order derivative defined as

$$\nabla^2 f = \frac{\partial^2 f}{\partial x^2} + \frac{\partial^2 f}{\partial y^2}. \tag{7.1-9}$$

As in the case of the gradient, Eq. (7.1-9) may be implemented in digital form in various ways. For a 3×3 region, the form most frequently encountered in practice is

$$\nabla^2 f = 4z_5 - (z_2 + z_4 + z_6 + z_8) \tag{7.1-10}$$

where the z's have been defined already. The basic requirement in defining the digital Laplacian is that the coefficient associated with the center pixel be positive and the coefficients associated with the outer pixels be negative (see Fig. 7.8a). Because the Laplacian is a derivative, the sum of the coefficients has to be zero. Hence the response is zero whenever the point in question and its neighbors have the same value. Figure 7.7 shows a spatial mask that can be used to implement Eq. (7.1-10).

Although, as indicated earlier, the Laplacian responds to transitions in intensity, it is seldom used in practice for edge detection for several reasons. As a second-order derivative, the Laplacian typically is unacceptably sensitive to noise. Moreover, the Laplacian produces double edges (see Fig. 7.4) and is unable to detect edge direction. For these reasons, the Laplacian usually plays the secondary role of detector for establishing whether a pixel is on the dark or light side of an edge. We demonstrate the usefulness of this property in Section 7.3.5.

(a)

(b)

(c)

(d)

Figure 7.6 (a) Original image; (b) result of applying the mask in Fig. 7.5(b) to obtain G_x; (c) result of using the mask in Fig. 7.5(c) to obtain G_y; (d) complete gradient image obtained by using Eq. (7.1-5).

A more general use of the Laplacian is in finding the *location* of edges using its zero-crossings property (see Fig. 7.4). This concept is based on convolving an image with the Laplacian of a 2-D Gaussian function of the form

$$h(x, y) = \exp\left(-\frac{x^2 + y^2}{2\sigma^2}\right) \tag{7.1-11}$$

where σ is the standard deviation (Marr and Hildreth [1980]). Let $r^2 = x^2 + y^2$. Then, from Eq. (7.1-9) the Laplacian of h (that is, the second derivative of h with respect to r) is

$$\nabla^2 h = \left(\frac{r^2 - \sigma^2}{\sigma^4}\right) \exp\left(-\frac{r^2}{2\sigma^2}\right). \tag{7.1-12}$$

Figure 7.8(a) shows a cross section of this circularly symmetric function. Note the smoothness of the function, its zero crossings at $r = \pm\sigma$, and the positive center and negative skirts. This shape is the model upon which Eq. (7.1-10) and the mask in Fig. 7.7 are based. When viewed in 3-D perspective with the vertical axis corresponding to intensity, Eq. (7.1-12) has a classical Mexican hat shape. Figure 7.8(b) shows this representation, but in image form. It can be shown (Problem 7.6) that the average value of the Laplacian operator $\nabla^2 h$ is zero. The same is true of a Laplacian image obtained by convolving this operator with a given image.

The discussion of Fig. 4.33 indicates that convolving an image with a function of the form shown in Fig. 7.8(b) blurs the image, with the degree of blurring being proportional to σ. Although this property has value in terms of noise reduction, the usefulness of Eq. (7.1-12) lies in its zero crossings.

Example: Consider Fig. 7.9(a), which is a simple image of resolution 320 × 320 pixels. Figure 7.9(b) shows the result of convolving this image with the function $\nabla^2 h$. The value of σ in this case is 4. In this result black represents the most negative values, and white represents the most positive values; thus mid grays represent zeros. Figure 7.9(c) shows a binary image created by setting all negative values in Fig. 7.9(b) to black and all positive values to white. From

0	−1	0
−1	4	−1
0	−1	0

Figure 7.7 *Mask used to compute the Laplacian.*

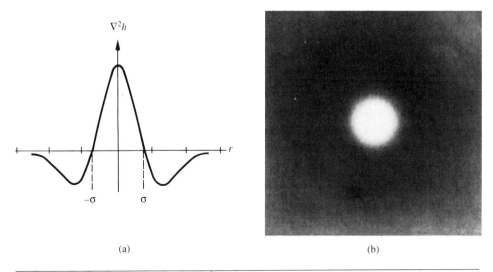

Figure 7.8 *(a) Cross section of $\nabla^2 h$; (b) $\nabla^2 h$ shown as an intensity function (image). (From Marr [1982].)*

this image identifying the zero crossings as the boundaries between black and white, as Fig. 7.9(d) shows, is a simple matter. Note that all principal edges in Fig. 7.9(a) are accurately located. ❑

The preceding discussion has one further implication: edge detection by gradient operations tends to work well in cases involving images with sharp intensity transitions and relatively low noise. Zero crossings offer an alternative in cases when edges are blurry or when a high noise content is present. The zero crossings offer reliable edge location, and the smoothing properties of $\nabla^2 h$ reduce the effects of noise. The price paid for these advantages is increased computational complexity and time.

7.1.4 Combined Detection

Using a multimask formulation makes possible development of a method to determine whether a pixel is most likely to be an isolated point or part of a line or an edge. The development becomes considerably more intuitive with use of a vector formulation. Let

$$\mathbf{w} = \begin{bmatrix} w_1 \\ w_2 \\ \vdots \\ w_9 \end{bmatrix} \qquad (7.1\text{-}13)$$

and

$$\mathbf{z} = \begin{bmatrix} z_1 \\ z_2 \\ \vdots \\ z_9 \end{bmatrix} \tag{7.1-14}$$

where w_i are the general coefficients of a 3×3 mask (see Fig. 7.1), and z_i are the corresponding gray levels, as discussed in Section 7.1.3. With this notation, the response of a mask in Eq. (7.1-1) is nothing more than the inner product of vectors $\mathbf{w}$ and $\mathbf{z}$. That is,

$$R = \sum_{i=1}^{9} w_i z_i$$
$$= \mathbf{w}^T \mathbf{z} \tag{7.1-15}$$

where the superscript T indicates vector transposition.

Let us assume for a moment that the masks have three, rather than nine, coefficients. In this case the vectors are 3-D and can be visualized without difficulty. Let us also assume that we have two masks designed to detect, say, edges and lines, and that the coefficients are such that the two corresponding vectors, denoted $\mathbf{w}_1$ and $\mathbf{w}_2$, are orthogonal and have unit length. In this case, the products $\mathbf{w}_1^T \mathbf{z}$ and $\mathbf{w}_2^T \mathbf{z}$ equal the projections of $\mathbf{z}$ onto the vectors $\mathbf{w}_1$ and $\mathbf{w}_2$, respectively. The reason is that, for $\mathbf{w}_1$,

$$\mathbf{w}_1^T \mathbf{z} = \|\mathbf{w}_1\| \, \|\mathbf{z}\| \cos \theta \tag{7.1-16}$$

where θ is the angle between the two vectors. But, as $\|\mathbf{w}_1\| = 1$,

$$\|\mathbf{z}\| \cos \theta = \mathbf{w}_1^T \mathbf{z} \tag{7.1-17}$$

which is the projection of $\mathbf{z}$ onto $\mathbf{w}_1$, as Fig. 7.10 shows. Similar comments apply to $\mathbf{w}_2$.

Now suppose that three orthogonal vectors of unit magnitude, $\mathbf{w}_1$, $\mathbf{w}_2$, and $\mathbf{w}_3$, correspond to three, 3-coefficient masks. The products $\mathbf{w}_1^T \mathbf{z}$, $\mathbf{w}_2^T \mathbf{z}$, and $\mathbf{w}_3^T \mathbf{z}$ represent the projections of $\mathbf{z}$ onto the vectors $\mathbf{w}_1$, $\mathbf{w}_2$, and $\mathbf{w}_3$. According to the above discussion, these products also represent the *individual* responses of the three masks. Suppose further that masks 1 and 2 are for lines and mask 3 is for edges. We want to answer the question: Is the region represented by $\mathbf{z}$ more like a line or more like an edge? Two masks represent lines but we are interested only in the line properties of $\mathbf{z}$, not the specific type of line present. Thus, we can answer the question by projecting $\mathbf{z}$ onto the subspace of $\mathbf{w}_1$ and

(a)

(b)

(c)

(d)

Figure 7.9 *(a) Original image; (b) result of convolving (a) with $\nabla^2 h$; (c) result of making (b) binary to simplify detection of zero crossings; (d) zero crossings. (From Marr [1982].)*

$\mathbf{w}_2$ (which in this case is a plane) and also onto $\mathbf{w}_3$. The angle between $\mathbf{z}$ and each of these two projections indicates whether $\mathbf{z}$ is closer to the line or the edge subspace. The geometric arrangement shown in Fig. 7.11 depicts this condition. The magnitude of the projection of $\mathbf{z}$ onto the plane determined by $\mathbf{w}_1$ and $\mathbf{w}_2$ is the quantity $[(\mathbf{w}_1^T\mathbf{z})^2 + (\mathbf{w}_2^T\mathbf{z})^2]^{1/2}$. The magnitude (norm) of $\mathbf{z}$ is

$$\|\mathbf{z}\| = [(\mathbf{w}_1^T\mathbf{z})^2 + (\mathbf{w}_2^T\mathbf{z})^2 + (\mathbf{w}_3^T\mathbf{z})^2]^{1/2}. \tag{7.1-18}$$

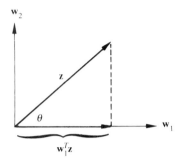

Figure 7.10   *Projection of* **z** *onto unit vector* **w**₁.

The angle between **z** and its projection onto this plane then is

$$\theta = \cos^{-1}\left\{\frac{[(\mathbf{w}_1^T\mathbf{z})^2 + (\mathbf{w}_2^T\mathbf{z})^2]^{1/2}}{[(\mathbf{w}_1^T\mathbf{z})^2 + (\mathbf{w}_2^T\mathbf{z})^2 + (\mathbf{w}_3^T\mathbf{z})^2]^{1/2}}\right\}$$

$$= \cos^{-1}\left\{\frac{\left[\sum_{i=1}^{2}(\mathbf{w}_i^T\mathbf{z})^2\right]^{1/2}}{\left[\sum_{j=1}^{3}(\mathbf{w}_j^T\mathbf{z})^2\right]^{1/2}}\right\} \tag{7.1-19}$$

$$= \cos^{-1}\left\{\frac{1}{\|\mathbf{z}\|}\left[\sum_{i=1}^{2}(\mathbf{w}_i^T\mathbf{z})^2\right]^{1/2}\right\}$$

where the last step follows from Eq. (7.1-18). A similar development would yield the angle of projection onto the **w**₃ subspace:

$$\phi = \cos^{-1}\left\{\frac{1}{\|\mathbf{z}\|}\left[\sum_{i=3}^{3}(\mathbf{w}_i^T\mathbf{z})^2\right]^{1/2}\right\} \tag{7.1-20}$$

$$= \cos^{-1}\left\{\frac{1}{\|\mathbf{z}\|}|\mathbf{w}_3^T\mathbf{z}|\right\}.$$

Thus, if $\theta < \phi$, the region represented by **z** is said to be closer to the characteristics of a line than of an edge.

For 3 × 3 masks, the problem becomes nine dimensional. The same concepts are still valid, but nine 9-D orthogonal vectors are needed to form a complete basis. The masks shown in Fig. 7.12 (proposed by Frei and Chen [1977]) satisfy this condition. The first four masks are suitable for detecting edges; the second set of four masks represents templates suitable for line detection; and the last mask (added to complete the bases) is proportional to the average of the pixels in the region at which the mask is located in an image.

For a 3×3 region represented by $\mathbf{z}$, and based on the assumption that the vectors $\mathbf{w}_i$, $i = 1, 2, \ldots, 9$, have been normalized, it follows from the preceding discussion that

$$p_e = \left[\sum_{i=1}^{4} (\mathbf{w}_i^T \mathbf{z})^2 \right]^{1/2} \tag{7.1-21}$$

$$p_l = \left[\sum_{i=5}^{8} (\mathbf{w}_i^T \mathbf{z})^2 \right]^{1/2} \tag{7.1-22}$$

and

$$p_a = \left| \mathbf{w}_9^T \mathbf{z} \right| \tag{7.1-23}$$

where p_e, p_l, and p_a are the magnitudes of the projections of $\mathbf{z}$ onto the edge, line, and average subspaces, respectively.

Similarly,

$$\theta_e = \cos^{-1} \left\{ \frac{1}{\|\mathbf{z}\|} \left[\sum_{i=1}^{4} (\mathbf{w}_i^T \mathbf{z})^2 \right]^{1/2} \right\} \tag{7.1-24}$$

$$\theta_l = \cos^{-1} \left\{ \frac{1}{\|\mathbf{z}\|} \left[\sum_{i=5}^{8} (\mathbf{w}_i^T \mathbf{z})^2 \right]^{1/2} \right\} \tag{7.1-25}$$

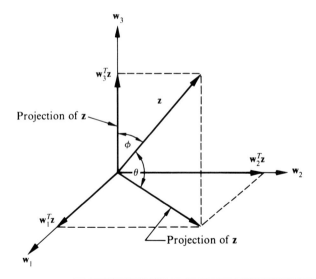

Figure 7.11 *Projections of* $\mathbf{z}$ *onto subspace (plane) determined by* $\mathbf{w}_1$ *and* $\mathbf{w}_2$, *and onto subspace* $\mathbf{w}_3$.

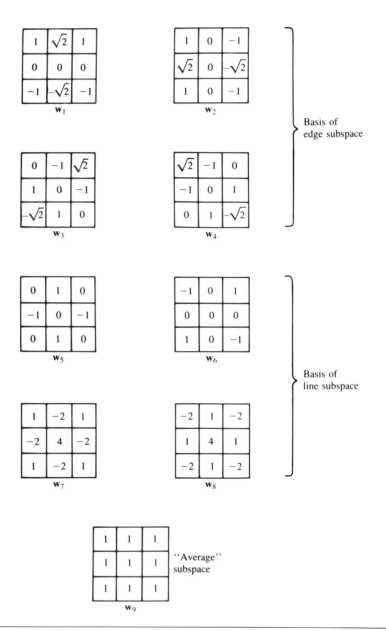

Figure 7.12   *Orthogonal masks (the **w**'s as shown are not normalized). (From Frei and Chen [1977].)*

and

$$\theta_a = \cos^{-1}\left\{\frac{1}{\|\mathbf{z}\|} \left|\mathbf{w}_9^T\mathbf{z}\right|\right\} \qquad (7.1\text{-}26)$$

where θ_e, θ_l and θ_a are the angles between $\mathbf{z}$ and its projections onto the edge, line, and average subspaces, respectively. These concepts, of course, can be extended directly to other bases and dimensions, as long as the basis vectors are orthogonal.

Example: The image shown in Fig. 7.13(a) is an aerial photograph of the site of a football stadium. Figures 7.13(b)–(j) show the magnitudes of the projections along the individual basis vectors obtained by using each of the masks in Fig. 7.12 and, for each position of the ith mask, computing a pixel value equal to $\left|\mathbf{w}_i^T\mathbf{z}\right|$. Figure 7.13(k) shows the magnitude of the projections onto the edge subspace [Eq. (7.1-21)], and Fig. 7.13(l) was formed from the magnitudes of the projections onto the line subspace [Eq. (7.1-22)]. In this example, the strongest responses were obtained with the edge subspace projections, indicating a strong edge content in the original image. ❏

7.2 EDGE LINKING AND BOUNDARY DETECTION ────────────

The techniques discussed in Section 7.1.4 detect intensity discontinuities. Ideally, these techniques should yield pixels lying only on the boundary between regions. In practice, this set of pixels seldom characterizes a boundary completely because of noise, breaks in the boundary from nonuniform illumination, and other effects that introduce spurious intensity discontinuities. Thus edge-detection algorithms typically are followed by linking and other boundary detection procedures designed to assemble edge pixels into meaningful boundaries. Several techniques are suited to this purpose.

7.2.1 Local Processing

One of the simplest approaches for linking edge points is to analyze the characteristics of pixels in a small neighborhood (say, 3×3 or 5×5) about every point (x, y) in an image that has undergone edge-detection. All points that are similar are linked, forming a boundary of pixels that share some common properties.

The two principal properties used for establishing similarity of edge pixels in this kind of analysis are (1) the strength of the response of the gradient operator used to produce the edge pixel, and (2) the direction of the gradient. The first property is given by the value of ∇f, as defined in Eq. (7.1-4) or (7.1-5). Thus an edge pixel with coordinates (x', y') and in the predefined

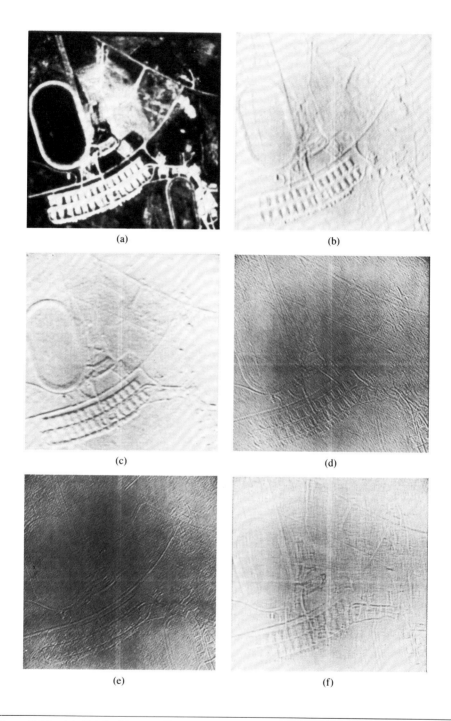

(a)

(b)

(c)

(d)

(e)

(f)

Figure 7.13 (a) Original image; (b)–(f) projections onto $\mathbf{w}_1$, $\mathbf{w}_2$, $\mathbf{w}_3$, $\mathbf{w}_4$, and $\mathbf{w}_5$ subspaces, respectively. (From Hall and Frei [1976].)

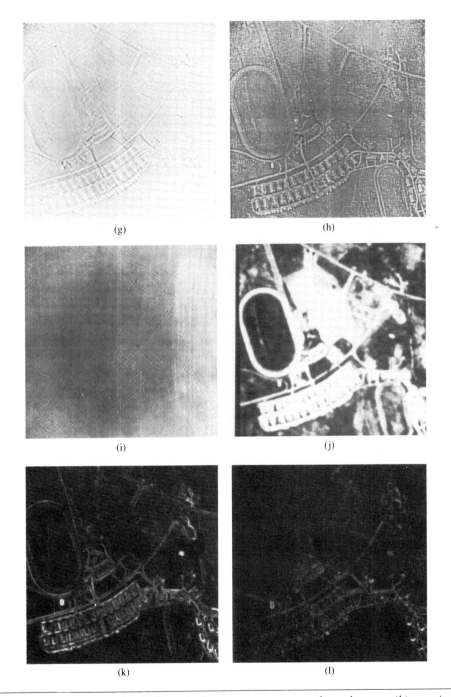

Figure 7.13 (Continued) (g)–(j) projections onto $\mathbf{w}_6$, $\mathbf{w}_7$, $\mathbf{w}_8$, and $\mathbf{w}_9$ subspaces; (k) magnitude of projection onto edge subspace; (l) magnitude of projection onto line subspace. (From Hall and Frei [1976].)

neighborhood of (x, y), is similar in magnitude to the pixel at (x, y) if

$$|\nabla f(x, y) - \nabla f(x', y')| \leq T \qquad (7.2\text{-}1)$$

where T is a nonnegative threshold.

The direction of the gradient vector is given by Eq. (7.1-6). Then, an edge pixel at (x', y') in the predefined neighborhood of (x, y) has an angle similar to the pixel at (x, y) if

$$|\alpha(x, y) - \alpha(x', y')| < A \qquad (7.2\text{-}2)$$

where A is an angle threshold. Note that the direction of the edge at (x, y), in reality, is perpendicular to the direction of the gradient vector at that point. However, for the purpose of comparing directions, Eq. (7.2-2) yields equivalent results.

A point in the predefined neighborhood of (x, y) is linked to the pixel at (x, y) if both magnitude and direction criteria are satisfied. This process is repeated for every location in the image. A record must be kept of linked points as the center of the neighborhood is moved from pixel to pixel. A simple bookkeeping procedure is to assign a different gray level to each set of linked edge pixels.

Example: To illustrate the foregoing procedure, consider Fig. 7.14(a), which shows an image of the rear of a vehicle. The objective is to find rectangles whose sizes makes them suitable candidates for license plates. The formation of these rectangles can be accomplished by detecting strong horizontal and vertical edges. Figures 7.14(b) and (c) show the components of the Sobel operators. Finally, Fig. 7.14(d) shows the results of linking all points that simultaneously had a gradient value greater than 25 and whose gradient directions did not differ by more than 15°. The horizontal lines were formed by sequentially applying these criteria to every row of Fig. 7.14(c), whereas a sequential column scan of Fig. 7.14(b) yielded the vertical lines. Further processing consisted of linking edge segments separated by small breaks and deleting isolated short segments.   ❏

7.2.2   Global Processing via the Hough Transform

In this section we consider linking points by determining whether they lie on a curve of specified shape. Unlike the local analysis method discussed in Section 7.2.1, we now consider global relationships between pixels.

Suppose that, for n points in an image, we want to find subsets of these points that lie on straight lines. One possible solution is first to find all lines determined by every pair of points and then find all subsets of points that are close to particular lines. The problem with this procedure is that it involves

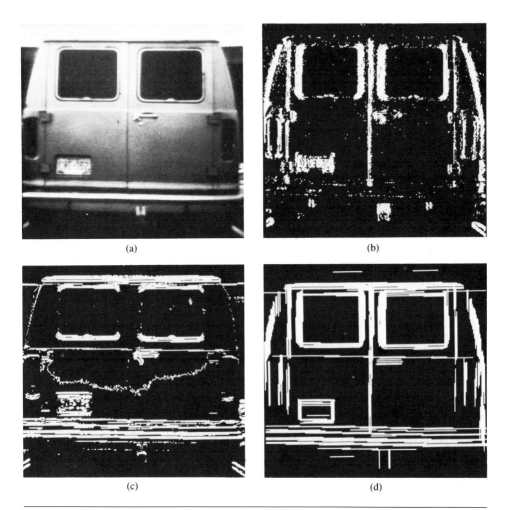

Figure 7.14 *(a) Input image; (b) G_y component of the gradient; (c) G_x component of the gradient; (d) result of edge linking. (Courtesy of Perceptics Corporation.)*

finding $n(n - 1)/2 \sim n^2$ lines and then performing $(n)(n(n - 1))/2 \sim n^3$ comparisons of every point to all lines. This approach is computationally prohibitive in all but the most trivial applications.

Hough [1962] proposed an alternative approach, commonly referred to as the *Hough transform*. Consider a point (x_i, y_i) and the general equation of a straight line in slope–intercept form, $y_i = ax_i + b$. Infinitely many lines pass through (x_i, y_i), but they all satisfy the equation $y_i = ax_i + b$ for varying values of a and b. However, writing this equation as $b = -x_ia + y_i$ and considering the *ab* plane (also called *parameter space*) yields the equation of a *single* line for a fixed pair (x_i, y_i). Furthermore, a second point (x_j, y_j) also has a line in parameter space associated with it, and this line intersects the line associated with (x_i, y_i) at (a', b'), where a' is the slope and b' the intercept of the line containing both (x_i, y_i) and (x_j, y_j) in the *xy* plane. In fact, all points contained on this line have lines in parameter space that intersect at (a', b'). Figure 7.15 illustrates these concepts.

The computational attractiveness of the Hough transform arises from subdivision of the parameter space into so-called *accumulator cells*, as illustrated in Fig. 7.16, where (a_{max}, a_{min}) and (b_{max}, b_{min}) are the expected ranges of slope and intercept values. The cell at coordinates (i, j), with accumulator value $A(i, j)$, corresponds to the square associated with parameter space coordinates (a_i, b_j). Initially, these cells are set to zero. Then, for every point (x_k, y_k) in the image plane, we let the parameter a equal each of the allowed subdivision values on the a axis and solve for the corresponding b using the equation $b = -x_k a + y_k$. The resulting b's are then rounded off to the nearest allowed value in the b axis. If a choice of a_p results in solution b_q, we let $A(p, q) = A(p, q) + 1$. At the end of this procedure, a value of M in $A(i, j)$ corresponds to M points in the *xy* plane lying on the line $y = a_i x + b_j$. The accuracy of the collinearity of these points is determined by the number of subdivisions in the *ab* plane.

Note that subdividing the a axis into K increments gives, for every point (x_k, y_k), K values of b corresponding to the K possible values of a. With n image points, this method involves nK computations. Thus the procedure just discussed is *linear* in n, and the product nK does not approach the number of computations discussed at the beginning of this section unless K approaches or exceeds n.

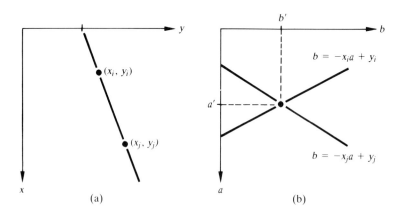

Figure 7.15   *(a) xy plane; (b) parameter space.*

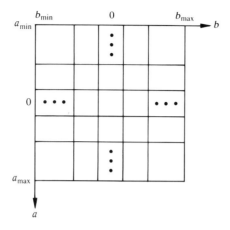

Figure 7.16 *Quantization of the parameter plane for use in the Hough transform.*

A problem with using the equation $y = ax + b$ to represent a line is that both the slope and intercept approach infinity as the line approaches the vertical. One way around this difficulty is to use the normal representation of a line:

$$x \cos \theta + y \sin \theta = \rho. \qquad (7.2\text{-}3)$$

Figure 7.17(a) shows the meaning of the parameters used in Eq. (7.2-3). The use of this representation in constructing a table of accumulators is identical to the method discussed for the slope–intercept representation. Instead of straight lines, however, the loci are sinusoidal curves in the $\rho\theta$ plane. As before, M collinear points lying on a line $x \cos \theta_j + y \sin \theta_j = \rho_i$ yields M sinusoidal curves that intersect at (ρ_i, θ_j) in the parameter space. Incrementing θ and solving for the corresponding ρ gives M entries in accumulator $A(i, j)$ associated with the cell determined by (ρ_i, θ_j). Figure 7.17(b) illustrates the subdivision of the parameter space.

The range of angle θ is $\pm 90°$, measured with respect to the x axis. Thus with reference to Fig. 7.17(a), a horizontal line has $\theta = 0°$, with ρ being equal to the positive x intercept. Similarly, a vertical line has $\theta = 90°$, with ρ being equal to the positive y intercept, or $\theta = -90°$, with ρ being equal to the negative y intercept.

Example: Figure 7.18 illustrates the Hough transform based on Eq. (7.2-3). Figure 7.18(a) shows an image with five labeled points. Each of these points is mapped onto the $\rho\theta$ plane, as shown in Fig. 7.18(b). The range of θ values is $\pm 90°$, and the range of the ρ axis is $\pm \sqrt{2}D$, where D is the distance between corners in the image. Unlike the transform based on using the slope–intercept, each of these curves has a different sinusoidal shape. (The horizontal line

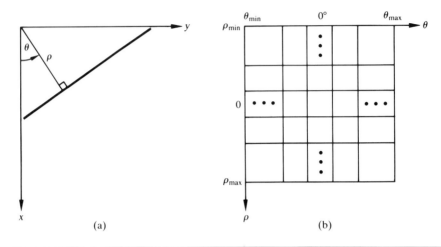

Figure 7.17   *(a) Normal representation of a line; (b) quantization of the $\rho\theta$ plane into cells.*

resulting from the mapping of point 1 is a special case of a sinusoid with zero amplitude.) A point at each extreme of the image was mapped, so the Hough transform of any other point in the image would lie between the limits shown in Fig. 7.18(b).

The collinearity detection property of the Hough transform is illustrated in Fig. 7.18(c). Point A denotes the intersection of the curves corresponding to points 1, 3, and 5 in the xy image plane. The location of point A indicates that these three points lie on a straight line passing through the origin ($\rho = 0$) and oriented at $-45°$. Similarly, the curves intersecting at point B in the parameter space indicate that points 2, 3, and 4 lie on a straight line oriented at $45°$, and whose distance from the origin is one-half the diagonal distance from the origin of the image to the opposite corner.

Finally, Fig. 7.18(d) indicates the fact that the Hough transform exhibits a reflective adjacency relationship at the right and left edges of the parameter space. This property, shown by the points marked A, B, and C in Fig. 7.18(d), is the result of the manner in which θ and ρ change sign at the $\pm90°$ boundaries.   ◻

Although the focus so far has been on straight lines, the Hough transform is applicable to any function of the form $g(\mathbf{v}, \mathbf{c}) = 0$, where $\mathbf{v}$ is a vector of coordinates and $\mathbf{c}$ is a vector of coefficients. For example, the points lying on the circle

$$(x - c_1)^2 + (y - c_2)^2 = c_3^2 \tag{7.2-4}$$

can be detected by using the approach just discussed. The basic difference is the presence of three parameters (c_1, c_2, and c_3), which results in a 3-D param-

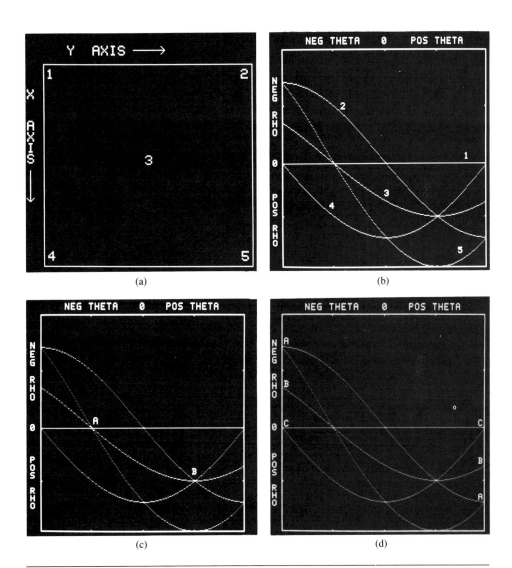

(a)

(b)

(c)

(d)

Figure 7.18 *Illustration of the Hough transform. (Courtesy of D. R. Cate, Texas Instruments, Inc.)*

eter space with cubelike cells and accumulators of the form $A(i, j, k)$. The procedure is to increment c_1 and c_2, solve for the c_3 that satisfies Eq. (7.2-4), and update the accumulator corresponding to the cell associated with the triplet (c_1, c_2, c_3). Clearly, the complexity of the Hough transform is strongly dependent on the number of coordinates and coefficients in a given functional representation. Further generalizations of the Hough transform to detect curves with no simple analytic representations are possible. These concepts, which are extensions of the material presented here, are treated in detail by Ballard [1981].

We now return to the edge-linking problem. An approach based on the Hough transform consists of (1) computing the gradient of an image, (2) specifying subdivisions in the $\rho\theta$ plane, (3) examining the counts of the accumulator cells for high pixel concentrations, and (4) examining the relation (principally for continuity) between pixels in a chosen cell. The concept of continuity in this case usually is based on computing the distance between disconnected pixels identified during traversal of the set of pixels corresponding to a given accumulator cell. A gap at any point is significant if the distance between that point and its closest neighbor exceeds a certain threshold. (See Section 2.4 for a discussion of connectivity, neighborhoods, and distance measures.)

Example: Consider Fig. 7.19(a), which shows an aerial infrared image containing two hangars and a runway. Figure 7.19(b) is a thresholded gradient image obtained using the Sobel operators discussed in Section 7.1.3 (note the small gaps in the borders of the runway). Figure 7.19(c) shows the linear Hough transform of the gradient image, and Fig. 7.19(d) shows (in white) the set of pixels linked according to the criteria that (1) they belonged to one of the three accumulator cells with the highest count, and (2) no gaps were longer than five pixels. Note the disappearance of the gaps as a result of linking.   ◻

7.2.3   Global Processing via Graph-Theoretic Techniques

The method discussed in Section 7.2.2 is based on obtaining a set of edge points through a gradient operation. As the gradient is a derivative, the operation is seldom suitable as a preprocessing step in situations characterized by high noise content. In this section we discuss a global approach based on representing edge segments in the form of a graph and searching the graph for low-cost paths that correspond to significant edges. This representation provides a rugged approach that performs well in the presence of noise. As might be expected, the procedure is considerably more complicated and requires more processing time than the methods discussed so far.

We begin the development with some basic definitions. A *graph* $G = (N, A)$ is a finite, nonempty set of nodes N, together with a set A of unordered pairs of distinct elements of N. Each pair (n_i, n_j) of A is called an *arc*. A graph in which the arcs are directed is called a *directed graph*. If an arc is directed

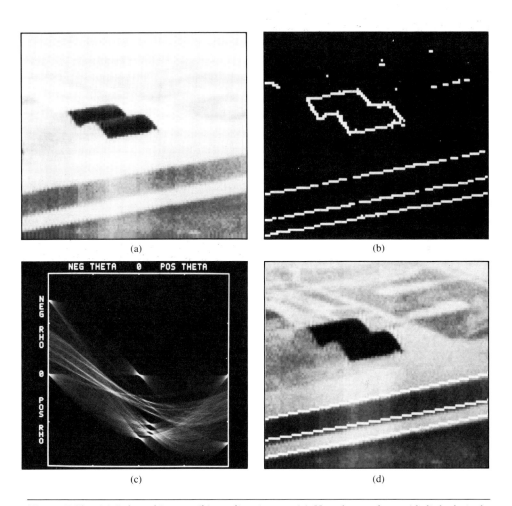

Figure 7.19 *(a) Infrared image; (b) gradient image; (c) Hough transform; (d) linked pixels. (Courtesy of D. R. Cate, Texas Instruments, Inc.)*

from node n_i to node n_j, then n_j is said to be a *successor* of its *parent* node n_i. The process of identifying the successors of a node is called *expansion* of the node. In each graph we define levels, such that level 0 consists of a single node, called the *start* node, and the nodes in the last level are called *goal* nodes. A *cost* $c(n_i, n_j)$ can be associated with every arc (n_i, n_j). A sequence of nodes n_1, $n_2, \ldots, n_k$ with each node n_i being a successor of node n_{i-1} is called a *path* from n_1 to n_k, and the cost of the path is

$$c = \sum_{i=2}^{k} c(n_{i-1}, n_i). \qquad (7.2\text{-}5)$$

Finally, an *edge element* is the boundary between two pixels p and q, such that p and q are 4-neighbors, as Fig. 7.20 illustrates. In this context, an *edge* is a sequence of edge elements.

We can illustrate how the foregoing concepts apply to edge detection with the 3×3 image shown in Fig. 7.21, where the outer numbers are pixel coordinates and the numbers in parentheses represent intensity. Each edge element defined by pixels p and q has an associated cost, defined as

$$c(p, q) = H - [f(p) - f(q)] \qquad (7.2\text{-}6)$$

where H is the highest intensity value in the image (7 in this case), $f(p)$ is the intensity value of p, and $f(q)$ is the intensity value of q. As indicated earlier, p and q are 4-neighbors.

Figure 7.22 shows the graph for this problem. Each node corresponds to an edge element, and an arc exists between two nodes if the two corresponding edge elements taken in succession can be part of an edge. The cost of each edge element, computed by using Eq. (7.2-6), is the arc leading into it, and goal nodes are shown as shaded rectangles. Each path between the start node and a goal node is a possible edge. For simplicity, the edge is assumed to start in the top row and terminate in the last row, so that the first element of an edge can be only $[(0, 0), (0, 1)]$ or $[(0, 1), (0, 2)]$ and the last element $[(2, 0), (2, 1)]$ or $[(2, 1), (2, 2)]$. The dashed lines represent the minimum-cost path, computed by using Eq. (7.2-5). Figure 7.23 shows the corresponding edge.

In general, the problem of finding a minimum-cost path is not trivial in terms of computation. Typically, the approach is to sacrifice optimality for the sake of speed, and the following algorithm represents a class of procedures that use heuristics in order to reduce the search effort. Let $r(n)$ be an estimate of the cost of a minimum-cost path from the start node s to a goal node, where the path is constrained to go through n. This cost can be expressed as the estimate of the cost of a minimum-cost path from s to n plus an estimate of the cost of that path from n to a goal node; that is,

$$r(n) = g(n) + h(n). \qquad (7.2\text{-}7)$$

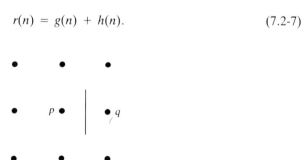

Figure 7.20   *Edge element between pixels p and q.*

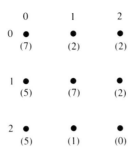

Figure 7.21   *A 3 × 3 image.*

Here, $g(n)$ can be chosen as the lowest cost path from s to n found so far, and $h(n)$ is obtained by using any available heuristic information (such as expanding only certain nodes based on previous costs in getting to that node). An algorithm that uses $r(n)$ as the basis for performing a graph search is as follows.

Step 1: Mark the start node OPEN and set $g(s) = 0$.

Step 2: If no node is OPEN exit with failure; otherwise, continue.

Step 3: Mark CLOSED the OPEN node n whose estimate $r(n)$ computed from Eq. (7.2-7) is smallest. (Ties for minimum r values are resolved arbitrarily, but always in favor of a goal node.)

Step 4: If n is a goal node, exit with the solution path obtained by tracing back through the pointers; otherwise, continue.

Step 5: Expand node n, generating all of its successors. (If there are no successors go to step 2.)

Step 6: If a successor n_i is not marked, set

$$r(n_i) = g(n) + c(n, n_i)$$

mark it OPEN, and direct pointers from it back to n.

Step 7: If a successor n_i is marked CLOSED or OPEN, update its value by letting

$$g'(n_i) = \min[g(n_i), g(n) + c(n, n_i)].$$

Mark OPEN those CLOSED successors whose g' values were thus lowered and redirect to n the pointers from all nodes whose g' values were lowered. Go to step 2.

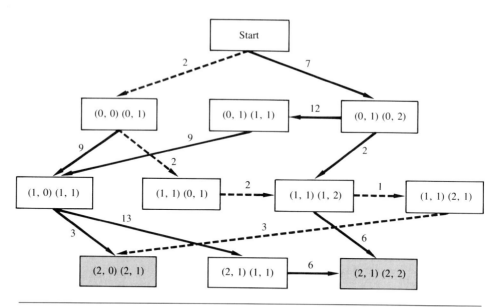

Figure 7.22 *Graph used for finding an edge in the image of Fig. 7.21. The pair (a, b)(c, d) in each box refers to points p and q, respectively. Note that p is assumed to be to the right of the path as the image is traversed from top to bottom. The dashed lines indicate the minimum-cost path. (Adapted from Martelli [1972].)*

In general, this algorithm does not guarantee a minimum-cost path; its advantage is speed via the use of heuristics. However, if $h(n)$ is a lower bound on the cost of the minimal-cost path from node n to a goal node, the procedure indeed yields an optimal path to a goal (Hart, Nilsson, and Raphael [1968]). If no heuristic information is available (that is, $h \equiv 0$), the procedure reduces to the *uniform-cost algorithm* of Dijkstra [1959].

Example: Figure 7.24 shows a typical result obtainable with this procedure. Figure 7.24(a) shows a noisy image, and Fig. 7.24(b) shows the result of edge

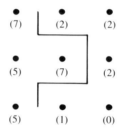

Figure 7.23 *Edge corresponding to the minimum-cost path in Fig. 7.22.*

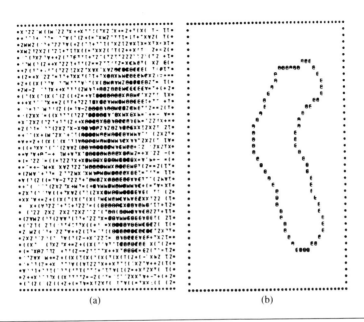

(a)   (b)

Figure 7.24 (a) Noisy image; (b) result of edge detection by using the heuristic graph search. (From Martelli [1976].)

segmentation by searching the corresponding graph for low-cost paths. Heuristics were brought into play by not expanding those nodes whose cost exceeded a certain threshold.   ❑

7.3 THRESHOLDING

Thresholding is one of the most important approaches to image segmentation. In this section, we develop various techniques for thresholding and discuss their merits and limitations.

7.3.1 Foundation

Suppose that the gray-level histogram shown in Fig. 7.25(a) corresponds to an image, $f(x, y)$, composed of light objects on a dark background, in such a way that object and background pixels have gray levels grouped into two dominant modes. One obvious way to extract the objects from the background is to select a threshold T that separates these modes. Then, any point (x, y) for which $f(x, y) > T$ is called an object point; otherwise, the point is called a background point. Figure 7.25(b) shows a slightly more general case of this approach. Here, three dominant modes characterize the image histogram (for example, two types of light objects on a dark background). The same basic approach classifies a point (x, y) as belonging to one object class if $T_1 < f(x, y) \leq T_2$, to the other

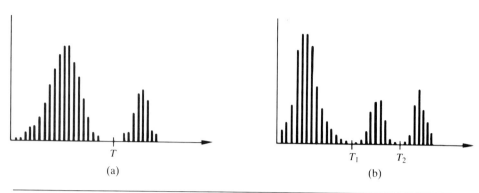

Figure 7.25 *Gray-level histograms that can be partitioned by (a) a single threshold and (b) multiple thresholds.*

object class if $f(x, y) > T_2$, and to the background if $f(x, y) \leq T_1$. This type of *multilevel thresholding* is generally less reliable than its single-threshold counterpart. The reason is the difficulty of establishing multiple thresholds that effectively isolate regions of interest, especially when the number of corresponding histogram modes is large. Typically, problems of this nature, if handled by thresholding, are best addressed by a single, variable threshold.

Based on the preceding discussion, thresholding may be viewed as an operation that involves tests against a function T of the form

$$T = T[x, y, p(x, y), f(x, y)] \tag{7.3-1}$$

where $f(x, y)$ is the gray level of point (x, y), and $p(x, y)$ denotes some local property of this point—for example, the average gray level of a neighborhood centered on (x, y). A thresholded image $g(x, y)$ is defined as

$$g(x, y) = \begin{cases} 1 & \text{if } f(x, y) > T \\ 0 & \text{if } f(x, y) \leq T. \end{cases} \tag{7.3-2}$$

Thus pixels labeled 1 (or any other convenient intensity level) correspond to objects, whereas pixels labeled 0 correspond to the background.

When T depends only on $f(x, y)$, the threshold is called *global*. (Figure 7.25a shows an example of such a threshold.) If T depends on both $f(x, y)$ and $p(x, y)$, the threshold is called *local*. If, in addition, T depends on the spatial coordinates x and y, the threshold is called *dynamic*.

7.3.2   The Role of Illumination

In Section 2.2 we stated that the formation of an image $f(x, y)$ may be viewed as the product of a reflectance component $r(x, y)$ and an illumination component $i(x, y)$. The purpose of this section is to discuss briefly the effect of illumination on image segmentation.

Consider the computer generated reflectance function shown in Fig. 7.26(a). The histogram of this function, shown in Fig. 7.26(b), is clearly bimodal and could be easily partitioned by placing a single threshold in the histogram valley. Multiplying the reflectance function in Fig. 7.26(a) by the illumination function shown in Fig. 7.26(c) yields the image $f(x, y)$ shown in Fig. 7.26(d). Figure 7.26(e) shows the histogram of this image. Note that the original valley was virtually eliminated, making segmentation by a single threshold an impossible task. Although we seldom have the reflectance function by itself to work with, this simple illustration shows that the reflective nature of objects and background could be such that they are easily separable. However, the image resulting from poor (in this case nonuniform) illumination could be quite difficult to segment.

The reason that the histogram in Fig. 7.26(e) is so corrupted can be explained with the aid of the discussion in Section 4.4.3. Taking the natural logarithm of $f(x, y) = i(x, y) r(x, y)$ yields the sum $z(x, y) = \ln f(x, y) = \ln i(x, y) + \ln r(x, y) = i'(x, y) + r'(x, y)$. From probability theory (Papoulis [1965]), if $i'(x, y)$ and $r'(x, y)$ are independent random variables, the histogram of $z(x, y)$ is given by the convolution of the histograms of $i'(x, y)$ and $r'(x, y)$. If $i(x, y)$ were constant, $i'(x, y)$ would be constant also, and its histogram would be a simple spike (like an impulse). The convolution of this impulselike function with the histogram of $r'(x, y)$ would leave the basic shape of this histogram virtually unchanged (see Fig. 3.15). But, if $i'(x, y)$ had a broader histogram (resulting from nonuniform illumination), the convolution process would smear the histogram of $r'(x, y)$, yielding a histogram for $z(x, y)$ whose shape could be quite different from that of the histogram of $r'(x, y)$. The degree of distortion depends on the broadness of the histogram of $i'(x, y)$, which in turn depends on the nonuniformity of the illumination function.

We have dealt with the logarithm of $f(x, y)$ instead of dealing with the image function directly, but the essence of the problem is clearly explained by using the logarithm to separate the illumination and reflectance components. This approach allows histogram formation to be viewed as a convolution process, thus explaining why a distinct valley in the histogram of the reflectance function could be virtually eliminated by improper illumination.

When access to the illumination source is available, a solution frequently used in practice to compensate for nonuniformity is to project the illumination pattern onto a constant, white reflective surface. This solution yields an image $g(x, y) = ki(x, y)$, where k is a constant that depends on the surface and $i(x, y)$ is the illumination pattern. Then, for any image $f(x, y) = i(x, y) r(x, y)$ obtained with the same illumination function, simply dividing $f(x, y)$ by $g(x, y)$ yields a normalized function $h(x, y) = f(x, y)/g(x, y) = r(x, y)/k$. Thus if $r(x, y)$ can be segmented by using a single threshold T, then $h(x, y)$ can also be segmented by using a single threshold of value T/k. Note that this method works well only if the illumination pattern produced by $i(x, y)$ does not change

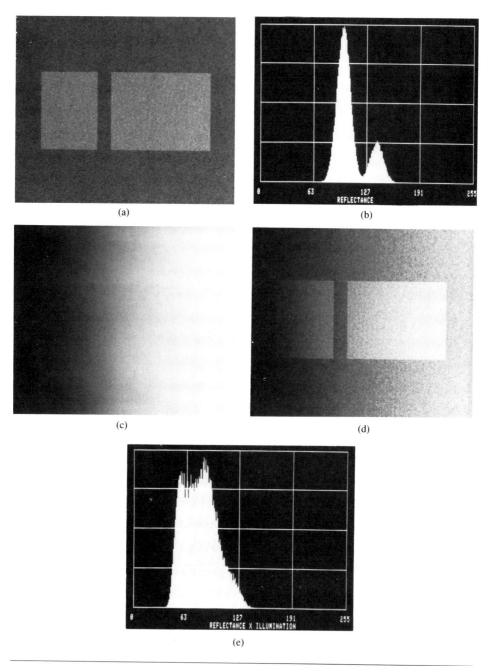

(a)

(b)

(c)

(d)

(e)

Figure 7.26 (a) Computer generated reflectance function; (b) histogram of reflectance function; (c) computer generated illumination function; (d) image produced by the product of the illumination and reflectance functions; (e) histogram of image.

446

from image to image. Typically, the normalization of $f(x, y)$ by $g(x, y)$ is carried out using an arithmetic-logic unit (ALU) processor, as discussed in Section 2.4.6.

7.3.3 Simple Global Thresholding

With reference to the discussion in Section 7.3.1, the simplest of all thresholding techniques is to partition the image histogram by using a single threshold, T, as illustrated in Fig. 7.25(a). Segmentation is then accomplished by scanning the image pixel by pixel and labeling each pixel as object or background, depending on whether the gray level of that pixel is greater or less than the value of T. As indicated earlier, the success of this method depends entirely on how well the histogram can be partitioned.

Figure 7.27 shows an example of global thresholding. Figure 7.27(a) shows a simple image, and Fig. 7.27(b) shows its histogram. Note that the range of gray levels is $[0, 255]$. Figure 7.27(b) shows the result of segmenting Fig. 7.27(a) by using a threshold $T = 90$, which achieved a "clean" segmentation by eliminating the shadows and leaving only the objects themselves. The objects of interest in this case are darker than the background, so any pixel with a gray level $\leq T$ was labeled black (0), and any pixel with a gray level $> T$ was labeled white (255). (The key objective is merely to generate a binary image, so the black–white relationship could be reversed.)

In practice, the type of global thresholding just described can be expected to be successful in highly controlled environments. One of the areas in which this often is possible is in industrial inspection applications, where illumination control usually is feasible. Recall from the discussion in Section 7.3.2 that illumination plays a crucial role in establishing the shape of the histogram in the resulting image.

7.3.4 Optimal Thresholding

Suppose that an image contains only two principal brightness regions. The histogram of such an image may be considered an estimate of the brightness probability density function, $p(z)$. This overall density function is the sum or mixture of two unimodal densities, one for the light and one for the dark regions in the image. Furthermore, the mixture parameters are proportional to the areas of the picture of each brightness. If the form of the densities is known or assumed, determining an optimal threshold (in terms of minimum error) for segmenting the image into the two brightness regions is possible.

Suppose that an image contains two values combined with additive Gaussian noise. The mixture probability density function is

$$p(z) = P_1 p_1(z) + P_2 p_2(z) \tag{7.3-3}$$

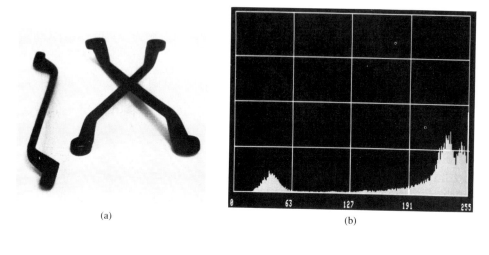

(a)

(b)

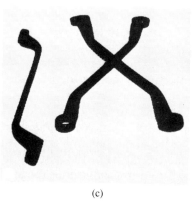

(c)

Figure 7.27 *Example of global thresholding: (a) original image and (b) its histogram; (c) result of segmentation with T = 90. (From Fu, Gonzalez, and Lee [1987].)*

which, for the Gaussian case, is

$$p(z) = \frac{P_1}{\sqrt{2\pi}\, \sigma_1} \exp\left[-\frac{(z - \mu_1)^2}{2\sigma_1^2}\right] + \frac{P_2}{\sqrt{2\pi}\, \sigma_2} \exp\left[-\frac{(z - \mu_2)^2}{2\sigma_2^2}\right] \quad (7.3\text{-}4)$$

where μ_1 and μ_2 are the mean values of the two brightness levels, σ_1 and σ_2 are the standard deviations about the means, and P_1 and P_2 are the a priori probabilities of the two levels. The constraint

$$P_1 + P_2 = 1 \quad (7.3\text{-}5)$$

must be satisfied, so the mixture density has five unknown parameters. If all the parameters are known, the optimal threshold is easily determined.

Suppose that the dark regions correspond to the background and the bright regions correspond to objects. In this case $\mu_1 < \mu_2$, and a threshold T may be defined so that all pixels with a gray level below T are considered background points and all pixels with a level above T are considered object points. The probability of (erroneously) classifying an object point as a background point is

$$E_1(T) = \int_{-\infty}^{T} p_2(z)\, dz. \tag{7.3-6}$$

Similarly, the probability of classifying a background point as an object point is

$$E_2(T) = \int_{T}^{\infty} p_1(z)\, dz. \tag{7.3-7}$$

Therefore the overall probability of error is

$$E(T) = P_2 E_1(T) + P_1 E_2(T). \tag{7.3-8}$$

To find the threshold value for which this error is minimal requires differentiating $E(T)$ with respect to T (using Liebnitz's rule) and equating the result to 0. Thus

$$P_1 p_1(T) = P_2 p_2(T). \tag{7.3-9}$$

Applying this result to the Gaussian density, taking logarithms, and simplifying, gives the quadratic equation

$$AT^2 + BT + C = 0 \tag{7.3-10}$$

where

$$
\begin{aligned}
A &= \sigma_1^2 - \sigma_2^2 \\
B &= 2(\mu_1 \sigma_2^2 - \mu_2 \sigma_1^2) \\
C &= \sigma_1^2 \mu_2^2 - \sigma_2^2 \mu_1^2 + 2\sigma_1^2 \sigma_2^2 \ln(\sigma_2 P_1 / \sigma_1 P_2).
\end{aligned}
\tag{7.3-11}
$$

The possibility of two solutions indicates that two threshold values may be required to obtain the optimal solution.

If the variances are equal, $\sigma^2 = \sigma_1^2 = \sigma_2^2$, a single threshold is sufficient:

$$T = \frac{\mu_1 + \mu_2}{2} + \frac{\sigma^2}{\mu_1 - \mu_2} \ln\left(\frac{P_2}{P_1}\right). \tag{7.3-12}$$

If the prior probabilities are equal, $P_1 = P_2$, the optimal threshold is the average of the means. The same holds for $\sigma = 0$. The determination of the optimal threshold may be similarly accomplished for other unimodal densities of known form, such as the Raleigh and log-normal densities.

A minimum mean square error approach may be used to estimate the parameters of an image from a histogram. For example, the mean square error between the mixture density $p(z)$ and the experimental histogram $h(z_i)$ is

$$e_{ms} = \frac{1}{n} \sum_{i-1}^{n} [p(z_i) - h(z_i)]^2 \qquad (7.3\text{-}13)$$

where an n-point histogram is assumed.

In general, analytically determining parameters that minimize this mean square error is not a simple matter. Even for the Gaussian case, the straight-forward computation of equating the partial derivatives to 0 leads to a set of simultaneous transcendental equations that usually can be solved only by numerical procedures. Because the gradient is easily computed, a conjugate gradient or Newton's method for simultaneous nonlinear equations may be used to minimize e_{ms}. With either of these iterative methods, starting values must be specified. Assuming the a priori probabilities to be equal may be sufficient. Starting values for the means and variances may be determined by detecting modes in the histogram or simply by dividing the histogram into two parts about its mean value, and computing means and variances of the two parts to be used as starting values.

Example: The following discussion of an approach developed by Chow and Kaneko [1972] for outlining boundaries of the left ventricle in cardioangiograms

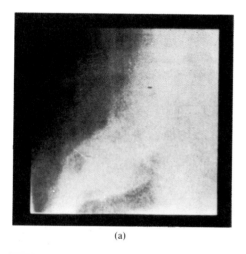
(a)

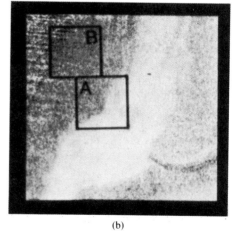
(b)

Figure 7.28 *A cardioangiogram before and after processing. (From Chow and Kaneko [1972].)*

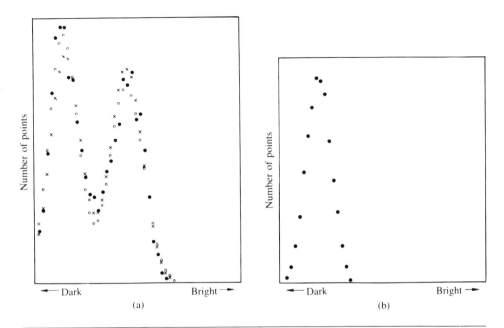

Figure 7.29 *Histograms (black dots) of regions A and B in Fig. 7.28(b). (From Chow and Kaneko [1972].)*

(that is, x-ray pictures of a heart that has been injected with a dye) illustrates optimal threshold selection.

Before thresholding, the images (of size 256×256 pixels) were first pre-processed by (1) taking the logarithm of every pixel to invert the exponential effects caused by radioactive absorption, (2) subtracting two images that were obtained before and after the dye agent was applied in order to remove the spinal column present in both images (see Section 4.2.3), and (3) averaging several angiograms to remove noise (see Section 4.2.4). Figure 7.28 shows a cardioangiogram before and after preprocessing (an explanation of the regions marked *A* and *B* follows).

In order to compute the optimal thresholds, each preprocessed image was subdivided into 49 regions by placing a 7×7 grid with 50 percent overlap over each image. Each of the 49 resulting overlapped regions contained 64×64 pixels. Figures 7.29(a) and 7.29(b) are the histograms of the regions marked *A* and *B* in Fig. 7.28(b). Note that the histogram for region *A* clearly is bimodal, indicating the presence of a boundary. The histogram for region *B*, however, is unimodal, indicating the absence of two markedly distinct regions.

After all 49 histograms were computed, a test of bimodality was performed to reject the unimodal histograms. The remaining histograms were then fitted by bimodal Gaussian density curves (see Eq. 7.3-4) using a conjugate gradient hill-climbing method to minimize the error function given in Eq. (7.3-13). The ×s and ○s in Fig. 7.29(a) are two fits to the histogram shown in black dots. The optimal thresholds were then obtained by using Eqs. (7.3.10) and (7.3-11).

At this stage of the process only the regions with bimodal histograms were assigned thresholds. The thresholds for the remaining regions were obtained by interpolating these thresholds. Then a second interpolation was carried out point by point by using neighboring threshold values so that, at the end of the procedure, every point in the image had been assigned a threshold. Finally, a binary decision was carried out for each pixel using the rule

$$f(x, y) = \begin{cases} 1 & \text{if } f(x, y) \geq T_{xy} \\ 0 & \text{otherwise} \end{cases}$$

where T_{xy} was the threshold assigned to location (x, y) in the image. [Note that these are dynamic thresholds, because they depend on the spatial coordinates (x, y).] Boundaries were then obtained by taking the gradient of the binary picture. Figure 7.30 shows the boundaries superimposed on the original image.   ❏

7.3.5 Threshold Selection Based on Boundary Characteristics

One of the most important aspects of threshold selection is the capability of reliably identifying the mode peaks in a given histogram. This capability is particularly important for automatic threshold selection in situations where

Figure 7.30 *Cardioangiogram showing superimposed boundaries. (From Chow and Kaneko [1972].)*

image characteristics can change over a broad range of intensity distributions. Based on the discussion in Sections 7.3.2–7.3.4, it is intuitively evident that the chances of selecting a "good" threshold should be considerably enhanced if the histogram peaks are tall, narrow, symmetric, and separated by deep valleys.

One approach for improving the shape of histograms is to consider only those pixels that lie on or near the boundary between objects and the background. An immediate and obvious improvement is that histograms would be less dependent on the relative sizes of objects and the background. For instance, the intensity histogram of an image composed of a large, nearly constant background area and one small object would be dominated by a large peak because of the high concentration of background pixels. But, if only the pixels on or near the boundary between the object and the background were used, the resulting histogram would have peaks of approximately the same height. In addition, the probability that any of those given pixels lies on an object would be approximately equal to the probability that it lies on the background, thus improving the symmetry of the histogram peaks. Finally, using pixels that satisfy some simple measures based on gradient and Laplacian operators has a tendency to deepen the valley between histogram peaks.

The principal problem with the approach just discussed is the implicit assumption that the boundary between objects and background is known. This information clearly is not available during segmentation, as finding a division between objects and background is precisely what segmentation is all about. However, from the material in Section 7.1.3, an indication of whether a pixel is on an edge may be obtained by computing its gradient. In addition, use of the Laplacian can yield information regarding whether a given pixel lies on the dark (background) or light (object) side of an edge. The average value of the Laplacian is 0 at the transition of an edge (see Fig. 7.4), so in practice the valleys of histograms formed from the pixels selected by a gradient/Laplacian criterion can be expected to be sparsely populated. This property produces the highly desirable deep valleys discussed earlier.

The gradient ∇f at any point (x, y) in an image is given by Eq. (7.1-4) or (7.1-5). Similarly, the Laplacian $\nabla^2 f$ is given by Eq. (7.1-10). These two quantities may be used to form a three-level image, as follows:

$$s(x, y) = \begin{cases} 0 & \text{if } \nabla f < T \\ + & \text{if } \nabla f \geq T \text{ and } \nabla^2 f \geq 0 \\ - & \text{if } \nabla f \geq T \text{ and } \nabla^2 f < 0 \end{cases} \qquad (7.3\text{-}14)$$

where the symbols 0, $+$, and $-$ represent any three distinct gray levels, T is a threshold, and the gradient and Laplacian are computed at every point (x, y). For a dark object on a light background, and with reference to Fig.

7.4(b), the use of Eq. (7.3-14) produces an image $s(x, y)$ in which all pixels that are not on an edge (as determined by ∇f to be less than T) are labeled 0, all pixels on the dark side of an edge are labeled $+$, and all pixels on the light side of an edge are labeled $-$. The symbols $+$ and $-$ in Eq. (7.3-14) are reversed for a light object on a dark background. Figure 7.31 shows the labeling produced by Eq. (7.3-14) for an image of a dark, underlined stroke written on a light background.

The information obtained by using this procedure can be used to generate a segmented, binary image in which 1's correspond to objects of interest and 0's correspond to the background. The transition (along a horizontal or vertical scan line) from a light background to a dark object must be characterized by the occurrence of a $-$ followed by a $+$ in $s(x, y)$. The interior of the object is composed of pixels that are labeled either 0 or $+$. Finally, the transition from the object back to the background is characterized by the occurrence of a $+$ followed by a $-$. Thus a horizontal or vertical scan line containing a section of an object has the following structure:

$$(\cdots)(-, +)(0 \text{ or } +)(+, -)(\cdots)$$

where $(\cdots)$ represents any combination of $+$, $-$, and 0. The innermost parentheses contain object points and are labeled 1. All other pixels along the

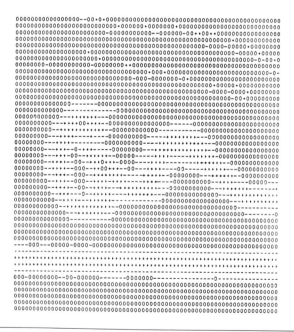

Figure 7.31 *Image of a handwritten stroke coded by using Eq. (7.3-14). (From White and Rohrer [1983].)*

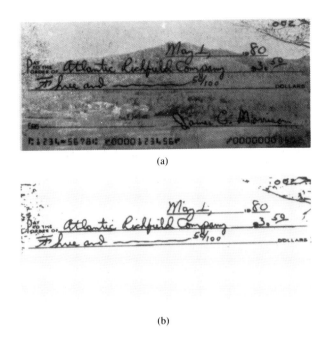

(a)

(b)

Figure 7.32 *(a) Original image; (b) segmented image. (From White and Rohrer [1983].)*

same scan line are labeled 0, with the exception of any other sequence of (0 or $+$) bounded by $(-, +)$ and $(+, -)$.

Example: Figure 7.32(a) shows an image of an ordinary scenic bank check. Figure 7.33 shows the histogram as a function of gradient values for pixels with gradients greater than 5. Note that this histogram has the properties discussed earlier. That is, it has two dominant modes that are symmetric, nearly of the same height, and are separated by a distinct valley. Finally, Fig. 7.32(b) shows the segmented image obtained by using Eq. (7.3-14) with T at or near the midpoint of the valley. The result was made binary by using the sequence analysis just discussed. Note that, although T is a constant threshold, its value was applied locally because the segmented image was generated by Eq. (7.3-14), which involves local gradient and Laplacian computations.   ❏

7.3.6 Thresholds Based on Several Variables

So far we have been concerned with thresholding a single intensity variable. In some cases, a sensor might make available more than one variable to characterize each pixel in an image. A notable example is color imaging, where red (R), green (G), and blue (B) components are used to form a composite

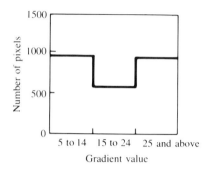

Figure 7.33 *Histogram of pixels with gradients greater than 5. (From White and Rohrer [1983].)*

color image (see Section 4.6.2). In this case, each pixel is characterized by three values, and constructing a 3-D "histogram" becomes possible. The basic procedure is the same as that used for one variable. For example, for three 16-level images corresponding to the RGB components, a $16 \times 16 \times 16$ grid (cube) is formed, and inserted in each cell of the cube is the number of pixels whose RGB components have intensities corresponding to the coordinates defining the location of that particular cell. Each entry can then be divided by the total number of pixels in the image to form a normalized histogram.

The concept of thresholding now becomes one of finding clusters of points in 3-D space. Suppose, for example, that K significant clusters of points are found in the histogram. The image can be segmented by assigning one intensity to pixels whose RGB components are closer to one cluster and another intensity to the other pixels in the image. This concept is easily extendable to more components and certainly to more clusters. The principal difficulty is that cluster seeking becomes an increasingly complex task as the number of variables increases. Cluster seeking methods can be found, for example, in the book by Tou and Gonzalez [1974].

Example: The image shown in Fig. 7.34(a) is a monochrome picture of a color photograph. The original color image was composed of three 16-level RGB images. The scarf was a vivid red, and the hair and facial colors were light and different in spectral characteristics from the window and other background features.

Figure 7.34(b) was obtained by thresholding about one of the histogram clusters. Note that the window, which in the monochrome picture is close in intensity to the hair, does not appear in the segmented image because of the use of multispectral characteristics to separate these two regions. Figure 7.34(c) was obtained by thresholding about a cluster close to the red axis. In this case only the scarf and part of a flower (also red) appeared in the segmented result.

The threshold used to obtain both results was a distance of one cell. Thus any pixel whose components were outside the cell enclosing the center of the cluster in question was classified as background (black). Pixels whose components placed them inside the cell were coded white.   ❏

Color segmentation can be based on any of the color models discussed in Section 4.6.2. For instance, hue and saturation are important properties in numerous applications dealing with the use of imaging for automated inspection. These properties are particularly important in attempts to emulate the equivalent function performed by human beings, such as in the inspection of fruits for ripeness or in the inspection of manufactured goods. As mentioned in Section 4.6.2, the HSI model is ideal for these types of applications because it is closely related to the way in which people describe the perception of color.

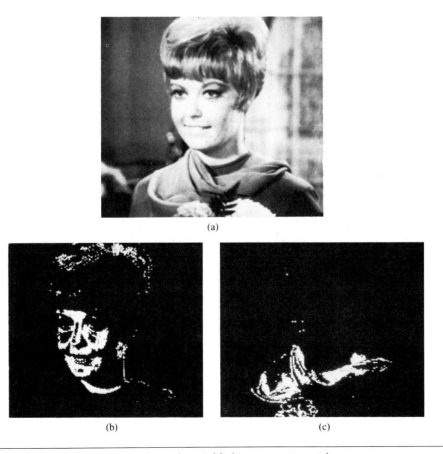

(a)

(b)   (c)

Figure 7.34 Segmentation by the multivariable histogram approach.

A segmentation approach using the hue and saturation components of a color signal also is particularly attractive, because it involves 2-D data clusters that are easier to analyze than, say, the 3-D clusters needed for RGB segmentation.

7.4 REGION-ORIENTED SEGMENTATION

The objective of segmentation is to partition an image into regions. In Sections 7.1 and 7.2 we approached this problem by finding boundaries between regions based on intensity discontinuities, whereas in Section 7.3 segmentation was accomplished via thresholds based on the distribution of pixel properties, such as intensity or color. In this section we discuss segmentation techniques that are based on finding the regions directly.

7.4.1 Basic Formulation

Let R represent the entire image region. We may view segmentation as a process that partitions R into n subregions, $R_1, R_2, \ldots, R_n$, such that

(a) $\bigcup\limits_{i=1}^{n} R_i = R$,

(b) R_i is a connected region, $i = 1, 2, \ldots, n,$

(c) $R_i \cap R_j = \phi$ for all i and $j, i \neq j,$

(d) $P(R_i) = $ TRUE for $i = 1, 2, \ldots, n,$ and

(e) $P(R_i \cup R_j) = $ FALSE for $i \neq j,$

where $P(R_i)$ is a logical predicate over the points in set R_i and ϕ is the null set.

Condition (a) indicates that the segmentation must be complete; that is, every pixel must be in a region. The second condition requires that points in a region must be connected (see Section 2.4.2 regarding connectivity). Condition (c) indicates that the regions must be disjoint. Condition (d) deals with the properties that must be satisfied by the pixels in a segmented region—for example $P(R_i) = $ TRUE if all pixels in R_i have the same intensity. Finally, condition (e) indicates that regions R_i and R_j are different in the sense of predicate P.

7.4.2 Region Growing by Pixel Aggregation

As its name implies, *region growing* is a procedure that groups pixels or subregions into larger regions. The simplest of these approaches is *pixel aggregation*, which starts with a set of "seed" points and from these grows regions by appending to each seed point those neighboring pixels that have similar properties (such as gray level, texture, color). To illustrate this procedure let us consider Fig. 7.35(a), where the numbers inside the cells represent gray-level values. Let the points with coordinates (3, 2) and (3, 4) be used as seeds. Using two starting points results in a segmentation consisting of, at most, two

	1	2	3	4	5
1	0	0	5	6	7
2	1	1	5	8	7
3	0	<u>1</u>	6	<u>7</u>	7
4	2	0	7	6	6
5	0	1	5	6	5

(a)

a	a	b	b	b
a	a	b	b	b
a	a	b	b	b
a	a	b	b	b
a	a	b	b	b

(b)

a	a	a	a	a
a	a	a	a	a
a	a	a	a	a
a	a	a	a	a
a	a	a	a	a

(c)

Figure 7.35 *Example of region growing using known starting points: (a) original image array; (b) segmentation result using an absolute difference of less than 3 between intensity levels; (c) result using an absolute difference of less than 8.*

regions: R_1 associated with seed (3, 2) and R_2 associated with seed (3, 4). The property P to be used to include a pixel in either region is that the absolute difference between the gray level of that pixel and the gray level of the seed be less than a threshold T. Any pixel that satisfies this property simultaneously for both seeds is (arbitrarily) assigned to region R_1. Figure 7.35(b) shows the result obtained using $T = 3$. In this case, the segmentation consists of two regions, where the points in R_1 are denoted a's and the points in R_2 by b's. Note that any starting point in either of these two resulting regions would yield the same result. However, choosing $T = 8$, would result in a single region, as Fig. 7.35(c) shows.

The preceding illustration, although simple in nature, points out some fundamental difficulties with region growing. Two immediate problems are the selection of initial seeds that properly represent regions of interest and the selection of suitable properties for including points in the various regions during the growing process. Selecting a set of one or more starting points often can be based on the nature of the problem. For example, in military applications of infrared imaging, targets of interest generally are hotter (and thus appear brighter) than the background. Choosing the brightest pixels then is a natural starting point for a region-growing algorithm. When a priori information is not available the procedure is to compute at every pixel the same set of properties that ultimately will be used to assign pixels to regions during the growing process. If the result of these computations shows clusters of values, the pixels whose properties place them near the centroid of these clusters can be used as seeds. For instance, in the preceding illustration, a gray-level histogram would show that points with intensity of 1 and 7 are the most predominant.

The selection of similarity criteria depends not only on the problem under consideration, but also on the type of image data available. For example, the analysis of land-use satellite imagery depends heavily on the use of color. This problem would be significantly more difficult to handle by using monochrome images alone. Unfortunately, the availability of multispectral and other complementary image data is the exception rather than the rule in image processing. Typically, region analysis must be carried out with a set of descriptors based on intensity and spatial properties (such as moments or texture) of a single image source. We discuss descriptors useful for region characterization in Section 8.3.

Descriptors alone can yield misleading results if connectivity or adjacency information is not used in the region-growing process. For example, visualize a random arrangement of pixels with only three distinct intensity values. Grouping pixels with the same intensity to form a "region" without paying attention to connectivity would yield a segmentation result that is meaningless in the context of this discussion.

Another problem in region growing is the formulation of a stopping rule. Basically, growing a region should stop when no more pixels satisfy the criteria for inclusion in that region. We mentioned that criteria such as intensity, texture, and color, are local in nature and do not take into account the "history" of region growth. Additional criteria that increase the power of a region-growing algorithm utilize the concept of size, likeness between a candidate pixel and the pixels grown so far (such as a comparison of the intensity of a candidate and the average intensity of the region), and the shape of the region being grown. The use of these types of descriptors is based on the assumption that a model of expected results is at least partially available.

Example: Figure 7.36(a) shows a section of a map containing a single seed point (a black dot). The criteria used for region growth were (1) that the absolute difference in gray level between the seed and a candidate point not exceed 10 percent of the difference between the minimum and maximum gray levels in the entire image (255 in this case), and (2) that any pixel added to the region be 8-connected to at least one pixel previously included in the region.

Figure 7.36(b) shows a region in the early stages of growth. Pixels with the same D_4 distance from the seed point were considered first. Increasing the value of this distance to expand growth resulted in a diamond-shaped region (see Section 2.4.5). Figure 7.36(c) shows the region in an intermediate stage of growth. Note how the diamond shape has been distorted as a result of hitting a boundary established by pixels that failed to satisfy the gray-level criterion. Finally, Fig. 7.36(d) shows the complete region grown by this technique. Although other pixels in neighboring regions satisfied the gray-level criterion, growth stopped because these pixels did not satisfy the connectivity criterion, owing to the separation caused by the dark border around the grown region. ❏

7.4.3 Region Splitting and Merging

The procedure just discussed grows regions from a set of seed points. An alternative is to subdivide an image initially into a set of arbitrary, disjointed regions and then merge and/or split the regions in an attempt to satisfy the conditions stated in Section 7.4.1. A split and merge algorithm that iteratively works toward satisfying these constraints is as follows.

Let R represent the entire image region and select a predicate P as discussed in Section 7.4.1. For a square image, one approach for segmenting R is to subdivide it successively into smaller and smaller quadrant regions so that, for any region R_i, $P(R_i)$ = TRUE. That is, if $P(R)$ = FALSE, divide the image into quadrants. If P is FALSE for any quadrant, subdivide that quadrant into subquadrants, and so on. This particular splitting technique has a convenient representation in the form of a so-called *quadtree* (that is, a tree in which each node has exactly four descendants), as illustrated in Fig. 7.37. Note that the root of the tree corresponds to the entire image and that each node corresponds to a subdivision. In this case, only R_4 was subdivided further.

If only splitting were used, the final partition likely would contain adjacent regions with identical properties. This drawback may be remedied by allowing

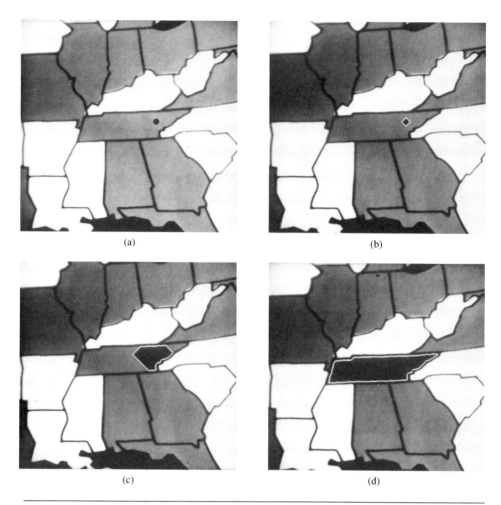

(a)   (b)

(c)   (d)

Figure 7.36   *(a) Original image showing seed point; (b) early stage of region growth; (c) intermediate stage of growth; (d) final region.*

merging, as well as splitting. Satisfying the constraints of Section 7.4.1 requires merging only adjacent regions whose combined pixels satisfy the predicate P; that is, two adjacent regions R_j and R_k are merged only if $P(R_j \cup R_k)$ = TRUE.

The preceding discussion may be summarized by the following procedure in which, at any step, we:

(1) split into four disjointed quadrants any region R_i where $P(R_i)$ = FALSE;

(2) merge any adjacent regions R_j and R_k for which $P(R_j \cup R_k)$ = TRUE; and

(3) stop when no further merging or splitting is possible.

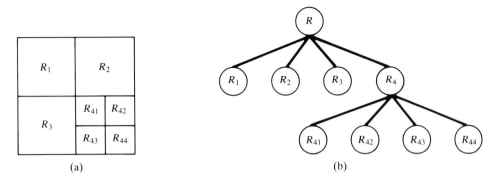

Figure 7.37 *(a) Partitioned image; (b) corresponding quadtree.*

Several variations of this basic approach are possible. For example, one possibility is to split the image initially into a set of square blocks. Further splitting is carried out as described, but merging is initially limited to groups of four blocks that are descendants in the quadtree representation and that satisfy the predicate *P*. When no further mergings of this type are possible, the procedure is terminated by one final merging of regions satisfying step 2. At this point, the merged regions may be of different sizes. The principal advantage of this approach is that it uses the same quadtree for splitting and merging, until the final merging step.

Example: Figure 7.38 illustrates the split and merge algorithm. The image consists of a single object and background. For simplicity, both the object and background have constant gray levels and $P(R_i)$ = TRUE if all pixels in R_i have the same intensity. Then, for the entire image region R, $P(R)$ = FALSE, so the image is split as shown in Fig. 7.38(a). In the next step, only the top left region satisfies the predicate so it is not changed, while the other three quadrants are split into subquadrants, as shown in Fig. 7.38(b). At this point several regions can be merged, with the exception of the two subquadrants

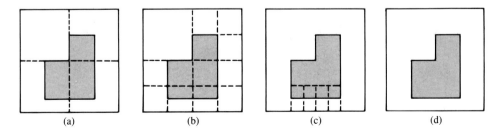

Figure 7.38 *Example of split-and-merge algorithm. (From Fu, Gonzalez, and Lee [1987].)*

that include the lower part of the object; these do not satisfy the predicate and must be split further. Figure 7.38(c) shows the results of the split and merge operation. At this point all regions satisfy P, and merging the appropriate regions from the last split operation yields the final, segmented result shown in Fig. 7.38(d).

Figure 7.39 shows a more practical example. In this case $P(R_i)$ = TRUE if at least 80 percent of the pixels in R_i have the property $|z_j - m_i| \leq 2\sigma_i$, where z_j is the gray level of the jth pixel in R_i, m_i is the mean gray level of that region, and σ_i is the standard deviation of the gray levels in R_i. If $P(R_i)$ = TRUE

(a)

(b)   (c)

Figure 7.39 (a) Original image; (b) result of split and merge procedure; (c) result of thresholding Fig. 7.39(b).

under this condition, the value of all the pixels in R_i were set equal to m_i. The result of applying this technique to the image in Fig. 7.39(a) is shown in Fig. 7.39(b). Note the shading effects in some corners of the image and near the leaf. The image shown in Fig. 7.39(c) was obtained by thresholding Fig. 7.39(b), with a threshold placed midway between the two principal peaks of the histogram. The shading (and the stem of the leaf) were eliminated as a result of thresholding.   ❏

As used in the preceding example, properties based on the mean and standard deviation of pixels in a region attempt to quantify the *texture* of a region (see Section 8.3.3 for a detailed discussion of texture). The concept of *texture segmentation* is based on using measures of texture for the predicates $P(R_i)$. That is, we can perform texture segmentation by any of the methods discussed in this section by specifying predicates based on texture content.

7.5 THE USE OF MOTION IN SEGMENTATION

Motion is a powerful cue used by human beings and animals to extract objects of interest from a background of irrelevant detail. In imaging applications, motion arises from a relative displacement between the sensing system and the scene being viewed, such as in robotic applications, autonomous navigation, and dynamic scene analysis. In the following sections we consider the use of motion in segmentation both spatially and in terms of the frequency domain.

7.5.1 Spatial Techniques

Basic approach

One of the simplest approaches for detecting changes between two image frames $f(x, y, t_i)$ and $f(x, y, t_j)$ taken at times t_i and t_j, respectively, is to compare the two images pixel by pixel. One procedure for doing this is to form a difference image. Suppose that we have a reference image containing only stationary components. Comparing this image against a subsequent image having the same environment but including a moving object results in the difference of the two images canceling the stationary components, leaving only nonzero entries that correspond to the nonstationary image components.

A difference image between two images taken at times t_i and t_j may be defined as

$$d_{ij}(x, y) = \begin{cases} 1 & \text{if } |f(x, y, t_i) - f(x, y, t_j)| > \theta \\ 0 & \text{otherwise} \end{cases} \tag{7.5-1}$$

where θ is a threshold. Note that $d_{ij}(x, y)$ has a 1 at spatial coordinates (x, y) only if the gray-level difference between the two images is appreciably different at those coordinates, as determined by the threshold θ.

In dynamic image analysis, all pixels in $d_{ij}(x, y)$ with value 1 are considered the result of object motion. This approach is applicable only if the two images are registered and the illumination is relatively constant within the bounds established by θ. In practice, 1-valued entries in $d_{ij}(x, y)$ often arise as a result of noise. Typically, these entries are isolated points in the difference image, and a simple approach to their removal is to form 4- or 8-connected regions of 1's in $d_{ij}(x, y)$ and then ignore any region that has less than a predetermined number of entries. Although it may result in ignoring small and/or slow-moving objects, this approach improves the chances that the remaining entries in the difference image actually are the result of motion.

Figure 7.40 illustrates these concepts. Figure 7.40(a) shows a reference image frame taken at time t_i and containing a single object of constant intensity that is moving with uniform velocity over a background surface, also of constant

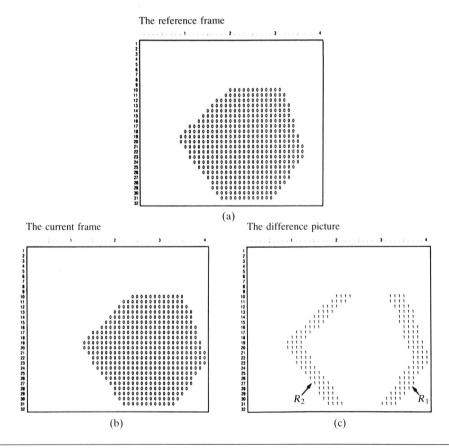

Figure 7.40 (a) Image taken at time t_i; (b) image taken at time t_j; (c) difference image. (From Jain [1981].)

intensity. Figure 7.40(b) shows a current frame taken at time t_j, and Fig. 7.40(c) shows the difference image computed using Eq. (7.5-1) with a threshold larger than the constant background intensity. Note that two disjoint regions were generated by the differencing process: one is the result of the leading edge and the other of the trailing edge of the moving object.

Accumulative differences

As already indicated, a difference image often contains isolated entries that are the result of noise. Although the number of these entries can be reduced or completely eliminated by a thresholded connectivity analysis, this filtering process can also remove small or slow-moving objects. Here, we address this problem by considering changes at a pixel location over several frames, thus introducing a "memory" into the process. The basic idea is to ignore changes that occur only sporadically over a frame sequence and can therefore be attributed to random noise.

Consider a sequence of image frames $f(x, y, t_1), f(x, y, t_2), \ldots , f(x, y, t_n)$, and let $f(x, y, t_1)$ be the reference image. An accumulative difference image is formed by comparing this reference image with every subsequent image in the sequence. A counter for each pixel location in the accumulative image is incremented every time a difference occurs at that pixel location between the reference and an image in the sequence. Thus when the kth frame is being compared with the reference, the entry in a given pixel of the accumulative image gives the number of times the gray level at that position was different from the corresponding pixel value in the reference image. Differences are established, for example, by the use of Eq. (7.5-1).

Figure 7.41 illustrates these concepts. Figures 7.41(a)–(e) show a rectangular object (described by 0's) that is moving to the right with a constant velocity of 1 pixel per frame. The images shown represent instants of time corresponding to 1-pixel displacements. Figure 7.41(a) shows the reference image frame, Figs. 7.41(b)–(d) are frames 2, 3, and 4 in the sequence, and Fig. 7.41(e) is the 11th frame. Figures 7.41(f)–(i) are the corresponding accumulative images, which may be explained as follows. In Fig. 7.41(f), the left-hand column of 1's is the result of differences between the object in Fig. 7.41(a) and the background in 7.41(b). The right-hand column of 1's is caused by differences between the background in the reference image and the leading edge of the moving object. By the time of the fourth frame (Fig. 7.41d), the first nonzero column of the accumulative difference image shows three counts, indicating three total differences between that column in the reference image and the corresponding column in the subsequent frames. Finally, Fig. 7.41(i) shows a total of 10 (represented by "A" in hexadecimal) changes at that location. A similar explanation applies to the other entries.

Often useful is consideration of three types of accumulative difference images: absolute (AADI), positive (PADI), and negative (NADI). The positive and negative quantities are obtained by using Eq. (7.5-1) without the absolute

```
     9
    10   00000000
    11   00000000
    12   00000000
(a) 13   00000000
    14   00000000
    15   00000000
    16
     9                              9
    10   00000000                  10   1     1
    11   00000000                  11   1     1
    12   00000000                  12   1     1
(b) 13   00000000                  13   1     1        (f)
    14   00000000                  14   1     1
    15   00000000                  15   1     1
    16                             16
     9                              9
    10   00000000                  10   21    21
    11   00000000                  11   21    21
    12   00000000                  12   21    21
(c) 13   00000000                  13   21    21        (g)
    14   00000000                  14   21    21
    15   00000000                  15   21    21
    16                             16
     9                              9
    10   00000000                  10   321   321
    11   00000000                  11   321   321
    12   00000000                  12   321   321
(d) 13   00000000                  13   321   321        (h)
    14   00000000                  14   321   321
    15   00000000                  15   321   321
    16                             16
     9                              9
    10          00000000           10   A98765438887654321
    11          00000000           11   A98765438887654321
    12          00000000           12   A98765438887654321
(e) 13          00000000           13   A98765438887654321      (i)
    14          00000000           14   A98765438887654321
    15          00000000           15   A98765438887654321
    16                             16
```

Figure 7.41 (a) Reference image frame; (b)–(e) frames 2, 3, 4, and 11; (f)–(i) accumulative difference images for frames 2, 3, 4, and 11 (the numbers 9–16 on the border are line references only and are not related to this discussion). (From Jain [1981].)

value and by using the reference frame instead of $f(x, y, t_i)$. If the gray levels of an object are numerically greater than the background and the difference is positive, it is compared against a positive threshold; if it is negative, the difference is compared against a negative threshold. This definition is reversed if the gray levels of the object are less than the background.

Example: Figures 7.42(a)–(c) show the AADI, PADI, and NADI for a 20 × 20 pixel object whose intensity is greater than the background and which is moving with constant velocity in a southeasterly direction. The spatial growth of the PADI stops when the object is displaced from its original position. In other words, when an object whose gray levels are greater than the background is completely displaced from its position in the reference image no new entries

```
?????????????????????
?????????????????????
?????????????????????
??988888888888888888811
??988888888888888888811
??988888888888888888811
??98877777777777777772211
??98877777777777777772211
??98877777777777777772211
??98877666666666666332211
??98877666666666666332211
??98877666666666666332211
??98877665555555555544332211
??98877665555555555544332211
??98877665555555555544332211
??98877665544444444445544332211
??98877665544444444445544332211
??98877665544444444445544332211
??98877665544333333336655443322211
??98877665544333333336655443322211
  11223344556666666666655443322211
  11223344556677777777665544332211
  11223344556677777777665544332211
  11223344556666666666655443322211
  11223344556677777777665544332211
  11223344556677777777665544332211
  11223344556666666666655443322211
  11223344556677777777665544332211
  11223344556677777777665544332211
  11223344556666666666655443322211
  11223344556666666666655443322211
  11223344556666666666655443322211
  11223344555555555555544332211
  11223344555555555555544332211
  11223344555555555555544332211
  11223344444444444444332211
  11223344444444444444332211
  11223344444444444444332211
  11223333333333333333332211
  11223333333333333333332211
  11223333333333333333332211
  11222222222222222222211
  11222222222222222222211
  11222222222222222222211
     111111111111111111111
     111111111111111111111
     111111111111111111111
```

(a)

```
9999999999999999999
9999999999999999999
9999999999999999999
99888888888888888888
99888888888888888888
99888888888888888888
99887777777777777777
99887777777777777777
99887777777777777777
99887766666666666666
99887766666666666666
99887766666666666666
99887766555555555555
99887766555555555555
99887766555555555555
99887766554444444444
99887766554444444444
99887766554444444444
99887766554433333333
99887766554433333333
```

(b)

```
                              11
                              11
                              11
                            2211
                            2211
                            2211
                          332211
                          332211
                          332211
                        44332211
                        44332211
                        44332211
                      554433221l
                      554433221l
                      554433221l
                    665544332211
                    665544332211
11223344556666666666655443322211
11223344556677777777665544332211
11223344556677777777665544332211
11223344556666666666655443322211
11223344556677777777665544332211
11223344556677777777665544332211
11223344556666666666655443322211
11223344556677777777665544332211
11223344556677777777665544332211
 11223344556666666666655443322211
 11223344556666666666655443322211
 11223344556666666666655443322211
  11223344555555555555544332211
  11223344555555555555544332211
  11223344555555555555544332211
   11223344444444444444332211
   11223344444444444444332211
   11223344444444444444332211
    11223333333333333333332211
    11223333333333333333332211
    11223333333333333333332211
     11222222222222222222211
     11222222222222222222211
     11222222222222222222211
      111111111111111111111
      111111111111111111111
      111111111111111111111
```

(c)

Figure 7.42 (a) Absolute, (b) positive, and (c) negative accumulative difference images for a 20 × 20 pixel object with intensity greater than the background and moving in a southeasterly direction. (From Jain [1983].)

are generated in the positive accumulative difference image. Thus when its growth stops, the PADI gives the initial location of the object in the reference frame. This property can be used to advantage in creating a reference from a dynamic sequence of images. Note in Fig. 7.42 that the AADI contains the regions of both the PADI and the NADI and that the entries in these images indicate the speed and direction of object movement. The images in Fig. 7.42 are shown in intensity-coded form in Fig. 7.43.   ❏

Establishing a reference image
A key to the success of the techniques discussed in the preceding two sections is having a reference image against which subsequent comparisons can be made. As indicated, the difference between two images in a dynamic imaging problem has the tendency to cancel all stationary components, leaving only image elements that correspond to noise and to the moving objects. The noise problem can be handled by the filtering approach mentioned earlier or by forming an accumulative difference image, as discussed in the preceding section.

In practice, obtaining a reference image with only stationary elements is not always possible, and building a reference from a set of images containing one or more moving objects becomes necessary. This necessity applies particularly to situations describing busy scenes or in cases where frequent updating is required. One procedure for generating a reference image is as follows. Consider the first image in a sequence to be the reference image. When a nonstationary component has moved completely out of its position in the reference frame, the corresponding background in the present frame can be duplicated in the location originally occupied by the object in the reference frame. When all moving objects have moved completely out of their original positions, a reference image containing only stationary components will have been created. Object displacement can be established by monitoring the growth of the PADI.

Example: Figures 7.44 and 7.45 illustrate the approach just discussed. Figure 7.44 shows two image frames of a traffic intersection. The first image is considered the reference, and the second depicts the same scene some time later. The principal moving features are the automobile moving from left to right and a pedestrian crossing the street in the bottom left of the picture. The moving automobile has been removed in Fig. 7.45(a); the pedestrian has been removed in Fig. 7.45(b).   ❏

7.5.2   Frequency Domain Techniques

In this section we consider the problem of determining motion estimates via a Fourier transform formulation. Consider a sequence $f(x, y, t)$, $t = 0, 1, \ldots,$ $T - 1$, of T digital image frames of size $M \times N$ generated by a stationary camera. We begin the development by assuming that all frames have a homogeneous background of zero intensity. The exception is a single, 1-pixel

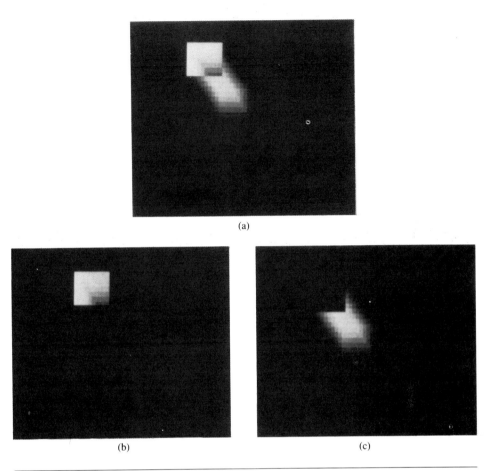

(a)

(b)   (c)

Figure 7.43 *Intensity-coded accumulative difference images for Fig. 7.42: (a) AADI, (b) PADI, and (c) NADI. (From Jain [1983].)*

object of unit intensity that is moving with constant velocity. Suppose that for frame one ($t = 0$) the image plane is projected onto the x axis; that is, the pixel intensities are summed across the columns. This operation yields a 1-D array with M entries that are 0, except at the location where the object is projected. Multiplying the components of the array by $\exp[j2\pi k_1 x\Delta t]$, $x = 0$, $1, \ldots, M - 1$, with the object at coordinates (x', y') at that instant of time, produces a sum equal to $\exp[j2\pi k_1 x'\Delta t]$. In this notation k_1 is a positive integer, and Δt is the time interval between frames.

Suppose that in frame two ($t = 1$) the object has moved to coordinates $(x' + 1, y')$; that is, it has moved 1 pixel parallel to the x axis; then, repeating the procedure yields the sum $\exp[j2\pi k_1(x' + 1)\Delta t]$. If the object continues to move 1 pixel location per frame, then, at any integer instant of time, the result

(a)   (b)

Figure 7.44 *Two image frames of a traffic scene. There are two principal moving objects: a white car in the middle of the picture and a pedestrian on the lower left. (From Jain [1981].)*

is $\exp[j2\pi k_1(x' + t)\Delta t]$, which, using Euler's formula, may be expressed as

$$\exp[j2\pi k_1(x' + t)\Delta t] = \cos[2\pi k_1(x' + t)\Delta t] + j\sin[2\pi k_1(x' + t)\Delta t] \quad (7.5\text{-}2)$$

for $t = 0, 1, \ldots, T - 1$. In other words, this procedure yields a complex sinusoid with frequency k_1. If the object were moving v_1 pixels (in the x direction) between frames, the sinusoid would have frequency $v_1 k_1$. Because t varies between 0 and $T - 1$ in integer increments, restricting k_1 to integer values causes the discrete Fourier transform of the complex sinusoid to have two peaks—one located at frequency $v_1 k_1$ and the other at $T - v_1 k_1$. This latter peak is the result of symmetry foldover, as discussed in Section 3.3.3, and may

(a)   (b)

Figure 7.45 *(a) Image with automobile removed and background restored; (b) image with pedestrian removed and background restored. The latter image can be used as a reference. (From Jain [1981].)*

be ignored. Thus a peak search in the Fourier spectrum yields $v_1 k_1$. Division of this quantity by k_1 yields v_1, which is the velocity component in the x direction, as the frame rate is assumed to be known. Similarly, projections onto the y axis would yield v_2, the component of velocity in the y direction.

A sequence of frames in which no motion takes place produces identical exponential terms, whose Fourier transform would consist of a single peak at a frequency of 0 (a single DC term). Therefore, because the operations discussed so far are linear, the general case involving one or more moving objects in an arbitrary static background would have a Fourier transform with a peak at DC corresponding to static image components and peaks at locations proportional to the velocities of the objects.

These concepts may be summarized by the following relations. For a sequence of T digital images of size $M \times N$, the sum of the weighted projections onto the x axis at any integer instant of time is

$$g_x(t, k_1) = \sum_{x=0}^{M-1} \sum_{y=0}^{N-1} f(x, y, t) e^{j2\pi k_1 x \Delta t} \qquad t = 0, 1, \ldots, T - 1. \qquad (7.5\text{-}3)$$

Similarly, the sum of the projections onto the y axis is

$$g_y(t, k_2) = \sum_{y=0}^{N-1} \sum_{x=0}^{M-1} f(x, y, t) e^{j2\pi k_2 y \Delta t} \qquad t = 0, 1, \ldots, T - 1 \qquad (7.5\text{-}4)$$

where k_1 and k_2 are positive integers.

The 1-D Fourier transforms of Eqs. (7.5-3) and (7.5-4), respectively, are

$$G_x(u_1, k_1) = \frac{1}{T} \sum_{t=0}^{T-1} g_x(t, k_1) e^{-j2\pi u_1 t/T} \qquad u_1 = 0, 1, \ldots, T - 1 \qquad (7.5\text{-}5)$$

and

$$G_y(u_2, k_2) = \frac{1}{T} \sum_{t=0}^{T-1} g_y(t, k_2) e^{-j2\pi u_2 t/T} \qquad u_2 = 0, 1, \ldots, T - 1. \qquad (7.5\text{-}6)$$

In practice, computation of these transforms is carried out using an FFT algorithm, as discussed in Section 3.4.

The frequency–velocity relationship is

$$u_1 = k_1 v_1 \qquad (7.5\text{-}7)$$

and

$$u_2 = k_2 v_2. \qquad (7.5\text{-}8)$$

In this formulation the unit of velocity is in pixels per total frame time. For example, $v_1 = 10$ is interpreted as a motion of 10 pixels in T frames. For frames that are taken uniformly, the actual physical speed depends on the frame rate and the distance between pixels. Thus if $v_1 = 10$, $T = 30$, the frame rate is two images per second, and the distance between pixels is 0.5 m, the actual physical speed in the x direction is

$$v_1 = (10 \text{ pixels})(0.5 \text{ m/pixel})(2 \text{ frames/sec})/(30 \text{ frames})$$
$$= 1/3 \text{ m/sec.}$$

The sign of the x component of the velocity is obtained by computing

$$S_{1x} = \left.\frac{d^2 \text{Re}[g_x(t, k_1)]}{dt^2}\right|_{t=n} \tag{7.5-9}$$

and

$$S_{2x} = \left.\frac{d^2 \text{Im}[g_x(t, k_1)]}{dt^2}\right|_{t=n} \tag{7.5-10}$$

Since g_x is sinusoidal, it can be shown that S_{1x} and S_{2x} will have the same sign at an arbitrary point in time n if the velocity component v_1 is positive. Conversely, opposite signs in S_{1x} and S_{2x} indicate a negative component. If either S_{1x} or S_{2x} is zero, we consider the next closest point in time, $t = n \pm \Delta t$. Similar comments apply to computing the sign of v_2.

Example: Figures 7.46–7.49 illustrate the effectiveness of the approach just derived. Figure 7.46 shows one of a 32-frame sequence of LANDSAT images

Figure 7.46   *LANDSAT frame. (From Cowart, Snyder, and Ruedger [1983].)*

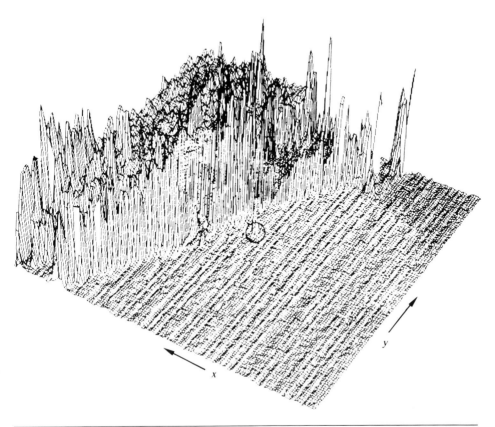

Figure 7.47 *Intensity plot of Fig. 7.46 with target circled. (From Rajala, Riddle, and Snyder [1983].)*

generated by adding white noise to a reference image. The sequence contains a superimposed target moving at 0.5 pixel per frame in the x direction and 1 pixel per frame in the y direction. The target, shown circled in Fig. 7.47, has a Gaussian intensity distribution spread over a small (9-pixel) area and is not easily discernible by eye. The results of computing Eqs. (7.5-5) and (7.5-6) with $k_1 = 6$ and $k_2 = 4$ are shown in Figs. 7.48 and 7.49, respectively. The peak at $u_1 = 3$ in Fig. 7.48 yields $v_1 = 0.5$ from Eq. (7.5-7). Similarly, the peak at $u_2 = 4$ in Fig. 7.49 yields $v_2 = 1.0$ from Eq. (7.5-8). ❏

Guidelines for the selection of k_1 and k_2 can be explained with the aid of Figs. 7.48 and 7.49. For instance, suppose that we had used $k_2 = 15$ instead of $k_2 = 4$. In that case the peaks in Fig. 7.49 would now be at $u_2 = 15$ and 17 because $v_2 = 1.0$, which would be a seriously aliased result. As discussed in Section 3.3.9, aliasing is caused by undersampling (too few frames in the present discussion, as the range of u is determined by T). Because $u = kv$, one possibility is to select k as the integer closest to $k = u_{max}/v_{max}$, where u_{max} is the aliasing frequency limitation established by T, and v_{max} is the maximum expected object velocity.

7.6 CONCLUDING REMARKS

Image segmentation is an essential preliminary step in most automatic pictorial pattern-recognition and scene-analysis problems. As indicated by the range of examples presented, the choice of one segmentation technique over another is dictated mostly by the peculiar characteristics of the problem being considered. The methods discussed in this chapter, although far from exhaustive, are representative of techniques commonly used in practice. The following references can be used as the basis for further study of this topic.

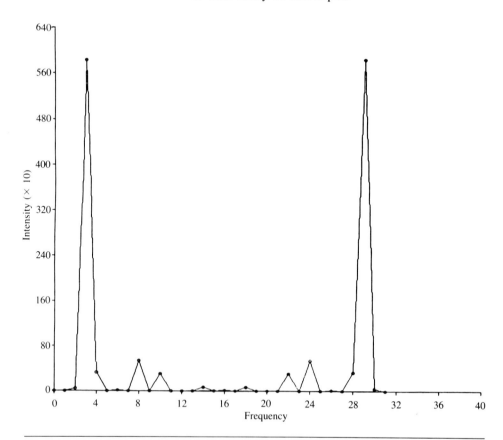

Figure 7.48 *Spectrum of Eq. (7.5-5) showing a peak at $u_1 = 3$. (From Rajala, Riddle, and Snyder [1983].)*

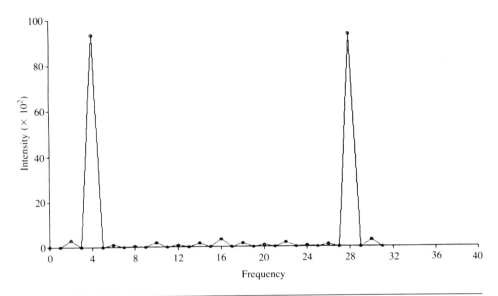

Figure 7.49 *Spectrum of Eq. (7.5-6) showing a peak at* $u_2 = 4$. *(From Rajala, Riddle, and Snyder [1983].)*

REFERENCES

Work dealing with the use of masks to detect gray-level discontinuities has a long history. Mask structures that complement the ones discussed in Section 7.1 are presented in early papers by Roberts [1965], Prewitt [1970], Kirsh [1971], and Robinson [1976]. A review article by Fram and Deutsch [1975] contains numerous masks and an evaluation of their performance. The discussion of the zero crossing properties of the Laplacian is based on a paper by Marr and Hildredth [1980] and the book by Marr [1982]. See also a paper by Clark [1989] on authenticating edges produced by zero crossing algorithms. Correction of parts of the Clark paper is given in Piech [1990]. A paper by Perona and Malik [1990] also is of interest. The vector formulation used for simultaneous detection of discontinuities is based on a paper by Frei and Chen [1977]; see also Park and Choi [1990]. Despite its long history, work on edge detection continues to be a topic of active research, as exemplified in the papers by Saito and Cunningham [1990], Haralick and Lee [1990], and Petrou and Kittler [1991].

For additional general reading on the fundamentals of mask detection and their use in image processing and computer vision, see the books by Rosenfeld and Kak [1982], Levine [1985], Fu, Gonzalez, and Lee [1987], and Jain [1989]. These books also provide additional details on the material presented in Section 7.2.1. The Hough transform (Section 7.2.2) was first proposed by P. V. C. Hough [1962] in a U.S. Patent, and later popularized by Duda and Hart [1972]. A generalization of the Hough transform for detecting arbitrary shapes has been proposed by Ballard [1981]. See also the papers by Hsu and Huang [1990] and Brummer [1991]. The material in Section 7.2.3 is based on two papers by Martelli [1972, 1976]. Another interesting approach based on a minimum-cost search is given by Ramer [1975]. For additional reading on graph searching techniques, see Nilsson [1971, 1980] and

Umeyama [1988]. A paper by Vuylsteke and Kittler [1990] dealing with edge labeling in the presence of noise also is of interest.

Thresholding is one of the earliest techniques developed for segmenting digital images. Some typical early references on this topic are the papers by Doyle [1962], Narasimhan and Fornago [1963], and Rosenfeld et al. [1965]. Survey papers by Weszka [1978], by Sahoo et al. [1988], and by Lee, Chung, and Park [1990] also are of interest. The optimal thresholding technique developed in Section 7.3.4 comes from Chow and Kaneko [1972]. The method presented in Section 7.3.5 is based on a paper by White and Rohrer [1983]. See also the papers by Perez and Gonzalez [1987], and by Parker [1991].

Early references on region-oriented segmentation are Muerle and Allen [1968] and Brice and Fennema [1970]. The review papers by Zucker [1976] and Fu and Mui [1981] establish some unifying concepts and discuss the merits of various segmentation techniques. The concept of a quadtree discussed in Section 7.4.3 was first proposed by Klinger [1972, 1976], who called this approach *regular decomposition*. See also the paper by Horowitz and Pavlidis [1974]. More recent developments in this area are exemplified by the discussions in Ballard and Brown [1982] and by results such as those presented by Grosky and Jain [1983] and Mark and Abel [1985]. An approach proposed by Haddon and Boyce [1990] for unifying region and boundary information for the purpose of segmentation and a segmentation method proposed by Pavlidis and Liow [1990] based on integrating region growing and edge detection also are of interest. Approaches based on the use of texture for image segmentation are exemplified by those reported by Rosenfeld and Kak [1982], Haralick and Shapiro [1985], and Bouman and Liu [1991]. Segmentation based on gray-scale morphological concepts (see Section 8.4) is beginning to show promise. Meyer and Beucher [1990] give a comprehensive overview of the use of morphology for image segmentation.

The material in Section 7.5.1 is based on two papers by Jain [1981, 1983]. The discussion in Section 7.5.2 is based on a technique developed by Rajala, Riddle, and Snyder [1983]. Other works of interest in dynamic image analysis are Aggarwal and Badler [1980], Thompson and Barnard [1981], Webb and Aggarwal [1981], Huang [1981], Yachida [1983], and Adiv [1985]. An interesting hardware implementation for computing motion parameters is given by Koch et al. [1988]. See Thompson [1989] for a collection of papers dealing with motion estimation and analysis. The papers by Shariat and Price [1990] and by Cumani et al. [1991] also are of interest.

PROBLEMS

7.1 A binary image contains straight lines oriented horizontally, vertically, at 45°, and at −45°. Give a set of 3 × 3 masks that can be used to detect 1-pixel-long breaks in these lines. Assume that the gray level of the lines is 1 and that the gray level of the background is 0.

7.2 What would Fig. 7.4 look like if, instead of using the edge model shown in that figure, you were to use a ramp model of an edge, as shown below?

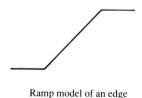

Ramp model of an edge

7.3 The results obtained by a single pass through an image of some 2-D masks can also be achieved by two passes using 1-D masks. For example, the result of using a 3 × 3 smoothing mask with coefficients 1/9 can also be obtained by first passing through an image the mask [1 1 1]. The result of this pass is then followed by a pass of the mask

$$\begin{bmatrix} 1 \\ 1 \\ 1 \end{bmatrix}$$

The final result is then scaled by 1/9. Show that the Sobel masks (Fig. 7.5) can be implemented by one pass of a *differencing* mask of the form $[-1\ 0\ 1]$ (or its vertical counterpart) followed by a *smoothing* mask of the form [1 2 1] (or its vertical counterpart).

7.4 Consider a binary image of size $N \times N$ pixels that contains a square of 1's of size $n \times n$ pixels at its center. The rest of the pixels in this image are background pixels labeled 0.

  a) Sketch the gradient of this image for the approximation given in Eq. (7.1-5). Assume that G_x and G_y are obtained by using the Sobel operators. Give the values of all pixels in the gradient image.

  b) Sketch the histogram of edge directions computed from Eq. (7.1-6). Be precise in labeling the height of each peak of the histogram.

  c) Sketch the Laplacian of the image for the approximation given in Eq. (7.1-10). Give the value of all pixels in the Laplacian image.

7.5 Show that the digital Laplacian given in Eq. (7.1-10) is proportional (by the factor ¼) to subtracting from $f(x, y)$ an average of the 4-neighbors of (x, y). (As indicated in Section 4.3.3, the process of subtracting a blurred version of $f(x, y)$ from itself is called *unsharp masking*.)

7.6 a) Prove that the average value of the Laplacian operator $\nabla^2 h$ given in Eq. (7.1-12) is zero.

  b) Prove that the average value of any image convolved with this operator also is zero.

  c) Would (b) be true in general for the approximation to the Laplacian given in Eq. (7.1-10)? Explain.

7.7 The Sobel gradient operators (Fig. 7.5) have their strongest response for vertical and horizontal edges. The so-called *compass gradient operators* of size 3 × 3 are designed to measure gradients of edges oriented in eight directions: E, NE, N, NW, W, SW, S, and SE. Give the form of these eight operators using coefficients valued 0, 1, or -1. Specify the gradient direction of each mask, keeping in mind that the gradient direction is orthogonal to the edge direction.

7.8 Specify the direction of the line(s) causing the strongest response in each of the line masks shown in Fig. 7.12. Assume that all lines are 1 pixel thick.

7.9 Propose a technique for detecting gaps of length ranging between 1 and L pixels in line segments of a gradient image. Assume that the background is constant, that all lines have been coded with the same intensity level, and that the lines are 1 pixel thick. Base your technique on 8-neighbor connectivity analysis (Section 2.4), rather than attempting to construct masks for detecting the gaps.

7.10 a) Explain why the Hough mapping of point 1 in Fig. 7.18(b) is a straight line.

b) Is this the only point that would produce this result?

c) Explain the reflective adjacency relationship illustrated in Fig. 7.18(d).

7.11 a) Develop a general procedure for obtaining the normal representation of a line from its slope–intercept equation $y = ax + b$.

b) Find the normal representation of the line $y = -2x + 1$.

7.12 An important area of application for image segmentation techniques is in processing images resulting from so-called bubble chamber events. These images arise from experiments in high-energy physics in which a beam of particles of known properties is directed onto a target of known nuclei. A typical event consists of incoming tracks, any one of which, in the event of a collision, branches out into secondary tracks of particles emanating from the point of collision. Propose a segmentation approach for detecting all tracks that contain at least 100 pixels and are angled at any of the following six directions off the horizontal: $\pm 25°$, $\pm 50°$, and $\pm 75°$. The allowable estimation error in any of these six directions is $\pm 5°$. For a track to be valid it must be at least 100 pixels long and not have more than three gaps, any of which cannot exceed 10 pixels. You may assume that the images have been preprocessed so that they are binary and that all tracks are 1 pixel wide, except at the point of collision from which they emanate. Your procedure should be able to differentiate between tracks that have the same direction but different origins.

7.13 a) Superimpose on Fig. 7.21 all the possible edges given by the graph in Fig. 7.22.

b) Compute the cost of the minimum-cost path.

7.14 Find the edge corresponding to the minimum-cost path in the subimage shown below, where the numbers in parentheses indicate intensity. Assume that the edge starts in the first column and ends in the last column.

	0	1	2
0	.	.	.
	(2)	(1)	(0)
1	.	.	.
	(1)	(1)	(7)
2	.	.	.
	(6)	(8)	(2)

7.15 Consider a noiseless image of size $N \times N$ whose first $N/2$ columns have gray level L_A and its remaining columns have gray level L_B, where $L_B > L_A$. The histogram of this image has only two peaks, of identical height, one located at L_A and the other at L_B. Segmenting this image into two halves based on its gray level content is a trivial task that can be accomplished by a single global threshold located between L_A and L_B. Suppose, however, that you multiply the image by a gray-scale wedge that varies from 0 on the left to K on the right, with $K > L_B$. What would the histogram of this new image look like? Label the various parts of this histogram clearly.

7.16 An image is composed of small, nonoverlapping blobs of mean gray level $m_1 = 150$ and variance $\sigma_1^2 = 400$ scattered on a background of mean $m_2 = 25$ and variance $\sigma_2^2 = 625$. All the blobs occupy approximately 20 percent of the image area. Propose a technique, based on thresholding, for segmenting the blobs out of the image.

7.17 Suppose that an image has the following intensity distributions, where $p_1(z)$ corresponds to the intensity of objects and $p_2(z)$ corresponds to the intensity of the background. Assume that $P_1 = P_2$ and find the optimal threshold between object and background pixels.

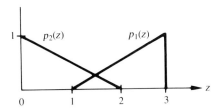

7.18 Start with Eq. (7.3-9) and derive Eqs. (7.3-10) and (7.3-11).

7.19 Derive Eq. (7.3-12) starting from Eqs. (7.3-10) and (7.3-11).

7.20 Consider the image in Problem 7.16 and propose a segmentation scheme based on region growing.

7.21 Segment the image shown below by using the split and merge procedure discussed in Section 7.4.3. Let $P(R_i) = $ TRUE if all pixels in R_i have the same intensity. Show the quadtree corresponding to your segmentation.

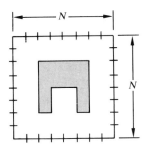

7.22 The speed of a bullet in flight is to be determined by high-speed imaging techniques. The method of choice involves the use of a flash that exposes the imaging surface of a TV camera for T sec. The bullet is 2.5 cm long, 1 cm wide, and its range of speed is 750 ± 250 m/sec. The camera optics produce an image in which the bullet occupies 10 percent of the horizontal resolution of a 256 × 256 digital image.

a) Determine the maximum value of T that will guarantee that the blur from motion does not exceed 1 pixel.

b) Determine the minimum number of frames per second that would have to be taken in order to guarantee that at least two complete images of the bullet are obtained during its path through the field of view of the camera.

c) Propose a segmentation procedure for automatically extracting the bullet from a sequence of frames.

d) Propose a method for automatically determining the speed of the bullet.

CHAPTER 8

REPRESENTATION AND DESCRIPTION

Well, but reflect; have we not several times
acknowledged that names rightly given are the
likenesses and images of the things which they
name?

Socrates

After an image has been segmented into regions by methods such as those discussed in Chapter 7, the resulting aggregate of segmented pixels usually are represented and described in a form suitable for further computer processing. Basically, representing a region involves two choices: (1) we can represent the region in terms of its external characteristics (its boundary), or (2) we can represent it in terms of its internal characteristics (the pixels comprising the region). Choosing a representation scheme, however, is only part of the task of making the data useful to a computer. The next task is to *describe* the region based on the chosen representation. For example, a region may be represented by its boundary with the boundary described by features such as its length, the orientation of the straight line joining the extreme points, and the number of concavities in the boundary.

Generally, an external representation is chosen when the primary focus is on shape characteristics. An internal representation is selected when the primary focus is on reflectivity properties, such as color and texture. In either case, the features selected as descriptors should be as insensitive as possible to variations such as changes in size, translation, and rotation. For the most part, the descriptors discussed in this chapter satisfy one or more of these properties.

8.1 REPRESENTATION SCHEMES

The segmentation techniques discussed in Chapter 7 yield raw data in the form of pixels along a boundary or pixels contained in a region. Although these data are sometimes used directly to obtain descriptors (as in determining the texture of a region), standard practice is to use schemes that compact the data into representations that are considerably more useful in the computation of descriptors. In this section we discuss various representation approaches.

8.1.1 Chain Codes

Chain codes are used to represent a boundary by a connected sequence of straight-line segments of specified length and direction. Typically, this representation is based on the 4- or 8-connectivity of the segments. The direction of each segment is coded by using a numbering scheme such as the ones shown in Fig. 8.1.

Digital images usually are acquired and processed in a grid format with equal spacing in the x and y directions, so a chain code could be generated by following a boundary in, say, a clockwise direction and assigning a direction to the segments connecting every pair of pixels. This method generally is unacceptable for two principal reasons: (1) the resulting chain of codes usually is quite long, and (2) any small disturbances along the boundary owing to noise or imperfect segmentation cause changes in the code that may not necessarily be related to the shape of the boundary.

An approach frequently used to circumvent the problems just discussed is to resample the boundary by selecting a larger grid spacing, as illustrated in Fig. 8.2(a). Then, as the boundary is traversed, a boundary point is assigned to each node of the large grid, depending on the proximity of the original boundary to that node, as shown in Fig. 8.2(b). The resampled boundary obtained in this way can then be represented by a 4- or 8-code, as shown in Figs. 8.2(c) and (d), respectively. The starting point in Fig. 8.2(c) is at the dot, and the boundary is the shortest allowable external 4-path in the grid of Fig.

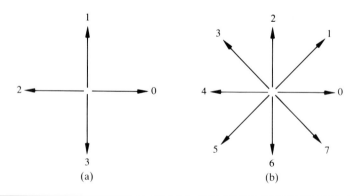

Figure 8.1 Directions for (a) 4-directional chain code and (b) 8-directional chain code.

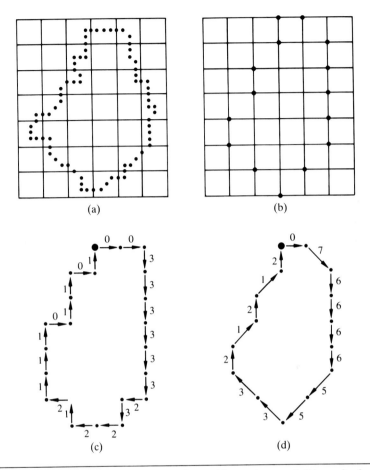

Figure 8.2 *(a) Digital boundary with resampling grid superimposed; (b) result of resampling; (c) 4-directional chain code; (d) 8-directional chain code.*

8.2(b). The boundary representation in Fig. 8.2(c) is the chain code 0033 . . . 01, and in Fig. 8.2(d) it is the code 076 . . . 12. As might be expected, the accuracy of the resulting code representation depends on the spacing of the sampling grid.

The chain code of a boundary depends on the starting point. However, the code can be normalized by a straightforward procedure: For a chain code generated by starting in an arbitrary position, we treat it as a circular sequence of direction numbers and redefine the starting point so that the resulting sequence of numbers forms an integer of minimum magnitude. We can also normalize for rotation by using the first difference of the chain code instead of the code itself. This difference is obtained simply by counting (counterclockwise) the number of directions that separate two adjacent elements of the code. For instance, the first difference of the 4-direction chain code 10103322 is 3133030. If we elect to treat the code as a circular sequence, then the first element of the difference is computed by using the transition between the last and first components of the chain. Here, the result is 33133030. Size normalization can be achieved by altering the size of the resampling grid.

These normalizations are exact only if the boundaries themselves are invariant to rotation and scale change, which, in practice, is seldom the case. For instance, the same object digitized in two different orientations will in general have different boundary shapes, with the degree of dissimilarity being proportional to image resolution. This effect can be reduced by selecting chain elements that are large in proportion to the distance between pixels in the digitized image or by orienting the resampling grid along the principal axes of the object to be coded, as discussed in Section 8.2.2.

8.1.2 Polygonal Approximations

A digital boundary can be approximated with arbitrary accuracy by a polygon. For a closed curve, the approximation is exact when the number of segments in the polygon is equal to the number of points in the boundary so that each pair of adjacent points defines a segment in the polygon. In practice, the goal of a polygonal approximation is to capture the essence of the boundary shape with the fewest possible polygonal segments. This problem in general is not trivial and can quickly turn into a time-consuming iterative search. However, several polygonal approximation techniques of modest complexity and processing requirements are well suited for image processing applications.

We begin the discussion of these techniques with a method for finding minimum perimeter polygons. The procedure is best explained by an example. Suppose that we enclose a boundary by a set of concatenated cells, as shown in Fig. 8.3(a). It helps to visualize this enclosure as two walls corresponding to the outside and inside boundaries of the strip of cells and think of the object boundary as a rubber band contained within the walls. If the rubber band is allowed to shrink, it takes the shape shown in Fig. 8.3(b), producing a polygon of minimum perimeter that fits the geometry established by the cell strip. If each cell encompasses only one point on the boundary, the error in each cell between the original boundary and the rubber-band approximation at most would be $\sqrt{2}d$, where d is the distance between pixels. This error can be reduced by half by forcing each cell to be centered on its corresponding pixel.

Merging techniques based on error or other criteria have been applied to the problem of polygonal approximation. One approach is to merge points along a boundary until the least square error line fit of the points merged so

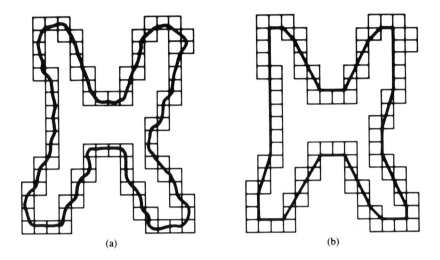

Figure 8.3 *(a) Object boundary enclosed by cells; (b) minimum perimeter polygon.*

far exceeds a preset threshold. When this condition occurs, the parameters of the line are stored, the error is set to 0, and the procedure is repeated, merging new points along the boundary until the error again exceeds the threshold. At the end of the procedure the intersections of adjacent line segments form the vertices of the polygon. One of the principal difficulties with this method is that vertices generally do not correspond to inflections (such as corners) in the boundary, because a new line is not started until the error threshold is exceeded. If, for instance, a long straight line were being tracked and it turned a corner, a number (depending on the threshold) of points past the corner would be absorbed before the threshold was exceeded. However, splitting along with merging may be used to alleviate this difficulty.

One approach to boundary segment *splitting* is to subdivide a segment successively into two parts until a given criterion is satisfied. For instance, a requirement might be that the maximum perpendicular distance from a boundary segment to the line joining its two end points not exceed a preset threshold. If it does, the farthest point becomes a vertex, thus subdividing the initial segment into two subsegments. This approach has the advantage of seeking prominent inflection points. For a closed boundary, the best starting points are usually the two farthest points in the boundary. For example, Fig. 8.4(a) shows an object boundary, and Fig. 8.4(b) shows a subdivision of this boundary (solid line) about its farthest points. The point marked c has the longest perpendicular distance from the top segment to line ab. Similarly, point d has the longest distance in the bottom segment. Figure 8.4(c) shows the result of using the splitting procedure with a threshold equal to 0.25 times the length of line ab.

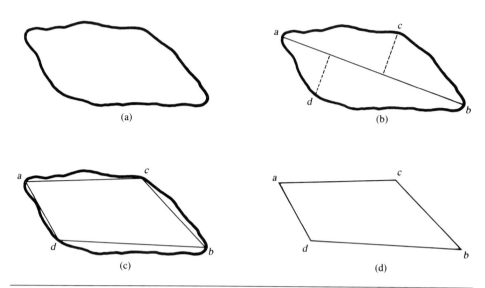

Figure 8.4 *(a) Original boundary; (b) boundary divided into segments based on distance computations; (c) joining of vertices; (d) resulting polygon.*

As no point in the new boundary segments has a perpendicular distance (to its corresponding straight-line segment) that exceeds this threshold, the procedure terminates with the polygon shown in Fig. 8.4(d).

8.1.3 Signatures

A signature is a 1-D functional representation of a boundary and may be generated in various ways. One of the simplest is to plot the distance from the centroid to the boundary as a function of angle, as illustrated in Fig. 8.5. Regardless of how a signature is generated, however, the basic idea is to reduce the boundary representation to a 1-D function, which presumably is easier to describe than the original 2-D boundary.

Signatures generated by the approach just described are invariant to translation, but they do depend on rotation and scaling. Normalization with respect to rotation can be achieved by finding a way to select the same starting point to generate the signature, regardless of the shape's orientation. One way to do so is to select the starting point as the point farthest from the centroid, if this point happens to be unique and independent of rotational aberrations for each shape of interest. Another way is to select the point on the principal eigen (major) axis farthest from the centroid (see Section 3.6). This method requires more computation, but it is more rugged because the direction of the major eigen axis is determined from the covariance matrix, which is based on all contour points. Yet another way is to obtain the chain code of the boundary and then use the approach discussed in Section 8.1.1, assuming that the coding is coarse enough that rotation does not affect its circularity.

Based on the assumptions of uniformity in scaling with respect to both axes and that sampling is taken at equal intervals of θ, changes in size of a shape result in changes in the amplitude values of the corresponding signature. One simple way to normalize for this result is to scale all functions so that they always span the same range of values, say, [0, 1]. The main advantage of this method is simplicity, but it has the potentially serious disadvantage that scaling of the entire function depends on only two values: the minimum and maximum. If the shapes are noisy, this dependence can be a source of error from object to object. A more rugged (but also more computationally intensive) approach is to divide each sample by the variance of the signature, assuming that the variance is not zero—as in the case of Fig. 8.5(a)—or so small that it creates computational difficulties. Use of the variance yields a variable scaling factor that is inversely proportional to changes in size and works much as automatic gain control does. Whatever the method used, the basic idea is to remove dependency on size but to preserve the fundamental shape of the waveforms.

Distance versus angle is, of course, not the only way to generate a signature. For example, the boundary could be traversed and the angle plotted between

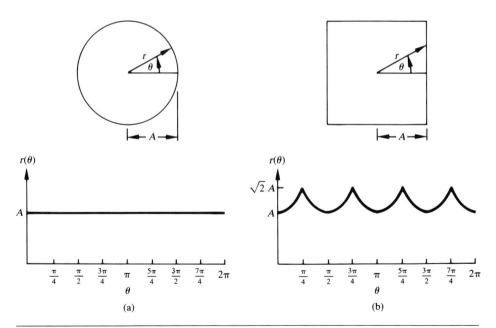

Figure 8.5   *Two simple boundary shapes and their corresponding distance-versus-angle signatures. In (a) $r(\theta)$ is constant, while in (b) $r(\theta) = A \sec \theta$. (From Fu, Gonzalez, and Lee [1987].)*

a line tangent to the boundary and a reference line as a function of position along the boundary. The resulting signature, although quite different from the $r(\theta)$ curve, would carry information about basic shape characteristics. For instance, horizontal segments in the curve would correspond to straight lines along the boundary, because the tangent angle would be constant there. A variation of this approach is to use the so-called *slope density function* as a signature. This function is simply a histogram of tangent-angle values. As a histogram is a measure of concentration of values, the slope density function responds strongly to sections of the boundary with constant tangent angles (straight or nearly straight segments) and has deep valleys in sections producing rapidly varying angles (corners or other sharp inflections).

8.1.4 Boundary Segments

Decomposing a boundary into segments often is useful. Decomposition reduces the boundary's complexity and thus simplifies the description process. This approach is particularly attractive when the boundary contains one or more significant concavities that carry shape information. In this case use of the convex hull of the region enclosed by the boundary is a powerful tool for robust decomposition of the boundary.

The *convex hull H* of an arbitrary set S is the smallest convex set containing S. The set difference $H - S$ is called the *convex deficiency D* of the set S. To envision how these concepts might be used to partition a boundary into meaningful segments, consider Fig. 8.6(a), which shows an object (set S) and its convex deficiency (shaded regions). The region boundary can be partitioned by following the contour of S and marking the points at which a transition is made into or out of a component of the convex deficiency. Figure 8.6(b) shows the result in this case. Note that in principle, this scheme is independent of region size and orientation.

In practice, digital boundaries tend to be irregular because of digitization, noise, and variations in segmentation. These effects usually result in a convex

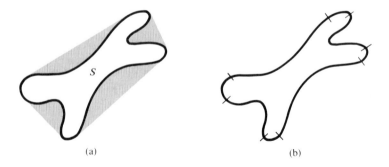

(a)   (b)

Figure 8.6   *(a) A region (S) and its convex deficiency (shaded); (b) partitioned boundary.*

deficiency that has small, meaningless components scattered randomly throughout the boundary. Rather than attempt to sort out these irregularities by postprocessing, common practice is to smooth a boundary prior to partitioning. There are a number of ways to do so. One way is to traverse the boundary and replace the coordinates of each pixel by the average coordinates of m of its neighbors along the boundary. This approach works for small irregularities, but it is time-consuming and difficult to control. Large values of m can result in excessive smoothing, whereas small values of m might not be sufficient in some segments of the boundary. A more rugged technique is to use a polygonal approximation, as discussed in Section 8.1.2, prior to finding the convex deficiency of a region. Regardless of the method used for smoothing, most digital boundaries of interest are simple polygons (polygons without self intersection). Graham and Yao [1983] give an algorithm for finding the convex hull of such polygons.

The concepts of a convex hull and its deficiency are equally useful for describing an entire region, as well as just its boundary. For example, description of a region might be based on its area and the area of its convex deficiency, the number of components in the convex deficiency, the relative location of these components, and so on. We develop an algorithm for finding the convex hull of a region in Section 8.4.4. References cited at the end of this chapter contain other formulations.

8.1.5   The Skeleton of a Region

An important approach to representing the structural shape of a plane region is to reduce it to a graph. This reduction may be accomplished by obtaining the *skeleton* of the region via a thinning (also called *skeletonizing*) algorithm. Thinning procedures play a central role in a broad range of problems in image processing, ranging from automated inspection of printed circuit boards to counting of asbestos fibers in air filters.

The skeleton of a region may be defined via the medial axis transformation (MAT) proposed by Blum [1967]. The MAT of a region R with border B is as follows. For each point p in R, we find its closest neighbor in B. If p has more than one such neighbor, it is said to belong to the *medial axis* (skeleton) of R. The concept of "closest" depends on the definition of a distance (see Section 2.4.5), and therefore the results of a MAT operation are influenced by the choice of a distance measure. Figure 8.7 shows some examples using the Euclidean distance.

Although the MAT of a region yields an intuitively pleasing skeleton, direct implementation of that definition is typically prohibitive computationally. Implementation potentially involves calculating the distance from every interior point to every point on the boundary of a region. Numerous algorithms have been proposed for improving computational efficiency while at the same time attempting to produce a medial axis representation of a region. Typically, these

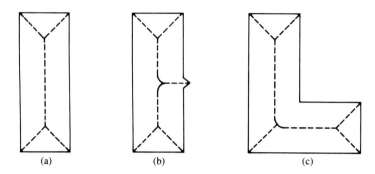

Figure 8.7 *Medial axes of three simple regions.*

are thinning algorithms that iteratively delete edge points of a region subject to the constraints that deletion of these points (1) does not remove end points, (2) does not break connectedness, and (3) does not cause excessive erosion of the region.

In this section we present an algorithm for thinning binary regions. Region points are assumed to have value 1 and background points to have value 0. The method consists of successive passes of two basic steps applied to the contour points of the given region, where a *contour point* is any pixel with value 1 and having at least one 8-neighbor valued 0. With reference to the 8-neighborhood definition shown in Fig. 8.8, step 1 flags a contour point p for deletion if the following conditions are satisfied:

(a) $2 \leqslant N(p_1) \leqslant 6$;

(b) $S(p_1) = 1$;   (8.1-1)

(c) $p_2 \cdot p_4 \cdot p_6 = 0$;

(d) $p_4 \cdot p_6 \cdot p_8 = 0$;

where $N(p_1)$ is the number of nonzero neighbors of p_1; that is,

$$N(p_1) = p_2 + p_3 + \cdots + p_8 + p_9 \qquad (8.1\text{-}2)$$

p_9	p_2	p_3
p_8	p_1	p_4
p_7	p_6	p_5

Figure 8.8 *Neighborhood arrangement used by the thinning algorithm.*

and $S(p_1)$ is the number of 0-1 transitions in the ordered sequence of p_2, p_3, . . . , p_8, p_9, p_2. For example, $N(p_1) = 4$ and $S(p_1) = 3$ in Fig. 8.9.

In step 2, conditions (a) and (b) remain the same, but conditions (c) and (d) are changed to

(c') $p_2 \cdot p_4 \cdot p_8 = 0$;   (8.1-3)

(d') $p_2 \cdot p_6 \cdot p_8 = 0$.

Step 1 is applied to every border pixel in the binary region under consideration. If one or more of conditions (a)–(d) are violated, the value of the point in question is not changed. If all conditions are satisfied the point is flagged for deletion. However, the point is not deleted until all border points have been processed. This delay prevents changing the structure of the data during execution of the algorithm. After step 1 has been applied to all border points, those that were flagged are deleted (changed to 0). Then, step 2 is applied to the resulting data in exactly the same manner as step 1.

Thus one iteration of the thinning algorithm consists of (1) applying step 1 to flag border points for deletion; (2) deleting the flagged points; (3) applying step 2 to flag the remaining border points for deletion; and (4) deleting the flagged points. This basic procedure is applied iteratively until no further points are deleted, at which time the algorithm terminates, yielding the skeleton of the region.

Condition (a) is violated when contour point p_1 has only one or seven 8-neighbors valued 1. Having only one such neighbor implies that p_1 is the end point of a skeleton stroke and obviously should not be deleted. Deleting p_1 if it had seven such neighbors would cause erosion into the region. Condition (b) is violated when it is applied to points on a stroke 1 pixel thick. Hence this condition prevents disconnection of segments of a skeleton during the thinning operation. Conditions (c) and (d) are satisfied simultaneously by the minimum set of values: ($p_4 = 0$ or $p_6 = 0$) or ($p_2 = 0$ and $p_8 = 0$). Thus with reference to the neighborhood arrangement in Fig. 8.8, a point that satisfies these conditions, as well as conditions (a) and (b), is an east or south boundary point or a northwest corner point in the boundary. In either case, p_1 is not part of the skeleton and should be removed. Similarly, conditions (c') and (d') are

0	0	1
1	p_1	0
1	0	1

Figure 8.9 *Illustration of conditions (a) and (b) in Eq. (8.1-1). In this case $N(p_1) = 4$ and $S(p_1) = 3$.*

satisfied simultaneously by the following minimum set of values: ($p_2 = 0$ *or* $p_8 = 0$) or ($p_4 = 0$ *and* $p_6 = 0$). These correspond to north or west boundary points, or a southeast corner point. Note that northeast corner points have $p_2 = 0$ and $p_4 = 0$ and thus satisfy conditions (c) and (d), as well as (c′) and (d′). The same is true for southwest corner points, which have $p_6 = 0$ and $p_8 = 0$.

Example: Figure 8.10(a) shows the result of applying step 1 of the thinning algorithm to the boundary of a simple region. The dots indicate the points flagged and subsequently removed at the end of step 1. Figure 8.10(b) shows the results obtained with step 2, and Fig. 8.10(c) shows the skeleton obtained after several iterations through these two steps. The skeleton of a region with less-regular properties is shown in Fig. 8.11. □

8.2 BOUNDARY DESCRIPTORS

8.2.1 Some Simple Descriptors

The *length* of a contour is one of its simplest descriptors. Simply counting the number of pixels along the contour gives a rough approximation of the length. For a chain-coded curve with unit spacing in both directions, the number of vertical and horizontal components plus $\sqrt{2}$ times the number of diagonal components gives the exact length.

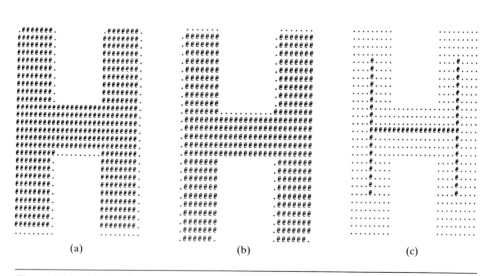

Figure 8.10   (a) Result of step 1 of the thinning algorithm during the first iteration through a region; (b) result of step 2; (c) final result. (From Zhang and Suen [1984].)

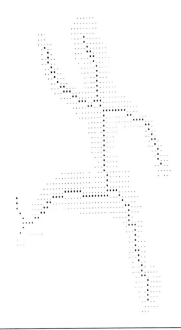

Figure 8.11 *Another example of thinning. (From Zhang and Suen [1984].)*

The *diameter* of a boundary B is defined as

$$\text{Diam}\ (B)\ =\ \max_{i,j}\ [D(p_i, p_j)] \qquad (8.2\text{-}1)$$

where D is a distance measure (see Section 2.4.5) and p_i and p_j are points on the boundary. The value of the diameter and the orientation of a line connecting the two extreme points that comprise the diameter (this line is called the *major axis* of the boundary) are useful descriptors of a boundary.

Curvature is defined as the rate of change of slope. In general, obtaining reliable measures of curvature at a point in a digital boundary is difficult because these boundaries tend to be locally "ragged." However, using the difference between the slopes of adjacent boundary segments (which have been represented as straight lines) as a descriptor of curvature at the point of intersection of the segments may prove helpful. For example, the vertices of boundaries such as those shown in Figs. 8.3(b) and 8.4(d) lend themselves well to curvature descriptions. As the boundary is traversed in the clockwise direction, a vertex point p is said to be part of a *convex* segment if the change in slope at p is nonnegative; otherwise, p is said to belong to a segment that is *concave*. The description of curvature at a point can be refined further by using ranges in the change of slope. For instance, p could be part of a nearly straight segment if the change is less than 10° or a *corner* point if the change exceeds 90°. Note, however, that these descriptors must be used with care because their interpretation depends on the length of the individual segments relative to the overall length of the boundary.

8.2.2 Shape Numbers

As explained in Section 8.1.1, the first difference of a chain-coded boundary depends on the starting point. The *shape number* of such a boundary, based on the 4-directional code of Fig. 8.1(a), is defined as the first difference of smallest magnitude. The *order n* of a shape number is defined as the number of digits in its representation. Moreover, n is even for a closed boundary, and its value limits the number of possible different shapes. Figure 8.12 shows all the shapes of order 4, 6, and 8, along with their chain-code representations, first differences, and corresponding shape numbers. Note that the first differences were computed by treating the chain codes as a circular sequence, as discussed in Section 8.1.1. Although the first difference of a chain code is independent of rotation, in general the coded boundary depends on the orientation of the grid. One way to normalize the grid orientation follows.

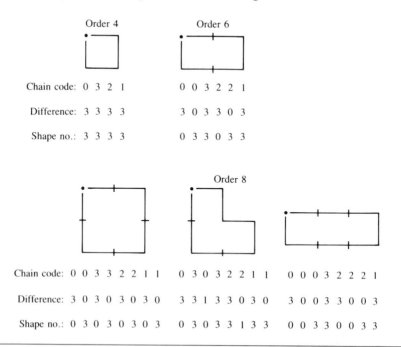

	Order 4		Order 6
Chain code:	0 3 2 1		0 0 3 2 2 1
Difference:	3 3 3 3		3 0 3 3 0 3
Shape no.:	3 3 3 3		0 3 3 0 3 3

			Order 8	
Chain code:	0 0 3 3 2 2 1 1	0 3 0 3 2 2 1 1	0 0 0 3 2 2 2 1
Difference:	3 0 3 0 3 0 3 0	3 3 1 3 3 0 3 0	3 0 0 3 3 0 0 3
Shape no.:	0 3 0 3 0 3 0 3	0 3 0 3 3 1 3 3	0 0 3 3 0 0 3 3

Figure 8.12 *All shapes of order 4, 6, and 8. The directions are from Fig. 8.1(a), and the dot indicates the starting point.*

As indicated previously, the *major axis* of a boundary is the straight-line segment joining the two points farthest from each other. The *minor axis* is perpendicular to the major axis and of such length that a box could be formed that just encloses the boundary. The ratio of the major to the minor axis is called the *eccentricity* of the boundary, and the rectangle just described is called the *basic rectangle*. In most cases a unique shape number will be obtained by aligning the chain-code grid with the sides of the basic rectangle.

In practice, for a desired shape order, we find the rectangle of order n whose eccentricity best approximates that of the basic rectangle and use this new rectangle to establish the grid size. For example, if $n = 12$, all the rectangles of order 12 (that is, those whose perimeter length is 12) are 2×4, 3×3, and 1×5. If the eccentricity of the 2×4 rectangle best matches the eccentricity of the basic rectangle for a given boundary, we establish a 2×4 grid centered on the basic rectangle and use the procedure outlined in Section 8.1.1 to obtain the chain code. The shape number follows from the first difference of this code, as indicated earlier. Although the order of the resulting shape number usually equals n because of the way the grid spacing was selected, boundaries with depressions comparable to this spacing sometimes yield shape numbers of order greater than n. In this case, we specify a rectangle of order lower than n and repeat the procedure until the resulting shape number is of order n.

Example: Suppose that $n = 18$ is specified for the boundary shown in Fig. 8.13(a). To obtain a shape number of this order requires following the steps just discussed. The first step is to find the basic rectangle, as shown in Fig. 8.13(b). The closest rectangle of order 18 is a 3×6 rectangle, requiring subdivision of the basic rectangle as shown in Fig. 8.13(c), where the chain-code directions are aligned with the resulting grid. The final step is to obtain the chain code and use its first difference to compute the shape number, as shown in Fig. 8.13(d). ❏

8.2.3 Fourier Descriptors

Figure 8.14 shows an N-point digital boundary in the xy plane. Starting at an arbitrary point (x_0, y_0), coordinate pairs (x_0, y_0), (x_1, y_1), (x_2, y_2), . . . , (x_{N-1}, y_{N-1}) are encountered in traversing the boundary, say, counterclockwise. These coordinates can be expressed in the form $x(k) = x_k$ and $y(k) = y_k$. With this notation, the boundary itself can be represented as the sequence of coordinates $s(k) = [x(k), y(k)]$, for $k = 0, 1, 2, . . . , N - 1$. Moreover, each coordinate pair can be treated as a complex number so that

$$s(k) = x(k) + jy(k) \qquad (8.2\text{-}2)$$

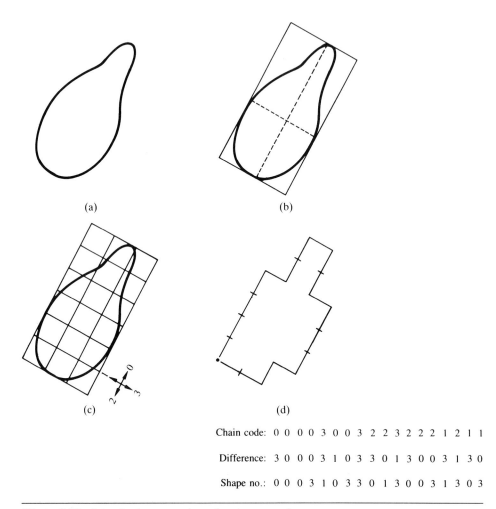

Chain code: 0 0 0 0 3 0 0 3 2 2 3 2 2 2 1 2 1 1

Difference: 3 0 0 0 3 1 0 3 3 0 1 3 0 0 3 1 3 0

Shape no.: 0 0 0 3 1 0 3 3 0 1 3 0 0 3 1 3 0 3

Figure 8.13 *Steps in the generation of a shape number.*

for $k = 0, 1, 2, \ldots, N - 1$. That is, the x axis is treated as the real axis and the y axis as the imaginary axis of a sequence of complex numbers. Although the interpretation of the sequence has been recast, the nature of the boundary itself has not been changed. Of course, this representation has one great advantage: It reduces a 2-D to a 1-D problem.

The discrete Fourier transform (DFT) of $s(k)$ is

$$a(u) = \frac{1}{N} \sum_{k=0}^{N-1} s(k) \exp[-j2\pi uk/N] \qquad (8.2\text{-}3)$$

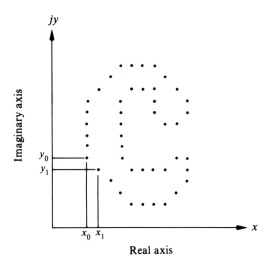

Figure 8.14 *A digital boundary and its representation as a complex sequence. The points* (x_0, y_0) *and* (x_1, y_1) *are (arbitrarily) the first two points in the sequence.*

for $u = 0, 1, 2, \ldots, N - 1$. The complex coefficients $a(u)$ are called the *Fourier descriptors* of the boundary. The inverse Fourier transform of the $a(u)$'s restores $s(k)$. That is,

$$s(k) = \sum_{u=0}^{N-1} a(u)\exp[j2\pi uk/N] \qquad (8.2\text{-}4)$$

for $k = 0, 1, 2, \ldots, N - 1$. Suppose, however, that instead of all the $a(u)$'s, only the first M coefficients are used. This is equivalent to setting $a(u) = 0$ for $u > M - 1$ in Eq. (8.2-4). The result is the following approximation to $s(k)$:

$$\hat{s}(k) = \sum_{u=0}^{M-1} a(u)\exp[j2\pi uk/N] \qquad (8.2\text{-}5)$$

for $k = 0, 1, 2, \ldots, N - 1$. Although only M terms are used to obtain each component of $\hat{s}(k)$, k still ranges from 0 to $N - 1$. That is, the same number of points exist in the approximate boundary, but not as many terms are used in the reconstruction of each point. If the number of points in the boundary is large, M generally is selected as an integer power of 2 so that an FFT algorithm can be used to expedite computation of the descriptors. Recall from discussions of the Fourier transform in Chapters 3 and 4 that high-frequency components account for fine detail, and low-frequency components determine global shape. Thus the smaller M becomes, the more detail is lost on the boundary.

Example: Figure 8.15 shows a square boundary consisting of $N = 64$ points and the results of using Eq. (8.2-5) to reconstruct this boundary for various values of M. Note that the value of M has to be about 8 before the reconstructed boundary looks more like a square than a circle. Next, note that little in the way of corner definition occurs until M is about 56, at which time the corner points begin to "break out" of the sequence. Finally, note that, when $M = 61$, the curves begin to straighten, which leads to an almost exact replica of the original one additional coefficient later. Thus a few low-order coefficients are able to capture gross shape, but many more high-order terms are required to define accurately sharp features such as corners and straight lines. This result

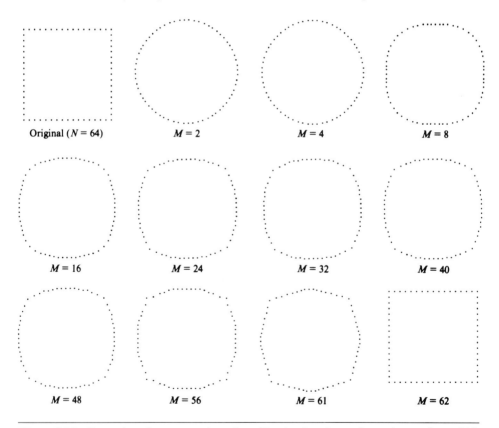

Figure 8.15   *Examples of reconstructions from Fourier descriptors for various values of M.*

is not unexpected in view of the role played by low- and high-frequency components in defining the shape of a region. ❏

    As demonstrated in the preceding example, a few Fourier descriptors can be used to capture the gross essence of a boundary. This property is valuable, because these coefficients carry shape information. Thus they can be used as the basis for differentiating between distinct boundary shapes, as we discuss in some detail in Chapter 9.

    We have stated several times that descriptors should be as insensitive as possible to translation, rotation, and scale changes. In cases where results depend on the order in which points are processed, an additional constraint is that descriptors should be insensitive to starting point. Fourier descriptors are not directly insensitive to these geometrical changes, but the changes can be related to simple transformations on the descriptors. For example, consider rotation and recall from elementary mathematical analysis that rotation of a point by an angle θ about the origin of the complex plane is accomplished by multiplying the point by $e^{j\theta}$. Doing so to every point of $s(k)$ rotates the entire sequence about the origin. The rotated sequence is $s(k)e^{j\theta}$, whose Fourier descriptors are

$$a_r(u) = \frac{1}{N} \sum_{k=0}^{N-1} s(k) \exp[j\theta] \exp[-j2\pi uk/N]$$
$$= a(u)e^{j\theta} \tag{8.2-6}$$

for $u = 0, 1, 2, \ldots, N - 1$. Thus rotation simply affects all coefficients equally by a multiplicative *constant* term $e^{j\theta}$.

    Table 8.1 summarizes the Fourier descriptors for a boundary sequence $s(k)$ that undergoes rotation, translation, scaling, and changes in starting point. The symbol Δ_{xy} is defined as $\Delta_{xy} = \Delta x + j\Delta y$, so the notation $s_t(k) = s(k) + \Delta_{xy}$ indicates redefining the sequence as

$$s_t(k) = [x(k) + \Delta x] + j[y(k) + \Delta y]. \tag{8.2-7}$$

Table 8.1 Some Basic Properties of Fourier Descriptors

Transformation	Boundary	Fourier Descriptor
Identity	$s(k)$	$a(u)$
Rotation	$s_r(k) = s(k)e^{j\theta}$	$a_r(u) = a(u)e^{j\theta}$
Translation	$s_t(k) = s(k) + \Delta_{xy}$	$a_t(u) = a(u) + \Delta_{xy}\,\delta(u)$
Scaling	$s_s(k) = \alpha s(k)$	$a_s(u) = \alpha a(u)$
Starting point	$s_p(k) = s(k - k_0)$	$a_p(u) = a(u)\,e^{-j2\pi k_0 u/N}$

In other words, translation consists of adding a constant displacement to all coordinates in the boundary. Note that translation has no effect on the descriptors, except for $k = 0$, which has the impulse function $\delta(k)$.[†] Finally, the expression $s_p(k) = s(k - k_0)$ means redefining the sequence as

$$s_p(k) = x(k - k_0) + jy(k - k_0) \tag{8.2-8}$$

which merely changes the starting point of the sequence to $k = k_0$ from $k = 0$. The last entry in Table 8.1 shows that a change in starting point affects all descriptors in a different (but known) way, in the sense that the term multiplying $a(u)$ depends on u.

8.2.4 Moments

The shape of boundary segments (and of signatures) can be described quantitatively by using moments. In order to see how this can be accomplished, consider Fig. 8.16(a), which shows the segment of a boundary, and Fig. 8.16(b), which shows the segment represented as a 1-D function $g(r)$ of an arbitrary variable r. Let us treat the amplitude of g as a random variable v and form an amplitude histogram $p(v_i)$, $i = 1, 2, \ldots, K$, where K is the number of discrete amplitude increments. Then, the nth moment of v about its mean is

$$\mu_n(v) = \sum_{i=1}^{K} (v_i - m)^n p(v_i) \tag{8.2-9}$$

where

$$m = \sum_{i=1}^{K} v_i p(v_i). \tag{8.2-10}$$

The quantity m is recognized as the mean or average value of v and μ_2 as its variance. Generally, only the first few moments are required to differentiate between signatures of clearly distinct shapes.

An alternative approach is to normalize $g(r)$ to unit area and treat it as a histogram. In this case, r becomes the random variable and the moments are

$$\mu_n(r) = \sum_{i=1}^{L} (r_i - m)^n g(r_i) \tag{8.2-11}$$

where

$$m = \sum_{i=1}^{L} r_i g(r_i). \tag{8.2-12}$$

[†] The Fourier transform of a constant is an impulse located at the origin. Recall that the impulse function is zero everywhere else.

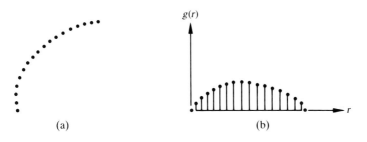

(a)   (b)

Figure 8.16   *(a) Boundary segment; (b) representation as a 1-D function.*

In this notation, L is the number of points on the boundary, and $\mu_n(r)$ is directly related to the shape of $g(r)$. For example, the second moment $\mu_2(r)$ measures the spread of the curve about the mean value of r and the third moment $\mu_3(r)$ measures its symmetry with reference to the mean. Both moment representations may be used simultaneously to describe a boundary segment or signature.

Basically, what we have accomplished is to reduce the description task to that of describing 1-D functions. Although moments are by far the most popular method, they are not the only descriptors that could be used for this purpose. For instance, another method involves computing the 1-D discrete Fourier transform given in Eq. (3.2-2), obtaining its spectrum, and using the first k components of the spectrum to describe $g(r)$. The advantage of moments over other techniques is that implementation of the former descriptors is straightforward and that they also carry a "physical" interpretation of boundary shape. The insensitivity of this approach to rotation is clear from Fig. 8.16. Size normalization, if desired, can be achieved by scaling the range of r.

8.3 REGIONAL DESCRIPTORS

8.3.1 Some Simple Descriptors

The *area* of a region is defined as the number of pixels contained within its boundary. The *perimeter* of a region is the length of its boundary. Although area and perimeter are sometimes used as descriptors, they apply primarily to situations in which the size of the objects of interest is invariant. A more frequent use of these two descriptors is in measuring *compactness* of a region, defined as (perimeter)^2/area. Compactness is a dimensionless quantity (and thus is insensitive to scale changes) and is minimal for a disk-shaped region. With the exception of errors introduced by rotation of a digital region, compactness also is insensitive to orientation.

The *principal axes* of a region are the eigenvectors of the covariance matrix obtained by using the pixels within the region as random variables (see Section 3.6). The two eigenvectors of the covariance matrix point in the directions of maximal region spread, subject to the constraint that they be orthogonal. The degree of spread is measured by the corresponding eigenvalues. Thus the principal spread and direction of a region can be described by the largest eigenvalue and its corresponding eigenvector. This type of description is insensitive to rotation but does depend on scale changes if eigenvalues are used to measure spread. One approach used frequently to compensate for this difficulty is to make the *ratio* of the large to the small eigenvalue as a descriptor.

Other simple measures used as region descriptors include the mean and median of the gray levels, the minimum and maximum gray-level values, and the number of pixels with values above and below the mean.

8.3.2 Topological Descriptors

Topological properties are useful for global descriptions of regions in the image plane. Simply defined, *topology* is the study of properties of a figure that are unaffected by any deformation, as long as there is no tearing or joining of the figure (sometimes these are called *rubber-sheet* distortions). For example, Fig. 8.17 shows a region with two holes. Thus if a topological descriptor is defined by the number of holes in the region, this property obviously will not be affected by a stretching or rotation transformation. In general, however, the number of holes will change if the region is torn or folded. Note that, as stretching affects distance, topological properties do not depend on the notion of distance or any properties implicitly based on the concept of a distance measure.

Another topological property useful for region description is the number of connected components. A connected component of a set is a subset of

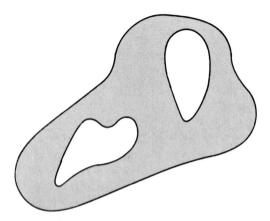

Figure 8.17 *A region with two holes.*

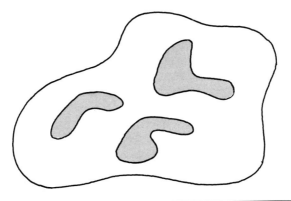

Figure 8.18   *A region with three connected components.*

maximal size such that any two of its points can be joined by a connected curve
lying entirely within the subset. Figure 8.18 shows a region with three connected
components. (See Sections 2.4.2 and 2.4.3 for a discussion of connected components and their labeling. We give a morphological algorithm for extracting
connected components in Section 8.4.4.)

The number of holes H and connected components C in a figure can be
used to define the *Euler number E*:

$$E = C - H. \qquad (8.3\text{-}1)$$

The Euler number is also a topological property. The regions shown in Fig.
8.19, for example, have Euler numbers equal to 0 and -1, respectively, because
the "A" has one connected component and one hole and the "B" one connected
component but two holes.

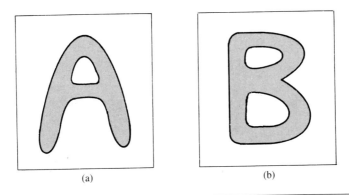

(a)   (b)

Figure 8.19   *Regions with Euler number equal to 0 and -1, respectively.*

Regions represented by straight-line segments (referred to as *polygonal networks*) have a particularly simple interpretation in terms of the Euler number. Figure 8.20 shows a polygonal network. Classifying interior regions of such a network into faces and holes often is important. Denoting the number of vertices by W, the number of edges by Q, and the number of faces by F gives the following relationship, called the *Euler formula*:

$$W - Q + F = C - H \qquad (8.3\text{-}2)$$

which, in view of Eq. (8.3-1), is related to the Euler number:

$$W - Q + F = C - H = E. \qquad (8.3\text{-}3)$$

The network shown in Fig. 8.20 has 7 vertices, 11 edges, 2 faces, 1 connected region, and 3 holes; thus

$$7 - 11 + 2 = 1 - 3 = -2.$$

Although topological concepts are rather general, they provide an additional feature that is often useful in characterizing regions in a scene.

8.3.3   Texture

An important approach to region description is to quantify its *texture* content. Although no formal definition of texture exists, intuitively this descriptor provides measures of properties such as smoothness, coarseness, and regularity

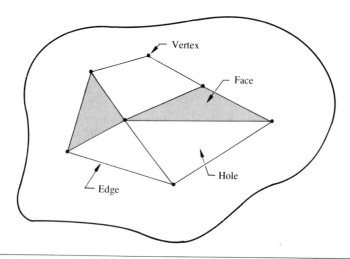

Figure 8.20   *A region containing a polygonal network.*

Figure 8.21 *Examples of (a) smooth, (b) coarse, and (c) regular textures. (From Fu, Gonzalez, and Lee [1987].)*

(Fig. 8.21 shows some examples). The three principal approaches used in image processing to describe the texture of a region are statistical, structural, and spectral. Statistical approaches yield characterizations of textures as smooth, coarse, grainy, and so on. Structural techniques deal with the arrangement of image primitives, such as the description of texture based on regularly spaced parallel lines. Spectral techniques are based on properties of the Fourier spectrum and are used primarily to detect global periodicity in an image by identifying high-energy, narrow peaks in the spectrum (see Sections 5.7 and 5.8).

Statistical approaches
One of the simplest approaches for describing texture is to use moments of the gray-level histogram of an image or region. Let z be a random variable denoting discrete image intensity and let $p(z_i)$, $i = 1, 2, \ldots, L$ be the corresponding histogram, where L is the number of distinct intensity levels. As indicated in Section 8.2.4, the nth moment of z about the mean is

$$\mu_n(z) = \sum_{i=1}^{L} (z_i - m)^n p(z_i) \tag{8.3-4}$$

where m is the mean value of z (the average intensity):

$$m = \sum_{i=1}^{L} z_i p(z_i). \tag{8.3-5}$$

Note from Eq. (8.3-4) that $\mu_0 = 1$ and $\mu_1 = 0$. The second moment [also called the *variance* and denoted $\sigma^2(z)$] is of particular importance in texture description. It is a measure of gray-level contrast that can be used to establish descriptors of relative smoothness. For example, the measure

$$R = 1 - \frac{1}{1 + \sigma^2(z)} \tag{8.3-6}$$

is 0 for areas of constant intensity [$\sigma^2(z) = 0$ if all z_i's have the same value] and approaches 1 for large values of $\sigma^2(z)$. The third moment is a measure of the skewness of the histogram while the fourth moment is a measure of its relative flatness. The fifth and higher moments are not so easily related to histogram shape, but they do provide further quantitative discrimination of texture content.

Measures of texture computed using only histograms suffer from the limitation that they carry no information regarding the relative position of pixels with respect to each other. One way to bring this type of information into the texture-analysis process is to consider not only the distribution of intensities, but also the positions of pixels with equal or nearly equal intensity values.

Let P be a position operator and let $\mathbf{A}$ be a $k \times k$ matrix whose element a_{ij} is the number of times that points with gray level z_i occur (in the position specified by P) relative to points with gray level z_j, with $1 \leqslant i, j \leqslant k$. For instance, consider an image with three gray levels, $z_1 = 0$, $z_2 = 1$, and $z_3 =$

2, as follows:

$$
\begin{array}{ccccc}
0 & 0 & 0 & 1 & 2 \\
1 & 1 & 0 & 1 & 1 \\
2 & 2 & 1 & 0 & 0 \\
1 & 1 & 0 & 2 & 0 \\
0 & 0 & 1 & 0 & 1
\end{array}
$$

Defining the position operator P as "one pixel to the right and one pixel below" yields the following 3×3 matrix $\mathbf{A}$:

$$
\mathbf{A} = \begin{bmatrix} 4 & 2 & 1 \\ 2 & 3 & 2 \\ 0 & 2 & 0 \end{bmatrix}
$$

where, for example, a_{11} (top left) is the number of times that a point with level $z_1 = 0$ appears one pixel location below and to the right of a pixel with the same gray level, and a_{13} (top right) is the number of times that a point with level $z_1 = 0$ appears one pixel location below and to the right of a point with gray level $z_3 = 2$. The size of $\mathbf{A}$ is determined strictly by the number of distinct gray levels in the input image. Thus application of the concepts discussed in this section usually requires that intensities be requantized into a few gray-level bands in order to keep the size of $\mathbf{A}$ manageable.

Let n be the total number of point pairs in the image that satisfy P (in the preceding example, $n = 16$). If a matrix $\mathbf{C}$ is formed by dividing every element of $\mathbf{A}$ by n, then c_{ij} is an estimate of the joint probability that a pair of points satisfying P will have values (z_i, z_j). The matrix $\mathbf{C}$ is called a *gray-level co-occurrence matrix*. Because $\mathbf{C}$ depends on P, the presence of given texture patterns may be detected by choosing an appropriate position operator. For instance, the operator used in the preceding example is sensitive to bands of constant intensity running at $-45°$. (Note that the highest value in $\mathbf{A}$ was $a_{11} = 4$, partially owing to a streak of points with intensity 0 and running at $-45°$.) More generally, the problem is to analyze a given $\mathbf{C}$ matrix in order to categorize the texture of the region over which $\mathbf{C}$ was computed. A set of descriptors useful for this purpose includes:

(1) maximum probability,

$$
\max_{i,j}(c_{ij})
$$

(2) element difference moment of order k,

$$
\sum_i \sum_j (i - j)^k c_{ij}
$$

(3) inverse element difference moment of order k,

$$\sum_i \sum_j c_{ij}/(i-j)^k \qquad i \neq j$$

(4) entropy,

$$-\sum_i \sum_j c_{ij} \log c_{ij}$$

(5) uniformity,

$$\sum_i \sum_j c_{ij}^2.$$

The basic idea is to characterize the "content" of $\mathbf{C}$ via these descriptors. For example, the first property gives an indication of the strongest response to P (as in the preceding example). The second descriptor has a relatively low value when the high values of $\mathbf{C}$ are near the main diagonal, because the differences $(i-j)$ are smaller there. The third descriptor has the opposite effect. The fourth descriptor is a measure of randomness, achieving its highest value when all elements of $\mathbf{C}$ are equal. Conversely, the fifth descriptor is lowest when the c_{ij}s are all equal.

One approach for using these descriptors is to "teach" a system representative descriptor values for a set of different textures. The texture of an unknown region is then subsequently determined by how closely its descriptors match those stored in the system memory. We discuss matching in more detail in Chapter 9.

Structural approaches
As mentioned at the beginning of this section, a second major category of texture description is based on structural concepts. Suppose that we have a rule of the form $S \rightarrow aS$, which indicates that the symbol S may be rewritten as aS (for example, three applications of this rule would yield the string $aaaS$). If a represents a circle (Fig. 8.22a) and the meaning of "circles to the right" is assigned to a string of the form $aaa \ldots$, the rule $S \rightarrow aS$ allows generation of the texture pattern shown in Fig. 8.22(b).

Suppose next that we add some new rules to this scheme: $S \rightarrow bA$, $A \rightarrow cA$, $A \rightarrow c$, $A \rightarrow bS$, $S \rightarrow a$, where the presence of a b means "circle down" and the presence of a c means "circle to the left." We can now generate a string of the form $aaabccbaa$ that corresponds to a 3×3 matrix of circles. Larger texture patterns, such as the one shown in Fig. 8.22(c) can be generated easily in the same way. (Note, however, that these rules can also generate structures that are not rectangular.)

The basic idea in the foregoing discussion is that a simple "texture primitive" can be used to form more complex texture patterns by means of some

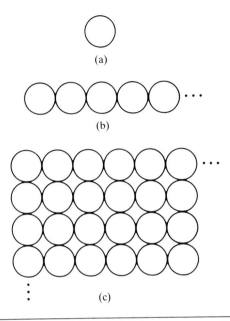

(a)

(b)

(c)

Figure 8.22 *(a) Texture primitive; (b) pattern generated by the rule S → aS; (c) 2-D texture pattern generated by this and other rules.*

rules that limit the number of possible arrangements of the primitive(s). These concepts lie at the heart of relational descriptions, a topic that we treat in considerably more detail in Section 8.5.

Spectral approaches

As indicated in Sections 5.7 and 5.8, the Fourier spectrum is ideally suited for describing the directionality of periodic or almost periodic 2-D patterns in an image. These global texture patterns, although easily distinguishable as concentrations of high-energy bursts in the spectrum, generally are quite difficult to detect with spatial methods because of the local nature of these techniques.

Here, we consider three features of the Fourier spectrum that are useful for texture description: (1) prominent peaks in the spectrum give the principal direction of the texture patterns; (2) the location of the peaks in the frequency plane gives the fundamental spatial period of the patterns; and (3) eliminating any periodic components via filtering leaves nonperiodic image elements, which can then be described by statistical techniques. Recall that the spectrum of a real image is symmetric about the origin, so only half of the frequency plane needs to be considered. Thus for the purpose of analysis, every periodic pattern is associated with only one peak in the spectrum, rather than two.

Detection and interpretation of the spectrum features just mentioned often are simplified by expressing the spectrum in polar coordinates to yield a function

$S(r, \theta)$, where S is the spectrum function and r and θ are the variables in this coordinate system. For each direction θ, $S(r, \theta)$ may be considered a 1-D function $S_\theta(r)$. Similarly, for each frequency r, $S_r(\theta)$ is a 1-D function. Analyzing $S_\theta(r)$ for a fixed value of θ yields the behavior of the spectrum (such as the presence of peaks) along a radial direction from the origin, whereas analyzing $S_r(\theta)$ for a fixed value of r yields the behavior along a circle centered on the origin.

A more global description is obtained by integrating (summing for discrete variables) these functions:

$$S(r) = \sum_{\theta=0}^{\pi} S_\theta(r) \tag{8.3-7}$$

and

$$S(\theta) = \sum_{r=1}^{R} S_r(\theta) \tag{8.3-8}$$

where R is the radius of a circle centered at the origin. For an $N \times N$ spectrum, R typically is chosen as $N/2$.

The results of Eqs. (8.3-7) and (8.3-8) constitute a pair of values $[S(r), S(\theta)]$ for each pair of coordinates (r, θ). By varying these coordinates, we can generate two 1-D functions, $S(r)$ and $S(\theta)$, that constitute a spectral-energy description of texture for an entire image or region under consideration. Furthermore, descriptors of these functions themselves can be computed in order to characterize their behavior quantitatively. Descriptors typically used for this purpose are the location of the highest value, the mean and variance of both the amplitude and axial variations (see Section 8.2.4), and the distance between the mean and the highest value of the function.

Example: Figure 8.23 illustrates the use of Eqs. (8.3-7) and (8.3-8) for global texture description. Figure 8.23(a) shows an image with periodic texture, and Fig. 8.23(b) shows its spectrum. Figures 8.23(c) and (d) show plots of $S(r)$ and $S(\theta)$, respectively. The plot of $S(r)$ is a typical structure, having high energy content near the origin and progressively lower values for higher frequencies. The plot of $S(\theta)$ shows prominent peaks at intervals of 45°, which clearly correspond to the periodicity in the texture content of the image.

As an illustration of how a plot of $S(\theta)$ could be used to differentiate between two texture patterns, Fig. 8.23(e) shows another image whose texture pattern is predominantly in the horizontal and vertical directions. Figure 8.23(f) shows the plot of $S(\theta)$ for the spectrum of this image. As expected, this plot

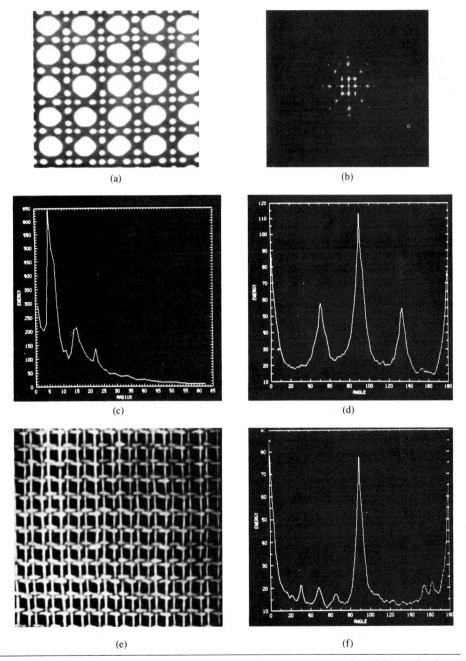

(a)

(b)

(c)

(d)

(e)

(f)

Figure 8.23 *(a) Image showing periodic texture; (b) spectrum; (c) plot of S(r); (d) plot of S(θ); (e) another image with a different type of periodic texture; (f) plot of S(θ). (Courtesy of D. Brzakovic, University of Tennessee.)*

shows high peaks at 90° intervals. Discriminating between the two texture patterns by analyzing their corresponding $S(\theta)$ waveforms would be straight forward. ❑

8.3.4 Moments

For a 2-D continuous function $f(x, y)$, the moment of order $(p + q)$ is defined as

$$m_{pq} = \int_{-\infty}^{\infty} \int_{-\infty}^{\infty} x^p y^q f(x, y) \, dx \, dy \tag{8.3-9}$$

for $p, q = 0, 1, 2, \ldots$.

A uniqueness theorem (Papoulis [1965]) states that if $f(x, y)$ is piecewise continuous and has nonzero values only in a finite part of the xy plane, moments of all orders exist and the moment sequence (m_{pq}) is uniquely determined by $f(x, y)$. Conversely, (m_{pq}) uniquely determines $f(x, y)$. The *central moments* can be expressed as

$$\mu_{pq} = \int_{-\infty}^{\infty} \int_{-\infty}^{\infty} (x - \bar{x})^p (y - \bar{y})^q f(x, y) \, dx \, dy \tag{8.3-10}$$

where

$$\bar{x} = \frac{m_{10}}{m_{00}} \quad \text{and} \quad \bar{y} = \frac{m_{01}}{m_{00}}.$$

For a digital image, Eq. (8.3-10) becomes

$$\mu_{pq} = \sum_{x} \sum_{y} (x - \bar{x})^p (y - \bar{y})^q f(x, y). \tag{8.3-11}$$

The central moments of order up to 3 are

$$\mu_{10} = \sum_{x} \sum_{y} (x - \bar{x})^1 (y - \bar{y})^0 f(x, y)$$

$$= m_{10} - \frac{m_{10}}{m_{00}} (m_{00})$$

$$= 0$$

$$\mu_{11} = \sum_{x} \sum_{y} (x - \bar{x})^1 (y - \bar{y})^1 f(x, y)$$

$$= m_{11} - \frac{m_{10} m_{01}}{m_{00}}$$

$$\mu_{20} = \sum_x \sum_y (x - \bar{x})^2 (y - \bar{y})^0 f(x, y)$$

$$= m_{20} - \frac{2m_{10}^2}{m_{00}} + \frac{m_{10}^2}{m_{00}} = m_{20} - \frac{m_{10}^2}{m_{00}}$$

$$\mu_{02} = \sum_x \sum_y (x - \bar{x})^0 (y - \bar{y})^2 f(x, y)$$

$$= m_{02} - \frac{m_{01}^2}{m_{00}}$$

$$\mu_{30} = \sum_x \sum_y (x - \bar{x})^3 (y - \bar{y})^0 f(x, y)$$

$$= m_{30} - 3\bar{x}m_{20} + 2\bar{x}^2 m_{10}$$

$$\mu_{12} = \sum_x \sum_y (x - \bar{x})^1 (y - \bar{y})^2 f(x, y)$$

$$= m_{12} - 2\bar{y}m_{11} - \bar{x}m_{02} + 2\bar{y}^2 m_{10}$$

$$\mu_{21} = \sum_x \sum_y (x - \bar{x})^2 (y - \bar{y})^1 f(x, y)$$

$$= m_{21} - 2\bar{x}m_{11} - \bar{y}m_{20} + 2\bar{x}^2 m_{01}$$

$$\mu_{03} = \sum_x \sum_y (x - \bar{x})^0 (y - \bar{y})^3 f(x, y)$$

$$= m_{03} - 3\bar{y}m_{02} + 2\bar{y}^2 m_{01}.$$

In summary,

$$\mu_{00} = m_{00} \qquad\qquad \mu_{11} = m_{11} - \bar{y}m_{10}$$

$$\mu_{10} = 0 \qquad\qquad \mu_{30} = m_{30} - 3\bar{x}m_{20} + 2m_{10}\bar{x}^2$$

$$\mu_{01} = 0 \qquad\qquad \mu_{12} = m_{12} - 2\bar{y}m_{11} - \bar{x}m_{02} + 2\bar{y}^2 m_{10}$$

$$\mu_{20} = m_{20} - \bar{x}m_{10} \qquad \mu_{21} = m_{21} - 2\bar{x}m_{11} - \bar{y}m_{20} + 2\bar{x}^2 m_{01}$$

$$\mu_{02} = m_{02} - \bar{y}m_{01} \qquad \mu_{03} = m_{03} - 3\bar{y}m_{02} + 2\bar{y}^2 m_{01}.$$

The *normalized central moments*, denoted η_{pq}, are defined as

$$\eta_{pq} = \frac{\mu_{pq}}{\mu_{00}^{\gamma}} \tag{8.3-12}$$

where

$$\gamma = \frac{p + q}{2} + 1 \tag{8.3-13}$$

for $p + q = 2, 3, \ldots$.

A set of seven *invariant moments* can be derived from the second and third moments:[†]

$$\phi_1 = \eta_{20} + \eta_{02} \tag{8.3-14}$$

$$\phi_2 = (\eta_{20} - \eta_{02})^2 + 4\eta_{11}^2 \tag{8.3-15}$$

$$\phi_3 = (\eta_{30} - 3\eta_{12})^2 + (3\eta_{21} - \eta_{03})^2 \tag{8.3-16}$$

$$\phi_4 = (\eta_{30} + \eta_{12})^2 + (\eta_{21} + \eta_{03})^2 \tag{8.3-17}$$

$$\phi_5 = (\eta_{30} - 3\eta_{12})(\eta_{30} + \eta_{12})[(\eta_{30} + \eta_{12})^2 \tag{8.3-18}$$
$$- 3(\eta_{21} + \eta_{03})^2] + (3\eta_{21} - \eta_{03})(\eta_{21} + \eta_{03})$$
$$[3(\eta_{30} + \eta_{12})^2 - (\eta_{21} + \eta_{03})^2]$$

$$\phi_6 = (\eta_{20} - \eta_{02})[(\eta_{30} + \eta_{12})^2 - (\eta_{21} + \eta_{03})^2] \tag{8.3-19}$$
$$+ 4\eta_{11}(\eta_{30} + \eta_{12})(\eta_{21} + \eta_{03})$$

$$\phi_7 = (3\eta_{21} - \eta_{03})(\eta_{30} + \eta_{12})[(\eta_{30} + \eta_{12})^2 \tag{8.3-20}$$
$$- 3(\eta_{21} + \eta_{03})^2] + (3\eta_{12} - \eta_{30})(\eta_{21} + \eta_{03})$$
$$[3(\eta_{30} + \eta_{12})^2 - (\eta_{21} + \eta_{03})^2].$$

This set of moments is invariant to translation, rotation, and scale change (Hu [1962]).

Example: The image shown in Fig. 8.24(a) was reduced to half size in Fig. 8.24(b), mirror-imaged in Fig. 8.24(c), and rotated by 2° and 45°, as shown in Figs. 8.24(d) and (e). The seven moment invariants given in Eqs. (8.3-14)–(8.3-20) were then computed for each of these images, and the logarithm of the results were taken to reduce the dynamic range. As Table 8.2 shows, the

Table 8.2   Moment Invariants for the Images in Figs. 8.24(a)–(e)

Invariant (Log)	Original	Half Size	Mirrored	Rotated 2°	Rotated 45°
ϕ_1	6.249	6.226	6.919	6.253	6.318
ϕ_2	17.180	16.954	19.955	17.270	16.803
ϕ_3	22.655	23.531	26.689	22.836	19.724
ϕ_4	22.919	24.236	26.901	23.130	20.437
ϕ_5	45.749	48.349	53.724	46.136	40.525
ϕ_6	31.830	32.916	37.134	32.068	29.315
ϕ_7	45.589	48.343	53.590	46.017	40.470

[†] Derivation of these results involves concepts that are beyond the scope of this discussion. The book by Bell [1965] and the paper by Hu [1962] contain detailed discussions of these concepts.

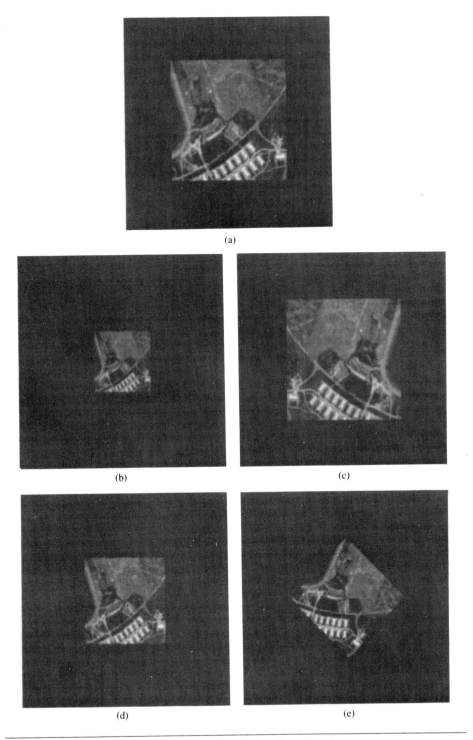

(a)

(b)

(c)

(d)

(e)

Figure 8.24 *Images used to demonstrate properties of moment invariants.*

results for Figs. 8.24(b)–(e) are in reasonable agreement with the invariants computed for the original image. The major cause of error can be attributed to the digital nature of the data.   ❑

8.4 MORPHOLOGY

The word *morphology* commonly denotes a branch of biology that deals with the form and structure of animals and plants. We use the same word here in the context of *mathematical morphology* as a tool for extracting image components that are useful in the representation and description of region shape, such as boundaries, skeletons, and the convex hull. We also are interested in morphological techniques for pre- or post-processing, such as morphological filtering, thinning, and pruning.

The language of mathematical morphology is *set theory*. As such, morphology offers a unified and powerful approach to numerous image processing problems. Sets in mathematical morphology represent the shapes of objects in an image. For example, the set of all black pixels in a binary image is a complete description of the image. In binary images, the sets in question are members of the 2-D integer space Z^2 (see Section 2.3.1), where each element of a set is a tuple (2-D vector) whose coordinates are the (x, y) coordinates of a black (by convention) pixel in the image. Gray-scale digital images can be represented as sets whose components are in Z^3. In this case, two components of each element of the set refer to the coordinates of a pixel, and the third corresponds to its discrete intensity value. Sets in higher dimensional spaces can contain other image attributes, such as color and time varying components.

In the following sections we develop and illustrate several important concepts in mathematical morphology. Although we discussed concepts such as the skeleton and boundary of a region earlier in this chapter, we revisit them here as special cases of a much larger set of morphological operations. Many of these operations can be formulated in terms of n-dimensional Euclidean space, E^n. However, we focus on binary images whose components are elements of Z^2. We discuss extensions to gray-scale images in Section 8.4.5.

8.4.1 Dilation and Erosion

We begin the discussion of morphological operations by treating in some detail two operations: *dilation* and *erosion*. They are the bases for most of the morphological operations discussed later.

Some basic definitions

Let A and B be sets in Z^2, with components $a = (a_1, a_2)$ and $b = (b_1, b_2)$, respectively. The *translation* of A by $x = (x_1, x_2)$, denoted $(A)_x$, is defined as

$$(A)_x = \{c \,|\, c = a + x, \quad \text{for } a \in A\}. \tag{8.4-1}$$

The *reflection* of B, denoted $\hat{B}$, is defined as

$$\hat{B} = \{x | x = -b, \quad \text{for } b \in B\}. \tag{8.4-2}$$

The *complement* of set A is

$$A^c = \{x | x \notin A\}. \tag{8.4-3}$$

Finally, the *difference* of two sets A and B, denoted $A - B$, is defined as

$$A - B = \{x | x \in A, x \notin B\} \quad = \quad A \cap B^c. \tag{8.4-4}$$

Example: Figure 8.25 illustrates the definitions just presented where the black dot identifies the origin of each set. Figure 8.25(a) shows a set A. Figure 8.25(b) shows the translation of A by $x = (x_1, x_2)$. Note that translation is accomplished by adding (x_1, x_2) to every element of A. Figure 8.25(c) shows a set B, and Fig. 8.25(d) shows its reflection about the origin. Finally, Fig. 8.25(e) shows a set A and its complement, and Fig. 8.25(f) shows the difference between the set A of Fig. 8.25(e) and the set B shown in Fig. 8.25(f). ❏

Dilation

With A and B as sets in Z^2 and $\varnothing$ denoting the empty set, the *dilation* of A by B, denoted $A \oplus B$, is defined as

$$A \oplus B = \{x | (\hat{B})_x \cap A \neq \varnothing\}. \tag{8.4-5}$$

Thus the dilation process consists of obtaining the reflection of B about its origin and then shifting this reflection by x. The dilation of A by B then is the set of all x displacements such that $\hat{B}$ and A overlap by at least one nonzero element. Based on this interpretation, Eq. (8.4-5) may be rewritten as

$$A \oplus B = \{x | [(\hat{B})_x \cap A] \subseteq A\}.$$

Set B is commonly referred to as the *structuring element* in dilation, as well as in other morphological operations.

Equation (8.4-5) is not the only definition of dilation in the current literature on morphology (see Problem 8.19 for two different, yet equivalent definitions). However, the preceding definition has a distinct advantage over other formulations in that it is more intuitive when the structuring element B is viewed

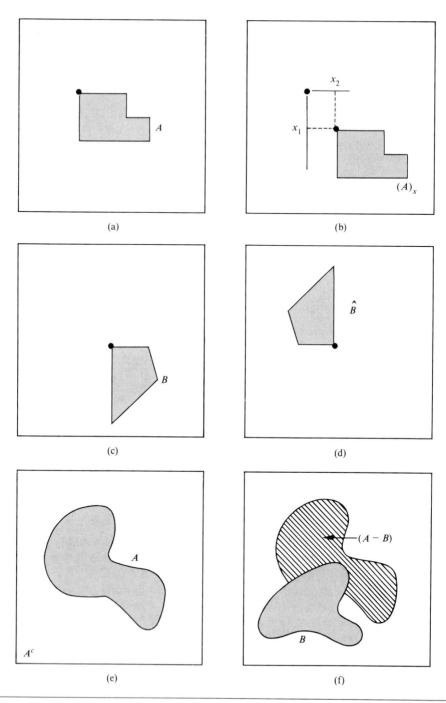

Figure 8.25 (a) Set A; (b) set A translated by point x; (c) set B; (d) reflection of B; (e) set A and its complement; (f) the difference of two sets (shown lined). The dot in each of the first four figures indicates the origin of the set.

as a convolution mask. Although dilation is based on set operations, whereas convolution is based on arithmetic operations, the basic process of "flipping" B about its origin and then successively displacing it so that it slides over set (image) A is analogous to the convolution process discussed in Sections 3.3.8 and 4.1.1.

Example: Figure 8.26(a) shows a simple set, and Fig. 8.26(b) shows a structuring element and its reflection. In this case the structuring element and its reflection are equal because B is symmetric with respect to its origin. The dashed line in Fig. 8.26(c) shows the original set for reference, and the solid line shows the limit beyond which any further displacements of the origin of $\hat{B}$ by x would cause the intersection of $\hat{B}$ and A to be empty. Thus all points inside this boundary constitute the dilation of A by B. Figure 8.26(d) shows a structuring element designed to achieve more dilation vertically than horizontally. Figure 8.26(e) shows dilation achieved with this element.   ❑

Erosion
For sets A and B in Z^2, the erosion of A by B, denoted $A \ominus B$, is defined as

$$A \ominus B = \{x | (B)_x \subseteq A\} \qquad (8.4\text{-}6)$$

which, in words, says that the erosion of A by B is the set of all points x such that B, translated by x, is contained in A. As in the case of dilation, Eq. (8.4-6) is not the only definition of erosion (see Problem 8.20 for two different, yet equivalent definitions). However, Eq. (8.4-6) usually is favored in practical implementations of morphology for the same reasons stated earlier in connection with Eq. (8.4-5).

Example: Figure 8.27 shows a process similar to that shown in Fig. 8.26. As before, set A is shown as a dashed line for reference in Fig. 8.27(c). There the solid line shows the limit beyond which further displacement of the origin of B would cause this set to cease being completely contained in A. Thus the locus of points within this boundary constitutes the erosion of A by B. Figure 8.27(d) shows an elongated structuring element, and Fig. 8.27(e) shows the erosion of A by this element. Note that the original set was eroded down to a line.   ❑

Dilation and erosion are duals of each other with respect to set complementation and reflection. That is,

$$(A \ominus B)^c = A^c \oplus \hat{B}. \qquad (8.4\text{-}7)$$

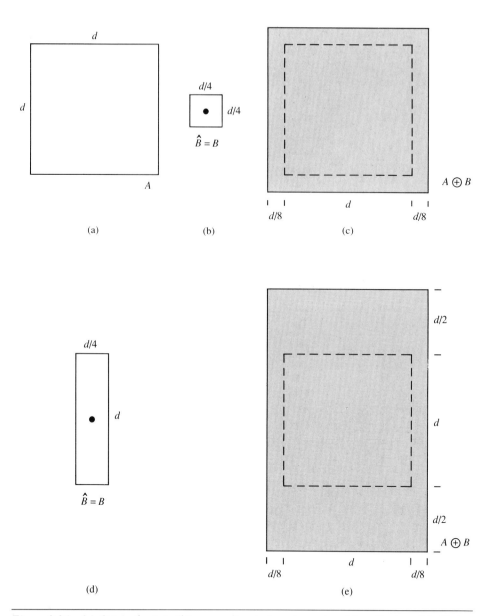

Figure 8.26 (a) Original set A; (b) square structuring element and its reflection; (c) dilation of A by B, shown shaded; (d) elongated structuring element; (e) dilation of A using this element.

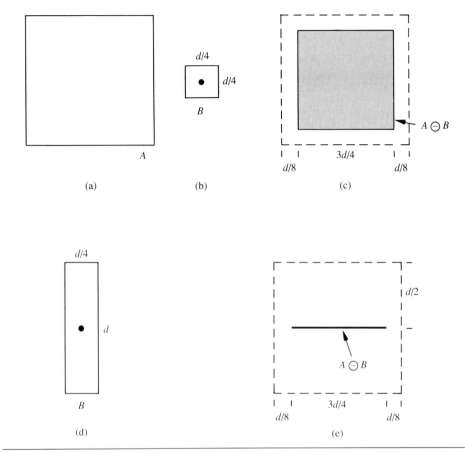

Figure 8.27 *(a) Original set A; (b) structuring element B; (c) erosion of A by B, shown shaded; (d) elongated structuring element; (e) erosion of A by this element.*

We proceed to prove this result formally in order to illustrate a typical approach for establishing the validity of morphological expressions. Starting with the definition of erosion, we have

$$(A \ominus B)^c = \{x \,|\, (B)_x \subseteq A\}^c.$$

If set $(B)_x$ is contained in set A, then $(B)_x \cap A^c = \varnothing$, in which case the preceding equation becomes

$$(A \ominus B)^c = \{x \,|\, (B)_x \cap A^c = \varnothing\}^c.$$

But the complement of the set of x's that satisfy $(B)_x \cap A^c = \emptyset$ is the set of x's such that $(B)_x \cap A^c \neq \emptyset$. Thus

$$(A \ominus B)^c = \{x \mid (B)_x \cap A^c \neq \emptyset\}$$
$$= A^c \oplus \hat{B}$$

where the last step follows from Eq. (8.4-5). This concludes the proof.

8.4.2   Opening and Closing

As we have seen, dilation expands an image and erosion shrinks it. In this section we discuss two other important morphological operations: opening and closing. *Opening* generally smooths the contour of an image, breaks narrow isthmuses, and eliminates thin protrusions. *Closing* also tends to smooth sections of contours but, as opposed to opening, it generally fuses narrow breaks and long thin gulfs, eliminates small holes, and fills gaps in the contour.

The opening of set A by structuring element B, denoted $A \circ B$, is defined as

$$A \circ B = (A \ominus B) \oplus B \tag{8.4-8}$$

which, in words, says that the opening of A by B is simply the erosion of A by B, followed by a dilation of the result by B.

The closing of set A by structuring element B, denoted $A \bullet B$, is defined as

$$A \bullet B = (A \oplus B) \ominus B \tag{8.4-9}$$

which, in words, says that the closing of A by B is simply the dilation of A by B, followed by the erosion of the result by B.

Example: Figure 8.28 illustrates opening and closing of a set A with a disk structuring element. Figure 8.28(a) shows the set, and Fig. 8.28(b) shows various positions of the disk structuring element during the erosion process which, when completed, resulted in the disjoint figure shown in Fig. 8.28(c). Note the elimination of the bridge between the two main sections. Its width was thin in relation to the diameter of the structuring element; that is, the structuring element could not be completely contained in this part of the set, thus violating the conditions of Eq. (8.4-6). The same also was true of the two rightmost members of the object. Figure 8.28(d) shows the process of dilating the eroded set, and Fig. 8.28(e) shows the final result of opening. Similarly, Figs. 8.28(f)–(i) show the results of closing A with the same structuring element. The result was to eliminate the small (in relation to B) bay on the left of the object. Note

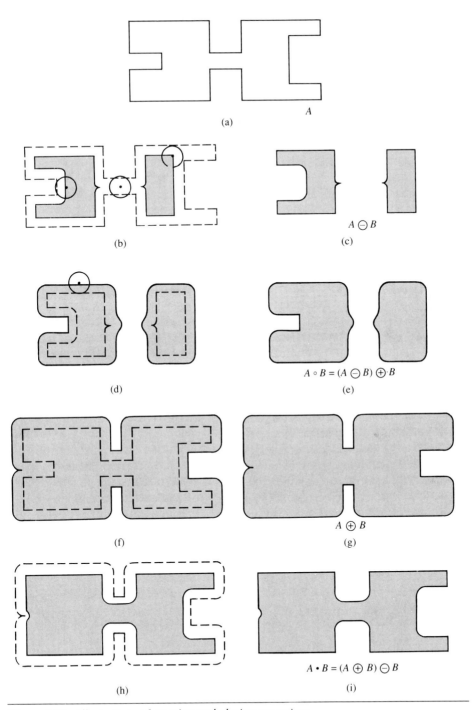

(a)

(b)

(c)

$A \ominus B$

(d)

(e)

$A \circ B = (A \ominus B) \oplus B$

(f)

(g)

$A \oplus B$

(h)

(i)

$A \bullet B = (A \oplus B) \ominus B$

Figure 8.28 *Illustrations of opening and closing operations.*

also the smoothing that resulted in parts of the object from both opening and closing the set A with a circular structuring element.   ◻

Opening and closing have a simple geometric interpretation. Suppose, for example, that we view the disk structuring element B as a (flat) "rolling ball." The boundary of $A \circ B$ is then given by the points on the boundary of B that reach the *farthest* into the boundary of A as B is rolled around the *inside* of this boundary. This interpretation yields Fig. 8.28(e) from Fig. 8.28(a). Note that all outward pointing corners were rounded, whereas inward pointing corners were not affected. Protruding elements where the ball did not fit were eliminated. This geometric *fitting* property of the opening operation leads to a set-theoretic formulation, which states that the opening of A by B is obtained by taking the union of all translates of B that fit into A. That is, opening can be expressed as a fitting process such that

$$A \circ B = \cup \{(B)_x \mid (B)_x \subset A\}.$$

Figure 8.29 illustrates this concept; a noncircular structuring element is used for variety.

Closing has a similar geometric interpretation, except that now, again using the rolling ball example, we roll B on the outside of the boundary (opening and closing are duals, so having to roll the ball on the outside is not unexpected). With this interpretation in mind, Fig. 8.28(i) follows easily from Fig. 8.28(a). Note that the inward pointing corners were rounded, whereas the outward pointing corners remained unchanged. The leftmost intrusion on the boundary of A was reduced in size significantly, because the ball did not fit there. Geometrically, a point z is an element of $A \bullet B$ if and only if $(B)_x \cap A \neq \emptyset$ for any translate of $(B)_x$ that contains z. Figure 8.30 illustrates this property.

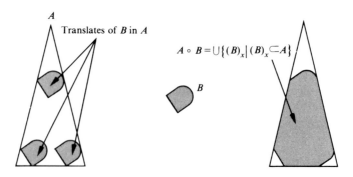

Figure 8.29   *"Fitting" characterization of opening. (Adapted from Giardina and Dougherty [1988].)*

Translates of B containing z. Each intersects A and, therefore, $z \in A \bullet B$

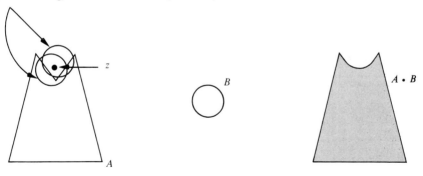

Figure 8.30   *Geometric interpretation of closing. Point z, contained in $(B)_z$, belongs to the closing, $A \bullet B$, if and only if $(B)_z \cap A \neq \emptyset$.*

As in the case of dilation and erosion, opening and closing are duals with respect to set complementation and reflection. That is,

$$(A \bullet B)^c = (A^c \circ \hat{B}). \tag{8.4-10}$$

We leave the proof of this result as an exercise.

The opening operation satisfies the following properties.

(i) $A \circ B$ is a subset (subimage) of A.

(ii) If C is a subset of D, then $C \circ B$ is a subset of $D \circ B$.

(iii) $(A \circ B) \circ B = A \circ B$.

Similarly, the closing operation satisfies the following properties.

(i) A is a subset (subimage) of $A \bullet B$.

(ii) If C is a subset of D, then $C \bullet B$ is a subset of $D \bullet B$.

(iii) $(A \bullet B) \bullet B = A \bullet B$.

These properties aid in understanding the results obtained when the opening and closing operations are used to construct morphological filters. Take, for instance, construction of a filter based on opening operations. With reference to the above properties: (*i*) the result will be a subset of the input; (*ii*) monotonicity will be preserved; and (*iii*) applying more than one opening operation has no effect on the result. This last property is sometimes called *idempotence*. Similar comments apply to closing operations.

Consider the simple binary image shown in Fig. 8.31(a), which consists of a rectangular object corrupted by noise. Here the noise manifests itself as dark

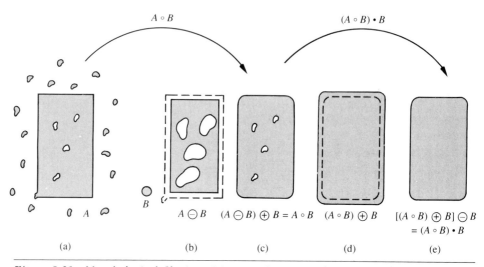

Figure 8.31 *Morphological filtering: (a) original, noisy image; (b) result of erosion; (c) opening of A; (d) result of performing dilation on the opening; (e) final result showing the closing of the opening. (Adapted from Giardina and Dougherty [1988].)*

elements (shaded) on a light background and as light voids on the dark object. Note that set A consists of the object and the background noise, with the noise inside the object creating inner boundaries through which the background shows. The objective is to eliminate the noise and its effects on the object, while distorting the object as little as possible. The morphological "filter" $(A \circ B) \bullet B$ can be used to accomplish this objective. Figure 8.31(c) shows the result of opening A with a disk structuring element larger than all noise components. Note that this operation took care of the background noise but did not affect the inner boundaries.

The background noise was eliminated in the erosion stage of opening because, in this idealized example, all noise components in the background are physically smaller than the structuring element. (Recall that erosion requires that the structuring element be completely contained in the set being eroded.) The size of the noise components inside the object increased in size (Fig. 8.31b), which was expected. The reason is that the voids in the object actually are inner boundaries that should increase in size as the object is eroded. Finally, Fig. 8.31(e) shows the result of morphologically closing Fig. 8.31(c). The inner boundaries were eliminated as a result of the dilation stage of the closing operation, as Fig. 8.31(d) shows.

8.4.3 Hit-or-Miss Transform

The morphological hit-or-miss transform is a basic tool for shape detection. We introduce this concept with the aid of Fig. 8.32, which shows a set A consisting of three shapes (subsets), denoted X, Y, and Z. The shading in

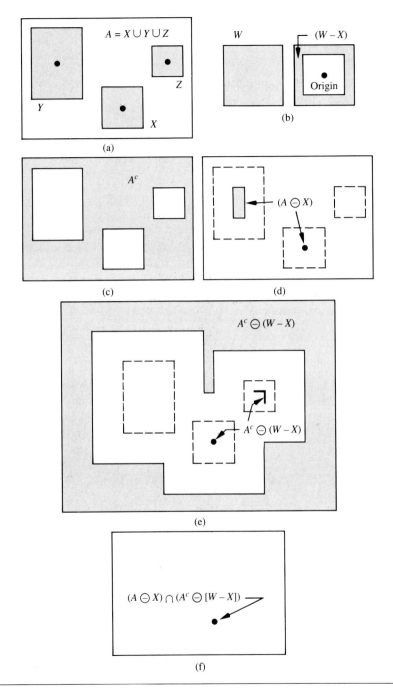

Figure 8.32 *(a) Set A; (b) a window, W, and the local background of X with respect to W,
(W − X); (c) complement of A; (d) erosion of A by X; (e) erosion of A^c by (W − X); (f)
intersection of (d) and (e), showing the location of the origin of X, as desired. It is instructive
to copy X and (W − X) on tracing paper and run these templates over A and A^c to verify
the results in (d) and (e).*

Figures 8.32(a)–(c) indicates the original sets, whereas the shading in Figures 8.32(d) and (e) indicates the result of morphological operations. The objective is to find the location of one of the shapes, say, X.

Let the origin of each shape be located at its center of gravity. If we enclose X by a small window, W, the *local background* of X with respect to W is the set difference $(W - X)$ shown in Fig. 8.32(b). Figure 8.32(c) shows the complement of A, which is needed later. Figure 8.32(d) shows the erosion of A by X (the dashed lines are included for reference). Recall that the erosion of A by X is the set of locations of the origin of X such that X is completely contained in A. Figure 8.32(e) shows the erosion of the complement of A by the local background set $(W - X)$; the outer shaded region is part of the erosion. We note from Figs. 8.32(d) and (e) that the set of locations for which X *exactly* fits inside A is the *intersection* of the erosion of A by X and the erosion of A^c by $(W - X)$ as shown in Fig. 8.32(f). This intersection is precisely the location sought. In other words, if B denotes the set composed of X and its background, the match (or set of matches) of B in A, denoted $A \circledast B$, is

$$A \circledast B = (A \ominus X) \cap [A^c \ominus (W - X)]. \tag{8.4-11}$$

We can generalize the notation somewhat by letting $B = (B_1, B_2)$, where B_1 is the set formed from elements of B associated with an object, and B_2 is the set of elements of B associated with the corresponding background. From the preceding discussion, $B_1 = X$ and $B_2 = (W - X)$. With this notation, Eq. (8.4-11) becomes

$$A \circledast B = (A \ominus B_1) \cap (A^c \ominus B_2). \tag{8.4-12}$$

By using the definition of set differences and the dual relationship between erosion and dilation, we can also write Eq. (8.4-12) as

$$A \circledast B = (A \ominus B_1) - (A \oplus \hat{B}_2). \tag{8.4-13}$$

Thus set $A \circledast B$ contains all the points at which, simultaneously, B_1 found a match ("hit") in A and B_2 found a match in A^c.

8.4.4   Some Basic Morphological Algorithms

With the preceding discussion as background, we are now ready to consider some practical uses of morphology. When dealing with binary images, the principal application of morphology is extracting image components that are useful in the representation and description of shape. In particular, we consider morphological algorithms for extracting boundaries, connected components, the convex hull, and the skeleton of a region. We also develop several methods (for region filling, thinning, thickening, and pruning) that are often used in conjunction with these algorithms as pre- or post-processing steps. Unlike the illustrations used previously in this section, most of those used in the rest of the discussion are "mini-images," designed to clarify the mechanics of each morphological process as we introduce it. The images are binary, with 1's shown shaded and 0's shown in white.

Boundary extraction

The boundary of a set A, denoted by $\beta(A)$, can be obtained by first eroding A by B, and then performing the set difference between A and its erosion. That is,

$$\beta(A) = A - (A \ominus B) \tag{8.4-14}$$

where B is a suitable structuring element.

Figure 8.33 illustrates the mechanics of boundary extraction. It shows a simple binary object, a structuring element B, and the result of using Eq. (8.4-14). Although the structuring element shown in Fig. 8.33(b) is among the most frequently used, it is by no means unique. For example, using a 5×5 structuring element of 1's would result in a boundary between 2 and 3 pixels thick. Note

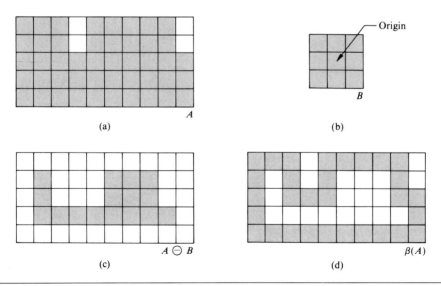

Figure 8.33 (a) Set A; (b) structuring element B; (c) A eroded by B; (d) boundary extracted by taking the set difference between A and its erosion.

that, when the origin of B is on the border of the set, part of the structuring element lies outside the set. The normal treatment of this condition is to implicitly assume that values outside the boundary of the set are 0.

Region filling

Next we develop a simple algorithm for region filling based on set dilations, complementation, and intersections. In Fig. 8.34, A denotes a set containing a subset whose elements are 8-connected boundary points of a region. Beginning with a point p inside the boundary, the objective is to fill the entire region with 1's.

Since, by assumption, all nonboundary points are labeled 0, we assign a value of 1 to p to start the procedure. The following procedure then fills the region with 1's:

$$X_k = (X_{k-1} \oplus B) \cap A^c \quad k = 1, 2, 3, \ldots \quad (8.4\text{-}15)$$

where $X_0 = p$, and B is the symmetric structuring element shown in Fig. 8.34(c). The algorithm terminates at iteration step k if $X_k = X_{k-1}$. The set union of X_k and A contains the filled set and its boundary.

The dilation process of Eq. (8.4-15) would fill the entire area if left unchecked. However, the intersection at each step with A^c limits the result to inside the region of interest (this type of delimiting process sometimes is called *conditional dilation*). The rest of Fig. 8.34 illustrates further the mechanics of Eq. (8.4-15). Although this example has only one subset, the concept clearly applies to any finite number of such subsets, so long as a point inside each boundary is given.

Extraction of connected components

We introduced the concept of connectivity in Section 2.4.2. In practice, extraction of connected components in a binary image is central to many automated image analysis applications. Let Y represent a connected component contained in a set A and assume that a point p of Y is known. Then, the following iterative expression yields all the elements of Y:

$$X_k = (X_{k-1} \oplus B) \cap A \quad k = 1, 2, 3, \ldots \quad (8.4\text{-}16)$$

where $X_0 = p$, and B is a suitable structuring element, as shown in Fig. 8.35. If $X_k = X_{k-1}$, the algorithm has converged and we let $Y = X_k$.

Equation (8.4-16) is similar in form to Eq. (8.4-15). The only difference is the use of A here instead of its complement, because all the elements sought (that is, the elements of the connected component) are labeled 1. The intersection with A at each iterative step eliminates dilations centered on elements labeled 0. Figure 8.35 illustrates the mechanics of Eq. (8.4-16). Note that the

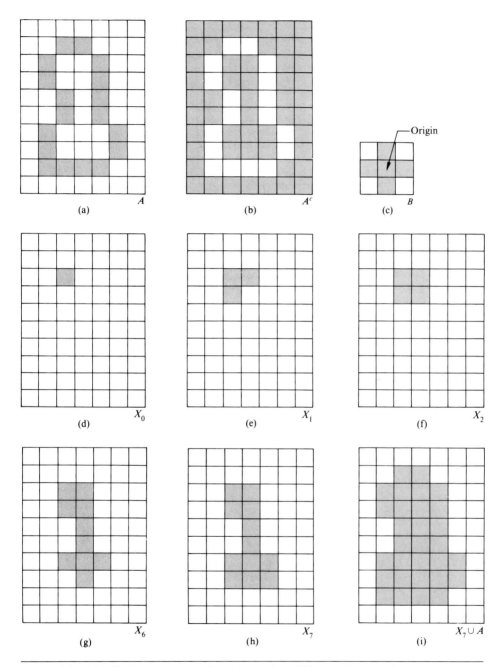

Figure 8.34 *(a) Set A containing a boundary subset; (b) complement of A; (c) structuring element B; (d) initial point inside the boundary; (e)–(h) various steps of Eq. (8.4-15); (i) final result, obtained by forming the set union of (a) and (h).*

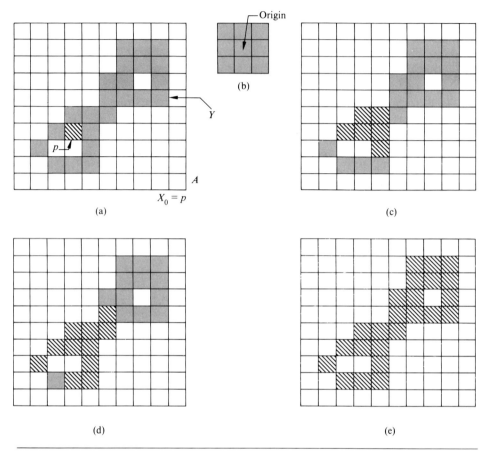

Figure 8.35 (a) Set A containing one connected component Y and initial point p (all shaded points are valued 1, but are shown different from p to indicate that they have not yet been found by the algorithm); (b) structuring element; (c) result of first iterative step; (d) result of second step; (e) final result.

shape of the structuring element assumes 8-connectivity between pixels. As in the region-filling algorithm, the results just discussed are applicable to any finite number of sets of connected components contained in A.

Convex hull

In Section 8.1.4 we introduced the convex hull of a set as a useful image descriptor. Here, we present a simple morphological algorithm for obtaining the convex hull, $C(A)$, of a set A. Let $B^i, i = 1, 2, 3, 4$, represent four structuring elements. The procedure consists of implementing the equation:

$$X_k^i = (X \circledast B^i) \cup A \qquad i = 1, 2, 3, 4 \quad \text{and} \quad k = 1, 2, 3, \ldots \qquad (8.4\text{-}17)$$

with $X_0^i = A$. Now let $D^i = X_{conv}^i$, where the subscript "conv" indicates convergence in the sense that $X_k^i = X_{k-1}^i$. Then, the convex hull of A is

$$C(A) = \bigcup_{i=1}^{4} D^i.$$
(8.4-18)

In other words, the procedure consists of iteratively applying the hit-or-miss transform to A with B^1; when no further changes occur, we perform the union with A and call the result D^1. The procedure is repeated with B^2 until no further changes occur, and so on. The union of the four resulting D's constitutes the convex hull of A.

Example: Figure 8.36 illustrates the procedure given in Eqs. (8.4-17) and (8.4-18). Figure 8.36(a) shows the structuring elements used to extract the convex hull (the origin of each element is at its center). Figure 8.36(b) shows a set A for which the convex hull is sought. Starting with $X_0^1 = A$ resulted after four iterations of Eq. (8.4-17) in the set shown in Fig. 8.36(c). Then, letting $X_0^2 = A$ and again using Eq. (8.4-17) resulted in the set shown in Fig. 8.36(d) (note that convergence was achieved in only two steps). The next two results were obtained in the same way. Finally, forming the union of the sets in Figs. 8.36(c), (d), (e), and (f) resulted in the convex hull shown in Fig. 8.36(g). The contribution of each structuring element is highlighted in the composite set shown in Fig. 8.36(h). ❑

Thinning

The thinning of a set A by a structuring element B, denoted $A \otimes B$, can be defined in terms of the hit-or-miss transform:

$$A \otimes B = A - (A \circledast B)$$
$$= A \cap (A \circledast B)^c.$$
(8.4-19)

A more useful expression for thinning A symmetrically is based on a *sequence* of structuring elements:

$$\{B\} = \{B^1, B^2, B^3, \ldots, B^n\}$$
(8.4-20)

where B^i is a rotated version of B^{i-1}. Using this concept, we now define thinning by a sequence of structuring elements as

$$A \otimes \{B\} = ((\ldots ((A \otimes B^1) \otimes B^2) \ldots) \otimes B^n).$$
(8.4-21)

In other words, the process is to thin A by *one pass* with B^1, then thin the result with one pass of B^2, and so on, until A is thinned with one pass of B^n. The entire process is repeated until no further changes occur.

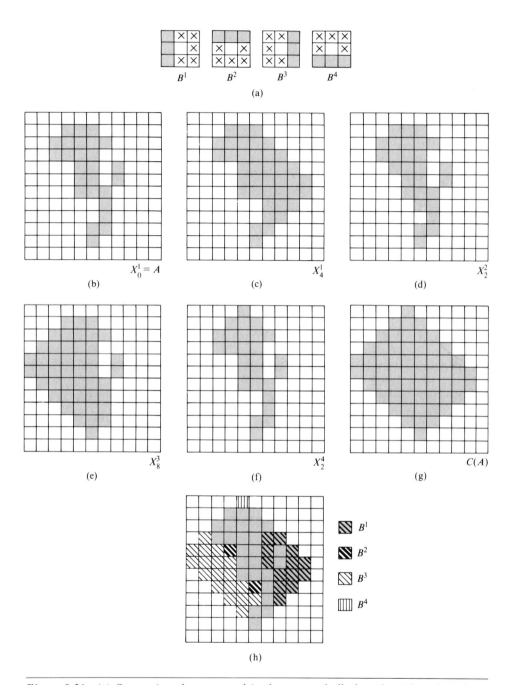

Figure 8.36 (a) Structuring elements used in the convex hull algorithm (the ×'s indicate "don't care," and B^i is a rotation of B^{i-1} by 90°; (b) set A; (c)–(f) results of convergence with the four structuring elements shown in (a); (g) convex hull; (h) convex hull showing the contribution of each structuring element.

Example: Figure 8.37(a) shows a set of structuring elements commonly used for thinning, and Fig. 8.37(b) shows a set A to be thinned by using the procedure just discussed. Figure 8.37(c) shows the result of thinning with one raster pass of A with B^1, and Figs. 8.37(d)–(k) show the results of passes with the other structuring elements. Convergence was achieved after the second pass of B^4.

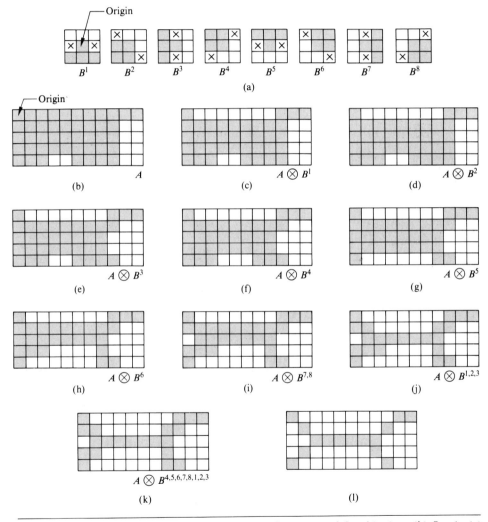

Figure 8.37 (a) Sequence of rotated structuring elements used for thinning; (b) Set A; (c) result of thinning with the first element; (d)–(i) results of thinning with the next seven elements (there was no change between the seventh and eighth elements); (j) result of using the first element again (there were no changes for the next two elements); (k) result after convergence; (l) conversion to m-connectivity.

Figure 8.37(k) shows the thinned result. Finally, Fig. 8.37(l) shows the thinned set converted to m-connectivity (see Section 2.4.2) to eliminate multiple paths.   ❏

Thickening

Thickening is the morphological dual of thinning and is defined by the expression

$$A \odot B = A \cup (A \circledast B) \tag{8.4-22}$$

where B is a structuring element suitable for thickening. As before, thickening can be defined as a sequential operation:

$$A \odot \{B\} = ((. . . ((A \odot B^1) \odot B^2) . . .) \odot B^n). \tag{8.4-23}$$

The structuring elements used for thickening have the same form as those shown in Fig. 8.37(a) in connection with thinning, but with all 1's and 0's interchanged. However, a separate algorithm for thickening is seldom used in practice. Instead, the usual procedure is to thin the background of the set in question and then complement the result. In other words, to thicken a set A, we form $C = A^c$, thin C, and then form C^c. Figure 8.38 illustrates this procedure.

Depending on the nature of A, this procedure may result in some disconnected points, as Fig. 8.38(d) shows. Hence thickening by this method usually is followed by a simple postprocessing step to remove disconnected points. Note from Fig. 8.38(c) that the thinned background forms a boundary for the thickening process. This useful feature is not present in the direct implementation of thickening using Eq. (8.4-23), and it is one of the principal reasons for using background thinning to accomplish thickening.

Skeletons

We introduced the concept of a skeleton and its extraction from a region in Section 8.1.5. Here, we approach this subject morphologically.

Lantuéjoul [1980] (see also Serra [1982] and Maragos [1987]) showed that the skeleton of a set (region) A can be expressed in terms of erosions and openings. That is, with $S(A)$ denoting the skeleton of A, it can be shown that

$$S(A) = \bigcup_{k=0}^{K} S_k(A) \tag{8.4-24}$$

with

$$S_k(A) = \bigcup_{k=0}^{K} \{(A \ominus kB) - [(A \ominus kB) \circ B]\} \tag{8.4-25}$$

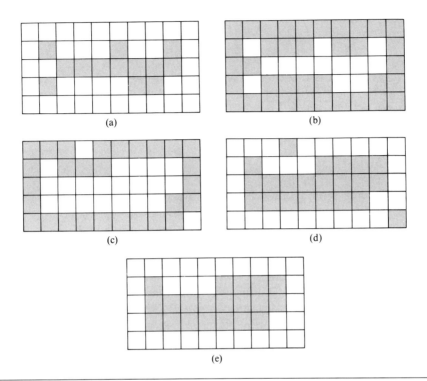

Figure 8.38 *Thickening via thinning of the background: (a) set A; (b) its complement; (c) result of thinning the complement of A; (d) thickened set obtained by complementing (c); (e) final result, showing removal of disconnected points.*

where B is a structuring element, $(A \ominus kB)$ indicates k successive erosions of A; that is

$$(A \ominus kB) = ((\ldots (A \ominus B) \ominus B) \ominus \ldots) \ominus B$$

k times, and K is the last iterative step before A erodes to an empty set. In other words,

$$K = \max \{k \mid (A \ominus kB) \neq \varnothing\}.$$

As before, the symbol $(\circ)$ is used to denote the opening operation in Eq. (8.4-25).

The formulation given in Eqs. (8.4-24) and (8.4-25) states that $S(A)$, the skeleton of A, can be obtained as the union of the *skeleton subsets* $S_k(A)$. Also, it can be shown that A can be reconstructed from these subsets by using the equation

$$A = \bigcup_{k=0}^{K} (S_k(A) \oplus kB) \tag{8.4-26}$$

where $(S_k(A) \oplus kB)$ denotes k successive dilations of $S_k(A)$; that is,

$$(S_k(A) \oplus kB) = ((\ldots (S_k(A) \oplus B) \oplus B) \oplus \ldots) \oplus B$$

k times, and the limit of the summation, K, is as before.

Example: Figure 8.39 illustrates the concepts just discussed. The first column shows the original set (at the top), and two erosions by the structuring element B. Note that one more erosion of A would yield the empty set, so $K = 2$ in this case. The second column shows the opening of the sets in the first column by B. These results are easily explained by the fitting characterization of the opening operation discussed in connection with Fig. 8.29. The third column simply contains the set differences between the first and second columns.

The fourth column contains two partial skeletons and the final result (at the bottom of the column). The final skeleton not only is thicker than it needs to be but, more important, it is not connected. This result is not unexpected, as nothing in the preceding formulation of the morphological skeleton guarantees connectivity. Morphology produces an elegant formulation in terms of erosions and openings of the given set. However, heuristic formulations such as the algorithm developed in Section 8.1.5 are needed if, as is usually the case, the skeleton must be maximally thin, connected, and minimally eroded.

The fifth column shows $S_0(A)$, $S_1(A) \oplus B$, and $(S_2(A) \oplus 2B) = (S_2(A) \oplus B) \oplus B$. Finally, the last column shows reconstruction of set A, which, according to Eq. (8.4-26), is the union of the dilated skeleton subsets shown in the fifth column.   ❏

Pruning

Pruning methods are an essential complement of thinning and skeletonizing algorithms, because these procedures tend to leave parasitic components that need to be cleaned up by postprocessing. We begin the discussion with a pruning problem and then develop a morphological solution based on the material introduced in the preceding sections. Thus we take advantage of what has been developed so far to illustrate how to go about solving a problem by combining several of the techniques discussed so far.

A common approach to the automated recognition of hand-printed characters is to analyze the shape of the skeleton of each character. These skeletons are often characterized by "spurs" (parasitic components), caused during erosion by nonuniformities in the strokes composing the characters. We develop a morphological technique for handling this problem, starting with the assumption that the length of a parasitic component does not exceed three pixels.

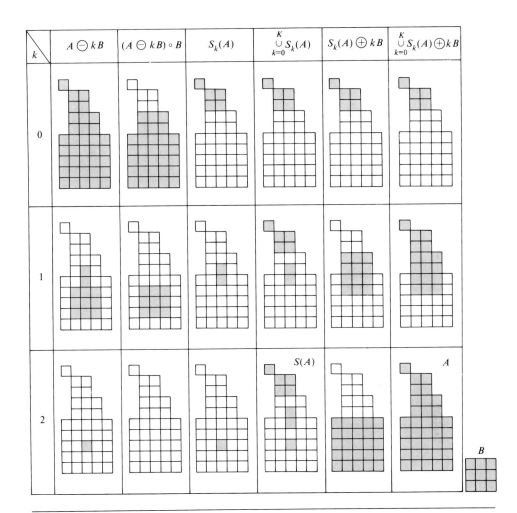

Figure 8.39 *An example of the implementation of Eqs. (8.4-24)–(8.4-26). The original set is shown at the top left, and its morphological skeleton is shown at the bottom of the fourth column. The reconstructed set is shown at the bottom of the sixth column.*

Figure 8.40(a) shows the skeleton of a hand-printed "a." The parasitic component on the leftmost part of the character is typical of what we are interested in removing. The solution is based on suppression of a parasitic branch by successively eliminating its end point. Of course, this also shortens (or eliminates) other branches in the character but, in the absence of other structural information, the assumption is that any branch with three or less pixels is to be eliminated. For an input set A, thinning A with a sequence of structuring elements designed to detect only end points achieves the desired

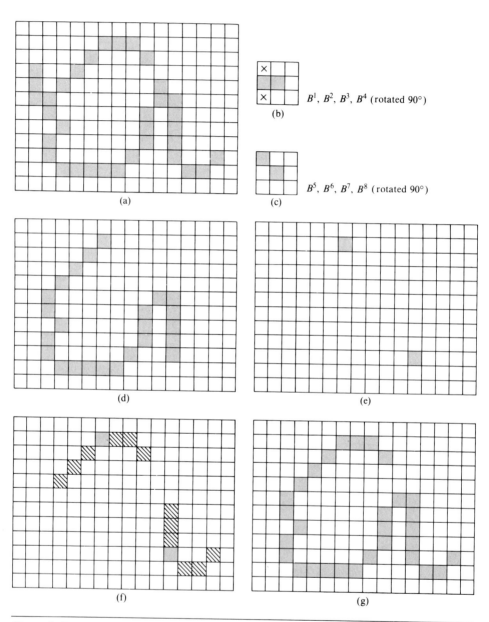

Figure 8.40 *Example of pruning: (a) original image; (b) and (c) structuring elements used for deleting (thinning) end points; (d) result of three cycles of thinning; (e) end points of (d); (f) dilation of end points conditioned on (a); (g) pruned image.*

result. That is, let

$$X_1 = A \otimes \{B\} \tag{8.4-27}$$

where $\{B\}$ denotes the sequence [see Eq. (8.4-20)] shown in Figs. 8.40(b) and (c). The sequence of structuring elements consists of two different structures, each of which is rotated 90° for a total of eight elements. The $\times$ in Fig. 8.40(b) signifies a "don't care" condition, in the sense that it does not matter whether the pixel in that location has a value of 0 or 1. Numerous results reported in the literature on morphology are based on the use of a *single* structuring element, similar to the one in Fig. 8.40(b), but having "don't care" conditions along the entire first column. This is incorrect. For example, this element would identify the point located in the eighth row, fourth column of Fig. 8.40(a) as an end point, thus eliminating it and breaking connectivity in the stroke.

Applying Eq. (8.4-27) to A three times yields the set X_1 shown in Fig. 8.40(d). The next step is to "restore" the character to its original form, but with the parasitic branches removed. To do so first requires forming a set X_2 containing all end points in X_1 (Fig. 8.40e):

$$X_2 = \bigcup_{k=1}^{8} (X_1 \circledast B^k) \tag{8.4-28}$$

where the B^k are the same end-point detectors used previously. The next step is dilation of the end points three times, using set A as a delimiter:

$$X_3 = (X_2 \oplus H) \cap A \tag{8.4-29}$$

where H is a 3×3 structuring element of 1's. As in the case of region filling and extraction of connected components, this type of conditional dilation prevents the creation of 1-valued elements outside the region of interest, as evidenced by the result shown in Fig. 8.40(f). Finally, the union of X_3 and X_1 yields the final result,

$$X_4 = X_1 \cup X_3 \tag{8.4-30}$$

as shown in Fig. 8.40(g).

In more complex scenarios, use of Eq. (8.4-29) sometimes picks up the "tips" of some parasitic branches. This condition can occur when the end points of these branches are near the skeleton. Although Eq. (8.4-27) may eliminate them, they can be picked up again during dilation because they are valid points in A. Unless entire parasitic elements are picked up again (a rare case if these elements are short with respect to valid strokes), detecting and eliminating them is easy because they are disconnected regions.

A natural thought at this juncture is that there must be easier ways to solve this problem. For example, we could just keep track of all deleted points and simply reconnect the appropriate points to all end points left after application of Eq. (8.4-27). This option is valid, but the advantage of the formulation presented is that the use of simple morphological constructs solved the entire problem. In practical situations when a set of such tools is available, the advantage is that no new algorithms have to be written. We simply combine the necessary morphological functions into a sequence of operations.

Table 8.3 summarizes the morphological results developed in this section. Figure 8.41 summarizes the basic types of structuring elements used.

Table 8.3   Summary of Morphological Results and Their Properties

Operation	Equation	Comments[†]
Translation	$(A)_x = \{c \mid c = a + x, \quad \text{for } a \in A\}$	Translates the origin of A to point x.
Reflection	$\hat{B} = \{x \mid x = -b, \quad \text{for } b \in B\}$	Reflects all elements of B about the origin of this set.
Complement	$A^c = \{x \mid x \notin A\}$	Set of points not in A.
Difference	$A - B = \{x \mid x \in A, x \notin B\} = A \cap B^c$	Set of points that belong to A but not to B.
Dilation	$A \oplus B = \{x \mid (\hat{B})_x \cap A \neq \varnothing\}$	"Expands" the boundary of A. (I)
Erosion	$A \ominus B = \{x \mid (B)_x \subseteq A\}$	"Contracts" the boundary of A. (I)
Opening	$A \circ B = (A \ominus B) \oplus B$	Smooths contours, breaks narrow isthmuses, and eliminates small islands and sharp peaks. (I)
Closing	$A \bullet B = (A \oplus B) \ominus B$	Smooths contours, fuses narrow breaks and long thin gulfs, and eliminates small holes. (I)
Hit-or-miss transform	$A \circledast B = (A \ominus B_1) \cap (A^c \ominus B_2)$ $= (A \ominus B_1) - (A \oplus \hat{B}_2)$	The set of points (coordinates) at which, simultaneously, B_1 found a match ("hit") in A and B_2 found a match in A^c.
Boundary extraction	$\beta(A) = A - (A \ominus B)$	Set of points on the boundary of set A. (I)
Region filling	$X_k = (X_{k-1} \oplus B) \cap A^c; \quad X_0 = p$ and $k = 1, 2, 3, \ldots$	Fills a region in A, given a point p in the region. (II)
Connected components	$X_k = (X_{k-1} \oplus B) \cap A; \quad X_0 = p$ and $k = 1, 2, 3, \ldots$	Finds a connected component Y in A, given a point p in Y. (I)

Table 8.3 (Continued)

Operation	Equation	Comments[†]
Convex hull	$X_k^i = (X_{k-1}^i \circledast B^i) \cup A$; $\quad i = 1, 2, 3, 4$, $k = 1, 2, 3, \ldots$, $X_0^i = A$, and $D^i = X_{\text{conv}}^i$ $C(A) = \bigcup_{i=1}^{4} D^i$	Finds the convex hull $C(A)$ of set A, where "conv" indicates convergence in the sense that $X_k^i = X_{k-1}^i$. (III)
Thinning	$A \otimes B = A - (A \circledast B)$ $= A \cap (A \circledast B)^c$ $A \circledast \{B\} = ((\ldots((A \otimes B^1) \otimes B^2) \ldots) \otimes B^n)$ $\{B\} = \{B^1, B^2, B^3, \ldots, B^n\}$	Thins set A. The first two equations give the basic definition of thinning. The last two equations shown denote thinning by a sequence of structuring elements. This method is normally used in practice. (IV)
Thickening	$A \odot B = A \cup (A \circledast B)$ $A \odot \{B\} = ((\ldots((A \odot B^1) \odot B^2) \ldots) \odot B^n)$	Thickens set A. (See preceding comments on sequences of structuring elements.) Uses (IV) with 0's and 1's reversed.
Skeletons	$S(A) = \bigcup_{k=0}^{K} S_k(A)$ $S_k(A) = \bigcup_{k=0}^{K} \{(A \ominus kB) - [(A \ominus kB) \circ B]\}$ $A = \bigcup_{k=0}^{K} (S_k(A) \oplus kB)$	Finds the skeleton $S(A)$ of set A. The last equation indicates that A can be reconstructed from its skeleton subsets $S_k(A)$. In all three equations, K is the value of the iterative step after which the set A erodes to the empty set. The notation $(A \ominus kB)$ denotes the kth iteration of successive erosion. (I)
Pruning	$X_1 = A \otimes \{B\}$ $X_2 = \bigcup_{k=1}^{8} (X_1 \circledast B^k)$ $X_3 = (X_2 \oplus H) \cap A$ $X_4 = X_1 \cup X_3$	X_4 is the result of pruning set A. The number of times that the first equation is applied to obtain X_1 must be specified. Structuring elements (V) are used for the first two equations. The third equation uses structuring element (I).

[†] The Roman numerals in parentheses refer to the structuring element(s) used in the morphological process (see Fig. 8.41).

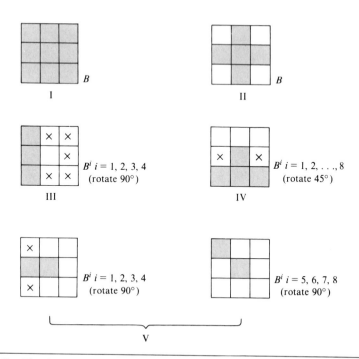

Figure 8.41 *The five basic types of structuring elements used in this section. The origin of each element is at its center and the ×'s indicate "don't care" values.*

Example: We conclude this section with a practical example illustrating the use of morphology in the early processing stages of a character recognition system capable of reading handwritten ZIP codes on U.S. mail.

Figure 8.42(a) shows the address portion of an envelope after image thresholding. An early processing step after the address field is located consists of extracting all connected components in the area encompassing this field (see Section 2.4.2 and the discussion earlier in this section for details on connected components). Each connected component is then enclosed by the smallest box that completely contains that component. The boxes and their contents then form the basis for part of the logic that deals with the extraction of the region containing the ZIP code. Figure 8.42(b) is a close-up of the region containing the ZIP code in this particular example. This case presents three problems: the first two characters (3 and 7) are joined, the first 1 is broken in the middle, and the loop of the numeral 2 is broken.

Joined characters can be detected in various ways after the ZIP code has been located. For instance, if analysis of the bounding boxes reveals less than five characters (or less than nine in the case of a "ZIP plus four"), the search for joined characters begins with measurement of the relative width of the boxes enclosing the characters (which at this point are being treated as connected components). An unusually wide box generally corresponds to two or more joined characters. A morphological approach for separating the joined characters consists of eroding the contents of a box until separate "character-like" regions result. For instance, the problem of the touching 3 and 7 was solved by five iterations of erosion performed in the box containing these characters. Figure 8.42(c) highlights the results, showing character separation. Note that erosion was performed *only* in the area where touching characters were suspected.

The problem of broken characters usually can be handled by dilation. In preprocessing, broken characters are suspected when, for example, boxes en-

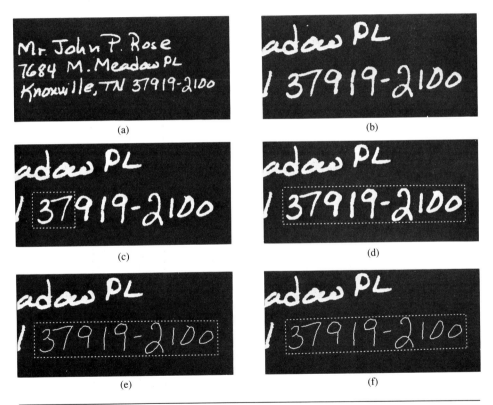

Figure 8.42 *(a) Thresholded address field; (b) close-up of ZIP code, showing touching and broken characters; (c) result after five iterations of erosion in a box enclosing the touching characters (characters are now disjoint); (d) result after three iterations of dilation on entire ZIP code field (breaks in the leftmost 1 and in the 2 bridged); (e) skeleton of (d), showing parasitic branches in the corner of the 7 and in one of the 0's; (f) result after seven iterations of pruning, showing removal of the parasitic branches. (Courtesy of Perceptics Corporation)*

closing some characters are small in relation to expected size or when two or more boxes form an unusual arrangement, such as being stacked. This latter condition revealed the presence of a broken character in the case of the 1 shown in Fig. 8.42(b). Assuming that the reason for such breaks is inconsistency in the width of the strokes leads to the expectation that other breaks might be present in the ZIP code field but did not result in separate connected components (such as the break in the 2). Thus, performing dilation on all characters makes sense, monitoring to see that new characters—or characters that were separated earlier—are not joined by the dilation process. Figure 8.42(d) shows the result after three dilations were performed on all the characters. Note that the gap in the middle of the broken 1 was bridged, as was the gap in the loop of the 2.

One of the principal approaches to structural character recognition is based on analysis of each character's skeleton. Figure 8.42(e) shows the skeletons of the ZIP code characters in Fig. 8.42(d), obtained by the algorithm developed in Section 8.1.5. Recall from the discussion of pruning that one of the problems with skeletons is the generation of parasitic branches. If not handled properly, they constitute a major source of error in character recognition. In this example, a small branch is present in the corner of the 7, and a major branch appears on the top of one of the zeros. The result of performing seven pruning passes eliminated both parasitic branches, as Fig. 8.42(f) shows. As indicated earlier, the number of pruning iterations is usually a heuristic choice. For instance, if the branch on the zero had been on the bottom right, the character could have been a Q, and completely deleting the branch would have caused an error. There is no sure way to get around this problem, other than to use contextual knowledge. In this example, we know that the character had to be a numeral because it was in the ZIP code field. In more complex situations (as in street addresses) the use of context involves correlating the ZIP code against street names valid for that code.   ❏

8.4.5 Extensions to Gray-Scale Images

In this section we extend to gray-scale images the basic operations of dilation, erosion, opening, and closing. We then use these operations to develop several basic gray-scale morphological algorithms. As in Section 8.4.4, our focus here is on the use of gray-scale morphology for extracting image components useful in the representation and description of shape. In particular, we develop algorithms for boundary extraction via a morphological gradient operation, and for region partitioning based on texture content. We also discuss algorithms for smoothing and enhancement, which often are useful as pre- or post-processing steps.

Throughout the discussions that follow, we deal with digital image functions of the form $f(x, y)$ and $b(x, y)$, where $f(x, y)$ is the input image and $b(x, y)$ is a structuring element, itself a subimage function. The assumption is that these functions are discrete in the sense introduced in Section 2.3.1. That is, if Z denotes the set of real integers, the assumption is that (x, y) are integers from $Z \times Z$ and that f and b are functions that assign a gray-level value (a real number from the set of real numbers, R) to each distinct pair of coordinates (x, y). If the gray levels also are integers, Z replaces R.

Dilation
Gray-scale dilation of f by b, denoted $f \oplus b$, is defined as

$$(f \oplus b)(s, t) = \max\{f(s - x, t - y) + b(x, y)|(s - x), (t - y) \in D_f; (x, y) \in D_b\}$$

$$(8.4\text{-}31)$$

where D_f and D_b are the domains of f and b, respectively. As before, b is the *structuring element* of the morphological process but note that b is now a function rather than a set.

The condition that the displacement parameters $(s - x)$ and $(t - y)$ have to be contained in the domain of f is analogous to the condition in the binary definition of dilation, where the two sets had to overlap by at least one element. Note also that the form of Eq. (8.4-31) is like that of 2-D convolution (Eq. 3.3-35), with the max operation replacing the sums of convolution and the addition replacing the products of convolution.

We illustrate the notation and mechanics of Eq. (8.4-31) by means of simple 1-D functions. For functions of one variable, Eq. (8.4-31) reduces to the expression

$$(f \oplus b)(s) = \max\{f(s - x) + b(x)|(s - x) \in D_f \text{ and } x \in D_b\}.$$

Recall from the discussion of convolution that $f(-x)$ is simply $f(x)$ flipped with respect to the origin of the x axis. As in convolution, the function $f(s - x)$ moves to the right for positive s, and to the left for negative s. The conditions that the value of $(s - x)$ has to be in the domain of f and that the value of x has to be in the domain of b, imply that f and b overlap. These conditions are analogous to the requirement in the binary definition of dilation, where the two sets had to overlap by at least one element. Finally, unlike in the binary case, f, rather than the structuring element b, is shifted. Equation (8.4-31) could be written so that b undergoes translation instead of f. However, if D_b is smaller than D_f (a condition almost always found in practice), the form given in Eq. (8.4-31) is simpler in terms of indexing and achieves the same result. Conceptually, f sliding by b is really no different than b sliding by f.

Dilation is commutative, so the alternative approach of interchanging f and b and using Eq. (8.4-31) can be utilized to compute $b \oplus f$. The result is the same, and b now is the function translated. However, erosion is not commutative, so this simple interchange of functions cannot be utilized. A different (and more complex) expression results from making b the function that is translated in both dilation and erosion. Thus for the sake of simplicity (and consistency with the literature), we elect to express dilation in the form of Eq. (8.4-31), keeping in mind that either approach is the same conceptually. An example is shown in Fig. 8.43.

Because dilation is based on choosing the maximum value of $f + b$ in a neighborhood defined by the shape of the structuring element, the general effect of performing dilation on a gray-scale image is two-fold: (1) if all the values of the structuring element are positive, the output image tends to be brighter than the input; and (2) dark details either are reduced or eliminated, depending on how their values and shapes relate to the structuring element used for dilation.

Erosion

Gray-scale erosion, denoted $f \ominus b$, is defined as

$$(f \ominus b)(s, t) = \min\{f(s + x, t + y) - b(x, y) | (s + x), (t + y) \in D_f; (x, y) \in D_b\}$$

$$(8.4\text{-}32)$$

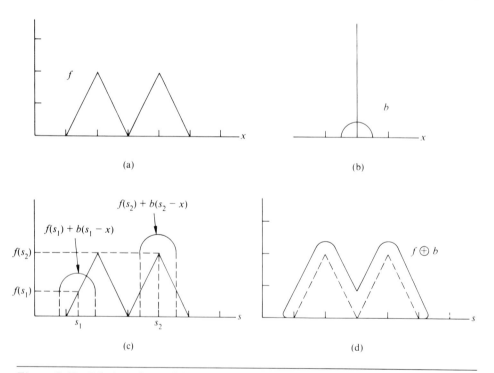

(a)   (b)

(c)   (d)

Figure 8.43 *Dilation obtained by sliding b past f. Mathematically, indexing is easier to implement by sliding f past b. The result, however, is the same. (Adapted from Giardina and Dougherty [1988].)*

where D_f and D_b are the domains of f and b, respectively. The condition that the displacement parameters $(s + x)$ and $(t + y)$ have to be contained in the domain of f is analogous to the condition in the binary definition of erosion, where the structuring element had to be completely contained by the set being eroded. Note that the form of Eq. (8.4-32) is like that of 2-D correlation (Eq. 3.3-39), with the min operation replacing the sums of correlation and subtraction replacing the products of correlation.

We illustrate the mechanics of Eq. (8.4-32) by eroding a simple 1-D function. For functions of one variable, the expression for erosion reduces to

$$(f \ominus b)(s) = \min\{f(s + x) - b(x) | (s + x) \in D_f \text{ and } x \in D_b\}.$$

As in correlation, the function $f(s + x)$ moves to the left for positive s and to the right for negative s. The requirements that $(s + x) \in D_f$ and $x \in D_b$ imply that the range of b is completely contained within the range of the displaced f. As noted above these requirements are analogous to those in the binary definition of erosion, where the structuring element had to be contained completely in the set being eroded.

Finally, unlike in the binary definition of erosion, f, rather than the structuring element b, is shifted. Equation (8.4-32) could be written so that b would be the function translated, resulting in a more complicated expression in terms of indexing. Because f sliding past b conceptually is the same as b sliding past f, the form of Eq. (8.4-32) is used for the reasons stated at the end of the discussion on dilation. Figure 8.44 shows the result of eroding the function of Fig. 8.43(a) by the structuring element of Fig. 8.43(b).

As Eq. (8.4-32) indicates, erosion is based on choosing the minimum value of $(f - b)$ in a neighborhood defined by the shape of the structuring element. The general effect of performing dilation on a gray-scale image is two-fold: (1)

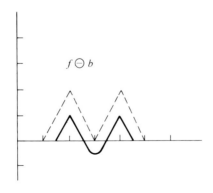

Figure 8.44 *Erosion of the function shown in Fig. 8.43(a) by the structuring element shown in Fig. 8.43(b). (Adapted from Giardina and Dougherty [1988].)*

if all the elements of the structuring element are positive, the output image tends to be darker than the input image; and (2) the effect of bright details in the input image that are smaller in "area" than the structuring element is reduced, with the degree of reduction being determined by the gray-level values surrounding the bright detail and by the shape and amplitude values of the structuring element itself.

As before, dilation and erosion are duals with respect to function complementation and reflection. That is,

$$(f \ominus b)^c(x, y) = (f^c \oplus \hat{b})(x, y) \tag{8.4-33}$$

where $f^c = -f(x, y)$ and $\hat{b} = b(-x, -y)$. Except as needed for clarity, we simplify the notation in the following discussions by omitting the arguments of all functions.

Example: Figure 8.45(a) shows a simple 512×512 gray-scale image, and Fig. 8.45(b) shows the result of dilating this image with a "flat-top" structuring element in the shape of a parallelepiped of unit height and size 5×5 pixels. Based on the preceding discussion, dilation is expected to produce an image that is brighter than the original and in which small, dark details have been reduced or eliminated. These effects clearly are visible in Fig. 8.45(b). Not only does the image appear brighter than the original, but the size of dark features, such as the nostrils and the dark components of the studded rein extending from the ears down to the neck, has been reduced. Figure 8.45(c) shows the result of eroding the original image. Note the opposite effect to dilation. The eroded image is darker, and the sizes of small, bright features (such as the studs on the rein) are reduced.   ❑

Opening and Closing
The expressions for opening and closing of gray-scale images have the same form as their binary counterparts. The opening of image f by image (structuring element) b, denoted $f \circ b$, is

$$f \circ b = (f \ominus b) \oplus b. \tag{8.4-34}$$

As in the binary case, opening is simply the erosion of f by b, followed by a dilation of the result by b. Similarly, the closing of f by b, denoted $f \bullet b$, is

$$f \bullet b = (f \oplus b) \ominus b. \tag{8.4-35}$$

The opening and closing for gray-scale images are duals with respect to complementation and reflection. That is,

$$(f \bullet b)^c = f^c \circ \hat{b}. \tag{8.4-36}$$

(a)

(b)

(c)

Figure 8.45 *(a) Original image; (b) result of dilation; (c) result of erosion. (Courtesy of A. Morris, Leica Cambridge, Ltd.)*

Because $f^c = -f(x, y)$, Eq. (8.4-36) also can be written as $-(f \cdot b) = (-f \circ \hat{b})$.

Opening and closing of images have a simple geometric interpretation. Suppose that we view an image function $f(x, y)$ in 3-D perspective (like a relief map), with the x and y axes being the usual spatial coordinates and the third axis being brightness (that is, values of f). In this representation, the image appears as a discrete surface whose value at any point (x, y) is that of f at those coordinates. Let us now assume that we want to open f by a spherical structuring element, b, and view this element as a "rolling ball." Then, the mechanics of opening f by b may be interpreted geometrically as the process of pushing the ball against the *underside* of the surface, while at the same time rolling it so that the entire underside of the surface is traversed. The opening, $f \circ b$, then is the surface of the highest points reached by any part of the sphere as it slides over the *entire* undersurface of f. Figure 8.46 illustrates this concept. Figure 8.46(a) shows a scan line of a gray-scale image as a continuous function to simplify the illustration. Figure 8.46(b) shows the rolling ball in various positions, and Fig. 8.46(c) shows the complete result of opening f by b along the

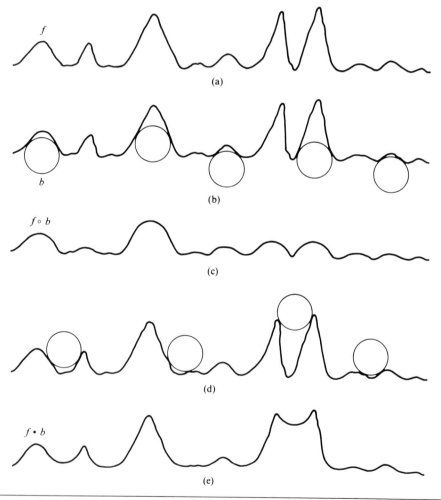

Figure 8.46   (a) A gray-scale scan line; (b) various locations of a rolling ball during opening; (c) result of opening; (d) various locations of the rolling ball during closing; (e) result of closing.

scan line. All the peaks that were narrow with respect to the diameter of the ball were reduced in amplitude and sharpness. In practical applications, opening operations usually are applied to remove small (with respect to the size of the structuring element) light details, while leaving the overall gray levels and larger bright features relatively undisturbed. The initial erosion removes the small details, but it also darkens the image. The subsequent dilation again increases the brightness of the image without reintroducing the details removed by erosion.

Figures 8.46(d) and (e) show the result of closing f by b. Here, the ball slides on top of the surface, and peaks essentially are left in their original form (so long as their separation at the narrowest point exceeds the diameter of the ball). In practical applications, closing is generally used to remove dark details from an image, while leaving bright features relatively undisturbed. The initial dilation removes the dark details and brightens the image, and the subsequent erosion darkens the image without reintroducing the details removed by dilation.

The opening operation satisfies the following properties:

(i) $(f \circ b) \hookleftarrow f$,

(ii) If $f_1 \hookleftarrow f_2$, then $(f_1 \circ b) \hookleftarrow (f_2 \circ b)$,

(iii) $(f \circ b) \circ b = f \circ b$.

The expression $u \hookleftarrow v$ is used to indicate that the domain of u is a subset of the domain of v and also that $u(x, y) \le v(x, y)$ for any (x, y) in the domain of u.

Similarly, the closing operation satisfies the following properties:

(i) $f \hookleftarrow (f \bullet b)$,

(ii) If $f_1 \hookleftarrow f_2$, then $(f_1 \bullet b) \hookleftarrow (f_2 \bullet b)$,

(iii) $(f \bullet b) \bullet b = f \bullet b$.

The usefulness of these expressions is similar to that of their binary counterparts. As in the binary case, properties *(ii)* and *(iii)* for both opening and closing often are called *increasing monotonicity* and *idempotence*, respectively.

Example: Figure 8.47(a) shows the result of opening the image in Fig. 8.45(a) with the same structuring element used there. Note the decreased sizes of the small, bright details, with no appreciable effect on the darker gray levels. Figure 8.47(b) shows the closing of Fig. 8.45(a). Note the decreased sizes of the small, dark details, with relatively little effect on the bright features. ❏

Some Applications of Gray-Scale Morphology

We conclude the discussion of morphological techniques by presenting in some detail various applications of the concepts developed in the preceding discussion. Unless stated otherwise, all the images shown are of size 512×512 and

 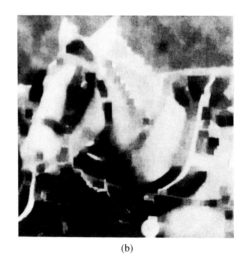

(a)   (b)

Figure 8.47 *(a) Opening and (b) closing of Fig. 8.45(a). (Courtesy of A. Morris, Leica Cambridge, Ltd.)*

were processed by using the structuring element discussed in connection with Fig. 8.45.

Morphological smoothing. One way to achieve smoothing is to perform a morphological opening followed by a closing. The net result of these two operations is to remove or attenuate both bright and dark artifacts or noise. Figure 8.48 shows a smoothed version of the original image shown in Fig. 8.45(a).

Morphological gradient. In addition to the operations discussed earlier in connection with the removal of small dark and bright artifacts, dilation and erosion often are used to compute the *morphological gradient* of an image, denoted g:

$$g = (f \oplus b) - (f \ominus b). \tag{8.4-37}$$

Figure 8.49 shows the result of computing the morphological gradient of the image shown in Fig. 8.45(a). As expected, the morphological gradient highlights sharp gray-level transitions in the input image. As opposed to gradients obtained using methods such as a Sobel operation, morphological gradients obtained using symmetrical structuring elements tend to depend less on edge directionality. The price paid for this advantage is a significant increase in computational requirements.

Top-hat transformation. The so called morphological *top-hat* transformation of an image, denoted h, is defined as

$$h = f - (f \circ b) \tag{8.4-38}$$

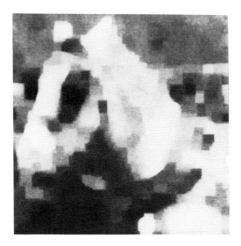

Figure 8.48 *Morphological smoothing of the image in Fig. 8.45(a). (Courtesy of A. Morris, Leica Cambridge, Ltd.)*

where, as before, f is the input image and b is the structuring element function. This transformation—which owes its original name to the use of a cylindrical or parallelepiped structuring element function with a flat top—is useful for enhancing detail in the presence of shading. Figure 8.50 shows the result of performing a top-hat transformation on the image of Fig. 8.45(a). Note the enhancement of detail in the background region below the lower part of the horse's head.

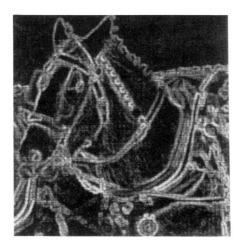

Figure 8.49 *Morphological gradient of the image in Fig. 8.45(a). (Courtesy of A. Morris, Leica Cambridge, Ltd.)*

Figure 8.50   *Result of performing a top-hat transformation on the image of Fig. 8.45(a). (Courtesy of A. Morris, Leica Cambridge, Ltd.)*

Textural segmentation. Figure 8.51(a) shows a simple gray-scale image composed of two texture regions. The region on the right consists of circular blobs of larger diameter than those on the left. The objective is to find the boundary between the two regions based on their textural content. Although various possible solutions based on the material in Chapter 7 may come immediately

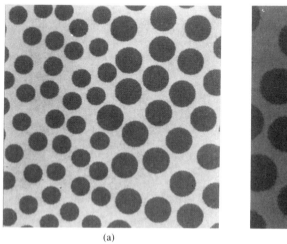

(a)

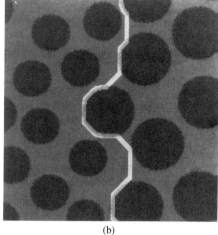

(b)

Figure 8.51   *(a) Original image; (b) segmentation boundary. (Courtesy of A. Morris, Leica Cambridge, Ltd.)*

to mind, a morphological approach utilizing closing and opening operations is particularly effective.

Because closing tends to remove dark details from an image, the procedure in this particular case is to close the input image by using successively larger structuring elements. When the size of the structuring element corresponds to that of the small blobs, they are removed from the image, leaving only a light background in the area previously occupied by them. At this point in the process, only the larger blobs and the light background on the left and between the large blobs themselves remain. Next, a single opening is performed with a structuring element that is large in relation to the separation between the large blobs. This operation removes the light patches between the blobs, leaving a dark region on the right consisting of the large dark blobs and the now equally dark patches between these blobs. At this point the process has produced a light region on the left and a dark region on the right. A simple threshold detection then yields the boundary between the two textural regions. Figure 8.51(b) shows the resulting boundary superimposed on the original image. It is instructive to work through this example in more detail using the rolling ball analogy described in Fig. 8.46.

Granulometry. Granulometry is a field that, among other things, deals with determining the size distribution of particles in an image. Figure 8.52(a) shows an image consisting of light objects of three different sizes. The objects not only are overlapping, but they also are too cluttered to enable detection of individual particles. Because the particles are bright with respect to the back-

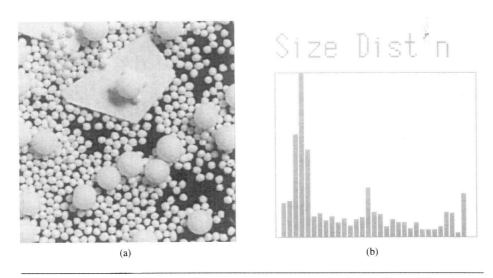

(a)   (b)

Figure 8.52 *(a) Original image consisting of overlapping particles; (b) size distribution. (Courtesy of A. Morris, Leica Cambridge, Ltd.)*

ground, the following morphological approach can be used to determine size distribution. Opening operations with structuring elements of increasing size are performed on the original image. The difference between the original image and its opening is computed after each pass with a different structuring element is completed. At the end of the process, these differences are normalized and then used to construct a histogram of particle-size distribution. This approach is based on the idea that opening operations of a particular size have the most effect on regions of the input image that contain particles of similar size. Thus a measure of the relative number of such particles is obtained by computing the difference between the input and output images. Figure 8.52(b) shows the resulting size distribution in this case. The histogram indicates the presence of three predominant particle sizes in the input image. This type of processing is useful for describing regions with a predominant particle-like character.

8.5   RELATIONAL DESCRIPTORS

The approaches discussed in Sections 8.2–8.4 generally apply to individual boundaries and regions of interest in an image. The next level of complexity in the description process is to organize these components to exploit any structural relationships that may exist between them.

We introduce this concept with the simple staircase structure shown in Fig. 8.53(a). Assume that this structure has been segmented out of an image and that we want to describe it in some formal way. By defining the two *primitive elements* a and b shown, we may code Fig. 8.53(a) in the form shown in Fig. 8.53(b). The most obvious property of the coded structure is the repetitiveness of the elements a and b. Therefore a simple description approach is to formulate

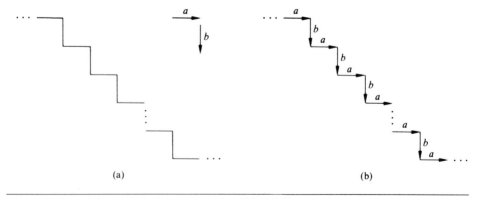

(a)   (b)

Figure 8.53   *(a) A simple staircase structure; (b) coded structure.*

a recursive relationship involving these primitive elements. One possibility is to use the *rewriting rules*:

(1) $S \rightarrow aA$,

(2) $A \rightarrow bS$, and

(3) $A \rightarrow b$,

where S and A are variables and the elements a and b are constants corresponding to the primitives defined previously. Rule 1 indicates that S, called the *starting symbol*, can be replaced by primitive a and variable A. This variable, in turn, can be replaced by b and S or by b alone. Replacing A with bS, leads back to the first rule and the procedure can be repeated. Replacing A with b terminates the procedure, because no variables remain in the expression. Figure 8.54 illustrates some sample derivations of these rules, where the numbers below the structures represent the order in which rules 1, 2, and 3 were applied. The relationship between a and b is preserved, because these rules force an a always to be followed by a b. Notably, these three simple rewriting rules can be used to generate (or describe) infinitely many "similar" structures. As we show in Chapter 9, this approach also has the advantage of a solid theoretical foundation.

Because strings are 1-D structures, their application to image description requires establishing an appropriate method for reducing 2-D positional relations to 1-D form. Most applications of strings to image description are based on the idea of extracting connected line segments from the objects of interest. One approach is to follow the contour of an object and code the result with segments of specified direction and/or length. Figure 8.55 illustrates this procedure.

Another, somewhat more general, approach is to describe sections of an image (such as small homogeneous regions) by directed line segments, which can be joined in other ways besides head-to-tail connections. Figure 8.56(a)

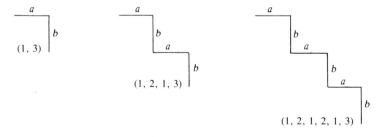

Figure 8.54 *Sample derivations for the rules $S \rightarrow aA$, $A \rightarrow bS$, and $A \rightarrow b$.*

Figure 8.55   *Coding a region boundary with directed line segments.*

illustrates this approach, and Fig. 8.56(b) shows some typical operations that
can be defined on abstracted primitives. Figure 8.56(c) shows a set of specific
primitives consisting of line segments defined in four directions, and Fig. 8.56(d)
shows a step-by-step generation of a specific shape, where $(\sim d)$ indicates the
primitive d with its direction reversed. Note that each composite structure has
a single head and a single tail. The result of interest is the last string, which
describes the complete structure.

   These types of strings are best suited to applications in which connectivity
of primitives can be expressed in a head-to-tail or other continuous manner.
The material in Chapter 9 requires an ability to deal with disjoint structures,
and one of the most useful approaches for doing so is to use tree descriptors.

   A *tree T* is a finite set of one or more nodes for which

(1) there is a unique node $ designated the *root*, and
(2) the remaining nodes are partitioned into m disjointed sets $T_1, \ldots, T_m$,
      each of which in turn is a tree called a *subtree* of T.

   The *tree frontier* is the set of nodes at the bottom of the tree (the *leaves*),
taken in order from left to right. For example, the following tree has root $
and frontier xy.

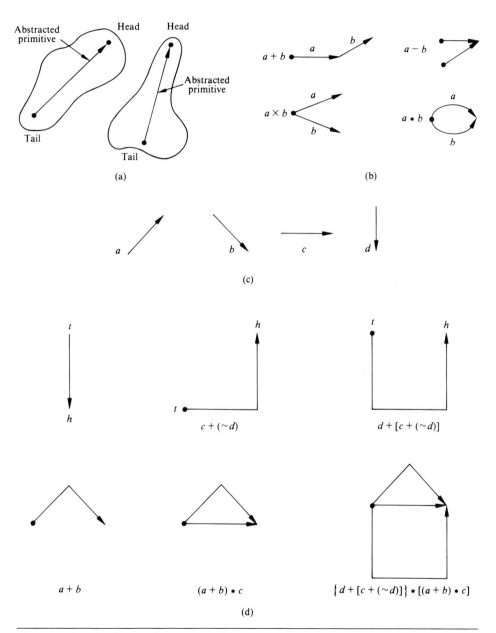

Figure 8.56 *(a) Abstracted primitives; (b) operations among primitives; (c) a set of specific primitives; (d) steps in building a structure.*

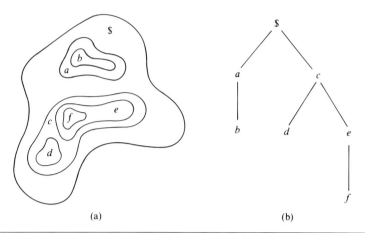

Figure 8.57 *(a) A simple composite region; (b) tree representation obtained by using the relationship "inside of."*

Generally, two types of information in a tree are important: (1) information about a node stored as a set of words describing the node, and (2) information relating a node to its neighbors stored as a set of pointers to those neighbors. As used in image description, the first type of information identifies a pattern primitive, whereas the second type defines the physical relationship of the primitive to other substructures. For example, Fig. 8.57(a) can be represented by a tree by using the relationship "inside of." Thus, if the root of the tree is denoted $, Fig. 8.57(a) shows that the first level of complexity involves a and c inside $, which produces two branches emanating from the root, as shown in Fig. 8.57(b). The next level involves b inside a and d and e inside c. Finally, f inside e completes the tree.

8.6 CONCLUDING REMARKS

The representation and description of objects or regions that have been seg-mented out of an image are early steps in the operation of most automated image analysis systems. The morphological concepts we discussed offer a pow-erful approach for extracting elements of these regions. These are useful in the representation and description of shape, such as boundaries, skeletons, and the convex hull. As indicated by the range of description techniques covered in this chapter, the problem under consideration dictates the choice of one method over another. The objective is to choose descriptors that "capture" essential differences between objects, or classes of objects, while maintaining as much independence as possible to changes in factors such as location, size, and orientation.

REFERENCES

The chain-code representation discussed in Section 8.1.1 was first proposed by Freeman [1961, 1974]. For further reading on polygonal approximations see the paper by Sklansky et al. [1972], the book by Pavlidis [1977], and a paper by Bengtsson and Eklundh [1991]. References for the discussion of signatures are Ambler et al. [1975], Nahim [1974], Ballard and Brown [1982], and Gupta and Srinath [1988]. Further information about algorithms for finding the convex hull and convex deficiency of a set is contained in Graham and Yao [1983] and Preparata and Shamos [1985]. The skeletonizing algorithm discussed in Section 8.1.5 is from Zhang and Suen [1984]. Some useful additional comments on the properties and implementation of this algorithm are included in a paper by Lu and Wang [1986]. A paper by Jang and Chin [1990] provides an interesting tie between the discussion in Section 8.1.5 and the morphological concept of thinning introduced in Section 8.4.4. Although some attempts have been made to use skeletons of gray-scale images (Dyer and Rosenfeld [1979], Salari and Siy [1984], Yu and Tsai [1990]), this type of representation usually is associated with binary data. Finding the extrema and other dominant points on digital boundaries plays an important role in several of the methods discussed in Sections 8.1 and 8.2. An algorithm proposed by Teh and Chin [1989] is of interest in this regard.

References for Section 8.2.1 are Shamos [1978], Fischler [1980], Toussaint [1982], and Rosenfeld and Kak [1982]. See also Mokhtarian and Mackworth [1986]. The discussion of shape numbers is based on the work of Bribiesca and Guzman [1980] and Bribiesca [1981]. An algorithm proposed by Freeman and Shapira [1975] for finding the basic rectangle of a closed, chain-coded curve also is of interest. References for Section 8.2.3 are Brill [1968], Zahn and Roskies [1972], and Persoon and Fu [1977]. See also Schalkoff [1989]. The material in Section 8.2.4 is based on elementary probability theory.

Additional details on the material in Sections 8.3.1 and 8.3.2 are presented in Duda and Hart [1973] and in Ballard and Brown [1982]. Texture descriptors have received a great deal of attention during the recent past. For further reading on the statistical aspects of texture see Haralick et al. [1973], Bajcsy and Lieberman [1976], Haralick [1979], and Cross and Jain [1983]. For structural texture see Lu and Fu [1978] and Tomita et al. [1982]. The discussion on spectral techniques is based on an early paper by Bajcsy [1973]. A paper by Wechsler [1980] provides a good survey of texture analysis. More recent applications of texture are described by Bouman and Liu [1991] and by Chen and Wang [1991]. The moment invariant approach discussed in Section 8.3.4 is from Hu [1962]. Additional information on this topic is contained in Bell [1965] and Wong and Hall [1978].

Basic references for the discussion in Section 8.4 are the books by Serra [1982, 1988], Giardina and Dougherty [1988], and Dougherty [1992]. Chapter 6 of a book by Pitas and Vanetsanopoulos [1990] also is of interest. The papers by Haralick et al. [1987] and Maragos [1987] provide a tutorial overview of morphological methods in image processing. Although morphological methods became an active topic of research in the United States from the mid-1980s onward, Golay's work in the mid- and late 1960s already had presented important elements of this subject (see, for example, Golay [1969] and a more recent paper by Preston

[1983]). A significant amount of work on binary and gray-scale morphology has been done in Europe since the early 1970s. The references in Serra [1982, 1988] provide an excellent guide to this body of work. A more recent paper by Meyer and Beucher [1990] gives an overview of the use of gray-scale morphology for solving segmentation problems. This paper is of interest as an extension of the basic gray-scale morphological concepts introduced in Section 8.4.5. The use of morphological filters for restoring binary images, as discussed in Schonfeld and Goutsias [1991], provides an additional example of the usefulness of the ideas introduced in Section 8.4. A basic tie between binary and gray-scale morphology is provided by the so-called *umbra homomorphism theorem*. Although development of this topic was beyond the scope of the discussion in Section 8.4, a deeper understanding of this subject can be gained by consulting the books by Serra [1982], Giardina and Dougherty [1988], and Dougherty [1992], as well as the paper by Haralick et al. [1987]. An approach for decomposing gray-scale morphological operations into binary morphological operations is given by Shih and Mitchell [1989]. Finally, references for Section 8.5 are Gonzalez and Thomason [1978] and Fu [1982].

PROBLEMS

8.1 a) Show that redefining the starting point of a chain code so that the resulting sequence of numbers forms an integer of minimum magnitude makes the code independent of the initial starting point on the boundary.

 b) Find the normalized starting point of the code 11076765543322.

8.2 a) Show that the first difference of a chain code normalizes it to rotation, as explained in Section 8.1.1.

 b) Compute the first difference of the code 0101030303323232212111.

8.3 a) Show that the rubber-band polygonal approximation approach discussed in Section 8.1.2 yields a polygon with minimum perimeter.

 b) Show that if each cell corresponds to a pixel on the boundary, the maximum possible error in that cell is $\sqrt{2}d$, where d is the grid distance between pixels.

8.4 a) Discuss the effect on the resulting polygon if the error threshold is set to zero in the merging method discussed in Section 8.1.2.

 b) What would be the effect on the splitting method?

8.5 a) Plot the signature of a square boundary using the tangent angle method discussed in Section 8.1.3.

 b) Repeat for the slope density function. Assume that the square is aligned with the x and y axes, and let the x axis be the reference line. Start at the corner closest to the origin.

8.6 Find the medial axis of (a) a circle, (b) a square, and (c) an equilateral triangle.

8.7 a) For each of the figures shown, discuss the action taken at point p by step 1 of the thinning algorithm presented in Section 8.1.5.

 b) Repeat for step 2. Assume that $p = 1$ in all cases.

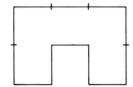

8.8 a) What is the order of the shape number for the figure shown?
   b) Obtain the shape number.

8.9 The procedure discussed in Section 8.2.3 for using Fourier descriptors consists of expressing the coordinates of a contour as complex numbers, taking the DFT of these numbers, and keeping only a few components of the DFT as descriptors of the boundary shape. The inverse DFT is then an approximation to the original contour. What class of contour shapes would have a DFT consisting of real numbers and how would the axis system in Fig. 8.14 have to be set up to obtain these real numbers?

8.10 Give the smallest number of moment descriptors needed to differentiate between the signatures of the figures shown in Fig. 8.5.

8.11 Find the Euler number of the characters 0, 1, 8, 9, and X.

8.12 You are to design an image processing system for detecting imperfections on the inside of certain solid plastic wafers. The wafers are examined by means of a low-energy x-ray imaging system, which yields images of 512×512 resolution with 8 bits per pixel. In the absence of imperfections, the images appear "bland," having a mean gray level of 100 with a noise variance of 400. The imperfections appear as bloblike regions in which the pixels have excursions in intensity of 50 gray levels or more about a mean of 100. A wafer is considered defective if such a region occupies an area exceeding 20×20 pixels in size. Propose an approach for solving this problem utilizing texture analysis.

8.13 Obtain the gray-level co-occurrence matrix of a 5×5 image composed of a checkerboard of alternating 1's and 0's if (a) the position operator P is defined as "one pixel to the right," and (b) "two pixels to the right." Assume that the top left pixel has value 0.

8.14 Consider a checkerboard image composed of alternating black and white squares, each of size $m \times m$. Give a position operator that would yield a diagonal co-occurrence matrix.

8.15 a) Sketch the dilation of a circle of radius r by a circular structuring element of radius $r/4$.

b) Use this structuring element to dilate a square of size $r \times r$.

c) Use the same structuring element to dilate an equilateral triangle with sides of size r.

d) Repeat (a)–(c) for erosion.

8.16 a) Repeat the dilation example shown in Figs. 8.26(d) and (e), but let the origin of the structuring element be located at its top left corner.

b) Repeat for erosion, and compare your result to Fig. 8.27(e).

8.17 Use the concepts introduced in Section 8.4 and develop a morphological algorithm for converting an 8-connected binary boundary to an m-connected boundary (see Section 2.4.2). An important requirement is that your algorithm cannot break connectivity. You may assume that the input boundary is fully connected and that it is 1 pixel thick (but it can have branching points).

8.18 Prove the validity of Eq. (8.4-10).

8.19 An alternative definition of dilation is

$$A \oplus B = \{c \in Z^2 | c = a + b, \quad \text{for some } a \in A \text{ and } b \in B\}.$$

a) Show that this definition and the definition in Eq. (8.4-5) are equivalent.

b) Show also that this definition is equivalent to yet another definition of dilation, $A \oplus B = \bigcup_{b \in B} (A)_b$. (This equation also is known as the *Minkowsky addition* of two sets.)

c) Show that $A \oplus B = \bigcup_{b \in B} (A)_b$ also is equivalent to the definition in Eq. (8.4-5).

8.20 An alternative definition of erosion is

$$A \ominus B = \{c \in Z^2 | c + b \in A, \quad \text{for every } b \in B\}.$$

a) Show that this definition is equivalent to the definition in Eq. (8.4-6).

b) Show also that this definition is equivalent to yet another definition of erosion, $A \ominus B = \bigcap_{b \in B} (A)_{-b}$. (If $-b$ is replaced with b, this expression is called the *Minkowsky subtraction* of two sets.)

c) Show that $A \ominus B = \bigcap_{b \in B} (A)_{-b}$ also is equivalent to the definition in Eq. (8.4-6).

8.21 Suppose that the image $f(x, y)$ and structuring element $b(x, y)$ in Eq. (8.4-31) both are rectangular, with domains D_f and D_b denoted ($[F_{x1}, F_{x2}], [F_{y1}, F_{y2}]$) and ($[B_{x1}, B_{x2}], [B_{y1}, B_{y2}]$), respectively. For example, the closed intervals $[F_{x1}, F_{x2}]$ and $[F_{y1}, F_{y2}]$ are the ranges of x and y in the x and y axes of the xy plane, where the function $f(x, y)$ is defined.

a) Assume that $(x, y) \in D_b$, and derive expressions for the intervals over which the displacement variables s and t can range to satisfy Eq. (8.4-31). These intervals in the s and t axes define the rectangular domain of $(f \oplus b)(s, t)$ in the st plane.

b) Repeat for erosion, as defined in Eq. (8.4-32).

8.22 A gray-scale image, $f(x, y)$, is corrupted by nonoverlapping noise spikes that can be modeled as small, cylindrical artifacts of radii $R_{min} \leq r \leq R_{max}$ and amplitude $A_{min} \leq a \leq A_{max}$.

a) Develop a morphological filtering approach for cleaning up the image.

b) Repeat (a), but now assume that there is overlapping of, at most, four noise spikes.

8.23 Give a spatial relationship and corresponding tree representation for a checkerboard pattern of black and white squares. Assume that the top left element is black, and that the root of the tree corresponds to that element. Your tree can have no more than two branches emanating from each node.

CHAPTER 9

RECOGNITION AND INTERPRETATION

One of the most interesting aspects of the world
is that it can be considered to be made up of
patterns. A pattern is essentially an arrangement.
It is characterized by the order of the elements
of which it is made, rather than by the intrinsic
nature of these elements.
Norbert Wiener

We conclude our coverage of digital image processing by developing several techniques for image recognition and interpretation. The material in this chapter is related primarily to applications requiring automated image analysis.

Image analysis is a process of discovering, identifying, and understanding patterns that are relevant to the performance of an image-based task. One of the principal goals of image analysis by computer is to endow a machine with the capability to approximate, in some sense, a similar capability in human beings. For example, in a system for automatically reading images of typed documents, the patterns of interest are alphanumeric characters, and the goal is to achieve character recognition accuracy that is as close as possible to the superb capability exhibited by human beings for performing such tasks.

Thus an automated image analysis system should be capable of exhibiting various degrees of intelligence. The concept of *intelligence* is somewhat vague, particularly with reference to a machine. However, conceptualizing various types of behavior generally associated with intelligence is not difficult. Several characteristics come immediately to mind: (1) the ability to extract pertinent information from a background of irrelevant details; (2) the capability to learn from examples and to generalize this knowledge so that it will apply in new and different circumstances; and (3) the ability to make inferences from incomplete information.

Image analysis systems with these characteristics can be designed and implemented for *limited* operational environments. However, we do not yet know how to endow these systems with a level of performance that comes even close to emulating human capabilities in performing general image analysis functions. Research in biological and computational systems continually is uncovering new and promising theories to explain human visual cognition. However, the state of the art in computerized image analysis for the most part is based on heuristic formulations tailored to solve specific problems. For example, some machines are capable of reading printed, properly formatted documents at speeds that are orders of magnitude faster than the speed that the most skilled human reader could achieve. However, systems of this type are highly specialized and thus have little or no extendability. That is, current theoretic and implementation limitations in the field of image analysis imply solutions that are highly problem dependent.

We indicated in Section 1.5 that the material in Chapters 1–3 deals with background topics, the material in Chapters 4–6 is useful for image preprocessing, and the material in Chapters 7–9 relates primarily to applications dealing with image analysis. This classification of functions, although appealing organizationally, should not be construed as implying that the material in Chapters 1–6 is not useful for image analysis. Image acquisition, enhancement, restoration, and compression are common in applications involving human *and* machine processing of digital image data. It will become evident in the following discussion that the design of image analysis systems requires knowledge of most of the material covered in this book.

9.1 ELEMENTS OF IMAGE ANALYSIS

Dividing the spectrum of techniques in image analysis into three basic areas is conceptually useful. These areas are (1) low-level processing, (2) intermediate-level processing, and (3) high-level processing. Although these subdivisions have no definitive boundaries, they do provide a useful framework for categorizing the various processes that are inherent components of an autonomous image analysis system. Figure 9.1 illustrates these concepts, with the overlapping dashed lines indicating that clear-cut boundaries between processes do not exist. For example, thresholding may be viewed as an enhancement (preprocessing) or a segmentation tool, depending on the application.

Low-level processing deals with functions that may be viewed as automatic reactions, requiring no intelligence on the part of the image analysis system. We treat image acquisition and preprocessing (Chapters 2–6) as low-level functions. This classification encompasses activities from the image formation process itself to compensations, such as noise reduction or image deblurring. Low-level functions may be compared to the sensing and adaptation processes that a person goes through when trying to find a seat immediately after entering a

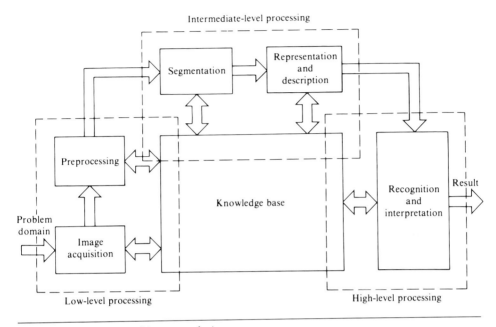

Figure 9.1 *Elements of image analysis.*

dark theater from bright sunlight. The (intelligent) process of finding an unoccupied seat cannot begin until a suitable image is available. The process followed by the brain in adapting the visual system to produce such an image is an automatic, unconscious reaction.

Intermediate-level processing deals with the task of extracting and characterizing components (say, regions) in an image resulting from a low-level process. As Fig. 9.1 indicates, intermediate-level processes encompass segmentation and description, using techniques such as those discussed in Chapters 7 and 8. Some capabilities for intelligent behavior have to be built into flexible segmentation procedures. For example, bridging small gaps in a segmented boundary involves more sophisticated elements of problem solving than mere low-level automatic reactions.

Finally, *high-level processing* involves recognition and interpretation, the principal subjects of this chapter. These two processes have a stronger resemblance to what generally is meant by the term *intelligent cognition*. The majority of techniques used for low- and intermediate-level processing encompass a reasonably well-defined set of theoretic formulations. However, as we venture into recognition, and especially into interpretation, our knowledge and understanding of fundamental principles becomes far less precise and much more speculative. This relative lack of understanding ultimately results in a formulation of constraints and idealizations intended to reduce task complexity to a manageable level. The end product is a system with highly specialized operational capabilities.

The material in the following sections deals with: (1) decision-theoretic methods for recognition, (2) structural methods for recognition, and (3) methods for image interpretation. Decision-theoretic recognition (Section 9.3) is based on representing patterns in vector form and then seeking approaches for grouping and assigning pattern vectors into different pattern classes. The principal approaches to decision-theoretic recognition are minimum distance classifiers, correlators, Bayes classifiers, and neural networks. In structural recognition (Section 9.4), patterns are represented in symbolic form (such as strings and trees), and recognition methods are based on symbol matching or on models that treat symbol patterns as sentences from an artificial language. Image interpretation (Section 9.5) deals with assigning meaning to an ensemble of recognized image elements. The predominant concept underlying image interpretation methodologies is the effective organization and use of knowledge about a problem domain. Current techniques for image interpretation are based on predicate logic, semantic networks, and production (in particular, *expert*) systems.

9.2   PATTERNS AND PATTERN CLASSES

As stated in Section 9.1, the ability to perform pattern recognition at some level is fundamental to image analysis. Here, a *pattern* is a quantitative or structural description of an object or some other entity of interest in an image. In general, a pattern is formed by one or more descriptors, such as those discussed in Chapter 8. In other words, a pattern is an arrangement of descriptors. (The name *features* is often used in the pattern recognition literature to denote descriptors.) A *pattern class* is a family of patterns that share some common properties. Pattern classes are denoted $\omega_1, \omega_2, \ldots, \omega_M$, where M is the number of classes. Pattern recognition by machine involves techniques for assigning patterns to their respective classes—automatically and with as little human intervention as possible.

The three principal pattern arrangements used in practice are vectors (for quantitative descriptions) and strings and trees (for structural descriptions). Pattern vectors are represented by bold lowercase letters, such as **x**, **y**, and **z**, and take the form:

$$\mathbf{x} = \begin{bmatrix} x_1 \\ x_2 \\ \vdots \\ x_n \end{bmatrix} \qquad (9.2\text{-}1)$$

where each component, x_i, represents the ith descriptor and n is the number of such descriptors. Pattern vectors are represented as columns (that is, $n \times 1$ matrices). Hence a pattern vector can be expressed in the form shown in Eq. (9.2-1) or in the equivalent form $\mathbf{x} = (x_1, x_2, \ldots, x_n)^T$, where T indicates transposition.

The nature of the components of a pattern vector $\mathbf{x}$ depends on the measurement technique used to describe the physical pattern itself. For example, suppose that we want to describe three types of iris flowers (*Iris setosa, virginica,* and *versicolor*) by measuring the widths and lengths of their petals. In this case, we would be dealing with 2-D vectors of the form:

$$\mathbf{x} = \begin{bmatrix} x_1 \\ x_2 \end{bmatrix} \tag{9.2-2}$$

where x_1 and x_2 correspond to petal length and width, respectively. The three pattern classes in this case, denoted ω_1, ω_2, and ω_3, correspond to the varieties *setosa, virginica,* and *versicolor,* respectively.

Because the petals of all flowers vary in width and length to some degree, the pattern vectors describing these flowers also will vary, not only between different classes, but also within a class. Figure 9.2 shows length and width measurements for several samples of each type of iris. After a set of measurements has been selected (two in this case), a pattern vector becomes the entire representation of each physical sample. Thus each flower in this case becomes a point in 2-D Euclidean space. We also note that measurements of petal width and length in this case adequately separated the class of *Iris setosa* from the other two but did not as successfully separate the *virginica* and *versicolor* types from each other. This result illustrates the classic *feature selection* problem, in which the degree of class separability depends strongly on the choice of pattern measurements selected for an application. We say considerably more about this issue in Section 9.3.3.

Figure 9.3 shows another example of pattern vector generation. In this case, we are interested in different types of noisy shapes, a sample of which is shown in Fig. 9.3(a). If we elect to describe each object by its signature (see Section 8.1.3), we would obtain 1-D signals of the form shown in Fig. 9.3(b). By sampling these functions at some specified interval values of θ, denoted θ_1, $\theta_2, \ldots, \theta_n$, we can form pattern vectors by letting $x_1 = r(\theta_1)$, $x_2 = r(\theta_2)$, $\ldots$, $x_n = r(\theta_n)$. These vectors become points in n-dimensional Euclidean space, and pattern classes become "clouds" in n dimensions.

Instead of using signature amplitudes directly, we could compute, say, the first n moments of a given signautre (Section 8.2.4) and use them as the components of the corresponding pattern vector. In fact, as may be evident by now, pattern vectors can be generated in numerous other ways. We present some of them throughout this chapter. For the moment, the key concept to

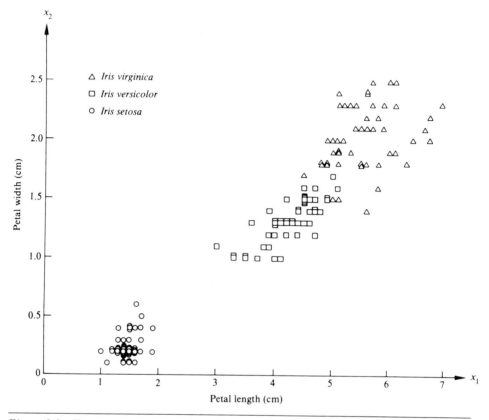

Figure 9.2   *Two measurements performed on three types of iris. (Adapted from Duda and Hart [1973].)*

keep in mind is that selecting the measurement or measurements on which to base each component of a pattern vector has a profound influence on the eventual performance of an image analysis system based on the pattern vector approach.

The techniques just described for generating pattern vectors yield pattern classes characterized by quantitative information. In some applications, pattern characteristics are best described by structural relationships. For example, fingerprint recognition is based on the interrelationships of print features called *minutiae*. These features are primitive components that describe fingerprint ridge properties, such as abrupt endings, branching, merging, and disconnected segments, together with their relative sizes and locations. Recognition problems of this type, in which not only quantitative measures about each feature but also the spatial relationships between the features determine class membership, generally are best solved by structural approaches.

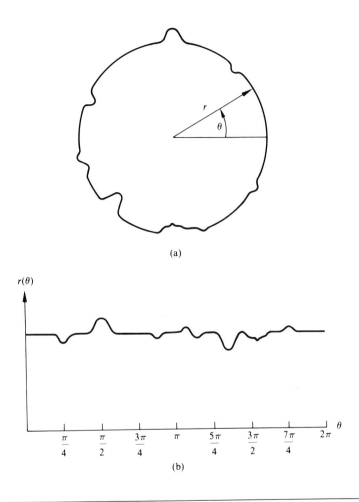

(a)

(b)

Figure 9.3 *A noisy object and its corresponding signature.*

Figure 9.4(a) shows a simple staircase pattern. This pattern could be sampled and expressed in terms of a pattern vector, similar to the approach used in Fig. 9.3. However, the basic structure, consisting of repetitions of two simple primitive elements, would be lost in this method of description. A more meaningful description would be to define the elements a and b and let the pattern be the string of symbols $w = \ldots ababab \ldots$, as shown in Fig. 9.4(b). The structure of this particular class of patterns is captured in this representation by requiring that connectivity be defined in a head-to-tail manner, and by allowing only alternating symbols. This structural construct is applicable to staircases of any length but excludes other types of structures that could be

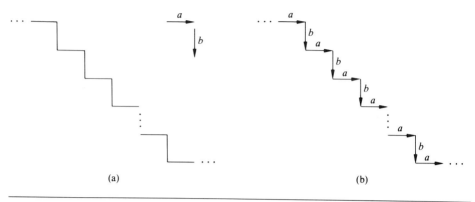

Figure 9.4 (a) Staircase structure; (b) structure coded in terms of the primitives a and b to yield the string representation . . . ababab. . . .

generated by other combinations of the primitives *a* and *b*. (Recall that more complex methods for generating pattern strings are discussed in Section 8.5.)

String representations adequately generate patterns of objects and other entities whose structure is based on relatively simple connectivity of primitives, usually associated with boundary shape. A more powerful approach for many applications is the use of tree descriptions, as defined in Section 8.5. Basically, most hierarchical ordering schemes lead to tree structures. For example, the aerial photograph in Fig. 9.5(a) depicts a scene composed of urban and rural land areas. Let us define the entire image area by the symbol $. The (upside

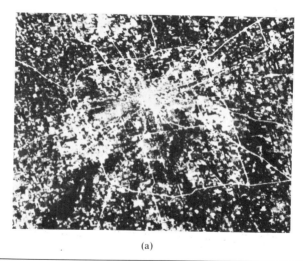

(a)

Figure 9.5 (a) Aerial photograph of urban and rural land areas; (b) tree representation. (From Brayer, Swain, and Fu [1977].)

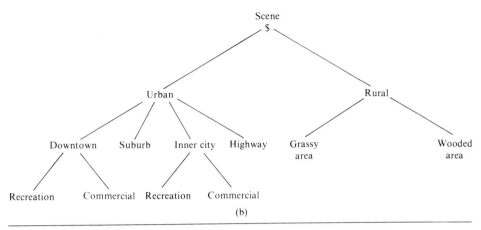

(b)

Figure 9.5 *con't.*

down) tree representation shown in Fig. 9.5(b) was obtained by using the structural relationship "composed of." Thus the root of the tree represents the entire scene. The next level indicates that the scene is composed of urban and rural areas. The rural area in turn is composed of grassy and wooded areas. The urban area can be subdivided into downtown, inner city, suburb and highway components. Finally, the downtown area is subdivided into recreational and commercial components. We can continue this type of subdivision until we reach the limit of our ability to resolve different regions in the image. We develop methods of using all the preceding pattern arrangements in the recognition stage of image analysis systems in the following two sections.

9.3   DECISION-THEORETIC METHODS

Decision-theoretic approaches to recognition are based on the use of *decision* (or *discriminant*) *functions*. Let $\mathbf{x} = (x_1, x_2, \ldots, x_n)^T$ represent an n-dimensional pattern vector, as discussed in Section 9.2. For M pattern classes $\omega_1, \omega_2, \ldots, \omega_M$, the basic problem in decision-theoretic pattern recognition is to find M decision functions $d_1(\mathbf{x}), d_2(\mathbf{x}), \ldots, d_M(\mathbf{x})$ with the property that, if a pattern $\mathbf{x}$ belongs to class ω_i, then

$$d_i(\mathbf{x}) > d_j(\mathbf{x}) \qquad j = 1, 2, \ldots, M; j \neq i. \qquad (9.3\text{-}1)$$

In other words, an unknown pattern $\mathbf{x}$ belongs to the ith pattern class if, upon substitution of $\mathbf{x}$ into all decision functions, $d_i(\mathbf{x})$ yields the largest numerical value. Ties are resolved arbitrarily.

The *decision boundary* separating class ω_i from ω_j is given by values of $\mathbf{x}$ for which $d_i(\mathbf{x}) = d_j(\mathbf{x})$ or, equivalently, by values of $\mathbf{x}$ for which

$$d_i(\mathbf{x}) - d_j(\mathbf{x}) = 0. \qquad (9.3\text{-}2)$$

Common practice is to identify the decision boundary between two classes by the single function $d_{ij}(\mathbf{x}) = d_i(\mathbf{x}) - d_j(\mathbf{x}) = 0$. Thus $d_{ij}(\mathbf{x}) > 0$ for patterns of class ω_i and $d_{ij}(\mathbf{x}) < 0$ for patterns of class ω_j.

The principal objective of the discussion in this section is to develop various approaches for finding decision functions that satisfy Eq. (9.3-1).

9.3.1 Matching

Minimum distance classifier

Suppose that each pattern class is represented by a *prototype* (or *mean*) vector:

$$\mathbf{m}_j = \frac{1}{N_j} \sum_{\mathbf{x} \in \omega_j} \mathbf{x} \qquad j = 1, 2, \ldots, M \qquad (9.3\text{-}3)$$

where N_j is the number of pattern vectors from class ω_j and the summation is taken over these vectors. One way to determine the class membership of an unknown pattern vector $\mathbf{x}$ is to assign it to the class of its closest prototype. Using the Euclidean distance to determine closeness reduces the problem to computing the distance measures:

$$D_j(\mathbf{x}) = \|\mathbf{x} - \mathbf{m}_j\| \qquad j = 1, 2, \ldots, M \qquad (9.3\text{-}4)$$

where $\|\mathbf{a}\| = (\mathbf{a}^T\mathbf{a})^{1/2}$ is the Euclidean norm. We then assign $\mathbf{x}$ to class ω_i if $D_i(\mathbf{x})$ is the smallest distance. That is, the smallest distance implies the best match in this formulation. It is not difficult to show (Problem 9.2) that this is equivalent to evaluating the functions

$$d_j(\mathbf{x}) = \mathbf{x}^T\mathbf{m}_j - \frac{1}{2}\mathbf{m}_j^T\mathbf{m}_j \qquad j = 1, 2, \ldots, M \qquad (9.3\text{-}5)$$

and assigning $\mathbf{x}$ to class ω_i if $d_i(\mathbf{x})$ yields the largest numerical value. This formulation agrees with the concept of a decision function, as defined in Eq. (9.3-1).

From Eqs. (9.3-2) and (9.3-5), the decision boundary between classes ω_i and ω_j for a minimum distance classifier is

$$d_{ij}(\mathbf{x}) = d_i(\mathbf{x}) - d_j(\mathbf{x}) \qquad\qquad\qquad (9.3\text{-}6)$$

$$= \mathbf{x}^T(\mathbf{m}_i - \mathbf{m}_j) - \frac{1}{2}(\mathbf{m}_i - \mathbf{m}_j)^T(\mathbf{m}_i - \mathbf{m}_j) = 0.$$

The surface given by Eq. (9.3-6) is the perpendicular bisector of the line segment joining $\mathbf{m}_i$ and $\mathbf{m}_j$ (see Problem 9.3). For $n = 2$, the perpendicular bisector is a line, for $n = 3$ it is a plane, and for $n > 3$ it is called a *hyperplane*.

Example: Figure 9.6 shows two pattern classes extracted from the iris samples in Fig. 9.2. The two classes, *Iris versicolor* and *Iris setosa*, denoted ω_1 and ω_2, respectively, have sample mean vectors $\mathbf{m}_1 = (4.3, 1.3)^T$ and $\mathbf{m}_2 = (1.5, 0.3)^T$.

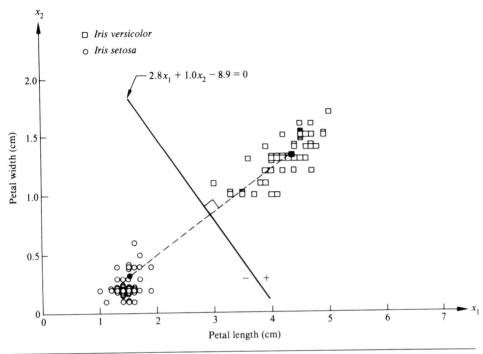

Figure 9.6 *Decision boundary of minimum distance classifier for the classes of Iris versicolor and Iris setosa.*

From Eq. (9.3-5), the decision functions are $d_1(\mathbf{x}) = \mathbf{x}^T\mathbf{m}_1 - \frac{1}{2}\mathbf{m}_1^T\mathbf{m}_1 = 4.3x_1 + 1.3x_2 - 10.1$ and $d_2(\mathbf{x}) = \mathbf{x}^T\mathbf{m}_2 - \frac{1}{2}\mathbf{m}_2^T\mathbf{m}_2 = 1.5x_1 + 0.3x_2 - 1.17$. From Eq. (9.3-6), the equation of the boundary becomes

$$d_{12}(\mathbf{x}) = d_1(\mathbf{x}) - d_2(\mathbf{x})$$
$$= 2.8x_1 + 1.0x_2 - 8.9 = 0.$$

Figure 9.6 shows a plot of this boundary (note that the patterns and the boundary are displaced vertically because the axes are not to the same scale). Substitution of any pattern from class ω_1 would yield $d_{12}(\mathbf{x}) > 0$. Conversely, any pattern from class ω_2 would yield $d_{12}(\mathbf{x}) < 0$. In other words, given an unknown pattern belonging to one of these two classes, the sign of $d_{12}(\mathbf{x})$ would be sufficient to determine the pattern's class membership. ❏

In practice, the minimum distance classifier works well when the distance between means is large compared to the spread or randomness of each class with respect to its mean. In Section 9.3.2 we show that the minimum distance classifier yields optimum performance (in terms of minimizing the average loss of misclassification) when the distribution of each class about its mean is in the form of a spherical "hypercloud" in n-dimensional pattern space.

The simultaneous occurrence of large mean separations and relatively small class spread occurs seldomly in practice unless the system designer controls the nature of the input. An excellent example is provided by systems designed to read stylized character fonts, such as the familiar American Banker's Association E-13B font character set. As Fig. 9.7 shows, this particular font set consists of 14 characters that were purposely designed on a 9 × 7 grid in order to facilitate their reading. The characters are usually printed in ink that contains finely ground magnetic material. Prior to being read, the ink is subjected to a magnetic field, which accentuates each character to simplify detection. In other words, the segmentation problem is solved by artificially highlighting each character.

The characters typically are scanned in a horizontal direction with a single-slit reading head that is narrower but taller than the characters. As the head

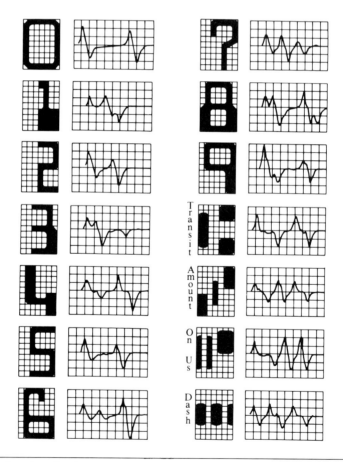

Figure 9.7 *American Bankers Association E-13B font character set and corresponding waveforms.*

moves across a character, it produces a 1-D electrical signal that is conditioned to be proportional to the rate of increase or decrease of the character area under the head. For example, consider the waveform associated with the number 0 in Fig. 9.7. As the reading head moves from left to right, the area seen by the head begins to increase, producing a positive derivative (a positive rate of change). As the head begins to leave the left leg of the 0, the area under the head begins to decrease, producing a negative derivative. When the head is in the middle zone of the character the area remains constant, producing a zero derivative. This pattern repeats itself as the head enters the right leg of the character. The design of the font ensures that the waveform of each character is distinct from that of all others. It also ensures that the peaks and zeros of each waveform occur approximately on the vertical lines of the background grid on which these waveforms are displayed, as shown in Fig. 9.7. The E-13B font has the property that sampling the waveforms only at these points yields enough information for their proper classification. The use of magnetized ink aids in providing clean waveforms, thus minimizing scatter.

Designing a minimum distance classifier for this application is straightforward. We simply store the sample values of each waveform and let each set of samples be represented as a prototype vector $\mathbf{m}_i$, $i = 1, 2, \ldots , 14$. When an unknown character is to be classified, the approach is to scan it in the manner previously described, express the grid samples of the waveform as a vector, $\mathbf{x}$, and identify its class by selecting the class of the prototype vector that yields the highest value in Eq. (9.3-5). High classification speeds can be achieved with analog circuits composed of resistor banks (see Problem 9.4).

Matching by correlation
We introduced the basic concept of image correlation in Section 3.3.8. Here, we consider it as the basis for finding matches of a subimage $w(x, y)$ of size $J \times K$ within an image $f(x, y)$ of size $M \times N$, where we assume that $J \leq M$ and $K \leq N$. Although the correlation approach can be formulated in vector form (see Problem 9.5), working directly with an image or subimage format is more intuitive (and traditional).

In its simplest form, the correlation between $f(x, y)$ and $w(x, y)$ is

$$c(s, t) = \sum_x \sum_y f(x, y)w(x - s, y - t) \tag{9.3-7}$$

where $s = 0, 1, 2, \ldots , M - 1, t = 0, 1, 2, \ldots , N - 1$, and the summation is taken over the image region where w and f overlap. Figure 9.8 illustrates the procedure, where we assume that the origin of $f(x, y)$ at its top left and the origin of $w(x, y)$ at its center. For any value of (s, t) inside $f(x, y)$, application of Eq. (9.3-7) yields one value of c. As s and t are varied, $w(x, y)$ moves around the image area, giving the function $c(s, t)$. The maximum value of $c(s, t)$ indicates the position where $w(x, y)$ best matches $f(x, y)$. Note that accuracy is lost for

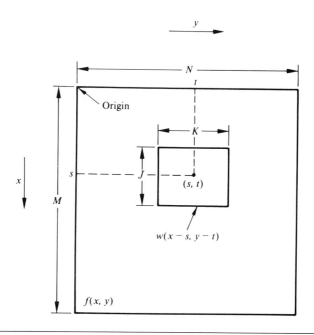

Figure 9.8 *Arrangement for obtaining the correlation of f(x, y) and w(x, y) at point (s, t).*

values of s and t near the edges of $f(x, y)$, with the amount of error being proportional to the size of $w(x, y)$.

The correlation function given in Eq. (9.3-7) has the disadvantage of being sensitive to changes in the amplitude of $f(x, y)$ and $w(x, y)$. For example, doubling all values of $f(x, y)$ doubles the value of $c(s, t)$. An approach frequently used to overcome this difficulty is to perform matching via the *correlation coefficient,* which is defined as

$$\gamma(s, t) = \frac{\sum_x \sum_y [f(x, y) - \bar{f}(x, y)][w(x - s, y - t) - \bar{w}]}{\left\{\sum_x \sum_y [f(x, y) - \bar{f}(x, y)]^2 \sum_x \sum_y [w(x - s, y - t) - \bar{w}]^2\right\}^{1/2}} \quad (9.3\text{-}8)$$

where $s = 0, 1, 2, \ldots, M - 1$, $t = 0, 1, 2, \ldots, N - 1$, $\bar{w}$ is the average value of the pixels in $w(x, y)$ (computed only once), $\bar{f}(x, y)$ is the average value of $f(x, y)$ in the region coincident with the current location of w, and the summations are taken over the coordinates common to both f and w. The correlation coefficient $\gamma(s, t)$ is scaled in the range -1 to 1, independent of scale changes in the amplitude of $f(x, y)$ and $w(x, y)$ (see Problem 9.5).

Example: Figure 9.9 illustrates the concepts just discussed. Figure 9.9(a) is $f(x, y)$ and Fig. 9.9(b) is $w(x, y)$. The correlation coefficient $\gamma(s, t)$ is shown as an image in Fig. 9.9(c). Note the higher value (intensity) of $\gamma(s, t)$ in the position where the best match between $f(x, y)$ and $w(x, y)$ was found. ☐

Although the correlation function can be normalized for amplitude changes via the correlation coefficient, obtaining normalization for changes in size and rotation can be difficult. Normalizing for size involves spatial scaling, a process that in itself adds a significant amount of computation. Normalizing for rotation is even more difficult. If a clue regarding rotation can be extracted from $f(x, y)$, then we simply rotate $w(x, y)$ so that it aligns itself with the degree of rotation in $f(x, y)$. However, if the nature of rotation is unknown, looking for the best match requires exhaustive rotations of $w(x, y)$. This procedure is impractical and, as a consequence, correlation seldom is used in cases when arbitrary or unconstrained rotation is present.

In Section 3.3.8 we mentioned that correlation also can be carried out in the frequency domain via the FFT. If f and w are the same size, this approach can be more efficient than direct implementation of correlation in the spatial domain. If Eq. (9.3-7) is used, w is usually much smaller than f. A trade-off estimate performed by Campbell [1969] indicates that, if the number of nonzero

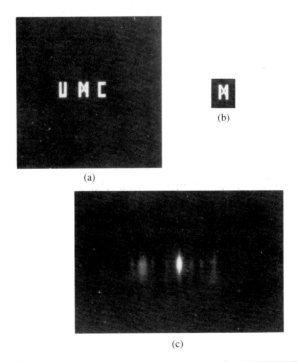

(b)

(a)

(c)

Figure 9.9 *Example of correlation. Note the brightness of $\gamma(s, t)$ at the position where the two letters match. (Adapted from Hall et al. [1971].)*

terms in w is less than 132 (a subimage of approximately 13×13 pixels), direct implementation of Eq. (9.3-7) is more efficient than the FFT approach. This number, of course, depends on the machine and algorithms used, but it does indicate approximate subimage size at which the frequency domain should be considered as an alternative. The correlation coefficient is considerably more difficult to implement in the frequency domain and is usually computed directly from Eq. (9.3-8).

9.3.2 Optimum Statistical Classifiers

Foundation

In this section we develop a probabilistic approach to recognition. As is true in most fields that deal with measuring and interpreting physical events, prob- ability considerations become important in pattern recognition because of the randomness under which pattern classes normally are generated. As shown in the following discussion, it is possible to derive a classification approach that is optimal in the sense that, on average, its use yields the lowest probability of committing classification errors.

The probability that a particular pattern $\mathbf{x}$ comes from class ω_i is denoted $p(\omega_i/\mathbf{x})$. If the pattern classifier decides that $\mathbf{x}$ came from ω_j when it actually came from ω_i, it incurs a loss, denoted L_{ij}. As pattern $\mathbf{x}$ may belong to any one of M classes under consideration, the average loss incurred in assigning $\mathbf{x}$ to class ω_j is

$$r_j(\mathbf{x}) = \sum_{k=1}^{M} L_{kj} p(\omega_k/\mathbf{x}). \tag{9.3-9}$$

Equation (9.3-9) often is called the *conditional average risk* or *loss* in decision-theory terminology.

From basic probability theory, $p(a/b) = [p(a)p(b/a)]/p(b)$. Using this expression, we write Eq. (9.3-9) in the form:

$$r_j(\mathbf{x}) = \frac{1}{p(\mathbf{x})} \sum_{k=1}^{M} L_{kj} p(\mathbf{x}/\omega_k) P(\omega_k) \tag{9.3-10}$$

where $p(\mathbf{x}/\omega_k)$ is the probability density function of the patterns from class ω_k and $P(\omega_k)$ is the probability of occurrence of class ω_k. Because $1/p(\mathbf{x})$ is positive and common to all the $r_j(\mathbf{x})$, $j = 1, 2, \ldots, M$, it can be dropped from Eq. (9.3-10) without affecting the relative order of these functions from the smallest to the largest value. The expression for the average loss then reduces to

$$r_j(\mathbf{x}) = \sum_{k=1}^{M} L_{kj} p(\mathbf{x}/\omega_k) P(\omega_k). \tag{9.3-11}$$

The classifier has M possible classes to choose from for any given unknown pattern. If it computes $r_1(\mathbf{x}), r_2(\mathbf{x}), \ldots, r_M(\mathbf{x})$ for each pattern $\mathbf{x}$, and assigns the pattern to the class with the smallest loss, the total average loss with respect to all decisions will be minimum. The classifier that minimizes the total average loss is called the *Bayes classifier*. Thus the Bayes classifier assigns an unknown pattern $\mathbf{x}$ to class ω_i if $r_i(\mathbf{x}) < r_j(\mathbf{x})$ for $j = 1, 2, \ldots, M; j \neq i$. In other words, $\mathbf{x}$ is assigned to class ω_i if

$$\sum_{k=1}^{M} L_{ki} p(\mathbf{x}/\omega_k) P(\omega_k) < \sum_{q=1}^{M} L_{qj} p(\mathbf{x}/\omega_q) P(\omega_q). \tag{9.3-12}$$

In many recognition problems, the loss for a correct decision is zero, and it has the same nonzero value (say, 1) for any incorrect decision. Under these conditions, the loss function becomes

$$L_{ij} = 1 - \delta_{ij} \tag{9.3-13}$$

where $\delta_{ij} = 1$ if $i = j$ and $\delta_{ij} = 0$ if $i \neq j$. Equation (9.3-13) indicates a loss of unity for incorrect decisions and a loss of zero for correct decisions. Substituting Eq. (9.3-13) into Eq. (9.3-11) yields

$$
\begin{aligned}
r_j(\mathbf{x}) &= \sum_{k=1}^{M} (1 - \delta_{kj}) p(\mathbf{x}/\omega_k) P(\omega_k) \\
&= p(\mathbf{x}) - p(\mathbf{x}/\omega_j) P(\omega_j).
\end{aligned}
\tag{9.3-14}
$$

The Bayes classifier then assigns a pattern $\mathbf{x}$ to class ω_i if

$$p(\mathbf{x}) - p(\mathbf{x}/\omega_i) P(\omega_i) < p(\mathbf{x}) - p(\mathbf{x}/\omega_j) P(\omega_j) \tag{9.3-15}$$

or, equivalently, if

$$p(\mathbf{x}/\omega_i) P(\omega_i) > p(\mathbf{x}/\omega_j) P(\omega_j) \qquad j = 1, 2, \ldots, M; j \neq i. \tag{9.3-16}$$

With reference to the discussion leading to Eq. (9.3-1), we see that the Bayes classifier for 0–1 loss functions is nothing more than implementation of decision functions of the form

$$d_j(\mathbf{x}) = p(\mathbf{x}/\omega_j) P(\omega_j) \qquad j = 1, 2, \ldots, M \tag{9.3-17}$$

where a pattern vector $\mathbf{x}$ is assigned to class ω_i if $d_i(\mathbf{x}) > d_j(\mathbf{x})$ for all $j \neq i$.

The decision functions given in Eq. (9.3-17) are optimal in that they minimize the average loss in misclassification. For this optimality to hold, however, the probability density functions of the patterns in each class, as well as the probability of occurrence of each class, must be known. The latter requirement usually is not a problem. For instance, if all classes are equally likely to occur, then $P(\omega_j) = 1/M$. Even if this relation is not true, these probabilities generally can be inferred from knowledge of the problem. Estimation of the probability density functions $p(\mathbf{x}/\omega_j)$ is another matter. If the pattern vectors, $\mathbf{x}$, are n-

dimensional, $p(\mathbf{x}/\omega_j)$ is a function of n variables, which, if its form is not known, requires methods from multivariate probability theory for its estimation. These methods are difficult to apply in practice, especially if the number of representative patterns from each class is not large or if the underlying form of the probability density functions is not well behaved. For these reasons, use of the Bayes classifier generally is based on the assumption of an analytic expression for the various density functions and then an estimation of the expression's parameters from sample patterns from each class. By far the most prevalent form assumed for $p(\mathbf{x}/\omega_j)$ is the Gaussian probability density function. The closer this assumption is to reality, the closer the Bayes classifier approaches the minimum average loss in classification.

Bayes classifier for Gaussian pattern classes

To begin, let us consider a 1-D problem ($n = 1$) involving two pattern classes ($M = 2$) governed by Gaussian densities, with means m_1 and m_2 and standard deviations σ_1 and σ_2, respectively. From Eq. (9.3-17) the Bayes decision functions have the form:

$$d_j(x) = p(x/\omega_j)P(\omega_j) \tag{9.3-18}$$

$$= \frac{1}{\sqrt{2\pi}\,\sigma_j} \exp\left[-\frac{(x - m_j)^2}{2\sigma_j^2} \right] P(\omega_j) \qquad j = 1, 2$$

where the patterns are now scalars, denoted by x. Figure 9.10 shows a plot of the probability density functions for the two classes. The boundary between the two classes is a single point, denoted x_0, such that $d_1(x_0) = d_2(x_0)$. If the two classes are equally likely to occur, $P(\omega_1) = P(\omega_2) = \frac{1}{2}$, and the decison boundary is the value of x_0 for which $p(x_0/\omega_1) = p(x_0/\omega_2)$. This point is the

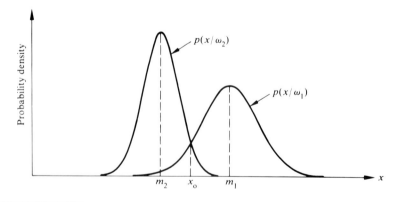

Figure 9.10 *Probability density functions for two 1-D pattern classes. The point x_0 is the decision boundary if the two classes are equally likely to occur.*

intersection of the two probability density functions, as shown in Fig. 9.10. Any pattern (point) to the right of x_o is classified as belonging to class ω_1. Similarly, any pattern to the left of x_o is classified as belonging to class ω_2. When the classes are not equally likely to occur, x_o moves to the left if class ω_1 is more likely to occur or, conversely, to the right if class ω_2 is more likely to occur. This result is to be expected, because the classifier is trying to minimize the loss of misclassification. For instance, in the extreme case, if class ω_2 never occurred, the classifier would never make a mistake by always assigning patterns to class ω_1 (that is, x_o would move to negative infinity).

In the n-dimensional case, the Gaussian density of the vectors in the jth pattern class has the form:

$$p(\mathbf{x}/\omega_j) = \frac{1}{(2\pi)^{n/2}|\mathbf{C}_j|^{1/2}} \exp\left[-\frac{1}{2}(\mathbf{x} - \mathbf{m}_j)^T \mathbf{C}_j^{-1}(\mathbf{x} - \mathbf{m}_j)\right] \qquad (9.3\text{-}19)$$

where each density is specified completely by its mean vector $\mathbf{m}_j$ and covariance matrix $\mathbf{C}_j$, which are defined as

$$\mathbf{m}_j = E_j\{\mathbf{x}\} \qquad (9.3\text{-}20)$$

and

$$\mathbf{C}_j = E_j\{(\mathbf{x} - \mathbf{m}_j)(\mathbf{x} - \mathbf{m}_j)^T\} \qquad (9.3\text{-}21)$$

where $E_j\{\cdot\}$ denotes the expected value of the argument over the patterns of class ω_j. In Eq. (9.3-19), n is the dimensionality of the pattern vectors, and $|\mathbf{C}_j|$ is the determinant of the matrix $\mathbf{C}_j$. Approximating the expected value E_j by the average value of the quantities in question yields an estimate of the mean vector and covariance matrix:

$$\mathbf{m}_j = \frac{1}{N_j} \sum_{\mathbf{x} \in \omega_j} \mathbf{x} \qquad (9.3\text{-}22)$$

and

$$\mathbf{C}_j = \frac{1}{N_j} \sum_{\mathbf{x} \in \omega_j} \mathbf{x}\mathbf{x}^T - \mathbf{m}_j\mathbf{m}_j^T \qquad (9.3\text{-}23)$$

where N_j is the number of pattern vectors from class ω_j, and the summation is taken over these vectors. Later in this section we give an example of how to use these two expressions.

The covariance matrix is symmetric and positive semidefinite. The diagonal element c_{kk} is the variance of the kth element of the pattern vectors. The off-diagonal element c_{jk} is the covariance of x_j and x_k. When the elements x_j and x_k are statistically independent, $c_{jk} = 0$. The multivariate Gaussian density function reduces to the product of the univariate Gaussian density of each element of $\mathbf{x}$ when the off-diagonal elements of the covariance matrix are zero.

According to Eq. (9.3-17), the Bayes decision function for class ω_j is $d_j(\mathbf{x}) = p(\mathbf{x}/\omega_j)P(\omega_j)$. However, because of the exponential form of the Gaussian density, working with the natural logarithm of this decision function is more convenient. In other words, we can use the form:

$$d_j(\mathbf{x}) = \ln[\,p(\mathbf{x}/\omega_j)P(\omega_j)]$$
$$= \ln p(\mathbf{x}/\omega_j) + \ln P(\omega_j). \tag{9.3-24}$$

This expression is equivalent to Eq. (9.3-17) in terms of classification performance because the logarithm is a monotonically increasing function. In other words, the numerical *order* of the decision functions in Eqs. (9.3-17) and (9.3-24) is the same. Substituting Eq. (9.3-19) into Eq. (9.3-24) yields

$$d_j(\mathbf{x}) = \ln P(\omega_j) - \frac{n}{2}\ln 2\pi - \frac{1}{2}\ln|\mathbf{C}_j| - \frac{1}{2}[(\mathbf{x} - \mathbf{m}_j)^T\mathbf{C}_j^{-1}(\mathbf{x} - \mathbf{m}_j)]. \tag{9.3-25}$$

The term $(n/2)\ln 2\pi$ is the same for all classes, so it can be eliminated from Eq. (9.3-25), which then becomes

$$d_j(\mathbf{x}) = \ln P(\omega_j) - \frac{1}{2}\ln|\mathbf{C}_j| - \frac{1}{2}[(\mathbf{x} - \mathbf{m}_j)^T\mathbf{C}_j^{-1}(\mathbf{x} - \mathbf{m}_j)] \tag{9.3-26}$$

for $j = 1, 2, \ldots, M$. Equation (9.3-26) represents the Bayes decision functions for Gaussian pattern classes under the condition of a 0–1 loss function.

The decision functions represented in Eq. (9.3-26) are hyperquadrics (quadratic functions in n-dimensional space), because no terms higher than the second degree in the components of $\mathbf{x}$ appear in the equation. Clearly, then, the best that a Bayes classifier for Gaussian patterns can do is to place a general second-order decision surface between each pair of pattern classes. If the pattern populations are truly Gaussian, however, no other surface would yield a lesser average loss in classification.

If all covariance matrices are equal, $\mathbf{C}_j = \mathbf{C}$, for $j = 1, 2, \ldots, M$—and dropping all terms independent of j—Eq. (9.3-26) becomes

$$d_j(\mathbf{x}) = \ln P(\omega_j) + \mathbf{x}^T\mathbf{C}^{-1}\mathbf{m}_j - \frac{1}{2}\mathbf{m}_j^T\mathbf{C}^{-1}\mathbf{m}_j \tag{9.3-27}$$

which are linear decision functions for $j = 1, 2, \ldots, M$.

If, in addition, $\mathbf{C} = \mathbf{I}$, where $\mathbf{I}$ is the identity matrix and $P(\omega_j) = 1/M$, for $j = 1, 2, \ldots, M$, then

$$d_j(\mathbf{x}) = \mathbf{x}^T\mathbf{m}_j - \frac{1}{2}\mathbf{m}_j^T\mathbf{m}_j \qquad j = 1, 2, \ldots, M. \tag{9.3-28}$$

Equation (9.3-28) represents the decision functions for a minimum distance classifier, as given in Eq. (9.3-5). Thus the minimum distance classifier is optimum in the Bayes sense if (1) the pattern classes are Gaussian, (2) all covariance matrices are equal to the identity matrix, and (3) all classes are equally likely to occur. Gaussian pattern classes satisfying these conditions are spherical clouds of identical shape in n dimensions (called *hyperspheres*). The minimum distance classifier establishes a hyperplane between every pair of classes, with the property that the hyperplane is the perpendicular bisector of the line segment joining the center of the pair of spheres. In two dimensions, the classes constitute circular regions, and the boundaries become lines that bisect the line segment joining the center of every pair of such circles.

Example: Figure 9.11 shows a simple arrangement of two pattern classes in three dimensions. We use these patterns to illustrate the mechanics of implementing the Bayes classifier, assuming that the patterns of each class are samples from a Gaussian distribution.

Applying Eq. (9.3-22) to the patterns of Fig. 9.11 yields

$$\mathbf{m}_1 = \frac{1}{4}\begin{bmatrix} 3 \\ 1 \\ 1 \end{bmatrix} \quad \text{and} \quad \mathbf{m}_2 = \frac{1}{4}\begin{bmatrix} 1 \\ 3 \\ 3 \end{bmatrix}$$

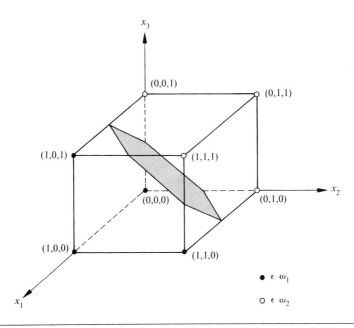

Figure 9.11 *Two simple pattern classes and their Bayes decision boundary.*

Similarly, applying Eq. (9.3-23) to the two pattern classes in turn yields two covariance matrices, which in this case are equal:

$$\mathbf{C}_1 = \mathbf{C}_2 = \frac{1}{16}\begin{bmatrix} 3 & 1 & 1 \\ 1 & 3 & -1 \\ 1 & -1 & 3 \end{bmatrix}$$

Because the covariance matrices are equal the Bayes decision functions are given by Eq. (9.3-27). If we assume that $P(\omega_1) = P(\omega_2) = \frac{1}{2}$, the $\ln P(\omega_i)$ term can be dropped, giving

$$d_j(\mathbf{x}) = \mathbf{x}^T\mathbf{C}^{-1}\mathbf{m}_j - \frac{1}{2}\mathbf{m}_j^T\mathbf{C}^{-1}\mathbf{m}_j$$

where

$$\mathbf{C}^{-1} = \begin{bmatrix} 8 & -4 & -4 \\ -4 & 8 & 4 \\ -4 & 4 & 8 \end{bmatrix}$$

Carrying out the expansion for $d_j(\mathbf{x})$ provides the decision functions:

$$d_1(\mathbf{x}) = 4x_1 - 1.5 \quad \text{and} \quad d_2(\mathbf{x}) = -4x_1 + 8x_2 + 8x_3 - 5.5.$$

The decision surface separating the two classes then is

$$d_1(\mathbf{x}) - d_2(\mathbf{x}) = 8x_1 - 8x_2 - 8x_3 + 4 = 0.$$

Figure 9.11 shows a section of this surface, where we note that the classes were separated effectively. ❏

One of the most successful applications of the Bayes classifier approach is in the classification of remotely sensed imagery generated by multispectral scanners aboard aircraft, satellites, and space stations. The voluminous image data generated by these platforms make automatic image classification and analysis a task of considerable interest in remote sensing. The applications of remote sensing are varied and include land use, crop inventory, crop disease detection, forestry, air and water quality monitoring, geological studies, weather prediction, and a score of other applications having environmental significance. The following example shows a typical application.

Example: A multispectral scanner responds to light in selected wavelength bands; for example: 0.40–0.44, 0.58–0.62, 0.66–0.72, and 0.80–1.00 microns

(10^{-6} m). These ranges are in the violet, green, red, and infrared bands, respectively. A region on the ground scanned in this manner produces four digital images, one image for each band. If the images are perfectly registered, a condition which is generally true in practice, they can be visualized as being stacked one behind the other, as Fig. 9.12 shows. Thus every point on the ground can be represented by a 4-element pattern vector of the form $\mathbf{x} = (x_1, x_2, x_3, x_4)^T$, where x_1 is a shade of violet, x_2 is a shade of green, and so on. If the images are of 512 × 512 resolution, each stack of four multispectral images can be represented by 262,144 pattern vectors.

The Gaussian Bayes classifier requires estimation of the mean vector and covariance matrix for each class. In remote sensing applications these estimates are obtained by collecting multispectral data for each region of interest and then using these samples, much as described in the preceding example. Figure 9.13(a) shows a typical image sensed remotely from an aircraft (this is a mono-chrome version of a multispectral original). In this particular case, the problem was to classify areas such as vegetation, water, and bare soil. Figure 9.13(b) shows the results of machine classification, using a Gaussian Bayes classifier, in the form of a computer printout. The arrows indicate some features of interest. Arrow 1 points to a corner of a field of green vegetation, and arrow 2 points to a river. Arrow 3 identifies a small hedgerow between two areas of bare soil. Arrow 4 indicates a tributary correctly identified by the system. Arrow 5 points to a small pond that is almost indistinguishable in Fig. 9.13(a). Comparing the original image with the computer output reveals recognition results that are very close to those that a human being would generate by visual analysis.   ❑

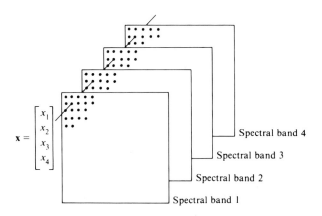

Figure 9.12   *Formation of a pattern vector from registered pixels of four digital images generated by a multispectral scanner.*

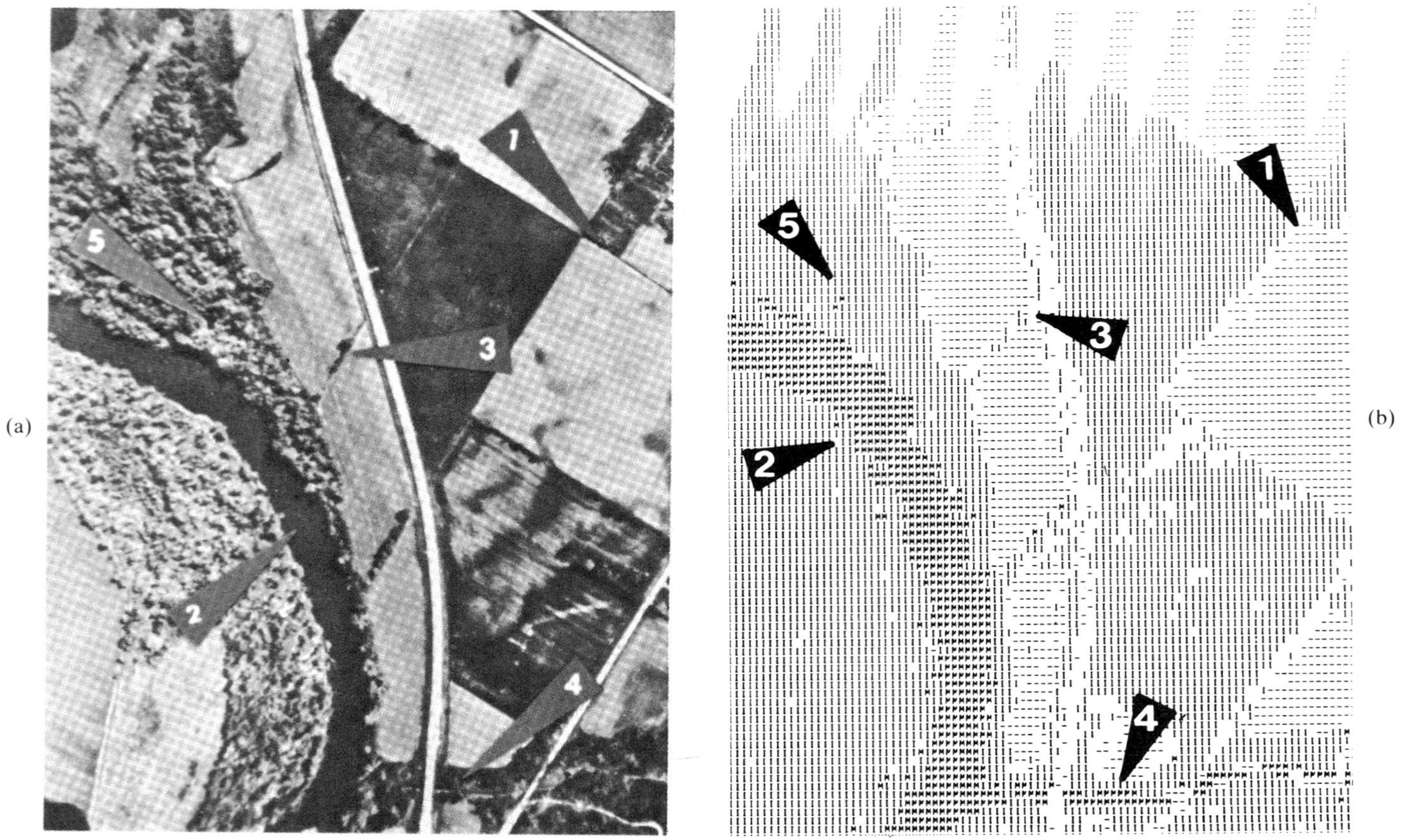

Figure 9.13 (a) Multispectral image; (b) printout of machine classification results using a Bayes classifier. (Courtesy of the Laboratory for Applications of Remote Sensing, Purdue University.)

Before beginning the next section, it is of interest to note that pixel-by-pixel classification of an image as described in the previous example segments the image into various classes. This approach is not unlike thresholding with several variables, as discussed briefly in Section 7.3.6.

9.3.3 Neural Networks

Background

The approaches discussed in the preceding two sections are based on the use of sample patterns to estimate certain statistical parameters of each pattern class. The minimum distance classifier is specified completely by the mean vector of each class. Similarly, the Bayes classifier for Gaussian populations is specified completely by the mean vector and covariance matrix of each class. The patterns (of *known* class membership) used to estimate these parameters usually are called *training patterns*, and a set of such patterns from each class is called a *training set*. The process by which a training set is used to obtain decision functions is called *learning* or *training*.

In the two approaches just discussed, training is a simple matter. The training patterns of each class are used in a straightforward manner to compute the parameters of the decision function corresponding to that class. After the parameters in question have been estimated, the structure of the classifier is fixed, and its eventual performance will depend on how well the actual pattern populations satisfy the underlying statistical assumptions made in the derivation of the classification method being used.

The statistical properties of the pattern classes in a problem often are unknown or cannot be estimated (recall our brief discussion in the preceding section regarding the difficulty of working with multivariate statistics). In practice, such decision-theoretic problems are best handled by methods that yield the required decision functions directly via training. Then, making assumptions regarding the underlying probability density functions or other probabilistic information about the pattern classes under consideration is unnecessary. In this section we discuss various approaches that meet this criterion.

The essence of the material that follows is the use of a multitude of elemental nonlinear computing elements (called *neurons*) organized as networks reminiscent of the way in which neurons are believed to be interconnected in the brain. The resulting models are referred to by various names, including *neural networks*, *neuro-computers*, *parallel distributed processing* (PDP) *models*, *neuromorphic systems*, *layered self-adaptive networks*, and *connectionist models*. Here, we use the name neural networks, or neural nets for short. We use these networks as vehicles for adaptively developing the coefficients of decision functions via successive presentations of training sets of patterns.

Interest in neural networks dates back to the early 1940s, as exemplified by the work of McCulloch and Pitts [1943]. They proposed neuron models in the form of binary threshold devices and stochastic algorithms involving sudden 0–1 and 1–0 changes of states in neurons as the bases for modeling neural systems. Subsequent work by Hebb [1949] was based on mathematical models that attempted to capture the concept of learning by reinforcement or association.

During the mid-1950s and early 1960s, a class of so-called *learning machines* originated by Rosenblatt [1957, 1962] caused significant excitement among researchers and practitioners of pattern recognition theory. The reason for the great interest in these machines, called *perceptrons*, was the development of mathematical proofs showing that perceptrons, when trained with linearly separable training sets, would converge to a solution in a finite number of iterative steps. The solution took the form of coefficients of hyperplanes capable of correctly separating the classes represented by patterns of the training set.

Unfortunately, the expectations following discovery of what appeared to be a well-founded theoretic model of learning soon met with disappointment. The basic perceptron and some of its generalizations at the time were simply inadequate for most pattern recognition tasks of practical significance. Subsequent attempts to extend the power of perceptron-like machines by considering multiple layers of these devices, although conceptually appealing, lacked effective training algorithms such as those that had created interest in the perceptron itself. The state of the field of learning machines in the mid-1960s was summarized by Nilsson [1965]. A few years later, Minsky and Papert [1969] presented a discouraging analysis of the limitation of perceptron-like machines. This view was held as late as the mid-1980s, as evidenced by comments by Simon [1986]. In this work, originally published in French in 1984, Simon dismisses the perceptron under the heading "Birth and Death of a Myth."

Recent results by Rumelhart, Hinton, and Williams [1986] dealing with the development of new training algorithms for multilayer perceptrons have changed matters considerably. Their basic method, often called the *generalized delta rule for learning by back-propagation*, provides an effective training method for multilayer machines. Although this training algorithm cannot be shown to converge to a solution in the sense of the analogous proof for the single-layer perceptron, the generalized delta rule has been used successfully in various problems of practical interest. This success has established multilayer perceptron-like machines as one of the principal models of neural networks currently in use.

Although developments such as new training rules for multilayer machines, the postulation of new models for neural networks, and some encouraging application results have sparked renewed interest in the branch of pattern recognition dealing with learning machines, research in this area is still in its infancy. The human brain has on the order of 100 billion neurons, organized in a complex network where individual neurons may be connected to several thousand other neurons. It is not yet understood how this massively parallel network, in which individual neurons fire at speeds measured in milliseconds (as compared with nanosecond speeds for off-the-shelf electronic components), can perform with amazing speed tasks such as the acquisition, storage, representation, retrieval, and analysis of highly complex sensory data. It is humbling to think of this exquisite data manipulation capability of the brain, and the way in which it allows us to construct mental images of people, places, or events based on fragments of information, such as a familiar sound or smell or simply the recollection of a calendar date.

In this context, current accomplishments in artificial neural networks pale by comparison. Thus the challenges ahead in this field of research are many. Our task here is to introduce several aspects of the state of the art in the implementation of multilayer neural networks. We begin by introducing the perceptron as a basic model of a neuron. We then discuss various aspects of training perceptrons under conditions of class separability and nonseparability. This material serves as the foundation for the development and illustration of the generalized delta rule for training multilayer neural networks.

Perceptron for two pattern classes
In its most basic form, the perceptron learns a linear decision function that dichotomizes two linearly separable training sets. Figure 9.14(a) shows schematically the perceptron model for two pattern classes. The response of this basic device is based on a weighted sum of its inputs; that is,

$$d(\mathbf{x}) = \sum_{i=1}^{n} w_i x_i + w_{n+1} \qquad (9.3\text{-}29)$$

which is a linear decision function with respect to the components of the pattern vectors (see Eq. 9.2-1). The coefficients w_i, $i = 1, 2, \ldots, n, n + 1$, called *weights*, modify the inputs before they are summed and fed into the threshold element. In this sense, weights are analogous to synapses in the human neural system. The function that maps the output of the summing junction into the final output of the device sometimes is called the *activation function*.

When $d(\mathbf{x}) > 0$ the threshold element causes the output of the perceptron to be $+1$, indicating that the pattern $\mathbf{x}$ was recognized as belonging to class ω_1. The reverse is true when $d(\mathbf{x}) < 0$. This mode of operation agrees with the comments made earlier in connection with Eq. (9.3-2) regarding the use of a single decision function for two pattern classes. When $d(\mathbf{x}) = 0$, $\mathbf{x}$ lies on the decision surface separating the two pattern classes, giving an indeterminate condition. The decision boundary implemented by the perceptron is obtained by setting Eq. (9.3-29) equal to zero:

$$d(\mathbf{x}) = \sum_{i=1}^{n} w_i x_i + w_{n+1} = 0 \qquad (9.3\text{-}30)$$

or

$$w_1 x_1 + w_2 x_2 + \ldots + w_n x_n + w_{n+1} = 0 \qquad (9.3\text{-}31)$$

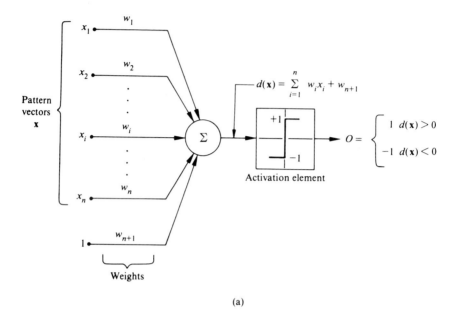

(a)

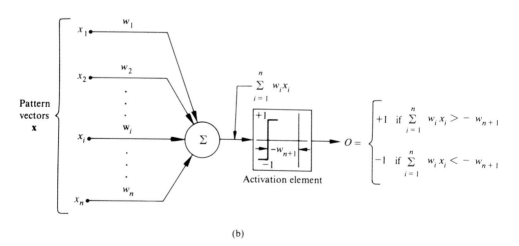

(b)

Figure 9.14 *Two equivalent representations of the perceptron model for two pattern classes.*

which is the equation of a hyperplane in n-dimensional pattern space. Geometrically, the first n coefficients establish the orientation of the hyperplane, whereas the last coefficient, w_{n+1}, is proportional to the perpendicular distance from the origin to the hyperplane. Thus if $w_{n+1} = 0$, the hyperplane goes through the origin of the pattern space. Similarly, if $w_j = 0$, the hyperplane is parallel to the x_j axis.

The output of the threshold element in Fig. 9.14(a) depends on the sign of $d(\mathbf{x})$. Instead of testing the entire function to determine whether it is positive or negative, we could test the summation part of Eq. (9.3-29) against the term w_{n+1}, in which case, the output of the system would be

$$O = \begin{cases} +1 & \text{if } \sum_{i=1}^{n} w_i x_i > -w_{n+1} \\[2em] -1 & \text{if } \sum_{i=1}^{n} w_i x_i < -w_{n+1}. \end{cases} \qquad (9.3\text{-}32)$$

This implementation is equivalent to Fig. 9.14(a) and is shown in Fig. 9.14(b), the only differences being that the threshold function is displaced by an amount $-w_{n+1}$ and that the constant unit input is no longer present. We return to the equivalence of these two formulations later in this section when we discuss implementation of multilayer neural networks.

Another formulation commonly found in practice is to augment the pattern vectors by appending an additional $(n+1)$st element, which is always equal to 1, regardless of class membership. That is, an augmented pattern vector $\mathbf{y}$ is created from a pattern vector $\mathbf{x}$ by letting $y_i = x_i$, $i = 1, 2, \ldots, n$, and appending the additional element $y_{n+1} = 1$. Equation (9.3-29) then becomes

$$\begin{aligned} d(\mathbf{y}) &= \sum_{i=1}^{n+1} w_i y_i \\ &= \mathbf{w}^T \mathbf{y} \end{aligned} \qquad (9.3\text{-}33)$$

where $\mathbf{y} = (y_1, y_2, \ldots, y_n, 1)^T$ is now an augmented pattern vector, and $\mathbf{w} = (w_1, w_2, \ldots, w_n, w_{n+1})^T$ is called the *weight vector*. This expression is usually more convenient in terms of notation. Regardless of the formulation used, however, the key problem is to find $\mathbf{w}$ by using a given training set of pattern vectors from each of two classes.

Training algorithms

The algorithms developed below are representative of the numerous approaches proposed over the years for training perceptrons.

Linearly separable classes. A simple, iterative algorithm for obtaining a solution weight vector for two linearly separable training sets follows. For two training sets of augmented pattern vectors belonging to pattern classes ω_1 and

ω_2, respectively, let $\mathbf{w}(1)$ represent the initial weight vector, which may be chosen arbitrarily. Then, at the kth iterative step; if $\mathbf{y}(k) \in \omega_1$ and $\mathbf{w}^T(k)\mathbf{y}(k) \leq 0$, replace $\mathbf{w}(k)$ by

$$\mathbf{w}(k + 1) = \mathbf{w}(k) + c\mathbf{y}(k) \qquad (9.3\text{-}34)$$

where c is a positive correction increment. But if $\mathbf{y}(k) \in \omega_2$ and $\mathbf{w}^T(k)\mathbf{y}(k) \geq 0$, replace $\mathbf{w}(k)$ with

$$\mathbf{w}(k + 1) = \mathbf{w}(k) - c\mathbf{y}(k). \qquad (9.3\text{-}35)$$

Otherwise, leave $\mathbf{w}(k)$ unchanged; that is, let

$$\mathbf{w}(k + 1) = \mathbf{w}(k). \qquad (9.3\text{-}36)$$

Simply stated, this algorithm makes a change in $\mathbf{w}$ only if the pattern being considered at the kth step in the training sequence is misclassified by the weight vector at that step. The correction increment c is assumed to be positive and, for now, to be constant. This algorithm sometimes is referred to as the *fixed increment correction rule*.

This training method clearly is based on a reward-and-punishment concept. The "reward" to the machine for correctly classifying a pattern is actually the absence of "punishment." In other words, if the machine classifies a pattern

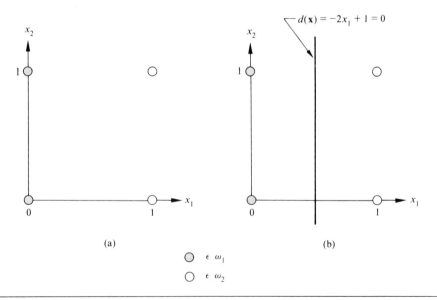

(a)   (b)

○ $\epsilon\ \omega_1$

○ $\epsilon\ \omega_2$

Figure 9.15 *Illustration of the perceptron training algorithm: (a) patterns belonging to two classes; (b) decision boundary determined by training.*

correctly, it is rewarded by the fact that no change is made in $\mathbf{w}$. However, if the machine misclassifies a pattern, it is punished by the fact that a change is made in the weight vector. Convergence of the algorithm occurs when the entire training set for both classes is cycled through the machine without any errors. The fixed increment correction rule converges in a finite number of steps if the two training sets of patterns are linearly separable. A proof of this result, sometimes called the *perceptron training theorem*, can be found in the books by Nilsson [1965], Duda and Hart [1973], and Tou and Gonzalez [1974].

Example: Consider the two training sets shown in Fig. 9.15(a), each consisting of two patterns. The training algorithm should be successful because the two training sets are linearly separable.

Before the algorithm is applied the patterns are augmented, yielding the training set $\{(0, 0, 1)^T, (0, 1, 1)^T\}$ for class ω_1 and $\{(1, 0, 1)^T, (1, 1, 1)^T\}$ for class ω_2. Letting $c = 1$, $\mathbf{w}(1) = \mathbf{0}$ and presenting the patterns in order results in the following sequence of steps:

$$\mathbf{w}^T(1)\mathbf{y}(1) = [0, 0, 0]\begin{bmatrix} 0 \\ 0 \\ 1 \end{bmatrix} = 0 \qquad \mathbf{w}(2) = \mathbf{w}(1) + \mathbf{y}(1) = \begin{bmatrix} 0 \\ 0 \\ 1 \end{bmatrix}$$

$$\mathbf{w}^T(2)\mathbf{y}(2) = [0, 0, 1]\begin{bmatrix} 0 \\ 1 \\ 1 \end{bmatrix} = 1 \qquad \mathbf{w}(3) = \mathbf{w}(2) = \begin{bmatrix} 0 \\ 0 \\ 1 \end{bmatrix}$$

$$\mathbf{w}^T(3)\mathbf{y}(3) = [0, 0, 1]\begin{bmatrix} 1 \\ 0 \\ 1 \end{bmatrix} = 1 \qquad \mathbf{w}(4) = \mathbf{w}(3) - \mathbf{y}(3) = \begin{bmatrix} -1 \\ 0 \\ 0 \end{bmatrix}$$

$$\mathbf{w}^T(4)\mathbf{y}(4) = [-1, 0, 0]\begin{bmatrix} 1 \\ 1 \\ 1 \end{bmatrix} = -1 \qquad \mathbf{w}(5) = \mathbf{w}(4) = \begin{bmatrix} -1 \\ 0 \\ 0 \end{bmatrix}$$

where corrections in the weight vector were made in the first and third steps because of misclassifications, as indicated in Eqs. (9.3-34) and (9.3-35). Because a solution has been obtained only when the algorithm yields a complete error-free iteration through all training patterns, the training set must be presented again. The machine learning process is continued by letting $\mathbf{y}(5) = \mathbf{y}(1)$, $\mathbf{y}(6) = \mathbf{y}(2)$, $\mathbf{y}(7) = \mathbf{y}(3)$, and $\mathbf{y}(8) = \mathbf{y}(4)$ and proceeding in the same manner. Convergence is achieved at $k = 14$, yielding the solution weight vector $\mathbf{w}(14) = (-2, 0, 1)^T$. The corresponding decision function is $d(\mathbf{y}) = -2y_1 + 1$. Going back to the original pattern space by letting $x_i = y_i$ yields $d(\mathbf{x}) = -2x_1 + 1$, which, when set equal to zero, becomes the equation of the decision boundary shown in Fig. 9.15(b).   ❑

Nonseparable classes. In practice, linearly separable pattern classes are the (rare) exception, rather than the rule. Consequently, a significant amount of research effort during the 1960s and 1970s went into development of techniques designed to handle nonseparable pattern classes. With recent advances in the training of neural networks, many of the methods dealing with nonseparable behavior have become merely items of historical interest. One of the early methods, however, is directly relevant to this discussion: the original delta rule. Known as the *Widrow–Hoff*, or *least mean square* (LMS) *delta rule* for training perceptrons, the method minimizes the error between the actual and desired response at any training step.

Consider the criterion function

$$J(\mathbf{w}) = \frac{1}{2}(r - \mathbf{w}^T\mathbf{y})^2 \tag{9.3-37}$$

where r is the desired response (that is, $r = +1$ if the augmented training pattern vector $\mathbf{y}$ belongs to class ω_1, and $r = -1$ if $\mathbf{y}$ belongs to class ω_2. The task is to adjust $\mathbf{w}$ incrementally in the direction of the negative gradient of $J(\mathbf{w})$ in order to seek the minimum of this function, which occurs when $r = \mathbf{w}^T\mathbf{y}$; that is, the minimum corresponds to correct classification. If $\mathbf{w}(k)$ represents the weight vector at the kth iterative step, a general gradient descent algorithm may be written as

$$\mathbf{w}(k + 1) = \mathbf{w}(k) - \alpha\left[\frac{\partial J(\mathbf{w})}{\partial \mathbf{w}}\right]_{\mathbf{w}=\mathbf{w}(k)} \tag{9.3-38}$$

where $\mathbf{w}(k + 1)$ is the new value of $\mathbf{w}$, and $\alpha > 0$ gives the magnitude of the correction. From Eq. (9.3-37),

$$\frac{\partial J(\mathbf{w})}{\partial \mathbf{w}} = -(r - \mathbf{w}^T\mathbf{y})\mathbf{y}. \tag{9.3-39}$$

Substituting this result into Eq. (9.3-38) yields

$$\mathbf{w}(k + 1) = \mathbf{w}(k) + \alpha[r(k) - \mathbf{w}^T(k)\mathbf{y}(k)]\mathbf{y}(k) \tag{9.3-40}$$

with the starting weight vector, $\mathbf{w}(1)$, being arbitrary. Making a correction only when a pattern is misclassified allows Eq. (9.3-40) to be expressed in the perceptron training algorithm form given in Eqs. (9.3-34)–(9.3-36).

By defining the change (delta) in weight vector as

$$\Delta\mathbf{w} = \mathbf{w}(k + 1) - \mathbf{w}(k) \tag{9.3-41}$$

we can write Eq. (9.3-40) in the form of a *delta correction algorithm:*

$$\Delta\mathbf{w} = \alpha e(k)\mathbf{y}(k) \tag{9.3-42}$$

where

$$e(k) = r(k) - \mathbf{w}^T(k)\mathbf{y}(k) \tag{9.3-43}$$

is the error committed with weight vector $\mathbf{w}(k)$ when pattern $\mathbf{y}(k)$ is presented.

Equation (9.3-43) gives the error with weight vector $\mathbf{w}(k)$. If we change it to $\mathbf{w}(k + 1)$, but leave the pattern the same, the error becomes

$$e(k) = r(k) - \mathbf{w}^T(k + 1)\mathbf{y}(k). \tag{9.3-44}$$

The change in error then is[7]

$$
\begin{aligned}
\Delta e &= [r(k) - \mathbf{w}^T(k + 1)\mathbf{y}(k)] - [r(k) - \mathbf{w}^T(k)\mathbf{y}(k)] \\
&= - [\mathbf{w}^T(k + 1) - \mathbf{w}^T(k)]\mathbf{y}(k) \\
&= - \Delta\mathbf{w}^T\mathbf{y}(k).
\end{aligned}
\tag{9.3-45}
$$

But $\Delta\mathbf{w} = \alpha e(k)\mathbf{y}(k)$, so

$$
\begin{aligned}
\Delta e &= - \alpha e(k)\mathbf{y}^T(k)\mathbf{y}(k) \\
&= - \alpha e(k)\|\mathbf{y}(k)\|^2.
\end{aligned}
\tag{9.3-46}
$$

Hence changing the weights reduces the error by a factor $\alpha\|\mathbf{y}(k)\|^2$. The next input pattern starts the new adaptation cycle, reducing the next error by a factor $\alpha\|\mathbf{y}(k + 1)\|^2$, and so on.

The choice of α controls stability and speed of convergence (Widrow and Stearns [1985]). Stability requires that $0 < \alpha < 2$. A practical range for α is $0.1 < \alpha < 1.0$. Although not shown here, the algorithm of Eq. (9.3-40) or Eqs. (9.3-42) and (9.3-43) converge to a solution that minimizes the mean square error over the patterns of the training set. When the pattern classes are separable, the solution given by the Widrow–Hoff procedure may or may not produce a separating hyperplane. That is, a mean square error solution does not imply a solution in the sense of the perceptron training theorem. This uncertainty is the price of using an algorithm that converges under both the separable and nonseparable cases in this particular formulation.

The two perceptron training algorithms discussed so far may be extended easily to cases involving more than two classes. Based on the historical com-

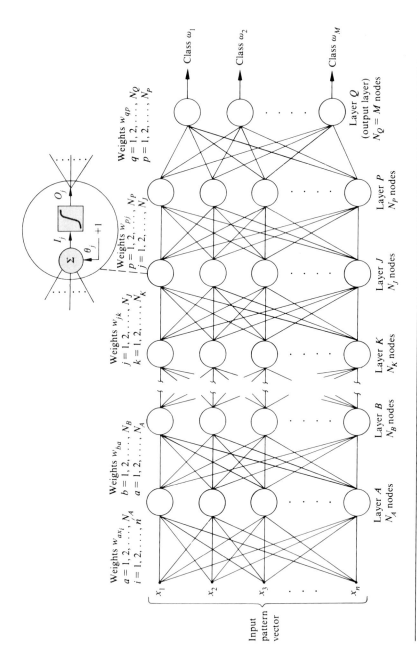

Figure 9.16 *Multilayer feedforward neural network model. The blowup shows the basic structure of each neuron element throughout the network. The offset θ_j is treated as just another weight.*

ments made at the beginning of this section, exploring these multiclass training algorithms here has little merit. Instead, we address multiclass training in the context of neural networks.

Multilayer feedforward neural networks
We can now tackle decision functions of multiclass pattern recognition problems, independent of whether or not the classes are separable, and involving architectures that consist of layers of perceptron computing elements.

Basic architecture. Figure 9.16 shows the system architecture of the neural network model under consideration. It consists of layers of structurally identical computing nodes (neurons) arranged so that the output of every neuron in one layer feeds into the input of every neuron in the next layer. The number of neurons in the first layer, called layer A, is N_A. Often, $N_A = n$, the dimensionality of the input pattern vectors. The number of neurons in the output layer, called layer Q, is denoted N_Q. The number N_Q equals M, the number of pattern classes that the neural network has been trained to recognize. The network recognizes a pattern vector **x** as belonging to class ω_m if the mth output of the network is "high" while all other outputs are "low."

As the blowup in Fig. 9.16 shows, each neuron has the same form as the perceptron model discussed earlier (see Fig. 9.14), with the exception that the hard-limiting activation function has been replaced by a soft-limiting "sigmoid" function. Differentiability along all paths of the neural network is required in the development of the training rule by back propagation. The following sigmoid activation function has the necessary differentiability:

$$h_j(I_j) = \frac{1}{1 + \exp[-(I_j + \theta_j)/\theta_o]} \tag{9.3-47}$$

where $I_j, j = 1, 2, \ldots, N_J$, represents the input to the activation element of each node in layer J of the network, θ_j is an offset, and θ_o controls the shape of the sigmoid function.

Equation (9.3-47) is plotted in Fig. 9.17, along with the limits for the "high" and "low" responses out of each node. Thus when this particular function is used, the system outputs a high reading for any value of I_j greater than θ_j. Similarly, the system outputs a low reading for any value of I_j less than θ_j. As Fig. 9.17 shows, the sigmoid activation function always is positive, and it can reach its limiting values of 0 and 1 only if the input to the activation element is infinitely negative or positive, respectively. For this reason, values near 0 and 1 (say, 0.05 and 0.95) define high and low values at the output of the neurons in Fig. 9.16. In principle, different types of activation functions could be used for different layers or even for different nodes in the same layer of a neural network. In practice, the usual approach is to use the same form of activation function throughout the network.

With reference to Fig. 9.14(b), the offset θ_j shown in Fig. 9.17 is analogous to the weight coefficient w_{n+1} in the earlier discussion of the perceptron. Implementation of this displaced threshold function can be done in the form of Fig. 9.14(a) by absorbing the offset θ_j as an additional coefficient that modifies a constant unity input to all nodes in the network. In order to follow the notation predominantly found in the literature, we do not show a separate constant input of $+1$ into all nodes of Fig. 9.16. Instead, this input and its modifying weight θ_j are integral parts of the network nodes. As noted in the blowup in Fig. 9.16, there is one such coefficient for each of the N_J nodes in layer J.

For the architecture shown in Fig. 9.16, the input to a node in any layer is the weighted sum of the outputs from the previous layer. Letting layer K denote the layer preceding layer J gives the input to the activation element of each node in layer J, denoted I_j:

$$I_j = \sum_{k=1}^{N_K} w_{jk} O_k \qquad (9.3\text{-}48)$$

for $j = 1, 2, \ldots, N_J$, where N_J is the number of nodes in layer J, N_K is the number of nodes in layer K, and w_{jk} are the weights modifying the outputs O_k of the nodes in layer K before they are fed into the nodes in layer J. The outputs of layer K are

$$O_k = h_k(I_k) \qquad (9.3\text{-}49)$$

for $k = 1, 2, \ldots, N_K$.

The subscript notation used in Eq. (9.3-48) is important, because we use it throughout the remainder of this section. First, note that I_j, $j = 1, 2, \ldots$,

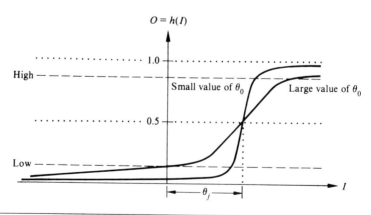

Figure 9.17   *The sigmoidal activation function of Eq. (9.3-47).*

N_J, represents the input to the *activation element* of the jth node in layer J. Thus I_1 represents the input to the activation element of the first (topmost) node in layer J, I_2 represents the input to the activation element of the second node in layer J, and so on. There are N_K inputs to every node in layer J, but *each* individual input can be weighted differently. Thus the N_K inputs to the first node in layer J are weighted by coefficients w_{1k}, $k = 1, 2, \ldots, N_K$; the inputs to the second node are weighted by coefficients w_{2k}, $k = 1, 2, \ldots, N_K$; and so on. Hence a total of $N_J \times N_K$ coefficients are necessary to specify the weighting of the outputs of layer K as they are fed into layer J. An additional N_J offset coefficients, θ_j, are needed to specify completely the nodes in layer J.

Substitution of Eq. (9.3-48) into (9.3-47) yields

$$h_j(I_j) = \cfrac{1}{1 + \exp\left[-\left(\sum_{k=1}^{N_K} w_{jk}O_k + \theta_j\right)\middle/\theta_o\right]} \tag{9.3-50}$$

which is the form of activation function used in the remainder of this section.

During training, adapting the neurons in the output layer is a simple matter, because the desired output of each node is known. The main problem in training a multilayer network lies in adjusting the weights in the so-called *hidden layers*, that is, in those other than the output layer.

Training by back propagation. We begin by concentrating on the output layer. The total squared error between the desired responses, r_q, and the corresponding actual responses, O_q, of nodes in (output) layer Q, is

$$E_Q = \frac{1}{2} \sum_{q=1}^{N_Q} (r_q - O_q)^2 \tag{9.3-51}$$

where N_Q is the number of nodes in output layer Q and the $\frac{1}{2}$ is used for convenience in notation for taking the derivative later.

The objective is to develop a training rule, similar to the delta rule, that allows adjustment of the weights in each of the layers in a way that seeks a minimum to an error function of the form shown in Eq. (9.3-51). As before, adjusting the weights in proportion to the partial derivative of the error with respect to the weights achieves this result. In other words,

$$\Delta w_{qp} = -\alpha \frac{\partial E_Q}{\partial w_{qp}} \tag{9.3-52}$$

where layer P precedes layer Q, Δw_{qp} is as defined in Eq. (9.3-42), and α is a positive correction increment.

The error E_Q is a function of the outputs, O_q, which in turn are functions of the inputs I_q. Using the chain rule, we evaluate the partial derivative of E_Q as follows:

$$\frac{\partial E_Q}{\partial w_{qp}} = \frac{\partial E_Q}{\partial I_q}\frac{\partial I_q}{\partial w_{qp}}. \tag{9.3-53}$$

From Eq. (9.3-48),

$$\frac{\partial I_q}{\partial w_{qp}} = \frac{\partial}{\partial w_{qp}}\sum_{p=1}^{N_P} w_{qp}\,O_p = O_p. \tag{9.3-54}$$

Substituting Eqs. (9.3-53) and (9.3-54) into Eq. (9.3-52) yields

$$\Delta w_{qp} = -\alpha\frac{\partial E_Q}{\partial I_q}O_p$$
$$= \alpha\,\delta_q O_p \tag{9.3-55}$$

where

$$\delta_q = -\frac{\partial E_Q}{\partial I_q}. \tag{9.3-56}$$

In order to compute $\partial E_Q/\partial I_q$, we use the chain rule to express the partial derivative in terms of the rate of change of E_Q with respect to O_q and the rate of change of O_q with respect to I_q. That is,

$$\delta_q = -\frac{\partial E_Q}{\partial I_q} = -\frac{\partial E_Q}{\partial O_q}\frac{\partial O_q}{\partial I_q}. \tag{9.3-57}$$

From Eq. (9.3-51),

$$\frac{\partial E_Q}{\partial O_q} = -(r_q - O_q) \tag{9.3-58}$$

and, from Eq. (9.3-49),

$$\frac{\partial O_q}{\partial I_q} = \frac{\partial}{\partial I_q}h_q(I_q) = h_q'(I_q) \tag{9.3-59}$$

Substituting Eqs. (9.3-58) and (9.3-59) into Eq. (9.3-57) gives

$$\delta_q = (r_q - O_q)h_q'(I_q) \tag{9.3-60}$$

which is proportional to the error quantity $(r_q - O_q)$. Substitution of Eqs. (9.3-56)–(9.3-58) into Eq. (9.3-55) finally yields

$$\Delta w_{qp} = \alpha(r_q - O_q)\, h'_q(I_q)O_p \qquad (9.3\text{-}61)$$
$$= \alpha\,\delta_q O_p.$$

After the function $h_q(I_q)$ has been specified, all the terms in Eq. (9.3-61) are known or can be observed in the network. In other words, upon presentation of any training pattern to the input of the network, we know what the desired response, r_q, of each output node should be. The value O_q of each output node can be observed as can I_q, the input to the activation elements of layer Q, and O_p, the output of the nodes in layer P. Thus we know how to adjust the weights that modify the links between the last and next-to-last layers in the network.

Continuing to work our way back from the output layer, let us now analyze what happens at layer P. Proceeding in the same manner yields

$$\Delta w_{pj} = \alpha(r_p - O_p)h'_p(I_p)O_j \qquad (9.3\text{-}62)$$
$$= \alpha\,\delta_p O_j$$

where the error term is

$$\delta_p = (r_p - O_p)h'_p(I_p). \qquad (9.3\text{-}63)$$

With the exception of r_p, all the terms in Eqs. (9.3-62) and (9.3-63) either are known or can be observed in the network. The term r_p makes no sense in an internal layer because we do not know what the response of an internal node in terms of pattern membership should be. We may specify what we want the response r to be only at the outputs of the network where final pattern classification takes place. If we knew that information at internal nodes, there would be no need for further layers. Thus we have to find a way to restate δ_p in terms of quantities that are known or that can be observed in the network.

Going back to Eq. (9.3-57), we write the error term for layer P as

$$\delta_p = -\frac{\partial E_P}{\partial I_p} = -\frac{\partial E_P}{\partial O_p}\frac{\partial O_p}{\partial I_p}. \qquad (9.3\text{-}64)$$

The term $\partial O_p/\partial I_p$ presents no difficulties. As before, it is

$$\frac{\partial O_p}{\partial I_p} = \frac{\partial h_p(I_p)}{\partial I_p} = h'_p(I_p) \qquad (9.3\text{-}65)$$

which is known once h_p is specified because I_p can be observed. The term that produced r_p was the derivative $\partial E_P/\partial O_p$, so this term must be expressed in a way that does not contain r_p. Using the chain rule, we write the derivative as

$$-\frac{\partial E_P}{\partial O_p} = -\sum_{q=1}^{NQ} \frac{\partial E_P}{\partial I_q} \frac{\partial I_q}{\partial O_p} = \sum_{q=1}^{NQ} \left(-\frac{\partial E_P}{\partial I_q}\right) \frac{\partial}{\partial O_p} \sum_{p=1}^{NP} w_{qp} O_p$$

$$= \sum_{q=1}^{NQ} \left(-\frac{\partial E_P}{\partial I_q}\right) w_{qp} \qquad\qquad (9.3\text{-}66)$$

$$= \sum_{q=1}^{NQ} \delta_q w_{qp}$$

where the last step follows from Eq. (9.3-56). Substituting Eqs. (9.3-65) and (9.3-66) into Eq. (9.3-64) yields the desired expression for δ_p:

$$\delta_p = h'_p(I_p) \sum_{q=1}^{NQ} \delta_q w_{qp} \qquad\qquad (9.3\text{-}67)$$

The factor δ_p can be computed now, because all its terms are known. Thus Eqs. (9.3-62) and (9.3-67) establish completely the training rule for layer P. The importance of Eq. (9.3-67) is that it computes δ_p from the quantities δ_q and w_{qp}, which are terms that were computed in the layer immediately following layer P. After the error term and weights have been computed for layer P, these quantities may be used similarly to compute the error and weights for the layer immediately preceding layer P. In other words, we have found a way to propagate the error back into the network, starting with the error at the output layer.

We may summarize and generalize the training procedure as follows. For any layers K and J, where layer K immediately precedes layer J, compute the weights w_{jk}, which modify the connections between these two layers, by using

$$\Delta w_{jk} = \alpha \, \delta_j O_k. \qquad\qquad (9.3\text{-}68)$$

If layer J is the output layer, δ_j is

$$\delta_j = (r_j - O_j) h'_j(I_j). \qquad\qquad (9.3\text{-}69)$$

If layer J is an internal layer and layer P is the next layer (to the right), then δ_j is given by

$$\delta_j = h'_j(I_j) \sum_{p=1}^{NP} \delta_p w_{jp} \qquad\qquad (9.3\text{-}70)$$

for $j = 1, 2, \ldots, N_J$.

Using the activation function in Eq. (9.3-50) with $\theta_o = 1$ yields

$$h'_j(I_j) = O_j(1 - O_j) \qquad\qquad (9.3\text{-}71)$$

in which case Eqs. (9.3-69) and (9.3-70) assume the following, particularly attractive forms:

$$\delta_j = (r_j - O_j)O_j(1 - O_j) \qquad (9.3\text{-}72)$$

for the output layer, and

$$\delta_j = O_j(1 - O_j) \sum_{p=1}^{N_P} \delta_p w_{jp} \qquad (9.3\text{-}73)$$

for internal layers. In both Eqs. (9.3-72) and (9.3-73), $j = 1, 2, \ldots, N_J$.

Equations (9.3-68)–(9.3-70) constitute the generalized delta rule for training the multilayer feedforward neural network of Fig. 9.16. The process starts with an arbitrary (but not all equal) set of weights throughout the network. Then, application of the generalized delta rule at any iterative step involves two basic phases. In the first phase, a training vector is presented to the network and is allowed to propagate through the layers to compute the output O_j for each node. The outputs O_q of the nodes in the output layer are then compared against their desired responses, r_q, to generate the error terms δ_q. The second phase involves a backward pass through the network during which the appropriate error signal is passed to each node and the corresponding weight changes are made. This procedure also applies to the bias weights θ_j, as discussed earlier in some detail. It simply is treated as an additional weight that modifies a unit input into the summing junction of every node in the network.

Common practice is to track the network error, as well as errors associated with individual patterns. In a successful training session, the network error decreases with the number of iterations and the procedure converges to a stable set of weights that exhibit only small fluctuations with additional training. The usual approach followed to establish whether a pattern has been classified correctly during training is to determine whether the response of the node in the output layer associated with the pattern class from which the pattern was obtained is high, while all the other nodes have outputs that are low, as defined earlier.

After the system has been trained, it classifies patterns using the parameters established during the training phase. In normal operation, all feedback operations are disconnected. Then, any input pattern is allowed to propagate through the various layers, and the pattern is classified as belonging to the class of the output node that was high, while all the others were low. If more than one output is labeled high, or if none of the outputs is so labeled, the choice is one of declaring a misclassification or simply assigning the pattern to the class of the output node with the highest numerical value.

Example: We illustrate how a neural network of the form shown in Fig. 9.16 was trained to recognize the four shapes shown in Fig. 9.18(a), as well as noisy versions of these shapes, samples of which are shown in Fig. 9.18(b).

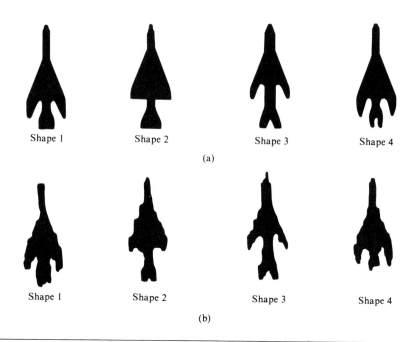

Shape 1   Shape 2   Shape 3   Shape 4

(a)

Shape 1   Shape 2   Shape 3   Shape 4

(b)

Figure 9.18 *(a) Reference shapes and (b) typical noisy shapes used in training the neural network of Fig. 9.19. (From Gupta et al. [1990].)*

Pattern vectors were generated by computing the normalized signatures of the shapes (see Section 8.1.3) and then obtaining 48 uniformly spaced samples of each signature. The resulting 48-dimensional vectors were the inputs to the three-layer feedforward neural network shown in Fig. 9.19. The number of neuron nodes in the first layer was chosen to be 48, corresponding to the dimensionality of the input pattern vectors. The 4 neurons in the third (output) layer correspond to the number of pattern classes, and the number of neurons in the middle layer was heuristically specified as 26 (the average of the number of neurons in the input and output layers). There are no known rules for specifying the number of nodes in the internal layers of a neural network, so this number generally is based either on prior experience or simply chosen arbitrarily and then refined by testing. In the output layer, the four nodes from top to bottom in this case represent classes ω_j, $j = 1, 2, 3$, and 4, respectively. After the network structure has been set, activation functions have to be selected for each unit and layer. All activation functions were selected to satisfy Eq. (9.3-50) so that, according to the earlier discussion, Eqs. (9.3-72) and (9.3-73) apply.

The training process was divided in two parts. In the first part, the weights were initialized to small random values with zero mean, and the network was then trained with pattern vectors corresponding to noise-free samples like the shapes shown in Fig. 9.18(a). The output nodes were monitored during training. The network was said to have learned the shapes from all four classes when, for any training pattern from class ω_i, the elements of the output layer yielded $O_i \geq 0.95$ and $O_q \leq 0.05$, for $q = 1, 2, \ldots, N_Q$; $q \neq i$. In other words, for any pattern of class ω_i, the output unit corresponding to that class had to be high (≥ 0.95) while, simultaneously, the output of all other nodes had to be low (≤ 0.05).

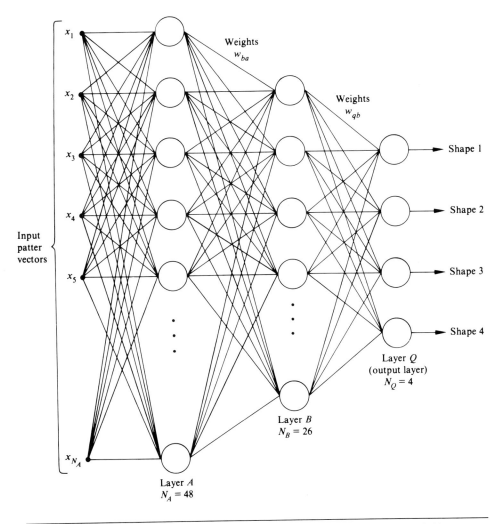

Figure 9.19   *Three-layer neural network used to recognize the shapes in Fig. 9.18.*

The second part of training was carried out with noisy samples, generated as follows. Each contour pixel in a noise-free shape was assigned a probability P of retaining its original coordinate in the image plane and a probability $R = 1 - P$ of being randomly assigned to the coordinates of one of its eight neighboring pixels. The degree of noise was increased by decreasing P (that is, increasing R). Two sets of noisy data were generated. The first consisted of 100 noisy patterns of each class generated by varying R between 0.1 and 0.6, giving a total of 400 patterns. This set, called the *test set*, was used to establish system performance after training.

Several noisy sets were generated for training the system with noisy data. The first set consisted of 10 samples for each class, generated by using $R_t = 0$, where R_t denotes a value of R used to generate training data. Starting with the weight vectors obtained in the first (noise-free) part of training, the system was allowed to go through a learning sequence with the new data set. Because $R_t = 0$ implies no noise, this retraining was an extension of the earlier, noise-free training. Using the resulting weights learned in this manner, the network was subjected to the test data set yielding the results shown by the curve labeled $R_t = 0$ in Fig. 9.20. The number of misclassified patterns divided by the total

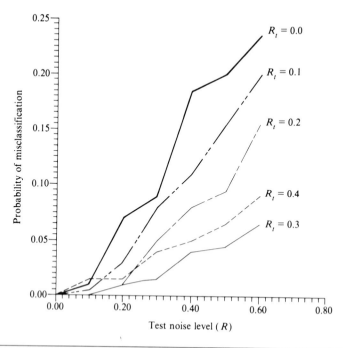

Figure 9.20 *Performance of the neural network as a function of noise level. (From Gupta et al. [1990].)*

number of patterns tested gives the probability of misclassification, which is a measure commonly used to establish network performance.

Next, starting with the weight vectors learned by using the data generated with $R_t = 0$, the system was retrained with a noisy data set generated with $R_t = 0.1$. The recognition performance was then established by running the test samples through the system again with the new weight vectors. Note the significant improvement in performance. Figure 9.20 shows the results obtained by continuing this retraining and retesting procedure for $R_t = 0.2, 0.3$, and 0.4. As expected if the system is learning properly, the probability of misclassifying patterns from the test set decreased as the value of R_t increased, because the system was being trained with noisier data for higher values of R_t. The one exception in Fig. 9.20 is the result for $R_t = 0.4$. The reason is the small number of samples used to train the system. That is, the network was not able to adapt itself sufficiently to the larger variations in shape at higher noise levels with the number of samples used. This hypothesis is verified by the results in Fig. 9.21, which show a lower probability of misclassification as the number of training samples was increased. Figure 9.21 also shows the curve for $R_t = 0.3$ from Fig. 9.20 for reference.

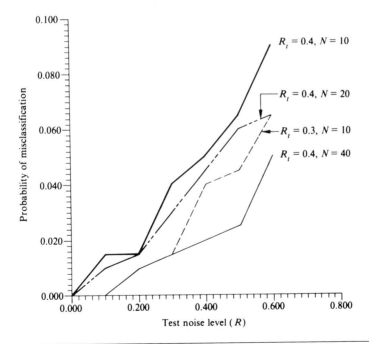

Figure 9.21 *Improvement in performance for $R_t = 0.4$ by increasing the number, N, of training patterns. Note the difference in scale from Fig. 9.20. (From Gupta et al. [1990].)*

The preceding results show that a three-layer neural network was capable of learning to recognize shapes corrupted by noise after a modest level of training. Even when trained with noise-free data (R_t = 0 in Fig. 9.20), the system was able to achieve a correct recognition level of close to 77 percent when tested with data highly corrupted by noise (R = 0.6 in Fig. 9.20). The recognition rate on the same data increased to about 99 percent when the system was trained with noisier data (R_t = 0.3 and 0.4). It is important to note that the system was trained by increasing its classification power via systematic, small incremental additions of noise. When the nature of the noise is known, this method is ideal for improving the convergence and stability properties of a neural network during learning. ❑

Complexity of decision surfaces. We have already established that a single-layer perceptron implements a hyperplane decision surface. A natural question at this point is: What is the nature of the decision surfaces implemented by a multilayer network, such as the model in Fig. 9.16? It is demonstrated in the following discussion that a three-layer network is capable of implementing arbitrarily complex decision surfaces composed of intersecting hyperplanes.

As a starting point, let us consider the two-input, two-layer network shown in Fig. 9.22(a). With two inputs, the patterns are two dimensional, and therefore, each node in the first layer of the network implements a line in 2-D space. We denote the high and low outputs of these two nodes 1 and 0, respectively. We assume that a 1 output indicates that the corresponding input vector to a node in the first layer lies on the positive side of the line. Then the possible combinations of outputs feeding the single node in the second layer are (1, 1), (1, 0), (0, 1), and (0, 0). If we define two regions, one for class ω_1 lying on the positive side of both lines, and the other for class ω_2 lying anywhere else, the

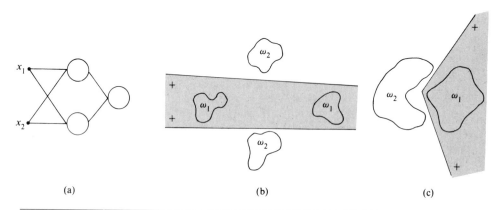

(a) (b) (c)

Figure 9.22 *(a) A two-input, two-layer, feedforward neural network; (b) and (c) examples of decision boundaries that can be implemented with this network.*

output node can classify any input pattern as belonging to one of these two regions simply by performing a logical AND operation. In other words, the output node responds with a 1, indicating class ω_1, only when both outputs from the first layer are 1. The AND operation can be performed by a neural node of the form discussed earlier if θ_j is set to a value in the half open interval $(1, 2]$. Thus if we assume 0 and 1 responses out of the first layer, the response of the output node will be high, indicating class ω_1, only when the sum performed by the neural node on the two outputs from the first layer is greater than 1. Figures 9.22(b) and (c) show how the network of Fig. 9.22(a) can successfully dichotomize two pattern classes that could not be separated by a single linear surface.

If the number of nodes in the first layer were increased to three, the network of Fig. 9.22(a) would implement a decision boundary consisting of the intersection of three lines. The requirement that class ω_1 lie on the positive side of all three lines would yield a convex region bounded by the three lines. In fact, an arbitrary open or closed convex region can be constructed simply by increasing the number of nodes in the first layer of a two-layer neural network.

The next logical step is to increase the number of layers to three. In this case the nodes of the first layer implement lines, as before. The nodes of the second layer then perform AND operations in order to form regions from the various lines. The nodes in the third layer assign class membership to the various regions. For instance, suppose that class ω_1 consists of two distinct regions, each of which is bounded by a different set of lines. Then two of the nodes in the second layer are for regions corresponding to the same pattern class. One of the output nodes needs to be able to signal the presence of that class when either of the two nodes in the second layer goes high. Assuming that high and low conditions in the second layer are denoted 1 and 0, respectively, this capability is obtained by making the output nodes of the network perform the logical OR operation. In terms of neural nodes of the form discussed earlier, we do so by setting θ_j to a value in the interval $[0, 1)$. Then, whenever at least one of the nodes in the second layer associated with that output node goes high (outputs a 1), the corresponding node in the output layer will go high, indicating that the pattern being processed belongs to the class associated with that node.

Figure 9.23 summarizes the preceding comments. Note in the third row that the complexity of decision regions implemented by a three-layer network is, in principle, arbitrary. In practice, a serious difficulty usually arises in structuring the second layer to respond correctly to the various combinations associated with particular classes. The reason is that lines do not just stop at their intersection with other lines, and, as a result, patterns of the same class may occur on both sides of lines in the pattern space. In practical terms, the second layer may have difficulty figuring out which lines should be included in the AND operation for a given pattern class—or it may even be impossible. The reference to the exclusive-OR problem in the third column of Fig. 9.23 deals

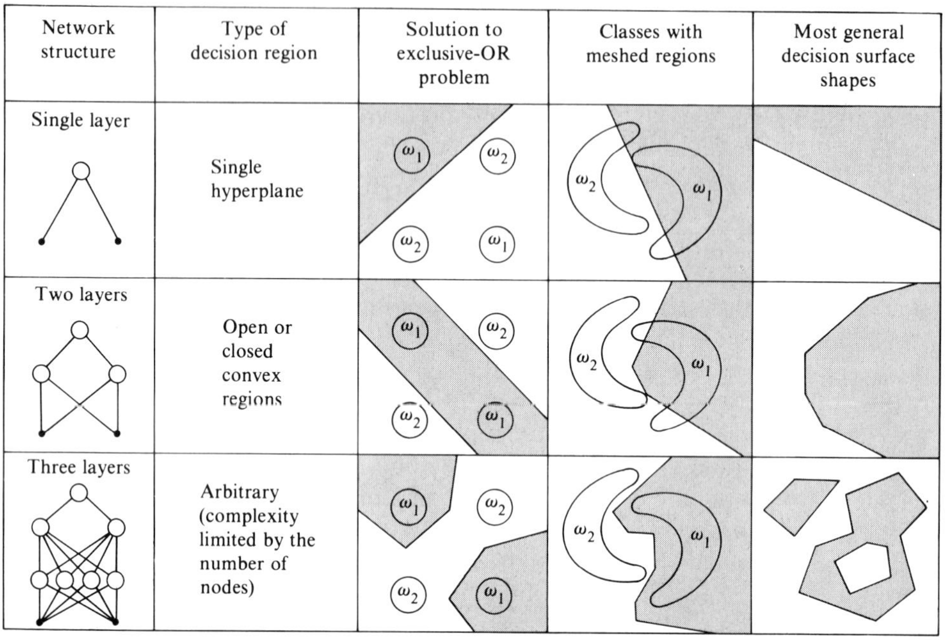

Network structure	Type of decision region	Solution to exclusive-OR problem	Classes with meshed regions	Most general decision surface shapes
Single layer	Single hyperplane			
Two layers	Open or closed convex regions			
Three layers	Arbitrary (complexity limited by the number of nodes)			

Figure 9.23   *Types of decision regions that can be formed by single- and multilayer feed-forward networks with one and two layers of hidden units and two inputs. (Adapted from Lippman [1987].)*

with the fact that, if the input patterns were binary, only four different patterns could be constructed in two dimensions. If the patterns are so arranged that class ω_1 consists of patterns $\{(0, 1), (1, 0)\}$ and class ω_2 consists of the patterns $\{(0, 0), (1, 1,)\}$, class membership of the patterns in these two classes is given by the exclusive-OR (XOR) logical function, which is 1 only when one or the other of the two variables is 1, and it is 0 otherwise. Thus an XOR value of 1 indicates patterns of class ω_1, and an XOR value of 0 indicates patterns of class ω_2.

The preceding discussion is generalized to n dimensions in a straightforward way: instead of lines, we deal with hyperplanes. A single-layer network implements a single hyperplane. A two-layer network implements arbitrary convex regions consisting of intersections of hyperplanes. A three-layer network implements decision surfaces of arbitrary complexity. The number of nodes used in each layer determines the complexity of the last two cases. The number of classes in the first case is limited to two. In the other two cases, the number of classes is arbitrary, because the number of output nodes can be selected to fit the problem at hand.

Considering the preceding comments, it is logical to ask: Why would anyone be interested in studying neural networks having more than three layers? After all, a three-layer network can implement decision surfaces of arbitrary complexity. The answer lies in the method used to train a network to utilize only three layers. The training rule for the network in Fig. 9.16 minimizes an error measure but says nothing about how to associate groups of hyperplanes with specific nodes in the second layer of a three-layer network of the type discussed earlier. In fact, the problem of how to perform trade-off analyses between the number of layers and the number of nodes in each layer remains unresolved in the field of neural networks. In practice, the trade-off is generally resolved by trial and error or by previous experience with a given problem domain.

9.4 STRUCTURAL METHODS

The techniques discussed in Section 9.3 deal with patterns quantitatively and largely ignore any structural relationships inherent in a pattern's shape. The structural methods discussed in this section, however, seek to achieve pattern recognition by capitalizing precisely on these types of relationships.

9.4.1 Matching Shape Numbers

A procedure analogous to the minimum distance concept introduced in Section 9.3.1 for pattern vectors can be formulated for the comparison of region boundaries that are described in terms of shape numbers. With reference to the discussion in Section 8.2.2, the *degree of similarity*, k, between two region boundaries (shapes), A and B, is defined as the largest order for which their shape numbers still coincide. For example, in the case of shape numbers of closed boundaries represented by 4-directional chain codes, A and B have a degree of similarity k if $s_4(A) = s_4(B)$, $s_6(A) = s_6(B)$, $s_8(A) = s_8(B)$, . . . , $s_k(A) = s_k(B)$, $s_{k+2}(A) \neq s_{k+2}(B)$, $s_{k+4}(A) \neq s_{k+4}(B)$, . . . , where s indicates shape number and the subscript indicates order. The *distance* between two shapes A and B is defined as the inverse of their degree of similarity:

$$D(A, B) = \frac{1}{k}. \tag{9.4-1}$$

This distance satisfies the following properties:

$$
\begin{aligned}
&D(A, B) \geq 0 \\
&D(A, B) = 0 \text{ iff } A = B \\
&D(A, C) \leq \max[D(A, B), D(B, C)].
\end{aligned}
\tag{9.4-2}
$$

Either k or D may be used to compare two shapes. If the degree of similarity is used, the larger k is, the more similar the shapes are (note that k is infinite for identical shapes). The reverse is true when the distance measure is used.

Example: Suppose that we have a shape F and want to find its closest match in a set of five other shapes (A, B, C, D, and E), as shown in Fig. 9.24(a). This problem is analogous to having five prototype shapes and trying to find the best match to a given unknown shape. The search may be visualized with the aid of the similarity tree shown in Fig. 9.24(b). The root of the tree corresponds to the lowest possible degree of similarity, which, for this example, is 4. The shapes are identical up to degree 8, with the exception of shape A, whose degree of similarity with respect to all other shapes is 6. Proceeding

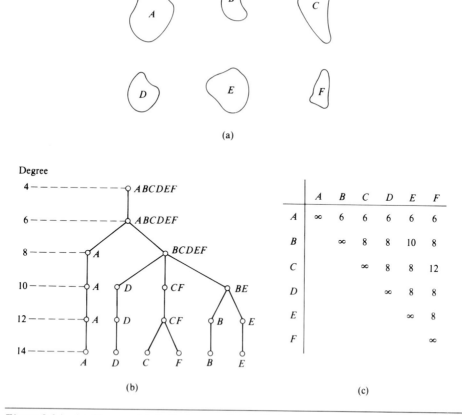

(a)

(b)

(c)

Figure 9.24 (a) Shapes; (b) similarity tree; (c) similarity matrix. (From Bribiesca and Guzman [1980].)

down the tree, we find that shape D has degree of similarity 8 with respect to all others, and so on. Shapes F and C match uniquely, having a higher degree of similarity than any other two shapes. At the other extreme, if A had been an unknown shape, all we could have said—using this method—is that A was similar to the other five shapes with degree of similarity 6. The same information can be summarized in the form of a *similarity matrix*, as shown in Fig. 9.24(c).   ❑

9.4.2 String Matching

Suppose that two region boundaries, A and B, are coded into strings (see Section 8.5) denoted $a_1a_2 \ldots a_n$ and $b_1b_2 \ldots b_m$, respectively. Let M represent the number of matches between the two strings, where a match occurs in the kth position if $a_k = b_k$. The number of symbols that do not match is

$$Q = \max(|A|, |B|) - M \qquad (9.4\text{-}3)$$

where $|arg|$ is the length (number of symbols) in the string representation of the argument. It can be shown that $Q = 0$ if and only if A and B are identical (see Problem 9.21).

A simple measure of similarity between A and B is the ratio

$$R = \frac{M}{Q} = \frac{M}{\max(|A|, |B|) - M}. \qquad (9.4\text{-}4)$$

Hence R is infinite for a perfect match and 0 when none of the symbols in A and B match ($M = 0$ in this case). Because matching is done symbol by symbol, the starting point on each boundary is important in terms of reducing the amount of computation. Any method that normalizes to, or near, the same starting point is helpful, so long as it provides a computational advantage over brute-force matching, which consists of starting at arbitrary points on each string and then shifting one of the strings (with wraparound) and computing Eq. (9.4-4) for each shift. The largest value of R gives the best match.

Example: Figures 9.25(a) and (b) show sample boundaries from each of two object classes, which were approximated by a polygonal fit (see Section 8.1.2). Figures 9.25(c) and (d) show the polygonal approximations corresponding to the boundaries shown in Figs. 9.25(a) and (b), respectively. Strings were formed from the polygons by computing the interior angle between segments as each polygon was traversed clockwise. Angles were coded into one of eight possible symbols, corresponding to 45° increments; that is, $\alpha_1: 0° < \theta \le 45°$; $\alpha_2: 45° < \theta \le 90°$; $\ldots$; $\alpha_8: 315° < \theta \le 360°$.

Figure 9.25(e) shows the results of computing the measure R for five samples of object 1 against themselves. The entries correspond to R values and, for

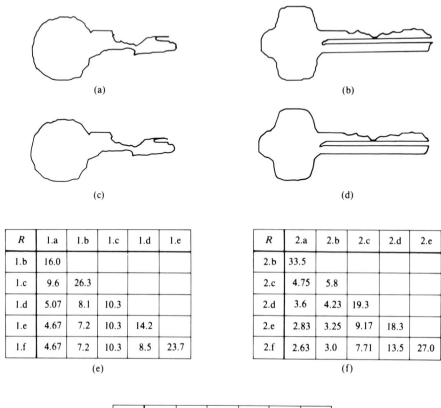

(a)   (b)

(c)   (d)

R	1.a	1.b	1.c	1.d	1.e
1.b	16.0				
1.c	9.6	26.3			
1.d	5.07	8.1	10.3		
1.e	4.67	7.2	10.3	14.2	
1.f	4.67	7.2	10.3	8.5	23.7

(e)

R	2.a	2.b	2.c	2.d	2.e
2.b	33.5				
2.c	4.75	5.8			
2.d	3.6	4.23	19.3		
2.e	2.83	3.25	9.17	18.3	
2.f	2.63	3.0	7.71	13.5	27.0

(f)

R	1.a	1.b	1.c	1.d	1.e	1.f
2.a	1.24	1.50	1.32	1.47	1.55	1.48
2.b	1.18	1.43	1.32	1.47	1.55	1.48
2.c	1.02	1.18	1.19	1.32	1.39	1.48
2.d	1.02	1.18	1.19	1.32	1.39	1.40
2.e	0.93	1.07	1.08	1.19	1.24	1.25
2.f	0.89	1.02	1.02	1.14	1.11	1.18

(g)

Figure 9.25   *(a) and (b) Sample boundaries of two different object classes; (c) and (d) their corresponding polygonal approximations; (e)–(g) tabulations of R. (Adapted from Sze and Yang [1981].)*

example, the notation 1.c refers to the third string from object class 1. Figure 9.25(f) shows the results of comparing the strings of the second object class against themselves. Finally, Fig. 9.25(g) shows a tabulation of R values obtained by comparing strings of one class against the other. Note that, here, all R values are considerably smaller than any entry in the two preceding tabulations, indicating that the R measure achieved a high degree of discrimination between the two classes of objects. For example, if the class membership of string 1.a had been unknown, the *smallest* value of R resulting from comparing this string against sample (prototype) strings of class 1 would have been 4.67. By contrast the *largest* value in comparing it against strings of class 2 would have been 1.24. This result would have led to the conclusion that string 1.a is a member of object class 1. This approach to classification is analogous to the minimum distance classifier introduced in Section 9.3.1. ❏

9.4.3 Syntactic Methods

Syntactic methods are among the most prevalent approaches for handling structural recognition problems. Basically, the idea behind syntactic pattern recognition is the specification of a set of pattern *primitives* (see Section 8.5), a set of rules (in the form of a *grammar*) that governs their interconnection, and a *recognizer* (called an *automaton*) whose structure is determined by the set of rules in the grammar. First we consider string grammars and automata and then extend these ideas to tree grammars and their corresponding automata. Recall that strings and trees are the principal structural pattern descriptors used in this book.

Syntactic recognition of strings
The following discussion is based on the assumption that the image regions or objects of interest have been expressed in string form by using the appropriate primitive elements, as discussed in Section 8.5.

String grammars. Suppose that we have two classes, ω_1 and ω_2, whose patterns are strings of primitives. We can interpret each primitive as being a symbol permissible in the *alphabet* of some *grammar*, where a grammar is a set of rules of syntax (hence the name syntactic recognition) that govern the generation of *sentences* formed from symbols of the alphabet. The set of sentences generated by a grammar, G, is called its *language* and is denoted $L(G)$. Here, sentences are strings of symbols (which in turn represent patterns), and languages correspond to pattern classes.

Consider two grammars, G_1 and G_2, whose rules of syntax are such that G_1 only allows generation of sentences that correspond to patterns from class ω_1, and that G_2 only allows generation of sentences corresponding to patterns from class ω_2. After two grammars with these properties have been established, the syntactic pattern recognition process, in principle, is straightforward. For a sentence representing an unknown pattern, the task is to decide in which language the pattern represents a valid sentence. If the sentence belongs to $L(G_1)$, we say that the pattern is from class ω_1. Similarly, the pattern is said to be from class ω_2 if the sentence is valid in $L(G_2)$. A unique decision cannot be made if the sentence belongs to both languages. A sentence that is invalid in both languages is rejected.

When there are more than two pattern classes, the syntactic classification approach is the same as described above, with the exception that more grammars (at least one per class) are involved in the process. For multiclass classification, a pattern belongs to class ω_i if it represents a valid sentence only of $L(G_i)$. As previously outlined, a unique decision cannot be made if a sentence belongs to languages of different classes. A sentence that is invalid over all languages is rejected.

When dealing with strings, we define a grammar as the 4-tuple

$$G = (N, \Sigma, P, S) \tag{9.4-5}$$

where

$$N = \text{a finite set of variables called } \textit{nonterminals}$$
$$\Sigma = \text{a finite set of constants called } \textit{terminals}$$
$$P = \text{a set of rewriting rules called } \textit{productions}$$
$$S \text{ in } N = \text{the } \textit{starting symbol}.$$

A requirement is that N and Σ be disjoint sets. In the following discussion, capital letters, $A, B, \ldots, S, \ldots$, denote nonterminals. Lowercase letters, $a, b, c, \ldots$, at the beginning of the alphabet denote terminals. Lowercase letters, v, w, x, y, z, toward the end of the alphabet denote strings of terminals. Lowercase Greek letters $\alpha, \beta, \theta, \ldots$, denote strings of mixed terminals and nonterminals. The *empty sentence* (the sentence with no symbols) is denoted λ. Finally, for a set V of symbols, the notation V^* denotes the set of all sentences composed of elements from V.

String grammars are characterized by the form of their productions. Of particular interest in syntactic pattern recognition are *regular grammars* and *context-free grammars*. Regular grammars have productions only of the form $A \rightarrow aB$ or $A \rightarrow a$, with A and B in N and a in Σ. Context-free grammars have productions only of the form $A \rightarrow \alpha$, with A in N and α in the set $(N \cup \Sigma)^* - \lambda$; that is, α can be any string composed of terminals and nonterminals, except the empty string.

Example: Suppose that the object shown in Fig. 9.26(a) is represented by its skeleton and that we define the primitives shown in Fig. 9.26(b) to describe the structure of this (and similar) skeletons. Consider the grammar $G = (N, \Sigma, P, S)$, with $N = \{A, B, S\}$, $\Sigma = \{a, b, c\}$, and $P = \{S \rightarrow aA, A \rightarrow bA,$

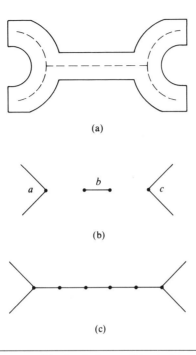

(a)

(b)

(c)

Figure 9.26   (a) Object represented by its skeleton; (b) primitives; (c) structure generated by using a regular string grammar.

$A \rightarrow bB$, $B \rightarrow c$}, where the terminals a, b, and c correspond to the primitives shown in Fig. 9.26(b). As indicated earlier, S is the starting symbol from which the strings of $L(G)$ are generated. For instance, applying the first production followed by two applications of the second production yields $S \Rightarrow aA \Rightarrow abA \Rightarrow abbA$, where ($\Rightarrow$) indicates a string derivation starting from S and using productions from the set P. The first production allowed rewriting S as aA, and the second production allowed rewriting A as bA. With a nonterminal in the string $abbA$, we can continue the derivation. For example, applying the second production two more times, followed by one application of the third production and one application of the fourth production, yields the string $abbbbbc$, which corresponds to the structure shown in Fig. 9.26(c). No nonterminals remain after application of the fourth production, so the derivation terminates when this production is used. The language generated by the rules of this grammar is $L(G) = \{ab^n c \mid n \geq 1\}$, where b^n indicates n repetitions of the symbol b. In other words, G is capable of generating *only* skeletons of the form shown in Fig. 9.26(c) but having arbitrary length.   ❑

Use of semantics.   In the preceding example we assumed that the interconnection between primitives takes place only at the dots shown in Fig. 9.26(b). In more complicated situations the rules of connectivity, as well as information regarding other factors (such as primitive length and direction), and the number of times a production can be applied, must be made explicit. This can be accomplished by using *semantic rules* stored in the *knowledge base* of Fig. 9.1. Basically, the syntax inherent in the production rules establishes the structure of an object, whereas semantics deal with its correctness. For example, the FORTRAN statement $A = B/C$ is syntactically correct, but it is semantically correct only if $C \neq 0$.

Suppose that we attach semantic information to the grammar discussed in the preceding example. The information can be attached to the production rules in the form shown in Table 9.1. By using semantic information, we are able to use a few rules of syntax to describe a broad (but limited as desired) class of patterns. For instance, by specifying the direction of θ in Table 9.1, we avoid having to specify primitives for each possible orientation. Similarly, by requiring that all primitives be oriented in the same direction, we eliminate from consideration nonsensical structures that deviate from the basic shapes typified by Fig. 9.26(a).

Automata as string recognizers. So far we have demonstrated that grammars are *generators* of patterns. In the following discussion we consider the problem of recognizing whether a pattern belongs to the language $L(G)$ generated by a grammar G. The basic concepts underlying syntactic recognition may be illustrated by the development of mathematical models of computing machines, called *automata*. Given an input pattern string, an automaton is capable of recognizing whether the pattern belongs to the language with which the automaton is associated. Here, we focus only on *finite automata*, which are the recognizers of languages generated by regular grammars.

A *finite automaton* is defined as the 5-tuple

$$A_f = (Q, \Sigma, \delta, q_0, F) \tag{9.4-6}$$

Table 9.1   Example of Semantic Information Attached to Production Rules

Production	Semantic Information
$S \rightarrow aA$	Connections to a are made only at the dot. The direction of a, denoted θ, is given by the direction of the perpendicular bisector of the line joining the end points of the two undotted segments. The line segments are 3 cm each.
$A \rightarrow bA$	Connections to b are made only at the dots. No multiple connections are allowed. The direction of b must be the same as the direction of a. The length of b is 0.25 cm. This production cannot be applied more than 10 times.
$A \rightarrow bB$	The direction of a and b must be the same. Connections must be simple and made only at the dots.
$B \rightarrow c$	The direction of c and a must be the same. Connections must be simple and made only at the dots.

where Q is a finite, nonempty set of *states*, Σ is a finite input *alphabet*, δ is a *mapping* from $Q \times \Sigma$ (the set of ordered pairs formed from elements of Q and Σ) into the collection of all subsets of Q, q_0 is the *starting state*, and F (a subset of Q) is a set of *final*, or *accepting, states*.

Example: Consider an automaton given by Eq. (9.4-6), with $Q = \{q_0, q_1, q_2\}$, $\Sigma = \{a, b\}$, $F = \{q_0\}$, and mappings given by $\delta(q_0, a) = \{q_2\}$, $\delta(q_0, b) = \{q_1\}$, $\delta(q_1, a) = \{q_2\}$, $\delta(q_1, b) = \{q_0\}$, $\delta(q_2, a) = \{q_0\}$, and $\delta(q_2, b) = \{q_1\}$. If, for example, the automaton is in state q_0 and an a is input, its state changes to q_2. Similarly, if a b is input next, the automaton changes to state q_1, and so on. The initial and final states are the same in this case.   ❏

Figure 9.27 shows a *state diagram* for the automaton just discussed. The state diagram consists of a node for each state and directed arcs showing the possible transitions between states. The final state is shown as a double circle, and each arc is labeled with the symbol that causes the transition between the states joined by that arc. In this case the initial and final states are the same. A string w of terminal symbols is said to be *accepted* or *recognized* by an automaton if, starting in state q_0, the sequence of symbols (encountered as w is scanned from left to right) causes the automaton to be in a final state after the last symbol from w has been scanned. For example, the automaton in Fig. 9.27 recognizes the string $w = abbabb$ but rejects the string $w = aabab$.

There is a one-to-one correspondence between regular grammars and finite automata. That is, a language is recognized by a finite automaton if and only if it is generated by a regular grammar. The design of a syntactic string recognizer based on the concepts discussed so far is a straightforward procedure, consisting of obtaining a finite automaton from a given regular grammar. Let

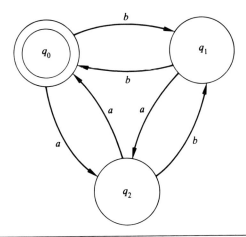

Figure 9.27   *A finite automaton.*

the grammar be denoted $G = (N, \Sigma, P, X_0)$, where $X_0 \equiv S$, and suppose that N is composed of X_0 plus n additional nonterminals $X_1, X_2, \ldots, X_n$. The set Q for the automaton is formed by introducing $n + 2$ states $\{q_0, q_1, \ldots, q_n, q_{n+1}\}$ such that q_i corresponds to X_i for $0 \leq i \leq n$, and q_{n+1} is the final state. The set of input symbols is identical to the set of terminals in G. The mappings in δ are obtained by using two rules based on the productions of G; namely, for each i and j, $0 \leq i \leq n$, $0 \leq j \leq n$:

1. If $X_i \rightarrow aX_j$ is in P, then $\delta(q_i, a)$ contains q_j.

2. If $X_i \rightarrow a$ is in P, then $\delta(q_i, a)$ contains q_{n+1}.

Conversely, given a finite automaton, $A_f = (Q, \Sigma, \delta, q_0, F)$, we obtain the corresponding regular grammar, $G = (N, \Sigma, P, X_0)$, by letting N consist of the elements of Q, with the starting symbol X_0 corresponding to q_0, and the productions of G obtained as follows:

1. If q_j is in $\delta(q_i, a)$, there is a production $X_i \rightarrow aX_j$ in P.

2. If a state in F is in $\delta(q_i, a)$, there is a production $X_i \rightarrow a$ in P.

The terminal set, Σ, is the same in both cases.

Example: The finite automaton for the grammar given in connection with Fig. 9.26 is obtained by writing the productions as $X_0 \rightarrow aX_1$, $X_1 \rightarrow bX_1$, $X_1 \rightarrow bX_2$, and $X_2 \rightarrow c$. Then, $A_f = (Q, \Sigma, \delta, q_0, F)$, with $Q = \{q_0, q_1, q_2, q_3\}$, $\Sigma = \{a, b, c\}$, $F = \{q_3\}$ and mappings $\delta(q_0, a) = \{q_1\}$, $\delta(q_1, b) = \{q_1, q_2\}$, $\delta(q_2, c) = \{q_3\}$. For completeness, we write $\delta(q_0, b) = \delta(q_0, c) = \delta(q_1, a) = \delta(q_1, c) = \delta(q_2, a) = \delta(q_2, b) = \emptyset$, where $\emptyset$ is the null set, indicating that these transitions are not defined for this automaton. ❑

Syntactic recognition of trees
Following a format similar to the preceding discussion for strings, we now expand the discussion to include tree descriptions of patterns. Again, we assume that the image regions or objects of interest have been expressed in the form of trees by using the appropriate primitive elements, as discussed in Section 8.5.

Tree grammars. A *tree grammar* is defined as the 5-tuple

$$G = (N, \Sigma, P, r, S) \tag{9.4-7}$$

where N and Σ, as before, are sets of nonterminals and terminals, respectively; S, contained in N, is the start symbol, which in general can be a tree; P is a set of productions of the form $T_i \rightarrow T_j$, where T_i and T_j are trees; and r is a *ranking function* that denotes the number of direct descendants (offspring) of a node whose label is a terminal in the grammar. Of particular relevance to our discussion are *expansive* tree grammars having productions of the form

$$X \rightarrow \underset{X_1 \ X_2 \ \cdots \ X_n}{k}$$

where $X_1, X_2, \ldots, X_n$ are nonterminals and k is a terminal.

Example: The skeleton of the structure shown in Fig. 9.28(a) can be generated by using a tree grammar with $N = \{X_1, X_2, X_3, S\}$ and $\Sigma = \{a, b, c, d, e\}$, where the terminals represent the primitives shown in Fig. 9.28(b). Assuming head-to-tail connectivity of the line primitives, and arbitrary connections to the circle along its circumference, the grammar under consideration has productions of the form:

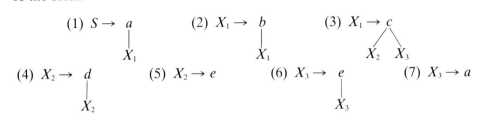

(1) $S \rightarrow \underset{X_1}{a}$ (2) $X_1 \rightarrow \underset{X_1}{b}$ (3) $X_1 \rightarrow \underset{X_2 \ X_3}{c}$

(4) $X_2 \rightarrow \underset{X_2}{d}$ (5) $X_2 \rightarrow e$ (6) $X_3 \rightarrow \underset{X_3}{e}$ (7) $X_3 \rightarrow a$

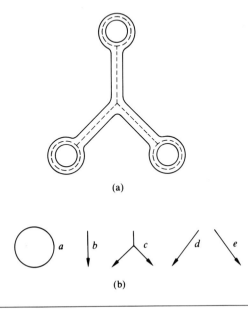

(a)

(b)

Figure 9.28 *(a) An object and (b) primitives used for representing the skeleton by means of a tree grammar.*

The ranking functions in this case are $r(a) = \{0, 1\}$, $r(b) = r(d) = r(e) = \{1\}$ and $r(c) = \{2\}$. Restricting application of productions 2, 4, and 6 to the same number of times would generate a structure in which all three legs have the same length. Similarly, requiring application of productions 4 and 6 the same number of times would produce a structure that is symmetrical about its vertical axis. This type of semantic information is similar to the earlier discussion in connection with Table 9.1 and the knowledge base of Fig. 9.1.   ❏

Tree automata. Whereas a conventional finite automaton scans an input string symbol by symbol from left to right, a tree automaton must begin simultaneously at each node on the frontier (the leaves taken in order from left to right) of an input tree and proceed along parallel paths toward the root. Specifically, a frontier-to-root automaton is defined as

$$A_t = (Q, F, \{f_k \mid k \in \Sigma\}) \tag{9.4-8}$$

where

Q is a finite set of states,

F, a subset of Q, is a set of final states, and

f_k is a relation in $Q^m \times Q$ such that m is a rank of k.

The notation Q^m indicates the Cartesian product of Q with itself m times: $Q^m = Q \times Q \times Q \times \ldots \times Q$. From the definition of the Cartesian product, we know that this expression means the set of all ordered m-tuples with elements from Q. For example, if $m = 3$, $Q^3 = Q \times Q \times Q = \{x, y, z \mid x \in Q, y \in Q, z \in Q\}$. Recall that a relation R from a set A to a set B is a subset of the Cartesian product of A and B; that is, $R \subseteq A \times B$. Thus a relation in $Q^m \times Q$ is simply a subset of the set $Q^m \times Q$.

For an expansive tree grammar, $G = (N, \Sigma, P, r, S)$, we construct the corresponding tree automaton by letting $Q = N$, with $F = \{S\}$ and, for each symbol a in Σ, defining a relation f_k such that $(X_1, X_2, \ldots, X_m, X)$ is in f_k if and only if there is in G a production

$$X \to k$$
$$X_1 \ X_2 \ \cdots \ X_m$$

For example, consider the simple tree grammar $G = (N, \Sigma, P, r, S)$, with $N = \{S, X\}$, $\Sigma = \{a, b, c, d\}$, productions

$$X \to a \qquad X \to b \qquad X \to c \qquad S \to d$$
$$\qquad\qquad\qquad\qquad\qquad\qquad X \qquad\qquad X \ \ X$$

and rankings $r(a) = \{0\}$, $r(b) = \{0\}$, $r(c) = \{1\}$, and $r(d) = \{2\}$. The corresponding tree automaton, $A_t = (Q, F, \{f_k \mid k \in \Sigma\})$, is specified by letting $Q = \{S, X\}$, $F = \{S\}$, and $\{f_k \mid k \in \Sigma\} = \{f_a, f_b, f_c, f_d\}$, where the relations are defined as

$$f_a = \{(\emptyset, X)\}, \text{ arising from production } X \to a$$
$$f_b = \{(\emptyset, X)\}, \text{ arising from production } X \to b$$
$$f_c = \{(X, X)\}, \text{ arising from production } X \to c$$
$$\qquad\qquad\qquad\qquad\qquad\qquad\qquad\qquad \overset{\displaystyle X}{\mid}$$

$$f_d = \{(X, X, S)\}, \text{ arising from production } S \to d$$

The interpretation of relation f_a is that a node labeled a with no offspring (hence the null symbol $\emptyset$) is assigned *state* X. The interpretation of f_c is that a node labeled c, with one offspring having state X, is assigned state X. The interpretation of relation f_d is that a node labeled d with two offspring, each having state X, is assigned state S.

In order to see how this tree automaton goes about recognizing a tree generated by the grammar discussed earlier, consider the tree shown in Fig. 9.29(a). Automaton A_t first assigns states to the frontier nodes a and b via

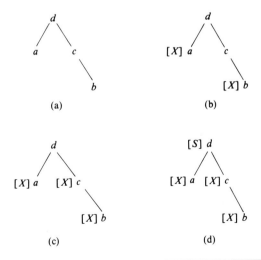

Figure 9.29 *Processing stages of a frontier-to-root tree automaton: (a) input tree; (b) state assignment to frontier nodes; (c) state assignment to intermediate nodes; (d) state assignment to root node. (From Gonzalez and Thomason [1978].)*

relations f_a and f_b, respectively. In this case, according to these two relations, state X is assigned to both leaves, as Fig. 9.29(b) shows. The automaton now moves up one level from the frontier and makes a state assignment to node c on the basis of f_c and the state of this node's offspring. The state assignment based on f_c again is X, as indicated in Fig. 9.29(c). Moving up one more level, the automaton encounters node d and, as its two offspring have been assigned states, relation f_d, which calls for assigning state S to node d, is used. Because this is the last node and the state S is in F, the automaton accepts (recognizes) the tree as being a valid member of the language of the tree grammar given earlier. Figure 9.29(d) shows the final representation of the state sequences followed along the frontier-to-root paths.

Example: An interesting application of tree grammars is the analysis of photographs from bubble chamber events. These photographs are taken during experiments in high-energy physics in which a beam of particles of known properties is directed onto a target of known nuclei. A typical event consists of tracks of secondary particles emanating from the point of collision, such as the example shown in Fig. 9.30. The incoming tracks are the horizontal parallel lines. Note the natural tree structure of the event near the middle of the photograph.

A typical experiment produces hundreds of thousands of photographs, many of which do not contain events of interest. Examining and categorizing these photographs is tedious and time-consuming for a human interpreter, thus creating a need for automatic processing algorithms and pattern recognition techniques.

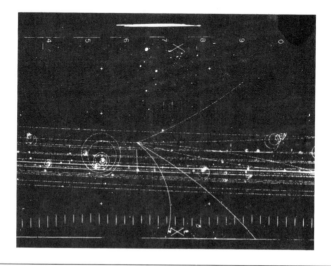

Figure 9.30 *A bubble chamber photograph. (From Fu and Bhargava [1973].)*

A grammar $G = (N, \Sigma, P, r, S)$ can be specified that generates trees representing events typical of those found in a hydrogen bubble chamber as a result of incoming positively charged particle streams. In this case, $N = \{S, X_1, X_2\}$, $\Sigma = \{a, b\}$, and the primitives a and b are interpreted as follows:

a: ⌒   *convex arc*

b: ⌣   *concave arc*

The productions in P are

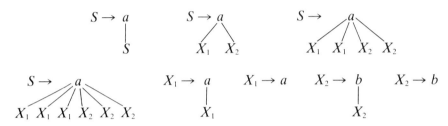

The rankings are $r(a) = \{0, 1, 2, 4, 6\}$ and $r(b) = \{0, 1\}$. The branching productions represent the number of tracks emanating from a collision, which occur in pairs and usually do not exceed six. Figure 9.31(a) shows the collision event in Fig. 9.30 segmented into convex and concave sections, and Fig. 9.31(b) shows the corresponding tree representation. This tree, as well as variations of it, can be generated by the grammar given above.

The tree automaton needed to recognize the types of trees just discussed is defined by using the procedure explained in the preceding discussion. Thus, $A_t = (Q, F, \{f_k \mid k \in \Sigma\})$ is specified by letting $Q = \{S, X_1, X_2\}$, $F = \{S\}$, and $\{f_k \mid k \in \Sigma\} = \{f_a, f_b\}$, where the relations are defined as $f_a = \{(S, S), (X_1, X_2, S), (X_1, X_1, X_2, X_2, S), (X_1, X_1, X_1, X_2, X_2, X_2, S), (X_1, X_1), (\varnothing, X_1)\}$, and $f_b = \{(X_2, X_2) (\varnothing, X_2)\}$. We leave it as an exercise to show that this automaton accepts the tree in Fig. 9.31(b). ❏

Learning

The syntactic recognition approaches introduced in the preceding discussion require specification of the appropriate automata (recognizers) for each class under consideration. In simple situations, inspection may yield the necessary automata. In more complicated cases, an algorithm for learning the automata from sample patterns (such as strings or trees) may be required. Because of the one-to-one correspondence between automata and grammars, the learning problem sometimes is posed in terms of learning grammars directly from sample patterns, a process usually called *grammatical inference*. In this section we focus on an algorithm for learning finite automata. The references at the end of this chapter provide a guide to methods for learning tree grammars and automata, as well as other syntactic recognition approaches.

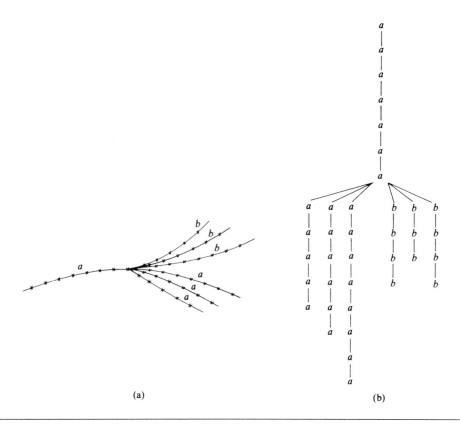

(a)   (b)

Figure 9.31   *(a) Coded event from Fig. 9.30; (b) corresponding tree representation. (From Fu and Bhargava [1973].)*

Suppose that all patterns of a class are generated by an *unknown* grammar G and that a finite set of samples R^+ with the property

$$R^+ \subseteq \{\alpha \mid \alpha \text{ in } L(G)\} \qquad (9.4\text{-}9)$$

is available. In the terminology introduced in Section 9.2, R^+, called a *positive sample set*, is simply a set of training patterns from the class associated with grammar G. The sample set R^+ is said to be *structurally complete* if each production in G is used to generate at least one element of R^+. We want to learn (synthesize) a finite automaton A_f that will accept the strings of R^+ and possibly some strings that resemble those of R^+.

Based on the definition of a finite automaton and the correspondence between G and A_f, it follows that $R^+ \subseteq \Sigma^*$, where Σ^* is the set of all strings composed of elements from Σ. Let z in Σ^* be a string such that zw is in R^+ for some w in Σ^*. For a positive integer k, we define the k tail of z with respect to R^+ as the set $h(z, R^+, k)$, where

$$h(z, R^+, k) = \{w \mid zw \text{ in } R^+, \mid w \mid \le k\}. \tag{9.4-10}$$

In other words, the k tail of z is the set of strings w with the properties (1) zw is in R^+, and (2) the length of w is less than or equal to k.

A procedure for learning an automaton $A_f(R^+, k) = (Q, \Sigma, \delta, q_0, F)$ from a sample set R^+ and a particular value of k consists of letting

$$Q = \{q \mid q = h(z, R^+, k) \text{ for } z \text{ in } \Sigma^*\} \tag{9.4-11}$$

and, for each a in Σ,

$$\delta(q, a) = \{q' \text{ in } Q \mid q' = h(za, R^+, k), \text{ with } q = h(z, R^+, k)\}. \tag{9.4-12}$$

In addition, we let

$$q_0 = h(\lambda, R^+, k) \tag{9.4-13}$$

and

$$F = \{q \mid q \text{ in } Q, \lambda \text{ in } q\} \tag{9.4-14}$$

where λ is the empty string (the string with no symbols). We note that $A_f(R^+, k)$ has as states subsets of the set of all k tails that can be constructed from R^+.

Example: Suppose that $R^+ = \{a, ab, abb\}$ and $k = 1$. The foregoing definition yields

$$
\begin{aligned}
z = \lambda, \qquad & h(\lambda, R^+, 1) = \{w \mid \lambda w \text{ in } R^+, \mid w \mid \le 1\} \\
& \qquad\qquad = \{a\} \\
& \qquad\qquad = q_0; \\
z = a, \qquad & h(a, R^+, 1) = \{w \mid aw \text{ in } R^+, \mid w \mid \le 1\} \\
& \qquad\qquad = \{\lambda, b\} \\
& \qquad\qquad = q_1; \\
z = ab, \qquad & h(ab, R^+, 1) = \{\lambda, b\} \\
& \qquad\qquad = q_1; \\
z = abb, \qquad & h(abb, R^+, 1) = \{\lambda\} \\
& \qquad\qquad = q_2.
\end{aligned}
$$

Other strings z in Σ^*, in this case, yield strings zw that do not belong to R^+, giving rise to a fourth state, denoted $q_\varnothing$, which corresponds to the condition that h is the null set. The states, therefore, are $q_0 = \{a\}$, $q_1 = \{\lambda, b\}$, $q_2 = \{\lambda\}$, and $q_\varnothing$, which give the set $Q = \{q_0, q_1, q_2, q_\varnothing\}$. Although the states are obtained as sets of symbols (k tails), only the state labels $q_0, q_1, \ldots$ are used in forming the set Q.

The next step is to obtain the transition functions. Since $q_0 = h(\lambda, R^+, 1)$, it follows that $\delta(q_0, a) = h(\lambda a, R^+, 1) = h(a, R^+, 1) = q_1$, and $\delta(q_0, b) = h(\lambda b, R^+, 1) = h(b, R^+, 1) = q_\varnothing$. Similarly, $q_1 = h(a, R^+, 1) = h(ab, R^+, 1)$ and $\delta(q_1, a) = h(aa, R^+, 1) = h(aba, R^+, 1) = q_\varnothing$. Also, $\delta(q_1, b) \supseteq h(ab, R^+, 1) = q_1$ and $\delta(q_1, b) \supseteq h(abb, R^+, 1) = q_2$; that is, $\delta(q_1, b) = \{q_1, q_2\}$. Following the procedure just described gives $\delta(q_2, a) = \delta(q_2, b) = \delta(q_\varnothing, a) = \delta(q_\varnothing, b) = q_\varnothing$.

The set of final states contains those states that have the empty string λ in their k-tail representation. In this case, $q_1 = \{\lambda, b\}$ and $q_2 = \{\lambda\}$, so $F = \{q_1, q_2\}$.

Based on these results, the inferred automaton is given by $A_f(R^+, 1) = (Q, \Sigma, \delta, q_0, F)$, where $Q = \{q_0, q_1, q_2, q_\varnothing\}$, $\Sigma = \{a, b\}$, $F = \{q_1, q_2\}$, and the transition functions are as given above. Figure 9.32 shows the state diagram. The automaton accepts strings of the form $a, ab, abb, \ldots, ab^n$. In other words, the procedure has identified iterative regularity on the symbol b. ☐

The preceding example clearly shows that the value of k controls the nature of the resulting automaton. The following properties exemplify the dependence of $A_f(R^+, k)$ on this parameter.

Property 1. $R^+ \subseteq L[A_f(R^+ \; k)]$ for all $k \geq 0$, where $L[A_f (R^+, k)]$ is the language accepted by $A_f(R^+, k)$.

Property 2. $L[A_f(R^+, k)] = R^+$ if k is equal to, or greater than, the length of the longest string in R^+; $L[A_f(R^+, k)] = \Sigma^*$ if $k = 0$.

Property 3. $L[A_f(R^+, k + 1)] \subseteq L[A_f(R^+, k)]$.

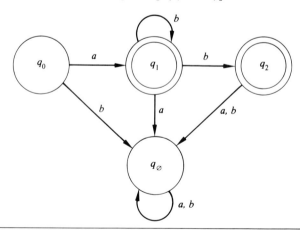

Figure 9.32 *State diagram for the finite automaton $A_f(R^+, 1)$ inferred from the sample set $R^+ = \{a, ab, abb\}$.*

Property 1 guarantees that $A_f(R^+, k)$ will, as a minimum, accept the strings in the sample set R^+. If k is equal to, or greater than, the length of the longest string in R^+, then by Property 2 the automaton will accept *only* the strings in R^+. If $k = 0$, $A_f(R^+, 0)$ will consist of one state $q_0 = \{\lambda\}$, which will act as both the initial and final state. The transition functions will then be of the form $\delta(q_0, a) = q_0$ for a in Σ. Therefore $L[A_f(R^+, 0)] = \Sigma^*$, and the automaton will accept the empty string λ and all strings composed of symbols from Σ. Finally, Property 3 indicates that the scope of the language accepted by $A_f(R^+, k)$ decreases as k increases.

These three properties allow control of the nature of $A_f(R^+, k)$ simply by varying the parameter k. If $L[A_f(R^+, k)]$ is a guess of the language L_0 from which the sample R^+ was chosen and if k is very small, this guess of L_0 will constitute a liberal inference that may include most or all of the strings in Σ^*. However, if k is equal to the length of the longest string in R^+, the inference will be conservative in the sense that $A_f(R^+, k)$ will accept only the strings contained in R^+. Figure 9.33 shows these concepts graphically.

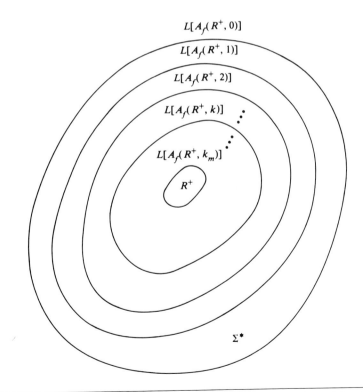

Figure 9.33 *Relationship between* $L[A_f(R^+, k)]$ *and* k. *The value of* k_m *is such that* $k_m \geq$ *(length of longest string in* R^+).

Example: Consider the set $R^+ = \{caaab, bbaab, caab, bbab, cab, bbb, cb\}$. For $k = 1$, following the same procedure used in the preceding example gives

1.	$z = \lambda,$	$h(\lambda, R^+, 1) = \{\varnothing\} = q_\varnothing;$
2.	$z = c,$	$h(z, R^+, 1) = \{b\} = q_1;$
3.	$z = ca,$	$h(z, R^+, 1) = \{b\} = q_1;$
4.	$z = cb,$	$h(z, R^+, 1) = \{\lambda\} = q_0;$
5.	$z = caa,$	$h(z, R^+, 1) = \{b\} = q_1;$
6.	$z = cab,$	$h(z, R^+, 1) = \{\lambda\} = q_0;$
7.	$z = caaa,$	$h(z, R^+, 1) = \{b\} = q_1;$
8.	$z = caab,$	$h(z, R^+, 1) = \{\lambda\} = q_0;$
9.	$z = caaab,$	$h(z, R^+, 1) = \{\lambda\} = q_0;$
10.	$z = b,$	$h(z, R^+, 1) = \{\varnothing\} = q_\varnothing;$
11.	$z = bb,$	$h(z, R^+, 1) = \{b\} = q_1;$
12.	$z = bba,$	$h(z, R^+, 1) = \{b\} = q_1;$
13.	$z = bbb,$	$h(z, R^+, 1) = \{\lambda\} = q_0;$
14.	$z = bbaa,$	$h(z, R^+, 1) = \{b\} = q_1;$
15.	$z = bbab,$	$h(z, R^+, 1) = \{\lambda\} = q_0;$
16.	$z = bbaab,$	$h(z, R^+, 1) = \{\lambda\} = q_0.$

The automaton is $A_f(R^+, 1) = (Q, \Sigma, \delta, q_0, F)$, with $Q = \{q_0, q_1, q_\varnothing\}$, $\Sigma = \{a, b, c\}$, $F = \{q_0\}$, and the transitions shown in the state diagram in Fig. 9.34. To be accepted by the automaton, a string must begin with a, b, or c and

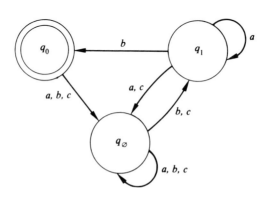

Figure 9.34 *State diagram for the automaton $A_f(R^+, 1)$ inferred from the sample set $R^+ = \{caaab, bbaab, caab, bbab, cab, bbb, cb\}$.*

end with a *b*. Also, strings with recursiveness in *a*, *b*, or *c* are accepted by $A_f(R^+, 1)$. ❑

The principal advantage of the preceding method is simplicity of implementation. The synthesis procedure can be simulated in a digital computer with a modest amount of effort. The main disadvantage is deciding on a proper value for *k*, although this problem is simplified to some degree by the three properties discussed earlier.

9.5 INTERPRETATION

So far we have been concerned primarily with individual processes, ranging from image acquisition and preprocessing to segmentation, description, and object recognition. In this section, we discuss the problem of using all the information generated by these processes in an attempt to *interpret* the contents of an image. In other words, we are interested in giving meaning to an image, a process which, in addition to interpretation, often is called *image understanding* or *scene analysis*. For consistency with earlier discussions, we continue to use the term *image interpretation*.

9.5.1 Background

Computerized image interpretation is an exceedingly complex process. Difficulties arise from both the large amount of data that must be processed and the lack of fundamental processing tools to get from what is given (an array of pixels) to the desired result (a detailing of image content). Thus with no general tools for performing unstructured image interpretation, we are forced to consider approaches that offer a reasonable chance of success. This constraint leads us to a two-phase compromise: (1) we limit the generality of the problem, and (2) we try to incorporate human knowledge into the process. Limiting the scope of the problem is, in principle, straightforward. When possible, we use all available means to limit unknown conditions in an attempt to simplify the problem at hand. When exercising control over problem variables is not possible, we are forced to limit the range (and accuracy) of expected results.

Incorporating human knowledge into an image interpretation task requires choice of a formalism in which to express this knowledge. The three principal approaches used are based on: (1) formal logic; (2) semantic networks; and (3) production systems. For the most part, logical systems are based on first-order predicate calculus, a language of symbolic logic in which a spectrum of statements ranging from simple facts to rather complex expressions can be expressed. Tools of predicate calculus allow knowledge to be expressed in terms of logical rules that can be used to prove (or disprove) the validity of logical expressions.

Semantic approaches represent knowledge in the form of so-called *semantic networks*, which are labeled, directed graphs. These graphs provide intuitive formulations in terms of relationships between elements of an image. In this type of formulation, objects are represented as nodes in a graph, and relationships between the objects are expressed as labeled arcs connecting the various nodes. As we demonstrate in Section 9.5.4, semantic networks provide a powerful approach for image interpretation.

Approaches based on *production* (also called *rule-based*) systems, have received the most attention in image interpretation applications. The reasons for this attention include the availability of numerous tools for development of such systems and the fact that human knowledge can be applied to these systems intuitively, straightforwardly, and incrementally. In particular, *expert systems*, which are restricted to *specific* task domains, are capable of addressing a wide range of applications in image processing.

9.5.2 Types of Knowledge

The subdivision of image processing functions in the three categories (low-, intermediate-, and high-level processing) detailed in Section 9.1 is valid for algorithms, but is not particularly useful in categorizing the various types of knowledge needed to carry out an image processing task. A much more useful categorization of knowledge is: (1) procedural knowledge, (2) visual knowledge, and (3) world knowledge.

Procedural knowledge deals with operations like selecting algorithms and setting parameters for these algorithms (for example, selecting threshold values). *Visual knowledge* deals with aspects of image formation, such as the knowledge that a shadow should be expected from oblique illumination of a 3-D object. *World knowledge* indicates overall knowledge about a problem domain. Examples of this type of knowledge include known relationships between objects in an image (for instance, in an aerial image of an airport, runways and taxiways intersect) and relationships between a scene and its environment (such as the fact that rain increases reflectivity of a road at night).

In general, procedural and visual knowledge are used for low- and intermediate-level processing, and world knowledge is used for high-level processing. In particular, world knowledge forms the basis for image interpretation tasks. Regardless of the type of knowledge, however, one of the most important aspects of representing knowledge for an image processing system is to make the representation as independent of the application as possible. Thus the idea is to avoid burying the knowledge in the code or hardware. Hence basic processing algorithms should be based on domain-independent knowledge, and knowledge about specific applications should be contained in the system's knowledge base and be as independent as possible of these algorithms.

9.5.3 Logical Systems (Predicate Calculus)

Predicate logic has evolved for more than a century into a comprehensive and well-documented body of knowledge that is useful for expressing propositions and for inferring new facts from a knowledge base of facts. One of the most powerful elements of this body of knowledge is the *first-order predicate calculus*, a system of logic capable of handling a broad range of mathematical expressions, as well as statements in a natural language, such as English.

Definitions

The elementary components of predicate calculus are *predicate symbols, function symbols, variable symbols*, and *constant symbols*. A predicate symbol represents a relation in the domain of discourse. For example, the statement "five is less than ten" can be expressed as LESSTHAN(five, ten), where LESSTHAN is a predicate symbol and five and ten are constant symbols.

Table 9.2 shows other examples. In these examples, a predicate symbol (such as MOTHER) identifies each predicate, which contains one or more arguments. The arguments may be *constants*, such as Mary, oceans, and Poe. Arguments also may be functions of other arguments. For example, MARRIED[father(John), mother(John)] represents the statement "John's father is married to John's mother." Here, John is a constant symbol, mother and father are function symbols, and MARRIED is a predicate symbol. In the last example in Table 9.2, BEHIND is a predicate symbol, and x and y are *variable symbols*.

Predicates such as those shown in Table 9.2 also are called *atoms*. Atoms can be combined by *logical connectives* to form *clauses*, as illustrated in Table 9.3. These logical connectives in Table 9.3 have the following familiar meanings: "$\wedge$" (AND), "$\vee$" (OR), "$\sim$" (NOT), and "$\Rightarrow$" (IMPLIES); $\forall x$, called the *universal quantifier*, is the familiar "for all x." Similarly, $\exists x$, called the *existential quantifier*, means "there exists an x." The first four examples in Table 9.3 deal with constant symbols, and the last two involve variable symbols. Logical expressions built by connecting other expressions by $\wedge$s ($\vee$s) are called *conjunctions* (*disjunctions*). Legitimate expressions of predicate calculus are called *well-formed formulas* (wffs).

Table 9.2 Examples of Predicates

Statement	Predicate
Mary is female	FEMALE(Mary)
Mary is mother	MOTHER(Mary)
Oceans are bigger than lakes	BIGGERTHAN(oceans, lakes)
Poe wrote *The Raven*	WRITE(Poe, *The Raven*)
x is behind y	BEHIND(x, y)

Table 9.3   Examples of Clauses

Statement	Clause
Mary is female and mother	FEMALE(Mary) $\wedge$ MOTHER(Mary)
Mary is male or Mary is female	MALE(Mary) $\vee$ FEMALE(Mary)
Mary is not a male	$\sim$MALE(Mary)
If Mary is a mother, Mary is female	MOTHER(Mary) $\Rightarrow$ FEMALE(Mary)
Everyone is male or female	$(\forall x)$[MALE(x) $\vee$ FEMALE(x)]
There is a person who wrote *Jaws*	$(\exists x)$WRITE$(x,$ *Jaws*$)$

A logical expression is said to be in *nonclausal form syntax* if it involves atoms, logical connectives, existential quantifiers, and universal quantifiers. A logical expression is said to be in *clausal form syntax* if it is of the form $(\forall x_1 x_2 \ldots x_k)[A_1 \wedge A_2 \wedge \ldots \wedge A_n \Rightarrow B_1 \vee B_2 \vee \ldots \vee B_m]$, where the A's and B's are atoms. The left and right parts of a clause are called its *condition* and its *conclusion*, respectively. When the condition side of the implication is null, an expression of the form $\Rightarrow P$ is interpreted to mean P. Conversely, the expression $P\Rightarrow$ is interpreted to mean $\sim P$.

Consider the statement "for every x, if x is a person and a parent, then x is either a mother or a father." In clausal syntax, this statement is written as

$$(\forall x)[\text{PERSON}(x) \wedge \text{PARENT}(x) \Rightarrow \text{MOTHER}(x) \vee \text{FATHER}(x)].$$

When written in nonclausal syntax, this expression becomes

$$(\forall x)[\sim\text{PERSON}(x) \vee \sim\text{PARENT}(x) \vee \text{MOTHER}(x) \vee \text{FATHER}(x)].$$

It is easily verified that these two expressions are equivalent (see Table 9.4). In fact, conversion from nonclausal to clausal form, and vice versa, always is possible. Therefore the two representations have equal expressive power.

Table 9.4 shows the relationships between the various logical connectives just introduced. The contents of the first five columns should be quite familiar

Table 9.4   Truth Table of Logical Connectives

A	B	$\sim A$	$A \wedge B$	$A \vee B$	$A \Rightarrow B$
T	T	F	T	T	T
T	F	F	F	T	F
F	T	T	F	T	T
F	F	T	F	F	T

from elementary logic. The implication operation may not be as familiar. The left side of an implication is called the *antecedent*, and the right side is called the *consequent*. Table 9.4 shows that an implication has value T if either the consequent has value T (regardless of the value of the antecedent) or if the antecedent has value F (regardless of the value of the consequent); otherwise the implication has value F. This definition—in which an implication is true whenever its antecedent is false—is a frequent source of confusion, because it can lead to some odd statements. For example, the representation in predicate calculus of the (nonsensical) sentence "If the Earth is square, then all animals are blue" has value T because the antecedent is false. In practice, this problem usually does not arise but keep in mind that logical implication does not always make sense in a natural language.

Example: The following predicate calculus representations illustrate the concepts introduced in the preceding discussion.

1. If an image is digital, then its pixels are discrete:

$$\text{DIGITAL(image)} \Rightarrow \text{DISCRETE(pixels)}.$$

2. All digital images have discrete pixels:

$$(\forall x)\{[\text{IMAGE}(x) \wedge \text{DIGITAL}(x)] \Rightarrow (\exists y)[\text{PIXEL-IN}(y, x) \wedge \text{DISCRETE}(y)]\}.$$

   In English, this expression reads: For all x, such that x is an image and x is digital, there exists a y such that y is a pixel in x, and y is discrete (note the use of variables).

3. Not all images are digital:

$$(\forall x)[\text{IMAGE}(x)] \Rightarrow (\exists y)[\text{IMAGE}(y) \wedge \sim\text{DIGITAL}(y)].$$

   This expression reads: For all x, if x is an image, then there exists a y such that y is an image and y is not digital.

4. Color digital images carry more information than monochrome digital images:

$$(\forall x)(\forall y)\{[\text{IMAGE}(x) \wedge \text{DIGITAL}(x) \wedge \text{COLOR}(x)] \wedge$$
$$[\text{IMAGE}(y) \wedge \text{DIGITAL}(y) \wedge \text{MONOCHROME}(y)] \Rightarrow \text{MOREINFO}(x, y)\}.$$

   This expression reads: For all x and for all y, if x is an image and x is color and x is digital and if y is an image and y is digital and y is monochrome, then x carries more information than y.   ❑

Some important equivalences

The validity of the following equivalences can be verified by using Table 9.4 and elementary logic:

$\sim(\sim A)$	is equivalent to	A.
$A \vee B$	is equivalent to	$\sim A \Rightarrow B$.

Contrapositive law

$A \Rightarrow B$	is equivalent to	$\sim B \Rightarrow \sim A$.

de Morgan's laws

$\sim(A \wedge B)$	is equivalent to	$\sim A \vee \sim B$.
$\sim(A \vee B)$	is equivalent to	$\sim A \wedge \sim B$.

Distributive laws

$A \wedge (B \vee C)$	is equivalent to	$(A \wedge B) \vee (A \wedge C)$.
$A \vee (B \wedge C)$	is equivalent to	$(A \vee B) \wedge (A \vee C)$.

Commutative laws

$A \wedge B$	is equivalent to	$B \wedge A$.
$A \vee B$	is equivalent to	$B \vee A$.

Associative laws

$(A \wedge B) \wedge C$	is equivalent to	$A \wedge (B \wedge C)$.
$(A \vee B) \vee C$	is equivalent to	$A \vee (B \vee C)$.

In addition,

$\sim(\forall x)P(x)$	is equivalent to	$(\exists x)[\sim P(x)]$.
$\sim(\exists x)P(x)$	is equivalent to	$(\forall x)[\sim P(x)]$.

These equivalences are quite useful for manipulating and simplifying logical expressions.

Inference by theorem proving

In predicate logic, rules of inference can be applied to certain wffs and sets of wffs to produce new wffs. The following are examples of inference rules, where the W's indicate wffs:

Modus Ponens

$$\text{From } W1 \wedge (W1 \Rightarrow W2) \quad \text{infer} \quad W2.$$

Modus Tollens

$$\text{From } \sim W2 \wedge (\sim W1 \Rightarrow W2) \quad \text{infer} \quad W1.$$

Projection

$$\text{From } W1 \wedge W2 \quad \text{infer} \quad W1.$$

Universal specialization

$$\text{From } (\forall x)W(x) \quad \text{infer} \quad W(c),$$

where c is a constant symbol, and the general statement "From F infer G" means that $F \Rightarrow G$ is always true (that is, F always implies G); this allows us to replace F by G in logical expressions.

Inference rules produce *derived* wffs from given wffs. In predicate calculus, derived wffs are called *theorems*, and the sequence of applications of inference rules used in the derivation constitutes a *proof* of the theorem. This concept is fundamental to our discussion, because numerous image interpretation tasks may be formulated in terms of theorem proving by using predicate calculus. In this way, rules of inference and a set of known facts can be used to deduce new facts or to prove the validity of a hypothesis.

In predicate calculus two basic methods may be used to prove the validity of logical expressions. The first is by direct manipulation of nonclausal forms, following a procedure similar to that used to prove mathematical expressions. The other is based on matching terms in expressions that are in clausal form. Both methods are illustrated in the following example.

Example: Suppose that we know the following facts: (1) the wastebasket is behind the desk, and (2) the chair is next to the desk. We assume that the following "physical" law holds in this case: (3) if x is behind y, then x is invisible. Facts (1) and (2) are problem specific, but assumption (3) is the type of knowledge that is problem independent. That is, so long as certain obvious conditions are satisfied, such as x has to be smaller than y, x has to lie completely behind y with respect to the location of the observer, and y has to be a solid object. We want to infer (prove)—using only the two facts and the assumption—that the wastebasket is invisible.

The two facts are of the form:

$$\text{BEHIND(wastebasket, desk)}$$

and

$$\text{NEXT-TO(chair, desk).}$$

Based on the statement of the problem, we know that these two facts are related by the logical connective $\wedge$:

$$\text{BEHIND(wastebasket, desk)} \wedge \text{NEXT-TO(chair, desk).}$$

The physical law in clausal form is

$$(\forall x, y)[\text{BEHIND}(x, y) \Rightarrow \text{INVISIBLE}(x)]$$

which is easily converted to nonclausal form by using the fact (from the preceding section) that $\sim A \Rightarrow B$ is equivalent to $A \vee B$. In other words, the foregoing expression in nonclausal form is

$$(\forall x, y)[\sim\text{BEHIND}(x, y) \vee \text{INVISIBLE}(x)].$$

We now express in conjunctive form all the knowledge we have about this problem:

(a) $(\forall x, y)\{\text{BEHIND}(\text{wastebasket, desk}) \wedge \text{NEXT-TO}(\text{chair, desk}) \wedge$
$$[\sim\text{BEHIND}(x, y) \vee \text{INVISIBLE}(x)]\}.$$

Substituting x by wastebasket and y by desk yields

(b) $\text{BEHIND}(\text{wastebasket, desk}) \wedge \text{NEXT-TO}(\text{chair, desk}) \wedge$
$$[\sim\text{BEHIND}(\text{wastebasket, desk}) \vee \text{INVISIBLE}(\text{wastebasket})].$$

By using the projection rule we *infer* the expression:

(c) $\text{BEHIND}(\text{wastebasket, desk}) \wedge$
$$[\sim\text{BEHIND}(\text{wastebasket, desk}) \vee \text{INVISIBLE}(\text{wastebasket})]$$

Using one of the distributive laws introduced in the preceding section gives $A \wedge (\sim A \vee B) = (A \wedge B)$. Thus we now have the reduced expression:

(d) $\text{BEHIND}(\text{wastebasket, desk}) \wedge \text{INVISIBLE}(\text{wastebasket})$.

Applying the projection rule again yields

(e) $\text{INVISIBLE}(\text{wastebasket})$.

Thus we have proved that the original expression given in (a) is completely equivalent to expression (e). In other words, we have *deduced* from the given information that the wastebasket is invisible.

We now proceed to prove the same result using a clausal representation. The method of proof in this representation consists of establishing that the *negation* of the clause that we want to prove is *inconsistent* with the facts, thus proving that the clause in question is true or valid. This seemingly backward way of doing things is the manner in which mechanical theorem provers usually work.

Based on the definitions presented earlier, we may express our knowledge about this problem in the following clausal form:

(a) $\Rightarrow\text{BEHIND}(\text{wastebasket, desk})$,

(b) $\Rightarrow\text{NEXT-TO}(\text{chair, desk})$,

(c) $(\forall x, y)[\text{BEHIND}(x, y) \Rightarrow \text{INVISIBLE}(x)]$,

and

(d) INVISIBLE(wastebasket)$\Rightarrow$.

Recall that we want to establish the inconsistency of the negation of the predicate INVISIBLE(wastebasket) which, based on the earlier definition, is represented as INVISIBLE(wastebasket)$\Rightarrow$.

After the elements of the problem have been expressed in clausal form, the idea is to match the left and right sides of different implications with the ultimate idea of arriving at the empty clause, which is a contradiction. The matching is performed by substituting variables in order to make atoms identical. After the matching, the derived clause, called the *resolvent*, consists of the unmatched left and right sides. The left part of (c) matches the right part of (a) if we substitute wastebasket for x and desk for y. The resolvent is

(e) $\Rightarrow$INVISIBLE(wastebasket).

However, the resolution of (d) and (e) is the empty clause, because the left side of (d) and the right side of (e) are identical. This result is a contradiction, which shows that the negation INVISIBLE(wastebasket)$\Rightarrow$ is invalid, thus proving the validity of the theorem INVISIBLE(wastebasket). ❏

A fundamental result in predicate calculus is that all true theorems are provable in finite time. An algorithmic (but inefficient) procedure for finding such proofs was first proposed by Herbrand [1930]. A much more efficient theorem-proving approach was discovered three decades later by Robinson [1965], who proposed a single rule of inference called *resolution*. Robinson showed that this single resolution rule preserves *completeness*, in the sense that all true theorems are provable, and *correctness*, in the sense that no false theorems are provable. As the preceding example shows, the rule of resolution, in principle, is simple. After the elements of the problem have been expressed in clausal form, the method seeks antecedents and consequents of different implications that can be matched. Matching is performed by substituting variables in order to make atoms identical. After matching, the derived clause, called the *resolvent*, consists of the unmatched left and right sides, as indicated earlier. Theorem proving now consists of resolving clauses with the objective of producing the empty clause, which is a contradiction. In practice, a significant part of the published literature on theorem proving deals with development of algorithms for the efficient discovery of resolvents in a given knowledge base.

Example: Suppose that the following information is part of the knowledge base of a system for interpreting aerial images:

1. All images of commercial airports contain runway(s).
2. All images of commercial airports contain airplanes.
3. All images of commercial airports contain building(s).
4. In a commercial airport, at least one building is a terminal building.
5. A building surrounded by airplanes such that the airplanes point to the building is a terminal building.

We condense this information into a "model" of a commercial airport in clause form as follows:

$$(\forall x)[\text{CONTAINS}(x, \text{runway(s)}) \wedge \text{CONTAINS}(x, \text{airplanes}) \wedge$$
$$\text{CONTAINS}(x, \text{building(s)}) \wedge \text{POINT-TO}(\text{airplanes},$$
$$\text{building(s)})] \Rightarrow \text{COMAIRPORT}(x).$$

The information given in (4) is not used directly in the model. Instead, its meaning is implicit in the two conditions in the model that require that there be building(s) and that airplanes point to building(s). The latter condition establishes a building as a terminal building.

Suppose that we are given the aerial image shown in Fig. 9.35(a) (the closeup in Fig. 9.35(b) gives a better idea of the level of detail in the image) and assume that we have a "recognition engine" capable of recognizing various objects in aerial photographs. We could approach the interpretation of Fig. 9.35(a) in two ways: (1) we could ask, "What is this an image of?" or (2) we could ask, "Is this an image of a commercial airport?" In general we cannot answer the first question with currently available techniques. The second question is still quite difficult to answer in general, but becomes easier to answer if we limit the domain of discourse. In particular, a *model-driven* approach in which the entities of interest are modeled as shown above has the significant advantage that it can be used to guide the operation of the recognition engine. Here, the engine has to be able to recognize three classes of objects: runways, airplanes, and buildings. If, as is usually the case, the altitude at which the image was taken is known, looking for these three types of objects is simplified even further, because relative-size scales may be used to guide the recognition process.

The output of a recognizer working on Fig. 9.35(a) and driven by the above model of a commercial airport would output information in the form: CONTAINS(image, runway), CONTAINS(image, airplanes), and CONTAINS (image, buildings). Further processing with the recognized objects would establish whether the clause POINT(airplanes, buildings) is true or false. If it is false, a procedure based on this simple model would stop. Otherwise, it would proceed to determine whether 9.35(a) is an image of a commercial airport by establishing the validity of the clause COMAIRPORT(image). Using theorem

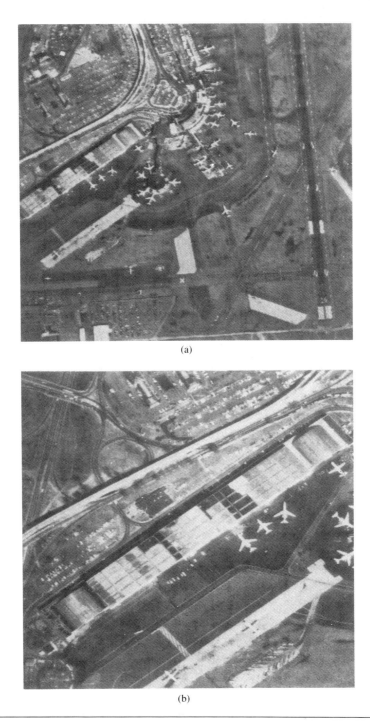

(a)

(b)

Figure 9.35 *(a) Aerial image of Washington National Airport; (b) detail. (From McKeown, Harvey, and McDermott [1985].)*

proving by resolution, we start with the following information, which has been extracted from the image:

  i. $\Rightarrow$CONTAINS(image, runway),

  ii. $\Rightarrow$CONTAINS(image, airplanes),

  iii. $\Rightarrow$CONTAINS(image, buildings),

  iv. $\Rightarrow$POINT-TO(airplanes, buildings),

and, finally, we have the negation of the clause we want to prove, or

  v. COMAIRPORT(image)$\Rightarrow$.

We begin by noting that, if we replace x by image, one of the clauses on the left side of the model matches the right side of (i). The resolvent then is

[CONTAINS(image, airplanes) $\wedge$ CONTAINS(image, buildings) $\wedge$

                POINT-TO(airplanes, buildings)] $\Rightarrow$ COMAIRPORT(image).

Similarly, one of the clauses on the left of the resolvent matches the right side of (ii). The new resolvent then is

[CONTAINS(image, buildings) $\wedge$ POINT-TO(airplanes, buildings)]

                                  $\Rightarrow$ COMAIRPORT(image).

Next, the application of (iii) and (iv) yields the resolvent

                $\Rightarrow$COMAIRPORT(image).

Finally, the resolution of this result and (v) yields the empty clause, thus producing a contradiction. This proves the validity of the clause COM-AIRPORT(image), indicating that the image is indeed an image of a commercial airport (that is, it matches our model of a commercial airport).   ❏

9.5.4 Semantic Networks

Semantic networks are labeled, directed graphs in which the nodes usually represent objects or variables and the arcs represent relationships between the nodes. Networks of this type have several advantages, including an intuitive and visually effective way of representing knowledge. In addition, because the basic representation is a graph, graph matching and labeling techniques may be used to manipulate the elements of a problem domain. Figure 9.36 shows a semantic network representation of the facts in the simple wastebasket problem.

Semantic networks offer an alternative way to perform interpretation tasks. Although there are numerous ways of using networks for this purpose, in this section we focus on networks used to represent and process knowledge ex-

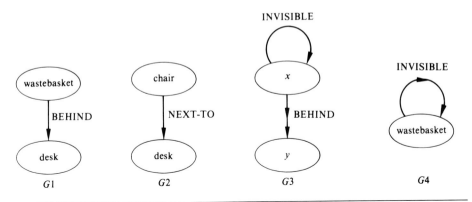

Figure 9.36 *Semantic graph partitions for the wastebasket problem.*

pressed in clausal form. This approach illustrates the basic concepts underlying the use of semantic networks and also helps maintain continuity in the discussion.

Constructing a semantic network from clausal expressions is straightforward. The idea is to represent each clause as a partition of the semantic network (that is, each clause is represented as a separate subgraph). The nodes of the network contain variables and constants (typically objects), and the labeled, directed arcs denote binary relationships between the nodes. An arc is drawn as an arrow with a single tip if it represents a relation in the conclusion (right) part of a clause and as a double-tipped arrow if it represents a relation in the condition (left) part of a clause. Figure 9.36 shows the graph partitions corresponding to expressions (a)–(d) of the wastebasket example. We convert a unary relation, such as INVISIBLE(x), into a binary relation (needed for consistency in the graph representations) by the notational trick INVISIBLE(x, x).

Performing inference with semantic networks of the form shown in Fig. 9.36 is simple and appealing conceptually. Graphs are merged by matching variables and constants, and double-tipped arrows cancel single-tipped arrows, along with their descendant nodes if they are equal. As in the preceding section, the objective is to get to an empty partition involving a negated clause established at the onset of the inference process. Figure 9.37 shows the result (denoted $G13$) of merging graph partitions $G1$ and $G3$ from Fig. 9.36. Merging $G13$ and $G4$ results in an empty partition, indicating (proving, as before) that the wastebasket is invisible.

Example: Let us return to the airport problem. Figure 9.38(a) shows our model of a commercial airport as a semantic network. Two different nodes are shown for "airplanes." It would have been equally correct to show a single airplanes node with an arc coming from x into it, labeled CONTAINS, and an arc labeled POINT-TO going into the buildings node. However, both conditions have to

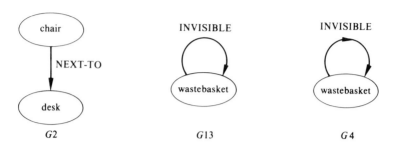

Figure 9.37 *Performing inference by merging graph partitions.*

be satisfied in order for the model itself to be satisfied, so showing two nodes labeled airplanes simplifies bookkeeping.

Figure 9.38(b) shows the facts extracted from the image in Fig. 9.35(a). Note the single-tipped arrows, which are a consequence of clausal representations (i)–(iv). Figure 9.38(d) shows the negation of the fact that we want to prove [causal representation (v)]. Figure 9.38(d) shows the model after the image data was substituted into it and the proper mergings were carried out. Finally, Fig. 9.38(e) shows that merging the graph partitions in Figs. 9.38(c) and (d) results in the empty partition, thus proving that the image in question is in fact an image of a commercial airport.   ❏

9.5.5   Production (Expert) Systems

Production systems offer an alternative approach to the types of inference discussed in Sections 9.5.3 and 9.5.4. As in predicate calculus and semantic networks, production systems require matching in order to identify which inference to make. However, the actions of a production system after a match has been found are much more general. In fact, actions of arbitrary complexity are allowed.

This flexibility of response has generated great interest in the development of production systems. In particular, expert systems have been used successfully in various applications, ranging from image processing and industrial inspection to medical diagnoses and process control. Expert systems are human-machine systems with specialized problem-solving expertise. Thus, the name *expert system* reflects the fact that these systems generally are based on knowledge obtained from people who are experts in a specified discipline.

Figure 9.39 shows the basic components of an expert system. The *language processor* serves as the communication interface between the user and the system. The user interacts with the expert system via a problem-oriented language, which usually is in a restricted English-like format. A graphic interface may be used to complement language communication. The language processor interprets inputs provided by the user and formats information generated by the system. The *justifier* explains the actions of the system to the user. For example, it answers questions about why a conclusion was reached or why an alternative was rejected. The justifier also plays a crucial role in the early design and debugging of an expert system.

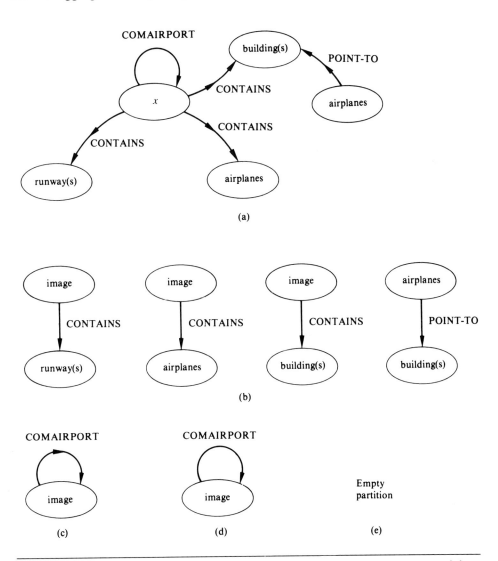

Figure 9.38 *(a) Semantic network model of commercial airport; (b) data extracted from aerial image in Fig. 9.35(a); (c) negation of fact to be proven; (d) result of substituting data into the model and merging; (e) result of merging (c) and (d).*

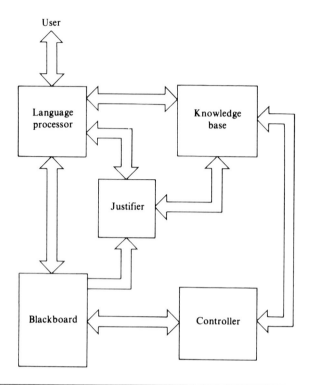

Figure 9.39 *Basic components of an expert system.*

The *blackboard* is working storage used to record items such as current data about a specific problem, working hypotheses, and intermediate decisions. The terms *temporary memory* and *short-term memory* often are used interchangeably to denote the blackboard. The *knowledge base* (a subset of the knowledge base in Fig. 9.1) contains procedural, visual, and world knowledge, as defined in Section 9.5.2. The degree to which the knowledge utilized by an expert system overlaps the knowledge used by other elements of an image processing system depends on the application. The knowledge base also contains the rules needed by the system to solve a problem. The *control mechanism* contains general problem-solving knowledge and conflict-resolution strategies. The general problem-solving knowledge, sometimes called an *inference engine*, embodies the essence of how to match rules, knowledge, algorithms, and currently known facts about a task in order to arrive at (or infer) a solution. That is, the control mechanism acts as the strategist in the selection and execution of tools to solve a problem. The conflict-resolution aspects of the control mechanism are called upon when two or more rules are triggered simultaneously. The way in which a conflict is resolved depends on the application, but some general approaches include *rule ordering*, whereby the rule with the highest priority is selected for firing (as defined later), and *recency ordering*, whereby the rule used most recently is the one allowed to fire. Rules in an expert system typically have the form

if (conditions) **then** (actions)

where the conditions and actions are expressed as conjunctive clauses. In other words, we read the above rule as: **if** condition 1 *and* condition 2 *and* . . . *and* condition *m* are true, **then** take action 1 *and* action 2 *and* . . . *and* action *k*.[†] For example, consider a sample rule for merging two regions in an image:

R(107) **if** the region sizes are small, *and* the regions are adjacent, *and*

the difference between their gray-level variances is small,

then merge the two regions.

The concepts of "small" and "adjacent" must be defined a priori and stored where the rules can get to the information when needed. This type of information is stored in the knowledge base. The regions are assumed to have been identified and their descriptors computed. That is, we assume that segmentation (Chapter 7) and description (Chapter 8) have taken place. Finally, this particular rule has three conditions but only one action. In practice, rules with multiple conditions leading to a single action are common in image processing systems.

When all the conditions in a rule are satisfied at the same time, the rule is said to be *triggered*. When the actions are performed the rule is said to be *fired*. The fact that a rule is triggered does not mean that the rule is automatically fired. More than one rule may be triggered by a particular set of conditions, in which case the system must enter a conflict-resolution stage to determine which rule takes precedence for firing. The idea is that only one rule is allowed to fire at a time.

The similarity between expert system rules of the form just described and the expressions in clause form discussed previously should be clear. In fact, expert rules usually are much easier to specify and read. For example, the physical law in the wastebasket problem discussed earlier may be expressed in rule form as

if object *x* is behind object *y*,

then object *x* is invisible.

[†]The word *and* in this context is the logical AND operator, denoted $\wedge$ in Sections 9.5.3 and 9.5.4. In expressing expert system rules, the use of *and* is not uncommon, because it is more English-like in appearance.

When specific facts are given, an expert system attempts to match those facts against conditions in the rule base. Matching of all conditions in a rule triggers the rule. If no conflicts arise, the action associated with that rule is activated, thus firing the rule. The action itself might be nothing more than a declarative statement, as in the above rule. With regard to the fact that "the wastebasket is behind the desk," the expert system would match wastebasket with x and desk with y, triggering the rule. The action in this case would be the statement: "wastebasket is invisible." The degree to which statements are accepted in English-like (or other natural language) formats depends on the sophistication of the expert system. Because expert systems tend to be "user friendly," interacting with them generally is much easier than with systems based on predicate logic or semantic networks.

Example: Let us consider an expert system formulation of the airport interpretation problem discussed earlier. The model expressed in rule form is as follows:

> **if** x is an image *and*
>
> x contains runway(s) *and*
>
> x contains airplanes *and*
>
> x contains building(s) *and*
>
> (some) airplanes point to building(s),
>
> **then** x is an image of a commercial airport.

In practice, the procedure of using this particular system to interpret an aerial image would begin with a query such as: Is this an image of an airport? In this case, the query would give the system its first fact: "x is an image." The controller would then attempt to match the conditions of those rules that start with: **if** x is an image. In this simple example, we need to determine only whether three other conditions are satisfied. The controller would manage all the resources in Fig. 9.1 that are necessary to look for instances of items in the image required to satisfy the rule conditions. For instance, the controller would initiate recognition procedures for finding runways in an image. These procedures would, in turn, need segmentation and description algorithms for extracting and characterizing candidate regions with the potential for being runways. Upon finding runways, the system would start looking for buildings, and so on. If all conditions are satisfied, the rule(s) would be triggered. If only one rule is triggered, no conflict-resolution would be required and the system would proceed to fire the rule which, in this case, would produce the result: "the image is an image of a commercial airport." ❏

The preceding example illustrates the basic mechanics followed by a typical expert system in trying to establish whether any of its rules are satisfied. In complex rule-based systems having hundreds, or even thousands, of rules, the principal challenges are searching for rules on which to attempt matches, keeping track of which rules are being processed at any one time, managing the resources available for image processing, and performing conflict resolution when needed. In the reference section that follows, we cite examples of expert systems that have been successful in a variety of restricted, but practical, image processing applications.

9.6   CONCLUDING REMARKS

Although the material in this chapter is introductory in nature, the topics covered are fundamental to understanding the state of the art in image recognition and interpretation. However, as may already be obvious, we have told only part of the story. The fields of image recognition and interpretation have been an active topic of research and development for many years and in a variety of disciplines. As a result, many thousands of articles and hundreds of books have documented an impressive number of approaches—some theoretic, others heuristic—proposed as solutions for various aspects of automated image analysis.

Despite this significant level of activity, the field remains a challenge. In particular, solutions of problems in image analysis are characterized by task-specific formulations, thus limiting the capability for advancement using the time-tried method of building a generalized body of results based on preceding accomplishments. For the foreseeable future, the design of image analysis systems will continue to require a mixture of art and science. In that sense, the material covered in this book may be viewed as a strong base upon which to build solutions to image processing problems in a broad spectrum of disciplines.

REFERENCES

General reading for the introductory discussion and the material in Section 9.1 are Ballard and Brown [1982], Fu, Gonzalez, and Lee [1987], Chang [1989], and Abidi, Eason, and Gonzalez [1991]. The material from Section 9.2 through the end of Section 9.3.2 is from pattern recognition theory. References for these sections are Duda and Hart [1973], Tou and Gonzalez [1974], Gonzalez and Thomason [1978] and Fu [1982]. Basic references for neural networks (Section 9.3.3) are the books by Rumelhart and McClelland [1986], McClelland and Rumelhart [1986], Pao [1989], Maren, Harston, and Pap [1990], Khanna [1990], and Freeman and Skapura [1991]. A special issue of *Computer* [1988] entitled "Artificial Neural Systems" contains several overview articles of interest. The example dealing with the recognition of distorted shapes is adapted from Gupta et al. [1990]. The material in Section 9.3.3 is introductory. In fact, the neural network model used in the discussion is one of numerous models proposed over the years. The books previously listed, in addition to a paper by Lippman [1987], give a good overview of the various models currently in use. The model covered in this chapter, however, is representative and is also used quite extensively in image processing.

The material in Section 9.4.1 is from Bribiesca and Guzman [1980], and the material in Section 9.4.2 is from Sze and Yang [1981]. References for Section 9.4.3 are Gonzalez and Thomason [1978] and Fu [1982]. The procedure for learning a finite automaton from sample strings is from Biermann and Feldman [1972]. For additional reading on the material of Section 9.5.1, see Chang [1989]. The various classifications of knowledge discussed in Section 9.5.2 are from Adimari et al. [1988]. References for Sections 9.5.3 and 9.5.4 are Ballard and Brown [1982], Nilsson [1971, 1980], and Chang [1989]. For an example of a comprehensive semantic network, see Niemann et al. [1990]. General references for Section 9.5.5 are Nilsson [1980] and Hayes-Roth et al. [1983]. As indicated in Section 9.5.5, rather complex expert systems have been built for performing image interpretation. A good example dealing with the use of expert systems for interpreting complex aerial photographs is given in the papers by McKeown, Harvey, and McDermott [1985] and by McKeown, Wilson, and Wixson [1989]. See also the book by Nagao and Takashi [1980], and a paper by Huertas, et al. [1990] in connection with this type of application. Other typical examples of the use of expert systems for image interpretation are Yuan and Lee [1987], in connection with the analysis of images of LSI (large-scale-integration) chips, Goodson and Lewis [1990], dealing with line extraction and identification in raster images, and Brzakovic et al. [1991] dealing with edge detection.

PROBLEMS

9.1 (a) Compute the decision functions of a minimum distance classifier for the patterns shown in Fig. 9.2.

   (b) Sketch the decision surfaces implemented by the decision functions in (a).

9.2 Show that Eqs. (9.3-4) and (9.3-5) perform the same function.

9.3 Show that the surface given by Eq. (9.3-6) is the perpendicular bisector of the line joining the n-dimensional points $\mathbf{m}_i$ and $\mathbf{m}_j$.

9.4 Show how the minimum distance classifier discussed in connection with Fig. 9.7 could be implemented by using M resistor banks (M is the number of classes), a summing junction at each bank (for summing currents), and a maximum selector capable of selecting the maximum of M inputs, where the inputs are currents.

9.5 Show that the correlation coefficient of Eq. (9.3-8) has values in the range $[-1, 1]$. (*Hint:* Express $\gamma(s, t)$ in vector form.)

9.6 An experiment produces binary images of blobs that are nearly elliptical in shape. The blobs are of three sizes, with the average values of the principal axes of the ellipses being (1.3, 0.7), (1.0, 0.5), and (0.75, 0.25). The dimensions of these axes vary $\pm 10\%$ about their average values. (A typical image containing these blobs is shown on the next page.) Develop an image analysis system capable of rejecting incomplete or overlapping ellipses and then classifying the remaining single ellipses into one of the three size classes given. Show your solution in block diagram form, giving specific details regarding the operation of each block. Solve the classification problem using a minimum distance classifier, indicating clearly how you would go about obtaining training samples and how you would use these samples to train the classifier.

9.7 Assume that the following pattern classes have Gaussian probability density functions: ω_1: $\{(0, 0)^T, (2, 0)^T, (2, 2)^T, (0, 2)^T\}$ and ω_2: $\{(4, 4)^T, (6, 4)^T, (6, 6)^T, (4, 6)^T\}$.

(a) Assume that $P(\omega_1) = P(\omega_2) = \frac{1}{2}$ and obtain the equation of the Bayes decision boundary between these two classes.

(b) Sketch the boundary.

9.8 Repeat Problem 9.7, but use the following pattern classes: ω_1: $\{(-1, 0)^T, (0, -1)^T, (1, 0)^T, (0, 1)^T\}$ and ω_2: $\{(-2, 0)^T, (0, -2)^T, (2, 0)^T, (0, 2)^T\}$. Observe that these classes are not linearly separable.

9.9 Repeat Problem 9.6, but use a Bayes classifier (assume Gaussian densities). Indicate clearly how you would go about obtaining training samples and how you would use these samples to train the classifier.

9.10 The Bayes decision functions $d_j(\mathbf{x}) = p(\mathbf{x}/\omega_j)P(\omega_j)$, $j = 1, 2, \ldots, M$, were derived using a 0–1 loss function. Prove that these decision functions minimize the probability of error. (*Hint:* The probability of error $p(e)$ is $1 - p(c)$, where $p(c)$ is the probability of being correct. For a pattern vector $\mathbf{x}$ belonging to class ω_i, $p(c/\mathbf{x}) = p(\omega_i/\mathbf{x})$. Find $p(c)$ and show that $p(c)$ is maximum [$p(e)$ is minimum] when $p(\mathbf{x}/\omega_i)P(\omega_i)$ is maximum.

9.11 (a) Apply the perceptron algorithm to the following pattern classes: ω_1: $\{(0, 0, 0)^T, (1, 0, 0)^T, (1, 0, 1)^T, (1, 1, 0)^T\}$; and ω_2: $\{(0, 0, 1)^T, (0, 1, 1)^T, (0, 1, 0)^T, (1, 1, 1)^T\}$. Let $c = 1$ and $\mathbf{w}(1) = (-1, -2, -2, 0)^T$.

(b) Sketch the decision surface obtained in (a). Show the pattern classes and indicate the positive side of the surface.

9.12 The perceptron algorithm given in Eqs. (9.3-34)–(9.3-36) can be expressed in a more concise form by multiplying the patterns of class ω_2 by -1, in which case the correction steps in the algorithm become $\mathbf{w}(k + 1) = \mathbf{w}(k)$, if $\mathbf{w}^T(k)\mathbf{y}(k) > 0$, and $\mathbf{w}(k + 1) = \mathbf{w}(k) + c\mathbf{y}(k)$ otherwise. This is one of several perceptron algorithm formulations that can be derived by starting from the general gradient descent equation

$$\mathbf{w}(k + 1) = \mathbf{w}(k) - c\left[\frac{\partial J(\mathbf{w}, \mathbf{y})}{\partial \mathbf{w}}\right]_{\mathbf{w} = \mathbf{w}(k)}$$

where $c > 0$, $J(\mathbf{w}, \mathbf{y})$ is a criterion function, and the partial derivative is evaluated at $\mathbf{w} = \mathbf{w}(k)$. Show that the perceptron algorithm formulation is obtainable from the general gradient descent procedure by using the criterion function $J(\mathbf{w}, \mathbf{y}) = \frac{1}{2}(|\mathbf{w}^T\mathbf{y}| - \mathbf{w}^T\mathbf{y})$, where $|\arg|$ is the absolute value of the argument. (*Note:* The partial derivative of $\mathbf{w}^T\mathbf{y}$ with respect to $\mathbf{w}$ equals $\mathbf{y}$.)

9.13 Prove that the perceptron training algorithm given in Eqs. (9.3-34)–(9.3-36) converges in a finite number of steps if the training pattern sets are linearly separable. [*Hint:* Multiply the patterns of class ω_2 by -1 and consider a nonnegative threshold, T, so that the perceptron training algorithm (with $c = 1$) is expressed as $\mathbf{w}(k + 1) = \mathbf{w}(k)$, if $\mathbf{w}^T(k)\mathbf{y}(k) > T$, and $\mathbf{w}(k + 1) = \mathbf{w}(k) + \mathbf{y}(k)$ otherwise. You may need to use the Cauchy–Schwartz inequality: $\|\mathbf{a}\|^2\|\mathbf{b}\|^2 \geq (\mathbf{a}^T\mathbf{b})^2$.]

9.14 Specify the structure and weights of a neural network capable of performing *exactly* the same function as a minimum distance classifier for two pattern classes in n-dimensional space.

9.15 Specify the structure and weights of a neural network capable of performing *exactly* the same function as a Bayes classifier for two pattern classes in n-dimensional space. The classes are Gaussian with different means but equal covariance matrices.

9.16 (a) Under what conditions are the neural networks in Problems 9.14 and 9.15 identical?
  (b) Would the generalized delta rule for multilayer feedforward neural networks developed in Section 9.3.3 yield this particular neural network if trained with a sufficiently large number of samples?

9.17 Two pattern classes in two dimensions are distributed in such a way that the patterns of class ω_1 lie randomly along a circle of radius r_1. Similarly, the patterns of class ω_2 lie randomly along a circle of radius r_2, where $r_2 = 2r_1$. Specify the structure of a neural network with the minimum number of layers and nodes needed to classify properly the patterns of these two classes.

9.18 Repeat Problem 9.6, but use a neural network. Indicate clearly how you would go about obtaining training samples and how you would use these samples to train the classifier. Select the simplest possible neural network which, in your opinion, is capable of solving the problem.

9.19 Show that the expression $h'_j(I_j) = O_j(1 - O_j)$ given in Eq. (9.3-71), where $h'_j(I_j) = \partial h_j(I_j)/\partial I_j$, follows from Eq. (9.3-50) with $\theta_o = 1$.

9.20 Show that the distance measure $D(A, B)$ of Eq. (9.4-1) satisfies the properties given in Eq. (9.4-2).

9.21 Show that $Q = \max(|A|, |B|) - M$ in Eq. (9.4-3) is 0 if and only if A and B are identical strings.

9.22 (a) Specify a finite automaton capable of recognizing pattern strings of the form ab^na.
  (b) Obtain the corresponding regular grammar from your solution in (a). (Do not solve by inspection.)

9.23 Give an expansive tree grammar for generating images consisting of alternating 1's and 0's in both spatial directions (in a checkerboard pattern). Assume that the top left element is a 1 and that all images terminate with a 1 as the bottom left element.

9.24 Use the learning procedure specified in Eqs. (9.4-9)–(9.4-14) to learn a finite automaton capable of recognizing strings of the form $ab^n a$, with $n > 0$. Start with the sample set {*aba, abba, abbba*}. If this set is insufficient for the algorithm to discover the iterative regularity of symbol b, add more sample strings until it can.

9.25 Show that the tree automaton given in connection with Fig. 9.30 accepts the tree given in Fig. 9.31(b).

9.26 Prove the validity of all the equivalences listed in Section 9.5.3 in the subsection entitled *Some important equivalences*.

9.27 Specify in English-like sentences the knowledge that would be required to classify all blobs in the images of Problem 9.6 into four basic categories: (1) complete, elliptical blobs; (2) incomplete, elliptical blobs; (3) complete, composite blobs; and (4) incomplete, composite blobs. Assume that images have been properly segmented into binary images in which every pixel is either an object or background pixel. In (2) and (4), *incomplete* means blobs that are partially outside the image area.

9.28 Use your answer to Problem 9.27 as the basis for a knowledge-based system that uses predicate logic and has the ability to classify all blobs into the four categories listed there. Specify clearly all image processing functions needed by the logic system to perform its task.

9.29 Repeat Problem 9.28, but instead use a semantic network. Specify clearly all required image processing functions needed by the system.

9.30 Based on your answer to Problem 9.27, give the rules of an expert system capable of classifying all blobs into the four categories listed there. Specify clearly all image processing functions needed by your expert system to perform its task.

9.31 A certain factory mass produces small American flags for sporting events. The quality assurance team has observed that, during periods of peak production, some printing machines have a tendency to drop (randomly) between one and three stars and one or two entire stripes. Aside from these errors, the flags are perfect in every other way. Although the flags containing errors represent a small percentage of total production, the plant manager decides to solve the problem. After much investigation, he concludes that visual automation is the most economical way to handle the problem. The basic specifications are as follows: The flags are approximately $3''$ by $5''$ in size, and they move lengthwise down the production line (individually, but with a $\pm 15°$ variation in orientation) at approximately $20''$/sec, with a separation between flags of approximately $2''$. (In all cases, "approximately" means $\pm 5\%$.) The plant manager hires you to design an image analysis system for each production line. You are told that cost and simplicity are important parameters in determining the viability of your approach. Design a complete system based on the model of Fig. 9.1 and document your solution (including assumptions) in a brief (but clear) written report addressed to the plant manager.

GENERATION OF HALFTONE IMAGES

As discussed in Section 1.4, the ideal method for displaying a digital image is via a monitor in which the intensity of each dot is proportional to the intensity of the corresponding pixel in the image being displayed. The gray-scale printing approaches discussed here provide an alternative when the only output means available is a bilevel device, such as a binary monitor, a line printer, or a laser printer. When used in conjunction with the coded images in Appendix B, these methods offer a useful avenue for experimenting with the various techniques discussed in the text and then outputting the results on generally available printing equipment.

The concept of interest is a technique called *halftoning*, which is the method used for printing gray-level pictures in newspapers, magazines, and books. The idea behind halftoning is quite simple. Consider a small resolution unit (say, a 0.02 × 0.02-in. square) that contains fine black detail on a white background. When viewed from a normal viewing distance (say, 10 in.), the eye integrates the contents of the square so that the viewer perceives only the average intensity of the area. This integration property of the eye is the basis for halftoning. The basic approach consists of imprinting on each (square) resolution unit a circle of ink whose size is inversely proportional to the intensity of the image in the area of the resolution unit. Figure A.1 shows an enlargement of a typical halftone pattern. Note that the dots are much smaller in the light areas of the image and get proportionally larger in darker regions. Newspaper halftones have a resolution of about 80 dots per inch (DPI), whereas book and magazine halftones have about double that resolution.

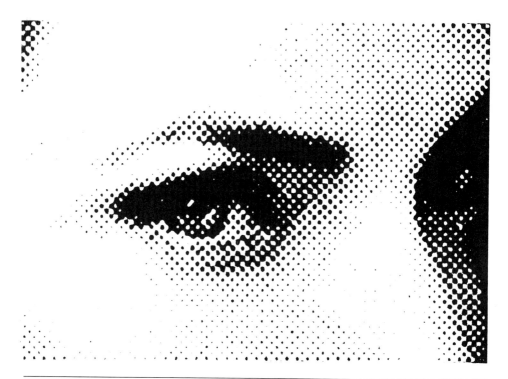

Figure A.1 *Enlarged halftone image.*

A halftone pattern may be approximated on a bilevel device in various ways. One of the simplest methods is to use character overstrikes. Figure A.2 shows a set of characters for achieving this result. In this particular case, five characters are used in various combinations to approximate 32 gray levels. Obviously, other combinations of characters besides the ones shown in Fig. A.2 are possible, so long as the characters used produce a reasonably smooth transition from black to white. The principal advantage of character overstriking is compactness, in the sense that only one character space is used to produce

```
MMMMMMHHHHHXHXOZWMNOS=I*++=:-.-
WWWWWW###*++----      =   -     -
####OO+-
OOO
+
```

█▓▒░▒▓█░░ # #̃#̃ # #̃ XHXⴲZWMNOS=I*++=:-.-   Gray levels

Figure A.2 *Overstrike characters used to obtain 32 gray levels. The 32nd character is a blank.*

a relatively large number of gray levels. Its principal disadvantage is that it tends to be slow. Generally, overstriking is the preferred technique when the output device is a line printer. Figure A.3 shows a gray-scale image printed by a line printer using the overstriking approach.

Another approach for halftoning on a bilevel device consists of forming various patterns of black dots within a white square area, with the idea of approximating the concept behind the halftoning approach for media printing, as discussed earlier. For example, a 2 × 2 pixel area of a bilevel device may be used to produce five gray levels, as shown in Fig. A.4. The advantage of this method, compared to overstriking, is speed. The principal disadvantage is that the resolution of the image being displayed is cut in half along each axis,

Figure A.3   *Image obtained by overstriking.*

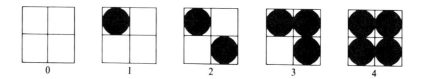

Figure A.4 *A 2 × 2 resolution region and corresponding dot patterns used to obtain five gray levels.*

because a square area of four pixels in the output device is needed to produce the gray level of a single pixel in the image.

A 3 × 3 area can be used to produce 10 gray levels using, for example, the dot patterns shown in Fig. A.5. Clearly, the price paid for increasing the number of gray levels is a two-thirds reduction in image resolution along each axis of the display. Thus an $n \times n$ group of bilevel pixels can produce $n^2 + 1$ gray levels. Designing dot patterns for use with this method involves two important considerations: First, the dots should be arranged so that conspicuous patterns are avoided in the printed image. For example, if the three dots corresponding to gray-level 3 in Fig. A.5 were arranged instead as a horizontal line in the center of the 3 × 3 area, a large area of constant gray-level 3 in the image would show two horizontal white lines, followed by a black line, followed by another two horizontal white lines, and so on. The patterns shown in Fig. A.5 tend to reduce such effects. Second, if a pixel in the pattern is black for gray level i, it should also be black for all levels $j > i$. This constraint reduces false contouring in the output image (see Section 2.3).

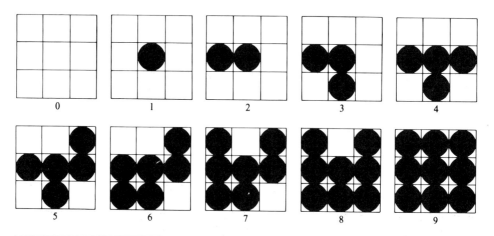

Figure A.5 *A 3 × 3 resolution region and corresponding dot patterns used to obtain 10 gray levels.*

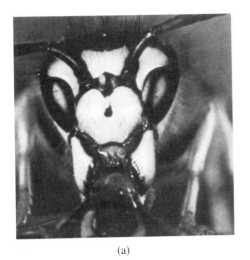

(a)   (b)

Figure A.6   *(a) A digital image; (b) result obtained from the halftone patterns of Fig. A.5.*

Figure A.6(b) shows an image printed with the dot patterns of Fig. A.5. The original image shown in Fig. A.6(a) was coded using these dot patterns and then output to an ordinary laser printer. The original image was of resolution 512 × 512 pixels, with 256 gray levels. The resolution of the coded image thus was reduced to 170 × 170 pixels, after allowing for the 3 × 3 gray-level regions needed to implement 10 gray levels. Although some false contouring is evident in Fig. A.6(b), this result would be acceptable for rough image processing work in the absence of a high-quality, gray-level output device.

CODED IMAGES

The following 64×64, 32-level images may be used as test data for many of the image processing concepts developed in the text. Along with each image is shown a coded array that contains an alphanumeric character for each pixel in the image. The range of these characters is 0–9 and $A–V$, which corresponds to 32 gray levels. The first step after reading the coded image into a computer is to convert the alphanumeric characters into numerical levels in the range 0 to 31. The resulting numerical array may be used in its original form or it may be corrupted, for example, by adding noise to each pixel. This flexibility allows generation of a variety of input data that may be used to illustrate the effects of image processing algorithms. The results before and after processing may be displayed on a standard bilevel device, such as a line printer, by using a program based on the concepts introduced in Appendix A.

Figure B.1   *Mona Lisa.*

Figure B.2   *Coded Mona Lisa.*

Figure B.3   *Characters.*

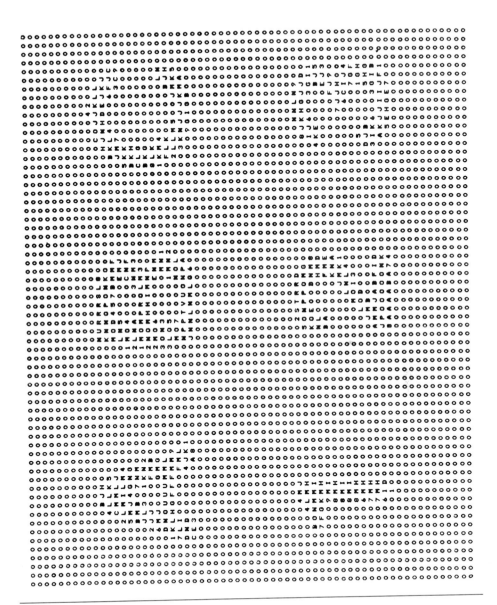

Figure B.4 *Coded characters.*

Figure B.5   *Lincoln.*

Figure B.6   *Coded Lincoln.*

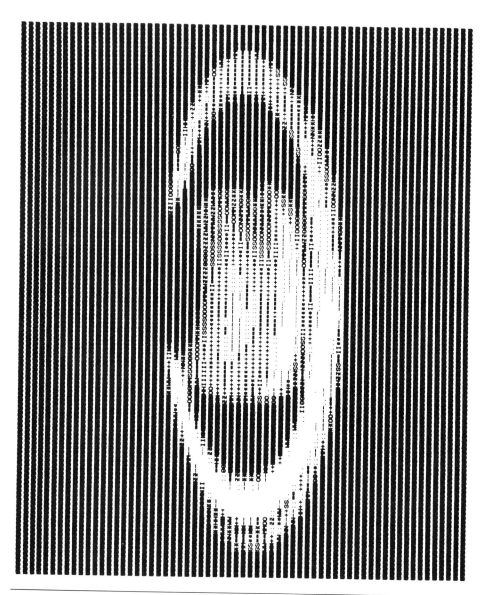

Figure B.7 *Saturn.*

Figure B.8 *Coded Saturn.*

Figure B.9   *Chromosomes.*

Figure B.10 *Coded chromosomes.*

Figure B.11   *Geometric figures.*

Figure B.12   *Coded geometric figures.*

BIBLIOGRAPHY

Abidi, M.A., Eason, R.O., and Gonzalez, R.C. [1991]. "Autonomous Robotics Inspection and Manipulation Using Multisensor Feedback." *IEEE Computer*, vol. 24, no. 4, pp. 17–31.

Abramson, N. [1963]. *Information Theory and Coding*, McGraw-Hill, New York.

Adimari, M., Masciangelo, S., Borghesi, L., and Vernazza, G. [1988]. "A Knowledge-Based Approach to Industrial Scene Analysis: Shadows and Reflexes Detection." In *Image Analysis and Processing II*, Cantoni, V. et al., eds., Plenum Press, New York, pp. 101–110.

Adiv, G. [1985]. "Determining Three-Dimensional Motion and Structure from Optical Flow Generated by Several Moving Objects." *IEEE Trans. Pattern Anal. Mach. Intell.*, vol. PAMI-7, no. 4, pp. 384–401.

Aggarwal, J.K., and Badler, N.I., eds. [1980]. "Motion and Time-Varying Imagery." *IEEE Trans. Pattern Anal. Mach. Intell.*, Special Issue, vol. PAMI-2, no. 6, pp. 493–588.

Ahmed, N., Natarajan, T., and Rao, K.R. [1974]. "Discrete Cosine Transforms." *IEEE Trans. Comp.*, vol. C-23, pp. 90–93.

Ahmed, N., and Rao, K.R. [1975]. *Orthogonal Transforms for Digital Signal Processing*, Springer-Verlag, New York.

Ambler, A.P., et al. [1975]. "A Versatile System for Computer Controlled Assembly." *Artificial Intell.*, vol. 6, no. 2, pp. 129–156.

Anderson, G.L., and Netravali, A.N. [1976]. "Image Restoration Based on a Subjective Criterion." *IEEE Trans. Syst. Man. Cyb.*, vol. SMC-6, no. 12, pp. 845–853.

Andrews, H.C. [1970]. *Computer Techniques in Image Processing*, Academic Press, New York.

Andrews, H.C. [1974]. "Digital Image Restoration: A Survey." *Computer J.*, vol. 7, no. 5, pp. 36–45.

Andrews, H.C., and Hunt, B.R. [1977]. *Digital Image Restoration*, Prentice-Hall, Englewood Cliffs, N.J.

Andrews, H.C., Tescher, A.G., and Kruger, R.P. [1972]. "Image Processing by Digital Computer." *IEEE Spectrum*, vol. 9, no. 7, pp. 20–32.

Ang, P.H., Ruetz, P.A., and Auld, D. [1991]. "Video Compression Makes Big Gains." *IEEE Spectrum*, vol. 28, no. 10, pp. 16–19.

Anuta, P.F. [1969]. "Digital Registration of Multispectral Video Imagery." *Soc. Photo-Optical Instrum. Engs.*, vol. 7, pp. 168–175.

Bajcsy, R. [1973]. "Computer Description of Textured Surfaces." *Proc. 1973 Int. Conf. Artificial Intell.*, Stanford, Calif., pp. 572–579.

Bajcsy, R., and Lieberman, L. [1976]. "Texture Gradient as a Depth Cue." *Comput. Graph. Image Proc.*, vol. 5, no. 1, pp. 52–67.

Ballard, D.H. [1981]. "Generalizing the Hough Transform to Detect Arbitrary Shapes." *Pattern Recognition*, vol. 13, no. 2, pp. 111–122.

Ballard, D.H., and Brown, C.M. [1982]. *Computer Vision*, Prentice-Hall, Englewood Cliffs, N.J.

Bates, R.H.T. and McDonnell, M.J. [1986]. *Image Restoration and Reconstruction*, Oxford University Press, New York.

Baumert, L.D., Golomb, S.W., and Hall, M., Jr. [1962]. "Discovery of a Hadamard Matrix of Order 92." *Bull. Am. Math. Soc.*, vol. 68, pp. 237–238.

Baylon, D.M., and Lim, J.S. [1990]. "Transform/Subband Analysis and Synthesis of Signals." *Tech. Report*, MIT Research Laboratory of Electronics, Cambridge, Mass.

Bell, E.T. [1965]. *Men of Mathematics*, Simon and Schuster, New York.

Bellman, R. [1970]. *Introduction to Matrix Analysis*, 2nd ed., McGraw-Hill, New York.

Bengtsson, A., and Eklundh, J.O. [1991]. "Shape Representation by Multiscale Contour Approximation." *IEEE Trans. Pattern Anal. Machine Intell.*, vol. 13, no. 1, pp. 85–93.

Berger, T. [1971]. *Rate Distortion Theory*, Prentice-Hall, Englewood Cliffs, N.J.

Bernstein, R. [1976]. "Digital Image Processing of Earth Observation Sensor Data." *IBM J. Res. Dev.*, vol. 20, no. 1, pp. 40–56.

Biberman, L.M. [1973]. "Image Quality." In *Perception of Displayed Information*, Biberman, L.M. ed., Plenum Press, New York.

Biermann, A.W., and Feldman, J.A. [1972]. "On the Synthesis of Finite-State Machines from Samples of Their Behavior." *IEEE Trans. Comput.*, vol. C-21, no. 6, pp. 592–597.

Billingsley, F.C., Goetz, A.F.H., and Lindsley, J.N. [1970]. "Color Differentiation by Computer Image Processing." *Photo. Sci. Eng.*, vol. 14, no. 1, pp. 28–35.

Bisignani, W.T., Richards, G.P., and Whelan, J.W. [1966]. "The Improved Grey Scale and Coarse-Fine PCM Systems: Two New Digital TV Bandwidth Reduction Techniques." *Proc. IEEE*, vol. 54, no. 3, pp. 376–390.

Blackman, E.S. [1968]. "Effects of Noise on the Determination of Photographic System Modulation Transfer Function." *Photogr. Sci. Eng.*, vol. 12, pp. 244–250.

Blackman, R.B., and Tukey, J.W. [1958]. *The Measurement of Power Spectra*, Dover Publications, New York.

Blahut, R.E. [1987]. *Principles and Practice of Information Theory*, Addison-Wesley, Reading, Mass.

Blum, H. [1967]. "A Transformation for Extracting New Descriptors of Shape." in *Models for the Perception of Speech and Visual Form*, Wathen-Dunn, W., ed., MIT Press, Cambridge, Mass.

Blume, H., and Fand, A. [1989]. "Reversible and Irreversible Image Data Compression Using the S-Transform and Lempel-Ziv Coding." *Proc. SPIE Medical Imaging III: Image Capture and Display*, vol. 1091, pp. 2–18.

Bouman, C., and Liu, B. [1991]. "Multiple Resolution Segmentation of Textured Images." *IEEE Trans. Pattern Anal. Machine Intell.*, vol. 13, no. 2, pp. 99–113.

Brayer, J.M., Swain, P.H., and Fu, K.S. [1977]. "Modeling of Earth Resources Satellite Data." *Syntactic Pattern Recognition Applications*, (K.S. Fu, ed.), Springer-Verlag, New York.

Bribiesca, E. [1981]. "Arithmetic Operations Among Shapes Using Shape Numbers." *Pattern Recog.*, vol. 13, no. 2, pp. 123–138.

Bribiesca, E., and Guzman, A. [1980]. "How to Describe Pure Form and How to Measure Differences in Shape Using Shape Numbers." *Pattern Recog.*, vol. 12, no. 2, pp. 101–112.

Brice, C.R., and Fennema, C.L. [1970]. "Scene Analysis Using Regions." *Artificial Intelligence,* vol. 1, pp. 205–226.

Brigham, E.O. [1974]. *The Fast Fourier Transform*, Prentice-Hall, Englewood Cliffs, N.J.

Brill, E.L. [1968]. "Character Recognition Via Fourier Descriptors." WESCON, Paper 25/3, Los Angeles, Calif.

Brown, J.L., Jr. [1960]. "Mean-Square Truncation Error in Series Expansions of Random Functions." *J. SIAM*, vol. 8, pp. 18–32.

Brummer, M.E. [1991]. "Hough Transform Detection of the Longitudinal Fissure in Tomographic Head Images." *IEEE Trans. Biomed. Images*, vol. 10, no. 1, pp. 74–83.

Brzakovic, D., Patton, R., and Wang, R. [1991]. "Rule-based Multi-template Edge Detection." *Comput. Vision, Graphics, Image Proc: Graphical Models and Image Proc.*, vol. 53, no. 3, pp. 258–268.

Budak, A. [1974]. *Passive and Active Network Analysis and Synthesis*, Houghton Mifflin, Boston.

Campbell, J.D. [1969]. "Edge Structure and the Representation of Pictures." Ph.D. dissertation, Dept. of Elec. Eng., University of Missouri, Columbia.

Candy, J.C., Franke, M.A., Haskell, B.G., and Mounts, F.W. [1971]. "Transmitting Television as Clusters of Frame-to-Frame Differences." *Bell Sys. Tech. J.*, vol. 50, pp. 1889–1919.

Cannon, T.M. [1974]. "Digital Image Deblurring by Non-Linear Homomorphic Filtering." Ph.D. Thesis, University of Utah.

Carlson, A.B. [1968]. *Communication Systems*, McGraw-Hill, New York.

Castleman, K.R. [1979]. *Digital Image Processing*, Prentice-Hall, Englewood Cliffs, N.J.

Chang, S.K. [1989]. *Principles of Pictorial Information Systems Design*, Prentice-Hall, Englewood Cliffs, N.J.

Chaudhuri, B.B. [1983]. "A Note on Fast Algorithms for Spatial Domain Techniques in Image Processing." *IEEE Trans. Syst. Man Cyb.*, vol. SMC-13, no. 6, pp. 1166–1169.

Chen, D., and Wang, L. [1991]. "Texture Features Based on Texture Spectrum." *Pattern Recog.*, vol. 24, no. 5, pp. 391–399.

Chen, P.H., and Wintz, P.A. [1976]. "Data Compression for Satellite Images." TR-EE-76-9, School of Electrical Engineering, Purdue University, West Lafayette, Ind.

Chow, C.K. and Kaneko, T. [1972]. "Automatic Boundary Detection of the Left Ventricle from Cineangiograms." *Comp. and Biomed. Res.*, vol. 5, pp. 388–410.

Clark, J.J. [1989]. "Authenticating Edges Produced by Zero-Crossing Algorithms." *IEEE Trans. Pattern Anal. Machine Intell.*, vol. 12, no. 8, pp. 830–831.

Clark, R.J. [1985]. *Transform Coding of Images*, Academic Press, New York.

Cochran, W.T., Cooley, J.W., et al. [1967]. "What Is the Fast Fourier Transform?" *IEEE Trans. Audio and Electroacoustics*, vol. AU-15, no. 2, pp. 45–55.

Computer [1974]. Special issue on digital image processing, vol. 7, no. 5.

Computer [1988]. Special issue on artificial neural systems, vol. 21, no. 3.

Cooley, J.W., Lewis, P.A.W., and Welch, P.D. [1967a]. "Historical Notes on the Fast Fourier Transform." *IEEE Trans. Audio and Electroacoustics*, vol. AU-15, no. 2, pp. 76–79.

Cooley, J.W., Lewis, P.A.W., and Welch, P.D. [1967b]. "Application of the Fast Fourier Transform to Computation of Fourier Integrals." *IEEE Trans. Audio and Electroacoustics*, vol. AU-15, no. 2, pp. 79–84.

Cooley, J.W., Lewis, P.A.W., and Welch, P.D. [1969]. "The Fast Fourier Transform and its Applications." *IEEE Trans. Educ.*, vol. E-12, no. 1, pp. 27–34.

Cooley, J.W., and Tukey, J.W. [1965]. "An Algorithm for the Machine Calculation of Complex Fourier Series." *Math. of Comput.*, vol. 19, pp. 297–301.

Cornsweet, T.N. [1970]. *Visual Perception*, Academic Press, New York.

Cowart, A.E., Snyder, W.E., and Ruedger, W.H. [1983]. "The Detection of Unresolved Targets Using the Hough Transform." *Comput. Vision Graph Image Proc.*, vol. 21, pp. 222–238.

Crimmins, T.R., and Brown, W.R. [1985]. "Image Algebra and Automatic Shape Recognition." *IEEE Trans. Aerospace and Electron. Syst.*, vol. AES-21, no. 1, pp. 60–69.

Cross, G.R., and Jain, A.K. [1983]. "Markov Random Field Texture Models." *IEEE Trans. Pattern Anal. Mach. Intell.*, vol. PAMI-5, no. 1, pp. 25–39.

Cumani, A., Guiducci, A., and Grattoni, P. [1991]. "Image Description of Dynamic Scenes." *Pattern Recog.*, vol. 24, no. 7, pp. 661–674.

Cutrona, L.J., and Hall, W.D. [1968]. "Some Considerations in Post-Facto Blur Removal." In *Evaluation of Motion-Degraded Images*, NASA Publ. SP-193, pp. 139–148.

Cutrona, L.J., Leith, E.N., and Palermo, C.J. [1960]. "Optical Data Processing and Filtering Systems." *IRE Trans. Info. Theory*, vol. IT-6, no. 3, pp. 386–400.

Danielson, G.C., and Lanczos, C. [1942]. "Some Improvements in Practical Fourier Analysis and Their Application to X-Ray Scattering from Liquids." *J. Franklin Institute*, vol. 233, pp. 365–380, 435–452.

Davenport, W.B., and Root, W.L. [1958]. *An Introduction to the Theory of Random Signals and Noise*, McGraw-Hill, New York.

Davis, L.S. [1975]. "A Survey of Edge Detection Techniques." *Comput. Graphics Image Proc.*, vol. 4, pp. 248–270.

Davis, L.S. [1982]. "Hierarchical Generalized Hough Transforms and Line-Segment Based Generalized Hough Transforms." *Pattern Recog.*, vol. 15, no. 4, pp. 277–285.

Davis, P.J. [1979]. *Circulant Matrices*, John Wiley & Sons, New York.

Davisson, L.D. [1972]. "Rate-Distortion Theory and Application." *Proc. IEEE*, vol. 60, pp. 800–808.

Delp, E.J., and Mitchell, O.R. [1979]. "Image Truncation using Block Truncation Coding." *IEEE Trans. Comm.*, vol. COM-27, pp. 1335–1342.

Deutsch, R. [1965]. *Estimation Theory*, Prentice-Hall, Englewood Cliffs, N.J.

Dijkstra, E. [1959]. "Note on Two Problems in Connection with Graphs." *Numerische Mathematik*, vol. 1, pp. 269–271.

Dougherty, E.R. [1992]. *An Introduction to Morphological Image Processing*, SPIE Press, Bellingham, Wash.

Doyle, W. [1962]. "Operations Useful for Similarity-Invariant Pattern Recognition." *J. ACM*, vol. 9, pp. 259–267.

Duan, J.R., and Wintz, P.A. [1974]. "Information Preserving Coding for Multispectral Scanner Data." TR-EE-74-15, School of Electrical Engineering, Purdue University, West Lafayette, Ind.

Duda, R.O., and Hart, P.E. [1972]. "Use of the Hough Transformation to Detect Lines and Curves in Pictures." *Comm. ACM*, vol. 15, no. 1, pp. 11–15.

Duda, R.O., and Hart, P.E. [1973]. *Pattern Classification and Scene Analysis*, John Wiley & Sons, New York.

Dudani, S.A., and Luk, A. [1977]. "Locating Straight-Edge Segments on Outdoor Scenes." *Proc. Conf. Pattern Recog. Image Proc.*, vol. 2, pp. 367–380.

Dyer, C.R. [1983]. "Gauge Inspection Using Hough Transforms." *IEEE Trans. Pattern Anal. Machine Intell.*, vol. PAMI-5, no. 6, pp. 621–623.

Dyer, C.R., and Rosenfeld, A. [1979]. "Thinning Algorithms for Grayscale Pictures." *IEEE Trans. Pattern Anal. Machine Intell.*, vol. PAMI-1, no. 1, pp. 88–89.

Elias, P. [1952]. "Fourier Treatment of Optical Processes." *J. Opt. Soc. Am.*, vol. 42, no. 2, pp. 127–134.

Elliott, D.F., and Rao, K.R. [1983]. *Fast Transforms: Algorithms and Applications*, Academic Press, New York.

Elsgolc, L.E. [1962]. *Calculus of Variations*, Addison-Wesley, Reading, Mass.

Equitz, W.H. [1989]. "A New Vector Quantization Clustering Algorithm." *IEEE Trans. Acous. Speech Signal Processing*, vol. ASSP-37, no. 10, pp. 1568–1575.

Essman, J., and Wintz, P.A. [1973]. "The Effects of Channel Errors in DPCM Systems and Comparison with PCM Systems." *IEEE Trans. on Comm.*, vol. 21, no. 8, pp. 867–877.

Evans, R.M. [1959]. *An Introduction to Color*, John Wiley & Sons, New York.

Falconer, D.G. [1970]. "Image Enhancement and Film Grain Noise." *Opt. Acta*, vol. 17, pp. 693–705.

Falconer, D.G. [1977]. "Target Tracking with the Hough Transform." *Proc. Asilomar Conf. Circ. Syst. Comput.*, vol. 11, pp. 249–252.

Fine, N.J. [1949]. "On the Walsh Functions." *Trans. Am. Math. Soc.*, vol. 65, pp. 373–414.

Fine, N.J. [1950]. "The Generalized Walsh Functions." *Trans. Am. Math. Soc.*, vol. 69, pp. 66–77.

Fischler, M.A. [1980]. "Fast Algorithms for Two Maximal Distance Problems with Applications to Image Analysis." *Pattern Recog.*, vol. 12, pp. 35–40.

Foley, J.D., and Van Dam, A. [1982]. *Fundamentals of Interactive Computer Graphics*, Addison-Wesley, Reading, Mass.

Fox, E.A. [1991]. "Advances in Interactive Digital Multimedia Systems." *Computer*, vol. 24, no. 10, pp. 9–21.

Fram, J.R., and Deutsch, E.S. [1975]. "On the Quantitative Evaluation of Edge Detection Schemes and Their Comparison with Human Performance." *IEEE Trans. Computers*, vol. C-24, no. 6, pp. 616–628.

Freeman, H. [1961]. "On the Encoding of Arbitrary Geometric Configurations." *IEEE Trans. Elec. Computers*, vol. EC-10, pp. 260–268.

Freeman, H. [1974]. "Computer Processing of Line Drawings." *Comput. Surveys*, vol. 6, pp. 57–97.

Freeman, H., and Shapira, R. [1975]. "Determining the Minimum-Area Encasing Rectangle for an Arbitrary Closed Curve." *Comm. ACM*, vol. 18, no. 7, pp. 409–413.

Freeman, J.A., and Skapura, D.M. [1991]. *Neural Networks: Algorithms, Applications, and Programming Techniques*, Addison-Wesley, Reading, Mass.

Frei, W., and Chen, C.C. [1977]. "Fast Boundary Detection: A Generalization and a New Algorithm." *IEEE Trans. Computers*, vol. C-26, no. 10, pp. 988–998.

Frendendall, G.L., and Behrend, W.L. [1960]. "Picture Quality—Procedures for Evaluating Subjective Effects of Interference." *Proc. IRE*, vol. 48, pp. 1030–1034.

Frieden, B.R. [1972]. "Restoring with Maximum Likelihood and Maximum Entropy." *J. Opt. Soc. Am.*, vol. 62, pp. 511–518.

Frieden, B.R. [1974]. "Image Restoration by Discrete Deconvolution of Minimal Length." *J. Opt. Soc. Am.*, vol. 64, pp. 682–686.

Fu, K.S. [1974]. *Syntactic Methods in Pattern Recognition*, Academic Press, New York.

Fu, K.S. [1982]. *Syntactic Pattern Recognition and Applications*, Prentice-Hall, Englewood Cliffs, N.J.

Fu, K.S., and Bhargava, B.K. [1973]. "Tree Systems for Syntactic Pattern Recognition." *IEEE Trans. Comput.*, vol. C-22, no. 12, pp. 1087–1099.

Fu, K.S., Gonzalez, R.C., and Lee, C.S.G. [1987]. *Robotics: Control, Sensing, Vision, and Intelligence*, McGraw-Hill, New York.

Fu, K.S., and Mui, J.K. [1981]. "A Survey of Image Segmentation." *Pattern Recog.*, vol. 13, no. 1, pp. 3–16.

Fu, K.S., and Rosenfeld, A. [1976]. "Pattern Recognition and Image Processing." *IEEE Trans. Computers*, vol. C-25, no. 12, pp. 1336–1346.

Gattis, J., and Wintz, P.A. [1971]. "Automated Techniques for Data Analysis and Transmission." TR-EE-71-37, School of Electrical Engineering, Purdue University, West Lafayette, Ind.

Gaven, J.V., Jr., Tavitian, J., and Harabedian, A. [1970]. "The Informative Value of Sampled Images as a Function of the Number of Gray Levels Used in Encoding the Images." *Phot. Sci. Eng.*, vol. 14, no. 1, pp. 16–20.

Gentleman, W.M. [1968]. "Matrix Multiplication and Fast Fourier Transformations." *Bell System Tech. J.*, vol. 47, pp. 1099–1103.

Gentleman, W.M., and Sande, G. [1966]. "Fast Fourier Transform for Fun and Profit." *Fall Joint Computer Conf.*, vol. 29, pp. 563–578, Spartan, Washington, D.C.

Gharavi, H., and Tabatabai, A. [1988]. "Sub-band Coding of Monochrome and Color Images." *IEEE Trans. Circuits Sys.*, vol. 35, no. 2, pp. 207–214.

Giardina, C.R., and Dougherty, E.R. [1988]. *Morphological Methods in Image and Signal Processing*, Prentice-Hall, Englewood Cliffs, N.J.

Gish, H., and Pierce, J.N. [1968]. "Asymptotically Efficient Quantizer." *IEEE Trans. Info. Theory*, vol. IT-14, pp. 676–683.

Golay, M.J.E. [1969]. "Hexagonal Parallel Pattern Transformations." *IEEE Trans. Comput.*, vol. C-18, pp. 733–740.

Goldmark, P.C., and Hollywood, J.M. [1951]. "A New Technique for Improving the Sharpness of Television Pictures," *Proc. IRE*, vol. 39, pp. 1314–1322.

Golomb, S.W., and Baumert, L.D. [1963]. "The Search for Hadamard Matrices." *Am. Math. Monthly*, vol. 70, pp. 27–31.

Gonzalez, R.C. [1972]. "Syntactic Pattern Recognition—Introduction and Survey." *Proc. Natl. Elec. Conf.*, vol. 27, pp. 27–31.

Gonzalez, R.C. [1985]. "Computer Vision." *Yearbook of Science and Technology*, McGraw-Hill, New York, pp. 128–132.

Gonzalez, R.C. [1985]. "Industrial Computer Vision." In *Advances in Information Systems Science*, Tou, J.T., ed., Plenum, New York, pp. 345–385.

Gonzalez, R.C. [1986]. "Image Enhancement and Restoration." In *Handbook of Pattern Recognition and Image Processing*, Young, T.Y. and Fu, K.S., eds., Academic Press, New York, pp. 191–213.

Gonzalez, R.C., Barrero, A., and Thomason, M.G. [1978]. "A Measure of Scene Content." *Proc. Pattern Recog. Image Proc. Conf.*, vol. 1, pp. 385–389.

Gonzalez, R.C., Edwards, J.J., and Thomason, M.G. [1976]. "An Algorithm for the Inference of Tree Grammars." *Int. J. Comput. Info. Sci.*, vol. 5, no. 2, pp. 145–163.

Gonzalez, R.C., and Fittes, B.A. [1975]. "Gray-Level Transformations for Interactive Image Enhancement." *Proc. Second Conf. Remotely Manned Syst.*, pp. 17–19.

Gonzalez, R.C., and Fittes, B.A. [1977]. "Gray-Level Transformations for Interactive Image Enhancement." *Mechanism and Machine Theory*, vol. 12, pp. 111–122.

Gonzalez, R.C., and Safabakhsh, R. [1982]. "Computer Vision Techniques for Industrial Applications." *Computer*, vol. 15, no. 12, pp. 17–32.

Gonzalez, R.C., and Thomason, M.G. [1978]. *Syntactic Pattern Recognition: An Introduction.* Addison-Wesley, Reading, Mass.

Gonzalez, R.C., Woods, R.E., and Swain, W.T. [1986]. "Digital Image Processing: An Introduction." *Digital Design*, vol. 16, no. 4, pp. 15–20.

Good, I.J. [1958]. "The Interaction Algorithm and Practical Fourier Analysis." *J. R. Stat. Soc. (Lond.)*, vol. B20, pp. 361–367; *Addendum*, vol. 22, 1960, pp. 372–375.

Goodman, J.W. [1968]. *Introduction to Fourier Optics*, McGraw-Hill, New York.

Goodson, K.J., and Lewis, P.H. [1990]. "A Knowledge-Based Line Recognition System." *Pattern Recog. Letters*, vol. 11, no. 4, pp. 295–304.

Graham, C.H., ed. [1965]. *Vision and Visual Perception*, John Wiley & Sons, New York.

Graham, D.N. [1967]. "Image Transmission by Two-Dimensional Contour Coding." *Proc. IEEE*, vol. 55, pp. 336–346.

Graham, R.E. [1958]. "Predictive Quantizing of Television Signals." *IRE Wescon Conv. Rec.*, vol. 2, pt. 2, pp. 147–157.

Graham, R.L., and Yao, F.F. [1983]. "Finding the Convex Hull of a Simple Polygon." *J. Algorithms*, vol. 4, pp. 324–331.

Gray, R.M. [1984]. "Vector Quantization." *IEEE Trans. Acous. Speech Signal Processing*, vol. ASSP-1, no. 2, pp. 4–29.

Green, W.B. [1983]. *Digital Image Processing—A Systems Approach*, Van Nostrand Reinhold, New York.

Gries, D. [1971]. *Compiler Construction for Digital Computers*, John Wiley & Sons, New York.

Grosky, W.I., and Jain, R. [1983]. "Optimal Quadtrees for Image Segments." *IEEE Trans. Pattern Anal. Machine Intell.*, vol. PAMI-5, no. 1, pp. 77–83.

Guillemin, E.A. [1949]. *The Mathematics of Circuit Analysis*, John Wiley & Sons, New York.

Gupta, L., Mohammad, R.S., and Tammana, R. [1990]. "A Neural Network Approach to Robust Shape Classification." *Pattern Recog.*, vol. 23, no. 6, pp. 563–568.

Gupta, L., and Srinath, M.D. [1988]. "Invariant Planar Shape Recognition Using Dynamic Alignment." *Pattern Recog.*, vol. 21, pp. 235–239.

Habibi, A. [1971]. "Comparison of Nth Order DPCM Encoder with Linear Transformations and Block Quantization Techniques." *IEEE Trans. Comm. Tech.*, vol. COM-19, no. 6, pp. 948–956.

Habibi, A. [1972]. "Two-Dimensional Bayesian Estimate of Images." *Proc. IEEE*, vol. 60, pp. 878–883.

Habibi, A. [1974]. "Hybrid Coding of Pictorial Data." *IEEE Trans. Comm.*, vol. COM-22, no. 5, pp. 614–624.

Habibi, A., and Wintz, P.A. [1971]. "Image Coding by Linear Transformations and Block Quantization." *IEEE Trans. Comm. Tech.*, vol. COM-19, pp. 50–62.

Hadamard, J. [1893]. "Resolution d'une Question Relative aux Determinants." *Bull. Sci. Math.*, Ser. 2, vol. 17, Part I, pp. 240–246.

Haddon, J.F., and Boyce, J.F. [1990]. "Image Segmentation by Unifying Region and Boundary Information." *IEEE Trans. Pattern Anal. Machine Intell.*, vol. 12, no. 10, pp. 929–948.

Hall, E.L. [1972]. "Automated Computer Diagnosis Applied to Lung Cancer." *Proc. 1972 Int. Conf. on Cybernetics Soc.*, New Orleans.

Hall, E.L. [1974]. "Almost Uniform Distributions for Computer Image Enhancement." *IEEE Trans. Computers*, vol. C-23, no. 2, pp. 207–208.

Hall, E.L. [1979]. *Computer Image Processing and Recognition*, Academic Press, New York.

Hall, E.L. et al. [1971]. "A Survey of Preprocessing and Feature Extraction Techniques for Radiographic Images." *IEEE Trans. Comput.*, vol. C-20, no. 9, pp. 1032–1044.

Hall, E.L., and Frei, W. [1976]. "Invariant Features for Quantitative Scene Analysis." Final Report, Contract F 08606-72-C-0008, Image Processing Institute, University of Southern California, Los Angeles.

Hamming, R.W. [1950]. "Error Detecting and Error Correcting Codes." *Bell Sys. Tech. J.*, vol. 29, pp. 147–160.

Hammond, J.L., and Johnson, R.S. [1962]. "Orthogonal Square-Wave Functions." *J. Franklin Inst.*, vol. 273, pp. 211–225.

Haralick, Haralick, R.M. [1979]. "Statistical and Structural Approaches to Texture." *Proc. 4th Int. Joint Conf. Pattern Recog.*, pp. 45–60.

Haralick, R.M., and Lee, J.S.J. [1990]. "Context Dependent Edge Detection and Evaluation." *Pattern Recog.*, vol. 23, no. 1–2, pp. 1–20.

Haralick, R.M., and Shapiro, L.G. [1985]. "Survey: Image Segmentation." *Comput. Vision, Graphics, Image Proc.*, vol. 29, pp. 100–132.

Haralick, R.M., Sternberg, S.R., and Zhuang, X. [1987]. "Image Analysis Using Mathematical Morphology." *IEEE Trans. Pattern Anal. Machine Intell.*, vol. PAMI-9, no. 4, pp. 532–550.

Haralick, R.M., Shanmugan, R., and Dinstein, I. [1973]. "Textural Features for Image Classification." *IEEE Trans Syst. Man Cyb.*, vol. SMC-3, no. 6, pp. 610–621.

Harmuth, H.F. [1968]. "A Generalized Concept of Frequency and Some Applications." *IEEE Trans. Info. Theory*, vol. IT-14, no. 3, pp. 375–382.

Harmuth, H.F. [1970]. *Transmission of Information by Orthogonal Signals*, Springer-Verlag, New York.

Harris, J.L. [1964]. "Resolving Power and Decision Theory." *J. Opt. Soc. Am.*, vol. 54, pp. 606–611.

Harris, J.L. [1966]. "Image Evaluation and Restoration." *J. Opt. Soc. Am.*, vol. 56, pp. 569–574.

Harris, J.L. [1968]. "Potential and Limitations of Techniques for Processing Linear Motion-Degraded Images." In *Eval. Motion Degraded Images*, NASA Publ. SP-193, pp. 131–138.

Hart, P.E., Nilsson, N.J., and Raphael, B. [1968]. "A Formal Basis for the Heuristic Determination of Minimum-Cost Paths." *IEEE Trans. Syst. Man Cyb*, vol. SMC-4, pp. 100–107.

Hayes-Roth, F., Waterman, D.A., and Lenat, D.B. [1983]. *Building Expert Systems*, Addison-Wesley, Reading, Mass.

Healy, D.J., and Mitchell, O.R. [1981]. "Digital Video Bandwidth Compression Using Block Truncation Coding." *IEEE Trans. Comm.*, vol. COM-29, no. 12, pp. 1809–1817.

Hebb, D.O. [1949]. *The Organization of Behavior: A Neuropsychological Theory*, John Wiley & Sons, New York.

Hecht, E., and Zajac, A. [1975]. *Optics*, Addison-Wesley, Reading, Mass.

Helstrom, C.W. [1967]. "Image Restoration by the Method of Least Squares." *J. Opt. Soc. Am.*, vol. 57, no. 3, pp. 297–303.

Henderson, K.W. [1964]. "Some Notes on the Walsh Functions." *IEEE Trans. Electronic Computers*, vol. EC-13, no. 1, pp. 50–52.

Herbrand, J. [1930]. "Recherches sur la Théorie de la Démontration." *Travaux de la Société des Sciences et des Lettres de Varsovie, Classe III, Sciences Mathématiques et Physiques*, no. 33.

Horn, B.K.P. [1986]. *Robot Vision*, McGraw-Hill, New York.

Horner, J.L. [1969]. "Optical Spatial Filtering with the Least-Mean-Square Error Filter." *J. Opt. Soc. Am.*, vol. 59, pp. 553–558.

Horowitz, M. [1957]. "Efficient Use of a Picture Correlator." *J. Opt. Soc. Am.*, vol. 47, p. 327.

Horowitz, S.L., and Pavlidis, T. [1974]. "Picture Segmentation by a Directed Split-and-Merge Procedure." *Proc. 2nd Int. Joint Conf. Pattern Recog.*, pp. 424–433.

Hotelling, H. [1933]. "Analysis of a Complex of Statistical Variables into Principal Components." *J. Educ. Psychol.*, vol. 24, pp. 417–441, 498–520.

Hough, P.V.C. [1962]. "Methods and Means for Recognizing Complex Patterns." U.S. Patent 3,069,654.

Hsu, C.C., and Huang, J.S. [1990]. "Partitioned Hough Transform for Ellipsoid Detection." *Pattern Recog.*, vol. 23, no. 3–4, pp. 275–282.

Hu, M.K. [1962]. "Visual Pattern Recognition by Moment Invariants." *IRE Trans. Info. Theory*, vol. IT-8, pp. 179–187.

Huang, T.S. [1965]. "PCM Picture Transmission." *IEEE Spectrum*, vol. 2, no. 12, pp. 57–63.

Huang, T.S. [1966]. "Digital Picture Coding." *Proc. Natl. Electron. Conf.*, pp. 793–797.

Huang, T.S. [1968]. "Digital Computer Analysis of Linear Shift-Variant Systems." in *Evaluation of Motion-Degraded Images*, NASA Publ. SP-193, pp. 83–87.

Huang, T.S. [1968]. "Run-length Coding and its Extensions." *EG&G Tech. Report*, No. B-3742. (Also in *Picture Bandwidth Compression*, Huang, T.S., and Tretiak, O.J., eds., [1972], Gordon and Breech, New York).

Huang, T.S., ed. [1975]. *Picture Processing and Digital Filtering*, Springer, New York.

Huang, T.S. [1981]. *Image Sequence Analysis*, Springer-Verlag, New York.

Huang, T.S., and Hussian, A.B.S. [1972]. "Facsimile Coding by Skipping White." *IEEE Trans. Comm.*, vol. COM-23, no. 12, pp. 1452–1466.

Huang, Y., and Schultheiss, P.M. [1963]. "Block Quantization of Correlated Gaussian Random Variables." *IEEE Trans. Commun. Syst.*, vol. CS-11, pp. 289–296.

Huang, T.S., and Tretiak, O.J. (eds.). [1972]. *Picture Bandwidth Compression*, Gordon and Breech, New York.

Huang, T.S., Yang, G.T., and Tang, G.Y. [1979]. "A Fast Two-Dimensional Median Filtering Algorithm." *IEEE Trans. Acoust., Speech, Sig. Proc.*, vol. ASSP-27, pp. 13–18.

Huertas, A., Cole. W., and Nevatia, R. [1990]. "Detecting Runways in Complex Airport Scenes." *Comput. Vision, Graphics, Image Proc.*, vol. 51, no. 2, pp. 107–145.

Huffman, D.A. [1952]. "A Method for the Construction of Minimum Redundancy Codes." *Proc. IRE*, vol. 40, no. 10, pp. 1098–1101.

Hummel, R.A. [1974]. "Histogram Modification Techniques." Technical Report TR-329, F-44620-72C-0062, Computer Science Center, University of Maryland, College Park, Md.

Hunt, B.R. [1971]. "A Matrix Theory Proof of the Discrete Convolution Theorem." *IEEE Trans. Audio and Electroacoust.*, vol. AU-19, no. 4, pp. 285–288.

Hunt, B.R. [1973]. "The Application of Constrained Least Squares Estimation to Image Restoration by Digital Computer." *IEEE Trans. Comput.*, vol. C-22, no. 9, pp. 805–812.

Hunter, R., and Robinson, A.H. [1980]. "International Digital Facsimile Coding Standards." *Proc. IEEE*, vol. 68, no. 7, pp. 854–867.

IEEE Trans. Circuits and Syst. [1975]. Special issue on digital filtering and image processing, vol. CAS-2, pp. 161–304.

IEEE Trans. Computers [1972]. Special issue on two-dimensional signal processing, vol. C-21, no. 7.

IEEE Trans. Comm. [1981]. Special issue on picture communication systems, vol. COM-29, no. 12.

IES Lighting Handbook [1972]. Illuminating Engineering Society Press, New York.

Jain, A.K. [1975]. "A Fast Karhunen–Loève Transform for a Class of Random Processes." *IEEE Trans. Commun.*, vol. COM-24, pp. 1023–1029.

Jain, A.K. [1979]. "A Sinusoidal Family of Unitary Transforms." *IEEE Trans. Pattern Anal. Machine Intell.*, vol. PAMI-1, no. 4, pp. 356–365.

Jain, A.K. [1981]. "Image Data Compression: A Review." *Proc. IEEE*, vol. 69, pp. 349–389.

Jain, A.K. [1989]. *Fundamentals of Digital Image Processing*, Prentice-Hall, Englewood Cliffs, N.J.

Jain, A.K., and Angel, E. [1974]. "Image Restoration, Modeling, and Reduction of Dimensionality." *IEEE Trans. Computers*, vol. C-23, pp. 470–476.

Jain, J.R., and Jain, A.K. [1981]. "Displacement Measurement and Its Application in Interframe Image Coding." *IEEE Trans. Comm.*, vol. COM-29, pp. 1799–1808.

Jain, R. [1981]. "Dynamic Scene Analysis Using Pixel-Based Processes." *Computer*, vol. 14, no. 8, pp. 12–18.

Jain, R. [1983]. "Segmentation of Frame Sequences Obtained by a Moving Observer." Report GMR-4247, General Motors Research Laboratories, Warren, Mich.

Jang, B.K., and Chin, R.T. [1990]. "Analysis of Thinning Algorithms Using Mathematical Morphology." *IEEE Trans. Pattern Anal. Machine Intell.*, vol. 12, no. 6, pp. 541–551.

Jayant, N.S., ed. [1976]. *Waveform Quantization and Coding*, IEEE Press, New York.

Kahaner, D.K. [1970]. "Matrix Description of the Fast Fourier Transform." *IEEE Trans. Audio Electroacoustics*, vol. AU-18, no. 4, pp. 442–450.

Kak, A.C., and Slaney, M. [1988]. *Principles of Computerized Tomographic Imaging*, IEEE Press, New York.

Karhunen, K. [1947]. "Über Lineare Methoden in der Wahrscheinlichkeitsrechnung." *Ann. Acad. Sci. Fennicae*, Ser. A137. (Translated by I. Selin in "On Linear Methods in Probability Theory." T-131, 1960, The RAND Corp., Santa Monica, Calif.)

Ketcham, D.J. [1976]. "Real-Time Image Enhancement Techniques." *Proc. Soc. Photo-Optical Instrum. Eng.*, vol. 74, pp. 120–125.

Khanna, T. [1990]. *Foundations of Neural Networks*, Addison-Wesley, Reading, Mass.

Kimme, C., Ballard, D.H., and Sklansky, J. [1975]. "Finding Circles by an Array of Accumulators." *Comm. ACM*, vol. 18, no. 2, pp. 120–122.

Kirsch, R. [1971]. "Computer Determination of the Constituent Structure of Biological Images." *Comput. Biomed. Res.*, vol. 4, pp. 315–328.

Kiver, M.S. [1965]. *Color Television Fundamentals*, McGraw-Hill, New York.

Klinger, A. [1972]. "Patterns and Search Statistics." In *Optimizing Methods in Statistics*, Rustagi, J.S., ed., Academic Press, New York, pp. 303–339.

Klinger, A. [1976]. "Experiments in Picture Representation Using Regular Decomposition." *Comput. Graphics Image Proc.*, vol. 5, pp. 68–105.

Knowlton, K. [1980]. "Progressive Transmission of Gray-Scale and Binary Pictures by Simple, Efficient, and Lossless Encoding Schemes." *Proc. IEEE*, vol. 68, no. 7, pp. 885–896.

Koch, C., Luo, J., and Mead, C. [1988]. "Computing Motion Using Analog and Resistive Networks." *Computer*, vol. 21, no. 3, pp. 52–63.

Kodak Plates and Films for Scientific Photography [1973]. Publication no. P-315, Eastman Kodak Co., Rochester, N.Y.

Kohler, R.J., and Howell, H.K. [1963]. "Photographic Image Enhancement by Superposition of Multiple Images." *Photogr. Sci. Eng.*, vol. 7, no. 4, pp. 241–245.

Koschman, A. [1954]. "On the Filtering of Nonstationary Time Series." *Proc. 1954 Natl. Electron. Conf.*, p. 126.

Kovasznay, L.S.G., and Joseph, H.M. [1953]. "Processing of Two-Dimensional Patterns by Scanning Techniques." *Science*, vol. 118, pp. 475–477.

Kovasznay, L.S.G., and Joseph, H.M. [1955]. "Image Processing." *Proc. IRE*, vol. 43, pp. 560–570.

Kramer, H.P., and Mathews, M.V. [1956]. "A Linear Coding for Transmitting a Set of Correlated Signals." *IRE Trans. Info. Theory*, vol. IT-2, pp. 41–46.

Kushnir, M., Abe, K., and Matsumoto, K. [1985]. "Recognition of Handprinted Hebrew Characters Using Features Selected in the Hough Transform Space." *Pattern Recog.*, vol. 18, no. 2, pp. 103–114.

Langdon, G.C., and Rissanen, J.J. [1981]. "Compression of Black–White Images with Arithmetic Coding." *IEEE Trans. Comm.*, vol. COM-29, no. 6, pp. 858–867.

Langford, M.J. [1984]. *The Darkroom Handbook*, Random House, New York.

Lantuéjoul, C. [1980]. "Skeletonization in Quantitative Metallography." In *Issues of Digital Image Processing*, Haralick, R.M., and Simon, J.C. (eds.), Sijthoff and Noordhoff, Groningen, The Netherlands.

Lawley, D.N., and Maxwell, A.E. [1963]. *Factor Analysis as a Statistical Method*, Butterworth, London.

Ledley, R.S. [1964]. "High-Speed Automatic Analysis of Biomedical Pictures." *Science*, vol. 146, no. 3461, pp. 216–223.

Ledley, R.S., et al. [1965]. "FIDAC: Film Input to Digital Automatic Computer and Associated Syntax-Directed Pattern Recognition Programming System." In *Optical and Electro-Optical Information Processing Systems*, Tippet, J., Beckowitz, D., Clapp, L., Koester, C., and Vanderburgh, A., Jr., eds., MIT Press, Cambridge, Mass., Chap. 33.

Lee, C.C. [1983]. "Elimination of Redundant Operations for a Fast Sobel Operator." *IEEE Trans. Syst. Man Cybern.*, vol. SMC-13, no. 3, pp. 242–245.

Lee, S.U., Chung, S.Y., and Park, R.H. [1990]. "A Comparative Performance Study of Several Global Thresholding Techniques for Segmentation." *Comput. Vision, Graphics, Image Proc.*, vol. 52, no. 2, pp. 171–190.

Legault, R.R. [1973]. "The Aliasing Problems in Two-Dimensional Sampled Imagery." In *Perception of Displayed Information*, Biberman, L.M., ed., Plenum Press, New York.

Lema, M.D., and Mitchell, O.R. [1984]. "Absolute Moment Block Truncation Coding and Its Application to Color Images." *IEEE Trans. Comm.*, vol. COM-32, no. 10, pp. 1148–1157.

Levine, M.D. [1985]. *Vision in Man and Machine*, McGraw-Hill, New York.

Limb, J.O., and Rubinstein, C.B. [1978]. "On the Design of Quantizers for DPCM Coders: A Functional Relationship Between Visibility, Probability, and Masking." *IEEE Trans. Comm.*, vol. COM-26, pp. 573–578.

Linde, Y., Buzo, A., and Gray, R.M. [1980]. "An Algorithm for Vector Quantizer Design." *IEEE Trans. Comm.*, vol. COM-28, no. 1, pp. 84–95.

Lipkin, B.S., and Rosenfeld, A., eds. [1970]. *Picture Processing and Psychopictorics*, Academic Press, New York.

Lippmann, R.P. [1987]. "An Introduction to Computing with Neural Nets." *IEEE ASSP Magazine*, vol. 4, pp. 4–22.

Loève, M. [1948]. "Fonctions Aléatoires de Second Ordre." in P. Lévy, *Processus Stochastiques et Mouvement Brownien*, Hermann, Paris.

Lohman, A.W., and Paris, D.P. [1965]. "Space-Variant Image Formation." *J. Opt. Soc. Am.*, vol. 55, pp. 1007–1013.

Lu, H.E., and Wang, P.S.P. [1986]. "A Comment on 'A Fast Parallel Algorithm for Thinning Digital Patterns.'" *Comm. ACM*, vol. 29, no. 3, pp. 239–242.

Lu, S.Y., and Fu, K.S. [1978]. "A Syntactic Approach to Texture Analysis." *Comput. Graph. Image Proc.*, vol. 7, no. 3, pp. 303–330.

MacAdam, D.P. [1970]. "Digital Image Restoration by Constrained Deconvolution." *J. Opt. Soc. Am.*, vol. 60, pp. 1617–1627.

Maragos, P. [1987]. "Tutorial on Advances in Morphological Image Processing and Analysis." Optical Engineering, vol. 26, no. 7, pp. 623–632.

Maren, A.J., Harston, C.T., and Pap, R.M. [1990]. *Handbook of Neural Computing Applications*, Academic Press, New York.

Mark, D.M., and Abel, D.J. [1985]. "Linear Quadtrees from Vector Representations of Polygons." *IEEE Trans. Pattern Anal. Machine Intell.*, vol. PAMI-7, no. 3, pp. 344–349.

Marr, D. [1982]. *Vision*, Freeman, San Francisco.

Marr, D., and Hildreth, E. [1980]. "Theory of Edge Detection." *Proc. R. Soc. Lond.*, vol. B207, pp. 187–217.

Martelli, A. [1972]. "Edge Detection Using Heuristic Search Methods." *Comput. Graphics Image Proc.*, vol. 1, pp. 169–182.

Martelli, A. [1976]. "An Application of Heuristic Search Methods to Edge and Contour Detection." *Comm. ACM*, vol. 19, no. 2, pp. 73–83.

Max, J. [1960]. "Quantizing for Minimum Distortion." *IRE Trans. Info. Theory*, vol. IT-6, pp. 7–12.

McClelland, J.L., and Rumelhart, D.E., eds. [1986]. *Parallel Distributed Processing: Explorations in the Microstructures of Cognition*, vol. 2: *Psychological and Biological Models*, the MIT Press, Cambridge, Mass.

McCulloch, W.S., and Pitts, W.H. [1943]. "A Logical Calculus of the Ideas Imminent in Nervous Activity." *Bulletin of Mathematical Biophysics*, vol. 5, pp. 115–133.

McFarlane, M.D. [1972]. "Digital Pictures Fifty Years Ago." *Proc. IEEE*, vol. 60, no. 7, pp. 768–770.

McGlamery, B.L. [1967]. "Restoration of Turbulence-Degraded Images." *J. Opt. Soc. Am.*, vol. 57, no. 3, pp. 293–297.

McKeown, D.M., Harvey, W.A., and McDermott, J. [1985]. "Rule-Based Interpretation of Aerial Imagery." *IEEE Trans. Pattern Anal. Machine Intell.*, vol. PAMI-7, no. 5, pp. 570–585.

McKeown, D.M., Wilson, A.H., and Wixson, L.E. [1989]. "Automatic Knowledge Acquisition for Aerial Image Interpretation." *Comput. Vision, Graphics, Image Proc.*, vol. 46, no. 1, pp. 37–81.

Mees, C.E.K., and James, T.H. [1966]. *The Theory of the Photographic Process*, Macmillan, New York.

Merlin, P.M., and Farber, D.J. [1975]. "A Parallel Mechanism for Detecting Curves in Pictures." *IEEE Trans. Comput.*, vol. C-24, no. 1, pp. 96–98.

Meyer, E.R., and Gonzalez, R.C. [1983]. "Spatial Techniques for Digital Image Enhancement and Restoration." *Proc. First South Afr. Symp. Digital Image Proc.*, Univ. of Natal, Durban, South Africa, pp. 137–182.

Meyer, F., and Beucher, S. [1990]. "Morphological Segmentation." *J. Visual Comm. and Image Representation*, vol. 1, no. 1, pp. 21–46.

Meyer, H., Rosdolsky, H.G., and Huang, T.S. [1973]. "Optimum Run Length Codes." *IEEE Trans. Comm.*, vol. COM-22, no. 6, pp. 826–835.

Minsky, M., and Papert, S. [1969]. *Perceptrons: An Introduction to Computational Geometry*, the MIT Press, Cambridge, Mass.

Mokhtarian, F., and Mackworth, A. [1986]. "A Scale-Based Description and Recognition of Planar Curves and Two-Dimensional Shapes." *IEEE Trans. Pattern Anal. Machine Intell.*, vol. PAMI-8, no. 1, pp. 34–43.

Moon, P. [1961]. *The Scientific Basis of Illuminating Engineering*, Dover, New York.

Mueller, P.F., and Reynolds, G.O. [1967]. "Image Restoration by Removal of Random Media Degradations." *J. Opt. Soc. Am.*, vol. 57, pp. 1338–1344.

Muerle, J.L., and Allen, D.C. [1968]. "Experimental Evaluation of Techniques for Automatic Segmentation of Objects in a Complex Scene." In *Pictorial Pattern Recognition*, (G.C. Cheng et al., eds.), Thompson, Washington, D.C.

Nagao, M., and Matsuyama, T. [1980]. *A Structural Analysis of Complex Aerial Photographs*, Plenum Press, New York.

Nahim, P.J. [1974]. "The Theory of Measurement of a Silhouette Description for Image Processing and Recognition." *Pattern Recog.*, vol. 6, no. 2, pp. 85–95.

Narasimhan, R., and Fornango, J.P. [1963]. "Some Further Experiments in the Parallel Processing of Pictures." *IEEE Trans. Elec. Computers*, vol. EC-12, pp. 748–750.

Narendra, P.M., and Fitch, R.C. [1981]. "Real-Time Adaptive Contrast Enhancement." *IEEE Trans. Pattern Anal. Mach. Intell.*, vol. PAMI-3, no. 6, pp. 655–661.

Nelson, C.N. [1971]. "Prediction of Densities in Fine Detail in Photographic Images." *Photogr. Sci. Eng.*, vol. 15, pp. 82–97.

Netravali, A.N. [1977]. "On Quantizers for DPCM Coding of Picture Signals." *IEEE Trans. Info. Theory*, vol. IT-23, no. 3, pp. 360–370.

Netravali, A.N., and Limb, J.O. [1980]. "Picture Coding: A Review." *Proc. IEEE*, vol. 68, no. 3, pp. 366–406.

Niemann, H., Sagerer, G.F., Schröder, S., and Kummert, F. [1990]. "ERNEST: A Semantic Network for Pattern Understanding." *IEEE Trans. Pattern Anal. Machine Intell.*, vol. 12, no. 9, pp. 883–905.

Nilsson, N.J. [1965]. *Learning Machines: Foundations of Trainable Pattern-Classifying Systems*, McGraw-Hill, New York.

Nilsson, N.J. [1971]. *Problem Solving Methods in Artificial Intelligence*, McGraw-Hill, New York.

Nilsson, N.J. [1980]. *Principles of Artificial Intelligence*, Tioga, Palo Alto, Calif.

Noble, B. [1969]. *Applied Linear Algebra*, Prentice-Hall, Englewood Cliffs, N.J.

O'Gorman, F., and Clowes, M.B. [1976]. "Finding Picture Edges Through Collinearity of Feature Points." *IEEE Trans. Comput.*, vol. C-25, no. 4, pp. 449–454.

O'Handley, D.A., and Green, W.B. [1972]. "Recent Developments in Digital Image Processing at the Image Processing Laboratory of the Jet Propulsion Laboratory." *Proc. IEEE*, vol. 60, no. 7, pp. 821–828.

Ohlander, R.B. [1975]. "Analysis of Natural Scenes." Ph.D. dissertation, Dept. of Computer Science, Carnegie-Mellon Univ., Pittsburgh.

O'Neill, E.L. [1956]. "Spatial Filtering in Optics." *IRE Trans. Info. Theory*, vol. IT-2, no. 2, pp. 56–65.

O'Neil, J.B. [1971]. "Entropy Coding in Speech and Television Differential PCM Systems." *IEEE Trans. Info. Theory*, vol. IT-17, pp. 758–761.

Oppenheim, A.V., and Schafer, R.W. [1975]. *Digital Signal Processing*, Prentice-Hall, Englewood Cliffs, N.J.

Oppenheim, A.V., Schafer, R.W., and Stockham, T.G., Jr. [1968]. "Nonlinear Filtering of Multiplied and Convolved Signals." *Proc. IEEE*, vol. 56, no. 8, pp. 1264–1291.

Paez, M.D., and Glisson, T.H. [1972]. "Minimum Mean-Square-Error Quantization in Speech PCM and DPCM Systems." *IEEE Trans. Comm.*, vol. COM-20, pp. 225–230.

Panter, P.F., and Dite, W. [1951]. "Quantization Distortion in Pulse Code Modulation with Nonuniform Spacing of Levels." *Proc. IRE*, vol. 39, pp. 44–48.

Pao, Y.H. [1989]. *Adaptive Pattern Recognition and Neural Networks*, Addison-Wesley, Reading, Mass.

Papoulis, A. [1962]. *The Fourier Integral and Its Applications*, McGraw-Hill, New York.

Papoulis, A. [1965]. *Probability, Random Variables, and Stochastic Processes*, McGraw-Hill, New York.

Papoulis, A. [1968]. *Systems and Transforms with Applications in Optics*, McGraw-Hill, New York.

Park, R.H., and Choi, W.Y. [1990]. "Comments on 'A Three-Module Strategy for Edge Detection.' " *IEEE Trans. Pattern Anal. Machine Intell.*, vol. 12, no. 2, pp. 23–24.

Parker, J.R. [1991]. "Gray Level Thresholding in Badly Illuminated Images." *IEEE Trans. Pattern Anal. Machine Intell.*, vol. 13, no. 8, pp. 813–819.

Pattern Recognition [1970]. Special issue on pattern recognition in photogrammetry, vol. 2, no. 4.

Pavlidis, T. [1972]. "Segmentation of Pictures and Maps Through Functional Approximation." *Comp. Graph. Image Proc.*, vol. 1, pp. 360–372.

Pavlidis, T. [1977]. *Structural Pattern Recognition*, Springer-Verlag, New York.

Pavlidis, T., and Liow, Y.T. [1990]. "Integrating Region Growing and Edge Detection." *IEEE Trans. Pattern Anal. Mach. Intell.*, vol. 12, no. 3, pp. 225–233.

Pearson, D.E. [1975]. *Transmission and Display of Pictorial Information*, John Wiley & Sons (Halsted Press), New York.

Pennebaker, W.B., Mitchell, J.L., Langdon, G.G., Jr., and Arps, R.B. [1988]. "An Overview of the Basic Principles of the Q-coder Adaptive Binary Arithmetic Coder." *IBM J. Res. Dev.*, vol. 32, no. 6, pp. 717–726.

Perez, A., and Gonzalez, R.C. [1987]. "An Iterative Thresholding Algorithm for Image Segmentation." *IEEE Trans. Pattern Anal. Machine Intell.*, vol. PAMI-9, no. 6, pp. 742–751.

Perona, P., and Malik, J. [1990]. "Scale-Space and Edge Detection Using Anisotropic Diffusion." *IEEE Trans. Pattern Anal. Machine Intell.*, vol. 12, no. 7, pp. 629–639.

Perrin, F.H. [1960]. "Methods of Appraising Photographic Systems." *J. SMPTE*, vol. 49, pp. 151–156 and 239–249.

Persoon, E., and Fu, K.S. [1977]. "Shape Discrimination Using Fourier Descriptors." *IEEE Trans. Systems Man Cyb.*, vol. SMC-7, no. 2, pp. 170–179.

Petrou, M., and Kittler, J. [1991]. "Optimal Edge Detector for Ramp Edges." *IEEE Trans. Pattern Anal. Machine Intell.*, vol. 13, no. 5, pp. 483–491.

Phillips, D.L. [1962]. "A Technique for the Numerical Solution of Certain Integral Equations of the First Kind." *J. Assoc. Comp. Mach.*, vol. 9, pp. 84–97.

Piech, M.A. [1990]. "Decomposing the Laplacian." *IEEE Trans. Pattern Anal. Machine Intell.*, vol. 12, no. 8, pp. 830–831.

Pitas, I., and Vanetsanopoulos, A.N. [1990]. *Nonlinear Digital Filters: Principles and Applications*, Kluger, Boston.

Pokorny, C.K., and Gerald, C.F. [1989]. *Computer Graphics: The Principles Behind the Art and Science*, Franklin, Beedle & Associates, Irvine, Calif.

Pratt, W.K. [1971]. "Spatial Transform Coding of Color Images." *IEEE Trans. Comm. Tech.*, vol. COM-19, no. 6, pp. 980–991.

Pratt, W.K. [1974]. "Correlation Techniques of Image Registration." *IEEE Trans. Aerospace and Elec. Syst.*, vol. AES-10, no. 3, pp. 353–358.

Pratt, W.K. [1978]. *Digital Image Processing*, John Wiley & Sons, New York.

Pratt, W.K. [1991]. *Digital Image Processing*, 2nd ed., John Wiley & Sons, New York.

Preparata, F.P., and Shamos, M.I. [1985]. *Computational Geometry: An Introduction*, Springer-Verlag, New York.

Preston, K. [1983]. "Cellular Logic Computers for Pattern Recognition." *Computer*, vol. 16, no. 1, pp. 36–47.

Prewitt, J.M.S. [1970]. "Object Enhancement and Extraction." in *Picture Processing and Psychopictorics*, Lipkin, B.S. and Rosenfeld, A., eds., Academic Press, New York.

Price, K.E. [1976]. "Change Detection and Analysis in Multispectral Images." Dept. of Computer Science, Carnegie-Mellon Univ., Pittsburgh.

Pritchard, D.H. [1977]. "U.S. Color Television Fundamentals—A Review." *IEEE Trans. Consumer Electronics*, vol. CE-23, no. 4, pp. 467–478.

Proc. IEEE [1967]. Special issue on redundancy reduction, vol. 55, no. 3.

Proc. IEEE [1972]. Special issue on digital picture processing, vol. 60, no. 7.

Proc. IEEE [1980]. Special issue on the encoding of graphics, vol. 68, no. 7.

Proc. IEEE [1985]. Special issue on visual communication systems, vol. 73, no. 2.

Proctor, C.W., and Wintz, P.A. [1971]. "Picture Bandwidth Reduction for Noisy Channels." TR-EE 71-30, School of Electrical Engineering, Purdue University, West Lafayette, Ind.

Rabbani, M., and Jones, P.W. [1991]. *Digital Image Compression Techniques*, SPIE Press, Bellingham, Wash.

Rajala, S.A., Riddle, A.N., and Snyder, W.E. [1983]. "Application of the One-Dimensional Fourier Transform for Tracking Moving Objects in Noisy Environments." *Comput. Vis. Graph. Image Proc.*, vol. 21, pp. 280–293.

Ramer, U. [1975]. "Extraction of Line Structures from Photographs of Curved Objects." *Comput. Graphics Image Proc.*, vol. 4, pp. 81–103.

Ready, P.J., and Wintz, P.A. [1973]. "Information Extraction, SNR Improvement, and Data Compression in Multispectral Imagery." *IEEE Trans. Comm.*, vol. COM-21, no. 10, pp. 1123–1131.

Rino, C.L. [1969]. "Bandlimited Image Restoration by Linear Mean-Square Estimation." *J. Opt. Soc. Am.*, vol. 59, pp. 547–553.

Riseman, E.A., and Arbib, M.A. [1977]. "Computational Techniques in Visual Systems. Part II: Segmenting Static Scenes." IEEE Computer Society Repository, R77–87.

Robbins, G.M., and Huang, T.S. [1972]. "Inverse Filtering for Linear Shift-Variant Imaging Systems." *Proc. IEEE*, vol. 60, pp. 862–872.

Roberts, L.G. [1965]. "Machine Perception of Three-Dimensional Solids." In *Optical and Electro-Optical Information Processing*, Tippet, J.T., ed., MIT Press, Cambridge, Mass.

Robinson, G.S. [1976]. "Detection and Coding of Edges Using Directional Masks." University of Southern California, Image Processing Institute, Report no. 660.

Robinson, J.A. [1965]. "A Machine-Oriented Logic Based on the Resolution Principle." *J. ACM*, vol. 12, no. 1, pp. 23–41.

Roese, J.A., Pratt, W.K., and Robinson, G.S. [1977]. "Interframe Cosine Transform Image Coding." *IEEE Trans. Comm.*, vol. COM-25, pp. 1329–1339.

Rosenblatt, F. [1959]. "Two Theorems of Statistical Separability in the Perceptron." In *Mechanisation of Thought Processes: Proc. of Symposium No. 10*, held at the National Physical Laboratory, November 1958, H.M. Stationery Office, London, vol. 1, pp. 421–456.

Rosenblatt, F. [1962]. *Principles of Neurodynamics: Perceptrons and the Theory of Brain Mechanisms*, Spartan, Washington, D.C.

Rosenfeld, A. [1969]. *Picture Processing by Computer*, Academic Press, New York.

Rosenfeld, A. [1972]. "Picture Processing." *Comput. Graph. Image Proc.*, vol. 1, pp. 394–416.

Rosenfeld, A. [1973]. "Progress in Picture Processing: 1969–71," *Comput. Surv.*, vol. 5, pp. 81–108.

Rosenfeld, A. [1974]. "Picture Processing: 1973," *Comput. Graph. Image Proc.*, vol. 3, pp. 178–194.

Rosenfeld, A. et al. [1965]. "Automatic Cloud Interpretation," *Photogrammetr. Eng.*, vol. 31, pp. 991–1002.

Rosenfeld, A., and Kak, A.C. [1982]. *Digital Picture Processing*, 2nd ed., Academic Press, New York.

Roth, W. [1968]. "Full Color and Three-Dimensional Effects in Radiographic Displays." *Investigative Radiol.*, vol. 3, pp. 56–60.

Rudnick, P. [1966]. "Note on the Calculation of Fourier Series." *Math. Comput.*, vol. 20, pp. 429–430.

Rumelhart, D.E., Hinton, G.E., and Williams, R.J. [1986]. "Learning Internal Representations by Error Propagation." In *Parallel Distributed Processing: Explorations in the Microstructures of Cognition*, vol. 1: *Foundations*, Rumelhart, D.E., et al. eds., MIT Press, Cambridge, Mass., pp. 318–362.

Rumelhart, D.E., and McClelland, J.L., eds. [1986]. *Parallel Distributed Processing: Explorations in the Microstructures of Cognition*, vol. 1: *Foundations*, MIT Press, Cambridge, Mass.

Runge, C. [1903]. *Zeit. für Math. and Physik*, vol. 48, p. 433.

Runge, C. [1905]. *Zeit. für Math. and Physik*, vol. 53, p. 117.

Runge, C., and König, H. [1924]. "Die Grundlehren der Mathematischen Wissenschaften." *Vorlesungen über Numerisches Rechnen*, vol. 11, Julius Springer, Berlin.

Rushforth, C.K., and Harris, R.W. [1968]. "Restoration, Resolution, and Noise." *J. Opt. Soc. Am.*, vol. 58, pp. 539–545.

Sahoo, P.K., Soltani, S., Wong, A.K.C., and Chan, Y.C. [1988]. "A Survey of Thresholding Techniques." *Comput. Vision, Graphics, Image Proc.*, vol. 4, pp. 233–260.

Saito, N., and Cunningham, M.A. [1990]. "Generalized E-Filter and its Application to Edge Detection." *IEEE Trans. Pattern Anal. Machine Intell.*, vol. 12, no. 8, pp. 814–817.

Sakrison, D.J., and Algazi, V.R. [1971]. "Comparison of Line-by-Line and Two-Dimensional Encoding of Random Images." *IEEE Trans. Info. Theory*, vol. IT-17, no. 4, pp. 386–398.

Salari, E., and Siy, P. [1984]. "The Ridge-Seeking Method for Obtaining the Skeleton of Digital Images." *IEEE Trans. Syst. Man Cyb.*, vol. SMC-14, no. 3, pp. 524–528.

Sawchuk, A.A. [1972]. "Space-Variant Image Motion Degradation and Restoration." *Proc. IEEE*, vol. 60, pp. 854–861.

Schalkoff, R.J. [1989]. *Digital Image Processing and Computer Vision*, John Wiley & Sons, New York.

Schonfeld, D., and Goutsias, J. [1991]. "Optimal Morphological Pattern Restoration from Noisy Binary Images." *IEEE Trans. Pattern Anal. Machine Intell.*, vol. 13, no. 1, pp. 14–29.

Schowengerdt, R.A. [1983]. *Techniques for Image Processing and Classification in Remote Sensing*, Academic Press, New York.

Schreiber, W.F. [1956]. "The Measurement of Third Order Probability Distributions of Television Signals." *IRE Trans. Info. Theory*, vol. IT-2, pp. 94–105.

Schreiber, W.F. [1967]. "Picture Coding." *Proc. IEEE*, (Special issue on Redundancy Reduction), vol. 55, pp. 320–330.

Schreiber, W.F., and Knapp, C.F. [1958]. "TV Bandwidth Reduction by Digital Coding." *Proc. IRE National Convention*, pt. 4, pp. 88–99.

Schutten, R.W., and Vermeij, G.F. [1980]. "The Approximation of Image Blur Restoration Filters by Finite Impulse Responses." *IEEE Trans. Pattern Anal. Mach. Intell.*, vol. PAMI-2, no. 2, pp. 176–180.

Schwartz, J.W., and Barker, R.C. [1966]. "Bit-Plane Encoding: A Technique for Source Encoding." *IEEE Trans. Aerosp. Elec. Systems*, vol. AES-2, no. 4, pp. 385–392.

Schwarz, R.E., and Friedland, B. [1965]. *Linear Systems*, McGraw-Hill, New York.

Scoville, F.W. [1965]. "The Subjective Effect of Brightness and Spatial Quantization." *Q. Rep.*, no. 78, MIT Research Laboratory of Electronics, Cambridge, Mass.

Seidman, J. [1972]. "Some Practical Applications of Digital Filtering in Image Processing." *Proc. Conf. Comput. Image Proc. Recog.*, University of Missouri, Columbia, vol. 2, pp. 9-1-1–9-1-16.

Selin, I. [1965]. *Detection Theory*, Princeton University Press, Princeton, N.J.

Serra, J. [1982]. *Image Analysis and Mathematical Morphology*, Academic Press, New York.

Serra, J., ed. [1988]. *Image Analysis and Mathematical Morphology*, vol. 2, Academic Press, New York.

Sezan, M.I., Rabbani, M., and Jones, P.W. [1989]. "Progressive Transmission of Images Using a Prediction/Residual Encoding Approach." *Opt. Eng.*, vol. 28, no. 5, pp. 556–564.

Shack, R.V. [1964]. "The Influence of Image Motion and Shutter Operation on the Photographic Transfer Function." *Appl. Opt.*, vol. 3, pp. 1171–1181.

Shamos, M.I. [1978]. "Computational Geometry." Ph.D. Thesis, Yale University, New Haven, Conn.

Shanks, J.L. [1969]. "Computation of the Fast Walsh-Fourier Transform." *IEEE Trans. Comput.*, vol. C-18, no. 5, pp. 457–459.

Shannon, C.E. [1948]. "A Mathematical Theory of Communication." *The Bell Sys. Tech. J.*, vol. XXVII, no. 3, pp. 379–423.

Shariat, H., and Price, K.E. [1990]. "Motion Estimation with More Than Two Frames." *IEEE Trans. Pattern Anal. Machine Intell.*, vol. 12, no. 5, pp. 417–434.

Shaw, A.C. [1970]. "Parsing of Graph-Representable Pictures." *J. ACM*, vol. 17, no. 3, pp. 453–481.

Sheppard, J.J., Jr. [1968]. *Human Color Perception*, Elsevier, New York.

Sheppard, J.J., Jr., Stratton, R.H., and Gazley, C., Jr. [1969]. "Pseudocolor as a Means of Image Enhancement." *Am. J. Optom. Arch. Am. Acad. Optom.*, vol. 46, pp. 735–754.

Shih, F.Y.C., and Mitchell, O.R. [1989]. "Threshold Decomposition of Gray-Scale Morphology into Binary Morphology." *IEEE Trans. Pattern Anal. Machine Intell.*, vol. 11, no. 1, pp. 31–42.

Shore, J.E. [1973]. "On the Application of Haar Functions." *IEEE Trans. Comm.*, vol. COM-21, pp. 209–216.

Simon, J.C. [1986]. *Patterns and Operators: The Foundations of Data Representations*, McGraw-Hill, New York.

Sklansky, J., Chazin, R.L., and Hansen, B.J. [1972]. "Minimum-Perimeter Polygons of Digitized Silhouettes." *IEEE Trans. Comput.*, vol. C-21, no. 3, pp. 260–268.

Slepian, D. [1967a]. "Linear Least-Squares Filtering of Distorted Images." *J. Opt. Soc. Am.*, vol. 57, pp. 918–922.

Slepian, D. [1967b]. "Restoration of Photographs Blurred by Image Motion." *BSTJ*, vol. 46, pp. 2353–2362.

Slepian, D., and Pollak, H.O. [1961]. "Prolate Spheroidal Wave Functions, Fourier Analysis, and Uncertainty–I." *Bell Sys. Tech. J.*, vol. 40, pp. 43–64.

Smith, A.R. [1978]. "Color Gamut Transform Pairs." *Proc. SIGGRAPH '78*, published as *Computer Graphics*, vol. 12, no. 3, pp. 12–19.

Smith, S.L. [1963]. "Color Coding and Visual Separability in Information Displays." *J. Appl. Psychol.*, vol. 47, pp. 358–364.

Snider, H.L. [1973]. "Image Quality and Observer Performance." In *Perception of Displayed Information*, Biberman, L.M., ed., Plenum Press, New York.

Som, S.C. [1971]. "Analysis of the Effect of Linear Smear." *J. Opt. Soc. Am.*, vol. 61, pp. 859–864.

Sondhi, M.M. [1972]. "Image Restoration: The Removal of Spatially Invariant Degradations." *Proc. IEEE*, vol. 60, no. 7, pp. 842–853.

Stark, H., ed. [1987]. *Image Recovery: Theory and Application*, Academic Press, New York.

Stevens, S.S. [1951]. *Handbook of Experimental Psychology*, John Wiley & Sons, New York.

Stockham, T.G., Jr. [1972]. "Image Processing in the Context of a Visual Model." *Proc. IEEE*, vol. 60, no. 7, pp. 828–842.

Storer, J.A., and Reif, J.H., eds. [1991]. *Proceedings of DDC '91*, IEEE Computer Society Press, Los Alamitos, Calif.

Stumpff, K. [1939]. *Tafeln und Aufgaben zur Harmonischen Analyse und Periodogrammrechnung*, Julius Springer, Berlin.

Sze, T.W., and Yang, Y.H. [1981]. "A Simple Contour Matching Algorithm." *IEEE Trans. Pattern Anal. Mach. Intell.*, vol. PAMI-3, no. 6, pp. 676–678.

Tanimoto, S.L. [1979]. "Image Transmission with Gross Information First." *Comput. Graphics Image Proc.*, vol. 9, pp. 72–76.

Tasto, M., and Wintz, P.A. [1971]. "Image Coding by Adaptive Block Quantization." *IEEE Trans. Comm. Tech.*, vol. COM-19, pp. 957–972.

Tasto, M., and Wintz, P.A. [1972]. "A Bound on the Rate-Distortion Function and Application to Images." *IEEE Trans. Info. Theory*, vol. IT-18, pp. 150–159.

Teh, C.H., and Chin, R.T. [1989]. "On the Detection of Dominant Points on Digital Curves." *IEEE Trans. Pattern Anal. Machine Intell.*, vol. 11, no. 8, pp. 859–872.

Thomas, J.B. [1969]. *Statistical Communication Theory*, John Wiley & Sons, New York.

Thomas, L.H. [1963]. "Using a Computer to Solve Problems in Physics." *Application of Digital Computers*, Ginn, Boston.

Thomason, M.G., and Gonzalez, R.C. [1975]. "Syntactic Recognition of Imperfectly Specified Patterns." *IEEE Trans. Comput.*, vol. C-24, no. 1, pp. 93–96.

Thompson, W.B. (ed.) [1989]. "Special Issue on Visual Motion." *IEEE Trans. Pattern Anal. Machine Intell.*, vol. 11, no. 5, pp. 449–541.

Thompson, W.B., and Barnard, S.T. [1981]. "Lower-Level Estimation and Interpretation of Visual Motion." *Computer*, vol. 14, no. 8, pp. 20–28.

Titchmarsh, E.C. [1948]. *Introduction to the Theory of Fourier Integrals*, Oxford University Press, New York.

Tomita, F., Shirai, Y., and Tsuji, S. [1982]. "Description of Texture by a Structural Analysis." *IEEE Trans. Pattern Anal. Mach. Intell.*, vol. PAMI-4, no. 2, pp. 183–191.

Toriwaki, J.I., Kato, N., and Fukumura, T. [1979]. "Parallel Local Operations for a New Distance Transformation of a Line Pattern and Their Applications." *IEEE Trans. System, Man, Cyb.*, vol. SMC-9, no. 10, pp. 628–643.

Tou, J.T., and Gonzalez, R.C. [1974]. *Pattern Recognition Principles*, Addison-Wesley, Reading, Mass.

Toussaint, G.T. [1982]. "Computational Geometric Problems in Pattern Recognition." In *Pattern Recognition Theory and Applications*, Kittler, J., Fu, K.S., and Pau, L.F., eds., Reidel, New York, pp. 73–91.

Trivedi, M.M., Chen, C., and Cress, D.H. [1990]. "Object Detection by Step-Wise Analysis of Spectral, Spatial, and Topographic Features," *Comput. Vision, Graphics, Image Proc.*, vol. 51, no. 3, pp. 235–255.

Twomey, S. [1963]. "On the Numerical Solution of Fredholm Integral Equations of the First Kind by the Inversion of the Linear System Produced by Quadrature." *J. Assoc. Comput. Mach.*, vol. 10, pp. 97–101.

Udpikar, V.R., and Raina, J.P. [1987]. "BTC Image Coding Using Vector Quantization." *IEEE Trans. Comm.*, vol. COM-35, no. 3, pp. 352–356.

Umeyama, S. [1988]. "An Eigendecomposition Approach to Weighted Graph Matching Problems." *IEEE Trans. Pattern Anal. Machine Intell.*, vol. 10, no. 5, pp. 695–703.

VanderBrug, G.J., and Rosenfeld, A. [1977]. "Two-Stage Template Matchings." *IEEE Trans. Comput.*, vol. C-26, no. 4, pp. 384–394.

Van Valkenburg, M.E. [1955]. *Network Analysis*, Prentice-Hall, Englewood Cliffs, N.J.

Vuylsteke, P., and Kittler, J. [1990]. "Edge-Labeling Using Dictionary-Based Relaxation." *IEEE Trans. Pattern Anal. Machine Intell.*, vol. 12, no. 2, pp. 165–181.

Walsh, J.L. [1923]. "A Closed Set of Normal Orthogonal Functions." *Am. J. Math.*, vol. 45, no. 1, pp. 5–24.

Walsh, J.W.T. [1958]. *Photometry*, Dover, New York.

Warshall, S. [1962]. "A Theorem on Boolean Matrices." *J. ACM*, vol. 9, no. 1, pp. 11–12.

Webb, J.A., and Aggarwal, J.K. [1981]. "Visually Interpreting the Motion of Objects in Space." *Computer*, vol. 14, no. 8, pp. 40–49.

Wechsler [1980]. "Texture Analysis—A Survey." *Signal Process*, vol. 2, pp. 271–280.

Wechsler, W., and Sklansky, J. [1977]. "Automatic Detection of Ribs in Chest Radiographs." *Pattern Recog.*, vol. 9, no. 1, pp. 21–28.

Weinberg, L. [1962]. *Network Analysis and Synthesis*, McGraw-Hill, New York.

Welch, T.A. [1984]. "A Technique for High-Performance Data Compression." *IEEE Computer*, vol. 17, no. 6, pp. 8–19.

Weszka, J.S. [1978]. "A Survey of Threshold Selection Techniques." *Comput. Graphics Image Proc.*, vol. 7, pp. 259–265.

Whelchel, J.E., Jr., and Guinn, D.F. [1968]. "The Fast Fourier-Hadamard Transform and its Use in Signal Representation and Classification." *Eascon 1968 Convention Record*, pp. 561–573.

White, J.M., and Rohrer, G.D. [1983]. "Image Thresholding for Optical Character Recognition and Other Applications Requiring Character Image Extraction." *IBM J. Res. Devel.*, vol. 27, no. 4, pp. 400–411.

Widrow, B. [1962]. "Generalization and Information Storage in Networks of 'Adaline' Neurons." In *Self-Organizing Systems 1962*, Yovitz, M.C. et al. (eds.), Spartan, Washington, D.C., pp. 435–461.

Widrow, B., and Hoff, M.E. [1960]. "Adaptive Switching Circuits." *1960 IRE WESCON Convention Record*, Part 4, pp. 96–104.

Widrow, B., and Stearns, S.D. [1985]. *Adaptive Signal Processing*, Prentice-Hall, Englewood Cliffs, N.J.

Wilkins, L.C., and Wintz, P.A. [1970]. "Studies on Data Compression, Part I: Picture Coding by Contours; Part II: Error Analysis of Run-Length Codes." TR-EE 70–17, School of Electrical Engineering, Purdue University, West Lafayette, Ind.

Williamson, J. [1944]. "Hadamard's Determinant Theorem and the Sum of Four Squares." *Duke Math. J.*, vol. 11, pp. 65–81.

Wintz, P.A. [1972]. "Transform Picture Coding." *Proc. IEEE*, vol. 60, no. 7, pp. 809–820.

Witten, I.H., Neal, R.M., and Cleary, J.G. [1987]. "Arithmetic Coding for Data Compression." *Comm. ACM*, vol. 30, no. 6, pp. 520–540.

Wolfe, G.J., and Mannos, J.L. [1979]. "Fast Median Filter Implementation." *Proc. Soc. Photo-Optical Inst. Eng.*, vol. 207, pp. 154–160.

Wong, R.Y., and Hall, E.L. [1978]. "Scene Matching with Invariant Moments." *Comput. Graph. Image Proc.*, vol. 8, pp. 16–24.

Wood, R.C. [1969]. "On Optimum Quantization." *IEEE Trans. Info. Theory*, vol. IT-15, pp. 248–252.

Woods, J.W., and O'Neil, S.D. [1986]. "Subband Coding of Images." *IEEE Trans. Acous. Speech Signal Proc.*, vol. ASSP-35, no. 5, pp. 1278–1288.

Woods, R.E., and Gonzalez, R.C. [1981]. "Real-Time Digital Image Enhancement." *Proc. IEEE*, vol. 69, no. 5, pp. 643–654.

Yachida, M. [1983]. "Determining Velocity Maps by Spatio-Temporal Neighborhoods from Image Sequences." *Comput. Vis. Graph. Image Proc.*, vol. 21, no. 2, pp. 262–279.

Yamazaki, Y., Wakahara, Y., and Teramura, H. [1976]. "Digital Facsimile Equipment 'Quick-FAX' Using a New Redundancy Reduction Technique." *NTC '76*, pp. 6.2-1–6.2-5.

Yates, F. [1937]. "The Design and Analysis of Factorial Experiments." Commonwealth Agricultural Bureaux, Farnam Royal, Burks, England.

Yu, S.S., and Tsai, W.H. [1990]. "A New Thinning Algorithm for Gray-Scale Images." *Pattern Recog.*, vol. 23, no. 10, pp. 1067–1076.

Yuan, M., and Li, J. [1987]. "A Production System for LSI Chip Anatomizing." *Pattern Recog. Letters*, vol. 5, no. 3, pp. 227–232.

Zahn, C.T., and Roskies, R.Z. [1972]. "Fourier Descriptors for Plane Closed Curves." *IEEE Trans. Comput.*, vol. C-21, no. 3, pp. 269–281.

Zhang, T.Y., and Suen, C.Y. [1984]. "A Fast Parallel Algorithm for Thinning Digital Patterns." *Comm. ACM*, vol. 27, no. 3, pp. 236–239.

Ziv, J., and Lempel, A. [1977]. "A Universal Algorithm for Sequential Data Compression." *IEEE Trans. Info. Theory*, vol. IT-23, no. 3, pp. 337–343.

Ziv, J., and Lempel, A. [1978]. "Compression of Individual Sequences Via Variable-Rate Coding." *IEEE Trans. Info. Theory*, vol. IT-24, no. 5, pp. 530–536.

Zucker, S.W. [1976]. "Region Growing: Childhood and Adolescence." *Comput. Graphics Image Proc.*, vol. 5, pp. 382–399.

INDEX